# Financial Management

FN 215

Sacred Heart University

Author: Eugene F. Brigham, Joel F. Houston

CENGAGE
Learning·

Australia • Brazil • Japan • Korea • Mexico • Singapore • Spain • United Kingdom • United States

**Financial Management: FN 215, Sacred Heart University**

Fundamentals of Financial Management
Eugene F. Brigham, Joel F. Houston

©2017 Cengage Learning. All rights reserved.

For product information and technology assistance, contact us at
**Cengage Learning Customer & Sales Support, 1-800-354-9706**

For permission to use material from this text or product,
submit all requests online at **cengage.com/permissions**
Further permissions questions can be emailed to
**permissionrequest@cengage.com**

This book contains select works from existing Cengage Learning resources and was produced by Cengage Learning Custom Solutions for collegiate use. As such, those adopting and/or contributing to this work are responsible for editorial content accuracy, continuity and completeness.

Compilation © 2017 Cengage Learning

ISBN:978-1-337-44700-3

**Cengage Learning**

Cengage Learning is a leading provider of customized learning solutions with office locations around the globe, including Singapore, the United Kingdom, Australia, Mexico, Brazil, and Japan. Locate your local office at:
**www.international.cengage.com/region.**

Cengage Learning products are represented in Canada by Nelson Education, Ltd.

For your lifelong learning solutions, visit **www.cengage.com/custom.**

Visit our corporate website at **www.cengage.com.**

# Brief Contents

I

# Preface

When the first edition of *Fundamentals* was published 38 years ago, we wanted to provide an introductory text that students would find interesting and easy to understand. *Fundamentals* immediately became the leading undergraduate finance text, and it has maintained that position ever since. However, over the years as *Fundamentals* got larger and larger, we heard more and more often that it was difficult to cover the entire book in a single term. These concerns led us to create *Fundamentals of Financial Management Concise* 21 years ago. When designing *Concise*, we had in mind those instructors who wanted to retain *Fundamentals'* depth and level but eliminate some less essential topics. As is the case with *Fundamentals*, our continuing goal is to produce a book and ancillary package that sets a new standard for finance textbooks.

Finance is an exciting and continually changing field. Since the last edition, many important changes have occurred within the global financial environment. In the midst of this changing environment, it is certainly an interesting time to be a finance student. In this latest edition, we highlight and analyze the events leading to these changes from a financial perspective. Although the financial environment is ever changing, the tried-and-true principles that the book has emphasized for nearly four decades are now more important than ever.

## Structure of the Book

Our target audience is a student taking his or her first, and perhaps only, finance course. Some of these students will decide to major in finance and go on to take courses in investments, money and capital markets, and advanced corporate finance. Others will choose marketing, management, or some other nonfinance business major. Still others will major in areas other than business and take finance plus a few other business courses to gain information that will help them in law, real estate, or other fields.

Our challenge has been to provide a book that serves all of these audiences well. We concluded that we should focus on the core principles of finance, including the basic topics of time value of money, risk analysis, and valuation. Moreover, we concluded that we should address these topics from two points of view: (1) that of an investor who is seeking to make intelligent investment choices and (2) that of a business manager trying to maximize the value of his or her firm's stock. Both investors and managers need to understand the same set of principles, so the core topics are important to students regardless of what they choose to do after they finish the course.

In planning the book's structure, we first listed the core topics in finance that are important to virtually everyone. Included were an overview of financial markets, methods used to estimate the cash flows that determine asset values, the time value of money, the determinants of interest rates, the basics of risk analysis, and the basics of bond and stock valuation procedures. We cover these core topics in the first nine chapters. Next, because most students in the course will probably work for a business firm, we want to show them how the core ideas are implemented in practice. Therefore, we go on to discuss cost of capital, capital budgeting, capital structure, dividend policy, working capital management, financial forecasting, and international operations.

Nonfinance majors sometimes wonder why they need to learn finance. As we have structured the book, it quickly becomes obvious to everyone why they need to understand time value, risk, markets, and valuation. Virtually all students enrolled in the basic course expect at some point to have money to invest, and they quickly realize that the knowledge gained from Chapters 1 through 9 will help them make better investment decisions. Moreover, students who plan to go into the business world soon realize that their own success requires that their firms be successful, and the topics covered in Chapters 10 through 17 will be helpful here. For example, good capital budgeting decisions require accurate forecasts from people in sales, marketing, production, and human resources, and nonfinancial people need to understand how their actions affect the firm's profits and future performance.

# Organization of the Chapters: A Valuation Focus

As we discuss in Chapter 1, in an enterprise system such as that of the United States, the primary goal of financial management is to maximize their firms' values. At the same time, we stress that managers should not do "whatever it takes" to increase the firm's stock price. Managers have a responsibility to behave ethically, and when striving to maximize value, they must abide by constraints such as not polluting the environment, not engaging in unfair labor practices, not breaking the antitrust laws, and the like. In Chapter 1, we discuss the concept of valuation, explain how it depends on future cash flows and risk, and show why value maximization is good for society in general. This valuation theme runs throughout the text.

Stock and bond values are determined in the financial markets, so an understanding of those markets is essential to anyone involved with finance. Therefore, Chapter 2 covers the major types of financial markets, the rates of return that investors have historically earned on different types of securities, and the risks inherent in these securities. This information is important for anyone working in finance, and it is also important for anyone who has or hopes to own any financial assets. In this chapter, we also highlight how this environment has changed in the aftermath of the financial crisis.

Asset values depend in a fundamental way on earnings and cash flows as reported in the accounting statements. Therefore, we review those statements in Chapter 3 and then, in Chapter 4, show how accounting data can be analyzed and used to measure how well a company has operated in the past and how well it is likely to perform in the future.

Chapter 5 covers the time value of money (TVM), perhaps the most fundamental concept in finance. The basic valuation model, which ties together cash flows, risk, and interest rates, is based on TVM concepts, and these concepts are used throughout the remainder of the book. Therefore, students should allocate plenty of time to studying Chapter 5.

Chapter 6 deals with interest rates, a key determinant of asset values. We discuss how interest rates are affected by risk, inflation, liquidity, the supply of and demand for capital in the economy, and the actions of the Federal Reserve. The discussion of interest rates leads directly to the topics of bonds in Chapter 7 and stocks in Chapters 8 and 9, where we show how these securities (and all other financial assets) are valued using the basic TVM model.

The background material provided in Chapters 1 through 9 is essential to both investors and corporate managers. These are "Finance" topics, not "Business" or "Corporate Finance" topics as those terms are commonly used. Thus, Chapters 1 through 9 concentrate on the concepts and models used to establish values, whereas Chapters 10 through 17 focus on specific actions managers can take to maximize their firms' values.

Because most business students don't plan to specialize in finance, they might think the "business finance" chapters are not particularly relevant to them. This is most decidedly not true, and in the later chapters we show that all really important business decisions involve every one of a firm's departments—marketing, accounting, production, and so on. Thus, although a topic such as capital budgeting can be thought of as a financial issue, marketing people provide inputs on likely unit sales and sales prices; manufacturing people provide inputs on costs; and so on. Moreover, capital budgeting decisions influence the size of the firm, its products, its profits, and its stock price, and those factors affect all of the firm's employees, from the CEO to the mail room staff.

# Innovations for the Ninth Edition

A great deal has happened in the financial markets and corporate America since the 8th edition was published. In this 9th edition, we have made several important changes to reflect this dynamic environment. Below, we provide a brief summary of the more significant changes.

1. Today's students are tomorrow's business and government leaders, and it is essential that they understand the key principles of finance, and the important role that financial markets and institutions have on our economy. Since the last edition, a number of key events have significantly influenced the financial markets and finance in general. Over the last few years, we have witnessed continued weakness in the economy following the global financial crisis of 2007 through 2009, the European debt crisis, Greece's continued financial difficulties, and growing unrest overseas. At the same time, the Federal Reserve's aggressive policy of quantitative easing (resulting in the injection of $4.5 trillion into the economy over a 5-year period) pushed interest rates to the lowest levels in years and is partially responsible for the dramatic run-up in the U.S. stock market that began in 2009. Throughout the 9th edition, we discuss these events and their implications for financial markets and corporate managers, and we use these examples to illustrate the importance of the key concepts covered in *Concise* for investors, businesses, and even government officials.

2. In the 9th edition, we also continue to highlight the important influences of increased globalization and changing technology. These influences have created new opportunities, but they have also generated new sources of risk for individuals and businesses. Since the last edition, we have seen, for example, Facebook, Twitter, Shake Shack, Uber, and Alibaba's initial public offerings, the rise of Bitcoin, several high-profile mergers, and the rise of corporate inversions—where U.S. companies pursue strategies to move their headquarters to lower-tax countries.

3. Instructors and students continually impress upon us the importance of having interesting and relevant real-world examples. Throughout the 9th edition, we have added several new examples where recent events help illustrate the key concepts covered in the text. We have added a number of new boxes discussing chapter concepts impacting real-world companies, such as: Chapter 2: "Initial Buzz Surrounding IPOs Doesn't Always Translate into Long-Lasting Success"; Chapter 6: "European Banks Confront the Reality of Negative Interest Rates"; Chapter 9: "Are 'Smart Beta' Funds a Smart Idea?"; and Chapter 12: "Google Puts a Time Limit on Its R&D Projects." We have also expanded and updated the many tables where we present real-world data, and we have revised the old Thomson One problems so that they can now be used with general Internet financial websites. To reflect this change, these problems are now called Taking a Closer Look. New Internet problems have been added in Chapters 6, 7, and 17. Finally, as is always the case, we have also made significant changes to many of the opening vignettes that precede each chapter.

4. We updated the tax discussion in Chapter 3 to reflect 2015 tax rates and tax law changes for tax returns due April 15, 2016. Impacts of these changes are discussed throughout the text, especially in the capital structure and dividend chapters. In addition, we have added discussion on Traditional and Roth IRAs. Finally, we added a few end-of-chapter problems on personal taxes.

5. To better reflect current market conditions, the interest rates in Section 8-4 (Relationship between Risk and Return) and in Section 9-6 (Valuing Nonconstant Growth Stocks) have been lowered, so the accompanying figures in those sections have been updated accordingly.

6. In Chapter 14, we added some current discussion on DRIPS for companies comprising the Dow Jones Industrial Average. In addition, we updated the discussion regarding the current stock repurchasing activity.

7. We updated the exchange rate data in Chapter 17 to reflect what's currently going on in the world. All figures and text discussion have been updated accordingly including "The Debt Crisis Hits Europe," "Hungry for a Big Mac?," "Measuring Country Risk," and "Investing in International Stocks" boxes.

8. Instructors and students have impressed upon us the importance of revising the end-of-chapter problems to facilitate the learning process. To this end, we have revised over 40%–50% of the end-of-chapter problems throughout the text. In addition, we revised the Integrated Cases for Chapters 8 and 9 to reflect lower returns currently existing in the market.

When revising the text, we always rely heavily on a team of reviewers who offer suggestions for making the text more readable and relevant to students. We give special thanks to these reviewers later in the preface; their comments and recommendations certainly helped us improve this 9th edition.

# Digital Solutions for the Ninth Edition

Changing technology and new ideas have had an exciting and dramatic influence on the ways we teach finance. Innovative instructors are developing and utilizing different classroom strategies, and new technology has allowed us to present key material in a more interesting and interactive fashion. As textbook authors, we think these new developments are tremendously exciting, and we have worked closely with our publisher's top team of innovative content and media developers, who have created a whole new set of revolutionary products for the 9th edition.

## MINDTAP™

MindTap™, Cengage Learning's fully online, highly personalized learning experience combines readings, multimedia activities, and assessments into a singular Learning Path. MindTap™ guides students through their course with ease and engagement with a Learning Path that includes an Interactive Chapter Reading, Problem Demonstrations, Blueprint Problems, and the Online Homework Assignment. Instructors can personalize the Learning Path for their students by customizing the robust suite of the *Concise* Ninth Edition resources and adding their own content via apps that integrate into the MindTap™ framework seamlessly with Learning Management Systems.

## BLUEPRINT PROBLEMS

Written by the authors and located within CengageNOW™, Aplia™, and Mind-Tap™, Blueprints teach students the fundamental finance concepts and their associated building blocks—going beyond memorization. By going through the problem step by step, they reinforce foundational concepts and allow students to demonstrate their understanding of the problem-solving process and business impact of each topic. Blueprints include rich feedback and explanations, providing students with an excellent learning resource to solidify their understanding.

## CONCEPTCLIPS

Embedded throughout the new interactive eReader, finance ConceptClips present fundamental key topics to students in an entertaining and memorable way via short animated video clips. Developed by Mike Brandl of The Ohio State University, these vocabulary animations provide students with a memorable auditory and visual representation of the important terminology for the course.

## PROBLEM WALK-THROUGHS

More than 100 Problem Walk-Through videos are embedded in the new inter-active MindTap eReader and online homework. Each video walks students through solving a problem from start to finish, and students can play and replay the tutorials as they work through homework assignments or prepare for quizzes and tests, almost as though they had an instructor by their side the whole time.

## APLIA™

Engage, prepare, and educate your students with this ideal online learning solution. Aplia™ Finance improves comprehension and outcomes by increasing student effort and engagement. Students stay on top of coursework with regularly scheduled homework assignments while automatic grading provides detailed, immediate feedback. Aplia™ assignments match the language, style, and structure of the text, which allows your students to apply what they learn directly to homework. Some of the features of Aplia™ include:

- MindTap™ eReader
- Auto-Graded Problem Sets
- Grade It Now
- Preparing for Finance Tutorials
- Finance in Action Modules
- Access to End-of-Chapter Problems, Blueprint Problems, and Test Bank
- Course Management System
- My Practice Reviews

For more information on how Aplia™ could benefit you, visit www.aplia .com/finance today!

## CENGAGENOW™

Designed by instructors for instructors, CengageNOW™ mirrors your natural workflow and provides time-saving, performance-enhancing tools for you and your students—all in one program! CengageNOW™ takes the best of current technology tools, including online homework management; fully customizable algorithmic end-of chapter problems and test bank; and course support materials such as online quizzing, videos, and tutorials to support your goals. With CengageNOW™, you can:

- Plan student assignments with an easy online homework management component.
- Manage your grade book with ease.
- Reinforce student comprehension with Personalized Study.
- Grade automatically for seamless, immediate results.

## COGNERO™ TESTING SOFTWARE

Cengage Learning Testing Powered by Cognero™ is a flexible, online system that allows you to author, edit, and manage test bank content from multiple Cengage Learning solutions; create multiple test versions in an instant; and deliver tests from your LMS, your classroom, or wherever you want. Revised to reflect concepts covered in the *Concise* Ninth Edition, the Cognero™ Test Bank is tagged according to Tier I (AACSB Business Program Interdisciplinary Learning Outcomes) and Tier II (Finance specific) topic, Bloom's Taxonomy, and difficulty level. In addition to these changes, we have also significantly updated and improved our more traditional ancillary package, which includes the Instructor's Manual, Test Bank, Study Guide, Excel Chapter Models, Excel Chapter Integrated Case Models, Excel Spreadsheet Problem Models, and PowerPoints for Chapter Integrated Cases.

# Acknowledgments

The book reflects the efforts of a great many people, both those who worked on *Concise* and our related books in the past and those who worked specifically on this 9th edition. First, we would like to thank Dana Aberwald Clark, who worked closely with us at every stage of the revision—her assistance was absolutely invaluable. Second, Susan Whitman provided great typing and logistical support.

Our colleagues John Banko, Roy Crum, Jim Keys, Andy Naranjo, M. Nimalendran, Jay Ritter, Mike Ryngaert, Craig Tapley, and Carolyn Takeda Brown have given us many useful suggestions over the years regarding the ancillaries and many parts of the book, including the integrated cases. We also benefited from the work of Mike Ehrhardt and Phillip Daves of the University of Tennessee, who worked with us on companion books.

We would also like to thank the following professors, whose reviews and comments on this and our earlier books contributed to this edition:

| | | | |
|---|---|---|---|
| Rebecca Abraham | Charles Barngrover | Waldo Born | Charles Chan |
| Robert Abraham | Sam Basu | Brian Boscaljon | Don Chance |
| Joe Adamo | Deborah Bauer | Steven Bouchard | Antony Chang |
| Robert Adams | Greg Bauer | Kenneth Boudreaux | Susan Chaplinsky |
| Mike Adler | Laura A. Beal | Rick Boulware | K. C. Chen |
| Cyrus Aleseyed | David Becher | Helen Bowers | Jay Choi |
| Sharif Ahkam | Bill Beedles | Oswald Bowlin | S. K. Choudhary |
| Syed Ahmad | Brian Belt | Don Boyd | Lal Chugh |
| Ed Altman | Moshe Ben-Horim | G. Michael Boyd | Peter Clarke |
| Bruce Anderson | Gary Benesh | Pat Boyer | Maclyn Clouse |
| Ron Anderson | Bill Beranek | Joe Brandt | Thomas S. Coe |
| Tom Anderson | Tom Berry | Elizabeth Brannigan | Bruce Collins |
| John Andrews | Al Berryman | Mary Broske | Mitch Conover |
| Bob Angell | Will Bertin | Christopher Brown | Margaret Considine |
| Vince Apilado | Scott Besley | David T. Brown | Phil Cooley |
| Harvey Arbalaez | Dan Best | Kate Brown | Joe Copeland |
| Kavous Ardalan | Mark S. Bettner | Larry Brown | David Cordell |
| Henry Arnold | Roger Bey | Todd A. Brown | Marsha Cornett |
| Tom Arnold | Gilbert W. Bickum | Bill Brueggeman | M. P. Corrigan |
| Bob Aubey | Dalton Bigbee | Paul Bursik | John Cotner |
| Gil Babcock | John Bildersee | Alva Butcher | Charles Cox |
| Peter Bacon | Kenneth G. Bishop | Bill Campsey | David Crary |
| Chung Baek | Laurence E. Blose | W. Thomas Carls | John Crockett Jr. |
| Bruce Bagamery | Russ Boisjoly | Bob Carlson | Julie Dahlquist |
| Kent Baker | Bob Boldin | Severin Carlson | Brent Dalrymple |
| Robert J. Balik | Keith Boles | David Cary | Bill Damon |
| Tom Bankston | Michael Bond | Steve Celec | Morris Danielson |
| Babu Baradwaj | Elizabeth Booth | Mary Chaffin | Joel Dauten |
| Les Barenbaum | Geof Booth | Rajesh Chakrabarti | Steve Dawson |

Sankar De
Fred Dellva
Jim DeMello
Chad Denson
James Desreumaux
Thomas Devaney
Bodie Dickerson
Bernard Dill
Gregg Dimkoff
Les Dlabay
Nathan Dong
Mark Dorfman
Tom Downs
Frank Draper
Anne M. Drougas
Gene Drzycimski
David A. Dubofsky
Dean Dudley
David Durst
Ed Dyl
Fred J. Ebeid
Daniel Ebels
Richard Edelman
Charles Edwards
Scott Ehrhorn
U. Elike
John Ellis
George Engler
Suzanne Erickson
Dave Ewert
John Ezzell
Olubunmi Faleye
L. Franklin Fant
John Farns
John Farris
David Feller
Richard J. Fendler
Michael Ferri
Jim Filkins
John Finnerty
Robert Fiore
Susan Fischer
Peggy Fletcher
Steven Flint
Russ Fogler
Jennifer Foo
Jennifer Frazier
Dan French
Harry Gallatin
Partha
    Gangopadhyay
John Garfinkel
Michael Garlington
David Garraty
Sharon H. Garrison
Jim Garven
Adam Gehr Jr.
Jim Gentry
Sudip Ghosh
Wafica Ghoul
Erasmo Giambona
Armand Gilinsky Jr.
Philip Glasgo

Rudyard Goode
Raymond Gorman
Walt Goulet
Bernie Grablowsky
Theoharry
    Grammatikos
Georg Grassmueck
Greg Gregoriou
Owen Gregory
Ed Grossnickle
John Groth
Alan Grunewald
Manak Gupta
Darryl Gurley
Sam Hadaway
Don Hakala
Gerald Hamsmith
Mahfuzul Haque
William Hardin
John Harris
Mary Hartman
Paul Hastings
Bob Haugen
Steve Hawke
Stevenson Hawkey
Del Hawley
Eric M. Haye
Robert Hehre
Brian Henderson
Kath Henebry
David Heskel
George Hettenhouse
Hans Heymann
Kendall Hill
Roger Hill
Tom Hindelang
Linda Hittle
Ralph Hocking
Robert P. Hoffman
J. Ronald Hoffmeister
Robert Hollinger
Jim Horrigan
John Houston
John Howe
Keith Howe
Stephen Huffman
Steve Isberg
Jim Jackson
Kevin T. Jacques
Keith Jakob
Vahan Janjigian
Narayanan
    Jayaraman
Benjamas
    Jirasakuldech
Zhenhn Jin
Kose John
Craig Johnson
Keith Johnson
Ramon Johnson
Steve Johnson
Ray Jones
Frank Jordan

Manuel Jose
Sally Joyner
Alfred Kahl
Gus Kalogeras
Rajiv Kalra
Ravi Kamath
John Kaminarides
Ashok Kapoor
Howard Keen
Michael Keenan
Bill Kennedy
Peppi M. Kenny
Carol Kiefer
Joe Kiernan
Richard Kish
Robert Kleiman
Erich Knehans
Don Knight
Ladd Kochman
Dorothy Koehl
Jaroslaw
    Komarynsky
Duncan Kretovich
Harold Krogh
Charles Kroncke
Don Kummer
Robert A. Kunkel
Reinhold Lamb
Christopher J.
    Lambert
Joan Lamm
Larry Lang
David Lange
P. Lange
Howard Lanser
Edward Lawrence
Martin Lawrence
Jerry M. Leabman
Rick LeCompte
Alice Lee
Wayne Lee
Jim LePage
Vance Lesseig
David E. LeTourneau
Denise Letterman
Jules Levine
John Lewis
Jason Lin
Chuck Linke
Yi Liu
Bill Lloyd
Susan Long
Robert L. Losey
Nancy L. Lumpkin
Yulong Ma
Fraser MacHaffie
Judy Maese
Bob Magee
Ileen Malitz
Bob Malko
Phil Malone
Abbas Mamoozadeh
Terry Maness

Chris Manning
Surendra
    Mansinghka
Timothy Manuel
Barry Marchman
Brian Maris
Terry Martell
David Martin
D. J. Masson
John Mathys
Ralph May
John McAlhany
Andy McCollough
Ambrose McCoy
Thomas McCue
Bill McDaniel
John McDowell
Charles McKinney
Robyn McLaughlin
James McNulty
Jeanette Medewitz-
    Diamond
Jamshid Mehran
Larry Merville
Rick Meyer
Jim Millar
Ed Miller
John Miller
Jill Misuraca
John Mitchell
Carol Moerdyk
Bob Moore
Scott B. Moore
Jose F. Moreno
Matthew Morey
Barry Morris
Gene Morris
Dianne R. Morrison
John K. Mullen
Chris Muscarella
David Nachman
Tim Nantell
Don Nast
Edward Nelling
Bill Nelson
Bob Nelson
Tom C. Nelson
William Nelson
Duong Nguyen
Bob Niendorf
Bruce Niendorf
Ben Nonnally Jr.
Tom O'Brien
William O'Connell
Dennis O'Connor
John O'Donnell
Jim Olsen
Robert Olsen
Dean Olson
Napoleon Overton
R. Daniel Pace
Darshana Palkar
Jim Pappas

Stephen Parrish
Helen Pawlowski
Barron Peake
Michael Pescow
Glenn Petry
Jim Pettijohn
Rich Pettit
Dick Pettway
Aaron Phillips
Hugo Phillips
Michael Phillips
H. R. Pickett
John Pinkerton
Gerald Pogue
Eugene Poindexter
R. Potter
Franklin Potts
R. Powell
Dianna Preece
Chris Prestopino
John Primus
Jerry Prock
Howard Puckett
Herbert Quigley
George Racette
Bob Radcliffe
David Rakowski
Narendar V. Rao
Allen Rappaport
Charles R. Rayhorn
Bill Rentz
Thomas Rhee
Ken Riener
Charles Rini
John Ritchie
Bill Rives
Pietra Rivoli
Antonio Rodriguez
James Rosenfeld
Stuart Rosenstein
E. N. Roussakis
Dexter Rowell
Saurav
    Roychoudhury

John Rozycki
Arlyn R. Rubash
Marjorie Rubash
Bob Ryan
Jim Sachlis
Abdul Sadik
Travis Sapp
Salil Sarkar
Thomas Scampini
Kevin Scanlon
Frederick Schadeler
Patricia L. Schaeff
David Schalow
Mary Jane Scheuer
David Schirm
Harold Schleef
Tom Schmidt
Oliver Schnusenberg
Robert Schwebach
Carol Schweser
John Settle
Alan Severn
James Sfiridis
Sol Shalit
Eliot H. Sherman
Frederic Shipley
Dilip Shome
Ron Shrieves
Neil Sicherman
J. B. Silvers
Sudhir Singh
Clay Singleton
Amit Sinha
Joe Sinkey
Stacy Sirmans
Greg Smersh
Jaye Smith
Patricia Smith
Patricia Matisz Smith
Dean S. Sommers
Don Sorensen
David Speairs
Michal Spivey
Ken Stanley

Kenneth Stanton
Ed Stendardi
Alan Stephens
Don Stevens
Glenn L. Stevens
Jerry Stevens
Lowell E. Stockstill
Glen Strasburg
David Suk
Katherine Sullivan
Kathie Sullivan
Timothy G. Sullivan
Philip Swensen
Bruce Swenson
Ernest Swift
Paul Swink
Eugene Swinnerton
Gary Tallman
Dular Talukdar
Dennis Tanner
T. Craig Tapley
Russ Taussig
John Teall
Richard Teweles
Ted Teweles
Madeline Thimmes
Samantha Thapa
Francis D. Thomas
Andrew Thompson
John Thompson
Thomas H.
    Thompson
Arlene Thurman
Dogan Tirtirogu
Janet Todd
Holland J. Toles
William Tozer
Emery Trahan
George Trivoli
Eric Tsai
George Tsetsekos
David Tufte
David Upton
Lloyd Valentine

Howard Van Auken
Pretorious Van den
    Dool
Pieter Vandenberg
Paul Vanderheiden
David O. Vang
JoAnn Vaughan
Jim Verbrugge
Patrick Vincent
Steve Vinson
Susan Visscher
John Wachowicz
John Walker
Joe Walker
Mike Walker
Elizabeth J. Wark
Sam Weaver
Marsha Weber
Al Webster
Shelton Weeks
Kuo-Chiang Wei
Bill Welch
Fred Weston
Richard Whiston
Jeffrey Whitworth
Norm Williams
Frank Winfrey
Tony Wingler
Ed Wolfe
Criss Woodruff
Don Woods
Yangru Wu
Robert Wyatt
Steve Wyatt
Sheng Yang
Elizabeth Yobaccio
Michael Yonan
David Zalewski
John Zietlow
Dennis Zocco
Sijing Zong
Kent Zumwalt

Special thanks are due to Shirley Love, Idaho State University, who wrote some chapter boxes relating to small-business issues; to Emery Trahan and Paul Bolster, Northeastern University, for their contributions; to Dilip Shome, Virginia Polytechnic Institute, who helped greatly with the capital structure chapter; to Dave Brown and Mike Ryngaert, University of Florida, who helped us with the bankruptcy material; to Roy Crum, Andy Naranjo, and Subu Venkataraman, who worked with us on the international materials; to Scott Below, East Carolina University, who developed the website information and references; to Laurie and Stan Eakins of East Carolina, who developed the Excel tutorial materials on the website; to Larry Wolken, Texas A&M University, who offered his hard work and advice for the development of the Lecture Presentation Software; and to Christopher Buzzard who helped us develop the Excel models, the website, and the PowerPoint presentations. Finally, we also want to acknowledge the contributions of the late Chris Barry, who wrote some of the chapter boxes in earlier editions.

Finally, the Cengage Learning staff, especially Mike Reynolds, Jana Lewis, Jessica Robbe, Scott Fidler, Adele Scholtz, Brad Sullender, and Heather Mooney, helped greatly with all phases of the book's development and production.

## Errors in the Textbook

At this point, most authors make a statement such as this: "We appreciate all the help we received from the people listed above; but any remaining errors are, of course, our own responsibility." And generally there are more than enough remaining errors! Having experienced difficulties with errors ourselves, both as students and instructors, we resolved to avoid this problem in *Concise*. As a result of our detection procedures, we are convinced that few errors remain, but primarily because we want to detect any errors that may have slipped by so that we can correct them in subsequent printings, we decided to offer a reward of $10 per error to the first person who reports it to us. For the purpose of this reward, errors are defined as misspelled words, nonrounding numerical errors, incorrect statements, and any other error that inhibits comprehension. Typesetting problems such as irregular spacing and differences of opinion regarding grammatical or punctuation conventions do not qualify for this reward. Given the ever-changing nature of the World Wide Web, changes in web addresses also do not qualify as errors, although we would like to learn about them. Finally, any qualifying error that has follow-through effects is counted as two errors only. Please report any errors to Joel Houston through e-mail at Concise@joelhouston.com or by regular mail at the address below.

## Conclusion

Finance is, in a real sense, the cornerstone of the enterprise system—good financial management is vitally important to the economic health of all firms and hence to the nation and the world. Because of its importance, finance should be widely and thoroughly understood, but this is easier said than done. The field is complex, and it undergoes constant change due to shifts in economic conditions. All of this makes finance stimulating and exciting, but challenging and sometimes perplexing. We sincerely hope that this 9th Edition of *Concise* will meet its own challenge by contributing to a better understanding of our financial system.

EUGENE F. BRIGHAM
JOEL F. HOUSTON
4723 N.W. 53rd Ave., Suite A
Gainesville, Florida 32653
Concise@joelhouston.com

November 2015

## Eugene F. Brigham  *University of Florida*

Dr. Eugene F. Brigham is Graduate Research Professor Emeritus at the University of Florida, where he has taught since 1971. Dr. Brigham received his MBA and PhD from the University of California–Berkeley and his undergraduate degree from the University of North Carolina. Prior to joining the University of Florida, Dr. Brigham held teaching positions at the University of Connecticut, the University of Wisconsin, and the University of California–Los Angeles. Dr. Brigham has served as president of the Financial Management Association and has written many journal articles on the cost of capital, capital structure, and other aspects of financial management. He has authored or co-authored 10 textbooks on managerial finance and managerial economics that are used at more than 1,000 universities in the United States and have been translated into 11 languages worldwide. He has testified as an expert witness in numerous electric, gas, and telephone rate cases at both federal and state levels. He has served as a consultant to many corporations and government agencies, including the Federal Reserve Board, the Federal Home Loan Bank Board, the U.S. Office of Telecommunications Policy, and the RAND Corporation. He spends his spare time on the golf course, enjoying time with his family and dogs, and tackling outdoor adventure activities, such as biking through Alaska.

## Joel F. Houston  *University of Florida*

Joel F. Houston is the John B. Hall Professor of Finance at the University of Florida. He received his MA and PhD from the Wharton School at the University of Pennsylvania, and his undergraduate degree from Franklin and Marshall College. Prior to his appointment at the University of Florida, Dr. Houston was an economist at the Federal Reserve Bank of Philadelphia. His research is primarily in the areas of corporate finance and financial institutions, and his work has been published in a number of top journals including the *Journal of Finance, Journal of Financial Economics, Journal of Business, Journal of Financial and Quantitative Analysis*, and *Financial Management*. Professor Houston also currently serves as an associate editor for the *Journal of Money, Credit and Banking, The Journal of Financial Services Research*, and *The Journal of Financial Economic Policy*. Since arriving at the University of Florida in 1987, he has received 20 teaching awards and has been actively involved in both undergraduate and graduate education. In addition to co-authoring leading textbooks in financial management, Dr. Houston has participated in management education programs for the PURC/World Bank Program, Southern Company, Exelon Corporation, and Volume Services America. He enjoys playing golf, working out, and spending time with his wife (Sherry), two children (Chris and Meredith), and daughter-in-law (Renae). He is an avid sports fan who follows the Florida Gators and the Pittsburgh Steelers, Pirates, and Penguins.

# Chapter 1

# An Overview of Financial Management

CHAPTER

Helen Sessions/Alamy

## Striking the Right Balance

In 1776, Adam Smith described how an "invisible hand" guides companies as they strive for profits, and that hand leads them to decisions that benefit society. Smith's insights led him to conclude that profit maximization is the right goal for a business and that the free enterprise system is best for society. But the world has changed since 1776. Firms today are much larger, they operate globally, they have thousands of employees, and they are owned by millions of stockholders. This makes us wonder if the "invisible hand" still provides reliable guidance: Should companies still try to maximize profits, or should they take a broader view and more balanced actions designed to benefit customers, employees, suppliers, and society as a whole?

Many academics and finance professionals today subscribe to the following modified version of Adam Smith's theory:

- A firm's principal financial goal should be to maximize the wealth of its stockholders, which means maximizing the value of its stock.

- Free enterprise is still the best economic system for society as a whole. Under the free enterprise framework, companies develop products and services that people want and that benefit society.

- However, some constraints are needed— firms should not be allowed to pollute the air and water, to engage in unfair employment practices, or to create monopolies that exploit consumers.

These constraints take a number of different forms. The first set of constraints is the costs that are assessed on companies if they take actions that harm society. Another set of constraints arises through the political process, where society imposes a wide range of regulations that are designed to keep companies from engaging in practices that are harmful to society. Properly imposed, these costs fairly transfer value to suffering parties and help create incentives that help prevent similar events from occurring in the future.

The recent financial crisis dramatically illustrates these points. We witnessed many Wall Street firms engaging in extremely risky activities that pushed the financial system to the brink of collapse in 2007 and 2008. Saving the financial system required a bailout of the banks and other financial companies, and that bailout imposed huge costs on taxpayers and helped push the economy into a deep recession. Apart from the huge costs imposed on society, the financial firms also paid a heavy price—a number of leading financial institutions saw a huge drop in their stock price, some failed and went out of business, and many Wall Street executives lost their jobs.

Arguably, these costs are not enough to prevent another financial crisis from occurring. Many maintain that the events surrounding the financial crisis illustrate that markets don't always work the way they should and that there is a need for stronger regulation of the financial sector. For example, in his recent books, Nobel Laureate Joseph Stiglitz makes a strong case for enhanced regulation. At the same time, others with a different political persuasion continue to express concerns about the costs of excessive regulation.

Beyond the financial crisis, there is a broader question of whether laws and regulations are enough to compel firms to act in society's interest. An increasing number of companies continue to recognize the need to maximize shareholder value, but they also see their mission as more than just making money for shareholders. Google's well-known corporate motto is "Don't Be Evil." Consistent with this mission, the company has its own in-house foundation that has made large investments in a wide range of philanthropic ventures worldwide.

Looking at another industry, Chipotle Mexican Grill has sought to balance societal and shareholder objectives. In the first paragraph of the company's letter to shareholders in its 2013 annual report, the company's co-CEOs Steve Ells and Monty Moran stated the company's mission:

> Chipotle's mission is to change the way people think about and eat fast food. At the heart of this lofty goal are two deeply held commitments. Our unique food culture results in our constant effort to find higher quality, more sustainable ingredients, along with better cooking techniques to prepare and serve the best tasting food possible. And our special people culture, which focuses on attracting and building teams of top performers empowered to achieve high standards, allows us to create an extraordinary dining experience for our customers and internally develop our future leaders to sustain our growth. Not coincidentally, these characteristics of our business are the primary drivers of our success and helped us deliver very strong results in 2013.

Later in the letter, Ells and Moran highlight the company's mission to provide "Food with Integrity"—this refers in part to their efforts to rely on organic food and sources where animals are treated respectfully. They also emphasize the high value they place on their employees and the efforts they impose to create a desirable work environment.

Over the past several years, consumers and investors alike have flocked to Chipotle. Between 2010 and 2014, the company's sales more than doubled and they now exceed $4 billion. Likewise, the company's stock price went from around $90 a share in early 2010 to above $700 a share in January 2015.

However, there have been some recent bumps in the road. Chipotle's stock price fell nearly 7% in February 2015, after the company reported weaker than expected sales growth for the fourth quarter of 2014. Some investors are also concerned that higher food prices and the company's push for quality ingredients have driven up their costs of production. So far, at least, Chipotle has been able to pass along some (but not all) of these costs to their customers in the form of higher prices.

Despite this recent setback, the company's outstanding performance during the last few years suggests that Chipotle's efforts to improve the welfare of its customers, employees, and surrounding communities has not compromised its ability to also increase shareholder value. Realistically, however, there will still be cases where companies face conflicts between their various constituencies—for example, a company may enhance shareholder value by laying off some workers, or a change in policy may improve the environment but reduce shareholder value. In these instances, managers have to balance these competing interests and different managers will clearly make different choices. At the end of the day, all companies struggle to find the right balance. Enlightened managers recognize that there is more to life than money, but it often takes money to do good things.

Sources: Kevin J. Delaney, "Google: From 'Don't Be Evil' to How to Do Good," *The Wall Street Journal*, January 18, 2008, pp. B1–B2; Joseph E. Stiglitz, *FreeFall: America, Free Markets, and the Sinking of the World Economy* (New York: W.W. Norton & Company, 2010); Joseph E. Stiglitz, *The Price of Inequality* (New York: W.W. Norton & Company, 2012); Spencer Jakab, "Ahead of the Tape: Chipotle Is an Expensive Burrito," *The Wall Street Journal* (online.wsj.com), February 2, 2015; and Chipotle Mexican Grill 2013 Annual Report and Proxy Statement (ir.chipotle.com/phoenix.zhtml?c=194775&p=irol-reportsAnnual).

# PUTTING THINGS IN PERSPECTIVE

This chapter will give you an idea of what financial management is all about. We begin the chapter by describing how finance is related to the overall business environment, by pointing out that finance prepares students for jobs in different fields of business, and by discussing the different forms of business organization. For corporations, management's goal should be to maximize shareholder wealth, which means maximizing the value of the stock. When we say "maximizing the value of the stock," we mean the "true, long-run value," which may be different from the current stock price. In the chapter, we discuss how firms must provide the right incentives for managers to focus on long-run value maximization. Good managers understand the importance of ethics, and they recognize that maximizing long-run value is consistent with being socially responsible.

When you finish this chapter, you should be able to:

- Explain the role of finance and the different types of jobs in finance.

- Identify the advantages and disadvantages of different forms of business organization.

- Explain the links between stock price, intrinsic value, and executive compensation.

- Identify the potential conflicts that arise within the firm between stockholders and managers and between stockholders and bondholders, and discuss the techniques that firms can use to mitigate these potential conflicts.

- Discuss the importance of business ethics and the consequences of unethical behavior.

## 1-1 What Is Finance?

Finance is defined by *Webster's Dictionary* as "the system that includes the circulation of money, the granting of credit, the making of investments, and the provision of banking facilities." Finance has many facets, which makes it difficult to provide one concise definition. The discussion in this section will give you an idea of what finance professionals do and what you might do if you enter the finance field after you graduate.

### 1-1A AREAS OF FINANCE

Finance as taught in universities is generally divided into three areas: (1) financial management, (2) capital markets, and (3) investments.

*Financial management*, also called corporate finance, focuses on decisions relating to how much and what types of assets to acquire, how to raise the capital needed to purchase assets, and how to run the firm so as to maximize its value. The same principles apply to both for-profit and not-for-profit organizations; and as the title suggests, much of this book is concerned with financial management.

*Capital markets* relate to the markets where interest rates, along with stock and bond prices, are determined. Also studied here are the financial institutions that supply capital to businesses. Banks, investment banks, stockbrokers, mutual funds, insurance companies, and the like bring together "savers" who have money to invest and businesses, individuals, and other entities that need capital for various purposes. Governmental organizations such as the Federal Reserve System, which regulates banks and controls the supply of money, and the Securities and Exchange Commission (SEC), which regulates the trading of stocks and bonds in public markets, are also studied as part of capital markets.

*Investments* relate to decisions concerning stocks and bonds and include a number of activities: (1) *Security analysis* deals with finding the proper values of individual securities (i.e., stocks and bonds). (2) *Portfolio theory* deals with the best way to structure portfolios, or "baskets," of stocks and bonds. Rational investors want to hold diversified portfolios in order to limit risks, so choosing a properly balanced portfolio is an important issue for any investor. (3) *Market analysis* deals with the issue of whether stock and bond markets at any given time are "too high," "too low," or "about right." Included in market analysis is *behavioral finance,* where investor psychology is examined in an effort to determine whether stock prices have been bid up to unreasonable heights in a speculative bubble or driven down to unreasonable lows in a fit of irrational pessimism.

Although we separate these three areas, they are closely interconnected. Banking is studied under capital markets, but a bank lending officer evaluating a business' loan request must understand corporate finance to make a sound decision. Similarly, a corporate treasurer negotiating with a banker must understand banking if the treasurer is to borrow on "reasonable" terms. Moreover, a security analyst trying to determine a stock's true value must understand corporate finance and capital markets to do his or her job. In addition, financial decisions of all types depend on the level of interest rates; so all people in corporate finance, investments, and banking must know something about interest rates and the way they are determined. Because of these interdependencies, we cover all three areas in this book.

## 1-1B FINANCE WITHIN AN ORGANIZATION

Most businesses and not-for-profit organizations have an organization chart similar to the one shown in Figure 1.1. The board of directors is the top governing body, and the chairperson of the board is generally the highest-ranking individual. The CEO comes next, but note that the chairperson of the board often also serves as the CEO. Below the CEO comes the chief operating officer (COO), who is often also designated as a firm's president. The COO directs the firm's operations, which include marketing, manufacturing, sales, and other operating departments. The chief financial officer (CFO), who is generally a senior vice president and the third-ranking officer, is in charge of accounting, finance, credit policy, decisions regarding asset acquisitions, and investor relations, which involves communications with stockholders and the press.

If the firm is publicly owned, the CEO and the CFO must both certify to the SEC that reports released to stockholders, and especially the annual report, are accurate. If inaccuracies later emerge, the CEO and the CFO could be fined or even jailed. This requirement was instituted in 2002 as a part of the **Sarbanes-Oxley Act**. The Act was passed by Congress in the wake of a series of corporate scandals involving now-defunct companies such as Enron and WorldCom, where investors, workers, and suppliers lost billions of dollars due to false information released by those companies.

## 1-1C FINANCE VERSUS ECONOMICS AND ACCOUNTING

Finance, as we know it today, grew out of economics and accounting. Economists developed the notion that an asset's value is based on the future cash flows the asset will provide, and accountants provided information regarding the likely size of those cash flows. People who work in finance need knowledge of both economics and accounting. Figure 1.1 illustrates that in the modern corporation, the accounting

*The duties of the CFO have broadened over the years. CFO magazine's online service,* **cfo.com***, is an excellent source of timely finance articles intended to help the CFO manage those new responsibilities.*

**Sarbanes-Oxley Act**
A law passed by Congress that requires the CEO and CFO to certify that their firm's financial statements are accurate.

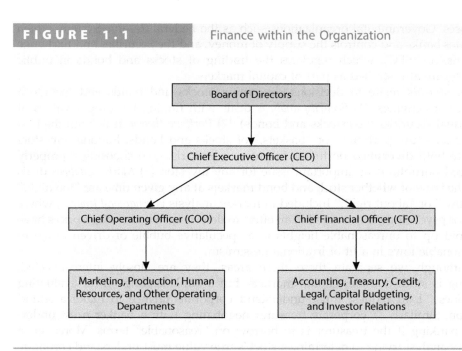

**FIGURE 1.1** — Finance within the Organization

department typically falls under the control of the CFO. This further illustrates the link among finance, economics, and accounting.

## SelfTest

What three areas of finance does this book cover? Are these areas independent of one another, or are they interrelated in the sense that someone working in one area should know something about each of the other areas? Explain.

Who is the CFO, and where does this individual fit into the corporate hierarchy? What are some of his or her responsibilities?

Does it make sense for not-for-profit organizations such as hospitals and universities to have CFOs? Why or why not?

What is the relationship among economics, finance, and accounting?

## 1-2 Jobs in Finance

To find information about different finance careers, go to **allbusinessschools.com/ business-careers/finance/ job-description**. This website provides information about different finance areas.

Finance prepares students for jobs in banking, investments, insurance, corporations, and government. Accounting students need to know marketing, management, and human resources; they also need to understand finance, for it affects decisions in all those areas. For example, marketing people propose advertising programs, but those programs are examined by finance people to judge the effects of the advertising on the firm's profitability. So to be effective in marketing, one needs to have a basic knowledge of finance. The same holds for management—indeed, most important management decisions are evaluated in terms of their effects on the firm's value.

It is also worth noting that finance is important to individuals regardless of their jobs. Some years ago most employees received pensions from their employers upon retirement, so managing one's personal investments was not critically important. That's no longer true. Most firms today provide "defined contribution" pension plans, where each year the company puts a specified amount of money into an account that belongs to the employee. The employee must decide how those funds are to be invested—how much should be divided among stocks, bonds, or money funds—and how much risk they're willing to take with their stock and bond investments. These decisions have a major effect on people's lives, and the concepts covered in this book can improve decision-making skills.

# 1-3 Forms of Business Organization

The basics of financial management are the same for all businesses, large or small, regardless of how they are organized. Still, a firm's legal structure affects its operations and thus should be recognized. There are four main forms of business organizations: (1) proprietorships, (2) partnerships, (3) corporations, and (4) limited liability companies (LLCs) and limited liability partnerships (LLPs). In terms of numbers, most businesses are proprietorships. However, based on the dollar value of sales, more than 80% of all business is done by corporations.[1] Because corporations conduct the most business and because most successful businesses eventually convert to corporations, we focus on them in this book. Still, it is important to understand the legal differences between types of firms.

A **proprietorship** is an unincorporated business owned by one individual. Going into business as a sole proprietor is easy—a person begins business operations. Proprietorships have three important advantages: (1) They are easy and inexpensive to form. (2) They are subject to few government regulations. (3) They are subject to lower income taxes than are corporations. However, proprietorships also have three important limitations: (1) Proprietors have unlimited personal liability for the business' debts, so they can lose more than the amount of money they invested in the company. You might invest $10,000 to start a business but be sued for $1 million if, during company time, one of your employees runs over someone with a car. (2) The life of the business is limited to the life of the individual who created it; and to bring in new equity, investors require a change in the structure of the business. (3) Because of the first two points, proprietorships have difficulty obtaining large sums of capital; hence, proprietorships are used primarily for small businesses. However, businesses are frequently started as proprietorships and then converted to corporations when their growth results in the disadvantages outweighing the advantages.

A **partnership** is a legal arrangement between two or more people who decide to do business together. Partnerships are similar to proprietorships in that they can be established relatively easily and inexpensively. Moreover, the firm's income is allocated on a pro rata basis to the partners and is taxed on an individual basis. This allows the firm to avoid the corporate income tax. However, all of the partners are generally subject to unlimited personal liability, which means that if a partnership goes bankrupt and any partner is unable to meet his or her pro rata share of the firm's liabilities, the remaining partners will be responsible for making good on the unsatisfied claims. Thus, the actions of a Texas partner can bring ruin to a millionaire New York partner who had nothing to do with the actions that led to the downfall of the company. Unlimited liability makes it difficult for partnerships to raise large amounts of capital.[2]

**Proprietorship**
An unincorporated business owned by one individual.

**Partnership**
An unincorporated business owned by two or more persons.

---

[1]Refer to *ProQuest Statistical Abstract of the United States: 2015*, Table 762: Number of Tax Returns, Receipts, and Net Income by Type of Business: 1990 to 2011, p. 515.

[2]Originally, there were just straightforward partnerships; but over the years, lawyers have created a number of variations. We leave the variations to courses on business law, but we note that the variations are generally designed to limit the liabilities of some of the partners. For example, a *limited partnership* has a general partner, who has unlimited liability, and one or more limited partners, whose liability is limited to the amount of their investment. This sounds great from the standpoint of limited liability; but the limited partners must cede sole control to the general partner, which means that they have almost no say in the way the firm is managed. With a corporation, the owners (stockholders) have limited liability, but they also have the right to vote and thus change management if they think that a change is in order. Note too that LLCs and LLPs, discussed later in this section, are increasingly used in lieu of partnerships.

**Corporation**
A legal entity created by a state, separate and distinct from its owners and managers, having unlimited life, easy transferability of ownership, and limited liability.

**S Corporations**
A special designation that allows small businesses that meet qualifications to be taxed as if they were a proprietorship or a partnership rather than a corporation.

**Limited Liability Company (LLC)**
A popular type of organization that is a hybrid between a partnership and a corporation.

**Limited Liability Partnership (LLP)**
Similar to an LLC but used for professional firms in the fields of accounting, law, and architecture. It provides personal asset protection from business debts and liabilities but is taxed as a partnership.

A **corporation** is a legal entity created by a state, and it is separate and distinct from its owners and managers. It is this separation that limits stockholders' losses to the amount they invested in the firm—the corporation can lose all of its money, but its owners can lose only the funds that they invested in the company. Corporations also have unlimited lives, and it is easier to transfer shares of stock in a corporation than one's interest in an unincorporated business. These factors make it much easier for corporations to raise the capital necessary to operate large businesses. Thus, companies such as Hewlett-Packard and Microsoft generally begin as proprietorships or partnerships, but at some point they find it advantageous to become a corporation.

A major drawback to corporations is taxes. Most corporations' earnings are subject to double taxation—the corporation's earnings are taxed; and then when its after-tax earnings are paid out as dividends, those earnings are taxed again as personal income to the stockholders. However, as an aid to small businesses, Congress created **S corporations**, which are taxed as if they were proprietorships or partnerships; thus, they are exempt from the corporate income tax. To qualify for S corporation status, a firm can have no more than 100 stockholders, which limits their use to relatively small, privately owned firms. Larger corporations are known as *C corporations*. The vast majority of small corporations elect S status and retain that status until they decide to sell stock to the public, at which time they become C corporations.

A **limited liability company (LLC)** is a popular type of organization that is a hybrid between a partnership and a corporation. A **limited liability partnership (LLP)** is similar to an LLC. LLPs are used for professional firms in the fields of accounting, law, and architecture, while LLCs are used by other businesses. Similar to corporations, LLCs and LLPs provide limited liability protection, but they are taxed as partnerships. Further, unlike limited partnerships, where the general partner has full control of the business, the investors in an LLC or LLP have votes in proportion to their ownership interest. LLCs and LLPs have been gaining in popularity in recent years, but large companies still find it advantageous to be C corporations because of the advantages in raising capital to support growth. LLCs/LLPs were dreamed up by lawyers; they are often structured in very complicated ways, and their legal protections often vary by state. So, it is necessary to hire a good lawyer when establishing one.

When deciding on its form of organization, a firm must trade off the advantages of incorporation against a possibly higher tax burden. However, for the following reasons, the value of any business other than a relatively small one will probably be maximized if it is organized as a corporation:

1. Limited liability reduces the risks borne by investors; and other things held constant, the lower the firm's risk, the higher its value.
2. A firm's value is dependent on its growth opportunities, which are dependent on its ability to attract capital. Because corporations can attract capital more easily than other types of businesses, they are better able to take advantage of growth opportunities.
3. The value of an asset also depends on its liquidity, which means the time and effort it takes to sell the asset for cash at a fair market value. Because the stock of a corporation is easier to transfer to a potential buyer than is an interest in a proprietorship or partnership, and because more investors are willing to invest in stocks than in partnerships (with their potential unlimited liability), a corporate investment is relatively liquid. This too enhances the value of a corporation.

## SelfTest

What are the key differences among proprietorships, partnerships, and corporations?

How are LLCs and LLPs related to the other forms of organization?

What is an S corporation, and what is its advantage over a C corporation? Why don't firms such as IBM, GE, and Microsoft choose S corporation status?

What are some reasons why the value of a business other than a small one is generally maximized when it is organized as a corporation?

Suppose you are relatively wealthy and are looking for a potential investment. You do not plan to be active in the business. Would you be more interested in investing in a partnership or in a corporation? Why?

# 1-4 The Main Financial Goal: Creating Value for Investors

In public corporations, managers and employees work on behalf of the shareholders who own the business, and therefore they have an obligation to pursue policies that promote stockholder value. While many companies focus on maximizing a broad range of financial objectives, such as growth, earnings per share, and market share, these goals should not take precedence over the main financial goal, which is to create value for investors. Keep in mind that a company's stockholders are not just an abstract group—they represent individuals and organizations who have chosen to invest their hard-earned cash into the company and who are looking for a return on their investment in order to meet their long-term financial goals, which might be saving for retirement, a new home, or a child's education.

If a manager is to maximize stockholder wealth, he or she must know how that wealth is determined. Throughout this book, we shall see that the value of any asset is the present value of the stream of cash flows that the asset provides to its owners over time. We discuss stock valuation in depth in Chapter 9, where we see that stock prices are based on cash flows expected in future years, not just in the current year. Thus, stock price maximization requires us to take a long-run view of operations. At the same time, managerial actions that affect a company's value may not immediately be reflected in the company's stock price.

## 1-4A DETERMINANTS OF VALUE

Figure 1.2 illustrates the situation. The top box indicates that managerial actions, combined with the economy, taxes, and political conditions, influence the level and riskiness of the company's future cash flows, which ultimately determine the company's stock price. As you might expect, investors like higher expected cash flows, but they dislike risk; so the larger the expected cash flows and the lower the perceived risk, the higher the stock's price.

The second row of boxes differentiates what we call "true" expected cash flows and "true" risk from "perceived" cash flows and "perceived" risk. By "true," we mean the cash flows and risk that investors would expect if they had all of the information that existed about a company. "Perceived" means what investors expect, given the limited information they have. To illustrate, in early 2001, investors had information that caused them to think Enron was highly profitable and would enjoy high and rising future profits. They also thought that actual results would be close to

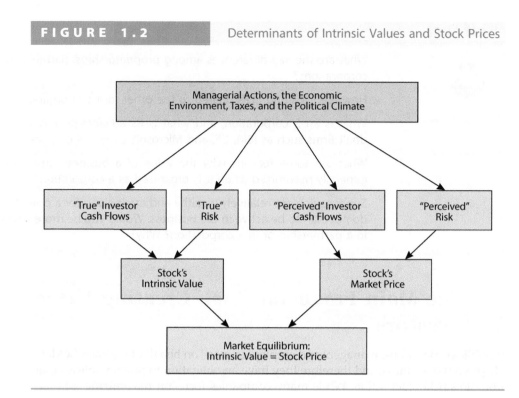

**FIGURE 1.2**   Determinants of Intrinsic Values and Stock Prices

### Intrinsic Value

An estimate of a stock's "true" value based on accurate risk and return data. The intrinsic value can be estimated, but not measured precisely.

### Market Price

The stock value based on perceived but possibly incorrect information as seen by the marginal investor.

### Marginal Investor

An investor whose views determine the actual stock price.

### Equilibrium

The situation in which the actual market price equals the intrinsic value, so investors are indifferent between buying and selling a stock.

the expected levels and hence that Enron's risk was low. However, true estimates of Enron's profits, which were known by its executives, but not the investing public, were much lower; and Enron's true situation was extremely risky.

The third row of boxes shows that each stock has an **intrinsic value**, which is an estimate of the stock's "true" value as calculated by a competent analyst who has the best available data, and a **market price**, which is the actual market price based on perceived but possibly incorrect information as seen by the **marginal investor**.[3] Not all investors agree, so it is the "marginal" investor who determines the actual price.

When a stock's actual market price is equal to its intrinsic value, the stock is in **equilibrium**, which is shown in the bottom box in Figure 1.2. When equilibrium exists, there is no pressure for a change in the stock's price. Market prices can—and do—differ from intrinsic values; but eventually, as the future unfolds, the two values tend to converge.

## 1-4B INTRINSIC VALUE

Actual stock prices are easy to determine—they can be found on the Internet and are published in newspapers every day. However, intrinsic values are estimates; and different analysts with different data and different views about the future form different estimates of a stock's intrinsic value. *Indeed, estimating intrinsic values is what security analysis is all about and is what distinguishes successful from unsuccessful investors.* Investing would be easy, profitable, and essentially riskless if we knew all stocks' intrinsic values; but, of course, we don't. We can estimate intrinsic values, but

---

[3]Investors at the margin are the ones who actually set stock prices. Some stockholders think that a stock at its current price is a good deal, and they would buy more if they had more money. Others think that the stock is priced too high, so they would not buy it unless the price dropped sharply. Still others think that the current stock price is about where it should be; so they would buy more if the price fell slightly, sell it if the price rose slightly, and maintain their current holdings unless something were to change. These are the marginal investors, and it is their view that determines the current stock price. We discuss this point in more depth in Chapter 9, where we discuss the stock market in detail.

**FIGURE 1.3**   Graph of Actual Prices versus Intrinsic Values

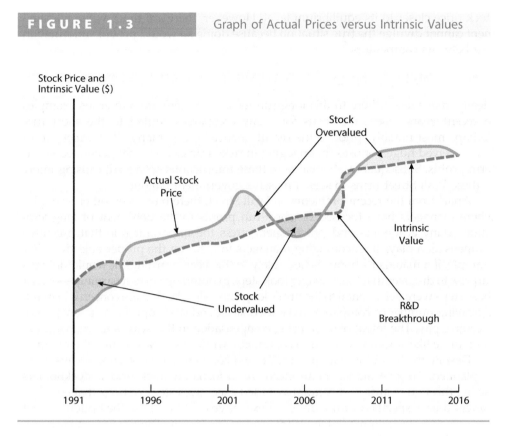

we can't be sure that we are right. A firm's managers have the best information about the firm's future prospects, so managers' estimates of intrinsic values are generally better than those of outside investors. However, even managers can be wrong.

Figure 1.3 graphs a hypothetical company's actual price and intrinsic value as estimated by its management over time.[4] The intrinsic value rises because the firm retains and reinvests earnings each year, which tends to increase profits. The value jumped dramatically in 2010, when a research and development (R&D) breakthrough raised management's estimate of future profits before investors had this information. The actual stock price tended to move up and down with the estimated intrinsic value; but investor optimism and pessimism, along with imperfect knowledge about the true intrinsic value, led to deviations between the actual prices and intrinsic values.

Intrinsic value is a long-run concept. *Management's goal should be to take actions designed to maximize the firm's intrinsic value, not its current market price.* Note, though, that maximizing the intrinsic value will maximize the *average* price over the long run, but not necessarily the current price at each point in time. For example, management might make an investment that lowers profits for the current year but raises expected future profits. If investors are not aware of the true situation, the stock price will be held down by the low current profit even though the intrinsic value was actually raised. Management should provide information that helps investors make better estimates of the firm's intrinsic value, which will keep the

---

[4]We emphasize that the intrinsic value is an estimate and that different analysts have different estimates for a company at any given time. Managers should also estimate their firm's intrinsic value and then take actions to maximize that value. They should try to help outside security analysts improve their intrinsic value estimates by providing accurate information about the company's financial position and operations, but without releasing information that would help its competitors.

stock price closer to its equilibrium level. However, there are times when management cannot divulge the true situation because doing so would provide information that helps its competitors.[5]

## 1-4C CONSEQUENCES OF HAVING A SHORT-RUN FOCUS

Ideally, managers adhere to this long-run focus, but there are numerous examples in recent years where the focus for many companies shifted to the short run. Perhaps most notably, prior to the recent financial crisis, many Wall Street executives received huge bonuses for engaging in risky transactions that generated short-term profits. Subsequently, the value of these transactions collapsed, causing many of these Wall Street firms to seek a massive government bailout.

Apart from the recent problems on Wall Street, there have been other examples where managers have focused on short-run profits to the detriment of long-term value. Many academics and practitioners stress the important role that executive compensation plays in encouraging managers to focus on the proper objectives. For example, if a manager's bonus is tied solely to this year's earnings, it would not be a surprise to discover that the manager took steps to pump up current earnings—even if those steps were detrimental to the firm's long-run value. With these concerns in mind, a growing number of companies have used stock and stock options as a key part of executive pay. The intent of structuring compensation in this way is for managers to think more like stockholders and to continually work to increase shareholder value.

Despite the best of intentions, stock-based compensation does not always work as planned. To give managers an incentive to focus on stock prices, stockholders (acting through boards of directors) awarded executives stock options that could be exercised on a specified future date. An executive could exercise the option on that date, receive stock, immediately sell it, and earn a profit. The profit was based on the stock price on the option exercise date, which led some managers to try to maximize the stock price on that specific date, not over the long run. That, in turn, led to some horrible abuses. Projects that looked good from a long-run perspective were turned down because they would penalize profits in the short run and thus lower the stock price on the option exercise day. Even worse, some managers deliberately overstated profits, temporarily boosted the stock price, exercised their options, sold the inflated stock, and left outside stockholders "holding the bag" when the true situation was revealed.

## SelfTest

What's the difference between a stock's current market price and its intrinsic value?

Do stocks have known and "provable" intrinsic values, or might different people reach different conclusions about intrinsic values? Explain.

Should managers estimate intrinsic values or leave that to outside security analysts? Explain.

If a firm could maximize either its current market price or its intrinsic value, what would stockholders (as a group) want managers to do? Explain.

Should a firm's managers help investors improve their estimates of the firm's intrinsic value? Explain.

---

[5]As we discuss in Chapter 2, many academics believe that stock prices embody all publicly available information—hence, that stock prices are typically reasonably close to their intrinsic values and thus at or close to equilibrium. However, almost no one doubts that managers have better information than the public at large, that at times stock prices and equilibrium values diverge, and thus that stocks can be temporarily undervalued or overvalued (as we suggest in Figure 1.3).

# 1-5 Stockholder–Manager Conflicts[6]

It has long been recognized that managers' personal goals may compete with shareholder wealth maximization. In particular, managers might be more interested in maximizing their own wealth than their stockholders' wealth; therefore, managers might pay themselves excessive salaries.

Effective executive compensation plans motivate managers to act in their stockholders' best interests. Useful motivational tools include (1) reasonable compensation packages, (2) firing of managers who don't perform well, and (3) the threat of hostile takeovers.

## 1-5A COMPENSATION PACKAGES

*Compensation packages* should be sufficient to attract and retain able managers, but they should not go beyond what is needed. Compensation policies need to be consistent over time. Also, compensation should be structured so that managers are rewarded on the basis of the stock's performance over the long run, not the stock's price on an option exercise date. This means that options (or direct stock awards) should be phased in over a number of years so that managers have an incentive to keep the stock price high over time. When the intrinsic value can be measured in an objective and verifiable manner, performance pay can be based on changes in intrinsic value. However, because intrinsic value is not observable, compensation must be based on the stock's market price—but the price used should be an average over time rather than on a specific date.

## 1-5B DIRECT STOCKHOLDER INTERVENTION

Years ago most stock was owned by individuals. Today, however, the majority of stock is owned by institutional investors such as insurance companies, pension funds, hedge funds, and mutual funds; and private equity groups are ready and able to step in and take over underperforming firms. These institutional money managers have the clout to exercise considerable influence over firms' operations. Given their importance, they have access to managers and can make suggestions about how the business should be run. In effect, institutional investors such as CalPERS (California Public Employees' Retirement System, with $300 billion of assets) and TIAA-CREF (Teachers Insurance and Annuity Association-College Retirement Equities Fund, a retirement plan originally set up for professors at private colleges that now has more than $600 billion of assets) act as lobbyists for the body of stockholders. When such large stockholders speak, companies listen. For example, Coca-Cola Co. revised its compensation package after hearing negative feedback from its largest stockholder, Warren Buffett.[7] Indeed, in 2015, Oracle Corp. is also facing pressure regarding executive compensation.

At the same time, any shareholder who has owned $2,000 of a company's stock for one year can sponsor a proposal that may be voted on at the annual stockholders' meeting, even if management opposes the proposal.[8] Although shareholder-sponsored proposals are nonbinding, the results of such votes are heard by top management.

---

[6]Conflicts between stockholders and managers, which are discussed in this section, and conflicts between stockholders and debtholders, which are discussed in the next section, are studied under the heading of "agency theory" in finance literature. The classic work on agency theory is Michael C. Jensen and William H. Meckling, "Theory of the Firm, Managerial Behavior, Agency Costs, and Ownership Structure," *Journal of Financial Economics*, vol. 3, no. 4 (October 1976), pp. 305–360.

[7]Anupreeta Das, Mike Esterl, and Joann S. Lublin, "Buffett Pressures Coca-Cola over Executive Pay," *The Wall Street Journal* (online.wsj.com), April 30, 2014; and Mark Melin, "Coca-Cola Changes Pay Plan, Warren Buffett Influence Credited," *ValueWalk* (www.valuewalk.com), October 1, 2014.

[8]Under current guidelines, shareholder proposals are restricted to governance issues, and shareholders are not allowed to vote directly on items that are considered to be "operating issues." However, the SEC recently adopted rules (resulting from the passage of the Dodd-Frank Act) mandating an advisory vote on CEO compensation at least once every three years.

# ARE CEOs OVERPAID?

In a 2014 survey of 300 large U.S. corporations, the Hay Group found that the median CEO received $13.6 million in total compensation (which includes salaries, bonuses, and long-term incentives such as stock options). Compared to 2013, total CEO compensation increased 13.5% during a year when corporate profits rose 4.5% and the median shareholder return was 16.6%. On the other hand, the average worker's pay raise was only 2.2%.

Arguably, media scrutiny and investor concerns about excessive compensation have led some companies to limit the compensation paid to their top executives. A further concern are the recent "Say on Pay" provisions in the 2010 Dodd-Frank Act, which give shareholders an ability to vote on whether they approve of the CEO's compensation package. While these votes are nonbinding, they have put pressure on firms who want to avoid the negative publicity surrounding a shareholder vote to reject the pay plan. As a result of these provisions, a substantial part of a CEO's pay is now tied to performance.

Many top CEOs still received extraordinarily high levels of total compensation. The top five highest paid CEOs were: Liberty Global's Michael T. Fries ($112.2 million), Microsoft's Satya Nadella ($84.3 million), Oracle's Larry Ellison ($67.3 million), Qualcomm's Steven Mollenkopf ($60.7 million), and CBS's Leslie Moonves ($57.2 million). At the same time, many CEOs who have received stock options in previous years have seen the value of these options increase dramatically because of the recent run-up in the stock market.

Looking at a longer time frame, average compensation levels are significantly higher than they were a decade ago. The large shifts in CEO compensation over time can often be attributed to the increased importance of stock options. Relatedly, over the past few years, a small number of CEOs have attracted attention by announcing that they are only going to accept a $1 cash salary. A recent study finds that shareholders of these firms don't do particularly well, but the CEOs' total compensation doesn't suffer since they instead receive offsetting compensation in the form of stock and stock options. The study concludes that the primary reason that these managers announce their $1 salary is to "employ camouflage in compensation schemes to avoid public outrage over excessive private benefits."[9] On the plus side, stock options provide CEOs with a powerful incentive to raise their companies' stock prices. Indeed, most observers believe there is a strong causal relationship between CEO compensation procedures and stock price performance.

Other critics argue that although performance incentives are entirely appropriate as a method of compensation, the overall level of CEO compensation is just too high. The critics ask such questions as these: Would these CEOs have been unwilling to take their jobs if they had been offered only half as many stock options? Would they have put forth less effort, and would their firms' stock prices have not increased as much? It is hard to say. Other critics lament that the exercise of stock options has dramatically increased the compensation of not only truly excellent CEOs, but it has also dramatically increased the compensation of some pretty average CEOs, who were lucky enough to have had the job during a stock market boom that raised the stock prices of even poor-performing companies. In addition, huge CEO salaries are widening the gap between top executives and middle management salaries leading to employee discontent and declining employee morale and loyalty.

As the current survey indicates, the shift to better align CEO pay with corporate performance is modest. Stock returns and corporate financial results are only two factors impacting CEO pay. The correlation between executive compensation and firm performance is not always strong. Other factors that influence CEO pay are the size of the firm (larger companies pay their CEOs more) and the type of industry (energy companies pay their CEOs more).

Sources: Louis Lavelle, Frederick F. Jespersen, and Michael Arndt, "Executive Pay," *BusinessWeek*, April 15, 2002, pp. 80–86; Jason Zweig, "A Chance to Veto a CEO's Bonus," *The Wall Street Journal* (online.wsj.com), January 29, 2011; Emily Chasan, "Early Say-On-Pay Results Show Rising Support, Few Failures," *The Wall Street Journal* (online.wsj.com), April 2, 2014; Joann S. Lublin, "How Much the Best-Performing and Worst-Performing CEOs Got Paid," *The Wall Street Journal* (online.wsj.com), June 24, 2015; and Chris Canipe and Sarah Slobin, "CEO Pay vs. Performance," *The Wall Street Journal* (online.wsj.com), June 24, 2015.

There has been an ongoing debate regarding how much influence shareholders should have through the proxy process. As a result of the passage of the Dodd-Frank Act, the SEC was given authority to make rules regarding shareholder access

---

[9]Gilberto R. Loureiro, Anil K. Makhija, and Dan Zhang, "The Ruse of a One-Dollar CEO Salary," Charles A. Dice Center Working Paper No. 2011-7 and Fisher College of Business Working Paper No. 2011-03-007, January 10, 2014. The paper is available at http://ssrn.com/abstract=1571823.

children to college, pay for a long-anticipated trip, and so forth. The shareholders elected a board of directors, which then selected Smith to run the company. Smith and the firm's other managers are working on behalf of the shareholders, and they were hired to pursue policies that enhance shareholder value.

Most managers understand that maximizing shareholder value does not mean that they are free to ignore the larger interests of society. Consider, for example, what would happen if Linda Smith narrowly focused on creating shareholder value, but in the process her company was unresponsive to its employees and customers, hostile to its local community, and indifferent to the effects its actions had on the environment. In all likelihood, society would impose a wide range of costs on the company. It may find it hard to attract top-notch employees, its products may be boycotted, it may face additional lawsuits and regulations, and it may be confronted with negative publicity. These costs would ultimately lead to a reduction in shareholder value. So clearly, when taking steps to maximize shareholder value, enlightened managers need to also keep in mind these society-imposed constraints.[13]

From a broader perspective, firms have a number of different departments, including marketing, accounting, production, human resources, and finance. The finance department's principal task is to evaluate proposed decisions and judge how they will affect the stock price and thus shareholder wealth. For example, suppose the production manager wants to replace some old equipment with new automated machinery that will reduce labor costs. The finance staff will evaluate that proposal and determine whether the savings seem to be worth the cost. Similarly, if marketing wants to spend $10 million advertising during the Super Bowl, the financial staff will evaluate the proposal, look at the probable increase in sales, and reach a conclusion as to whether the money spent will lead to a higher stock price. Most significant decisions are evaluated in terms of their financial consequences, but astute managers recognize that they also need to take into account how these decisions affect society at large.

Interestingly, some companies have taken more explicit steps to recognize the broader needs of society. A fairly small but rapidly growing number of companies have become certified as "B" or "benefit" corporations. While these companies are still focused on making a profit, they are committed to putting other stakeholders such as employees, customers, and their communities on an equal footing with shareholders. In order to qualify as a B corporation, the company must subject itself to an annual audit in which its practices regarding social responsibility, corporate governance, and transparency are reviewed. A recent *Time* magazine article points out that 26 states now provide a legal framework for companies to be certified as a B corporation. The article also estimates that roughly 1,200 companies (mostly small) companies have qualified as B corporations.[14]

As you might imagine, there is a very wide range of opinions regarding the appropriate balance between the interests of shareholders and other societal stakeholders. For example, a mutual fund manager attracted a lot of attention when he characterized shareholder wealth maximization as the "world's dumbest idea." Later on, a high-profile columnist for *The Wall Street Journal* offered a strong criticism of this viewpoint, and laid out his argument for why maximizing shareholder value is the appropriate goal.[15] While these arguments will no doubt

---

[13]A recent study highlights the various factors that motivate corporate managers to make socially responsible investments. Refer to Richard Borghesi, Joel F. Houston, and Andy Naranjo, "Corporate Socially Responsible Investments: CEO Altruism, Reputation, and Shareholder Interests," *Journal of Corporate Finance*, vol. 26 (June 2014), pp. 164–181.

[14]Refer to Bill Saporito, "Making Good, Plus a Profit: A New Type of Company Lures Activist Entrepreneurs," *Time*, March 23, 2015, p. 22.

[15]Refer to Holman W. Jenkins, Jr., "Are Shareholders Obsolete?" *The Wall Street Journal* (online.wsj.com), January 2, 2015.

continue, there is a broader consensus that emphasizes that maximizing shareholder value doesn't mean that corporate managers should ignore other societal interests. Indeed, our discussion in this chapter is meant to illustrate that companies striving to increase shareholder value have to be ever mindful of these broader interests.

## Self*Test*

Is maximizing shareholder value inconsistent with being socially responsible? Explain.

When Boeing decides to invest $5 billion in a new jet airliner, are its managers certain of the project's effects on Boeing's future profits and stock price? Explain.

# 1-8 Business Ethics

As a result of the financial scandals occurring during the past decade, there has been a strong push to improve *business ethics*. This is occurring on many fronts—actions begun by former New York Attorney General and former Governor Elliot Spitzer and others who sued companies for improper acts; Congress's passing of the Sarbanes-Oxley Act of 2002 to impose sanctions on executives who sign financial statements later found to be false; Congress's passing of the Dodd-Frank Act to implement an aggressive overhaul of the U.S. financial regulatory system aimed at preventing reckless actions that would cause another financial crisis; and business schools trying to inform students about proper versus improper business actions.

As noted earlier, companies benefit from having good reputations and are penalized by having bad ones; the same is true for individuals. Reputations reflect the extent to which firms and people are ethical. *Ethics* is defined in *Webster's Dictionary* as "standards of conduct or moral behavior." Business ethics can be thought of as a company's attitude and conduct toward its employees, customers, community, and stockholders. A firm's commitment to business ethics can be measured by the tendency of its employees, from the top down, to adhere to laws, regulations, and moral standards relating to product safety and quality, fair employment practices, fair marketing and selling practices, the use of confidential information for personal gain, community involvement, and the use of illegal payments to obtain business.

## 1-8A WHAT COMPANIES ARE DOING

Most firms today have strong written codes of ethical behavior; companies also conduct training programs to ensure that employees understand proper behavior in different situations. When conflicts arise involving profits and ethics, ethical considerations sometimes are so obviously important that they dominate. In other cases, however, the right choice is not clear. For example, suppose that Norfolk Southern's managers know that its coal trains are polluting the air; but the amount of pollution is within legal limits, and further reduction would be costly. Are the managers ethically bound to reduce pollution? Similarly, several years ago Merck's research indicated that its Vioxx pain medicine might be causing heart attacks. However, the evidence was not overly strong, and the product was clearly helping some patients. Over time, additional tests produced stronger evidence that Vioxx did pose a health risk. What should Merck have done, and when should Merck have done it? If the company released negative but perhaps incorrect information, this announcement would have hurt sales and possibly prevented some patients benefitting from the product. If the company delayed the release of this additional information, more patients might have suffered irreversible harm. At what point should Merck have made the potential problem known to the public? There are no obvious answers to questions such as these; but companies must deal with them, and a failure to handle them properly can lead to severe consequences.

## 1-8B CONSEQUENCES OF UNETHICAL BEHAVIOR

Over the past few years, ethical lapses have led to a number of bankruptcies. The collapses of Enron and WorldCom as well as the accounting firm Arthur Andersen dramatically illustrate how unethical behavior can lead to a firm's rapid decline. In all three cases, top executives came under fire because of misleading accounting practices that led to overstated profits. Enron and WorldCom executives were busily selling their stock at the same time they were recommending the stock to employees and outside investors. These executives reaped millions before the stock declined, while lower-level employees and outside investors were left "holding the bag." Some of these executives are now in jail, and Enron's CEO had a fatal heart attack while awaiting sentencing after being found guilty of conspiracy and fraud. Moreover, Merrill Lynch and Citigroup, which were accused of facilitating these frauds, were fined hundreds of millions of dollars.

In other cases, companies avoid bankruptcy but face a damaging blow to their reputation. Safety concerns tarnished Toyota's once-sterling reputation for reliability. Ethical questions were raised regarding when the company's senior management became aware of the problems and whether they were forthcoming in sharing these concerns with the public. Similarly, GM executives are currently under fire for their delay in addressing defective ignition switches, which have been connected to 57 deaths and the recall of 2.6 million vehicles.

In April 2010, the SEC brought forth a civil fraud suit against Goldman Sachs. The SEC contended that Goldman Sachs misled its investors when it created and marketed securities that were backed by subprime mortgages. In July 2010, Goldman Sachs ultimately reached a settlement where it agreed to pay $550 million. While just one example, many believe that too many Wall Street executives in recent years have been willing to compromise their ethics. In May 2011, Raj Rajaratnam, the founder of the hedge fund Galleon Group LLC, was convicted of securities fraud and conspiracy in one of the government's largest insider trading cases. Mr. Rajaratnam traded on information (worth approximately $63.8 million) from insiders at technology companies and others in the hedge fund industry. On October 13, 2011, he was sentenced to 11 years in prison. On March 14, 2014, the Federal Deposit Insurance Corporation (FDIC) sued 16 big banks (including Bank of America, Citigroup, and JPMorgan Chase) for actively manipulating the London Interbank Offered Rate (the LIBOR rate) to make additional profits on their trades. This is particularly important because the LIBOR rate is used to set the terms in many financial contracts. The banks are accused of rigging LIBOR from August 2007 to mid-2011. Five of the banks, Barclay's, RBS, UBS, Deutsche Bank, and Rabobank of the Netherlands, together have paid $5 billion to settle the charges and avoid criminal prosecution if they meet certain conditions.

The perception of widespread improper actions has caused many investors to lose faith in American business and to turn away from the stock market, which makes it difficult for firms to raise the capital they need to grow, create jobs, and stimulate the economy. So, unethical actions can have adverse consequences far beyond the companies that perpetrate them.

All this raises a question: Are *companies* unethical, or is it just a few of their employees? That was a central issue that came up in the case of Arthur Andersen, the accounting firm that audited Enron, WorldCom, and several other companies that committed accounting fraud. Evidence showed that relatively few of Andersen's accountants helped perpetrate the frauds. Its top managers argued that while a few rogue employees did bad things, most of the firm's 85,000 employees, and the firm itself, were innocent. The U.S. Justice Department disagreed, concluding that the firm was guilty because it fostered a climate where unethical behavior was permitted and that Andersen used an incentive system that made such behavior profitable to both the perpetrators and the firm. As a result, Andersen was put out of business, its partners lost millions of dollars, and its 85,000 employees lost their jobs. In most other cases, individuals, rather than firms, were tried; and though the firms survived, they suffered damage to their reputations, which greatly lowered their future profit potential and value.

## 1-8C HOW SHOULD EMPLOYEES DEAL WITH UNETHICAL BEHAVIOR?

Far too often the desire for stock options, bonuses, and promotions drives managers to take unethical actions such as fudging the books to make profits in the manager's division look good, holding back information about bad products that would depress sales, and failing to take costly but needed measures to protect the environment. Generally, these acts don't rise to the level of an Enron or a WorldCom, but they are still bad. If questionable things are going on, who should take action and what should that action be? Obviously, in situations such as Enron and WorldCom, where fraud was being perpetrated at or close to the top, senior managers knew about the illegal activities. In other cases, the problem is caused by a mid-level manager trying to boost his or her unit's profits and thus his or her bonus. In all cases, though, at least some lower-level employees are aware of what's happening; they may even be ordered to take fraudulent actions. Should the lower-level employees obey their boss's orders; refuse to obey those orders; or report the situation to a higher authority, such as the company's board of directors, the company's auditors, or a federal prosecutor?

In the WorldCom and Enron cases, it was clear to a number of employees that unethical and illegal acts were being committed; but in cases such as Merck's Vioxx product, the situation was less clear. Because early evidence that Vioxx led to heart attacks was weak and evidence of its pain reduction was strong, it was probably not appropriate to sound an alarm early on. However, as evidence accumulated, at some point the public needed to be given a strong warning, or the product should have been taken off the market. But judgment comes into play when deciding on what action to take and when to take it. If a lower-level employee thinks that a product should be pulled, but the boss disagrees, what should the employee do? If an employee decides to report the problem, trouble may ensue regardless of the merits of the case. If the alarm is false, the company will have been harmed, and nothing will have been gained. In that case, the employee will probably be fired. Even if the employee is right, his or her career may still be ruined because many companies (or at least bosses) don't like "disloyal, troublemaking" employees.

Such situations arise fairly often, ranging from accounting fraud to product liability and environmental cases. Employees jeopardize their jobs if they come forward over their bosses' objections. However, if they don't speak up, they may suffer emotional problems and contribute to the downfall of their companies and the accompanying loss of jobs and savings. Moreover, if employees obey orders regarding actions they know are illegal, they may end up going to jail. Indeed, in most of the scandals that have gone to trial, the lower-level people who physically entered the bad data received longer jail sentences than the bosses who presumably gave the directives. So employees can be "stuck between a rock and a hard place," that is, doing what they should do and possibly losing their jobs versus going along with the boss and possibly ending up in jail. This discussion shows why ethics is such an important consideration in business and in business schools—and why we are concerned with it in this book.

## Self Test

How would you define *business ethics*?

Can a firm's executive compensation plan lead to unethical behavior? Explain.

Unethical acts are generally committed by unethical people. What are some things companies can do to help ensure that their employees act ethically?

# TYING IT ALL TOGETHER

This chapter provides a broad overview of financial management. *Management's primary goal should be to maximize the long-run value of the stock, which means the intrinsic value as measured by the stock's price over time.* To maximize value, firms must develop products that consumers want, produce the products efficiently, sell them at competitive prices, and observe laws relating to corporate behavior. If firms are successful at maximizing the stock's value, they will also be contributing to social welfare and citizens' well-being.

Businesses can be organized as proprietorships, partnerships, corporations, limited liability companies (LLCs), or limited liability partnerships (LLPs). The vast majority of all business is done by corporations, and the most successful firms become corporations, which explains the focus on corporations in this book.

The primary tasks of the CFO are (1) to make sure the accounting system provides "good" numbers for internal decision making and for investors, (2) to ensure that the firm is financed in the proper manner, (3) to evaluate the operating units to make sure they are performing in an optimal manner, and (4) to evaluate all proposed capital expenditures to make sure they will increase the firm's value. In the remainder of this book, we discuss exactly how financial managers carry out these tasks.

## Self-Test Questions and Problems

(Solutions Appear in Appendix A)

**ST-1  KEY TERMS**   Define each of the following terms:

a. Sarbanes-Oxley Act
b. Proprietorship; partnership; corporation
c. S corporation; limited liability company (LLC); limited liability partnership (LLP)
d. Intrinsic value; market price
e. Marginal investor; equilibrium
f. Corporate raider; hostile takeover
g. Stockholder wealth maximization
h. Business ethics

## Questions

1-1   What is a firm's intrinsic value? Its current stock price? Is the stock's "true" long-run value more closely related to its intrinsic value or to its current price?

1-2   When is a stock said to be in equilibrium? Why might a stock at any point in time not be in equilibrium?

1-3   Suppose three honest individuals gave you their estimates of Stock X's intrinsic value. One person is your current roommate, the second person is a professional security analyst with an excellent reputation on Wall Street, and the third person is Company X's CFO. If the three estimates differed, in which one would you have the most confidence? Why?

1-4 Is it better for a firm's actual stock price in the market to be under, over, or equal to its intrinsic value? Would your answer be the same from the standpoints of stockholders in general and a CEO who is about to exercise a million dollars in options and then retire? Explain.

1-5 If a company's board of directors wants management to maximize shareholder wealth, should the CEO's compensation be set as a fixed dollar amount, or should the compensation depend on how well the firm performs? If it is to be based on performance, how should performance be measured? Would it be easier to measure performance by the growth rate in reported profits or the growth rate in the stock's intrinsic value? Which would be the better performance measure? Why?

1-6 What are the various forms of business organization? What are the advantages and disadvantages of each?

1-7 Should stockholder wealth maximization be thought of as a long-term or a short-term goal? For example, if one action increases a firm's stock price from a current level of $20 to $25 in 6 months and then to $30 in 5 years, but another action keeps the stock at $20 for several years but then increases it to $40 in 5 years, which action would be better? Think of some specific corporate actions that have these general tendencies.

1-8 What are some actions that stockholders can take to ensure that management's and stockholders' interests are aligned?

1-9 The president of Southern Semiconductor Corporation (SSC) made this statement in the company's annual report: "SSC's primary goal is to increase the value of our common stockholders' equity." Later in the report, the following announcements were made:

a. The company contributed $1.5 million to the symphony orchestra in Birmingham, Alabama, its headquarters city.

b. The company is spending $500 million to open a new plant and expand operations in China. No profits will be produced by the Chinese operation for 4 years, so earnings will be depressed during this period versus what they would have been had the decision been made not to expand in China.

c. The company holds about half of its assets in the form of U.S. Treasury bonds, and it keeps these funds available for use in emergencies. In the future, though, SSC plans to shift its emergency funds from Treasury bonds to common stocks.

Discuss how SSC's stockholders might view each of these actions and how the actions might affect the stock price.

1-10 Investors generally can make one vote for each share of stock they hold. TIAA-CREF is the largest institutional shareholder in the United States; therefore, it holds many shares and has more votes than any other organization. Traditionally, this fund has acted as a passive investor, just going along with management. However, in 1993, it mailed a notice to all 1,500 companies whose stocks it held that henceforth it planned to actively intervene if, in its opinion, management was not performing well. Its goal was to improve corporate performance to boost the prices of the stocks it held. It also wanted to encourage corporate boards to appoint a majority of independent (outside) directors; and it stated that it would vote against any directors of firms that "don't have an effective, independent board that can challenge the CEO."

In the past, TIAA-CREF responded to poor performance by "voting with its feet," which means selling stocks that were not doing well. However, by 1993, that position had become difficult to maintain for two reasons. First, the fund invested a large part of its assets in "index funds," which hold stocks in accordance with their percentage value in the broad stock market. Furthermore, TIAA-CREF owns such large blocks of stocks in many companies that if it tried to sell out, doing so would severely depress the prices of those stocks. Thus, TIAA-CREF is locked in to a large extent, which led to its decision to become a more active investor.

a. Is TIAA-CREF an ordinary shareholder? Explain.

b. Due to its asset size, TIAA-CREF owns many shares in a number of companies. The fund's management plans to vote those shares. However, TIAA-CREF is owned by many thousands of investors. Should the fund's managers vote its shares, or should it pass those votes, on a pro rata basis, back to its own shareholders? Explain.

1-11 Edmund Enterprises recently made a large investment to upgrade its technology. Although these improvements won't have much effect on performance in the short run, they are expected to reduce future costs significantly. What effect will this investment have on Edmund Enterprises' earnings per share this year? What effect might this investment have on the company's intrinsic value and stock price?

1-12 Suppose you were a member of Company X's board of directors and chairperson of the company's compensation committee. What factors should your committee consider when setting the CEO's compensation? Should the compensation consist of a dollar salary, stock options that depend on the firm's performance, or a mix of the two? If "performance" is to be considered, how should it be measured? Think of both theoretical and practical (i.e., measurement) considerations. If you were also a vice president of Company X, might your actions be different than if you were the CEO of some other company?

1-13 Suppose you are a director of an energy company that has three divisions—natural gas, oil, and retail (gas stations). These divisions operate independently from one another, but all division managers report to the firm's CEO. If you were on the compensation committee, as discussed in Question 1-12, and your committee was asked to set the compensation for the three division managers, would you use the same criteria as that used for the firm's CEO? Explain your reasoning.

1-14 Bedrock Company has $70 million in debt and $30 million in equity. The debt matures in 1 year and has a 10% interest rate, so the company is promising to pay back $77 million to its debtholders 1 year from now.

The company is considering two possible investments, each of which will require an upfront cost of $100 million. Each investment will last for 1 year, and the payoff from each investment depends on the strength of the overall economy. There is a 50% chance that the economy will be weak and a 50% chance it will be strong.

Here are the expected payoffs (all dollars are in millions) from the two investments:

| | Payoff in 1 Year If the Economy Is Weak | Payoff in 1 Year If the Economy Is Strong | Expected Payoff |
|---|---|---|---|
| Investment L | $90.00 | $130.00 | $110.00 |
| Investment H | 50.00 | 170.00 | 110.00 |

Note that the two projects have the same expected payoff, but Project H has higher risk. The debtholders always get paid first and the stockholders receive any money that is available after the debtholders have been paid.

Assume that if the company doesn't have enough funds to pay off its debtholders 1 year from now, then Bedrock will declare bankruptcy. If bankruptcy is declared, the debtholders will receive all available funds, and the stockholders will receive nothing.

a. Assume that the company selects Investment L. What is the expected payoff to the firm's debtholders? What is the expected payoff to the firm's stockholders?

b. Assume that the company selects Investment H. What is the expected payoff to the firm's debtholders? What is the expected payoff to the firm's stockholders?

c. Would the debtholders prefer that the company's managers select Project L or Project H? Briefly explain your reason.

d. Explain why the company's managers, acting on behalf of the stockholders, might select Project H, even though it has greater risk.

e. What actions can debtholders take to protect their interests?

## Solutions to Self-Test Questions and Problems

**ST-1**   Refer to the marginal glossary definitions or relevant chapter sections to check your responses.

# Chapter 2

# Financial Markets and Institutions

Jemal Countess/Getty Images Entertainment/Getty Images

## The Economy Depends on a Strong Financial System

History shows that a strong financial system is a necessary ingredient for a growing and prosperous economy. Companies raising capital to finance capital expenditures and investors saving to accumulate funds for future use require well-functioning financial markets and institutions.

Over the past few decades, changing technology and improving communications have increased cross-border transactions and expanded the scope and efficiency of the global financial system. Companies routinely raise funds throughout the world to finance projects all around the globe. Likewise, with the click of a mouse an individual investor in Pittsburgh can deposit funds in a European bank or purchase a mutual fund that invests in Chinese securities.

These innovations helped spur global economic growth by providing capital to an increasing number of individuals throughout the world. Along the way, the financial industry

attracted a lot of talented people who created, marketed, and traded a large number of new financial products. However, despite their benefits many of these same factors led to excesses that culminated in the financial crisis of 2007 and 2008.

In the aftermath of the crisis, the financial sector is slowly recovering, but its effects continue to linger. The crisis also reaffirmed how changes in the value of financial assets can quickly spill over and affect other parts of the economy. For example, a 2014 article in *The Wall Street Journal* described how a dramatic drop in many of the leading hot tech stocks (Facebook, King Digital Entertainment—the maker of Candy Crush Saga, Netflix, Yelp, and Twitter) suddenly made it more difficult for new start-ups to raise money in the initial public offering (IPO) market. A year later in early 2015, at least two of the stocks (Netflix and Facebook) were showing renewed signs of life.

Moreover, there are signs that both the overall economy and the IPO market are beginning to rebound. For example, in January 2015 the burger chain Shake Shack had a stronger than expected IPO, and clients from Goldman Sachs Group put $1.6 billion into Uber, a mobile-app-based transportation network. But arguably the most dramatic event was when the Chinese online retailer Alibaba raised $25 billion in September 2014. This turned out to be the largest global IPO in history.

These recent events notwithstanding, managers and investors don't operate in a vacuum—they make decisions within a large and complex financial environment. This environment includes financial markets and institutions, tax and regulatory policies, and the state of the economy. The environment both determines the available financial alternatives and affects the outcome of various decisions. Thus, it is crucial that investors and financial managers have a good understanding of the environment in which they operate.

Sources: Michael J. De La Merced, "Shake Shack More Than Doubles Its I.P.O. Price in Market Debut," *The New York Times* (http://dealbook.nytimes.com), January 30, 2015; Mike Isaac and Michael J. De La Merced, "Uber Closes $1.6 Billion in Financing," *The New York Times* (http://dealbook.nytimes.com), January 21, 2015; and Ryan Mac, "Alibaba Claims Title for Largest Global IPO Ever with Extra Share Sales," *Forbes* (www.forbes.com), September 22, 2014.

# PUTTING THINGS IN PERSPECTIVE

In Chapter 1, we saw that a firm's primary financial goal is to maximize long-run shareholder value. Shareholder value is ultimately determined in the financial markets; so if financial managers are to make good decisions, they must understand how these markets operate. In addition, individuals make personal investment decisions; so they too need to know something about financial markets and the institutions that operate in those markets. Therefore, in this chapter, we describe the markets where capital is raised, securities are traded, and stock prices are established and the institutions that operate in these markets. We will also discuss the concept of market efficiency and demonstrate how efficient markets help promote the effective allocation of capital.

In recent years, the dramatic price swings in the financial markets that have become increasingly common have led many to question whether markets are always efficient. In response, there has been increased interest in *behavioral finance theory*. This theory focuses on how psychological factors influence individual decisions (sometimes in perverse ways), and the resulting impact these decisions have on financial markets.

When you finish this chapter, you should be able to:

- Identify the different types of financial markets and financial institutions, and explain how these markets and institutions enhance capital allocation.

- Explain how the stock market operates, and list the distinctions between the different types of stock markets.

- Explain how the stock market has performed in recent years.

- Discuss the importance of market efficiency, and explain why some markets are more efficient than others.

- Develop a simple understanding of behavioral finance.

*For additional information regarding the financial crisis, students can refer to* **stlouisfed.org/Financial-Crisis.** *Another good source can be found at* **fcic.law.stanford.edu,** *which focuses on the Financial Crisis Inquiry Commission.*

## 2-1 The Capital Allocation Process

Businesses, individuals, and governments often need to raise capital. For example, Carolina Power & Light Energy (CP&L) forecasts an increase in the demand for electricity in North and South Carolina, so it will build a new power plant to meet those needs. Because CP&L's bank account does not contain the $1 billion necessary to pay for the plant, the company must raise this capital in the financial markets. Similarly, the proprietor of a San Francisco hardware store wants to expand into appliances. Where will he get the money to buy the initial inventory of TV sets, washers, and freezers? Or suppose the Johnson family wants to buy a home that costs $200,000, but they have only $50,000 in savings. Where will they obtain the additional $150,000? The city of New York needs $200 million to build a new sewer plant. Where can it obtain this money? Finally, the federal government needs more money than it receives from taxes. Where will the extra money come from?

On the other hand, some individuals and firms have incomes that exceed their current expenditures, in which case they have funds available to invest. For example, Carol Hawk has an income of $36,000, but her expenses are only $30,000. That leaves her with $6,000 to invest. Similarly, Microsoft has accumulated roughly $90.3 billion of cash and marketable securities. What can Microsoft do with this money until it is needed in the business?

People and organizations with surplus funds are saving today in order to accumulate funds for some future use. Members of a household might save to pay for their children's education and the parents' retirement, while a business might save to fund future investments. Those with surplus funds expect to earn a return on their investments, while people and organizations that need capital understand that they must pay interest to those who provide that capital.

In a well-functioning economy, capital flows efficiently from those with surplus capital to those who need it. This transfer can take place in the three ways described in Figure 2.1.

<table>
<tr><td>FIGURE 2.1</td><td>Diagram of the Capital Formation Process for Business</td></tr>
</table>

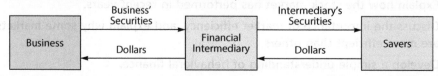

1. Direct Transfers

2. Indirect Transfers through Investment Bankers

3. Indirect Transfers through a Financial Intermediary

1. *Direct transfers* of money and securities, as shown in the top section, occur when a business sells its stocks or bonds directly to savers, without going through any type of financial institution. The business delivers its securities to savers, who, in turn, give the firm the money it needs. This procedure is used mainly by small firms, and relatively little capital is raised by direct transfers.

2. As shown in the middle section, transfers may also go through an investment bank (iBank) such as Morgan Stanley, which *underwrites* the issue. An underwriter facilitates the issuance of securities. The company sells its stocks or bonds to the investment bank, which then sells these same securities to savers. The businesses' securities and the savers' money merely "pass through" the investment bank. However, because the investment bank buys and holds the securities for a period of time, it is taking a risk—it may not be able to resell the securities to savers for as much as it paid. Because new securities are involved and the corporation receives the sale proceeds, this transaction is called a *primary market transaction*.

3. Transfers can also be made through a *financial intermediary* such as a bank, an insurance company, or a mutual fund. Here the intermediary obtains funds from savers in exchange for its securities. The intermediary uses this money to buy and hold businesses' securities, and the savers hold the intermediary's securities. For example, a saver deposits dollars in a bank, receiving a certificate of deposit; then the bank lends the money to a business in the form of a mortgage loan. Thus, intermediaries literally create new forms of capital—in this case, certificates of deposit, which are safer and more liquid than mortgages and thus better for most savers to hold. The existence of intermediaries greatly increases the efficiency of money and capital markets.

Often the entity needing capital is a business (and specifically a corporation); but it is easy to visualize the demander of capital being a home purchaser, a small business, or a government unit. For example, if your uncle lends you money to fund a new business, a direct transfer of funds will occur. Alternatively, if you borrow money to purchase a home, you will probably raise the funds through a financial intermediary such as your local commercial bank or mortgage banker. That banker could sell your mortgage to an investment bank, which then might use it as collateral for a bond that is purchased by a pension fund.

In a global context, economic development is highly correlated with the level and efficiency of financial markets and institutions.[1] It is difficult, if not impossible, for an economy to reach its full potential if it doesn't have access to a well-functioning financial system. In a well-developed economy like that of the United States, an extensive set of markets and institutions has evolved over time to facilitate the efficient allocation of capital. To raise capital efficiently, managers must understand how these markets and institutions work; and individuals need to know how the markets and institutions work to earn high rates of returns on their savings.

## Self *Test*

Name three ways capital is transferred between savers and borrowers.

Why are efficient capital markets necessary for economic growth?

---

[1]For a detailed review of the evidence linking financial development to economic growth, see Ross Levine, "Finance and Growth: Theory and Evidence," Chapter 12 in *Handbook of Economic Growth*, edited by Philippe Aghion and Steven Durlauf (Amsterdam: Elsevier Science, 2005).

# 2-2 Financial Markets

People and organizations wanting to borrow money are brought together with those who have surplus funds in the *financial markets*. Note that *markets* is plural; there are many different financial markets in a developed economy such as that of the United States. We describe some of these markets and some trends in their development.

## 2-2A TYPES OF MARKETS

Different financial markets serve different types of customers or different parts of the country. Financial markets also vary depending on the maturity of the securities being traded and the types of assets used to back the securities. For these reasons, it is useful to classify markets along the following dimensions:

1. *Physical asset markets versus financial asset markets. Physical asset markets* (also called "tangible" or "real" asset markets) are for products such as wheat, autos, real estate, computers, and machinery. *Financial asset markets,* on the other hand, deal with stocks, bonds, notes, and mortgages. Financial markets also deal with *derivative securities* whose values are *derived* from changes in the prices of other assets. A share of Ford stock is a "pure financial asset," while an option to buy Ford shares is a derivative security whose value depends on the price of Ford stock.

2. *Spot markets versus futures markets.* **Spot markets** are markets in which assets are bought or sold for "on-the-spot" delivery (literally, within a few days). **Futures markets** are markets in which participants agree today to buy or sell an asset at some future date. For example, a farmer may enter into a futures contract in which he agrees today to sell 5,000 bushels of soybeans 6 months from now at a price of $9.75 a bushel. To continue that example, a food processor that needs soybeans in the future may enter into a futures contract in which it agrees to buy soybeans 6 months from now. Such a transaction can reduce, or *hedge*, the risks faced by both the farmer and the food processor.

3. *Money markets versus capital markets.* **Money markets** are the markets for short-term, highly liquid debt securities. The New York, London, and Tokyo money markets are among the world's largest. **Capital markets** are the markets for intermediate- or long-term debt and corporate stocks. The New York Stock Exchange, where the stocks of the largest U.S. corporations are traded, is a prime example of a capital market. There is no hard-and-fast rule, but in a description of debt markets, *short-term* generally means less than 1 year, *intermediate-term* means 1 to 10 years, and *long-term* means more than 10 years.

4. *Primary markets versus secondary markets.* **Primary markets** are the markets in which corporations raise new capital. If GE were to sell a new issue of common stock to raise capital, a primary market transaction would take place. The corporation selling the newly created stock, GE, receives the proceeds from the sale in a primary market transaction. **Secondary markets** are markets in which existing, already outstanding securities are traded among investors. Thus, if Jane Doe decided to buy 1,000 shares of GE stock, the purchase would occur in the secondary market. The New York Stock Exchange is a secondary market because it deals in outstanding, as opposed to newly issued, stocks and bonds. Secondary markets also exist for mortgages, other types of loans, and other financial assets. The corporation whose securities are being traded is not involved in a secondary market transaction and thus does not receive funds from such a sale.

**Spot Markets**
The markets in which assets are bought or sold for "on-the-spot" delivery.

**Futures Markets**
The markets in which participants agree today to buy or sell an asset at some future date.

**Money Markets**
The financial markets in which funds are borrowed or loaned for short periods (less than one year).

**Capital Markets**
The financial markets for stocks and for intermediate- or long-term debt (one year or longer).

**Primary Markets**
Markets in which corporations raise capital by issuing new securities.

**Secondary Markets**
Markets in which securities and other financial assets are traded among investors after they have been issued by corporations.

5. *Private markets versus public markets.* **Private markets**, where transactions are negotiated directly between two parties, are differentiated from **public markets**, where standardized contracts are traded on organized exchanges. Bank loans and private debt placements with insurance companies are examples of private market transactions. Because these transactions are private, they may be structured in any manner to which the two parties agree. By contrast, securities that are traded in public markets (for example, common stock and corporate bonds) are held by a large number of individuals. These securities must have fairly standardized contractual features because public investors do not generally have the time and expertise to negotiate unique, nonstandardized contracts. Broad ownership and standardization result in publicly traded securities being more liquid than tailor-made, uniquely negotiated securities.

> **Private Markets**
> Markets in which transactions are worked out directly between two parties.
>
> **Public Markets**
> Markets in which standardized contracts are traded on organized exchanges.

Other classifications could be made, but this breakdown shows that there are many types of financial markets. Also note that the distinctions among markets are often blurred and unimportant except as a general point of reference. For example, it makes little difference if a firm borrows for 11, 12, or 13 months, that is, whether the transaction is a "money" or "capital" market transaction. You should be aware of the important differences among types of markets, but don't be overly concerned about trying to distinguish them at the boundaries.

A healthy economy is dependent on efficient funds transfers from people who are net savers to firms and individuals who need capital. Without efficient transfers, the economy could not function: Carolina Power & Light Energy could not raise capital, so Raleigh's citizens would have no electricity; the Johnson family would not have adequate housing; Carol Hawk would have no place to invest her savings; and so forth. Obviously, the level of employment and productivity (i.e., the standard of living) would be much lower. Therefore, it is essential that financial markets function efficiently—not only quickly, but also inexpensively.

Table 2.1 is a listing of the most important instruments traded in the various financial markets. The instruments are arranged in ascending order of typical length of maturity. As we go through this book, we will look in more detail at many of the instruments listed in Table 2.1. For example, we will see that there are many varieties of corporate bonds, ranging from "plain vanilla" bonds to bonds that can be converted to common stocks to bonds whose interest payments vary depending on the inflation rate. Still, the table provides an overview of the characteristics and costs of the instruments traded in the major financial markets.

## 2-2B RECENT TRENDS

Financial markets have experienced many changes in recent years. Technological advances in computers and telecommunications, along with the globalization of banking and commerce, have led to deregulation, which has increased competition throughout the world. As a result, there are more efficient, internationally linked markets, which are far more complex than what existed a few years ago. While these developments have been largely positive, they have also created problems for policymakers. With these concerns in mind, Congress and regulators have moved to reregulate parts of the financial sector following the 2007–2008 financial crisis. The box titled "Changing Technology Has Transformed Financial Markets" on page 34 illustrates some dramatic examples of how changing technology has transformed financial markets in recent years.

**TABLE 2.1**   Summary of Major Market Instruments, Market Participants, and Security Characteristics

| Instrument (1) | Market (2) | Major Participants (3) | Riskiness (4) | Original Maturity (5) | Interest Rate on 3/5/15[a] (6) |
|---|---|---|---|---|---|
| | | | **Security Characteristics** | | |
| U.S. Treasury bills | Money | Sold by U.S. Treasury to finance federal expenditures | Default-free, close to riskless | 91 days to 1 year | 0.02% |
| Bankers' acceptances | Money | A firm's note, but one guaranteed by a bank | Low degree of risk if guaranteed by a strong bank | Up to 180 days | 0.23% |
| Commercial paper | Money | Issued by financially secure firms to large investors | Low default risk | Up to 270 days | 0.14% |
| Negotiable certificates of deposit (CDs) | Money | Issued by major money-center commercial banks to large investors | Default risk depends on the strength of the issuing bank | Up to 1 year | 0.20% |
| Money market mutual funds | Money | Invest in Treasury bills, CDs, and commercial paper; held by individuals and businesses | Low degree of risk | No specific maturity (instant liquidity) | 0.42% |
| Eurodollar market time deposits | Money | Issued by banks outside the United States | Default risk depends on the strength of the issuing bank | Up to 1 year | 0.15% |
| Consumer credit, including credit card debt | Money | Issued by banks, credit unions, and finance companies to individuals | Risk is variable | Variable | Variable, but average APR is 11.10%–16.40% |
| U.S. Treasury notes and bonds | Capital | Issued by U.S. government | No default risk, but price will decline if interest rates rise; hence, there is some risk | 2 to 30 years | 0.65% on 2-year to 2.71% on 30-year bonds |
| Mortgages | Capital | Loans to individuals and businesses secured by real estate; bought by banks and other institutions | Risk is variable; risk is high in the case of subprime loans | Up to 30 years | 3.36% adjustable 5-year rate, 3.94% 30-year fixed rate |
| State and local government bonds | Capital | Issued by state and local governments; held by individuals and institutional investors | Riskier than U.S. government securities but exempt from most taxes | Up to 30 years | 3.68% 20-year bonds, mixed quality debt |

*(Continued)*

TABLE 2.1 Summary of Major Market Instruments, Market Participants, and Security Characteristics

| Instrument (1) | Market (2) | Major Participants (3) | Riskiness (4) | Security Characteristics | | |
|---|---|---|---|---|---|---|
| | | | | Original Maturity (5) | Interest Rate on 3/5/15[a] (6) | |
| Corporate bonds | Capital | Issued by corporations; held by individuals and institutional investors | Riskier than U.S. government securities but less risky than preferred and common stocks; varying degree of risk within bonds depends on strength of issuer | Up to 40 years[b] | 3.71% on AAA bonds, 4.58% on BBB bonds | |
| Leases | Capital | Similar to debt in that firms can lease assets rather than borrow and then buy the assets | Risk similar to corporate bonds | Generally 3 to 20 years | Similar to bond yields | |
| Preferred stocks | Capital | Issued by corporations to individuals and institutional investors | Generally riskier than corporate bonds but less risky than common stock | Unlimited | 5.75% to 9.5% | |
| Common stocks[c] | Capital | Issued by corporations to individuals and institutional investors | Riskier than bonds and preferred stock; risk varies from company to company | Unlimited | NA | |

Notes:

[a]The yields reported are from The Wall Street Journal (online.wsj.com), March 5, 2015, and Board of Governors of the Federal Reserve System, "Selected Interest Rates (Daily)," www.federalreserve.gov/releases/H15/update. Money market rates assume a 3-month maturity.

[b]A few corporations have issued 100-year bonds; however, the majority has issued bonds with maturities that are less than 40 years.

[c]While common stocks do not pay interest, they are expected to provide a "return" in the form of dividends and capital gains. Historically, stock returns have averaged between 9% and 12% a year, but they can be much higher or lower in a given year. Of course, if you purchase a stock, your actual return may be considerably higher or lower than these historical averages.

## Changing Technology Has Transformed Financial Markets

In recent years, changing technology has created numerous innovations and has dramatically transformed the operation of financial markets. Here are just a few interesting examples:

- Changing technology has created a whole class of firms that use computer algorithms to buy and sell securities, often at speeds less than a second. The trades conducted by these high-frequency trading (HFT) firms now represent a very significant fraction of the total trading volume in a given day. Proponents argue that these HFT firms generate liquidity, which helps reduce transactions costs and makes it easier for other investors to get in and out of the market. Critics argue that these activities can create market instability and that HFT firms often engage in trades that are self-serving to their own interests, to the detriment of other investors. A recent best-selling book by Michael Lewis, titled *Flash Boys*, attracted a lot of attention for its highly critical depiction of HFT firms.

- Changing technology has changed the way that many people pay for transactions. Many of us rarely use cash anymore and instead often rely on debit and credit cards for payment. Others often use electronic commerce services such as PayPal to make online payments. More recently, there has been a growing interest in Bitcoin—a virtual currency that involves no intermediary and has no fees.[2] Although intriguing, many are concerned that the lack of regulation makes Bitcoin an attractive vehicle for illegal transactions and that investors in the currency lack any legal protection against fraudulent activities.[3]

- Changing technology has allowed some individuals and firms to bypass intermediaries and directly raise money from investors to help fund various projects. This activity is referred to as *crowdfunding*. Two leading examples of these platforms include Kickstarter and Indiegogo.[4]

Globalization has exposed the need for greater cooperation among regulators at the international level, but the task is not easy. Factors that complicate coordination include (1) the different structures in nations' banking and securities industries; (2) the trend toward financial services conglomerates, which obscures developments in various market segments; and (3) the reluctance of individual countries to give up control over their national monetary policies. Still, regulators are unanimous about the need to close the gaps in the supervision of worldwide markets.

Another important trend in recent years has been the increased use of **derivatives**. A derivative is any security whose value is *derived* from the price of some other "underlying" asset. An option to buy IBM stock is a derivative, as is a contract to buy Japanese yen six months from now. The value of the IBM option depends on the price of IBM's stock and the value of the Japanese yen "future" depends on the exchange rate between yen and dollars. The market for derivatives has grown faster than any other market in recent years, providing investors with new opportunities but also exposing them to new risks.

*Derivatives*

Any financial asset whose value is derived from the value of some other "underlying" asset.

---

[2]For a concise review of Bitcoin, see Tal Yellin, Dominic Aratari, and Jose Pagliery, "What Is Bitcoin?" *CNN Money* (money.cnn.com), January 2014.

[3]Despite these concerns, many believe that Bitcoin would become an important part of the global economy. See, for example, a recent article by Paul Vigna and Michael J. Casey, "BitBeat: The Fed's Surprisingly Warm Take on Bitcoin," *The Wall Street Journal* (blogs.wsj.com), May 19, 2014.

[4]For a discussion of the role that these groups play in the funding process, see "Where Do Crowdfunding Platforms Fit in Venture Capital?" *The Wall Street Journal* (blogs.wsj.com), May 2, 2014.

To illustrate the growing importance of derivatives, consider the case of *credit default swaps.*[5] Credit default swaps are contracts that offer protection against the default of a particular security. Suppose a bank wants to protect itself against the default of one of its borrowers. The bank could enter into a credit default swap where it agrees to make regular payments to another financial institution. In return, that financial institution agrees to insure the bank against losses that would occur if the borrower defaulted.

Derivatives can be used to reduce risks or to speculate. Suppose a wheat processor's costs rise and its net income falls when the price of wheat rises. The processor could reduce its risk by purchasing derivatives—wheat futures—whose value increases when the price of wheat rises. This is a *hedging operation,* and its purpose is to reduce risk exposure. Speculation, on the other hand, is done in the hope of high returns; but it raises risk exposure. For example, several years ago Procter & Gamble disclosed that it lost $150 million on derivative investments. More recently, losses on mortgage-related derivatives helped contribute to the credit collapse in 2008.

If a bank or any other company reports that it invests in derivatives, how can one tell if the derivatives are held as a hedge against something like an increase in the price of wheat or as a speculative bet that wheat prices will rise? The answer is that it is very difficult to tell how derivatives are affecting the firm's risk profile. In the case of financial institutions, things are even more complicated—the derivatives are generally based on changes in interest rates, foreign exchange rates, or stock prices; and a large international bank might have tens of thousands of separate derivative contracts. The size and complexity of these transactions concern regulators, academics, and members of Congress. Former Fed Chairperson Alan Greenspan noted that in theory, derivatives should allow companies to better manage risk, but that it is not clear whether recent innovations have "increased or decreased the inherent stability of the financial system."

## SelfTest

Distinguish between physical asset markets and financial asset markets.

What's the difference between spot markets and futures markets?

Distinguish between money markets and capital markets.

What's the difference between primary markets and secondary markets?

Differentiate between private and public markets.

Why are financial markets essential for a healthy economy and economic growth?

## 2-3 Financial Institutions

Direct funds transfers are common among individuals and small businesses and in economies where financial markets and institutions are less developed. But large businesses in developed economies generally find it more efficient to enlist the services of a financial institution when it comes time to raise capital.

---

[5]A 2010 article in *The New York Times* reported that this market had grown from $900 billion in 2000 to more than $30 trillion in 2008. The article also describes how credit default swaps helped contribute to the 2007–2008 financial crises in the United States and Europe. Refer to "Times Topics: Credit Default Swaps," *The New York Times* (topics.nytimes.com), March 10, 2010.

In the United States and other developed nations, a set of highly efficient financial intermediaries has evolved. Their original roles were generally quite specific, and regulation prevented them from diversifying. However, in recent years regulations against diversification have been largely removed; and today the differences between institutions have become blurred. Still, there remains a degree of institutional identity. Therefore, it is useful to understand the major categories of financial institutions. Keep in mind, though, that one company can own a number of subsidiaries that engage in the different functions described next.

**Investment Bank**

An organization that underwrites and distributes new investment securities and helps businesses obtain financing.

1. **Investment banks** traditionally help companies raise capital. They (1) help corporations design securities with features that are currently attractive to investors, (2) buy these securities from the corporation, and (3) resell them to savers. Because the investment bank generally guarantees that the firm will raise the needed capital, the investment bankers are also called *underwriters*. The recent credit crisis has had a dramatic effect on the investment banking industry. Bear Stearns collapsed and was later acquired by JP Morgan, Lehman Brothers went bankrupt, and Merrill Lynch was forced to sell out to Bank of America. The two "surviving" major investment banks (Morgan Stanley and Goldman Sachs) received Federal Reserve approval to become commercial bank holding companies.

**Commercial Bank**

The traditional department store of finance serving a variety of savers and borrowers.

2. **Commercial banks,** such as Bank of America, Citibank, Wells Fargo, and JP Morgan Chase, are the traditional "department stores of finance" because they serve a variety of savers and borrowers. Historically, commercial banks were the major institutions that handled checking accounts and through which the Federal Reserve System expanded or contracted the money supply. Today, however, several other institutions also provide checking services and significantly influence the money supply. Note too that the larger banks are generally part of financial services corporations as described next.[6]

**Financial Services Corporation**

A firm that offers a wide range of financial services, including investment banking, brokerage operations, insurance, and commercial banking.

3. **Financial services corporations** are large conglomerates that combine many different financial institutions within a single corporation. Most financial services corporations started in one area but have now diversified to cover most of the financial spectrum. For example, Citigroup owns Citibank (a commercial bank), an investment bank, a securities brokerage organization, insurance companies, and leasing companies.

4. *Credit unions* are cooperative associations whose members are supposed to have a common bond, such as being employees of the same firm. Members' savings are loaned only to other members, generally for auto purchases, home improvement loans, and home mortgages. Credit unions are often the cheapest source of funds available to individual borrowers.

5. *Pension funds* are retirement plans funded by corporations or government agencies for their workers and administered primarily by the trust departments of commercial banks or by life insurance companies. Pension funds invest primarily in bonds, stocks, mortgages, and real estate.

6. *Life insurance companies* take savings in the form of annual premiums; invest these funds in stocks, bonds, real estate, and mortgages; and make payments to the beneficiaries of the insured parties. In recent years, life insurance companies have also offered a variety of tax-deferred savings plans designed to provide benefits to participants when they retire.

---

[6]Two other institutions that were important a few years ago were *savings and loan associations* and *mutual savings banks*. Most of these organizations have now been merged into commercial banks.

7. **Mutual funds** are corporations that accept money from savers and then use these funds to buy stocks, long-term bonds, or short-term debt instruments issued by businesses or government units. These organizations pool funds and thus reduce risks by diversification. They also achieve economies of scale in analyzing securities, managing portfolios, and buying and selling securities. Different funds are designed to meet the objectives of different types of savers. Hence, there are bond funds for those who prefer safety, stock funds for savers who are willing to accept significant risks in the hope of higher returns, and **money market funds** that are used as interest-bearing checking accounts.

   Another important distinction exists between actively managed funds and indexed funds. *Actively managed funds* try to outperform the overall markets, whereas *indexed funds* are designed to simply replicate the performance of a specific market index. For example, the portfolio manager of an actively managed stock fund uses his or her expertise to select what he or she thinks will be the best-performing stocks over a given time period. By contrast, an index fund that tracks the S&P 500 index will simply hold the basket of stocks that comprise the S&P 500. Both types of funds provide investors with valuable diversification, but actively managed funds typically have much higher fees—in large part, because of the extra costs involved in trying to select stocks that will (hopefully) outperform the market. In any given year, the very best actively managed funds will outperform the market index, but many will do worse than the overall market—even before taking into account their higher fees. Furthermore, it is extremely difficult to predict which actively managed funds will beat the market in a particular year. For this reason, many academics and practitioners have encouraged investors to rely more heavily on indexed funds.[7]

   There are literally thousands of different mutual funds with dozens of different goals and purposes. Excellent information on the objectives and past performances of the various funds are provided in publications such as *Value Line Investment Survey* and *Morningstar Mutual Funds*, which are available in most libraries and on the Internet.

8. *Exchange Traded Funds (ETFs)* are similar to regular mutual funds and are often operated by mutual fund companies. ETFs buy a portfolio of stocks of a certain type—for example, the S&P 500 or media companies or Chinese companies—and then sell their own shares to the public. ETF shares are generally traded in the public markets, so an investor who wants to invest in the Chinese market, for example, can buy shares in an ETF that holds stocks in that particular market.

9. *Hedge funds* are also similar to mutual funds because they accept money from savers and use the funds to buy various securities, but there are some important differences. While mutual funds (and ETFs) are registered and regulated by the Securities and Exchange Commission (SEC), hedge funds are largely unregulated. This difference in regulation stems from the fact that mutual funds typically target small investors, whereas hedge funds typically have large minimum investments (often exceeding $1 million) and are marketed primarily to institutions and individuals with high net worths. Hedge funds received their name because they traditionally were used when an individual was trying to hedge risks. For example, a hedge

*Mutual Funds*
Organizations that pool investor funds to purchase financial instruments and thus reduce risks through diversification.

*Money Market Funds*
Mutual funds that invest in short-term, low-risk securities and allow investors to write checks against their accounts.

---

[7]Refer to Mark Hulbert, "The Index Funds Win Again," *The New York Times* (www.nytimes.com), February 21, 2009; and Rick Ferri, "Index Fund Portfolios Reign Superior," *Forbes* (www.forbes.com), August 20, 2012.

fund manager who believes that interest rate differentials between corporate and Treasury bonds are too large might simultaneously buy a portfolio of corporate bonds and sell a portfolio of Treasury bonds. In this case, the portfolio would be "hedged" against overall movements in interest rates, but it would perform especially well if the spread between these securities became smaller.

However, some hedge funds take on risks that are considerably higher than that of an average individual stock or mutual fund. For example, in 1998, Long-Term Capital Management (LTCM), a high-profile hedge fund (whose managers included several well-respected practitioners as well as two Nobel Prize–winning professors who were experts in investment theory), made some incorrect assumptions and "blew up."[8] LTCM had many billions of dollars under management, and it owed large amounts of money to a number of banks. To avert a worldwide crisis, the Federal Reserve orchestrated a buyout of the firm with a group of New York banks.

Table 2.2 lists the 10 largest hedge funds as of January 2, 2015. As evidence of their growing importance, each of these funds controls more than $25 billion in assets. As hedge funds have become more popular, many of them have begun to lower their minimum investment requirements. Perhaps not surprisingly, their rapid growth and shift toward smaller investors have also led to a call for more regulation.

10. *Private equity companies* are organizations that operate much like hedge funds; but rather than purchasing some of the stock of a firm, private equity players buy and then manage entire firms. Most of the money used to buy the target companies is borrowed. While private equity activity slowed around the financial crisis, over the past decade a number of high-profile companies (including Harrah's Entertainment, Albertson's, Neiman Marcus, and Clear Channel) have been acquired by private equity firms. More recently in 2013, two major deals were announced. Berkshire Hathaway (and its chairman Warren Buffett) partnered with the private equity firm 3G Capital to acquire H.J. Heinz Co. on June 7, 2013, for $28 billion. On October 29, 2013, Dell

Ten Largest Hedge Funds as of January 2, 2015     **TABLE 2.2**

| Fund | Assets under Management ($ in billions) |
| --- | --- |
| Bridgewater Associates | 169.5 |
| AQR Capital Management | 64.9 |
| Man Investments | 50.0 |
| Och-Ziff Capital Management Group | 47.2 |
| Standard Life Investments | 35.3 |
| BlackRock Alternative Investors | 31.8 |
| Winton Capital Management | 31.1 |
| Viking Global Investors | 30.3 |
| Millennium Management | 29.2 |
| Lone Pine Capital | 29.0 |

Source: Michelle Jones, "Biggest Hedge Funds Nab (Almost) All of the Assets," *ValueWalk* (www.valuewalk .com), May 27, 2015.

---

[8]See Franklin Edwards, "Hedge Funds and the Collapse of Long-Term Capital Management," *Journal of Economic Perspectives*, vol. 13, no. 2 (Spring 1999), pp. 189–210, for a thoughtful review of the implications of the collapse of Long-Term Capital Management.

Computer completed its deal to go private with the assistance of the private equity firm, Silver Lake Partners, for $24.9 billion. Other leading private equity firms include The Carlyle Group, Kohlberg Kravis Roberts, and The Blackstone Group.

With the exception of hedge funds and private equity companies, financial institutions are regulated to ensure the safety of these institutions and to protect investors. Historically, many of these regulations—which have included a prohibition on nationwide branch banking, restrictions on the types of assets the institutions could purchase, ceilings on the interest rates they could pay, and limitations on the types of services they could provide—tended to impede the free flow of capital and thus hurt the efficiency of the capital markets. Recognizing this fact, policymakers took several steps during the 1980s and 1990s to deregulate financial services companies. For example, the restriction barring nationwide branching by banks was eliminated in 1999.

Many believed that excessive deregulation and insufficient supervision of the financial sector was partially responsible for the 2007–2008 financial crisis. With these concerns in mind, Congress passed the Dodd-Frank Act. The legislation's main goals are to create a new agency for consumer protection, work to increase the transparency of derivative transactions, and force financial institutions to take steps to limit excessive risk taking and to hold more capital.

Panel A of Table 2.3 lists the 10 largest U.S. bank holding companies, and Panel B shows the leading world banking companies. Among the world's 10 largest, only one is based in the United States. While U.S. banks have grown dramatically as a result of recent mergers, they are still small by global standards. Panel C of the table lists the 10 leading global IPO underwriters in terms of dollar volume of new equity issues. Seven of the top underwriters are also listed as major commercial banks or are part of bank holding companies shown in Panels A and B, which confirms the continued blurring of distinctions between different types of financial institutions.

Largest Banks and Underwriters    **TABLE 2.3**

| Panel A<br>U.S. Bank Holding<br>Companies[a] | Panel B<br>World Banking<br>Companies[b] | Panel C<br>Leading Global IPO<br>Underwriters[c] |
| --- | --- | --- |
| JPMorgan Chase & Co. | Industrial & Commercial Bank of China Ltd (China) | Credit Suisse |
| Bank of America Corp. | China Construction Bank Corporation (China) | Morgan Stanley |
| Citigroup Inc. | BNP Paribas SA (France) | Citi |
| Wells Fargo & Co. | Agricultural Bank of China Ltd (China) | BofA Merrill Lynch |
| Goldman Sachs Group, Inc. | Bank of China Ltd (China) | Goldman Sachs |
| Morgan Stanley | Deutsche Bank AG (Germany) | JPMorgan |
| General Electric Capital Corp. | Barclays Bank PLC (UK) | Barclays |
| U.S. Bancorp | Credit Agricole SA (France) | Jefferies & Co. |
| Bank of New York Mellon Corp. | Japan Post Bank Co. Ltd (Japan) | Deutsche Bank |
| PNC Financial Services Group, Inc. | JPMorgan Chase Bank National Assoc. (USA) | Piper Jaffray |

*Notes:*

[a] Ranked by total assets as of December 31, 2014.
  Source: National Information Center, www.ffiec.gov/nicpubweb/nicweb/Top50Form.aspx.

[b] Ranked by total assets from balance sheet information available on November 25, 2014.
  Source: www.accuity.com/useful-links/bank-rankings.

[c] Ranked by dollar amount raised through new IPO issues in 2014. For this ranking, the lead underwriter (manager) is given credit for the entire issue.
  Source: www.renaissancecapital.com/ipohome/underwriter/urankings.aspx?list=proceeds&nav=f&StartDate=1/1/2014&EndDate=12/31/2014.

# SECURITIZATION HAS DRAMATICALLY TRANSFORMED THE BANKING INDUSTRY

At one time, commercial banking was a simpler business than it is today. A typical bank received money from its depositors and used it to make loans. In the vast majority of cases, the banker held the loan on its books until it matured. Because they originated the loan and continued to hold it on their books, the banks generally knew the risks involved. However, because banks often had limited funding, there was a cap on the number of loans they could hold on their books. And because most of the loans were made to individuals and businesses in their local market, banks were less able to spread their risk.

To address these concerns, financial engineers came up with the idea of securitizing loans. This is a process whereby an agent (such as an investment bank) creates an entity that buys a large number of loans from a wide range of banks and then issues securities that are backed by the loan payments. Securitization began in the 1970s when government-backed entities purchased pools of home mortgages and then issued securities backed by the cash flows from the diversified portfolio of mortgages. In many respects, securitization was a tremendous innovation. Banks no longer had to hold their mortgages, so they could quickly convert the originated loan to cash, enabling them to redeploy their capital to make other loans. At the same time, the newly created securities gave investors an opportunity to invest in a diversified portfolio of home mortgages. In addition, these securities traded on the open market so that investors were able to easily buy and sell them as their circumstances and views of the mortgage markets changed over time.

Over the last few decades, this process has accelerated. Bankers have securitized different types of loans into all types of different securities. One notable example is *collateralized debt obligations (CDOs)*, where an entity issues several classes of securities backed by a portfolio of loans. For example, an investment bank purchases $100 million of mortgage loans from banks and mortgage brokers throughout the country. The investment bank uses the collateral to create $100 million in new securities, which are divided into three classes (often referred to as *tranches*). The Class A bonds have the first claim on the cash flows from the mortgages. Because they have the first claim, they are the least risky and are rated AAA by the rating agencies. The Class B bonds get paid after the Class A bonds are paid, but they too will generally have a high rating. Finally, the Class C bonds get paid. Because they are last in line, they will have the highest risk, but they will also sell for the lowest price. If the underlying mortgages perform well, the C bonds will realize the highest returns, but they will suffer the most if the underlying mortgages don't perform well.

CDOs backed by pools of higher risk (subprime) mortgages played a major role in the 2007–2008 financial crisis. During the housing boom, financial institutions and mortgage brokers originated a large number of new mortgages, and investment bankers hungry for fees were more than happy to create new CDOs backed by these subprime mortgages. The securities created through these CDOs were sold primarily to other commercial and investment banks and to other financial institutions, such as hedge funds, mutual funds, and pension funds. Buoyed by the mistaken belief that housing prices would never fall, many viewed these securities as solid investments, and they received additional comfort from the fact that they were highly rated.

When the housing market collapsed, the value of these securities plummeted, destroying the balance sheets of many financial institutions. Making matters worse, it became very hard to value these securities because they were backed by such a large, diverse pool of mortgages. Not sure what they had on their books, many institutions tried to sell these securities at the same time, and the "rush to the exit" further depressed prices, causing the cycle to deepen.

Following the crisis, many have looked to reform the securitization business, and others have criticized the rating agencies for routinely assigning high credit ratings to what in hindsight were extremely risky securities. At the same time, an article in *Barron's* highlights the important role that securitization plays in the capital markets and raises concerns that the economy won't thrive again until the securitization business recovers.

Source: David Adler, "A Flat Dow for 10 Years? Why It Could Happen," *Barron's* (online.barrons.com), December 28, 2009.

## Self Test

What's the difference between a commercial bank and an investment bank?

List the major types of financial institutions, and briefly describe the primary function of each.

What are some important differences between mutual funds, Exchange Traded Funds, and hedge funds? How are they similar?

# 2-4 The Stock Market

As noted earlier, outstanding, previously issued securities are traded in the secondary markets. By far, the most active secondary market—and the most important one to financial managers—is the *stock market*, where the prices of firms' stocks are established. Because the primary goal of financial managers is to maximize their firms' stock prices, knowledge of the stock market is important to anyone involved in managing a business.

There are a number of different stock markets. The two leaders are NYSE Euronext and NASDAQ. NYSE Euronext was formed through the 2007 merger of the New York Stock Exchange (NYSE) and Euronext, which at the time was the largest European exchange. Stocks are traded using a variety of market procedures, but there are two basic types: (1) *physical location exchanges,* which include the NYSE and several regional stock exchanges, and (2) *electronic dealer-based markets,* which include the NASDAQ, the less formal over-the-counter market, and the recently developed electronic communications networks (ECNs).

(See the box titled "The NYSE and NASDAQ Go Global.") Because the physical location exchanges are easier to describe and understand, we discuss them first.

## 2-4A PHYSICAL LOCATION STOCK EXCHANGES

**Physical location exchanges** are tangible entities. Each of the larger exchanges occupies its own building, allows a limited number of people to trade on its floor, and has an elected governing body—its board of governors. Members of the NYSE formerly had "seats" on the exchange, although everybody stood. Today the seats have been exchanged for trading licenses, which are auctioned to member organizations and cost about $50,000 per year. Most of the larger investment banks operate *brokerage departments.* They purchase seats on the exchanges and designate one or more of their officers as members. The exchanges are open on all normal working days, with the members meeting in a large room equipped with telephones and other electronic equipment that enable each member to communicate with his or her firm's offices throughout the country.

Like other markets, security exchanges facilitate communication between buyers and sellers. For example, Goldman Sachs (the fifth-largest brokerage firm) might receive an order from a customer who wants to buy shares of GE stock. Simultaneously, Morgan Stanley (the second-largest brokerage firm) might receive an order from a customer wanting to sell shares of GE. Each broker communicates electronically with the firm's representative on the NYSE. Other brokers throughout the country are also communicating with their own exchange members. The exchange members with *sell orders* offer the shares for sale, and they are bid for by the members with *buy orders.* Thus, the exchanges operate as *auction markets.*[9]

> **Physical Location Exchanges**
> Formal organizations having tangible physical locations that conduct auction markets in designated ("listed") securities.

---

[9]The NYSE is actually a modified auction market wherein people (through their brokers) bid for stocks. Originally—in 1792—brokers would literally shout, "I have 100 shares of Erie for sale; how much am I offered?" and then sell to the highest bidder. If a broker had a buy order, he or she would shout, "I want to buy 100 shares of Erie; who'll sell at the best price?" The same general situation still exists, although the exchanges now have members known as *specialists* who facilitate the trading process by keeping an inventory of shares of the stocks in which they specialize. If a buy order comes in at a time when no sell order arrives, the specialist will sell some inventory. Similarly, if a sell order comes in, the specialist will buy and add to inventory. The specialist sets a *bid price* (the price the specialist will pay for the stock) and an *ask price* (the price at which shares will be sold out of inventory). The bid and ask prices are set at levels designed to keep the inventory in balance. If many buy orders start coming in because of favorable developments, or many sell orders come in because of unfavorable events, the specialist will raise or lower prices to keep supply and demand in balance. Bid prices are somewhat lower than ask prices, with the difference, or *spread,* representing the specialist's profit margin. Special facilities are available to help institutional investors such as mutual or pension funds sell large blocks of stock without depressing their prices. In essence, brokerage houses that cater to institutional clients will purchase blocks (defined as 10,000 or more shares) and then resell the stock to other institutions or individuals. Also, when a firm has a major announcement that is likely to cause its stock price to change sharply, it will ask the exchange to halt trading in its stock until the announcement has been made and the resulting information has been digested by investors.

## GLOBAL PERSPECTIVES

### *The NYSE and NASDAQ Go Global*

Advances in computers and telecommunications that spurred consolidation in the financial services industry have also promoted online trading systems that bypass the traditional exchanges. These systems, which are known as *electronic communications networks (ECNs)*, use electronic technology to bring buyers and sellers together. The rise of ECNs accelerated the move toward 24-hour trading. U.S. investors who wanted to trade after the U.S. markets closed could utilize an ECN, thus bypassing the NYSE and NASDAQ.

Recognizing the new threat, the NYSE and NASDAQ took action. First, both exchanges went public, which enabled them to use their stock as "currency" that could be used to buy ECNs and other exchanges across the globe. For example, NASDAQ acquired the Philadelphia Stock Exchange, several ECNs, and 25% of the London Stock Exchange; and it is actively seeking to merge with other exchanges around the world. The NYSE took similar actions, including a merger with the largest European exchange, Euronext, to form NYSE Euronext and then acquiring the American Stock Exchange (AMEX).

More recently, the NYSE Euronext itself became a takeover target, when it was recently acquired by the Intercontinental Exchange (ICE). The deal combined ICE's futures, over-the-counter, and derivatives trading with the NYSE's stock trading. The takeover received final regulatory approval in 2013. On June 24, 2014, ICE spun off Euronext.

These actions illustrate the growing importance of global trading, especially electronic trading. Indeed, many pundits have concluded that the floor traders who buy and sell stocks on the NYSE and other physical exchanges will soon become a thing of the past. That may or may not be true, but it is clear that stock trading will continue to undergo dramatic changes in the upcoming years. To find a wealth of up-to-date information on the NYSE and NASDAQ, go to Google (or another search engine) and do NYSE history and NASDAQ history searches.

Sources: John McCrank and Luke Jeffs, "ICE to Buy NYSE Euronext for $8.2 Billion" www.reuters.com, December 20, 2012; Inti Landauro, "ICE Plans Euronext IPO," *The Wall Street Journal* (online.wsj.com), May 27, 2014; and Alex Gavrish, "Euronext NV: Recent Spin-Off Warrants Further Monitoring," *ValueWalk* (www.valuewalk.com), August 25, 2014.

## 2-4B OVER-THE-COUNTER (OTC) AND THE NASDAQ STOCK MARKETS

**Over-the-Counter (OTC) Market**

A large collection of brokers and dealers, connected electronically by telephones and computers, that provides for trading in unlisted securities.

Although the stocks of most large companies trade on the NYSE, a larger number of stocks trade off the exchange in what was traditionally referred to as the **over-the-counter (OTC) market**. An explanation of the term *over-the-counter* will help clarify how this term arose. As noted earlier, the exchanges operate as auction markets—buy and sell orders come in more or less simultaneously, and exchange members match these orders. When a stock is traded infrequently, perhaps because the firm is new or small, few buy and sell orders come in, and matching them within a reasonable amount of time is difficult. To avoid this problem, some brokerage firms maintain an inventory of such stocks and stand prepared to make a market for them. These "dealers" buy when individual investors want to sell, and they sell part of their inventory when investors want to buy. At one time, the inventory of securities was kept in a safe; and the stocks, when bought and sold, were literally passed over the counter.

**Dealer Markets**

Include all facilities that are needed to conduct security transactions not conducted on the physical location exchanges.

Today these markets are often referred to as **dealer markets**. A dealer market includes all facilities that are needed to conduct security transactions, but the transactions are not made on the physical location exchanges. The dealer market system consists of (1) the relatively few *dealers* who hold inventories of these securities and who are said to "make a market" in these securities; (2) the thousands of brokers who act as *agents* in bringing the dealers together with investors; and (3) the computers, terminals, and electronic networks that provide a communication link between dealers and brokers. The dealers who make a market in a particular stock quote the price at which they will pay for the stock (the *bid price*) and the price at which they will sell shares (the *ask price*). Each dealer's prices, which are adjusted as supply and demand conditions change, can be seen on computer screens across the world. The *bid-ask spread,* which is the difference between bid and ask prices, represents the dealer's markup, or profit. The dealer's risk increases when the stock is more volatile or when the stock trades infrequently. Generally, we would expect volatile, infrequently traded stocks to have wider spreads in order to compensate the dealers for assuming the risk of holding them in inventory.

Brokers and dealers who participate in the OTC market are members of a self-regulatory body known as the *Financial Industry Regulatory Authority* (FINRA), which licenses brokers and oversees trading practices. The computerized network used by FINRA is known as NASDAQ, which originally stood for "National Association of Securities Dealers Automated Quotations."

NASDAQ started as a quotation system, but it has grown to become an organized securities market with its own listing requirements. Over the past decade, the competition between the NYSE and NASDAQ has become increasingly fierce. As noted earlier, the NASDAQ has invested in the London Stock Exchange and other market makers, while the NYSE merged with Euronext (which was later spun off) and was purchased by Intercontinental Exchange—further adding to the competition. Because most of the larger companies trade on the NYSE, the market capitalization of NYSE-traded stocks is much higher than for stocks traded on NASDAQ.

Interestingly, many high-tech companies such as Microsoft, Google, and Intel have remained on NASDAQ even though they meet the listing requirements of the NYSE. At the same time, however, other high-tech companies have left NASDAQ for the NYSE. Despite these defections, NASDAQ's growth over the past decade has been impressive. In the years ahead, competition between NASDAQ and NYSE will no doubt remain fierce.

## Self*Test*

What are the differences between the physical location exchanges and the NASDAQ stock market?

What is the bid-ask spread?

# 2-5 The Market for Common Stock

Some companies are so small that their common stocks are not actively traded; they are owned by relatively few people, usually the companies' managers. These firms are said to be *privately owned,* or **closely held, corporations**; and their stock is called *closely held stock.* In contrast, the stocks of most large companies are owned by thousands of investors, most of whom are not active in management. These companies are called **publicly owned corporations**, and their stock is called *publicly held stock.*

## 2-5A TYPES OF STOCK MARKET TRANSACTIONS

We can classify stock market transactions into three distinct categories:

1.  *Outstanding shares of established publicly owned companies that are traded: the secondary market.* Allied Food Products, the company we study in Chapters 3 and 4, has 50 million shares of stock outstanding. If the owner of 100 shares sells his or her stock, the trade is said to have occurred in the *secondary market.* Thus, the market for outstanding shares, or *used shares,* is the secondary market. The company receives no new money when sales occur in this market.

*Closely Held Corporation*
A corporation that is owned by a few individuals who are typically associated with the firm's management.

*Publicly Owned Corporation*
A corporation that is owned by a relatively large number of individuals who are not actively involved in the firm's management.

2. *Additional shares sold by established publicly owned companies: the primary market.* If Allied Food decides to sell (or issue) an additional 1 million shares to raise new equity capital, this transaction is said to occur in the *primary market.*[10]

3. *Initial public offerings made by privately held firms: the IPO market.* Whenever stock in a closely held corporation is offered to the public for the first time, the company is said to be **going public**. The market for stock that is just being offered to the public is called the **initial public offering (IPO) market.**[11] In the summer of 2004, Google sold shares to the public for the first time at $85 per share. By March 2015, the stock was selling for more than $575. In 2006, McDonald's owned Chipotle Mexican Grill. McDonald's then sold its shares to the public for about $47.50 to raise capital to support its core business; and by March 2015, Chipotle's stock price was more than $670. In some more recent examples, General Motors (GM) went public as part of its reorganization following its government bailout. In May 2011, the professional-networking site LinkedIn Corp. created excitement when shares of its IPO more than doubled during its first day of trading. In 2013, Twitter went public at an offer price of $26 per share; a day later its price had jumped to an intra-day high above $50 per share. In March 2015, its price has cooled off a bit and is in the neighborhood of $47 per share. And, of course, Alibaba's initial stock price on September 19, 2014, was $68 but by close its price had risen 38% to $93.89. In early March 2015, its price has simmered somewhat to around $85 per share.

The number of new IPOs rises and falls with the stock market. When the market is strong, many companies go public to bring in new capital and to give their founders an opportunity to cash out some of their shares. As you might expect, not all IPOs are as well received as Google, Chipotle, and LinkedIn. The most striking example is Facebook, which had the largest and highest-profile IPO of 2012. Amid much fanfare, the company went public on May 18, 2012, at a price of $38 per share. In the two weeks after the IPO, the stock had fallen to below $28, and just a few months later in September, the price reached a low of $17.55. By year-end 2012, the stock rebounded to $26.62, which was still 30% below the initial offering price. So, although Facebook raised a lot of money through its IPO, its initial investors did not quickly realize the big return that many were looking to capture. However, it is important to note that despite its rocky start, investors who continued to hold Facebook stock did quite well. In contrast, the box, titled "Initial Buzz Surrounding IPOs Doesn't Always Translate into Long-Lasting Success," demonstrates Twitter's disappointing post-IPO performance, despite a much higher first day return.

Even if you are able to identify a "hot" issue, it is often difficult to purchase shares in the initial offering. These deals are often *oversubscribed*, which means that the demand for shares at the offering price exceeds the number of shares issued. In such instances, investment bankers favor large institutional investors (who are their best customers); and small investors find it hard, if not impossible, to get in on the ground floor. They can buy the stock in the aftermarket; but evidence suggests that when an investor does not get in on the ground floor, over the long run IPOs often

*Going Public*

The act of selling stock to the public at large by a closely held corporation or its principal stockholders.

*Initial Public Offering (IPO) Market*

The market for stocks of companies that are in the process of going public.

*For information on IPOs, refer to Professor Jay Ritter's (University of Florida) web page* **site.warrington.ufl .edu/ritter/ipo-data/.**

---

[10]Allied has 60 million shares authorized but only 50 million outstanding; thus, it has 10 million authorized but unissued shares. If it had no authorized but unissued shares, management could increase the authorized shares by obtaining stockholders' approval, which would generally be granted without any arguments.

[11]A number of years ago Coors, the beer company, offered some of its shares to the public. These shares were designated Class B, and they were nonvoting. The Coors family retained the founders' shares, called Class A stock, which carried full voting privileges. This illustrates how the managers of a company can use different classes of shares to maintain control.

# INITIAL BUZZ SURROUNDING IPOs DOESN'T ALWAYS TRANSLATE INTO LONG-LASTING SUCCESS

A recent article in *Fortune* cautions IPO investors: "Don't be fooled by the drama of first-day performance." The article suggests that there is not always a strong correlation between the market's initial reaction to an IPO and the stock's longer-run performance. As a case in point, *Fortune* compares the post-IPO performance of Facebook and Twitter. As we mention in the text, Facebook's stock slid sharply in the aftermath of its IPO. However, since then Facebook's stock has impressively rebounded. By contrast, Twitter's IPO generated a lot of initial buzz, but since then the stock has languished. The chart below illustrates Twitter's post-IPO struggles and highlights the major events the company faced after going public.

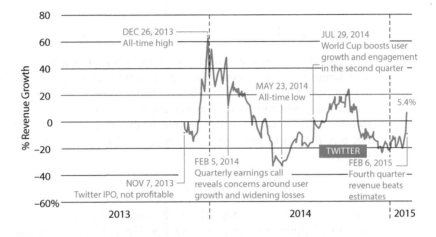

Source: Erin Griffith, "The Tale of Two IPOs: Facebook and Twitter," *Fortune* (www.fortune.com), February 19, 2015.

underperform the overall market.[12] Other critics point out that when an IPO's price dramatically jumps the first day of trading, this implies that the underwriter set the price too low and failed to maximize the issuer's potential proceeds by "leaving money on the table." [13]

Google's highly publicized IPO attracted attention because of its size (Google raised $1.67 billion in stock) and because of the way the sale was conducted. Rather than having the offer price set by its investment bankers, Google conducted a Dutch auction, where individual investors placed bids for shares directly. In a *Dutch auction*, the actual transaction price is set at the highest price (the clearing price) that causes all of the offered shares to be sold. Investors who set their bids at or above the clearing price received all of the shares they subscribed to at the offer price, which turned out to be $85. While Google's IPO was in many ways precedent setting, few companies going public since then have been willing or able to use the Dutch auction method to allocate their IPO shares.

It is important to recognize that firms can go public without raising any additional capital. For example, the Ford Motor Company was once owned exclusively by the Ford family. When Henry Ford died, he left a substantial part of his

---

[12]See Jay R. Ritter, "The Long-Run Performance of Initial Public Offerings," *Journal of Finance*, vol. 46, no. 1 (March 1991), pp. 3–27.

[13]See, for example, the online column by Professor Hersh Shefrin, "Why Twitter's IPO Was Really a Failure," *Forbes* (www.forbes.com), November 8, 2013.

stock to the Ford Foundation. When the Foundation later sold some of the stock to the general public, the Ford Motor Company went public, even though the company itself raised no capital in the transaction.

## SelfTest

Differentiate between closely held and publicly owned corporations.

Differentiate between primary and secondary markets.

What is an IPO?

What is a Dutch auction, and what company used this procedure for its IPO?

# 2-6 Stock Markets and Returns

Anyone who has invested in the stock market knows that there can be (and generally are) large differences between *expected* and *realized* prices and returns. Figure 2.2 shows how total realized portfolio returns have varied from year to year. As logic would suggest (and as is demonstrated in Chapter 9), a stock's expected return as estimated by investors at the margin is always positive; otherwise, investors would not buy the stock. However, as Figure 2.2 shows, in some years, actual returns are negative.

### 2-6A STOCK MARKET REPORTING

Up until a few years ago, the best source of stock quotations was the business section of daily newspapers such as *The Wall Street Journal*. One problem with newspapers, however, is that they report yesterday's prices. Now it is possible to obtain quotes throughout the day from a wide variety of Internet sources. One of the best is Yahoo!'s finance.yahoo.com; Figure 2.3 shows a detailed quote for Twitter, Inc. (TWTR) for March 9, 2015. As the heading shows, Twitter is traded on the NYSE under the symbol TWTR. The information right below the company name and ticker symbol shows the real-time quote at 12:03 p.m. EDT of $47.62, which is up $0.87 (or 1.87%) from the previous day's close. Twitter stock closed on Friday, March 6, 2015, at $46.75 per share and it opened for trading on Monday, March 9, 2015, at $47.22 per share. As of noon March 9, 2015, Twitter's stock had

**FIGURE 2.2**   S&P 500 Index, Total Returns: Dividend Yield + Capital Gain or Loss, 1968–2014

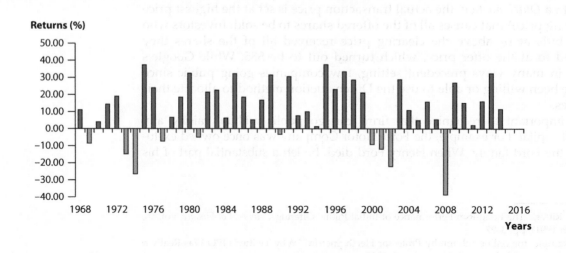

Source: Data taken from various issues of *The Wall Street Journal* "Investment Scoreboard" section.

| FIGURE 2.3 | Stock Quote for Twitter, Inc., March 9, 2015 |
|---|---|

**Twitter, Inc. (TWTR)** - NYSE  ★ Watchlist

**47.62** ↑0.87 (1.87%)  12:03PM EDT - Nasdaq Real Time Price

| | | | |
|---|---|---|---|
| Prev Close: | 46.75 | Day's Range: | 47.13–48.08 |
| Open: | 47.22 | 52wk Range: | 29.51–55.99 |
| Bid: | 47.83 × 200 | Volume: | 7,531,031 |
| Ask: | 47.84 × 900 | Avg Vol (3m): | 20,498,600 |
| 1y Target Est: | 53.00 | Market Cap: | 30.36B |
| Beta: | N/A | P/E (ttm): | N/A |
| Earnings Date: | Apr 27–May 1 (Est.) | EPS (ttm): | −0.96 |
| | | Div & Yield: | N/A (N/A) |

Twitter, Inc. Common Stock ■ TWTR  Mar 9, 12:03pm EDT

Source: Twitter, Inc. (TWTR), finance.yahoo.com.

traded from a low of $47.13 to a high of $48.08 and the price range during the past 52 weeks was between $29.51 and $55.99.

The next three lines give the bid (buy) and ask (sell) price range for the stock—the difference between the two represents the dealer's spread or profit. (In this example, a buyer had offered to purchase 200 shares at a bid price of $47.83, and a seller was offering to sell 900 shares at an ask price of $47.84.) The 1-year target estimate represents the median 1-year target price as forecasted by analysts covering the stock. As of noon March 9, 7,531,031 shares of stock had traded hands. Twitter's average daily trading volume (based on the past 3 months) was 20,498,600 shares, so just based on half a day, trading on this day looks to be below the average daily trading volume. The total value of all of Twitter's stock, called its market cap, was $30.36 billion.

The last three lines report other market information for Twitter. The beta for the company is not shown. The firm's next earnings announcement is estimated between April 27th and May 1st. Twitter's P/E ratio (price per share divided by the most recent 12 months' earnings) is not shown, and its earnings per share for the most recent 12 months was −$0.96. Twitter doesn't pay a dividend so the dividend and yield information is shown as N/A (not applicable).

In Figure 2.3, the chart to the right plots the stock price during the day; however, the links below the chart allow you to pick different time intervals for plotting data. As you can see, Yahoo! provides a great deal of information in its detailed quote; and even more detail is available on the screen page below the basic quote information.

## 2-6B STOCK MARKET RETURNS

In Chapters 8 and 9, we discuss in detail how a stock's rate of return is calculated, what the connection is between risk and returns, and what techniques analysts use to value stocks. However, it is useful at this point to give you an idea of how stocks have performed in recent years. Figure 2.2 shows how the returns on large U.S. stocks have varied over the past years, and the box titled "Measuring the Market" provides information on the major U.S. stock market indices and their performances since the mid-1990s.

The market trend has been strongly up since 1968, but by no means does it go up every year. Indeed, as we can see from Figure 2.2, the overall market was down

# MEASURING THE MARKET

Stock market indexes are designed to show the performance of the stock market. However, there are many stock indexes, and it is difficult to determine which index best reflects market actions. Some are designed to represent the entire stock market, some track the returns of certain industry sectors, and others track the returns of small-cap, mid-cap, or large-cap stocks. In addition, there are indexes for different countries. We discuss here the three leading U.S. indexes. These indexes are used as a benchmark for comparing individual stocks with the overall market, for measuring the trend in stock prices over time, and for determining how various economic factors affect the market.

## Dow Jones Industrial Average

Unveiled in 1896 by Charles H. Dow, the Dow Jones Industrial Average (DJIA) began with just 10 stocks, was expanded in 1916 to 20 stocks, and then was increased to 30 stocks in 1928, when the editors of *The Wall Street Journal* began adjusting the index for stock splits and making periodic substitutions. Recently, Apple replaced AT&T on the DJIA, recognizing the importance of computer technology and social media companies. Today the DJIA still includes 30 companies. They represent about a fifth of the market value of all U.S. stocks, and all are leading companies in their industries and widely held by individual and institutional investors. Visit djaverages.com to get more information about the DJIA. You can find out how it is calculated, the companies that make up the DJIA, and more history about the DJIA. In addition, a DJIA time line shows various historical events.

## S&P 500 Index

Created in 1926, the S&P 500 Index is widely regarded as the standard for measuring large-cap U.S. stock market performance. The stocks in the S&P 500 are selected by the Standard & Poor's Index Committee, and they are the leading companies in the leading industries. It is weighted by each stock's market value, so the largest companies have the greatest influence. The S&P 500 is one of the most commonly used benchmarks for the U.S. stock market. Index funds designed to mirror the same performance of the index have grown in number and size over the last decade. The number of index funds has more than quadrupled in the last decade, and assets in stock index funds have grown over 85% during the past five years.

## NASDAQ Composite Index

The NASDAQ Composite Index measures the performance of all stocks listed on the NASDAQ. Currently, it includes approximately 2,700 companies; and because many companies in the technology sector are traded on the computer-based NASDAQ exchange, this index is generally regarded as an economic indicator of the high-tech industry. Apple, Microsoft, Google, Facebook, and Intel are the five largest NASDAQ companies, and they make up a high percentage of the index's value-weighted market capitalization. For this reason, substantial movements in the same direction by these five companies can move the entire index.

## Recent Performance

The accompanying figure plots the value that an investor would now have if he or she had invested $1 in each of the three indexes on January 1, 1995, through January 1, 2015. The returns on the three indexes are compared with an investment strategy that invests only in 1-year Treasury bills (T-bills). During the last 20 years, the average annualized returns of these indexes ranged from 7.6% for the S&P 500 to 9.5% for the NASDAQ. (The Dow's annualized return during this same period was 7.8%).

### Growth of a $1 Investment Made on January 1, 1995, through January 1, 2015

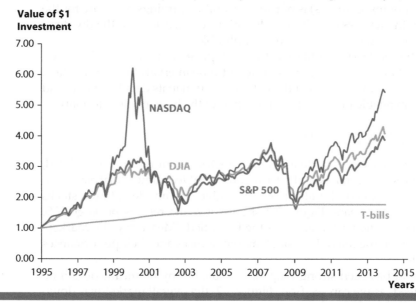

in 10 of the last 47 years, including the three consecutive years of 2000–2002. The stock prices of individual companies have likewise gone up and down.[14] Of course, even in bad years, some individual companies do well; so "the name of the game" in security analysis is to pick the winners. Financial managers attempt to do this, but they don't always succeed. In subsequent chapters, we will examine the decisions managers make to increase the odds that their firms will perform well in the marketplace.

## SelfTest

Would you expect a portfolio that consisted of the NYSE stocks to be more or less risky than a portfolio of NASDAQ stocks?

If we constructed a chart like Figure 2.2 for a typical S&P 500 stock, do you think it would show more or less volatility? Explain.

# 2-7 Stock Market Efficiency

To begin this section, consider the following definitions:

- *Market price:* The current price of a stock. For example, the Internet showed that on one day, Twitter's stock traded at $47.62. The market price had varied from $47.13 to $48.08 during that same day as buy and sell orders came in.

- *Intrinsic value:* The price at which the stock would sell if all investors had all knowable information about a stock. This concept was discussed in Chapter 1, where we saw that a stock's intrinsic value is based on its expected future cash flows and its risk. Moreover, the market price tends to fluctuate around the intrinsic value; and the intrinsic value changes over time as the company succeeds or fails with new projects, competitors enter or exit the market, and so forth. We can guess (or estimate) Twitter's intrinsic value, but different analysts will reach somewhat different conclusions.

- *Equilibrium price:* The price that balances buy and sell orders at any given time. When a stock is in equilibrium, the price remains relatively stable until new information becomes available and causes the price to change.

- *Efficient market:* A market in which prices are close to intrinsic values and stocks seem to be in equilibrium.

When markets are efficient, investors can buy and sell stocks and be confident that they are getting good prices. When markets are inefficient, investors may be afraid to invest and may put their money "under the pillow," which will lead to a poor allocation of capital and economic stagnation. From an economic standpoint, market efficiency is good.

---

[14]If we constructed a graph like Figure 2.2 for individual stocks rather than for the index, far greater variability would be shown. Also, if we constructed a graph like Figure 2.2 for bonds, it would have similar ups and downs, but the bars would be far smaller, indicating that gains and losses on bonds are generally much smaller than those on stocks. Above-average bond returns occur in years when interest rates decline, losses occur when interest rates rise sharply, but interest payments tend to stabilize bonds' total returns. We discuss bonds in detail in Chapter 7.

Academics and financial professionals have studied the issue of market efficiency.[15] As generally happens, some people think that markets are highly efficient, some think that markets are highly inefficient, and others think that the issue is too complex for a simple answer. With this point in mind, it is interesting to note that the 2013 Nobel Prize in Economics was awarded to three distinguished scholars (Eugene Fama, Lars Hansen, and Robert Shiller) for their "empirical analysis of asset prices." Professor Hansen was cited for his work in developing statistical models for testing the rationality of markets. Also, acknowledging the validity of different views in this area, the Nobel Committee saw fit to simultaneously recognize Professor Fama (a pioneer in developing efficient market theory) and Professor Shiller (a noted skeptic of market efficiency).

Those who believe that markets are efficient note that there are 100,000 or so full-time, highly trained professional analysts and traders operating in the market. Many have PhDs in physics, chemistry, and other technical fields in addition to advanced degrees in finance. Moreover, there are fewer than 3,000 major stocks; so if each analyst followed 30 stocks (which is about right, as analysts tend to focus on a specific industry), on average, 1,000 analysts would be following each stock. Further, these analysts work for organizations such as Goldman Sachs, JPMorgan Chase, and Deutsche Bank or for Warren Buffett and other billionaire investors who have billions of dollars available to take advantage of bargains. Also, the SEC has disclosure rules that, combined with electronic information networks, means that new information about a stock is received by all analysts at about the same time, causing almost instantaneous revaluations. All of these factors help markets to be efficient and cause stock prices to move toward their intrinsic values.

However, other people point to data that suggest that markets are not very efficient. For example, on May 6, 2010, the Dow Jones Index fell nearly 1,000 points only to rebound rapidly by the end of the day.[16] In 2000, Internet stocks rose to phenomenally high prices, and then fell to zero or close to it the following year. No truly important news was announced that could have caused either of these changes; and if the market was efficient, it's hard to see how such drastic changes could have occurred. Another situation that causes people to question market efficiency is the apparent ability of some analysts to consistently outperform the market over long periods. Warren Buffett comes to mind, but there are others. If markets are truly efficient, then each stock's price should be close to its intrinsic value. That would make it hard for any analyst to consistently pick stocks that outperform the market.

The following diagram sums up where most observers seem to be today. There is an "efficiency continuum," with the market for some companies' stocks being highly efficient and the market for other stocks being highly inefficient. The key factor is the size of the company—the larger the firm, the more analysts tend to follow it and thus the faster new information is likely to be reflected in the stock's price. Also, different companies communicate better

---

[15]The general name for these studies is the *efficient markets hypothesis*, or *EMH*. It was, and still is, a hypothesis that needs to be proved or disproved empirically. In the literature, researchers identified three levels of efficiency: *weak form,* which contends that information on past stock price movements cannot be used to predict future stock prices; *semi-strong form,* which contends that all publicly available information is immediately incorporated into stock prices (i.e., that one cannot analyze published reports and then beat the market); and *strong form,* which contends that even company insiders, with inside information, cannot earn abnormally high returns.

[16]Regulators are investigating the causes of this dramatic decline, and are particularly focusing on the role played by computerized trading. Refer to Tom Lauricella, Scott Patterson, and Carolyn Cui, "Computer Trading Is Eyed," *The Wall Street Journal* (online.wsj.com), May 8, 2010.

with analysts and investors; and the better the communications, the more efficient the market for the stock.

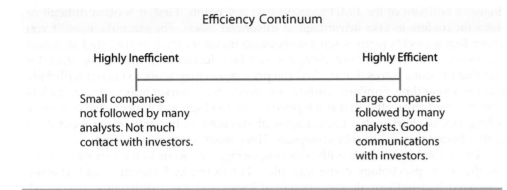

Efficiency Continuum

Highly Inefficient

Highly Efficient

Small companies not followed by many analysts. Not much contact with investors.

Large companies followed by many analysts. Good communications with investors.

As an investor, would you prefer to purchase a stock whose price was determined in an efficient or an inefficient market? If you thought you knew something that others didn't know, you might prefer inefficient markets. But if you thought that those physics PhDs with unlimited buying power and access to company CEOs might know more than you, you would probably prefer efficient markets, where the price you paid was likely to be the "right" price. From an economic standpoint, it is good to have efficient markets in which everyone is willing to participate. So the SEC and other regulatory agencies should do everything they can to encourage market efficiency.

Thus far we have been discussing the market for individual stocks. But the notion of efficiency applies to the pricing of all assets. For example, the dramatic rise and subsequent collapse of housing prices in many U.S. markets suggests that there was a lot of inefficiency in these markets. It is also important to realize that the level of market efficiency also varies over time. In one respect, we might expect that lower transactions costs and the increasing number of analysts would cause markets to become increasingly efficient over time. However, the recent housing bubble and the previous bubble for Internet stocks provides some contrary evidence. Indeed, these recent events have caused many experts to look for alternative reasons for this apparent irrational behavior. A lot of their research looks for psychologically based explanations, which we discuss in the next section.

## 2-7A BEHAVIORAL FINANCE THEORY

The *efficient markets hypothesis (EMH)* remains one of the cornerstones of modern finance theory. It implies that, on average, asset prices are about equal to their intrinsic values. The logic behind the EMH is straightforward. If a stock's price is "too low," rational traders will quickly take advantage of this opportunity and buy the stock, pushing prices up to the proper level. Likewise, if prices are "too high," rational traders will sell the stock, pushing the price down to its equilibrium level. Proponents of the EMH argue that these forces keep prices from being systematically wrong.

Although the logic behind the EMH is compelling, many events in the real world seem inconsistent with the hypothesis, which has spurred a growing field called *behavioral finance*. Rather than assuming that investors are rational, behavioral finance theorists borrow insights from psychology to better understand how irrational behavior can be sustained over time. Pioneers in this field include psychologists Daniel Kahneman, Amos Tversky, and Richard Thaler.

Their work has encouraged a growing number of scholars to work in this promising area of research.[17]

Professor Thaler and his colleague Nicholas Barberis argue that behavioral finance's criticism of the EMH rests on two key points. First, it is often difficult or risky for traders to take advantage of mispriced assets. For example, even if you know that a stock's price is too low because investors have overreacted to recent bad news, a trader with limited capital may be reluctant to purchase the stock for fear that the same forces that pushed the price down may work to keep it artificially low for a long time. Similarly, during the recent stock market bubble, many traders who believed (correctly) that stock prices were too high lost a great deal of money selling stocks short in the early stages of the bubble, because prices went even higher before they eventually collapsed. Thus, mispricings may persist.

The second point deals with why mispricings can occur in the first place. Here insights from psychology come into play. For example, Kahneman and Tversky suggested that individuals view potential losses and gains differently. If you ask average individuals whether they would rather have $500 with certainty or flip a fair coin and receive $1,000 if a head comes up and nothing if a tail comes up, most would prefer the certain $500, which suggests an aversion to risk. However, if you ask people whether they would rather pay $500 with certainty or flip a coin and pay $1,000 if it's a head and nothing if it's a tail, most would indicate that they prefer to flip the coin. Other studies suggest that people's willingness to take a gamble depends on recent performance. Gamblers who are ahead tend to take on more risk, whereas those who are behind tend to become more conservative.

These experiments suggest that investors and managers behave differently in down markets than they do in up markets, which might explain why those who made money early in the stock market bubble continued to invest their money in the market even as prices went ever higher. Other evidence suggests that individuals tend to overestimate their true abilities. For example, a large majority of people (upward of 90% in some studies) believe that they have above-average driving ability and above-average ability to get along with others. Barberis and Thaler point out that:

> *Overconfidence may in part stem from two other biases, self-attribution bias and hindsight bias. Self-attribution bias refers to people's tendency to ascribe any success they have in some activity to their own talents, while blaming failure on bad luck rather than on their ineptitude. Doing this repeatedly will lead people to the pleasing, but erroneous, conclusion that they are very talented. For example, investors might become overconfident after several quarters of investing success [Gervais and Odean (2001)]. Hindsight bias is the tendency of people to believe, after an event has occurred, that they predicted it before it happened. If people think they predicted the past better than they actually did, they may also believe that they can predict the future better than they actually can.[18]*

---

[17]Five noteworthy sources for students interested in behavioral finance are George Akerlof and Robert Shiller, *Animal Spirits: How Human Psychology Drives the Economy, and Why It Matters for Global Capitalism* (Princeton, NJ: Princeton University Press, 2009); Richard Thaler and Cass Sunstein, *Nudge: Improving Decisions about Health, Wealth, and Happiness* (New Haven, CT: Yale University Press, 2008); Richard H. Thaler, Editor, *Advances in Behavioral Finance* (New York: Russell Sage Foundation, 1993); Hersh Shefrin, "Behavioral Corporate Finance," *Journal of Applied Corporate Finance*, vol. 14, no. 3 (Fall 2001), pp. 113–125; and Nicholas Barberis and Richard Thaler, "A Survey of Behavioral Finance," Chapter 18 in *Handbook of the Economics of Finance*, edited by George Constantinides, Milt Harris, and René Stulz (New York: Elsevier/North-Holland, 2003). Students interested in learning more about the efficient markets hypothesis should consult Burton G. Malkiel, *A Random Walk Down Wall Street: The Time-Tested Strategy for Successful Investing*, 9th edition (New York: W.W. Norton & Company, 2007).

[18]Nicholas Barberis and Richard Thaler, "A Survey of Behavioral Finance," Chapter 18 in *Handbook of the Economics of Finance*, edited by George Constantinides, Milt Harris, and René Stulz (New York: Elsevier/North-Holland, 2003).

Behavioral finance has been studied in both the corporate finance and investments areas. For example, Mark Grinblatt and Matti Keloharju conducted a recent study demonstrating that investors who are characterized as being overconfident and prone to "seeking sensations" trade more frequently.[19] Likewise, a study by Ulrike Malmendier of Stanford and Geoffrey Tate of Wharton found that overconfidence leads managers to overestimate their ability and thus the profitability of their projects.[20] This may explain why so many corporate projects fail to live up to their stated expectations.

## 2-7B CONCLUSIONS ABOUT MARKET EFFICIENCY

As noted previously, if the stock market is efficient, it is a waste of time for most people to seek bargains by analyzing published data on stocks. That follows because if stock prices already reflect all publicly available information, they will be fairly priced; and a person can beat the market only with luck or inside information. So rather than spending time and money trying to find undervalued stocks, it would be better to buy an index fund designed to match the overall market as reflected in an index such as the S&P 500. However, if we worked for an institution with billions of dollars, we would try to find undervalued stocks or companies because even a small undervaluation would amount to a great deal of money when investing millions rather than thousands. Also, markets are more efficient for individual stocks than for entire companies; so for investors with enough capital, it does make sense to seek out badly managed companies that can be acquired and improved. Note, though, that a number of private equity players are doing exactly that; so the market for entire companies may soon be as efficient as that for individual stocks.

However, even if markets are efficient and all stocks and companies are fairly priced, an investor should still be careful when selecting stocks for his or her portfolio. Most importantly, the portfolio should be diversified, with a mix of stocks from various industries along with some bonds and other fixed-income securities. We will discuss diversification in greater detail in Chapter 8, but it is an important consideration for most individual investors.

## SelfTest

What does it mean for a market to be "efficient"?

Is the market for all stocks equally efficient? Explain.

Why is it good for the economy that markets be efficient?

Is it possible that the market for individual stocks could be highly efficient, but the market for whole companies could be less efficient? Explain.

What is behavioral finance? What are the implications of behavioral finance for market efficiency?

---

[19]Mark Grinblatt and Matti Keloharju: "Sensation Seeking, Overconfidence, and Trading Activity," *The Journal of Finance*, vol. LXIV, no. 2 (April 2009), pp. 549–578.
[20]Ulrike Malmendier and Geoffrey Tate, "CEO Overconfidence and Corporate Investment," Stanford Graduate School of Business Research Paper #1799, June 2004.

# TYING IT ALL TOGETHER

In this chapter, we provided a brief overview of how capital is allocated and discussed the financial markets, instruments, and institutions used in the allocation process. We discussed physical location exchanges and electronic markets for common stocks, stock market reporting, and stock indexes. We demonstrated that security prices are volatile—investors expect to make money, which they generally do over time; but losses can be large in any given year. Finally, we discussed the efficiency of the stock market and developments in behavioral finance. After reading this chapter, you should have a general understanding of the financial environment in which businesses and individuals operate, realize that actual returns are often different from expected returns, and be able to read stock market quotations from business newspapers or various Internet sites. You should also recognize that the theory of financial markets is a "work in progress," and much work remains to be done.

## Self-Test Questions and Problems

(Solutions Appear in Appendix A)

ST-1 **KEY TERMS** Define each of the following terms:
a. Spot markets; futures markets
b. Money markets; capital markets
c. Primary markets; secondary markets
d. Private markets; public markets
e. Derivatives
f. Investment banks (iBanks); commercial banks; financial services corporations
g. Mutual funds; money market funds
h. Physical location exchanges; over-the-counter (OTC) market; dealer market
i. Closely held corporation; publicly owned corporation
j. Going public; initial public offering (IPO) market
k. Efficient markets hypothesis (EMH)
l. Behavioral finance

## Questions

2-1 How does a cost-efficient capital market help reduce the prices of goods and services?

2-2 Describe the different ways in which capital can be transferred from suppliers of capital to those who are demanding capital.

2-3 Is an initial public offering an example of a primary or a secondary market transaction? Explain.

2-4 Indicate whether the following instruments are examples of money market or capital market securities.

    a. U.S. Treasury bills
    b. Long-term corporate bonds
    c. Common stocks
    d. Preferred stocks
    e. Dealer commercial paper

2-5 What would happen to the U.S. standard of living if people lost faith in the safety of the financial institutions? Explain.

2-6 What types of changes have financial markets experienced during the last two decades? Have they been perceived as positive or negative changes? Explain.

2-7 Differentiate between dealer markets and stock markets that have a physical location.

2-8 Identify and briefly compare the two leading stock exchanges in the United States today.

2-9 Briefly explain what is meant by the term *efficiency continuum*.

2-10 Explain whether the following statements are true or false.

    a. Derivative transactions are designed to increase risk and are used almost exclusively by speculators who are looking to capture high returns.
    b. Hedge funds typically have large minimum investments and are marketed to institutions and individuals with high net worths.
    c. Hedge funds have traditionally been highly regulated.
    d. The New York Stock Exchange is an example of a stock exchange that has a physical location.
    e. A larger bid-ask spread means that the dealer will realize a lower profit.

# INTEGRATED CASE

## SMYTH BARRY & COMPANY

2-1 **FINANCIAL MARKETS AND INSTITUTIONS** Assume that you recently graduated with a degree in finance and have just reported to work as an investment adviser at the brokerage firm of Smyth Barry & Co. Your first assignment is to explain the nature of the U.S. financial markets to Michelle Varga, a professional tennis player who recently came to the United States from Mexico. Varga is a highly ranked tennis player who expects to invest substantial amounts of money through Smyth Barry. She is very bright; therefore, she would like to understand in general terms what will happen to her money. Your boss has developed the following questions that you must use to explain the U.S. financial system to Varga.

    a. What are the three primary ways in which capital is transferred between savers and borrowers? Describe each one.
    b. What is a market? Differentiate between the following types of markets: physical asset markets versus financial asset markets, spot markets versus futures markets, money markets versus capital markets, primary markets versus secondary markets, and public markets versus private markets.
    c. Why are financial markets essential for a healthy economy and economic growth?
    d. What are derivatives? How can derivatives be used to reduce risk? Can derivatives be used to increase risk? Explain.

e. Briefly describe each of the following financial institutions: investment banks, commercial banks, financial services corporations, pension funds, mutual funds, exchange traded funds, hedge funds, and private equity companies.

f. What are the two leading stock markets? Describe the two basic types of stock markets.

g. If Apple Computer decided to issue additional common stock, and Varga purchased 100 shares of this stock from Smyth Barry, the underwriter, would this transaction be a primary or a secondary market transaction? Would it make a difference if Varga purchased previously outstanding Apple stock in the dealer market? Explain.

h. What is an initial public offering (IPO)?

i. What does it mean for a market to be efficient? Explain why some stock prices may be more efficient than others.

j. After your consultation with Michelle, she wants to discuss these two possible stock purchases:

1. While in the waiting room of your office, she overheard an analyst on a financial TV network say that a particular medical research company just received FDA approval for one of its products. On the basis of this "hot" information, Michelle wants to buy many shares of that company's stock. Assuming the stock market is highly efficient, what advice would you give her?

2. She has read a number of newspaper articles about a huge IPO being carried out by a leading technology company. She wants to purchase as many shares in the IPO as possible and would even be willing to buy the shares in the open market immediately after the issue. What advice do you have for her?

k. How does behavioral finance explain the real-world inconsistencies of the efficient markets hypothesis (EMH)?

# Financial Statements, Cash Flow, and Taxes

Diana Haronis/Getty Images

## Unlocking the Valuable Information in Financial Statements

In Chapter 1, we said that managers should make decisions that enhance long-term shareholder value, and they should be less concerned about short-term accounting measures such as earnings per share. With that important point in mind, you might reasonably wonder why are we now going to talk about accounting and financial statements. The simple answer is financial statements convey a lot of useful information that helps corporate managers assess the company's strengths and weaknesses and gauge the expected impact of various proposals. Good managers must have a solid understanding of the key financial statements. Outsiders also rely heavily on financial statements when deciding whether they want to buy the company's stock, lend money to the company, or enter into a long-term business relationship with the company.

At first glance, financial statements can be overwhelming—but if we know what we are looking for, we can quickly learn a great deal about a company after a quick review of its financial statements. Looking at the balance sheet we can see how large a company is, the types of assets it holds, and how it finances those assets. Looking at the income statement, we can see if the company's sales increased or declined and whether the company made a profit. Glancing at the statement of cash flows, we can see if the company made any new investments, if it raised funds through financing, repurchased debt or equity, or paid dividends.

For example, in early 2015, Whole Foods released its first quarter financial statements. The news was good. The company announced higher than expected earnings per share, and the stock market responded positively. Its reported sales were $4.7 billion, which was nearly 10% higher than the $4.2 billion reported a year earlier. During the first quarter, Whole Foods also announced a 4.5% increase in same-store sales, and that it had opened nine new stores. Reviewing the company's 2014 annual report at the end of its fiscal year (September 28, 2014), Whole Foods showed total assets of $5.7 billion and total liabilities of $1.9 billion on its balance sheet. Finally, looking at the statement of cash flows, we see that the cash generated from its operating activities ($1.088 billion) exceeded the $484 million spent on investing activities. However, Whole Foods' overall cash position declined by $100 million because of the cash the company used to pay dividends and to repurchase common stock.

While we can learn a lot from a quick tour of the financial statements, a good financial analyst does not just accept these numbers at face value. The analyst digs deeper to see what's really driving the numbers and uses his or her intuition and knowledge of the industry to help assess the company's future direction. Keep in mind that just because a company reports great numbers doesn't mean that you should purchase the stock. In the case of Whole Foods, its stock price did rise after it announced its better-than-expected financial numbers for the first quarter. However, as is always the case, analysts have mixed feelings about the stock's future direction. It's these types of disagreements that make finance interesting, and as always, time will tell whether the optimists (the bulls) or the pessimists (the bears) are correct.

 PUTTING THINGS IN PERSPECTIVE

A manager's primary goal is to maximize shareholder value, which is based on the firm's future cash flows. But how do managers decide which actions are most likely to increase those flows, and how do investors estimate future cash flows? The answers to both questions lie in a study of financial statements that publicly traded firms must provide to investors. Here *investors* include both institutions (banks, insurance companies, pension funds, and the like) and individuals like you.

Much of the material in this chapter deals with concepts you covered in a basic accounting course. However, the information is important enough to warrant a review. Also, in accounting you probably focused on how accounting statements are made; the focus here is on how investors and managers *interpret* and *use* them. Accounting is the basic language of business, so everyone engaged in business needs a good working knowledge of it. It is used to "keep score"; and if investors and managers do not know the score, they won't know whether their actions are appropriate. If you took midterm exams but were not told your scores, you would have a difficult time knowing whether you needed to improve. The same idea holds in business. If a firm's managers—whether they work in marketing, human resources, production, or finance—do not understand financial statements, they will not be able to judge the effects of their actions, which will make it hard for the firm to survive, much less to have a maximum value.

When you finish this chapter you should be able to:

- List each of the key financial statements and identify the kinds of information they provide to corporate managers and investors.

- Estimate a firm's free cash flow and explain why free cash flow has such an important effect on firm value.

- Discuss the major features of the federal income tax system.

# 3-1 Financial Statements and Reports

**Annual Report**

A report issued annually by a corporation to its stockholders. It contains basic financial statements as well as management's analysis of the firm's past operations and future prospects.

The **annual report** is the most important report that corporations issue to stockholders, and it contains two types of information.[1] First, there is a verbal section, often presented as a letter from the chairperson, which describes the firm's operating results during the past year and discusses new developments that will affect future operations. Second, the report provides these four basic financial statements:

1. The *balance sheet,* which shows what assets the company owns and who has claims on those assets as of a given date—for example, December 31, 2016.

2. The *income statement,* which shows the firm's sales and costs (and thus profits) during some past period—for example, 2016.

3. The *statement of cash flows,* which shows how much cash the firm began the year with, how much cash it ended up with, and what it did to increase or decrease its cash.

4. The *statement of stockholders' equity,* which shows the amount of equity the stockholders had at the start of the year, the items that increased or decreased equity, and the equity at the end of the year.

These statements are related to one another; and taken together they provide an accounting picture of the firm's operations and financial position.

The quantitative and verbal materials are equally important. The firm's financial statements report *what has actually happened* to its assets, earnings, and dividends over the past few years, whereas management's verbal statements attempt to explain why things turned out the way they did and what might happen in the future.

For discussion purposes, we use data for Allied Food Products, a processor and distributor of a wide variety of food products, to illustrate the basic financial statements. Allied was formed in 1985, when several regional firms merged; it has grown steadily while earning a reputation as one of the best firms in its industry. Allied's earnings dropped from $121.8 million in 2015 to $117.5 million in 2016. Management reported that the drop resulted from losses associated with a drought as well as increased costs due to a three-month strike. However, management then went on to describe a more optimistic picture for the future, stating that full operations had been resumed, that several unprofitable businesses had been eliminated, and that 2017 profits were expected to rise sharply. Of course, an increase in profitability may not occur; and analysts should compare management's past statements with subsequent results. In any event, *the information contained in the annual report can be used to help forecast future earnings and dividends.* Therefore, investors are very interested in this report.

We should note that Allied's financial statements are relatively simple and straightforward; we also omitted some details often shown in the statements. Allied finances with only debt and common stock—it has no preferred stock, convertibles, or complex derivative securities. Also, the firm has made no acquisitions that resulted in goodwill that must be carried on the balance sheet. Finally, all of its assets are used in its basic business operations; hence, no non-operating assets must be pulled out when we evaluate its operating performance. We deliberately chose such a company because this is an introductory text; as such, we want to explain the basics of financial analysis, not wander into arcane accounting matters that are best left to accounting and security analysis courses. We do point out some of the pitfalls that can be encountered when trying to interpret accounting statements, but we leave it to advanced courses to cover the intricacies of accounting.

---

[1]Firms also provide quarterly reports, but these are much less comprehensive than the annual report. In addition, larger firms file even more detailed statements with the Securities and Exchange Commission (SEC), giving breakdowns for each major division or subsidiary. These reports, called *10-K reports,* are made available to stockholders upon request to a company's corporate secretary. In this chapter, we focus on annual data—balance sheets at the ends of years and income statements for entire years rather than for shorter time periods.

# GLOBAL PERSPECTIVES

## *Global Accounting Standards: Will It Ever Happen?*

For the past decade, global accounting standards to improve financial reporting to investors and users of that information seemed all but certain. In 2005, the EU required the adoption of International Financial Reporting Standards (IFRS), and in 2007, the SEC eliminated the requirement for companies reporting under IFRS to reconcile their financial statements to U.S. Generally Accepted Accounting Principles (GAAP). To date, 120 countries have adopted IFRS. However, on July 13, 2012, the SEC staff issued a report that failed to recommend IFRS for U.S. adoption. The ultimate decision will be up to the SEC commission. On December 6, 2014, at an AICPA (American Institute of Certified Public Accountants) national conference, SEC chief accountant, James Schnurr, stated that he was open to dialogue about the best way to achieve high-quality financial information and comparability.

The effort to internationalize accounting standards began in 1973 with the formation of the International Accounting Standards Committee. However, in 1998, it became apparent that a full-time rule-making body with global representation was necessary; so the International Accounting Standards Board (IASB) was established. The IASB was charged with the responsibility for creating a set of IFRS. The "convergence" process began in earnest in September 2002 with the "Norwalk Agreement," in which the Financial Accounting Standards Board (FASB) and IASB undertook a short-term project to remove individual differences between the FASB's U.S. GAAP and IFRS and agreed to coordinate their activities. The process was meant to narrow gaps between the two standards, with the intention of making the transition for companies simpler and less expensive.

Obviously, the globalization of accounting standards is a huge endeavor—one that involves compromises between the IASB and FASB. However, in recent years the momentum behind this goal has diminished. Despite the best of intentions, progress toward consolidation was slowed by the 2007–2008 financial crisis and the resulting global recession. In addition, the leasing and financial instruments impairment projects progressed slowly, and the chairs of both the FASB and IASB left their positions. It has become apparent that the cost to companies, both large and small, for switching from GAAP to IFRS will be significant. Finally, the SEC has been given the task of implementing the Dodd–Frank financial reform law—limiting its ability to focus on adopting global accounting standards. However, despite the slow progress, in May 2014, the IASB and FASB issued a converged standard on revenue recognition from contracts with customers, sending a signal to capital markets that converged standards are possible. In addition, the SEC chief accountant expressed his desire to see a converged lease accounting standard in the not so distant future, since the basic lease model used by the IASB and FASB is similar.

The United States is an important economy, and without its participation it will be difficult to truly have global accounting standards. Although this report is a setback, many CFOs and accounting professionals still expect the SEC to come out with an American version of IFRS to coexist with GAAP. The FASB and IASB remain committed to improving U.S. GAAP and IFRS and achieving their convergence. Global accounting standards are probably inevitable—it's just a question of time.

Sources: Lee Berton, "All Accountants Soon May Speak the Same Language," *The Wall Street Journal*, August 29, 1995, p. A15; James Turley (CEO, Ernst & Young), "Mind the GAAP," *The Wall Street Journal*, November 9, 2007, p. A18; David M. Katz "The Path to Global Standards?" CFO.com, January 28, 2011; "Global Accounting Standards: Closing the GAAP," *The Economist* (economist.com), vol. 404, July 21, 2012; Joe Adler, "Is Effort to Unify Accounting Regimes Falling Apart?" *American Banker*, vol. 177, no. 145, July 30, 2012; Kathleen Hoffelder, "SEC Report Backs Away from Convergence," *CFO Magazine* (cfo.com/magazine), September 1, 2012; Ken Tysiac, "Still in Flux: Future of IFRS in U.S. Remains Unclear after SEC Report," *Journal of Accountancy* (journalofaccountancy.com), September 2012; and Tammy Whitehouse, "Ten Years on, Convergence Movement Starting to Wane," *Compliance Week* (complianceweek.com), October 2, 2012.

## Self Test

What is the annual report, and what two types of information does it provide?

What four financial statements are typically included in the annual report?

Why is the annual report of great interest to investors?

## 3-2 The Balance Sheet

The balance sheet is a "snapshot" of a firm's position at a specific point in time. Figure 3.1 shows the layout of a typical **balance sheet**. The left side of the statement shows the assets that the company owns, and the right side shows the firm's liabilities and *stockholders' equity*, which are claims against the firm's assets. As Figure 3.1 shows, assets are divided into two major categories: current assets and fixed, or long-term,

**Balance Sheet**
A statement of a firm's financial position at a specific point in time.

**FIGURE 3.1**     A Typical Balance Sheet

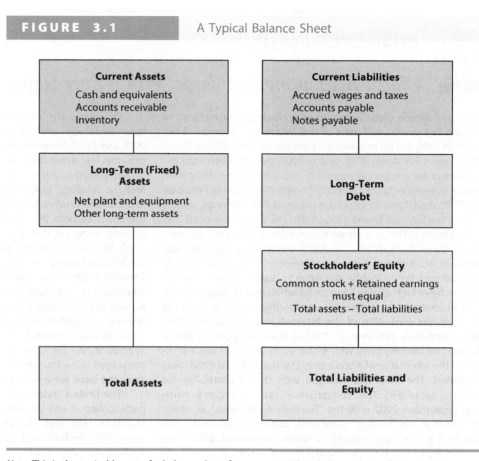

*Note:* This is the typical layout of a balance sheet for one year. When balance sheets for two or more years are shown, assets are listed in the top section; liabilities and equity, in the bottom section. See Table 3.1 for an illustration.

assets. Current assets consist of assets that should be converted to cash within one year, and they include cash and cash equivalents, accounts receivable, and inventory.[2] Long-term assets are assets expected to be used for more than one year; they include plant and equipment in addition to intellectual property such as patents and copyrights. Plant and equipment is generally reported net of accumulated depreciation. Allied's long-term assets consist entirely of net plant and equipment, and we often refer to them as "net fixed assets."

The claims against assets are of two basic types—liabilities (or money the company owes to others) and stockholders' equity. Current liabilities consist of claims that must be paid off within one year, including accounts payable, accruals (total of accrued wages and accrued taxes), and notes payable to banks and other short-term lenders that are due within one year. Long-term debt includes bonds that mature in more than a year.

**Stockholders' equity** can be thought of in two ways. First, it is the amount that stockholders paid to the company when they bought shares the company

*Stockholders' Equity*

It represents the amount that stockholders paid the company when shares were purchased and the amount of earnings the company has retained since its origination.

---

[2]Allied and most other companies hold some currency in addition to a bank checking account. They may also hold short-term interest-bearing securities that can be sold and thus converted to cash immediately with a simple telephone call. These securities are called "cash equivalents," and they are generally included with checking account balances for financial reporting purposes. If a company owns stocks or other marketable securities that it regards as short-term investments, these items will be shown separately on the balance sheet. Allied does not hold any marketable securities other than cash equivalents.

sold to raise capital, in addition to all of the earnings the company has retained over the years:[3]

**Stockholders' equity = Paid-in capital + Retained earnings**

The **retained earnings** are not just the earnings retained in the latest year—they are the cumulative total of all of the earnings the company has earned and retained during its life.

Stockholders' equity can also be thought of as a residual:

**Stockholders' equity = Total assets − Total liabilities**

*Retained Earnings*
They represent the cumulative total of all earnings kept by the company during its life.

If Allied had invested surplus funds in bonds backed by subprime mortgages and the bonds' value fell below their purchase price, the true value of the firm's assets would have declined. The amount of its liabilities would not have changed—the firm would still owe the amount it had promised to pay its creditors. Therefore, the reported value of the common equity must decline. The accountants would make a series of entries, and the result would be a reduction in retained earnings—and thus in common equity. In the end, assets would equal liabilities and equity, and the balance sheet would balance. This example shows why common stock is more risky than bonds—any mistake that management makes has a big impact on the stockholders. Of course, gains from good decisions also go to the stockholders; so with risk come possible rewards.

Assets on the balance sheet are listed by the length of time before they will be converted to cash (inventories and accounts receivable) or used by the firm (fixed assets). Similarly, claims are listed in the order in which they must be paid: Accounts payable must generally be paid within a few days, accruals must also be paid promptly, notes payable to banks must be paid within one year, and so forth, down to the stockholders' equity accounts, which represent ownership and need never be "paid off."

## 3-2A ALLIED'S BALANCE SHEET

Table 3.1 shows Allied's year-end balance sheets for 2016 and 2015. From the 2016 statement, we see that Allied had $2 billion of assets—half current and half long term. These assets were financed with $310 million of current liabilities, $750 million of long-term debt, and $940 million of common equity. Comparing the balance sheets for 2016 and 2015, we see that Allied's assets grew by $320 million and its liabilities and equity necessarily grew by that same amount. Assets must, of course, equal liabilities and equity; otherwise, the balance sheet does not balance.

Several additional points about the balance sheet should be noted:

1. *Cash versus other assets.* Although assets are reported in dollar terms, only the cash and equivalents account represents actual spendable money. Accounts receivable represent credit sales that have not yet been collected. Inventories show the cost of raw materials, work in process, and finished goods. Net fixed assets represent the cost of the buildings and equipment used in operations minus the depreciation that has been taken on these assets. At the end of 2016, Allied has $10 million of cash; hence, it could write checks totaling that amount. The noncash assets should generate cash over time, but they do not represent cash in hand. And the cash they would bring in if they were sold today could be higher or lower than the values reported on the balance sheet.

---

[3]On Allied's balance sheet, we simply show a common stock line representing the "paid-in" capital of stockholders when they purchased common shares of stock.

**TABLE 3.1**        Allied Food Products: December 31 Balance Sheets (Millions of Dollars)

|  | 2016 | 2015 |
|---|---|---|
| *Assets* |  |  |
| Current assets: |  |  |
|    Cash and equivalents | $ 10 | $ 80 |
|    Accounts receivable | 375 | 315 |
|    Inventories | 615 | 415 |
|   Total current assets | $1,000 | $ 810 |
| Net fixed assets: |  |  |
|   Net plant and equipment (cost minus depreciation) | 1,000 | 870 |
| Other assets expected to last more than a year | 0 | 0 |
| Total assets | $2,000 | $1,680 |
| *Liabilities and Equity* |  |  |
| Current liabilities: |  |  |
|    Accounts payable | $ 60 | $ 30 |
|    Accruals | 140 | 130 |
|    Notes payable | 110 | 60 |
|   Total current liabilities | $ 310 | $ 220 |
| Long-term bonds | 750 | 580 |
| Total liabilities | $1,060 | $ 800 |
| Common equity: |  |  |
|    Common stock (50,000,000 shares) | $ 130 | $ 130 |
|    Retained earnings | 810 | 750 |
|   Total common equity | $ 940 | $ 880 |
| Total liabilities and equity | $2,000 | $1,680 |

*Notes:*

1. Inventories can be valued by several different methods, and the method chosen can affect both the balance sheet value and the cost of goods sold, and thus net income, as reported on the income statement. Similarly, companies can use different depreciation methods. The methods used must be reported in the notes to the financial statements, and security analysts can make adjustments when they compare companies if they think the differences are material.
2. Book value per share: Total common equity/Shares outstanding $= \$940/50 = \$18.80$.
3. A relatively few firms use preferred stock, which we discuss in Chapter 9. Preferred stock can take several different forms, but it is generally like debt because it pays a fixed amount each year. However, it is like common stock because a failure to pay the preferred dividend does not expose the firm to bankruptcy. If a firm does use preferred stock, it is shown on the balance sheet between total debt and common stock. There is no set rule on how preferred stock should be treated when financial ratios are calculated—it could be considered as debt or as equity. Bondholders often think of it as equity, while stockholders think of it as debt because it is a fixed charge. In truth, preferred stock is a hybrid, somewhere between debt and common equity.

**Working Capital**
Current assets.

2. *Working capital.* Current assets are often called **working capital** because these assets "turn over"; that is, they are used and then replaced throughout the year. When Allied buys inventory items on credit, its suppliers, in effect, lend it the money used to finance the inventory items. Allied could have borrowed from its bank or sold stock to obtain the money, but it received the funds from its suppliers. These loans are shown as accounts payable, and they typically are "free" in the sense that they do not bear interest. Similarly, Allied pays its workers every two weeks and pays taxes quarterly; so Allied's labor force and taxing authorities provide it with loans equal to its accrued wages and taxes. In addition to these "free" sources of short-term credit, Allied borrows from its bank on a short-term basis. These bank loans are shown as notes payable. Although accounts payable and accruals do not bear interest, Allied pays interest on funds obtained from the bank. The total of accounts payable, accruals, and

notes payable represent current liabilities on its balance sheet. If we subtract current liabilities from current assets, the difference is called **net working capital**:

$$\text{Net working capital} = \text{Current assets} - \text{Current liabilities}$$
$$= \$1{,}000 - \$310 = \$690 \text{ million}$$

*Net Working Capital*
Current assets minus current liabilities.

Current liabilities include accounts payable, accruals, and notes payable to the bank. Financial analysts often make an important distinction between the "free" liabilities (accruals and accounts payable) and interest-bearing notes payable (which incur interest expense that is included as a financing cost on the firm's income statement). With this distinction in mind, analysts often focus on **net operating working capital (NOWC)** which differs from net working capital because interest-bearing notes payable are subtracted from current liabilities:

*Net Operating Working Capital (NOWC)*
Current assets minus non-interest-bearing current liabilities.

$$\begin{array}{c}\text{Net operating}\\ \text{working capital (NOWC)}\end{array} = \begin{array}{c}\text{Current}\\ \text{assets}\end{array} - \left(\begin{array}{c}\text{Current}\\ \text{liabilities}\end{array} - \begin{array}{c}\text{Notes}\\ \text{payable}\end{array}\right) \qquad \blacktriangledown \quad 3.1$$

$$= \$1{,}000 - (\$310 - \$110) = \$800 \text{ million}$$

Note that Allied's "free," or non-interest-bearing, current liabilities in 2016 total $200 million ($310 million in current liabilities less the $110 million in interest-bearing notes payable).

## quick question

**QUESTION:**

Refer to Allied's balance sheets shown in Table 3.1 to answer the following questions:
a.  What was Allied's net working capital on December 31, 2015?
b.  What was Allied's net operating working capital on December 31, 2015?

**ANSWER:**

a.  Net working capital$_{2015}$ = Current assets$_{2015}$ − Current liabilities$_{2015}$

   Net working capital$_{2015}$ = \$810 − \$220 = **\$590 million**

b.  $\begin{array}{c}\text{Net operating}\\ \text{working capital}_{2015}\end{array} = \begin{array}{c}\text{Current}\\ \text{assets}_{2015}\end{array} - \left(\begin{array}{c}\text{Current}\\ \text{liabilities}_{2015}\end{array} - \begin{array}{c}\text{Notes}\\ \text{payable}_{2015}\end{array}\right)$

   $\begin{array}{c}\text{Net operating}\\ \text{working capital}_{2015}\end{array} = \$810 - (\$220 - \$60)$

   $\begin{array}{c}\text{Net operating}\\ \text{working capital}_{2015}\end{array} = \$810 - \$160 =$ **\$650 million**

3.  *Total debt versus total liabilities.* A company's total debt includes both its short-term and long-term interest-bearing liabilities. Total liabilities equal total debt plus the company's "free" (non-interest bearing) liabilities. Allied's short-term debt is shown as notes payable on its balance sheet:[4]

$$\text{Total debt} = \text{Short-term debt} + \text{Long-term debt}$$
$$= \$110 + \$750 = \$860 \text{ million}$$

$$\text{Total liabilities} = \text{Total debt} + (\text{Accounts payable} + \text{Accruals})$$
$$= \$860 + (\$60 + \$140) = \$1{,}060 \text{ million} = \$1.06 \text{ billion}$$

---

[4]Companies also include the portion of their long-term bonds that is currently due as part of short-term debt.

### quick question

**QUESTION:**

Refer to Allied's balance sheets shown in Table 3.1. What was Allied's total debt on December 31, 2015?

**ANSWER:**

Total debt$_{2015}$ = Short-term debt$_{2015}$ + Long-term debt$_{2015}$

Total debt$_{2015}$ = \$60 + \$580 = **\$640 million**

4. *Other sources of funds.* Most companies (including Allied) finance their assets with a combination of short-term debt, long-term debt, and common equity. Some companies also use "hybrid" securities such as preferred stock, convertible bonds, and long-term leases. Preferred stock is a hybrid between common stock and debt, while convertible bonds are debt securities that give the bondholder an option to exchange their bonds for shares of common stock. In the event of bankruptcy, debt is paid off first, and then preferred stock. Common stock is last, receiving a payment only when something remains after the debt and preferred stock are paid off.[5]

5. *Depreciation.* Most companies prepare two sets of financial statements—one is based on Internal Revenue Service (IRS) rules and is used to calculate taxes; the other is based on GAAP and is used for reporting to investors. Firms often use accelerated depreciation for tax purposes but straight-line depreciation for stockholder reporting. Allied uses accelerated depreciation for both.[6]

6. *Market values versus book values.* Companies generally use GAAP to determine the values reported on their balance sheets. In most cases, these accounting numbers (or "book values") are different from what the assets would sell for if they were offered for sale (or "market values"). For example, Allied purchased its headquarters in Chicago in 1991. Under GAAP, the company must report the value of this asset at its historical cost (what it originally paid for the building in 1991) less accumulated depreciation. Given that Chicago real estate prices have increased over the last 24 years (even considering the impact of the recent recession on real estate values), the market value of the building is higher than its book value. Other assets' market values also differ from their book values.

---

[5]These other forms of financing are discussed in greater detail in Chapter 20, "Hybrid Financing: Preferred Stock, Warrants, and Convertibles," from Brigham and Daves, *Intermediate Financial Management*, 12th edition (Mason, OH: Cengage Learning, 2016).

[6]Depreciation over an asset's life is equal to the asset's cost, but accelerated depreciation results in higher initial depreciation charges—and thus lower taxable income—than straight line. Due to the time value of money, it is better to delay taxes; so most companies use accelerated depreciation for tax purposes. Either accelerated or straight line can be used for stockholder reporting. Allied is a relatively conservative company; hence, it uses accelerated depreciation for stockholder reporting. Had Allied elected to use straight line for stockholder reporting, its 2016 depreciation expense would have been \$25 million lower, the \$1 billion shown for "net plant" on its balance sheet would have been \$25 million higher, and its reported income would also have been higher.

Depreciation is also important in capital budgeting, where we make decisions regarding new investments in fixed assets. We will have more to say about depreciation in Chapter 12, when we discuss capital budgeting.

We can also see from Table 3.1 that the book value of Allied's common equity at the end of 2016 was $940 million. Because 50 million shares were outstanding, the book value per share was $940/50 = $18.80. However, the market value of the common stock was $23.06. As is true for most companies in 2016, shareholders are willing to pay more than book value for Allied's stock. This occurs in part because the values of assets have increased due to inflation and in part because shareholders expect earnings to grow. Allied, like most other companies, has learned how to make investments that will increase future profits.

> *Apple provides an example of a company with very strong future prospects, and as a result, in early 2015 its market value was more than six times its book value. On the other hand, if a company has problems, its market value can fall below its book value. For example, SkyWest, a regional airline that has struggled in recent years, saw its stock trading around $15 a share at a time early in 2015 when its book value per share exceeded $27.*

7. *Time dimension.* The balance sheet is a snapshot of the firm's financial position *at a point in time*—for example, on December 31, 2016. Thus, we see that on December 31, 2015, Allied had $80 million of cash; but that balance fell to $10 million by year-end 2016. The balance sheet changes every day as inventories rise and fall, as bank loans are increased or decreased, and so forth. A company such as Allied, whose business is seasonal, experiences especially large balance sheet changes during the year. Its inventories are low just before the harvest season but high just after the fall crops have been harvested and processed. Similarly, most retailers have large inventories just before Christmas but low inventories (and high accounts receivable) just after Christmas. We will examine the effects of these changes in Chapter 4, when we compare companies' financial statements and evaluate their performance.

## CASH HOLDINGS AND NET OPERATING WORKING CAPITAL: A CLOSER LOOK

To help keep things simple, our definition of net operating working capital (NOWC) assumes that all of the firm's current assets (including cash) are used for normal operating purposes. Although this assumption may be reasonable, there are clear instances where firms hold more cash than they need to run their day-to-day operations. For example, at December 31, 2014, Microsoft had more than $90.2 billion in cash and short-term investments!

In practice, if a financial analyst believes that some of the firm's cash is being held for non-operating purposes, he or she would subtract these excess cash holdings from the firm's current assets when calculating net operating working capital, as follows:

$$\text{NOWC} = (\text{Current assets} - \text{``Excess'' cash})$$
$$- (\text{Current liabilities} - \text{Notes payable})$$

To illustrate, if we make the extreme assumption that all of Allied's $10 million in cash is held for non-operating purposes, then this $10 million in excess cash would be subtracted from its current assets, and its NOWC would be calculated as $790 million instead of the $800 million calculated earlier. Although the difference for Allied is fairly small, assumptions about the level of excess cash become much more important when analyzing companies with very large cash holdings. However, unless otherwise noted, throughout this text we will assume that a firm's cash balance is used solely for operating purposes.

# THE BALANCE SHEET OF AN AVERAGE AMERICAN HOUSEHOLD

Balance sheets are not unique to corporations. Every entity—including state and local governments, nonprofit agencies, and individual households—has a balance sheet.

We can learn a lot about a household's financial well-being by looking at its balance sheet. Although obviously every household is different, economists can use available data to estimate the balance sheet of an average American household.

For example, in 2009, James Kwak posted his calculations of the average household balance sheet on his popular website *The Baseline Scenario* (baselinescenario.com), which provides interesting commentary on a variety of current economic and financial issues. The underlying data for his calculations came from the Federal Reserve Board's *Survey of Consumer Finances.*

A summary of Kwak's calculations for 2004, 2007, and 2009 are shown below. Although his calculations were only meant to give a broad picture of recent trends, they produce some interesting findings:

- The largest asset of the average household is its primary residence.

- The average American household does not have a large amount of savings in place for retirement.

- Perhaps somewhat surprisingly, average household debt levels have not increased dramatically in recent years.

- Average household net worth increased slightly from 2004 to 2007, but declined sharply from 2007 to 2009. The decline in net worth was due to two reasons: The sharp decline in the housing market reduced the value of the average home and the sharp decline in the stock market reduced the value of the average amount of retirement savings.

Likewise, a Federal Reserve study (*2010 Survey of Consumer Finances*) highlighted the deterioration in household finances due to the financial crisis and resulting recession. The average family's pre-tax income fell 5.6%, and the average family's net worth dropped nearly 40% during the period 2007–2010. Indeed, at the end of 2010, the average family's net worth stood at the same level that was observed in 1992—so in effect, the recent decline wiped out about 18 years' worth of savings and investment.

Although not broken down on a per-household level, updated information on aggregate household finances is on the Federal Reserve website. For example, numbers released in March 2015 indicate that aggregate household balance sheets have strengthened somewhat since 2010. Indeed, household net worth from 2010 through 2014 increased by almost 33%. These improvements reflect that many households have made progress in reducing their debt level. Household levels of net worth have also improved because of the surge in home prices and the large run-up in the stock market during this time period.[7]

| | 2004 | 2007 | 2009 |
|---|---|---|---|
| Income | $ 47,500 | $ 47,300 | $ 47,300 |
| *Assets* | | | |
| Bank accounts | 3,300 | 2,700 | 2,700 |
| Retirement savings | 19,000 | 23,900 | 17,900 |
| Vehicles | 14,400 | 14,600 | 14,600 |
| Primary residence | 148,300 | 150,000 | 125,400 |
| Total assets | $185,000 | $191,200 | $ 160,600 |
| *Liabilities* | | | |
| Mortgage on primary residence | $ 84,800 | $ 88,700 | $ 88,700 |
| Installment loans | 11,800 | 12,800 | 12,800 |
| Credit cards | 2,400 | 2,400 | 2,400 |
| Total liabilities | $ 99,000 | $103,900 | $ 103,900 |
| *Net worth* | $ 86,000 | $ 87,300 | $ 56,700 |

*Note*: See Kwak's posting on *The Baseline Scenario* for more details about the methods that he used in his calculations.

Sources: James Kwak, "Tracking the Household Balance Sheet," *The Baseline Scenario* (baselinescenario.com), February 15, 2009; William R. Emmons and Bryan J. Noeth, "Unsteady Progress: Income Trends in the Federal Reserve's Survey of Consumer Finances," Federal Reserve Bank of St. Louis, *In the Balance*, no. 2, 2012 (www.stlouisfed.org); Charles Riley, "Family Net Worth Plummets Nearly 40%," *CNN Money* (money.cnn.com), June 12, 2012; and "Financial Accounts of the United States," *Federal Reserve Statistical Release*, March 12, 2015.

[7]Refer to www.federalreserve.gov/releases/z1/current/z1r-5.pdf, Table B.101 "Balance Sheet of Households and Nonprofit Organizations (1)," March 12, 2015.

## SelfTest

What is the balance sheet, and what information does it provide?

How is the order in which items are shown on the balance sheet determined?

Explain in words the difference between net working capital and net operating working capital.

Explain in words the difference between total debt and total liabilities.

What items on Allied's December 31 balance sheet would probably be different from its June 30 values? Would these differences be as large if Allied were a grocery chain rather than a food processor? Explain.

# 3-3 The Income Statement

Table 3.2 shows Allied's 2015 and 2016 **income statements**. Net sales are shown at the top of the statement; then operating costs, interest, and taxes are subtracted to obtain the net income available to common shareholders. We also show earnings and dividends per share, in addition to some other data, at the bottom of Table 3.2. Earnings per share (EPS) is often called "the bottom line," denoting that of all items on the income statement, EPS is the one that is most important to stockholders. Allied earned $2.35 per share in 2016, down from $2.44 in 2015. In spite of the decline in earnings, the firm still increased the dividend from $1.06 to $1.15.

A typical stockholder focuses on the reported EPS, but professional security analysts and managers differentiate between *operating* and *non-operating* income. **Operating income** is derived from the firm's regular core business—in Allied's case, from producing and selling food products. Moreover, it is calculated before deducting interest expenses and taxes, which are considered to be non-operating costs. Operating income is also called EBIT, or earnings before interest and taxes. Here is its equation:

*Income Statements*
Reports summarizing a firm's revenues, expenses, and profits during a reporting period, generally a quarter or a year.

*Operating Income*
Earnings from operations before interest and taxes (i.e., EBIT).

$$\text{Operating income (or EBIT)} = \text{Sales revenues} - \text{Operating costs}$$
$$= \$3{,}000.0 - \$2{,}716.2$$
$$= \$283.8 \text{ million}$$

3.2

This figure must, of course, match the one reported on the income statement.

Different firms have different amounts of debt, different tax carrybacks and carryforwards, and different amounts of non-operating assets such as marketable securities. These differences can cause two companies with identical operations to report significantly different net incomes. For example, suppose two companies have identical sales, operating costs, and assets. However, one company uses some debt, and the other uses only common equity. Despite their identical operating performances, the company with no debt (and therefore no interest expense) would report a higher net income because no interest was deducted from its operating income. Consequently, if you want to compare two companies' operating performances, it is best to focus on their operating income.[8]

---

[8]Operating income is important for several reasons. Managers are generally compensated based on the performance of the units they manage. A division manager can control his or her division's performance, but not the firm's capital structure policy or other corporate decisions. Second, if one firm is considering acquiring another, it will be interested in the value of the target firm's operations; that value is determined by the target firm's operating income. Third, operating income is normally more stable than total income, as total income can be heavily influenced by write-offs of bonds backed by subprime mortgages and the like. Therefore, analysts focus on operating income when they estimate firms' long-run stock values.

| TABLE 3.2 | Allied Food Products: Income Statements for Years Ending December 31 (Millions of Dollars, Except for Per-Share Data) |

|  | 2016 | 2015 |
| --- | --- | --- |
| Net sales | $3,000.0 | $2,850.0 |
| Operating costs except depreciation and amortization | 2,616.2 | 2,497.0 |
| Depreciation and amortization | 100.0 | 90.0 |
| Total operating costs | $2,716.2 | $2,587.0 |
| Operating income, or earnings before interest and taxes (EBIT) | $ 283.8 | $ 263.0 |
| Less interest | 88.0 | 60.0 |
| Earnings before taxes (EBT) | $ 195.8 | $ 203.0 |
| Taxes (40%) | 78.3 | 81.2 |
| Net income | $ 117.5 | $ 121.8 |
| | | |
| *Here are some related items:* | | |
| Total dividends | $ 57.5 | $ 53.0 |
| Addition to retained earnings = Net income − Total dividends | $ 60.0 | $ 68.8 |
| | | |
| *Per-share data:* | | |
| Common stock price | $ 23.06 | $ 26.00 |
| Earnings per share (EPS)[a] | $ 2.35 | $ 2.44 |
| Dividends per share (DPS)[a] | $ 1.15 | $ 1.06 |
| Book value per share (BVPS)[a] | $ 18.80 | $ 17.60 |

*Notes:*

[a]Allied has 50 million shares of common stock outstanding. Note that EPS is based on net income available to common stockholders. Calculations of EPS, DPS, and BVPS for 2016 are as follows:

$$\text{Earnings per share} = \text{EPS} = \frac{\text{Net income}}{\text{Common shares outstanding}} = \frac{\$117,500,000}{50,000,000} = \$2.35$$

$$\text{Dividends per share} = \text{DPS} = \frac{\text{Dividends paid to common stockholders}}{\text{Common shares outstanding}} = \frac{\$57,500,000}{50,000,000} = \$1.15$$

$$\text{Book value per share} = \text{BVPS} = \frac{\text{Total common equity}}{\text{Common shares outstanding}} = \frac{\$940,000,000}{50,000,000} = \$18.80$$

When a firm has options or convertibles outstanding or it recently has issued new common stock, a more comprehensive EPS, "diluted EPS," is calculated. Its calculation is a bit more complicated, but you may refer to any financial accounting text for a discussion.

**Depreciation**

The charge to reflect the cost of assets depleted in the production process. Depreciation is not a cash outlay.

**Amortization**

A noncash charge similar to depreciation except that it represents a decline in value of intangible assets.

From Allied's income statement, we see that its operating income increased from $263.0 million in 2015 to $283.8 million in 2016, or by $20.8 million. However, its 2016 net income declined. This decline occurred because it increased its debt in 2016, and the $28 million increase in interest lowered its net income.

Taking a closer look at the income statement, we see that depreciation and amortization are important components of operating costs. Recall from accounting that **depreciation** is an annual charge against income that reflects the estimated dollar cost of the capital equipment and other tangible assets that were depleted in the production process. **Amortization** amounts to the same thing except that it represents the decline in value of intangible assets such as patents, copyrights, trademarks, and goodwill. Because depreciation and amortization are so similar, they are generally lumped together for purposes of financial analysis on the income statement and for other purposes. They both write off, or allocate, the costs of assets over their useful lives.

Even though depreciation and amortization are reported as costs on the income statements, they are not cash expenses—cash was spent in the past, when the assets being written off were acquired, but no cash is paid out to cover depreciation and amortization. Therefore, managers, security analysts, and bank loan officers who are concerned with the amount of cash a company is generating often calculate **EBITDA**, an acronym for earnings before interest, taxes, depreciation, and amortization. Allied has no amortization charges, so Allied's depreciation and amortization expense consists entirely of depreciation. In 2016, Allied's EBITDA was $383.8 million.

**EBITDA**
Earnings before interest, taxes, depreciation, and amortization.

Although the balance sheet represents a snapshot in time, the income statement reports on operations *over a period of time.* For example, during 2016, Allied had sales of $3 billion and its net income was $117.5 million. Income statements are prepared monthly, quarterly, and annually. The quarterly and annual statements are reported to investors, while the monthly statements are used internally by managers for planning and control purposes.

Finally, note that the income statement is tied to the balance sheet through the retained earnings account on the balance sheet. Net income as reported on the income statement less dividends paid is the retained earnings for the year (e.g., 2016). Those retained earnings are added to the cumulative retained earnings from prior years to obtain the year-end 2016 balance for retained earnings. The retained earnings for the year are also reported in the statement of stockholders' equity. All four of the statements provided in the annual report are interrelated.

## Self*Test*

Why is earnings per share called "the bottom line"? What is EBIT, or operating income?

What is EBITDA?

Which is more like a snapshot of the firm's operations—the balance sheet or the income statement? Explain your answer.

## 3-4 Statement of Cash Flows

Net income as reported on the income statement is not cash; and in finance, "cash is king." Management's goal is to maximize the price of the firm's stock; and the value of any asset, including a share of stock, is based on the cash flows the asset is expected to produce. Therefore, managers strive to maximize the cash flows available to investors. The **statement of cash flows**, as shown in Table 3.3, is the accounting report that shows how much cash the firm is generating. The statement is divided into four sections, and we explain it on a line-by-line basis.[9]

*Statement of Cash Flows*
A report that shows how items that affect the balance sheet and income statement affect the firm's cash flows.

Here is a line-by-line explanation of the statement shown in Table 3.3:

a.  *Operating activities.* This section deals with items that occur as part of normal ongoing operations.

b.  *Net income.* The first operating activity is net income, which is the first source of cash. If all sales were for cash, if all costs required immediate cash payments, and if the firm were in a static situation, net income would equal

---

[9]Allied's statement of cash flows is relatively simple because it is a relatively uncomplicated company. Many cash flow statements are more complex; but if you understand Table 3.3, you should be able to follow more complex statements.

**TABLE 3.3**     Allied Food Products: Statement of Cash Flows for 2016 (Millions of Dollars)

| | | 2016 |
|---|---|---|
| a. | **I. Operating Activities** | |
| b. | Net income | $117.5 |
| c. | Depreciation and amortization | 100.0 |
| d. | Increase in inventories | (200.0) |
| e. | Increase in accounts receivable | (60.0) |
| f. | Increase in accounts payable | 30.0 |
| g. | Increase in accrued wages and taxes | 10.0 |
| h. | Net cash provided by (used in) operating activities | ($ 2.5) |
| i. | **II. Long-Term Investing Activities** | |
| j. | Additions to property, plant, and equipment | ($230.0) |
| k. | Net cash used in investing activities | ($230.0) |
| l. | **III. Financing Activities** | |
| m. | Increase in notes payable | $ 50.0 |
| n. | Increase in bonds | 170.0 |
| o. | Payment of dividends to stockholders | (57.5) |
| p. | Net cash provided by financing activities | $162.5 |
| q. | **IV. Summary** | |
| r. | Net decrease in cash (Net sum of I, II, and III) | ($ 70.0) |
| s. | Cash and equivalents at the beginning of the year | 80.0 |
| t. | Cash and equivalents at the end of the year | $ 10.0 |

*Note*: Here and throughout the book parentheses are sometimes used to denote negative numbers.

cash from operations. However, these conditions don't hold, so net income is not equal to cash from operations. Adjustments shown in the remainder of the statement must be made.

c. *Depreciation and amortization.* The first adjustment relates to depreciation and amortization. Allied's accountants subtracted depreciation (it has no amortization expense), which is a noncash charge, when they calculated net income. Therefore, depreciation must be added back to net income when cash flow is determined.

d. *Increase in inventories.* To make or buy inventory items, the firm must use cash. It may receive some of this cash as loans from its suppliers and workers (payables and accruals); but ultimately, any increase in inventories requires cash. Allied increased its inventories by $200 million in 2016. That amount is shown in parentheses on line d because it is negative (i.e., a use of cash). If Allied had reduced its inventories, it would have generated positive cash.

e. *Increase in accounts receivable.* If Allied chooses to sell on credit when it makes a sale, it will not immediately get the cash that it would have received had it not extended credit. To stay in business, it must replace the inventory that it sold on credit; but it won't yet have received cash from the credit sale. So if the firm's accounts receivable increase, this will amount to a use of cash. Allied's receivables rose by $60 million in 2016, and that use of cash is shown as a negative number on line e. If Allied had reduced its receivables, this would be shown as a positive cash flow.

(Once cash is received for the sale, the accompanying accounts receivable will be eliminated.)

f.  *Increase in accounts payable.* Accounts payable represent a loan from suppliers. Allied bought goods on credit, and its payables increased by $30 million this year. That is treated as a $30 million increase in cash on line f. If Allied had reduced its payables, that would have required, or used, cash. Note that as Allied grows, it will purchase more inventories. That will give rise to additional payables, which will reduce the amount of new outside funds required to finance inventory growth.

g.  *Increase in accrued wages and taxes.* The same logic applies to accruals as to accounts payable. Allied's accruals increased by $10 million this year, which means that in 2016, it borrowed an additional $10 million from its workers and taxing authorities. So this represents a $10 million cash inflow.

h.  *Net cash provided by operating activities.* All of the previous items are part of normal operations—they arise as a result of doing business. When we sum them, we obtain the net cash flow from operations. Allied had positive flows from net income, depreciation, and increases in payables and accruals; but it used cash to increase inventories and to carry receivables. The net result was that operations led to a $2.5 million net cash outflow.

i.  *Long-term investing activities.* All activities involving long-term assets are covered in this section. Allied had only one long-term investment activity—the acquisition of some fixed assets, as shown on line j. If Allied had sold some fixed assets, its accountants would have reported it in this section as a positive amount (i.e., as a cash inflow).

j.  *Additions to property, plant, and equipment.* Allied spent $230 million on fixed assets during the current year. This is an outflow; therefore, it is shown in parentheses. If Allied had sold some of its fixed assets, this would have been a cash inflow.[10]

k.  *Net cash used in investing activities.* Because Allied had only one investment activity, the total on this line is the same as that on the previous line.

l.  *Financing activities.* Allied's financing activities are shown in this section.

m.  *Increase in notes payable.* Allied borrowed an additional $50 million from its bank this year, which was a cash inflow. When Allied repays the loan, this will be an outflow.

n.  *Increase in bonds (long-term debt).* Allied borrowed an additional $170 million from long-term investors this year, issuing bonds in exchange for cash. This is shown as an inflow. When the bonds are repaid by the firm some years hence, this will be an outflow.

o.  *Payment of dividends to stockholders.* Dividends are paid in cash, and the $57.5 million that Allied paid to stockholders is shown as a negative amount.

p.  *Net cash provided by financing activities.* The sum of the three financing entries, which is a positive $162.5 million, is shown here. These funds were used to help pay for the $230 million of new plant and equipment and to help cover the deficit resulting from operations.

q.  *Summary.* This section summarizes the change in cash and cash equivalents over the year.

---

[10]The number on line j is "gross" investment, or total expenditures. It is also equal to the change in net plant and equipment (from the balance sheet) plus depreciation, as shown on line c: Gross investment = Net investment + Depreciation = $130 + $100 = $230.

# MASSAGING THE CASH FLOW STATEMENT

Profits as reported on the income statement can be "massaged" by changes in depreciation methods, inventory valuation procedures, and so on, but "cash is cash," so management can't mess with the cash flow statement, right? Nope—wrong. A 2005 article in *The Wall Street Journal* ("Little Campus Lab Shakes Big Firms") described how Ford, General Motors, and several other companies overstated their operating cash flows, the most important section of the cash flow statement. Indeed, GM reported more than twice as much cash from operations as it really generated, $7.6 billion versus a true $3.5 billion. When GM sold cars to a dealer on credit, it created an account receivable, which should be shown in the "Operating Activities" section as a use of cash. However, GM classified these receivables as an investing activity. That decision more than doubled its reported cash flow from operations. It didn't affect the end-of-year cash balance, but it made operations look stronger than they really were.

If Allied Foods, in Table 3.3, had done this, the $60 million increase in receivables, which is correctly shown as a use of cash, would have been shifted to the "Investing Activities" section, causing Allied's cash provided by operations to rise from −$2.5 million to +$57.5 million. That would have made Allied look better to investors and credit analysts, but it would have been just smoke and mirrors.

GM's treatment was first reported by Charles Mulford, a professor at Georgia Tech. The SEC then sent GM a letter requiring it to change its procedures. The company issued a statement saying it thought that it was acting in accordance with GAAP but that it would reclassify its accounts in the future. GM's action was not in the league of WorldCom's or Enron's fraudulent accounting practices, but it does show that companies sometimes do things to make their statements look better than they really are.

Source: Based on Diya Gullapalli, "Little Campus Lab Shakes Big Firms," *The Wall Street Journal*, March 1, 2005, p. C3.

r. *Net decrease in cash.* The net sum of the operating activities, investing activities, and financing activities is shown here. These activities resulted in a $70 million net decrease in cash during 2016, mainly due to expenditures on new fixed assets.

s. *Cash and equivalents at the beginning of the year.* Allied began the year with $80 million of cash, which is shown here.

t. *Cash and equivalents at the end of the year.* Allied ended the year with $10 million of cash, the $80 million it started with minus the $70 million net decrease that occurred during the year. Clearly, Allied's cash position is weaker than it was at the beginning of the year.

Allied's statement of cash flows should be of concern to its managers and investors. The company was able to cover the small operating deficit and the large investment in fixed assets by borrowing and reducing its beginning balances of cash and equivalents. However, the firm can't continue to do this indefinitely. In the long run, Section I needs to show positive operating cash flows. In addition, we would expect Section II to show expenditures on fixed assets that are about equal to (1) its depreciation charges (to replace worn out fixed assets), along with (2) some additional expenditures to provide for growth. Section III would normally show some net borrowing in addition to a "reasonable" amount of dividends.[11] Finally, Section IV should show a reasonably stable year-to-year cash balance. These conditions don't hold for Allied, so some actions should be taken to correct the situation. We will consider corrective actions in Chapter 4, when we analyze the firm's financial statements.

---

[11]The average company pays out about one-third of its earnings as dividends, but there is a great deal of variation between companies, depending on each company's needs for retained earnings to support growth. We cover dividends in detail in Chapter 14.

## SelfTest

What is the statement of cash flows, and what are some questions it answers?

Identify and briefly explain the four sections shown in the statement of cash flows.

If during the year a company has high cash flows from its operations, does this mean that cash on its balance sheet will be higher at the end of the year than it was at the beginning of the year? Explain.

## 3-5 Statement of Stockholders' Equity

Changes in stockholders' equity during the accounting period are reported in the **statement of stockholders' equity**. Table 3.4 shows that Allied earned $117.5 million during 2016, paid out $57.5 million in common dividends, and plowed $60 million back into the business. Thus, the balance sheet item "Retained earnings" increased from $750 million at year-end 2015 to $810 million at year-end 2016.[12]

Note that "retained earnings" represents a *claim against assets*, not assets per se. Stockholders allow management to retain earnings and reinvest them in the business, use retained earnings for additions to plant and equipment, add to inventories, and the like. Companies *do not* just pile up cash in a bank account. *Thus, retained earnings as reported on the balance sheet do not represent cash and are not "available" for dividends or anything else.*[13]

*Statement of Stockholders' Equity*
A statement that shows by how much a firm's equity changed during the year and why this change occurred.

Allied Food Products: Statement of Stockholders' Equity, December 31, 2016 (Millions of Dollars)  **TABLE 3.4**

|  | COMMON STOCK | | Retained Earnings | Total Stockholders' Equity |
|---|---|---|---|---|
|  | Shares (000) | Amount |  |  |
| Balances, December 31, 2015 | 50,000 | $130.0 | $750.0 | $880.0 |
| 2016 Net income |  |  | 117.5 |  |
| Cash dividends |  |  | (57.5) |  |
| Addition to retained earnings |  |  |  | 60.0 |
| Balances, December 31, 2016 | 50,000 | $130.0 | $810.0 | $940.0 |

---

[12]If they had been applicable, columns would have been used to show Additional Paid-in Capital and Treasury Stock. Also, additional rows would have contained information on such things as new issues of stock, treasury stock acquired or reissued, stock options exercised, and unrealized foreign exchange gains or losses.

[13]Cash (as of the balance sheet date) is found in the cash account, an asset account. A positive number in the retained earnings account indicates only that the firm has in the past earned income and has not paid it all out as dividends. Even though a company reports record earnings and shows an increase in retained earnings, it still may be short of cash if it is using its available cash to purchase current and fixed assets to support growth. The same situation holds for individuals. You might own a new BMW (no loan), many clothes, and an expensive stereo (hence, have a high net worth); but if you had only $0.23 in your pocket plus $5.00 in your checking account, you would still be short of cash.

## SelfTest

What information does the statement of stockholders' equity provide?

Why do changes in retained earnings occur?

Explain why the following statement is true: The retained earnings account reported on the balance sheet does not represent cash and is not "available" for dividend payments or anything else.

# 3-6 Uses and Limitations of Financial Statements

As we mentioned in the opening vignette to this chapter, financial statements provide a great deal of useful information. You can inspect the statements and answer a number of important questions such as these: How large is the company? Is it growing? Is it making or losing money? Is it generating cash through its operations, or are operations actually losing cash?

At the same time, investors need to be cautious when they review financial statements. Although companies are required to follow GAAP, managers still have a lot of discretion in deciding how and when to report certain transactions. (For an example, see the box in Section 3-4, "Massaging the Cash Flow Statement," on GM's treatment of receivables.)

Consequently, two firms in exactly the same situation may report financial statements that convey different impressions about their financial strength. Some variations may stem from legitimate differences of opinion about the correct way to record transactions. In other cases, managers may choose to report numbers in a manner that helps them present either higher or more stable earnings over time. As long as they follow GAAP, such actions are legal, but these differences make it difficult for investors to compare companies and gauge their true performances. In particular, watch out if senior managers receive bonuses or other compensation based on earnings in the short run—they may try to boost short-term reported income to boost their bonuses.

Unfortunately, there have also been cases where managers disregarded GAAP and reported fraudulent statements. One blatant example of cheating involved WorldCom, which reported asset values that exceeded their true value by about $11 billion. This led to an understatement of costs and a corresponding overstatement of profits. Enron is another high-profile example. It overstated the value of certain assets, reported those artificial value increases as profits, and transferred the assets to subsidiary companies to hide the true facts. Enron's and WorldCom's investors eventually learned what was happening, and the companies were forced into bankruptcy. Many of their top executives went to jail; the accounting firm that audited their books was forced out of business; and investors lost billions of dollars.

After the Enron and WorldCom fiascos, Congress in 2002 passed the Sarbanes-Oxley Act (SOX), which required companies to improve their internal auditing standards and required the CEO and CFO to certify that the financial statements were properly prepared. The SOX bill also created a new watchdog organization to help make sure that the outside accounting firms were doing their jobs.

More recently, a serious debate has arisen regarding the appropriate accounting for complicated investments held by financial institutions. In the recent financial crisis, many of these investments (particularly those related to subprime mortgages) turned out to be worth a lot less than their stated book value. Currently, regulators and other policy makers are struggling to come up with the best way to account for and regulate many of these "toxic assets."[14]

Finally, keep in mind that even if investors receive accurate accounting data, it is cash flows, not accounting income, that matters most. Similarly, as we shall see in Chapters 11 and 12, when managers make capital budgeting decisions on which projects to accept, their focus should be on cash flow.

## Self Test

Can investors be confident that if the financial statements of different companies are accurate and are prepared in accordance with GAAP, the data reported by one company will be comparable to the data provided by another?

Why might different companies account for similar transactions in different ways?

## 3-7  Free Cash Flow

Thus far, we have focused on financial statements as they are prepared by accountants. However, accounting statements are designed primarily for use by creditors and tax collectors, not for managers and stock analysts. Therefore, corporate decision makers and security analysts often modify accounting data to meet their needs. The most important modification is the concept of **free cash flow (FCF)**, defined as "the amount of cash that could be withdrawn without harming a firm's ability to operate and to produce future cash flows." Here is the equation used to calculate free cash flow:

**Free Cash Flow (FCF)**
The amount of cash that could be withdrawn without harming a firm's ability to operate and to produce future cash flows.

$$FCF = \left[ EBIT(1-T) + \begin{matrix} Depreciation \\ and\ amortization \end{matrix} \right] - \left[ \begin{matrix} Capital \\ expenditures \end{matrix} + \begin{matrix} \Delta Net\ operating \\ working\ capital \end{matrix} \right] \qquad 3.3$$

The first term represents the amount of cash that the firm generates from its current operations. EBIT $(1 - T)$ is often referred to as **NOPAT**, or **net operating profit after taxes**. Depreciation and amortization are added back because these are noncash expenses that reduce EBIT but do not reduce the amount of cash the company has available to pay its investors. The second bracketed term indicates the amount of cash that the company is investing in its fixed assets (capital expenditures) and operating working capital in order to sustain ongoing operations. A positive level of FCF indicates that the firm is generating more than enough cash to finance current investments in fixed assets and working capital. By contrast, negative free cash flow means that the company does not have sufficient internal funds to finance investments in fixed assets and working capital, and that it will have to raise new money in the capital markets in order to pay for these investments.

**Net Operating Profit After Taxes (NOPAT)**
The profit a company would generate if it had no debt and held only operating assets.

*Consider the case of Home Depot. The first bracketed term in Equation 3.3 represents the amount of cash that Home Depot is generating from its existing stores. The second bracketed term represents the amount of cash that the company is spending this period to construct new stores. When Home Depot opens a new store, it needs cash to purchase the land and construct the building—these are capital expenditures, and they lead to a corresponding increase in the firm's fixed assets on the balance sheet. However, when it opens a new store, the company also needs to increase its net operating working capital. In*

---

[14]On May 12, 2011, the FASB and IASB jointly issued new guidance regarding how fair value measurement should be applied where its use is already required. It does not extend the use of fair value accounting.

*particular, the company needs to stock the store with new inventory. Part of this inventory may be financed through accounts payable—for example, a supplier might ship Home Depot some flashlights today and allow Home Depot to pay for them later. In this case, there would be no increase in net operating working capital because the increase in current assets exactly equals the increase in current liabilities. Other portions of their inventory may not have offsetting accounts payable, so there will be an increase in net operating working capital, and the company must come up with the cash today in order to pay for this increase. Putting everything together, the company as a whole is generating positive free cash flow if the money generated from operating existing stores exceeds the money required to build new stores.*

Looking at Allied's key financial statements, we can collect the pieces that we need to calculate its free cash flow. First, we can obtain Allied's EBIT and depreciation and amortization expense from the income statement. Looking at Table 3.2, we see that Allied's 2016 operating income (EBIT) was $283.8 million. Because Allied's tax rate is 40%, it follows that its NOPAT = EBIT$(1 - T)$ = $283.8$(1 - 0.4)$ = $170.3 million. We also see that Allied's depreciation and amortization expense in 2016 was $100 million.

Allied's capital expenditures (the cash used to purchase new fixed assets) can be found under the investment activities on the Statement of Cash Flows. Looking at Table 3.3, we see that Allied's capital expenditures in 2016 totaled $230 million.[15] Finally, we need to calculate the change in net operating working capital ($\Delta$NOWC). Recall that NOWC is current assets minus non-interest-bearing current liabilities (where non-interest-bearing current liabilities are calculated as current liabilities minus notes payable). We showed earlier that Allied's NOWC for 2016 was:

$$\text{NOWC}_{2016} = \$1{,}000 - (\$310 - \$110) = \$800 \text{ million}$$

Likewise, its NOWC for 2015 can be calculated as:

$$\text{NOWC}_{2015} = \$810 - (\$220 - \$60) = \$650 \text{ million}$$

Thus, Allied's change in net operating working capital ($\Delta$NOWC) = $150 million ($800 million − $650 million). Putting everything together, we can now calculate Allied's 2016 free cash flow:

$$\text{FCF} = \left[ \text{EBIT}(1 - T) + \begin{array}{c} \text{Depreciation} \\ \text{and amortization} \end{array} \right] - \left[ \begin{array}{c} \text{Capital} \\ \text{expenditures} \end{array} + \begin{array}{c} \Delta\text{Net operating} \\ \text{working capital} \end{array} \right]$$

$$\text{FCF}_{2016} = [\$170.3 + \$100] - [\$230 + \$150]$$

$$= -\$109.7 \text{ million}$$

Allied's FCF is negative, which is not good. Note, though, that the negative FCF is largely attributable to the $230 million expenditure for a new processing plant. This plant is large enough to meet production for several years, so another new plant will not be needed until 2020. Therefore, Allied's FCF for 2017 and the next few years should increase, which means that Allied's financial situation is not as bad as the negative FCF might suggest.

Most rapidly growing companies have negative FCFs—the fixed assets and working capital needed to support a firm's rapid growth generally exceed cash flows from its existing operations. This is not bad, provided a firm's new investments are eventually profitable and contribute to its FCF.

---

[15]Alternatively, we can calculate Allied's capital expenditures by looking at changes in net fixed assets on the balance sheet between 2015 and 2016 and then adding back depreciation and amortization for 2016. In this example, Allied's net fixed assets increased $130 million (from $870 million in 2015 to $1 billion in 2016), and its depreciation and amortization totaled $100 million in 2016. Consequently, gross capital expenditures were $130 million + $100 million = $230 million.

## quick question

**QUESTION:**

A company has EBIT of $30 million, depreciation of $5 million, and a 40% tax rate. It needs to spend $10 million on new fixed assets and $15 million to increase its current assets. It expects its accounts payable to increase by $2 million, its accruals to increase by $3 million, and its notes payable to increase by $8 million. The firm's current liabilities consist of only accounts payable, accruals, and notes payable. What is its free cash flow?

**ANSWER:**

First, you need to determine the $\Delta$Net operating working capital ($\Delta$NOWC):

$\Delta$NOWC = $\Delta$Current assets − ($\Delta$Current liabilities − $\Delta$Notes payable)
$\Delta$NOWC = $15 − ($13 − $8)
$\Delta$NOWC = $15 − $5 = $10 million.

Now, you can solve for free cash flow (FCF):

FCF = [EBIT(1−T)+Depreciation and amortization] − [Capital expenditures + $\Delta$NOWC]
FCF = [$30(1 − 0.4) + $5] − [$10 + $10]
FCF = [$18 + $5] − $20
**FCF = $3 million**

# FREE CASH FLOW IS IMPORTANT FOR BUSINESSES BOTH SMALL AND LARGE

Free cash flow is important to large companies like Allied Foods. Security analysts use FCF to help estimate the value of the stock, and Allied's managers use it to assess the value of proposed capital budgeting projects and potential merger candidates. Note, though, that the concept is also relevant for small businesses.

Assume that your aunt and uncle own a small pizza shop and that their accountant prepares their financial statements. The income statement shows their accounting profit for each year. Although they are certainly interested in this number, what they probably care more about is how much money they can take out of the business each year to maintain their standard of living. Let's assume that the shop's net income for 2016 was $75,000. However, your aunt and uncle had to spend $50,000 to refurbish the kitchen and restrooms.

So although the business is generating a great deal of "profit," your aunt and uncle can't take much money out because they have to put money back into the pizza shop. Stated another way, their free cash flow is much less than their net income. The required investments could be so large that they even exceed the money made from selling pizza. In this case, your aunt and uncle's free cash flow would be negative. If so, this means they must find funds from other sources just to maintain their pizza business.

As astute business owners, your aunt and uncle recognize that their restaurant investments, such as updating the kitchen and restrooms, are nonrecurring; and if nothing else happens unexpectedly, your aunt and uncle should be able to take more cash out of the business in future years, when their free cash flow increases. But some businesses never seem to produce cash for their owners—they consistently generate positive net income, but this net income is swamped by the amount of cash that has to be plowed back into the business.

Thus, when it comes to valuing the pizza shop (or any business small or large), what really matters is the amount of free cash flow that the business generates over time. Looking ahead, your aunt and uncle face competition from national chains that are moving into the area. To meet the competition, your aunt and uncle will have to modernize the dining room. This will again drain cash from the business and reduce its free cash flow, although the hope is that it will enable them to increase sales and free cash flow in the years ahead. As we will see in Chapters 11 and 12, which cover capital budgeting, evaluating projects require us to estimate whether the future increases in free cash flow are sufficient to more than offset the initial project cost. Therefore, the free cash flow calculation is critical to a firm's capital budgeting analysis.

Many analysts regard FCF as being the single most important number that can be developed from accounting statements, even more important than net income. After all, FCF shows how much cash the firm can distribute to its investors. We discuss FCF again in Chapter 9, which covers stock valuation, and in Chapters 11 and 12, which cover capital budgeting.

## Self Test

What is free cash flow (FCF)?

Why is FCF an important determinant of a firm's value?

## 3-8 MVA and EVA

Items reported on the financial statements reflect historical, in-the-past, values, not current market values, and there are often substantial differences between the two. Changes in interest rates and inflation affect the market value of the company's assets and liabilities but often have no effect on the corresponding book values shown in the financial statements. Perhaps, more importantly, the market's assessment of value takes into account its ongoing assessment of current operations as well as future opportunities. For example, it cost Microsoft very little to develop its first operating system, but that system turned out to be worth many billions that were not shown on its balance sheet. For a given level of debt, these increases in asset value also lead to a corresponding increase in the market value of equity.

To illustrate, consider the following situation. A firm was started with $1 million of assets at book value (historical cost), $500,000 of which was provided by bondholders, and $500,000 by stockholders (50,000 shares purchased at $10 per share). However, this firm became very successful; the market value of the firm's equity is now worth $19.5 million, and its current stock price is $19,500,000/50,000 = $390 per share. Clearly the firm's managers have done a marvelous job for the stockholders.

The accounting statements do not reflect market values, so they are not sufficient for purposes of evaluating managers' performance. To help fill this void, financial analysts have developed two additional performance measures, the first of which is **MVA**, or **market value added**.[16] MVA is simply the difference between the market value of a firm's equity and the book value as shown on the balance sheet, with market value found by multiplying the stock price by the number of shares outstanding. For our hypothetical firm, MVA is $19.5 million − $0.5 million = $19 million.

*Market Value Added (MVA)*

The excess of the market value of equity over its book value.

For Allied, which has 50 million shares outstanding and a stock price of $23.06, the market value of the equity is $1,153 million versus a book value, as shown on the balance sheet in Table 3.1, of $940 million. Therefore, Allied's MVA is $1,153 − $940 = $213 million. This $213 million represents the difference between the money Allied's stockholders have invested in the corporation since its founding—including retained earnings—versus the cash they could receive if they sold the business. The higher its MVA, the better the job management is doing for the firm's shareholders. Boards of directors often look at MVA when deciding on the compensation a firm's

---

[16]The concepts of EVA and MVA were developed by Joel Stern and Bennett Stewart, co-founders of the consulting firm Stern Stewart & Company. Stern Stewart copyrighted the terms *MVA* and *EVA*, so other consulting firms have given other names to these values. Still, MVA and EVA are the terms most commonly used in practice. For more on MVA and EVA, see G. Bennett Stewart, *The Quest for Value* (New York: HarperCollins, 1991, 1999).

managers deserve. Note, though, that just as all ships rise in a rising tide, most firms' stock prices rise in a rising stock market, so a positive MVA may not be entirely attributable to management performance.

A related concept, **economic value added (EVA)**, sometimes called "economic profit," is closely related to MVA and is found as follows:[17]

**Economic Value Added (EVA)**

Excess of NOPAT over capital costs.

$$\text{EVA} = \begin{array}{c}\text{Net operating profit}\\\text{after taxes}\\\text{(NOPAT)}\end{array} - \begin{array}{c}\text{Annual dollar}\\\text{cost of}\\\text{capital}\end{array}$$

3.4

$$= \text{EBIT}(1 - T) - \left(\begin{array}{c}\text{Total}\\\text{invested}\\\text{capital}\end{array} \times \begin{array}{c}\text{After-tax}\\\text{percentage}\\\text{cost of capital}\end{array}\right)$$

Companies create value (and realize positive EVA) if the benefits of their investments exceed the cost of raising the necessary capital. Total invested capital represents the amount of money that the company has raised from debt, equity, and any other sources of capital (such as preferred stock). The annual dollar cost of capital is total invested capital multiplied by the after-tax percentage cost of this capital. So, for example, if the company has raised $1 million in capital, and the current cost of capital is 10%, the annual dollar cost of capital would be $100,000. The funds raised from this capital are invested in a variety of net fixed assets and net operating working capital. In any given year, NOPAT is the amount of money that these investments have generated for the company's investors after paying for operating costs and taxes—in this regard it represents the benefits of capital investments.

EVA is an estimate of a business's true economic profit for a given year, and it often differs sharply from accounting net income. The main reason for this difference is that although accounting income takes into account the cost of debt (the company's interest expense), it does not deduct for the cost of equity capital. By contrast, EVA takes into account the total dollar cost of all capital, which includes both the cost of debt and equity capital.

If EVA is positive, then after-tax operating income exceeds the cost of the capital needed to produce that income, and management's actions are adding value for stockholders. Positive EVA on an annual basis will help ensure that MVA is also positive. Note that whereas MVA applies to the entire firm, EVA can be determined for divisions as well as for the company as a whole, so it is useful as a guide to "reasonable" compensation for divisional as well as top corporate managers.

## Self Test

Define the terms *market value added (MVA)* and *economic value added (EVA)*.

How does EVA differ from accounting net income?

---

[17]Another top consulting company, McKinsey & Company, uses the term *economic profit*. Its definition of economic profit is:

(Total invested capital) × (Return on invested capital − Cost of capital)

Because the return on invested capital is [EBIT(1 − T)]/Total invested capital, you can show with a little bit of algebra that EVA and economic profit are identical.

# 3-9 Income Taxes

The IRS website is **www.irs .gov**. Here you can find current filing information and current credits and deductions information, and order needed forms and publications.

**Progressive**

A tax system where the tax rate is higher on higher incomes. The personal income tax in the United States, which ranges from 0% on the lowest incomes to 39.6% on the highest incomes, is progressive.

**Marginal Tax Rate**

The tax rate applicable to the last unit of a person's income.

**Average Tax Rate**

Taxes paid divided by taxable income.

**Capital Gain**

The profit from the sale of a capital asset for more than its purchase price.

**Capital Loss**

The loss from the sale of a capital asset for less than its purchase price.

Individuals and corporations pay out a significant portion of their income as taxes, so taxes are important in both personal and corporate decisions. We summarize the key aspects of the U.S. tax system for individuals in this section and for corporations in the next section, using 2015 data. The details of our tax laws change fairly often—annually for items that are indexed for inflation—but the basic nature of the tax system is likely to remain intact.

## 3-9A INDIVIDUAL TAXES

Individuals pay taxes on wages and salaries, on investment income (dividends, interest, and profits from the sale of securities), and on the profits of proprietorships and partnerships. The tax rates are **progressive**—that is, the higher one's income, the larger the percentage paid in taxes. Table 3.5 provides the 2015 tax rates that taxpayers will pay for tax returns due April 15, 2016.

Taxable income is defined as "gross income less a set of exemptions and deductions." When filing a tax return in 2016 for the tax year 2015, taxpayers received an exemption of $4,000 for each dependent, including the taxpayer, which reduces taxable income. However, this exemption is indexed to rise with inflation, and the exemption is phased out (taken away) for high-income taxpayers. Also, certain expenses, including mortgage interest paid, state and local income taxes paid, and charitable contributions, can be deducted and thus be used to reduce taxable income; but again, high-income taxpayers lose most of these deductions.

The **marginal tax rate** is defined as "the tax rate on the last dollar of income." Marginal rates begin at 10% and rise to 39.6%. Note, though, that when consideration is given to the phase-out of exemptions and deductions, to Social Security and Medicare taxes, and to state taxes, the marginal tax rate may actually exceed 50%. Average tax rates can be calculated from the data in Table 3.5. For example, if a single individual had taxable income of $38,000, his or her tax bill would be $5,156.25 + ($38,000 − $37,450)(0.25) = $5,156.25 + $137.50 = $5,293.75. Her **average tax rate** would be $5,293.75/$38,000 = 13.9% versus a marginal rate of 25%. If she received a raise of $1,000, bringing her income to $39,000, she would have to pay $250 of it as taxes; so her after-tax raise would be $750.

Note too that *interest income* received by individuals from corporate securities is added to other income and thus is taxed at federal rates going up to 39.6%, plus state taxes.[18] *Capital gains and losses,* on the other hand, are treated differently. Assets such as stocks, bonds, and real estate are defined as *capital assets.* When you buy a capital asset and later sell it for more than you paid, you earn a profit that is called a **capital gain**; when you suffer a loss, it is called a **capital loss**. If you held the asset for a year or less, you will have a *short-term capital gain or loss,* while if you held it for more than a year, you will have a *long-term capital gain or loss.* Thus, if you buy 100 shares of Disney stock for $80 per share and sell them for $90 per share, you have a capital gain of 100 × $10, or $1,000. However, if you sell the stock for $70 per share, you will have a $1,000 capital loss. Depending on how long you hold the stock, you will have a short-term or long-term capital gain or loss.[19] If you sell the stock for exactly $80 per share, you make neither a gain nor a loss; so no tax is due.

---

[18]Under U.S. tax laws, interest on most state and local government bonds, called municipals or "munis," is not subject to federal income taxes. This has a significant effect on the values of munis and on their rates of return. We discuss rates and returns in Chapter 8.

[19]If you have a *net* capital loss (your capital losses exceed your capital gains) for the year, you can deduct up to $3,000 of this loss against your other income (for example, salary, interest, and dividends).

2015 Individual Tax Rates    **TABLE 3.5**

**Single Individuals**

| If Your Taxable Income Is | You Pay This Amount on the Base of the Bracket | Plus This Percentage on the Excess over the Base (Marginal Rate) | Average Tax Rate at Top of Bracket |
|---|---|---|---|
| Up to $9,225 | $ 0 | 10.0% | 10.0% |
| $9,225–$37,450 | 922.50 | 15.0 | 13.8 |
| $37,450–$90,750 | 5,156.25 | 25.0 | 20.4 |
| $90,750–$189,750 | 18,481.25 | 28.0 | 24.3 |
| $189,750–$411,500 | 46,075.25 | 33.0 | 29.0 |
| $411,500–$413,200 | 119,401.25 | 35.0 | 29.0 |
| Over $413,200 | 119,996.25 | 39.6 | 39.6 |

**Married Couples Filing Joint Returns**

| If Your Taxable Income Is | You Pay This Amount on the Base of the Bracket | Plus This Percentage on the Excess over the Base (Marginal Rate) | Average Tax Rate at Top of Bracket |
|---|---|---|---|
| Up to $18,450 | $ 0 | 10.0% | 10.0% |
| $18,450–$74,900 | 1,845.00 | 15.0 | 13.8 |
| $74,900–$151,200 | 10,312.50 | 25.0 | 19.4 |
| $151,200–$230,450 | 29,387.50 | 28.0 | 22.4 |
| $230,450–$411,500 | 51,577.50 | 33.0 | 27.1 |
| $411,500–$464,850 | 111,324.00 | 35.0 | 28.0 |
| Over $464.850 | 129,996.50 | 39.6 | 39.6 |

*Notes:*

1. These are the 2015 tax rates that will be paid on tax returns due April 15, 2016. The income ranges at which each tax rate takes effect are indexed with inflation, so they change each year.

2. The average tax rates are always below the marginal rates, but in 2015 the average at the top of the brackets approaches 39.6% as taxable income rises without limit.

3. In 2015, a *personal exemption* of $4,000 per person or dependent could be deducted from gross income to determine taxable income. Thus, a husband and wife with two children would have a 2015 exemption of 4 × 4,000 = 16,000. The exemption increases with inflation, but if gross income exceeds certain limits, the exemption is phased out, and this has the effect of raising the effective tax rate on incomes over the specified limit. In addition, taxpayers can claim *itemized deductions* for charitable contributions and certain other items, but these deductions are also phased out for high-income taxpayers. In addition, there are Social Security and Medicare taxes. These additional situations and payroll taxes push the 2015 effective tax rate up well above 39.6%.

A short-term capital gain is taxed at the same rate as ordinary income. However, long-term capital gains are taxed differently. For most taxpayers, the rate on long-term capital gains is only 15%. Thus, if in 2015, you were in the 35% tax bracket, any short-term capital gains you earned would be taxed just like ordinary income; but your long-term capital gains would only be taxed at 15%. However, the tax rate on long-term capital gains is 20% for taxpayers in the 39.6% tax bracket. In addition, high-income taxpayers may incur a 3.8% unearned income Medicare contribution tax applied to their capital gains and other net investment income. So, the highest tax rate that could apply on short-term capital gains that are taxed at ordinary rates is 43.4% compared to 23.8% on long-term capital gains. Even for individuals at these top tax brackets, the tax rate on long-term capital gains still remains considerably lower than the tax rate on ordinary income.

Beginning in 2013, the maximum tax rate on *qualified dividends* increased to 20% for taxpayers in the 39.6% tax bracket.[20] However, for most taxpayers the top tax rate on qualified dividends is 15%. Because corporations pay dividends out of earnings that have already been taxed, there is *double taxation of corporate income*—income is first taxed at the corporate rate; and when what is left is paid out as dividends, it is taxed again. This double taxation motivated Congress to tax dividends at a lower rate than the rate on ordinary income.

Tax rates on dividends and capital gains have varied over time, but they have generally been lower than rates on ordinary income. Congress wants the economy to grow. For growth, we need investment in productive assets; and low capital gains and dividend tax rates encourage investment. Individuals with money to invest understand the tax advantages associated with making equity investments in newly formed companies versus buying bonds, so new ventures have an easier time attracting capital under the tax system. All in all, lower capital gains and dividend tax rates stimulate capital formation and investment.

As you might imagine, over the years Congress has frequently adjusted the tax code for individuals to promote certain activities. For example, Individual Retirement Accounts (IRAs) have encouraged individuals to save more for retirement. There are two main types of IRAs, **Traditional IRAs** and **Roth IRAs**. In each case, investors receive valuable tax benefits as long as the money is held in their account until age $59^1/_2$. Qualified contributions to a Traditional IRA are tax deductible, and the income and capital gains on the investments within the account are not taxed until the money is withdrawn after age $59^1/_2$. On the other hand, contributions to a Roth IRA are not tax deductible (they come out of after-tax dollars), but from that point forward, neither the future income nor the capital gains from the investments are taxed. In each case, investors in IRAs face penalties if they withdraw funds before age $59^1/_2$, unless there is a qualifying exception—for example, investors in a Roth IRA can withdraw up to $10,000 from their account to help pay for a first-time home without facing a penalty.

As a very rough rule of thumb, Roth IRAs are more attractive for those individuals who believe that their tax rates will increase over time—either because they think their income will increase as they age and/or because they think Congress will raise overall tax rates in the future. For this reason, many younger investors who expect higher pay (and therefore higher tax rates!) over time tend to select Roth IRAs. Indeed, a Vanguard analyst in a recent article in *The Wall Street Journal* estimates that investors under 30 years old allocate 92% of their IRA funds into Roth accounts. But as you might expect, one size doesn't fit all, and it is important to review the specific eligibility requirements, potential penalties, and distribution policies before making any investments. Fortunately, there are a lot of great online resources that summarize the relative benefits and drawbacks with both Traditional and Roth IRAs.[21]

One other tax feature should be addressed—the **Alternative Minimum Tax (AMT)**. The AMT was created in 1969 because Congress learned that 155 millionaires with high incomes paid no taxes because they had so many tax shelters from items such as depreciation on real estate and municipal bond interest. Under the AMT law, people must calculate their tax under the "regular" system and then under the AMT system, where many deductions are added back to income and then taxed

---

*Traditional IRAs*

Individual retirement arrangements in which qualified contributions are tax deductible and income and capital gains on investments within the account are not taxed until the money is withdrawn after age $59^1/_2$.

*Roth IRAs*

Individual retirement arrangements in which contributions are not tax deductible but the future income and capital gains within these accounts are not taxed if the money is withdrawn after age $59^1/_2$.

*Alternative Minimum Tax (AMT)*

Created by Congress to make it more difficult for wealthy individuals to avoid paying taxes through the use of various deductions.

---

[20]For a dividend to be "qualified," the investor must have owned the stock for more than 60 days during a 121-day period that begins 60 days prior to the ex-dividend date. We discuss dividends in Chapter 14; however, for now, understand that the ex-dividend date is the date when the right to the current dividend leaves the stock.

[21]For additional information regarding IRAs refer to Laura Saunders, "Is a Roth Account Right for You?" *The Wall Street Journal* (online.wsj.com), December 19, 2014; and David Wolpe, "All about IRAs," *The Motley Fool* (www.fool.com/money/allaboutiras/allaboutiras.htm).

at a special AMT rate. For many years, the AMT was not indexed for inflation; and literally millions of taxpayers found themselves subject to this very complex tax.[22]

New tax legislation also increased health care taxes for single taxpayers earning more than $200,000 and married taxpayers earning more than $250,000. These taxpayers will incur an additional 0.9% Medicare tax and a 3.8% net investment income tax on certain types of investment income.

## 3-9B CORPORATE TAXES

The corporate tax structure, shown in Table 3.6, is relatively simple. To illustrate, if a firm had $65,000 of taxable income, its tax bill would be $11,250:

$$\text{Taxes} = \$7,500 + 0.25(\$15,000)$$
$$= \$7,500 + \$3,750 = \$11,250$$

Its average tax rate would be $11,250/$65,000 = 17.3%. Note that corporate income above $18,333,333 has an average and marginal tax rate of 35%.

### Interest and Dividends Received by a Corporation

Corporations earn most of their income from operations, but they may also own securities—bonds and stocks—and receive interest and dividend income. Interest income received by a corporation is taxed as ordinary income at regular corporate tax rates. *However, dividends are taxed more favorably: 70% of dividends received is excluded from taxable income,* whereas *the remaining 30% is taxed at the ordinary tax rate.*[23] Thus, a corporation earning more than $18,333,333 and paying a 40% marginal federal plus state tax rate would normally pay only $(0.30)(0.4) = 0.12 = 12\%$ of its dividend income as taxes. If this firm had $10,000 in pretax dividend income, its after-tax dividend income would be $8,800:

$$\text{After-tax income} = \text{Pretax income}(1 - T) = \$10,000(1 - 0.12) = \$8,800$$

2015 Corporate Tax Rates  **TABLE 3.6**

| If a Corporation's Taxable Income Is | It Pays This Amount on the Base of the Bracket | Plus This Percentage on the Excess over the Base (Marginal Rate) | Average Tax Rate at Top of Bracket |
|---|---|---|---|
| Up to $50,000 | $ 0 | 15% | 15.0% |
| $50,000–$75,000 | 7,500 | 25 | 18.3 |
| $75,000–$100,000 | 13,750 | 34 | 22.3 |
| $100,000–$335,000 | 22,250 | 39 | 34.0 |
| $335,000–$10,000,000 | 113,900 | 34 | 34.0 |
| $10,000,000–$15,000,000 | 3,400,000 | 35 | 34.3 |
| $15,000,000–$18,333,333 | 5,150,000 | 38 | 35.0 |
| Over $18,333,333 | 6,416,667 | 35 | 35.0 |

---

[22]Beginning in 2013, the AMT exemption amounts are indexed to inflation. In 2015, the AMT exemption amounts are $53,600 for single taxpayers, $83,400 for those married and filing jointly, and $41,700 for those married and filing separately. The corporate AMT exemption is $40,000 and is phased out with alternative minimum taxable income between $150,000 and $310,000.

[23]The exclusion depends on the percentage of the paying company's stock the receiving company owns. If it owns 100% (hence, the payer is a subsidiary), all of the dividend will be excluded. If it owns less than 20%, which is the case if the stock held is just an investment, 70% will be excluded. Also, state tax rules vary; but in our example, we assume that Allied also has a state tax exclusion.

The rationale behind this exclusion is that when a corporation receives dividends and then pays out its own after-tax income as dividends to its stockholders, the dividends received are subjected to triple taxation: (1) The original corporation is taxed. (2) The second corporation is taxed on the dividends it receives. (3) The individuals who receive the final dividends are taxed again. This explains the 70% intercorporate dividend exclusion.

Suppose a firm has excess cash that it does not need for operations, and it plans to invest this cash in marketable securities. The tax factor favors stocks, which pay dividends, rather than bonds, which pay interest. For example, suppose Allied had $100,000 to invest, and it could buy bonds that paid 8% interest, or $8,000 per year, or stock that paid 7% in dividends, or $7,000. Allied is in the 40% federal-plus-state tax bracket. Therefore, if Allied bought bonds and received interest, its tax on the $8,000 of interest would be 0.4($8,000) = $3,200, and its after-tax income would be $4,800. If it bought stock, its tax would be $7,000(0.12) = $840, and its after-tax income would be $6,160. *Other factors might lead Allied to invest in bonds, but when the investor is a corporation, the tax factor favors stock investments.*

### Interest and Dividends Paid by a Corporation

A firm like Allied can finance its operations with either debt or stock. If a firm uses debt, it must pay interest, whereas if it uses stock, it is expected to pay dividends. *Interest paid can be deducted from operating income to obtain taxable income, but dividends paid cannot be deducted.* Therefore, Allied would need $1 of pretax income to pay $1 of interest; but because it is in the 40% federal-plus-state tax bracket, it must earn $1.67 of pretax income to pay $1 of dividends:

$$\frac{\text{Pretax income needed}}{\text{to pay \$1 of dividends}} = \frac{\$1}{1 - \text{Tax rate}} = \frac{\$1}{0.60} = \$1.67$$

Working backward, if Allied has $1.67 in pretax income, it must pay $0.67 in taxes [(0.4)($1.67) = $0.67]. This leaves it with after-tax income of $1.00.

Table 3.7 shows the situation for a firm with $10 million of assets, sales of $5 million, and $1.5 million of earnings before interest and taxes (EBIT). As shown in column 1, if the firm were financed entirely by bonds and if it made interest payments of $1.5 million, its taxable income would be zero; taxes would be zero; and its investors would receive the entire $1.5 million. (The term *investors* includes both stockholders and bondholders.) However, as shown in column 2, if the firm had no debt and was therefore financed entirely by stock, all of the $1.5 million of EBIT would be taxable income to the corporation; the tax would be

**TABLE 3.7**      Returns to Investors under Bond and Stock Financing

|  | Use Bonds (1) | Use Stocks (2) |
|---|---|---|
| Sales | $5,000,000 | $5,000,000 |
| Operating costs | 3,500,000 | 3,500,000 |
| Earnings before interest and taxes (EBIT) | $1,500,000 | $1,500,000 |
| Interest | 1,500,000 | 0 |
| Taxable income | $        0 | $1,500,000 |
| Federal-plus-state taxes (40%) | 0 | 600,000 |
| After-tax income | $        0 | $  900,000 |
| Income to investors | $1,500,000 | $  900,000 |
| Rate of return on $10 million of assets | 15.0% | 9.0% |

$1,500,000(0.40) = $600,000; and investors would receive only $0.9 million versus $1.5 million under debt financing. Therefore, the rate of return to investors on their $10 million investment is much higher when debt is used.

Of course, it is generally not possible to finance exclusively with debt; and the risk of doing so would offset the benefits of the higher expected income. *Still, the fact that interest is a deductible expense has a profound effect on the way businesses are financed—the corporate tax system favors debt financing over equity financing.* This point is discussed in more detail in Chapters 10 and 13.[24]

## Corporate Capital Gains

Before 1987, corporate long-term capital gains were taxed at lower rates than corporate ordinary income; so the situation was similar for corporations and individuals. Currently, though, corporations' capital gains are taxed at the same rates as their operating income.

## Corporate Loss Carryback and Carryforward

Ordinary corporate operating losses can be carried back (**carryBack**) to each of the preceding 2 years and carried forward (**carryForward**) for the next 20 years and used to offset taxable income in those years. For example, an operating loss in 2016 could be carried back and used to reduce taxable income in 2014 and 2015, it also could be carried forward, if necessary, and used in 2017, 2018, up until 2036. The loss is applied to the earliest year first, then to the next earliest year, and so forth, until losses have been used up or the 20-year carryforward limit has been reached.

To illustrate, suppose Company X had $2 million of pretax profits (taxable income) in 2014 and 2015 and then in 2016, it lost $12 million. Its federal-plus-state tax rate is 40%. As shown in Table 3.8, Company X would use the carryback feature to recompute its taxes for 2014, using $2 million of the 2016 operating losses to reduce the 2014 pretax profit to zero. This would permit it to recover the taxes paid in 2014. Therefore, in 2016, it would receive a refund of its 2014 taxes because of the loss experienced in 2016. Because $10 million of the unrecovered losses would still be available, X would repeat this procedure for 2015. Thus, in 2016, the company would pay zero taxes for 2016 and would receive a refund for taxes paid in 2014 and 2015. It would still

*Carryback*
Ordinary corporate operating losses can be carried backward for 2 years and carried forward for 20 years to offset taxable income in a given year.

*Carryforward*
Ordinary corporate operating losses can be carried backward for 2 years and carried forward for 20 years to offset taxable income in a given year.

Calculation of Loss Carryback and Carryforward for 2014–2015 Using a $12 Million 2016 Loss    **TABLE 3.8**

|  | 2014 | 2015 |
|---|---|---|
| Original taxable income | $ 2,000,000 | $ 2,000,000 |
| Carryback credit | −2,000,000 | −2,000,000 |
| Adjusted profit | $          0 | $          0 |
| Taxes previously paid (40%) | 800,000 | 800,000 |
| Difference = Tax refund | $    800,000 | $    800,000 |

Total refund check received in 2017: $800,000 + $800,000 = $1,600,000.

Amount of loss carryforward available for use in 2017–2036:

| | |
|---|---|
| 2016 loss | $12,000,000 |
| Carryback losses used | 4,000,000 |
| Carryforward losses still available | $ 8,000,000 |

[24]A company could, in theory, refrain from paying dividends to help prevent its stockholders from having to pay taxes on dividends received. The IRS has a rule against the *improper accumulation of retained earnings.* However, in our experience, it is easy for firms to justify retaining earnings; and we have never seen a firm have a problem with the improper accumulation rule.

have $8 million of unrecovered losses to carry forward, subject to the 20-year limit. This $8 million could be used until the entire $12 million loss had been used to offset taxable income. The purpose of permitting this loss treatment is to avoid penalizing corporations whose incomes fluctuate substantially from year to year.

## Consolidated Corporate Tax Returns

If a corporation owns 80% or more of another corporation's stock, it can aggregate income and file one consolidated tax return. This allows the losses of one company to be used to offset the profits of another. (Similarly, one division's losses can be used to offset another division's profits.) No business wants to incur losses; but tax offsets make it more feasible for large, multidivisional corporations to undertake risky new ventures or ventures that will suffer losses during a developmental period.

## Taxation of Small Businesses: S Corporations

*S Corporation*

A small corporation that, under Subchapter S of the Internal Revenue Code, elects to be taxed as a proprietorship or a partnership yet retains limited liability and other benefits of the corporate form of organization.

As we noted in Chapter 1, the Tax Code allows small businesses that meet certain conditions to be set up as corporations and thus receive the benefits of the corporate form of organization—especially limited liability—yet still be taxed as proprietorships or partnerships rather than as corporations. These corporations are called **S Corporations**. (Regular corporations are called C corporations.) If a corporation elects to set up as an S corporation, all of its income is reported as personal income by its stockholders, on a pro rata basis, and thus is taxed at the stockholders' individual rates. Because the income is taxed only once, this is an important benefit to the owners of small corporations in which all or most of the income earned each year will be distributed as dividends. The situation is similar for LLCs.

## Depreciation

Depreciation plays an important role in income tax calculations—the larger the depreciation, the lower the taxable income, the lower the tax bill, and thus the higher the operating cash flow. Congress specifies the life over which assets can be depreciated for tax purposes and the depreciation methods that can be used. We discuss in detail how depreciation is calculated and how it affects income and cash flows when we study capital budgeting.

## SelfTest

Explain this statement: Our tax rates are progressive.

What's the difference between marginal and average tax rates?

What's the AMT, and what is its purpose?

What's a muni bond, and how are these bonds taxed?

What are long-term capital gains? Are they taxed like other income? Explain.

How does our tax system influence the use of debt financing by corporations?

What is the logic behind allowing tax loss carrybacks/carryforwards?

Differentiate between S and C corporations.

# TYING IT ALL TOGETHER

The primary purposes of this chapter were to describe the basic financial statements, to present background information on cash flows, to differentiate between cash flow and accounting income, and to provide an overview of the federal income tax system. In the next chapter, we build on this information to analyze a firm's financial statements and to determine its financial health.

## Self-Test Questions And Problems

(Solutions Appear in Appendix A)

**ST-1** **KEY TERMS** Define each of the following terms:

a. Annual report; balance sheet; income statement; statement of cash flows; statement of stockholders' equity
b. Stockholders' equity; retained earnings; working capital; net working capital; net operating working capital (NOWC); total debt
c. Depreciation; amortization; operating income; EBITDA; free cash flow (FCF)
d. Net operating profit after taxes (NOPAT)
e. Market value added (MVA); economic value added (EVA)
f. Progressive tax; marginal tax rate; average tax rate
g. Tax loss carryback; carryforward; alternative minimum tax (AMT)
h. Traditional IRAs; Roth IRAs
i. Capital gain (loss)
j. S corporation

**ST-2** **NET INCOME AND CASH FLOW** Last year Rattner Robotics had $5 million in operating income (EBIT). Its depreciation expense was $1 million, its interest expense was $1 million, and its corporate tax rate was 40%. At year-end, it had $14 million in current assets, $3 million in accounts payable, $1 million in accruals, $2 million in notes payable, and $15 million in net plant and equipment. Rattner uses only debt and common equity to fund its operations. (In other words, Rattner has no preferred stock on its balance sheet.) Rattner had no other current liabilities. Assume that Rattner's only noncash item was depreciation.

a. What was the company's net income?
b. What was its net operating working capital (NOWC)?
c. What was its net working capital (NWC)?
d. Rattner had $12 million in net plant and equipment the prior year. Its net operating working capital has remained constant over time. What is the company's free cash flow (FCF) for the year that just ended?
e. Rattner has 500,000 common shares outstanding, and the common stock amount on the balance sheet is $5 million. The company has not issued or repurchased common stock during the year. Last year's balance in retained earnings was $11.2 million, and the firm paid out dividends of $1.2 million during the year. Develop Rattner's end-of-year statement of stockholders' equity.
f. If the firm's stock price at year-end is $52, what is the firm's market value added (MVA)?
g. If the firm's after-tax percentage cost of capital is 9%, what is the firm's EVA at year-end?

## Questions

**3-1** What four financial statements are contained in most annual reports?

**3-2** Who are some of the basic users of financial statements, and how do they use them?

**3-3** If a "typical" firm reports $20 million of retained earnings on its balance sheet, could its directors declare a $20 million cash dividend without having any qualms about what they were doing? Explain your answer.

**3-4** Explain the following statement: Although the balance sheet can be thought of as a snapshot of a firm's financial position *at a point in time*, the income statement reports on operations *over a period of time*.

**3-5** Financial statements are based on generally accepted accounting principles (GAAP) and are audited by CPA firms. Do investors need to worry about the validity of those statements? Explain your answer.

**3-6** Refer to the box titled, "The Balance Sheet of an 'Average' American Household" when answering parts a and b.

    a. Based on this evidence, did the financial position of the average household improved during 2004–2007? During 2007–2010? During 2010–2014? Explain your answers.

    b. What do you think the average household balance sheet looks like today? Explain your answer.

**3-7** What is free cash flow? If you were an investor, why might you be more interested in free cash flow than net income?

**3-8** Would it be possible for a company to report negative free cash flow and still be highly valued by investors; that is, could a negative free cash flow ever be viewed optimistically by investors? Explain your answer.

**3-9** How are management's actions incorporated in EVA and MVA? How are EVA and MVA interconnected?

**3-10** Explain the following statement: Our tax rates are progressive.

**3-11** What does *double taxation of corporate income* mean? Could income ever be subject to *triple* taxation? Explain your answer.

**3-12** How does the deductibility of interest and dividends by the paying corporation affect the choice of financing (i.e., the use of debt versus equity)?

## Problems

**Easy Problems 1–8**

**3-1** **BALANCE SHEET** The assets of Dallas & Associates consist entirely of current assets and net plant and equipment. The firm has total assets of $2.5 million and net plant and equipment equals $2 million. It has notes payable of $150,000, long-term debt of $750,000, and total common equity of $1.5 million. The firm does have accounts payable and accruals on its balance sheet. The firm only finances with debt and common equity, so it has no preferred stock on its balance sheet.

    a. What is the company's total debt?

    b. What is the amount of total liabilities and equity that appears on the firm's balance sheet?

    c. What is the balance of current assets on the firm's balance sheet?

    d. What is the balance of current liabilities on the firm's balance sheet?

    e. What is the amount of accounts payable and accruals on its balance sheet? (Hint: Consider this as a single line item on the firm's balance sheet.)

    f. What is the firm's net working capital?

    g. What is the firm's net operating working capital?

    h. What is the explanation for the difference in your answers to parts f and g?

**3-2** **INCOME STATEMENT** Byron Books Inc. recently reported $13 million of net income. Its EBIT was $20.8 million, and its tax rate was 35%. What was its interest expense?

(Hint: Write out the headings for an income statement, and fill in the known values. Then divide $13 million of net income by $(1 - T) = 0.65$ to find the pretax income. The difference between EBIT and taxable income must be interest expense. Use this same procedure to complete similar problems.)

**3-3   INCOME STATEMENT**   Patterson Brothers recently reported an EBITDA of $7.5 million and net income of $2.1 million. It had $2.0 million of interest expense, and its corporate tax rate was 30%. What was its charge for depreciation and amortization?

**3-4   STATEMENT OF STOCKHOLDERS' EQUITY**   In its most recent financial statements, Nessler Inc. reported $75 million of net income and $825 million of retained earnings. The previous retained earnings were $784 million. How much in dividends were paid to shareholders during the year? Assume that all dividends declared were actually paid.

**3-5   MVA**   Harper Industries has $900 million of common equity on its balance sheet; its stock price is $80 per share; and its market value added (MVA) is $50 million. How many common shares are currently outstanding?

**3-6   MVA**   Over the years, Masterson Corporation's stockholders have provided $34,000,000 of capital when they purchased new issues of stock and allowed management to retain some of the firm's earnings. The firm now has 2,000,000 shares of common stock outstanding, and the shares sell at a price of $28 per share. How much value has Masterson's management added to stockholder wealth over the years, that is, what is Masterson's MVA?

**3-7   EVA**   Barton Industries has operating income for the year of $3,500,000 and a 36% tax rate. Its total invested capital is $20,000,000 and its after-tax percentage cost of capital is 8%. What is the firm's EVA?

**3-8   PERSONAL TAXES**   Susan and Stan Britton are a married couple who file a joint income tax return, where the tax rates are based on the tax tables presented in the chapter. Assume that their taxable income this year was $375,000.

a.  What is their federal tax liability?
b.  What is their marginal tax rate?
c.  What is their average tax rate?

**Intermediate Problems 9–14**

**3-9   BALANCE SHEET**   Which of the following actions are most likely to directly increase cash as shown on a firm's balance sheet? Explain and state the assumptions that underlie your answer.

a.  It issues $4 million of new common stock.
b.  It buys new plant and equipment at a cost of $3 million.
c.  It reports a large loss for the year.
d.  It increases the dividends paid on its common stock.

**3-10   STATEMENT OF STOCKHOLDERS' EQUITY**   Electronics World Inc. paid out $22.4 million in total common dividends and reported $144.7 million of retained earnings at year-end. The prior year's retained earnings were $95.5 million. What was the net income? Assume that all dividends declared were actually paid.

**3-11   EVA**   For 2016, Gourmet Kitchen Products reported $22 million of sales and $19 million of operating costs (including depreciation). The company has $15 million of total invested capital. Its after-tax cost of capital is 10%, and its federal-plus-state income tax rate was 36%. What was the firm's economic value added (EVA), that is, how much value did management add to stockholders' wealth during 2016?

**3-12   STATEMENT OF CASH FLOWS**   Hampton Industries had $39,000 in cash at year-end 2015 and $11,000 in cash at year-end 2016. The firm invested in property, plant, and equipment totaling $210,000. Cash flow from financing activities totaled +$120,000.

a.  What was the cash flow from operating activities?
b.  If accruals increased by $15,000, receivables and inventories increased by $50,000, and depreciation and amortization totaled $25,000, what was the firm's net income?

**3-13** **STATEMENT OF CASH FLOWS** You have just been hired as a financial analyst for Barrington Industries. Unfortunately, company headquarters (where all of the firm's records are kept) has been destroyed by fire. So, your first job will be to recreate the firm's cash flow statement for the year just ended. The firm had $100,000 in the bank at the end of the prior year, and its working capital accounts except cash remained constant during the year. It earned $5 million in net income during the year but paid $800,000 in dividends to common shareholders. Throughout the year, the firm purchased $5.5 million of machinery that was needed for a new project. You have just spoken to the firm's accountants and learned that annual depreciation expense for the year is $450,000; however, the purchase price for the machinery represents additions to property, plant, and equipment before depreciation. Finally, you have determined that the only financing done by the firm was to issue long-term debt of $1 million at a 6% interest rate. What was the firm's end-of-year cash balance? Recreate the firm's cash flow statement to arrive at your answer.

**3-14** **FREE CASH FLOW** Arlington Corporation's financial statements (dollars and shares are in millions) are provided here.

**Balance Sheets as of December 31**

| Assets | 2016 | 2015 |
|---|---|---|
| Cash and equivalents | $ 15,000 | $ 14,000 |
| Accounts receivable | 35,000 | 30,000 |
| Inventories | 33,320 | 27,000 |
| Total current assets | $ 83,320 | $ 71,000 |
| Net plant and equipment | 48,000 | 46,000 |
| Total assets | $131,320 | $117,000 |
| *Liabilities and Equity* | | |
| Accounts payable | $ 10,100 | $ 9,000 |
| Accruals | 8,000 | 6,000 |
| Notes payable | 7,000 | 5,050 |
| Total current liabilities | $ 25,100 | $ 20,050 |
| Long-term bonds | 20,000 | 20,000 |
| Total liabilities | $ 45,100 | $ 40,050 |
| Common stock (4,000 shares) | 40,000 | 40,000 |
| Retained earnings | 46,220 | 36,950 |
| Common equity | $ 86,220 | $ 76,950 |
| Total liabilities and equity | $131,320 | $117,000 |

**Income Statement for Year Ending December 31, 2016**

| | |
|---|---|
| Sales | $210,000 |
| Operating costs excluding depreciation and amortization | 160,000 |
| EBITDA | $ 50,000 |
| Depreciation & amortization | 6,000 |
| EBIT | $ 44,000 |
| Interest | 5,350 |
| EBT | $ 38,650 |
| Taxes (40%) | 15,460 |
| Net income | $ 23,190 |
| Dividends paid | $ 13,920 |

a. What was net operating working capital for 2015 and 2016?
b. What was Arlington's 2016 free cash flow?
c. Construct Arlington's 2016 statement of stockholders' equity.
d. What was Arlington's 2016 EVA? Assume that its after-tax cost of capital is 10%.
e. What was Arlington's MVA at year-end 2016? Assume that its stock price at December 31, 2016, was $25.

**Challenging Problems 15–18**

**3-15  INCOME STATEMENT** Edmonds Industries is forecasting the following income statement:

| | |
|---|---|
| Sales | $10,000,000 |
| Operating costs excluding depreciation & amortization | 5,500,000 |
| EBITDA | $ 4,500,000 |
| Depreciation and amortization | 1,200,000 |
| EBIT | $ 3,300,000 |
| Interest | 500,000 |
| EBT | $ 2,800,000 |
| Taxes (40%) | 1,120,000 |
| Net income | $ 1,680,000 |

The CEO would like to see higher sales and a forecasted net income of $2,100,000. Assume that operating costs (excluding depreciation and amortization) are 55% of sales and that depreciation and amortization and interest expenses will increase by 6%. The tax rate, which is 40%, will remain the same. (Note that while the tax rate remains constant, the taxes paid will change.) What level of sales would generate $2,100,000 in net income?

**3-16  FINANCIAL STATEMENTS** The Davidson Corporation's balance sheet and income statement are provided here.

**Davidson Corporation: Balance Sheet as of December 31, 2016**
**(Millions of Dollars)**

| Assets | | Liabilities and Equity | |
|---|---|---|---|
| Cash and equivalents | $ 15 | Accounts payable | $ 120 |
| Accounts receivable | 515 | Accruals | 280 |
| Inventories | 880 | Notes payable | 220 |
| Total current assets | $1,410 | Total current liabilities | $ 620 |
| Net plant and equipment | 2,590 | Long-term bonds | 1,520 |
| | | Total liabilities | $2,140 |
| | | Common stock (100 million shares) | 260 |
| | | Retained earnings | 1,600 |
| | | Common equity | $1,860 |
| Total assets | $4,000 | Total liabilities and equity | $4,000 |

**Davidson Corporation: Income Statement for Year Ending December 31, 2016**
**(Millions of Dollars)**

| | |
|---|---|
| Sales | $6,250 |
| Operating costs excluding depreciation and amortization | 5,230 |
| EBITDA | $1,020 |
| Depreciation & amortization | 220 |
| EBIT | $ 800 |
| Interest | 180 |
| EBT | $ 620 |
| Taxes (40%) | 248 |
| Net income | $ 372 |
| Common dividends paid | $ 146 |
| Earnings per share | $ 3.72 |

a. Construct the statement of stockholders' equity for December 31, 2016. No common stock was issued during 2016.
b. How much money has been reinvested in the firm over the years?
c. At the present time, how large a check could be written without it bouncing?
d. How much money must be paid to current creditors within the next year?

3-17    **FREE CASH FLOW**   Financial information for Powell Panther Corporation is shown here.

**Powell Panther Corporation: Income Statements for Year Ending December 31**
**(Millions of Dollars)**

|  | 2016 | 2015 |
|---|---|---|
| Sales | $1,200.0 | $1,000.0 |
| Operating costs excluding depreciation and amortization | 1,020.0 | 850.0 |
| EBITDA | $ 180.0 | $ 150.0 |
| Depreciation & amortization | 30.0 | 25.0 |
| Earnings before interest and taxes (EBIT) | $ 150.0 | $ 125.0 |
| Interest | 21.7 | 20.2 |
| Earnings before taxes (EBT) | $ 128.3 | $ 104.8 |
| Taxes (40%) | 51.3 | 41.9 |
| Net income | $ 77.0 | $ 62.9 |

**Powell Panther Corporation: Balance Sheets as of December 31**
**(Millions of Dollars)**

|  | 2016 | 2015 |
|---|---|---|
| *Assets* | | |
| Cash and equivalents | $ 12.0 | $ 10.0 |
| Accounts receivable | 180.0 | 150.0 |
| Inventories | 180.0 | 200.0 |
| Total current assets | $372.0 | $360.0 |
| Net plant and equipment | 300.0 | 250.0 |
| Total assets | $672.0 | $610.0 |
| | | |
| *Liabilities and Equity* | | |
| Accounts payable | $108.0 | $ 90.0 |
| Accruals | 72.0 | 60.0 |
| Notes payable | 67.0 | 51.5 |
| Total current liabilities | $247.0 | $201.5 |
| Long-term bonds | 150.0 | 150.0 |
| Total liabilities | $397.0 | $351.5 |
| Common stock (50 million shares) | 50.0 | 50.0 |
| Retained earnings | 225.0 | 208.5 |
| Common equity | $275.0 | $258.5 |
| Total liabilities and equity | $672.0 | $610.0 |

a. What was net operating working capital for 2015 and 2016?
b. What was the 2016 free cash flow?
c. How would you explain the large increase in 2016 dividends?

3-18    **PERSONAL TAXES**   Mary Jarvis is a single individual who is working on filing her tax return for the previous year. She has assembled the following relevant information:

• She received $82,000 in salary.
• She received $12,000 of dividend income.

- She received $5,000 of interest income on Home Depot bonds.
- She received $22,000 from the sale of Disney stock that was purchased 2 years prior to the sale at a cost of $9,000.
- She received $10,000 from the sale of Google stock that was purchased 6 months prior to the sale at a cost of $7,500.
- Mary receives one exemption ($4,000), and she has allowable itemized deductions of $7,500. These amounts will be deducted from her gross income to determine her taxable income.

Assume that her tax rates are based on the tax tables presented in the chapter.

a. What is Mary's federal tax liability?
b. What is her marginal tax rate?
c. What is her average tax rate?

# Comprehensive/Spreadsheet Problem

3-19    **FINANCIAL STATEMENTS, CASH FLOW, AND TAXES**   Laiho Industries's 2015 and 2016 balance sheets (in thousands of dollars) are shown.

|  | 2016 | 2015 |
|---|---|---|
| Cash | $102,850 | $ 89,725 |
| Accounts receivable | 103,365 | 85,527 |
| Inventories | 38,444 | 34,982 |
| Total current assets | $244,659 | $210,234 |
| Net fixed assets | 67,165 | 42,436 |
| Total assets | $311,824 | $252,670 |
| Accounts payable | $ 30,761 | $ 23,109 |
| Accruals | 30,477 | 22,656 |
| Notes payable | 16,717 | 14,217 |
| Total current liabilities | $ 77,955 | $ 59,982 |
| Long-term debt | 76,264 | 63,914 |
| Total liabilities | $154,219 | $123,896 |
| Common stock | 100,000 | 90,000 |
| Retained earnings | 57,605 | 38,774 |
| Total common equity | $157,605 | $128,774 |
| Total liabilities and equity | $311,824 | $252,670 |

a. Sales for 2016 were $455,150,000, and EBITDA was 15% of sales. Furthermore, depreciation and amortization were 11% of net fixed assets, interest was $8,575,000, the corporate tax rate was 40%, and Laiho pays 40% of its net income as dividends. Given this information, construct the firm's 2016 income statement.
b. Construct the statement of stockholders' equity for the year ending December 31, 2016, and the 2016 statement of cash flows.
c. Calculate 2015 and 2016 net operating working capital (NOWC) and 2016 free cash flow (FCF).
d. If Laiho increased its dividend payout ratio, what effect would this have on corporate taxes paid? What effect would this have on taxes paid by the company's shareholders?
e. Assume that the firm's after-tax cost of capital is 10.5%. What is the firm's 2016 EVA?
f. Assume that the firm's stock price is $22 per share and that at year-end 2016 the firm has 10 million shares outstanding. What is the firm's MVA at year-end 2016?

# INTEGRATED CASE

## D'LEON INC., PART I

**3-20** **FINANCIAL STATEMENTS AND TAXES** Donna Jamison, a 2011 graduate of the University of Florida, with 4 years of banking experience, was recently brought in as assistant to the chairperson of the board of D'Leon Inc., a small food producer that operates in north Florida and whose specialty is high-quality pecan and other nut products sold in the snack foods market. D'Leon's president, Al Watkins, decided in 2015 to undertake a major expansion and to "go national" in competition with Frito-Lay, Eagle, and other major snack foods companies. Watkins believed that D'Leon's products were of higher quality than the competition's; that this quality differential would enable it to charge a premium price; and that the end result would be greatly increased sales, profits, and stock price.

The company doubled its plant capacity, opened new sales offices outside its home territory, and launched an expensive advertising campaign. D'Leon's results were not satisfactory, to put it mildly. Its board of directors, which consisted of its president, vice president, and major stockholders (all of whom were local businesspeople), was most upset when directors learned how the expansion was going. Unhappy suppliers were being paid late; and the bank was complaining about the deteriorating situation and threatening to cut off credit. As a result, Watkins was informed that changes would have to be made—and quickly; otherwise, he would be fired. Also, at the board's insistence, Donna Jamison was brought in and given the job of assistant to Fred Campo, a retired banker who was D'Leon's chairperson and largest stockholder. Campo agreed to give up a few of his golfing days and help nurse the company back to health, with Jamison's help.

Jamison began by gathering the financial statements and other data given in Tables IC 3.1, IC 3.2, IC 3.3, and IC 3.4. Assume that you are Jamison's assistant. You must help her answer the following questions for Campo. (Note: We will continue with this case in Chapter 4, and you will feel more comfortable with the analysis there. But answering these questions will help prepare you for Chapter 4. Provide clear explanations.)

a. What effect did the expansion have on sales, after-tax operating income, net operating working capital (NOWC), and net income?

b. What effect did the company's expansion have on its free cash flow?

c. D'Leon purchases materials on 30-day terms, meaning that it is supposed to pay for purchases within 30 days of receipt. Judging from its 2016 balance sheet, do you think that D'Leon pays suppliers on time? Explain, including what problems might occur if suppliers are not paid in a timely manner.

d. D'Leon spends money for labor, materials, and fixed assets (depreciation) to make products—and spends still more money to sell those products. Then the firm makes sales that result in receivables, which eventually result in cash inflows. Does it appear that D'Leon's sales price exceeds its costs per unit sold? How does this affect the cash balance?

e. Suppose D'Leon's sales manager told the sales staff to start offering 60-day credit terms rather than the 30-day terms now being offered. D'Leon's competitors react by offering similar terms, so sales remain constant. What effect would this have on the cash account? How would the cash account be affected if sales doubled as a result of the credit policy change?

f. Can you imagine a situation in which the sales price exceeds the cost of producing and selling a unit of output, yet a dramatic increase in sales volume causes the cash balance to decline? Explain.

g. Did D'Leon finance its expansion program with internally generated funds (additions to retained earnings plus depreciation) or with external capital? How does the choice of financing affect the company's financial strength?

h. Refer to Tables IC 3.2 and IC 3.4. Suppose D'Leon broke even in 2016 in the sense that sales revenues equaled total operating costs plus interest charges. Would the asset expansion have caused the company to experience a cash shortage that required it to raise external capital? Explain.

i. If D'Leon starts depreciating fixed assets over 7 years rather than 10 years, would that affect (1) the physical stock of assets, (2) the balance sheet account for fixed assets, (3) the company's reported net income, and (4) the company's cash position? Assume that the same depreciation method is used for stockholder reporting and for tax calculations and that the accounting change has no effect on assets' physical lives.

j. Explain how earnings per share, dividends per share, and book value per share are calculated and what they mean. Why does the market price per share not equal the book value per share?

k. Explain briefly the tax treatment of (1) interest and dividends paid, (2) interest earned and dividends received, (3) capital gains, and (4) tax loss carrybacks and carryforwards. How might each of these items affect D'Leon's taxes?

Balance Sheets    TABLE IC 3.1

|  | 2016 | 2015 |
|---|---|---|
| **Assets** | | |
| Cash | $ 7,282 | $ 57,600 |
| Accounts receivable | 632,160 | 351,200 |
| Inventories | 1,287,360 | 715,200 |
| Total current assets | $1,926,802 | $1,124,000 |
| Gross fixed assets | 1,202,950 | 491,000 |
| Less accumulated depreciation | 263,160 | 146,200 |
| Net fixed assets | $ 939,790 | $ 344,800 |
| Total assets | $2,866,592 | $1,468,800 |
| **Liabilities and Equity** | | |
| Accounts payable | $ 524,160 | $ 145,600 |
| Accruals | 489,600 | 136,000 |
| Notes payable | 636,808 | 200,000 |
| Total current liabilities | $1,650,568 | $ 481,600 |
| Long-term debt | 723,432 | 323,432 |
| Common stock (100,000 shares) | 460,000 | 460,000 |
| Retained earnings | 32,592 | 203,768 |
| Total equity | $ 492,592 | $ 663,768 |
| Total liabilities and equity | $2,866,592 | $1,468,800 |

**TABLE IC 3.2**　　　　　　Income Statements

| | 2016 | 2015 |
|---|---|---|
| Sales | $6,034,000 | $3,432,000 |
| Cost of goods sold | 5,528,000 | 2,864,000 |
| Other expenses | 519,988 | 358,672 |
| Total operating costs excluding depreciation and amortization | $6,047,988 | $3,222,672 |
| Depreciation and amortization | 116,960 | 18,900 |
| EBIT | ($ 130,948) | $ 190,428 |
| Interest expense | 136,012 | 43,828 |
| EBT | ($ 266,960) | $ 146,600 |
| Taxes (40%) | (106,784)[a] | 58,640 |
| Net income | ($ 160,176) | $ 87,960 |
| | | |
| EPS | ($ 1.602) | $ 0.880 |
| DPS | $ 0.110 | $ 0.220 |
| Book value per share | $ 4.926 | $ 6.638 |
| Stock price | $ 2.25 | $ 8.50 |
| Shares outstanding | 100,000 | 100,000 |
| Tax rate | 40.00% | 40.00% |
| Lease payments | $ 40,000 | $ 40,000 |
| Sinking fund payments | 0 | 0 |

[a]The firm had sufficient taxable income in 2014 and 2015 to obtain its full tax refund in 2016.

**TABLE IC 3.3**　　　　　　Statement of Stockholders' Equity, 2016

| | Common Stock | | Retained Earnings | Total Stockholders' Equity |
|---|---|---|---|---|
| | Shares | Amount | | |
| Balances, December 31, 2015 | 100,000 | $460,000 | $203,768 | $ 663,768 |
| 2016 Net income | | | (160,176) | |
| Cash dividends | | | (11,000) | |
| Addition (subtraction) to retained earnings | | | | (171,176) |
| Balances, December 31, 2016 | 100,000 | $460,000 | $ 32,592 | $ 492,592 |

Statement of Cash Flows, 2016    **TABLE IC 3.4**

**Operating Activities**

| | |
|---|---:|
| Net income | ($ 160,176) |
| Depreciation and amortization | 116,960 |
| Increase in accounts payable | 378,560 |
| Increase in accruals | 353,600 |
| Increase in accounts receivable | (280,960) |
| Increase in inventories | (572,160) |
| Net cash provided by operating activities | ($ 164,176) |

**Long-Term Investing Activities**

| | |
|---|---:|
| Additions to property, plant, and equipment | ($ 711,950) |
| Net cash used in investing activities | ($ 711,950) |

**Financing Activities**

| | |
|---|---:|
| Increase in notes payable | $ 436,808 |
| Increase in long-term debt | 400,000 |
| Payment of cash dividends | (11,000) |
| Net cash provided by financing activities | $ 825,808 |

**Summary**

| | |
|---|---:|
| Net decrease in cash | ($ 50,318) |
| Cash at beginning of year | 57,600 |
| Cash at end of year | $ 7,282 |

# TAKING A CLOSER LOOK

## EXPLORING WHOLE FOODS' FINANCIAL STATEMENTS

*Use online resources to work on this chapter's questions. Please note that website information changes over time, and these changes may limit your ability to answer some of these questions.*

Over the past decade, Whole Foods Market, Inc., has become an increasingly familiar part of the urban landscape. As of November 5, 2014, the company had 401 stores in the United States, Canada, and the United Kingdom.

Using financial websites such as finance.yahoo.com and money.msn.com, you can access a wealth of financial information for companies such as Whole Foods. By entering the company's ticker symbol, WFM, you will be able to access a great deal of useful information, including a summary of what Whole Foods does (Profile), a chart of its recent stock price (Interactive Chart), EPS estimates (Earnings), recent news stories (Headlines), and a list of key financial data and ratios (Key Ratios).

In researching a company's operating performance, a good place to start is the recent stock price performance. From an interactive chart, you can obtain a chart of the company's stock price performance and compare it to the overall market (as measured by the S&P 500 index) between 2010 and 2015. As you can see, Whole Foods has had its ups and downs. But the company's overall performance has been quite strong during the past 5 years, and it has beaten the overall market handily.

You can also find Whole Foods' recent financial statements (Financials). Typically, you can find annual balance sheets, income statements, and cash flow statements for 3 to 5 years. Quarterly information is also available.

## DISCUSSION QUESTIONS

1. Looking at the most recent year available, what is the amount of total assets on Whole Foods' balance sheet? What percentage is fixed assets, such as plant and equipment? What percentage is current assets? How much has the company grown over the years that are shown?

2. Does Whole Foods have very much long-term debt? What are the chief ways in which Whole Foods has financed assets?

3. Looking at the statement of cash flows, what factors can explain the change in the company's cash position over the last couple of years?

4. Looking at the income statement, what are the company's most recent sales and net income? Over the past several years, what has been the sales growth rate? What has been the growth rate in net income?

5. Over the past few years, has there been a strong correlation between stock price performance and reported earnings? Explain. (Hint: Change the Interactive Stock Chart so that it corresponds to the same number of years shown for the financial statements.)

## Solutions to Self-Test Questions and Problems

**ST-1**   Refer to the marginal glossary definitions or relevant chapter sections to check your responses.

**ST-2**   a.

| | |
|---|---|
| EBIT | $5,000,000 |
| Interest | 1,000,000 |
| EBT | $4,000,000 |
| Taxes 40% | 1,600,000 |
| Net income | $2,400,000 |

b.   Current liabilities = Accounts payable + Accruals + Notes payable
$$= \$3,000,000 + \$1,000,000 + \$2,000,000$$
$$= \$6,000,000$$

NOWC = Current assets − (Current liabilities − Notes payable)
$$= \$14,000,000 - (\$6,000,000 - \$2,000,000)$$
$$= \$10,000,000$$

c.   NWC = Current assets − Current liabilities
$$= \$14,000,000 - \$6,000,000$$
$$= \$8,000,000$$

d.   $\text{FCF} = \Big(\text{EBIT}(1-\text{T}) + \text{Depreciation}\Big) - \Big(\begin{array}{c}\text{Capital} \\ \text{expenditures}\end{array} + \begin{array}{c}\text{Increase in net operating} \\ \text{working capital}\end{array}\Big)$

$$= [\$5,000,000(0.6) + \$1,000,000] - [\$4,000,000 + 0]$$
$$= \$4,000,000 - \$4,000,000$$
$$= \$0$$

Note that capital expenditures are equal to the change in net plant and equipment plus the annual depreciation expense.

e.   Rattner's end-of-year Statement of Stockholders' Equity is calculated as follows:

**Statement of Stockholders' Equity**

| | Common Stock | | Retained | Total Stockholders' |
|---|---|---|---|---|
| | Shares | Amount | Earnings | Equity |
| Balances, beginning of year | 500,000 | $5,000,000 | $11,200,000 | $16,200,000 |
| Net income | | | 2,400,000 | |
| Cash dividends | | | −1,200,000 | |
| Addition to retained earnings | | | | 1,200,000 |
| Balances, end of year | 500,000 | $5,000,000 | $12,400,000 | $17,400,000 |

f.   MVA = ($P_0$ × Number of shares) − Book value of equity
$$= (\$52 \times 500,000) - \$17,400,000$$
$$= \$8,600,000$$

g. Before we can calculate the firm's EVA, we need to calculate the firm's total invested capital. We know that the firm uses no preferred stock, and we know that Assets = Liabilities + Equity. From the information provided in the problem we know:

|  |  | Accounts payable | $ 3,000,000 |
|---|---|---|---|
|  |  | Accruals | 1,000,000 |
|  |  | Notes payable | 2,000,000 |
| Current assets | $14,000,000 | Current liabilities | $ 6,000,000 |
|  |  | Long-term debt | ? |
| Net fixed assets | 15,000,000 | Common equity | 17,400,000 |
| Total assets | $29,000,000 | Total liabilities & equity | $29,000,000 |

We calculated common equity in part e, so the only value we don't know on the balance sheet is long-term debt. However, we have enough information to calculate it:

**Long-term debt  = $29,000,000 − $17,400,000 − $6,000,000**
**Long-term debt  = $5,600,000**

Now, we can find the firm's total invested capital:

**Total invested capital = Notes payable + Long-term debt + Common equity**
**Total invested capital = $2,000,000 + $5,600,000 + $17,400,000**
**Total invested capital = $25,000,000**

Now, we can calculate the firm's EVA:

**EVA = EBIT(1 − T) − [Total invested capital × After-tax % cost of capital]**
**EVA = $5,000,000(0.6) − [$25,000,000 × 0.09]**
**EVA = $3,000,000 − $2,250,000 = $750,000**

## Answers to Selected End-of-Chapter Problems

**3-2**  $800,000
**3-4**  $34,000,000
**3-6**  $22,000,000
**3-8**  a. $99,279
     b. 33%
     c. 26.47%
**3-10** $71,600,000
**3-12** a. $62,000
     b. $72,000
**3-14** a. $\text{NOWC}_{2015} = \$56,000; \text{NOWC}_{2016} = \$65,220$
     b. $15,180
     c. CS = $40,000; RE = $46,220
     d. EVA = $15,078
     e. MVA = $13,780
**3-16** a. $\text{RE}_{2015} = \$1,374$ million
     b. $1,600 million
     c. $15 million
     d. $620 million
**3-18** a. $19,043.75
     b. $25%
     c. 18.49%

## Selected Equations and Tables

Stockholders' equity = Paid-in capital + Retained earnings

Stockholders' equity = Total assets − Total liabilities

Net working capital = Current assets − Current liabilities

Net operating working capital = (Current assets − Excess cash)

$$- \text{ (Current liabilities − Notes payable)}$$

Total debt = Short-term debt + Long-term debt

Total liabilities = Total debt + Accounts payable + Accruals

Operating income (or EBIT) = Sales revenues − Operating costs

$$\text{FCF} = (\text{EBIT}(1 - T) + \text{Depreciation}) - \left( \begin{array}{c} \text{Capital} \\ \text{expenditures} \end{array} + \begin{array}{c} \Delta\text{Net operating} \\ \text{working capital} \end{array} \right)$$

$$\text{MVA} = (P_0 \times \text{Shares outstanding}) - \text{Book value of total common equity}$$

$$\text{EVA} = \text{EBIT}(1 - T) - \left( \begin{array}{ccc} \text{Total} & & \text{After-tax} \\ \text{invested} & \times & \text{percentage} \\ \text{capital} & & \text{cost of capital} \end{array} \right)$$

### 2015 Individual Tax Rates: Single Individuals

| If Your Taxable Income Is | You Pay This Amount on the Base of the Bracket | Plus This Percentage on the Excess over the Base (Marginal Rate) | Average Tax Rate at Top of Bracket |
|---|---|---|---|
| Up to $9,225 | $        0 | 10.0% | 10.0% |
| $9,225–$37,450 | 922.50 | 15.0 | 13.8 |
| $37,450–$90,750 | 5,156.25 | 25.0 | 20.4 |
| $90,750–$189,750 | 18,481.25 | 28.0 | 24.3 |
| $189,750–$411,500 | 46,075.25 | 33.0 | 29.0 |
| $411,500–$413,200 | 119,401.25 | 35.0 | 29.0 |
| Over $413,200 | 119,996.25 | 39.6 | 39.6 |

### Married Couples Filing Joint Returns

| If Your Taxable Income Is | You Pay This Amount on the Base of the Bracket | Plus This Percentage on the Excess over the Base (Marginal Rate) | Average Tax Rate at Top of Bracket |
|---|---|---|---|
| Up to $18,450 | 0 | 10.0% | 10.0% |
| $18,450–$74,900 | 1,845.00 | 15.0 | 13.8 |
| $74,900–$151,200 | 10,312.50 | 25.0 | 19.4 |
| $151,200–$230,450 | 29,387.50 | 28.0 | 22.4 |
| $230,450–$411,500 | 51,577.50 | 33.0 | 27.1 |
| $411,500–$464,850 | 111,324.00 | 35.0 | 28.0 |
| Over $464,850 | 129,996.50 | 39.6 | 39.6 |

### 2015 Corporate Tax Rates

| If a Corporation's Taxable Income Is | You Pay This Amount on the Base of the Bracket | Plus This Percentage on the Excess over the Base (Marginal Rate) | Average Tax Rate at Top of Bracket |
|---|---|---|---|
| Up to $50,000 | $        0 | 15% | 15.0% |
| $50,000–$75,000 | 7,500 | 25 | 18.3 |
| $75,000–$100,000 | 13,750 | 34 | 22.3 |
| $100,000–$335,000 | 22,250 | 39 | 34.0 |
| $335,000–$10,000,000 | 113,900 | 34 | 34.0 |
| $10,000,000–$15,000,000 | 3,400,000 | 35 | 34.3 |
| $15,000,000–$18,333,333 | 5,150,000 | 38 | 35.0 |
| Over $18,333,333 | 6,416,667 | 35 | 35.0 |

# Analysis of Financial Statements

## Can You Make Money Analyzing Stocks?

For many years, a debate has raged over this question. Some argue that the stock market is highly efficient and that all available information regarding a stock is already reflected in its price. The "efficient market advocates" point out that there are thousands of smart, well-trained analysts working for institutions with billions of dollars. These analysts have access to the latest information, and they spring into action—buying or selling—as soon as a firm releases any information that has a bearing on its future profits. The "efficient market advocates" also point out that few mutual funds, which hire good people and pay them well, actually beat the averages. If these experts earn only average returns, how can the rest of us expect to beat the market?

Others disagree, arguing that analysis can pay off. They point out that some fund managers perform better than average year after year. Also, they note that some "activist" investors analyze firms carefully, identify those with weaknesses that appear to be correctable, and then persuade their managers to take actions to improve the firms' performances.

Arguably, the world's best-known investor is Warren Buffett. Through his company Berkshire Hathaway, Buffett has made significant investments in a number of well-known companies, including Coca-Cola, American Express, DIRECTV, IBM, and Wells Fargo. Buffett is well known for taking a long-run view of things. His value-investing approach, which borrows heavily from the ideas espoused decades ago by Benjamin Graham, looks for stocks trading at prices that are significantly lower than their estimated intrinsic value. Value investors rely heavily on the type of analysis described in this chapter to assess a company's strengths and weaknesses and to derive the key inputs for their estimates of intrinsic value.

Berkshire Hathaway's performance under Buffett's management has been nothing short of amazing. A recent article in *Fortune* calculates that in the 50 years that Buffett has been at the helm (1964–2014), Berkshire Hathaway has provided its investors with a staggering total return of 1,826,163%, which translates into a compound annual return of 21.6%! And so far, Buffett is showing no signs of slowing down. Always looking for new opportunities, in June 2013, Berkshire Hathaway partnered with private equity firm 3G Capital and acquired H.J. Heinz Company for $28 billion. A year later in November 2014, Buffett saw what he thought was another good opportunity. In that transaction, Berkshire purchased the Duracell battery unit from Procter and Gamble. And in March 2015, he once again combined forces with 3G Capital

to help finance the merger between Heinz and Kraft Foods. In each case, Buffett purchased a well-established brand that he believes has even greater potential for improvement.

So, although many people regard financial statements as "just accounting," they really are much more. As you will see in this chapter, these statements provide a wealth of information that can be used for a wide variety of purposes by managers, investors, lenders, customers, suppliers, and regulators. An analysis of its statements can highlight a company's strengths and shortcomings, and this information can be used by management to improve the company's performance and by others to predict future results.

Sources: Carol J. Loomis, "Grading Berkshire after 50 Years under Buffett: How Does a 1,826,163% Stock Rise Sound?" *Fortune* (www.fortune.com), February 28, 2015; and Jonathan Stempel and Devika Krishna Kumar, "Buffett's Berkshire Hathaway Buys P&G's Duracell," *Reuters* (www.reuters .com), November 13, 2014.

 # PUTTING THINGS IN PERSPECTIVE

**The primary goal of financial management is to maximize shareholders' wealth, not accounting measures such as net income or earnings per share (EPS). However, accounting data influence stock prices, and these data can be used to see why a company is performing the way it is and where it is heading. Chapter 3 described the key financial statements and showed how they change as a firm's operations change. Now, in Chapter 4, we show how the statements are used by managers to improve the firm's stock price; by lenders to evaluate the likelihood that borrowers will be able to pay off loans; and by security analysts to forecast earnings, dividends, and stock prices.**

**If management is to maximize a firm's value, it must take advantage of the firm's strengths and correct its weaknesses. Financial analysis involves (1) comparing the firm's performance to that of other firms in the same industry and (2) evaluating trends in the firm's financial position over time. These studies help managers identify deficiencies and take corrective actions. In this chapter, we focus on how managers and investors evaluate a firm's financial position. Then, in later chapters, we examine the types of actions managers can take to improve future performance and thus increase the firm's stock price.**

**When you finish this chapter, you should be able to**

- **Explain what ratio analysis is.**
- **List the five groups of ratios and identify, calculate, and interpret the key ratios in each group.**
- **Discuss each ratio's relationship to the balance sheet and income statement.**
- **Discuss why return on equity (ROE) is the key ratio under management's control and how the other ratios impact ROE, and explain how to use the DuPont equation for improving ROE.**
- **Compare a firm's ratios with those of other firms (benchmarking) and analyze a given firm's ratios over time (trend analysis).**
- **Discuss the tendency of ratios to fluctuate over time (which may or may not be problematic); explain how they can be influenced by accounting practices as well as other factors; and explain why they must be used with care.**

# 4-1 Ratio Analysis

Ratios help us evaluate financial statements. For example, at the end of 2016, Allied Food Products had $860 million of interest-bearing debt and interest charges of $88 million, while Midwest Products had $52 million of interest-bearing debt and interest charges of $4 million. Which company is stronger? The burden of these debts and the companies' ability to repay them can best be evaluated by comparing each firm's total debt to its total capital and comparing interest expense to the income and cash available to pay that interest. Ratios are used to make such comparisons. We calculate Allied's ratios for 2016 using data from the balance sheets and income statements given in Tables 3.1 and 3.2. We also evaluate the ratios relative to food industry averages, using data in millions of dollars.[1] As you will see, we can calculate many different ratios, with different ones used to examine different aspects of the firm's operations. You will get to know some ratios by name, but it's better to understand what they are designed to do than to memorize names and equations.

We divide the ratios into five categories:

1. *Liquidity ratios,* which give an idea of the firm's ability to pay off debts that are maturing within a year.

2. *Asset management ratios,* which give an idea of how efficiently the firm is using its assets.

3. *Debt management ratios,* which give an idea of how the firm has financed its assets as well as the firm's ability to repay its long-term debt.

4. *Profitability ratios,* which give an idea of how profitably the firm is operating and utilizing its assets.

5. *Market value ratios,* which give an idea of what investors think about the firm and its future prospects.

Satisfactory liquidity ratios are necessary if the firm is to continue operating. Good asset management ratios are necessary for the firm to keep its costs low and thus its net income high. Debt management ratios indicate how risky the firm is and how much of its operating income must be paid to bondholders rather than stockholders. Profitability ratios combine the asset and debt management categories and show their effects on ROE. Finally, market value ratios tell us what investors think about the company and its prospects.

All of the ratios are important, but different ones are more important for some companies than for others. For example, if a firm borrowed too much in the past and its debt now threatens to drive it into bankruptcy, the debt ratios are key. Similarly, if a firm expanded too rapidly and now finds itself with excess inventory and manufacturing capacity, the asset management ratios take center stage. The ROE is always important; but a high ROE depends on maintaining liquidity, on efficient asset management, and on the proper use of debt. Managers are, of course, vitally concerned with the stock price; but managers have little direct control over

---

[1]Financial statement data for most publicly traded firms can be obtained from the Internet. Free sites that provide this information include Google Finance (google.com/finance) and Yahoo! Finance (finance.yahoo.com). These sites provide financial statements, which can be copied to an Excel file and used to create your own ratios; but the websites also provide calculated ratios.

In addition to the ratios discussed in this chapter, financial analysts often employ a tool known as *common size analysis.* To form a *common size balance sheet,* simply divide each asset, liability, and equity item by total assets and then express the results as percentages. To develop a *common size income statement,* divide each income statement item by sales. The resultant percentage statements can be compared with statements of larger or smaller firms or with those of the same firm over time. One would normally obtain the basic statements from a source such as Google Finance and copy them to Excel, so constructing common size statements is quite easy. Note too that industry average data are generally given as percentages, which make them easy to compare with a firm's own common size statements. We provide Allied Food Products's common size statements in Web Appendix 4A.

the stock market's performance, while they do have control over their firm's ROE. So ROE tends to be the main focal point.

# 4-2 Liquidity Ratios

The liquidity ratios help answer this question: Will the firm be able to pay off its debts as they come due and thus remain a viable organization? If the answer is no, liquidity must be addressed.

*Liquid Asset*

An asset that can be converted to cash quickly without having to reduce the asset's price very much.

*Liquidity Ratios*

Ratios that show the relationship of a firm's cash and other current assets to its current liabilities.

*Current Ratio*

This ratio is calculated by dividing current assets by current liabilities. It indicates the extent to which current liabilities are covered by those assets expected to be converted to cash in the near future.

A **liquid asset** is one that trades in an active market and thus can be quickly converted to cash at the going market price. As shown in Table 3.1 in Chapter 3, Allied has $310 million of current liabilities that must be paid off within the coming year. Will it have trouble meeting that obligation? A full liquidity analysis requires the use of a cash budget, which we discuss in Chapter 15; however, by relating cash and other current assets to current liabilities, ratio analysis provides a quick and easy-to-use measure of liquidity. Two of the most commonly used **liquidity ratios** are discussed below.

## 4-2A CURRENT RATIO

The primary liquidity ratio is the **current ratio**, which is calculated by dividing current assets by current liabilities:

$$\text{Current ratio} = \frac{\text{Current assets}}{\text{Current liabilities}}$$

$$= \frac{\$1,000}{\$310} = 3.2\times$$

$$\text{Industry average} = 4.2\times$$

Current assets include cash, marketable securities, accounts receivable, and inventories. Allied's current liabilities consist of accounts payable, accrued wages and taxes, and short-term notes payable to its bank, all of which are due within one year.

If a company is having financial difficulty, it typically begins to pay its accounts payable more slowly and to borrow more from its bank, both of which increase current liabilities. If current liabilities are rising faster than current assets, the current ratio will fall; and this is a sign of possible trouble. Allied's current ratio is 3.2, which is well below the industry average of 4.2. Therefore, its liquidity position is somewhat weak, but by no means desperate.[2]

Although industry average figures are discussed later in some detail, note that an industry average is not a magic number that all firms should strive to maintain; in fact, some very well-managed firms may be above the average, while other good firms are below it. However, if a firm's ratios are far removed from the averages for its industry, an analyst should be concerned about why this variance occurs. Thus, a deviation from the industry average should signal the analyst (or management) to check further. Note too that a high current ratio generally indicates a very strong, safe liquidity position; it might also indicate that the firm has too much old inventory that will have to be written off and too many old accounts receivable that may turn into bad debts. Or the high current ratio might indicate that the firm has too much cash, receivables, and inventory relative to its sales, in which case these assets are not being managed efficiently. So it is always necessary to thoroughly examine the full set of ratios before forming a judgment as to how well the firm is performing.

---

[2]Because current assets should be convertible to cash within a year, it is likely that they could be liquidated at close to their stated value. With a current ratio of 3.2, Allied could liquidate current assets at only 31% of book value and still pay off current creditors in full: $1/3.2 = 0.31$, or 31%. Note also that $0.31(\$1,000) = \$310$, the current liabilities balance.

# FINANCIAL ANALYSIS ON THE INTERNET

A wide range of valuable financial information is available on the Internet. With just a couple of clicks, an investor can find the key financial statements for most publicly traded companies.

Suppose you are thinking of buying some Disney stock, and you want to analyze its recent performance. Here's a partial (but by no means complete) list of sites you can access to get started:

- One source is Yahoo! Finance (finance.yahoo.com). Here you will find updated market information along with links to a variety of research sites. Enter a stock's ticker symbol, and you will see the stock's current price along with recent news about the company. Click "Key Statistics" to find a report on the company's key financial ratios. Links to the company's financials (income statement, balance sheet, and statement of cash flows) can also be found. Yahoo! Finance also has a list of insider transactions that tell you whether a company's CEO and other key insiders are buying or selling the company's stock. In addition, the site has a message board where investors share opinions about the company and a link is provided to the company's filings with the Securities and Exchange Commission (SEC). Note also that, in most cases, a more complete listing of SEC filings can be found at the SEC website (sec.gov).

- Two other websites with similar information are Google Finance (google.com/finance) and *MSN Money* (money.msn .com). After entering a stock's ticker symbol, you will see the current stock price and a list of recent news stories. At either of these sites, you will find links to a company's financial statements and key ratios, as well as other information including analyst ratings, historical charts, earnings estimates, and a summary of insider transactions.

- Other sources for up-to-date market information are CNNMoney.com (money.cnn.com), Zacks Investment Research (zacks.com), and MarketWatch (marketwatch.com), part of *The Wall Street Journal* Digital Network. On these sites, you also can obtain stock quotes, financial statements, links to Wall Street research and SEC filings, company profiles, and charts of a firm's stock price over time.

- CNBC (cnbc.com) is another good source of financial information. Here, you enter a firm's ticker symbol to obtain the firm's stock price and fundamentals like its market cap, beta, and dividend yield. You can also chart a firm's stock price and obtain news about the company, earnings history and estimates, industry peer comparisons, and quarterly or annual financial statements.

- Seekingalpha.com provides stock price quotes; fundamentals like EPS, P/E, and dividend yield information as well as stock price charts. In addition, you can obtain breaking news on any stocks you've listed in your portfolio or any that you wish to follow.

- If you're looking for data on bond yields, key money rates, and currency rates, Bloomberg (bloomberg.com) is an excellent source for this type of information.

- Another good place to look is Reuters (reuters.com). Here you can find links to analysts' research reports along with the key financial statements.

- A valuable subscriber website from *Value Line Investment Survey* (valueline.com) provides industry-specific and detailed company income statement data, capital structure data, returns data, EPS, book value per share, cash flow per share, and other investment data.

- If you're interested in obtaining baseline values on individual stocks, you will find ValuePro (valuepro.net) helpful. It identifies key financial numbers used to obtain a stock's value and allows the user to make changes and see their impact on the stock's value.

- After accumulating all of this information, you may want to look at a site that provides opinions regarding the direction of the overall market and a particular stock. Two popular sites are The Motley Fool (fool.com) and The Street (thestreet.com).

- A popular source is *The Wall Street Journal* website (online.wsj .com). It is a great resource, but you have to subscribe to access the full range of materials.

When analyzing ratios using different sources, it is important that you understand how each source calculates a particular ratio. Differences among sources could be attributable to timing differences (using an average number versus a trailing 12-month number) or to different definitions. It is quite possible that, if you were to examine the same ratio for a particular company, you might see different values for the same ratio depending on the source chosen. You can often click "Help" within the particular website and search for the site's specific finance glossary to determine how ratios are defined. Keep this in mind when conducting ratio analysis.

This list is just a small subset of the information available online and available to you to work the end-of-chapter Internet exercises Taking a Closer Look. Sites come and go and change their content over time. In addition, new and interesting sites are constantly being added to the Internet.

## 4-2B QUICK, OR ACID TEST, RATIO

**Quick (Acid Test) Ratio**
This ratio is calculated by deducting inventories from current assets and then dividing the remainder by current liabilities.

The second liquidity ratio is the **quick**, or **acid test, ratio**, which is calculated by deducting inventories from current assets and then dividing the remainder by current liabilities:

$$\text{Quick, or acid test, ratio} = \frac{\text{Current assets} - \text{Inventories}}{\text{Current liabilities}}$$

$$= \frac{\$385}{\$310} = 1.2\times$$

$$\text{Industry average} = 2.2\times$$

Inventories are typically the least liquid of a firm's current assets; and if sales slow down, they might not be converted to cash as quickly as expected.[3] Also, inventories are the assets on which losses are most likely to occur in the event of liquidation. Therefore, the quick ratio, which measures the firm's ability to pay off short-term obligations without relying on the sale of inventories, is important.

The industry average quick ratio is 2.2, so Allied's 1.2 ratio is relatively low. Still, if the accounts receivable can be collected, the company can pay off its current liabilities even if it has trouble disposing of its inventories.

## Self Test

What are the characteristics of a liquid asset? Give examples of some liquid assets.

What question are the two liquidity ratios designed to answer?

Which is the least liquid of the firm's current assets?

A company has current liabilities of $500 million, and its current ratio is 2.0. What is the total of its current assets? **($1,000 million)** If this firm's quick ratio is 1.6, how much inventory does it have? **($200 million)** (Hint: To answer this problem and some of the other problems in this chapter, write out the equation for the ratio in the question, insert the given data, and solve for the missing value.) Examples:

Current ratio = 2.0 = CA/CL = CA/$500, so CA = 2($500) = $1,000.
Quick ratio = 1.6 = (CA − Inventories)/CL = ($1,000 − Inventories)/$500, so $1,000 − Inventories = 1.6($500) and Inventories = $1,000 − $800 = $200.

## 4-3 Asset Management Ratios

**Asset Management Ratios**
A set of ratios that measure how effectively a firm is managing its assets.

The second group of ratios, the **asset management ratios**, measure how effectively the firm is managing its assets. These ratios answer this question: Does the amount of each type of asset seem reasonable, too high, or too low in view of current and projected sales? These ratios are important because when Allied and other companies acquire assets, they must obtain capital from banks or other sources and capital is expensive. Therefore, if Allied has too many assets, its cost of capital will be too

---

[3]Some companies also report "Other current assets" on their balance sheet. Our definition of the quick ratio would implicitly assume that these other current assets could be easily converted to cash. As an alternative measure, some analysts define the quick ratio as:

(Cash and equivalents + Accounts receivable)/Current liabilities

This alternative measure assumes that the other current assets cannot be easily converted to cash. In the case of Allied, because it has no other current assets, the two measures would yield the same number.

high, which will depress its profits. On the other hand, if its assets are too low, profitable sales will be lost. So Allied must strike a balance between too many and too few assets, and the asset management ratios will help it strike this proper balance.

## 4-3A INVENTORY TURNOVER RATIO

"Turnover ratios" divide sales by some asset: Sales/Various assets. As the name implies, these ratios show how many times the particular asset is "turned over" during the year. Here is the **inventory turnover ratio**:

$$\text{Inventory turnover ratio} = \frac{\text{Sales}}{\text{Inventories}}$$
$$= \frac{\$3,000}{\$615} = 4.9\times$$
$$\text{Industry average} = 10.9\times$$

As a rough approximation, each item of Allied's inventory is sold and restocked, or "turned over," 4.9 times per year. *Turnover* is a term that originated many years ago with the old Yankee peddler who would load up his wagon with pots and pans, and then go off on his route to peddle his wares. The merchandise was called working capital because it was what he actually sold, or "turned over," to produce his profits, whereas his "turnover" was the number of trips he took each year. Annual sales divided by inventory equaled turnover, or trips per year. If he made 10 trips per year, stocked 100 pots and pans, and made a gross profit of $5 per item, his annual gross profit was $(100)(\$5)(10) = \$5,000$. If he went faster and made 20 trips per year, his gross profit doubled, other things held constant. So his turnover directly affected his profits.

Allied's inventory turnover of 4.9 is much lower than the industry average of 10.9. This suggests that it is holding too much inventory. Excess inventory is, of course, unproductive and represents an investment with a low or zero rate of return. Allied's low inventory turnover ratio also makes us question its current ratio. With such a low turnover, the firm may be holding obsolete goods that are not worth their stated value.[4]

Note that sales occur over the entire year, whereas the inventory figure is for one point in time. For this reason, it might be better to use an average inventory measure.[5] If the business is highly seasonal or if there has been a strong upward or downward sales trend during the year, it is especially useful to make an adjustment. Allied's sales are not growing especially fast though; and to maintain comparability with industry averages, we used year-end rather than average inventories.

## 4-3B DAYS SALES OUTSTANDING

Accounts receivable are evaluated by the **days sales outstanding (DSO) ratio**, also called the average collection period (ACP).[6] It is calculated by dividing accounts receivable by the average daily sales to find how many days' sales are tied up in

*Inventory Turnover Ratio*
This ratio is calculated by dividing sales by inventories.

*Days Sales Outstanding (DSO) Ratio*
This ratio is calculated by dividing accounts receivable by average sales per day. It indicates the average length of time the firm must wait after making a sale before it receives cash.

---

[4]Our measure of inventory turnover is frequently used by established compilers of financial ratio statistics such as *Value Line* (valueline.com) and *Morningstar* (morningstar.com). However, you should recognize that other sources calculate inventory using cost of goods sold in place of sales in the formula's numerator. The rationale for this alternative measure is that sales are stated at market prices; so if inventories are carried at cost, as they generally are, the calculated turnover overstates the true turnover ratio. Therefore, it might be more appropriate to use cost of goods sold in place of sales in the formula's numerator. When evaluating and comparing financial ratios from various sources, it is important to understand how those sources are specifically calculating financial ratios.

[5]Preferably, the average inventory value should be calculated by summing the monthly figures during the year and dividing by 12. If monthly data are not available, the beginning and ending figures can be added and then divided by 2. Both methods adjust for growth, but not for seasonal effects.

[6]We could use the receivables turnover to evaluate receivables. Allied's receivables turnover is $3,000/$375 = 8\times$. However, the DSO ratio is easier to interpret and judge.

receivables. Thus, the DSO represents the average length of time the firm must wait after making a sale before receiving cash. Allied has 46 days' sales outstanding, well above the 36-day industry average:

$$\text{DSO} = \begin{array}{c} \text{Days} \\ \text{sales} \\ \text{outstanding} \end{array} = \frac{\text{Receivables}}{\text{Average sales per day}} = \frac{\text{Receivables}}{\text{Annual sales}/365}$$

$$= \frac{\$375}{\$3,000/365} = \frac{\$375}{\$8.2192} = 45.625 \text{ days} \approx 46 \text{ days}$$

$$\text{Industry average} = 36 \text{ days}$$

The DSO can be compared with the industry average, but it is also evaluated by comparing it with Allied's credit terms. Allied's credit policy calls for payment within 30 days. So the fact that 46 days' sales are outstanding, not 30 days', indicates that Allied's customers, on average, are not paying their bills on time. This deprives the company of funds that could be used to reduce bank loans or some other type of costly capital. Moreover, the high average DSO indicates that if some customers are paying on time, quite a few must be paying very late. Late-paying customers often default, so their receivables may end up as bad debts that can never be collected.[7] Note too that the trend in the DSO over the past few years has been rising, but the credit policy has not been changed. This reinforces our belief that Allied's credit manager should take steps to collect receivables faster.

## 4-3C FIXED ASSETS TURNOVER RATIO

**Fixed Assets Turnover Ratio**
The ratio of sales to net fixed assets.

The **fixed assets turnover ratio**, which is the ratio of sales to net fixed assets, measures how effectively the firm uses its plant and equipment:

$$\text{Fixed assets turnover ratio} = \frac{\text{Sales}}{\text{Net fixed assets}}$$

$$= \frac{\$3,000}{\$1,000} = 3.0\times$$

$$\text{Industry average} = 2.8\times$$

Allied's ratio of 3.0 times is slightly above the 2.8 industry average, indicating that it is using its fixed assets at least as intensively as other firms in the industry. Therefore, Allied seems to have about the right amount of fixed assets relative to its sales.

Potential problems may arise when interpreting the fixed assets turnover ratio. Recall that fixed assets are shown on the balance sheet at their historical costs less depreciation. Inflation has caused the value of many assets that were purchased in the past to be seriously understated. Therefore, if we compare an old firm whose fixed assets have been depreciated with a new company with similar operations that acquired its fixed assets only recently, the old firm will probably have the higher fixed assets turnover ratio. However, this would be more reflective of the age of the assets than of inefficiency on the part of the new firm. The accounting profession is trying to develop procedures for making financial statements reflect current values rather than historical values, which would help us make better comparisons. However, at the moment, the problem still exists; so financial analysts must recognize this problem and deal with it judgmentally. In Allied's case, the issue is not serious because all firms in the industry have been expanding at about the same rate; hence, the balance sheets of the comparison firms are reasonably comparable.[8]

---

[7]For example, if further analysis along the lines suggested in Part 6 of this text (Working Capital Management) indicates that 85% of the customers pay in 30 days, for the DSO to average 46 days, the remaining 15% must be paying, on average, in 136.67 days. Paying that late suggests financial difficulties. A DSO of 46 days would alert a good analyst of the need to dig deeper.

[8]Refer to FASB Accounting Standards Codification Topic 255, Changing Prices, for a discussion of the effects of inflation on financial statements. ASC 255 references FAS 89, Financial Reporting and Changing Prices, issued in December 1986.

## 4-3D TOTAL ASSETS TURNOVER RATIO

The final asset management ratio, the **total assets turnover ratio**, measures the turnover of all of the firm's assets, and it is calculated by dividing sales by total assets:

$$\text{Total assets turnover ratio} = \frac{\text{Sales}}{\text{Total assets}}$$
$$= \frac{\$3,000}{\$2,000} = 1.5\times$$
$$\text{Industry average} = 1.8\times$$

**Total Assets Turnover Ratio**

This ratio is calculated by dividing sales by total assets.

Allied's ratio is somewhat below the industry average, indicating that it is not generating enough sales given its total assets. We just saw that Allied's fixed assets turnover is in line with the industry average; so the problem is with its current assets, inventories and accounts receivable, whose ratios were below the industry standards. Inventories should be reduced and receivables collected faster, which would improve operations.

## Self Test

Write the equations for four ratios that are used to measure how effectively a firm manages its assets.

If one firm is growing rapidly and another is not, how might this distort a comparison of their inventory turnover ratios?

If you wanted to evaluate a firm's DSO, with what could you compare it?

How might the different ages of firms distort comparisons of their fixed assets turnover ratios?

A firm has annual sales of $100 million, $20 million of inventory, and $30 million of accounts receivable. What is its inventory turnover ratio? **(5×)** What is its DSO? **(109.5 days)**

# 4-4 Debt Management Ratios

The use of debt will increase, or "leverage up," a firm's ROE if the firm earns more on its assets than the interest rate it pays on debt. However, debt exposes the firm to more risk than if it financed only with equity. In this section we discuss **debt management ratios**.

Table 4.1 illustrates the potential benefits and risks associated with debt.[9] Here we analyze two companies that are identical except for how they are financed. Firm U (for *Unleveraged*) has no debt; thus, it uses 100% common equity. Firm L (for *Leveraged*) obtained 50% of its capital as debt at an interest rate of 10%. Both firms have $100 of assets, and their sales are expected to range from a high of $150 down to $75 depending on business conditions. Some of their operating costs (e.g., rent and the president's salary) are fixed and will be

**Debt Management Ratios**

A set of ratios that measure how effectively a firm manages its debt.

---

[9]We discuss ROE in more depth later in this chapter, and we examine the effects of leverage in detail in Chapter 13. The relationship between various debt management ratios and bond ratings is discussed in Chapter 7 and illustrated in Table 7.4.

**TABLE 4.1**     The Effects of Financial Leverage

### Firm U—Unleveraged (No Debt)

| Current assets | $ 50 | Debt | $ 0 |
|---|---|---|---|
| Fixed assets | 50 | Common equity | 100 |
| Total assets | $100 | Total liabilities and equity | $100 |

| | | State of the Economy | | |
|---|---|---|---|---|
| | | **Good** | **Expected** | **Bad** |
| Sales revenues | | $150.0 | $100.0 | $75.0 |
| Operating costs | Fixed | 45.0 | 45.0 | 45.0 |
| | Variable | 60.0 | 40.0 | 30.0 |
| Total operating costs | | 105.0 | 85.0 | 75.0 |
| Operating income (EBIT) | | $ 45.0 | $ 15.0 | $ 0.0 |
| Interest (Rate = 10%) | | 0.0 | 0.0 | 0.0 |
| Earnings before taxes (EBT) | | $ 45.0 | $ 15.0 | $ 0.0 |
| Taxes (Rate = 40%) | | 18.0 | 6.0 | 0.0 |
| Net income (NI) | | $ 27.0 | $ 9.0 | $ 0.0 |
| $ROE_U$ | | 27.0% | 9.0% | 0.0% |

### Firm L—Leveraged (Some Debt)

| Current assets | $ 50 | Debt | $ 50 |
|---|---|---|---|
| Fixed assets | 50 | Common equity | 50 |
| Total assets | $100 | Total liabilities and equity | $100 |

| | | State of the Economy | | |
|---|---|---|---|---|
| | | **Good** | **Expected** | **Bad** |
| Sales revenues | | $150.0 | $100.0 | $ 75.0 |
| Operating costs | Fixed | 45.0 | 45.0 | 45.0 |
| | Variable | 60.0 | 40.0 | 30.0 |
| Total operating costs | | 105.0 | 85.0 | 75.0 |
| Operating income (EBIT) | | $ 45.0 | $ 15.0 | $ 0.0 |
| Interest (Rate = 10%) | | 5.0 | 5.0 | 5.0 |
| Earnings before taxes (EBT) | | $ 40.0 | $ 10.0 | −$ 5.0 |
| Taxes (Rate = 40%) | | 16.0 | 4.0 | 0.0 |
| Net income (NI) | | $ 24.0 | $ 6.0 | −$ 5.0 |
| $ROE_L$ | | 48.0% | 12.0% | −10.0% |

the same regardless of the level of sales, while other costs (e.g., manufacturing labor and materials costs) vary with sales.[10]

Notice that everything is the same in the table for the leveraged and unleveraged firms down through operating income—thus, their EBITs are the same in each state of the economy. However, things differ below operating income. Firm U has no debt, it pays no interest, its taxable income is the same as its operating income, it

---

[10]The financial statements do not show the breakdown between fixed and variable operating costs, but companies can and do make this breakdown for internal purposes. Of course, the distinction is not always clear because a fixed cost in the very short run can become a variable cost over a longer time horizon. It's interesting to note that companies are moving toward making more of their costs variable, using such techniques as increasing bonuses rather than base salaries, switching to profit-sharing plans rather than fixed pension plans, and outsourcing various operations.

pays a 40% state and federal tax rate, and its net income ranges from $27 under good conditions down to $0 under bad conditions. When U's net income is divided by its common equity, its ROEs range from 27% to 0% depending on the state of the economy.

Firm L has the same EBIT as U under each state of the economy, but L uses $50 of debt with a 10% interest rate; so it has $5 of interest charges regardless of the economy. This $5 is deducted from EBIT to arrive at taxable income; taxes are taken out; and the result is net income, which ranges from $24 to −$5 depending on conditions.[11] At first, it looks as though Firm U is better off under all conditions, but this is not correct—we need to consider how much the two firms' stockholders have invested. Firm L's stockholders have put up only $50; so when that investment is divided into net income, we see that their ROE under good conditions is a whopping 48% (versus 27% for U) and is 12% (versus 9% for U) under expected conditions. However, L's ROE falls to −10% under bad conditions, which means that Firm L would go bankrupt if those conditions persisted for several years.

Thus, firms with relatively high debt ratios typically have higher expected returns when the economy is normal, but lower returns and possibly bankruptcy if the economy goes into a recession. Therefore, decisions about the use of debt require firms to balance higher expected returns against increased risk. Determining the optimal amount of debt is a complicated process, and we defer a discussion of that subject until Chapter 13. For now, we simply look at two procedures that analysts use to examine the firm's debt. (1) They check the balance sheet to determine the proportion of total funds represented by debt. (2) They review the income statement to see the extent to which interest is covered by operating profits.

## 4-4A TOTAL DEBT TO TOTAL CAPITAL

The ratio of **total debt to total capital** measures the percentage of the firm's capital provided by debtholders:

$$\frac{\text{Total debt}}{\text{Total capital}} = \frac{\text{Total debt}}{\text{Total debt} + \text{Equity}}$$

$$= \frac{\$110 + \$750}{\$1,800} = \frac{\$860}{\$1,800} = 47.8\%$$

Industry average = 36.4%

*Total Debt to Total Capital*
The ratio of total debt to total capital.

Recall from Chapter 3 that total debt includes all short-term and long-term interest-bearing debt, but it does not include operating items such as accounts payable and accruals. Allied has total debt of $860 million, which consists of $110 million in short-term notes payable and $750 million in long-term bonds. Its total capital is $1.80 billion: $860 million of debt plus $940 million in total equity. To keep things simple, unless we say otherwise, we will generally refer to the total debt to total capital ratio as the company's *debt ratio*.[12] Creditors prefer low debt ratios because the lower the ratio, the greater the cushion against creditors' losses in the event of

---

[11]As we discussed in the last chapter, firms can carry losses back or forward for several years. Therefore, if firm L had profits and thus paid taxes in 2015, it could carry-back the 2016 loss under bad conditions and receive a credit (a check from the government). In Table 4.1, we disregard the carryback/carryforward provision.

[12]Two other debt ratios are often used in financial analysis:

1. Some analysts like to look at a broader debt ratio that includes all total liabilities (including accounts payables and accruals) divided by total assets. For Allied, the total liabilities-to-assets ratio is 53% ($1,060 million divided by $2,000 million), while the industry average is 40%.
2. Another measure, the debt-to-equity ratio equals total debt divided by total equity. Allied's debt-to-equity ratio is $860 million/$940 million = 91.5%.

liquidation. Stockholders, on the other hand, may want more leverage because it can magnify expected earnings, as we saw in Table 4.1.

Allied's debt ratio is 47.8%, which means that its creditors have supplied roughly half of its total funds. As we will discuss in Chapter 13, a number of factors affect a company's optimal debt ratio. Nevertheless, the fact that Allied's debt ratio exceeds the industry average by a large amount raises a red flag, and this will make it relatively costly for Allied to borrow additional funds without first raising more equity. Creditors will be reluctant to lend the firm more money, and management would probably be subjecting the firm to too high a risk of bankruptcy if it sought to borrow a substantial amount of additional funds.

## 4-4B TIMES-INTEREST-EARNED RATIO

**Times-Interest-Earned (TIE) Ratio**

The ratio of earnings before interest and taxes (EBIT) to interest charges; a measure of the firm's ability to meet its annual interest payments.

The **times-interest-earned (TIE) ratio** is determined by dividing earnings before interest and taxes (EBIT in Table 3.2) by the interest charges:

$$\text{Times-interest-earned (TIE) ratio} = \frac{\text{EBIT}}{\text{Interest charges}}$$
$$= \frac{\$283.8}{\$88} = 3.2\times$$
$$\text{Industry average} = 6.0\times$$

The TIE ratio measures the extent to which operating income can decline before the firm is unable to meet its annual interest costs. Failure to pay interest will bring legal action by the firm's creditors and probably result in bankruptcy. Note that earnings before interest and taxes, rather than net income, are used in the numerator. Because interest is paid with pretax dollars, the firm's ability to pay current interest is not affected by taxes.

Allied's interest is covered 3.2 times. The industry average is 6 times, so Allied is covering its interest charges by a much lower margin of safety than the average firm in the industry. Thus, the TIE ratio reinforces our conclusion from the debt ratio, namely, that Allied would face difficulties if it attempted to borrow additional money.[13]

## SelfTest

How does the use of financial leverage affect stockholders' control position?

How does the U.S. tax structure influence a firm's willingness to finance with debt?

How does the decision to use debt involve a risk-versus-return trade-off?

Explain the following statement: Analysts look at both balance sheet and income statement ratios when appraising a firm's financial condition.

Name two ratios that are used to measure financial leverage and write their equations.

---

[13] Another commonly used debt management ratio, using earnings before interest, taxes, depreciation, and amortization (EBITDA), is the EBITDA coverage ratio calculated as:

$$\text{EBITDA coverage ratio} = \frac{\text{EBITDA} + \text{Lease payments}}{\text{Interest} + \text{Principal payments} + \text{Lease payments}}$$

This ratio is more complete than the TIE ratio because it recognizes that depreciation and amortization expenses are not cash expenses, and thus are available to service debt, and that lease payments and principal repayments on debt are fixed charges. For more on this ratio, see E. F. Brigham and P. R. Daves, *Intermediate Financial Management*, 12th edition (Mason, OH: Cengage Learning, 2016), Chapter 7.

# 4-5 Profitability Ratios

Accounting statements reflect events that happened in the past, but they also provide clues about what's really important—that is, what's likely to happen in the future. The liquidity, asset management, and debt ratios covered thus far tell us something about the firm's policies and operations. Now we turn to the **profitability ratios**, which reflect the net result of all of the firm's financing policies and operating decisions.

**Profitability Ratios**
A group of ratios that show the combined effects of liquidity, asset management, and debt on operating results.

## 4-5A OPERATING MARGIN

The **operating margin**, calculated by dividing operating income (EBIT) by sales, gives the operating profit per dollar of sales:

$$\text{Operating margin} = \frac{\text{EBIT}}{\text{Sales}}$$
$$= \frac{\$283.8}{\$3,000} = 9.5\%$$
$$\text{Industry average} = 10.0\%$$

*Operating Margin*
This ratio measures operating income, or EBIT, per dollar of sales; it is calculated by dividing operating income by sales.

Allied's 9.5% operating margin is below the industry average of 10.0%. This subpar result indicates that Allied's operating costs are too high. This is consistent with the low inventory turnover and high days sales outstanding ratios that we calculated earlier.

## 4-5B PROFIT MARGIN

The **profit margin**, also sometimes called the *net profit margin*, is calculated by dividing net income by sales:

$$\text{Profit margin} = \frac{\text{Net income}}{\text{Sales}}$$
$$= \frac{\$117.5}{\$3,000} = 3.9\%$$
$$\text{Industry average} = 5.0\%$$

*Profit Margin*
This ratio measures net income per dollar of sales and is calculated by dividing net income by sales.

Allied's 3.9% profit margin is below the industry average of 5.0%, and this subpar result occurred for two reasons. First, Allied's operating margin was below the industry average because of the firm's high operating costs. Second, the profit margin is negatively impacted by Allied's heavy use of debt. To see this second point, recognize that net income is *after interest*. Suppose two firms have identical operations in the sense that their sales, operating costs, and operating income are identical. However, one firm uses more debt; hence, it has higher interest charges. Those interest charges pull down its net income; and because sales are identical, the result is a relatively low profit margin for the firm with more debt. We see then that Allied's operating inefficiency and its high debt ratio combine to lower its profit margin below the food processing industry average. It also follows that when two companies have the same operating margin but different debt ratios, we can expect the company with a higher debt ratio to have a lower profit margin.

Note too that while a high return on sales is good, we must also be concerned with turnover. If a firm sets a very high price on its products, it may earn a high return on each sale but fail to make many sales. It might generate a high profit margin but realize low sales, and hence experience a low net income. We will see shortly how, through the use of the DuPont equation, profit margins, the use of debt, and turnover ratios interact to affect overall stockholder returns.

## 4-5C RETURN ON TOTAL ASSETS

**Return on Total Assets (ROA)**
The ratio of net income to total assets.

Net income divided by total assets gives us the **return on total assets (ROA)**:

$$\text{Return on total assets (ROA)} = \frac{\text{Net income}}{\text{Total assets}}$$
$$= \frac{\$117.5}{\$2,000} = 5.9\%$$
$$\text{Industry average} = 9.0\%$$

Allied's 5.9% return is well below the 9.0% industry average. This is not good—it is obviously better to have a higher than a lower return on assets. Note, though, that a low ROA can result from a conscious decision to use a great deal of debt, in which case high interest expenses will cause net income to be relatively low. That is part of the reason for Allied's low ROA. Never forget—you must look at a number of ratios, see what each suggests, and then look at the overall situation before you judge the performance of a company and consider what actions it should undertake to improve.

## 4-5D RETURN ON COMMON EQUITY

**Return on Common Equity (ROE)**
The ratio of net income to common equity; measures the rate of return on common stockholders' investment.

Another important accounting ratio is the **return on common equity (ROE)**, which is found as follows:

$$\text{Return on common equity (ROE)} = \frac{\text{Net income}}{\text{Common equity}}$$
$$= \frac{\$117.5}{\$940} = 12.5\%$$
$$\text{Industry average} = 15.0\%$$

Stockholders expect to earn a return on their money, and this ratio tells how well they are doing in an accounting sense. Allied's 12.5% return is below the 15.0% industry average, but not as far below as the return on total assets. This somewhat better ROE results from the company's greater use of debt, a point discussed earlier in the chapter.

## 4-5E RETURN ON INVESTED CAPITAL

**Return on Invested Capital (ROIC)**
The ratio of after-tax operating income to total invested capital; it measures the total return that the company has provided for its investors.

The **return on invested capital (ROIC)** measures the total return that the company has provided for its investors:

$$\text{Return on invested capital (ROIC)} = \frac{\text{EBIT}(1 - T)}{\text{Total invested capital}}$$
$$= \frac{\text{EBIT}(1 - T)}{\text{Debt} + \text{Equity}} = \frac{\$170.3}{\$1,800} = 9.5\%$$
$$\text{Industry average} = 10.8\%$$

ROIC differs from ROA in two ways. First, its return is based on total invested capital rather than total assets. Second, in the numerator it uses after-tax operating income (NOPAT) rather than net income. The key difference is that net income subtracts the company's after-tax interest expense and therefore represents the total amount of income available to shareholders, while NOPAT is the amount of funds available to pay both stockholders and debtholders.

## quick question

**QUESTION:**

A company has $20 billion of sales and $1 billion of net income. Its total assets are $10 billion. The company's total assets equal total invested capital, and its capital consists of half debt and half common equity. The firm's interest rate is 5%, and its tax rate is 40%.

1. What is its profit margin?

2. What is its ROA?

3. What is its ROE?

4. What is its ROIC?

5. Would this firm's ROA increase if it used less leverage? (The size of the firm does not change.)

**ANSWER:**

a. Profit margin $= \dfrac{\text{Net income}}{\text{Sales}} = \dfrac{\$1\,\text{billion}}{\$20\,\text{billion}} = 5\%.$

b. ROA $= \dfrac{\text{Net income}}{\text{Total assets}} = \dfrac{\$1\,\text{billion}}{\$10\,\text{billion}} = 10\%.$

c. ROE $= \dfrac{\text{Net income}}{\text{Common equity}} = \dfrac{\$1\,\text{billion}}{\$5\,\text{billion}} = 20\%.$

d. First, we need to calculate the firm's EBIT by working up the firm's income statement:

| | | |
|---|---|---|
| EBIT | $1,916,666,667 | EBT + Interest |
| Interest | 250,000,000 | 0.05 × 0.5 × $10,000,000,000 |
| EBT | $1,666,666,667 | $1,000,000,000/(1 − 0.4) |
| Taxes (40%) | 666,666,667 | EBT × 0.4 |
| Net income | $1,000,000,000 | |

$$\text{ROIC} = \dfrac{\text{EBIT}(1-T)}{\text{Total invested capital}} = \dfrac{\$1,916,666,667(0.6)}{\$10,000,000,000} = 11.5\%.$$

e. If the company used less debt, it would increase net income because interest expense would be reduced. Because assets would not change and net income increases, ROA will increase.

## 4-5F BASIC EARNING POWER (BEP) RATIO

The **basic earning power (BEP) ratio** is calculated by dividing operating income (EBIT) by total assets:

$$\text{Basic earning power (BEP)} = \dfrac{\text{EBIT}}{\text{Total assets}}$$

$$= \dfrac{\$283.8}{\$2,000} = 14.2\%$$

Industry average $= 18.0\%$

*Basic Earning Power (BEP) Ratio*
This ratio indicates the ability of the firm's assets to generate operating income; it is calculated by dividing EBIT by total assets.

This ratio shows the raw earning power of the firm's assets before the influence of taxes and debt, and it is useful when comparing firms with different debt and tax situations. Because of its low turnover ratios and poor profit margin on sales, Allied has a lower BEP ratio than the average food processing company.

## SelfTest

Identify six profitability ratios, and write their equations.

Why does the use of debt lower the profit margin and the ROA?

Using more debt lowers profits and thus the ROA. Why doesn't debt have the same negative effect on the ROE?

A company has a 10% ROA. Assume that a company's total assets equal total invested capital, and that the company has no debt, so its total invested capital equals total equity. What are the company's ROE and ROIC? **(10%, 10%)**

# 4-6 Market Value Ratios

**Market Value Ratios**

Ratios that relate the firm's stock price to its earnings and book value per share.

ROE reflects the effects of all of the other ratios, and it is the single best accounting measure of performance. Investors like a high ROE, and high ROEs are correlated with high stock prices. However, other things come into play. For example, financial leverage generally increases the ROE but also increases the firm's risk; so if a high ROE is achieved by using a great deal of debt, the stock price might end up lower than if the firm had been using less debt and had a lower ROE. We use the final set of ratios—the **market value ratios**, which relate the stock price to earnings and book value price—to help address this situation. If the liquidity, asset management, debt management, and profitability ratios all look good, and if investors think these ratios will continue to look good in the future, the market value ratios will be high; the stock price will be as high as can be expected; and management will be judged as having done a good job.

The market value ratios are used in three primary ways: (1) by investors when they are deciding to buy or sell a stock, (2) by investment bankers when they are setting the share price for a new stock issue (an IPO), and (3) by firms when they are deciding how much to offer for another firm in a potential merger.

### 4-6A PRICE/EARNINGS RATIO

**Price/Earnings (P/E) Ratio**

The ratio of the price per share to earnings per share; shows the dollar amount investors will pay for $1 of current earnings.

The **price/earnings (P/E) ratio** shows how much investors are willing to pay per dollar of reported profits. Allied's stock sells for $23.06; so with an EPS of $2.35, its P/E ratio is 9.8×:

$$\text{Price/Earnings (P/E) ratio} = \frac{\text{Price per share}}{\text{Earnings per share}}$$

$$= \frac{\$23.06}{\$2.35} = 9.8\times$$

$$\text{Industry average} = 11.3\times$$

As we will see in Chapter 9, P/E ratios are relatively high for firms with strong growth prospects and little risk but low for slowly growing and risky firms. Allied's P/E ratio is below its industry average; so this suggests that the company is regarded as being relatively risky, as having poor growth prospects, or both.[14]

P/E ratios vary considerably over time and across firms.[15] In March 2015, the S&P 500's P/E ratio was 21.4×. At this same point in time, Yahoo! Inc. had a P/E of 5.89×,

---

[14]Security analysts also look at the price-to-free-cash-flow ratio. In addition, analysts consider the PEG, or P/E-to-growth, ratio where the P/E is divided by the firm's forecasted growth rate. Allied's growth rate as forecasted by a number of security analysts for the next 5 years is 7.0%, so its PEG = 9.8/7.0 = 1.4×. The lower the ratio, the better; and most firms have ratios in the range of 1.0× to 2.0×. We note, though, that P/E ratios jump around from year to year because earnings and forecasted growth rates fluctuate. Like other ratios, PEG ratios are interesting, but must be interpreted with care and judgment.

[15]On his website (www.econ.yale.edu/~shiller/data.htm), Professor Robert Shiller reports the annual P/E ratio of the overall stock market dating back to 1871. His calculations show that the historical average P/E ratio for the market has been 16.6×, and it has ranged from 4.8× to 44.2×.

while Under Armour, Inc., a rapidly growing apparel company, had a P/E of 82.61×. Moreover, once high-flying growth stocks such as Intel and Exxon Mobil (both of which a decade ago had P/E ratios above 20) have seen their P/Es fall below 14× as they become larger, more stable companies with fewer growth opportunities.

## 4-6B MARKET/BOOK RATIO

The ratio of a stock's market price to its book value gives another indication of how investors regard the company. Companies that are well regarded by investors—which means low risk and high growth—have high M/B ratios. For Allied, we first find its book value per share:

$$\text{Book value per share} = \frac{\text{Common equity}}{\text{Shares outstanding}}$$

$$= \frac{\$940}{50} = \$18.80$$

We then divide the market price per share by the book value per share to get the **market/book (M/B) Ratio**, which for Allied is 1.2×:

$$\text{Market/Book (M/B) ratio} = \frac{\text{Market price per share}}{\text{Book value per share}}$$

$$= \frac{\$23.06}{\$18.80} = 1.2\times$$

$$\text{Industry average} = 1.7\times$$

*Market/Book (M/B) Ratio*

The ratio of a stock's market price to its book value.

Investors are willing to pay less for a dollar of Allied's book value than for one of an average food processing company. This is consistent with our other findings. M/B ratios typically exceed 1.0, which means that investors are willing to pay more for stocks than the accounting book values of the stocks. This situation occurs primarily because asset values, as reported by accountants on corporate balance sheets, do not reflect either inflation or goodwill. Assets purchased years ago at pre-inflation prices are carried at their original costs even though inflation might have caused their actual values to rise substantially; and successful companies' values rise above their historical costs, whereas unsuccessful ones have low M/B ratios.[16] This point is demonstrated by Google and Bank of America: In March 2015, Google's M/B ratio was 3.61× while Bank of America's was only 0.76×. Google's stockholders now have $3.61 in market value per $1.00 of equity, whereas Bank of America's stockholders have only $0.76 for each dollar they invested.

## Self*Test*

Describe two ratios that relate a firm's stock price to its earnings and book value per share and write their equations.

In what sense do these market value ratios reflect investors' opinions about a stock's risk and expected future growth?

What does the price/earnings (P/E) ratio show? If one firm's P/E ratio is lower than that of another firm, what factors might explain the difference?

How is book value per share calculated? Explain how inflation and R&D programs might cause book values to deviate from market values.

---

[16]The second point is known as *survivor bias*. Successful companies survive and are reflected in the averages, whereas unsuccessful companies vanish, and their low numbers are not reflected in the averages.

# 4-7 Tying the Ratios Together: The DuPont Equation

**DuPont Equation**

A formula that shows that the rate of return on equity can be found as the product of profit margin, total assets turnover, and the equity multiplier. It shows the relationships among asset management, debt management, and profitability ratios.

We have discussed many ratios, so it would be useful to see how they work together to determine the ROE. For this, we use the **DuPont equation**, a formula developed by the chemical giant's financial staff in the 1920s. It is shown here for Allied and the food processing industry:

$$
\begin{aligned}
\text{ROE} &= \quad\quad\text{ROA} \quad\quad\quad \times \text{Equity multiplier} \\
&= \text{Profit margin} \times \text{Total assets turnover} \times \text{Equity multiplier} \\
&= \frac{\text{Net income}}{\text{Sales}} \times \frac{\text{Sales}}{\text{Total assets}} \times \frac{\text{Total assets}}{\text{Total common equity}} \\
&= \frac{\$117.5}{\$3,000} \times \frac{\$3,000}{\$2,000} \times \frac{\$2,000}{\$940} \\
&= 3.92\% \times 1.5 \text{ times} \times 2.13 \text{ times} = 12.5\%
\end{aligned}
$$

$$\text{Industry} = 5.0\% \times 1.8 \text{ times} \times 1.67 \text{ times} = 15.0\%$$

▼ 4.1

- The first term, the profit margin, tells us how much the firm earns on its sales. This ratio depends primarily on costs and sales prices—if a firm can command a premium price and hold down its costs, its profit margin will be high, which will help its ROE.

- The second term is the total assets turnover. It is a "multiplier" that tells us how many times the profit margin is earned each year—Allied earned 3.92% on each dollar of sales, and its assets were turned over 1.5 times each year; so its return on assets was 3.92% × 1.5 = 5.9%. Note, though, that this entire 5.9% belongs to the common stockholders—the bondholders earned a return in the form of interest, and that interest was deducted before we calculated net income to stockholders. So the whole 5.9% return on assets belongs to the stockholders. Therefore, the return on assets must be adjusted upward to obtain the return on equity.

- That brings us to the third term, the equity multiplier, which is the adjustment factor. Allied's assets are 2.13 times its equity, so we must multiply the 5.9% return on assets by the 2.13× equity multiplier to arrive at its ROE of 12.5%.[17]

Note that ROE as calculated using the DuPont equation is identical to Allied's ROE, 12.5%, which we calculated earlier. What's the point of going through all of the steps required to implement the DuPont equation to find ROE? The answer is that the DuPont equation helps us see *why* Allied's ROE is only 12.5% versus 15.0% for the industry. First, its profit margin is below average, which indicates that its costs are not being controlled as well as they should be and that it cannot charge premium prices. In addition, because it uses more debt than most companies, its high interest charges also reduce its profit margin. Second, its total assets turnover is below the industry average, which indicates that it has more assets than it needs. Finally, because its equity multiplier is relatively high, its heavy use of debt offsets to some extent its low profit margin and turnover. However, the high debt ratio exposes Allied to above-average bankruptcy risk; so it might want to cut back on its financial leverage. But if it reduced its debt to the same level as the average firm in

---

[17]The equity multiplier relates to the firm's use of debt. The industry equity multiplier can be obtained by using the industry ROE and ROA. The equity multiplier = Total assets divided by common equity. ROE = Net income/Common equity and ROA = Net income/ Total assets. So, ROE ÷ ROA = Equity multiplier as shown below:

$$\frac{\text{ROE}}{\text{ROA}} = \frac{\text{NI}}{\text{Equity}} \div \frac{\text{NI}}{\text{Assets}} = \frac{\text{NI}}{\text{Equity}} \times \frac{\text{Assets}}{\text{NI}} = \frac{\text{Assets}}{\text{Equity}} = \text{Equity multiplier.}$$

# MICROSOFT EXCEL: A TRULY ESSENTIAL TOOL

Microsoft Excel is an essential tool for anyone dealing with business issues—not just finance and accounting professionals but also lawyers, marketers, auto sales managers, government employees, and many others. Indeed, anyone who works with numbers will be more efficient and productive if they know the basics of Excel, so it's a necessity for anyone who hopes to hold a managerial position.

As you go through this book, you will see that Excel is used in four main ways:

**1.** *As a financial calculator.* Excel can add, subtract, multiply, and divide, and it can retain results from one operation for use in subsequent operations. For example, we created the financial statements in Chapter 3 with Excel, and we use it to analyze those statements in the current chapter. We could have done this with a calculator or pencil and paper, but it was a lot easier with Excel. As we will see throughout the text, Excel also has a large number of built-in financial functions that can be used to simply calculate the answers to a wide range of financial problems. For example, using Excel, it is straightforward to calculate the return on an investment, the price of a bond, or the value of a project.

**2.** *To modify the work when things change.* Suppose your boss asked you to create the statements in Chapter 3, but when you finished she said, "Thanks, but the accounting department just informed us that inventories in 2016 were overstated by $100 million, which means that total assets were also overstated. To make the balance sheet balance, we must reduce retained earnings, common equity, and total claims against assets. Please make those adjustments and give me a revised set of statements before the board meeting tomorrow morning."

If you were working with a calculator, you'd be looking at an all-nighter, but with Excel you could make just one change—reduce 2016 inventories by $100 million—and Excel would instantly revise the statements. If your company had two people working on problems like this, who would get promoted and who would get a pink slip?

**3.** *Sensitivity analysis.* We use ratios to analyze financial statements and assess how well a company is managed, and if weaknesses are detected management can make changes to improve the situation. For example, Allied's return on equity (ROE), a key determinant of its stock price, is below the industry average. ROE depends on a number of factors, including the level of inventories, and using Excel one can see how ROE would change if inventories were increased or decreased. Then, management can investigate alternative inventory policies to see how they would impact profits and the ROE. In theory, one could do this analysis with a calculator, but this would be inefficient, and in a competitive world efficiency is essential to survival.

**4.** *Risk assessments.* Sensitivity analysis can be used to assess the risk inherent in different policies. For example, *forecasted* returns on equity are generally higher if a firm increases its debt, but the more debt the firm carries, the worse the effects of an economic downturn. We can use Excel to quantify the effects of changing economic conditions with different amounts of debt, and thus the probability that the firm will go bankrupt in a recession. Many firms learned about this during the 2007–2009 recession, so the survivors are now more interested than ever in risk models.

This listing gives you an idea of what Excel can do and why it is important in business today. We illustrate it throughout the book, and you should make an effort to understand how to use it. The Excel chapter models can be found on the text's website, www.cengagebrain.com. You will find an understanding of Excel very helpful when you begin interviewing for a job.[18]

its industry without any other changes, its ROE would decline significantly, to $3.92\% \times 1.5 \times 1.67 = 9.8\%$.[19]

Allied's management can use the DuPont equation to help identify ways to improve its performance. Focusing on the profit margin, its marketing people can study the effects of raising sales prices or of introducing new products with higher margins. Its cost accountants can study various expense items and, working with engineers, purchasing agents, and other operating personnel, seek ways to cut costs.

---

[18]It is often impractical for professors to test students on their ability to integrate Excel into financial management, so some students conclude that knowing more about Excel won't help them on tests and thus they ignore it. That's unfortunate, and we can only say that there's more to school than grades alone, and in the long run knowing something about Excel is one of the most valuable tools you can learn in school.

[19]The ROE reduction would actually be somewhat less because if debt were lowered, interest payments would also decline, which would raise Allied's profit margin. Allied's analysts determined that the net effect of a reduction in debt would still be a significant reduction in ROE.

The credit manager can investigate ways to speed up collections, which would reduce accounts receivable and therefore improve the quality of the total assets turnover ratio. And the financial staff can analyze the effects of alternative debt policies, showing how changes in leverage would affect both the expected ROE and the risk of bankruptcy.

As a result of this analysis, Ellen Jackson, Allied's chief executive officer (CEO), undertook a series of moves that are expected to cut operating costs by more than 20%. Jackson and Allied's other executives have a strong incentive to improve the firm's financial performance—their compensation depends on how well the company operates.

## SelfTest

Write the equation for the DuPont equation.

What is the equity multiplier, and why is it used?

How can management use the DuPont equation to analyze ways of improving the firm's performance?

## 4-8 Potential Misuses of ROE

Although ROE is an important measure of performance, we know that managers should strive to maximize shareholder wealth. If a firm takes steps that improve its ROE, does that mean that shareholder wealth will also be increased? The answer is "not necessarily." Indeed, three problems are likely to arise if a firm relies too heavily on ROE to measure performance.

First, ROE does not consider risk. Shareholders care about ROE, but they also care about risk. To illustrate, consider two divisions within the same firm. Division S has stable cash flows and a predictable 15% ROE. Division R has a 16% expected ROE, but its cash flows are quite risky; so the expected ROE may not materialize. If managers were compensated solely on the basis of ROE and if the expected ROEs were actually achieved during the coming year, Division R's manager would receive a higher bonus than S's, even though S might actually be creating more value for shareholders as a result of its lower risk. Similarly, financial leverage can increase expected ROE, but more leverage means higher risk; so raising ROE through the use of leverage may not be good.

Second, ROE does not consider the amount of invested capital. To illustrate, consider a company that is choosing between two mutually exclusive projects. Project A calls for investing $50,000 at an expected ROE of 50%, while Project B calls for investing $1,000,000 at a 45% ROE. The projects are equally risky, and the company's cost of capital is 10%. Project A has the higher ROE, but it is much smaller. Project B should be chosen because it would add more to shareholder wealth.

Third, a focus on ROE can cause managers to turn down profitable projects. For example, suppose you manage a division of a large firm and the firm determines bonuses solely on the basis of ROE. You project that your division's ROE for the year will be an impressive 45%. Now you have an opportunity to invest in a large, low-risk project with an estimated ROE of 35%, which is well above the firm's 10% cost of capital. Even though this project is extremely profitable, you might still be reluctant to undertake it because it would reduce your division's average ROE and therefore your year-end bonus.

# ECONOMIC VALUE ADDED (EVA) VERSUS NET INCOME

As we mentioned in Chapter 3, economic value added (EVA) is a measure of how much management has added to shareholders' wealth during the year. To better understand the idea behind EVA, let's look at Allied's 2016 numbers (in millions). Allied's total invested capital consists of $110 of notes payable, $750 of long-term debt, and $940 of common equity, totaling $1,800. Debt represents 47.78% of this total, and common equity is 52.22% of this total. Later in the text we discuss how to calculate the cost of Allied's capital; but for now, to simplify things, we estimate its capital cost at 10%. Thus, the firm's total dollar cost of capital (which includes both debt and common equity) per year is $0.10 \times \$1,800 = \$180$.

Now let's look at Allied's income statement. Its operating income, EBIT, is $283.8; and its interest expense is $88.0. Therefore, its taxable income is $\$283.8 - \$88.0 = \$195.8$. Taxes equal 40% of taxable income, or $0.4\,(\$195.8) = \$78.3$; so the firm's net income is $117.5. Its return on equity, ROE, is $\$117.5\,/\,\$940 = 12.5\%$.

Given this data, we can now calculate Allied's EVA. The basic formula for EVA (as discussed in Chapter 3) is as follows:

$$EVA = EBIT(1-T) - \left(\begin{array}{c}\text{Total} \\ \text{invested capital}\end{array}\right) \times \left(\begin{array}{c}\text{After-tax} \\ \text{cost of capital}\end{array}\right)$$

$$= \$283.8(1 - 0.40) - (\$1,800)(0.10)$$

$$= \$170.3 - \$180$$

$$= -\$9.7$$

This negative EVA indicates that Allied's shareholders actually earned $9.7 million less than they could have earned elsewhere by investing in other stocks with the same risk as Allied. To see where this −$9.7 comes from, let's trace what happened to the money:

- The firm generated $283.8 of operating income.

- $78.3 went to the government to pay taxes, leaving $205.5 available for investors—stockholders and bondholders.

- $88.0 went to the bondholders in the form of interest payments, thus leaving $117.5 for the stockholders.

- However, Allied's shareholders must also earn a return on the equity capital they have invested in the firm, because they could have invested in other companies of comparable risk. We call this the cost of Allied's equity.

- Once Allied's shareholders are "paid" their return, the firm comes up $9.7 million short—that's the economic value management added, and it is negative. In a sense, Allied's management created *negative* wealth because it provided shareholders with a lower return than they could have earned on alternative investments with the same risk as Allied's stock.

- In practice, it is often necessary to make several adjustments to arrive at a "better" measure of EVA. The adjustments deal with non-operating assets, leased assets, depreciation, and other accounting details that we leave for discussion in advanced finance courses.

### The Connection between ROE and EVA

EVA is different from traditional accounting profit *because EVA reflects the cost of equity as well as the cost of debt.* Indeed, using the previous example, we could also express EVA as net income minus the dollar cost of equity:

$$EVA = \text{Net income} - (\text{Equity} \times \text{Cost of equity})$$

This expression above could be rewritten as follows:

$$EVA = (\text{Equity})(\text{Net income}/\text{Equity} - \text{Cost of equity})$$

which can be rewritten as:

$$EVA = \text{Equity}(ROE - \text{Cost of equity})$$

This last expression implies that EVA depends on three factors: rate of return, as reflected in ROE; risk, which affects the cost of equity; and size, which is measured by the equity employed. Recall that earlier in this chapter, we said that shareholder value depends on risk, return, and capital invested. This final equation illustrates that point.

These three examples suggest that a project's ROE must be combined with its size and risk to determine its effect on shareholder value, as we illustrate in the diagram below:

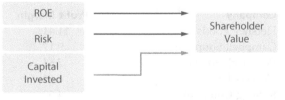

We will discuss this in more depth when we consider capital budgeting, where we look in detail at how projects are selected so as to maximize stock prices and consequently shareholder value.

## SelfTest

If a firm takes steps that increase its expected future ROE, does this necessarily mean that the stock price will also increase? Explain.

# 4-9 Using Financial Ratios to Assess Performance

Although financial ratios help us evaluate financial statements, it is often hard to evaluate a company by just looking at the ratios. For example, if you see that a company has a current ratio of 1.2, it is hard to know if that is good or bad, unless you put the ratio in its proper perspective. Allied's management could look at industry averages; it could compare itself to specific companies or "benchmarks"; and it can analyze the trends in each ratio. We look at all three approaches in this section.

## 4-9A COMPARISON TO INDUSTRY AVERAGE

As we have done for Allied, one way to assess performance is to compare the company's key ratios to the industry averages. Table 4.2 provides a summary of the ratios we have discussed in this chapter. This table is useful as a quick reference, and the calculated ratios and accompanying comments give a good sense of Allied's strengths and weaknesses relative to the average food processing company. To give you a further sense of some "real-world" ratios, Table 4.3 provides a list of ratios for a number of different industries in March 2015.

## 4-9B BENCHMARKING

**Benchmarking**
The process of comparing a particular company with a subset of top competitors in its industry.

Ratio analysis involves comparisons with industry average figures, but Allied and many other firms also compare themselves with a subset of top competitors in their industry. This is called **benchmarking**, and the companies used for the comparison are called benchmark companies. Allied's management benchmarks against Campbell Soup, a leading manufacturer of canned soups; Tyson Foods, a processor of chicken, beef, and pork products; J&J Snack Foods, a manufacturer of nutritional snack foods; ConAgra Foods, a packaged food company that supplies frozen potatoes and other vegetables to commercial customers; Flowers Foods, a producer of bakery and snack-food goods; Hershey Foods, a producer of chocolates and non-chocolate confectionary products; and Kellogg Company, a manufacturer of ready-to-eat cereals and convenience foods. Ratios are calculated for each company, then listed in descending order as shown below for the profit margin (the firms' latest 12 months' results reported by *MSN Money* (money.msn.com) as of March 17, 2015):

| Company | Profit Margin |
|---|---|
| Hershey Foods | 11.41% |
| Campbell Soup | 9.17 |
| J&J Snack Foods | 7.61 |
| Flowers Foods | 4.69 |
| Kellogg Company | 4.33 |
| **Allied Food Products** | **3.92** |
| Tyson Foods | 2.32 |
| ConAgra Foods | 2.28 |

Allied Food Products: Summary of Financial Ratios (Millions of Dollars)   **TABLE 4.2**

| Ratio | Formula | Calculation | Ratio | Industry Average | Comment |
|-------|---------|-------------|-------|------------------|---------|
| **Liquidity** | | | | | |
| Current | $\dfrac{\text{Current assets}}{\text{Current liabilities}}$ | $\dfrac{\$1,000}{\$310}$ | = 3.2× | 4.2× | Poor |
| Quick | $\dfrac{\text{Current assets} - \text{Inventories}}{\text{Current liabilities}}$ | $\dfrac{\$385}{\$310}$ | = 1.2× | 2.2× | Poor |
| **Asset Management** | | | | | |
| Inventory turnover | $\dfrac{\text{Sales}}{\text{Inventories}}$ | $\dfrac{\$3,000}{\$615}$ | = 4.9× | 10.9× | Poor |
| Days sales outstanding (DSO) | $\dfrac{\text{Receivables}}{\text{Annual sales}/365}$ | $\dfrac{\$375}{\$8.2192}$ | = 46 days | 36 days | Poor |
| Fixed assets turnover | $\dfrac{\text{Sales}}{\text{Net fixed assets}}$ | $\dfrac{\$3,000}{\$1,000}$ | = 3.0× | 2.8× | OK |
| Total assets turnover | $\dfrac{\text{Sales}}{\text{Total assets}}$ | $\dfrac{\$3,000}{\$2,000}$ | = 1.5× | 1.8× | Somewhat low |
| **Debt Management** | | | | | |
| Total debt to total capital | $\dfrac{\text{Total debt}}{\text{Total capital}}$ | $\dfrac{\$860}{\$1,800}$ | = 47.8% | 36.4% | High (risky) |
| Times-interest-earned (TIE) | $\dfrac{\text{Earnings before interest and taxes (EBIT)}}{\text{Interest charges}}$ | $\dfrac{\$283.8}{\$88}$ | = 3.2× | 6.0× | Low (risky) |
| **Profitability** | | | | | |
| Operating margin | $\dfrac{\text{Operating income (EBIT)}}{\text{Sales}}$ | $\dfrac{\$283.8}{\$3,000}$ | = 9.5% | 10.0% | Low |
| Profit margin | $\dfrac{\text{Net income}}{\text{Sales}}$ | $\dfrac{\$117.5}{\$3,000}$ | = 3.9% | 5.0% | Poor |
| Return on total assets (ROA) | $\dfrac{\text{Net income}}{\text{Total assets}}$ | $\dfrac{\$117.5}{\$2,000}$ | = 5.9% | 9.0% | Poor |
| Return on common equity (ROE) | $\dfrac{\text{Net income}}{\text{Common equity}}$ | $\dfrac{\$117.5}{\$940}$ | = 12.5% | 15.0% | Poor |
| Return on invested capital (ROIC) | $\dfrac{\text{EBIT}(1 - T)}{\text{Total invested capital}}$ | $\dfrac{\$170.3}{\$1,800}$ | = 9.5% | 10.8% | Poor |
| Basic earning power (BEP) | $\dfrac{\text{Earnings before interest and taxes (EBIT)}}{\text{Total assets}}$ | $\dfrac{\$283.8}{\$2,000}$ | = 14.2% | 18.0% | Poor |
| **Market Value** | | | | | |
| Price/Earnings (P/E) | $\dfrac{\text{Price per share}}{\text{Earnings per share}}$ | $\dfrac{\$23.06}{\$2.35}$ | = 9.8× | 11.3× | Low |
| Market/Book (M/B) | $\dfrac{\text{Market price per share}}{\text{Book value per share}}$ | $\dfrac{\$23.06}{\$18.80}$ | = 1.2× | 1.7× | Low |

The benchmarking setup makes it easy for Allied's management to see exactly where it stands relative to the competition. As the data show, Allied is near the bottom of its benchmark group relative to its profit margin, so it has lots of room for improvement. Other ratios are analyzed similarly.

Comparative ratios are available from a number of sources, including both Yahoo! Finance and MSN Money. Useful ratios are also compiled by Value Line, Dun and Bradstreet (D&B), and the Risk Management Association, which is the national association of bank loan officers. Also, financial statement data for thousands of publicly owned corporations are available on other Internet sites, and as brokerage houses, banks, and other financial institutions have access to these data, security analysts can and do generate comparative ratios tailored to their specific needs.

Each of the data-supplying organizations uses a somewhat different set of ratios designed for its own purposes. For example, D&B deals mainly with small firms,

**TABLE 4.3**     Key Financial Ratios for Selected Industries[a]

| Industry Name | Current Ratio | Inventory Turnover[b] | Total Assets Turnover | LT Debt/ LT Capital[c] | Net Profit Margin | Return on Assets | Return on Equity |
|---|---|---|---|---|---|---|---|
| Aerospace/defense | 1.25 | 3.04 | 0.87 | 40.48% | 7.76% | 6.75% | 27.38% |
| Apparel stores | 1.64 | 4.83 | 1.94 | 40.12 | 7.66 | 14.88 | 40.65 |
| Auto manufacturing—major | 1.21 | 10.67 | 0.69 | 43.18 | 5.84 | 4.02 | 12.94 |
| Beverage (soft drink) | 1.06 | 7.35 | 0.66 | 45.95 | 12.37 | 8.17 | 25.15 |
| Electronics—diversified | 2.58 | 4.70 | 0.52 | 21.88 | 17.44 | 9.09 | 15.39 |
| Food wholesalers | 2.63 | 14.23 | 3.03 | 55.56 | 1.84 | 5.59 | 15.68 |
| Grocery stores | 0.83 | 14.46 | 3.48 | 53.92 | 1.68 | 5.85 | 22.73 |
| Health services—specialized | 1.69 | 9.59 | 0.95 | 89.22 | 4.99 | 4.76 | 66.14 |
| Lodging | 0.97 | 10.71 | 0.66 | 76.58 | 6.85 | 4.50 | 29.12 |
| Newspapers | 0.91 | 123.92 | 0.42 | 35.06 | 4.66 | 1.94 | 4.07 |
| Paper and paper products | 1.56 | 6.95 | 0.91 | 62.69 | 3.22 | 2.92 | 12.86 |
| Railroad | 1.22 | 9.23 | 0.43 | 37.50 | 20.86 | 8.95 | 22.33 |
| Restaurant | 1.31 | 28.76 | 0.97 | 53.70 | 14.92 | 14.45 | 36.01 |
| Retail (department stores) | 1.34 | 2.88 | 1.38 | 51.92 | 3.68 | 5.06 | 19.40 |
| Scientific and technical instruments | 1.41 | 5.72 | 0.51 | 38.65 | 10.03 | 5.13 | 10.56 |
| Sporting goods | 0.73 | 21.78 | 0.47 | 29.08 | 13.08 | 6.12 | 10.73 |
| Steel and iron | 1.99 | 5.44 | 0.33 | 40.48 | −8.43 | −2.80 | −8.34 |
| Tobacco (cigarettes) | 1.00 | 1.65 | 0.69 | 131.55 | 25.37 | 17.54 | −184.32 |

*Notes:*

[a]The ratios presented are averages for each industry. Ratios for the individual companies are also available.

[b]The inventory turnover ratio in this table is calculated as the company's latest 12 months of cost of sales divided by the average of its inventory for the last quarter and the comparable year earlier quarter.

[c]LT debt/LT capital is calculated as LT debt/(LT debt + Equity) by using MSN's Debt/Equity ratio as follows:

$$\frac{D/E}{(1 + D/E)}$$

Source: Data obtained from *MSN Money*, Key Ratios (money.msn.com), March 17, 2015.

many of which are proprietorships, and it sells its services primarily to banks and other lenders. Therefore, D&B is concerned largely with the creditor's viewpoint, and its ratios emphasize current assets and liabilities, not market value ratios. So, when you select a comparative data source, you should be sure that your emphasis is similar to that of the agency whose ratios you plan to use. Additionally, there are often definitional differences in the ratios presented by different sources, so before using a source, be sure to verify the exact definitions of the ratios to ensure consistency with your own work.

## 4-9C TREND ANALYSIS

**Trend Analysis**

An analysis of a firm's financial ratios over time; used to estimate the likelihood of improvement or deterioration in its financial condition.

As a final comparison, Allied compares its ratios to its own past levels. It is important to analyze trends in ratios as well as their absolute levels, for trends give clues as to whether a firm's financial condition is likely to improve or to deteriorate. To do a **trend analysis**, simply plot a ratio over time, as shown in Figure 4.1. This graph shows that Allied's ROE has been declining since 2013 even though the industry average has been relatively stable. All the other ratios could be analyzed similarly, and such an analysis can be quite useful in gaining insights as to why the ROE behaved as it did.

**FIGURE 4.1**     Rate of Return on Common Equity, 2012–2016

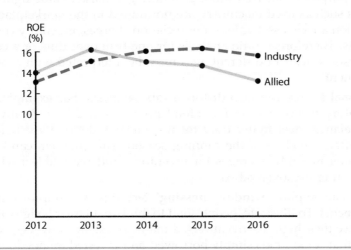

## SelfTest

Why might railroads have such low total assets turnovers and food wholesalers and grocery stores such high turnovers?

If competition causes all companies to have similar ROEs in the long run, would companies with high turnovers tend to have high or low profit margins? Explain your answer.

Why are comparative ratio analyses useful?

How does one do a trend analysis?

What important information does a trend analysis provide?

## 4-10 Uses and Limitations of Ratios

As noted earlier, ratio analysis is used by three main groups: (1) *managers,* who use ratios to help analyze, control, and thus improve their firms' operations; (2) *credit analysts,* including bank loan officers and bond rating analysts, who analyze ratios to help judge a company's ability to repay its debts; and (3) *stock analysts,* who are interested in a company's efficiency, risk, and growth prospects. In later chapters, we will look more closely at the basic factors that underlie each ratio. Note, though, that while ratio analysis can provide useful information concerning a company's operations and financial condition, it does have limitations. Some potential problems are listed here:

1. Many firms have divisions that operate in different industries; and for such companies, it is difficult to develop a meaningful set of industry averages. Therefore, ratio analysis is more useful for narrowly focused firms than for multidivisional ones.

2. Most firms want to be better than average, so merely attaining average performance is not necessarily good. As a target for high-level performance, it is best to focus on the industry leaders' ratios. Benchmarking helps in this regard.

*To find information about a company quickly, link to* **reuters.com/finance**. *Here you can find company profiles and snapshots, and stock price quotes, as well as share information, key ratios, and comparative ratios.*

3. Inflation has distorted many firms' balance sheets—book values are often different from market values. Market values would be more appropriate for most purposes, but we cannot generally get market value figures because assets such as used machinery are not traded in the marketplace. Further, inflation affects asset values, depreciation charges, inventory costs, and thus profits. Therefore, a ratio analysis for one firm over time or a comparative analysis of firms of different ages must be interpreted with care and judgment.

4. Seasonal factors can also distort a ratio analysis. For example, the inventory turnover ratio for a food processor will be radically different if the balance sheet figure used for inventory is the one just before, versus just after, the close of the canning season. This problem can be mitigated by using monthly averages for inventory (and receivables) when calculating turnover ratios.

**"Window Dressing" Techniques**

Techniques employed by firms to make their financial statements look better than they really are.

5. Firms can employ **"window dressing" techniques** to improve their financial statements. To illustrate, people tend to think that larger hedge funds got large because their high returns attracted many investors. However, we learned in 2007 that some funds simply borrowed and invested money to increase their apparent size. One fund, Wharton Asset Management, reported $2 billion "under management," but it had actually attracted less than $100 million of investors' capital.

6. Different accounting practices can distort comparisons. As noted earlier, inventory valuation and depreciation methods can affect financial statements and thus distort comparisons among firms. Also, if one firm leases much of its productive equipment, its fixed assets turnover may be artificially high because leased assets often do not appear on the balance sheet. At the same time, the liability associated with the lease may not appear as debt, keeping the debt ratio low, even though failure to make lease payments can bankrupt the firm. Therefore, leasing can artificially improve both turnover and the debt ratios. The accounting profession has taken steps to reduce this problem, but it still can cause distortions.

7. It is difficult to generalize about whether a particular ratio is "good" or "bad." For example, a high current ratio may indicate a strong liquidity position, which is good, but it can also indicate excessive cash, which is bad because excess cash in the bank is a nonearning asset. Similarly, a high fixed assets turnover ratio may indicate that the firm uses its assets efficiently, but it could also indicate that the firm is short of cash and cannot afford to make needed fixed asset investments.

8. Firms often have some ratios that look "good" and others that look "bad," making it difficult to tell whether the company is, on balance, strong or weak. To deal with this problem, banks and other lending organizations often use statistical procedures to analyze the *net effects* of a set of ratios and to classify firms according to their probability of getting into financial trouble.[20]

We see then that ratio analysis is useful, but analysts should be aware of the problems just listed and make adjustments as necessary. Ratio analysis conducted in a mechanical, unthinking manner is dangerous; but used intelligently and with good judgment, it can provide useful insights into firms' operations. Your judgment

---

[20]The technique used is discriminant analysis. The seminal work on this subject was undertaken by Edward I. Altman, "Financial Ratios, Discriminant Analysis, and the Prediction of Corporate Bankruptcy," *Journal of Finance*, vol. 23, no. 4 (September 1968), pp. 589–609.

# LOOKING FOR WARNING SIGNS WITHIN THE FINANCIAL STATEMENTS

Financial scandals have spurred a renewed interest in financial accounting, and analysts now scour companies' financial statements to see if trouble is lurking. This renewed interest has led to a list of red flags to consider when reviewing a company's financial statements. For example, after conferring with New York University Accounting Professor Baruch Lev, *Fortune* magazine's Shawn Tully identified the following warning signs:

• Year after year a company reports restructuring charges and/or write-downs. This practice raises concerns because companies can use write-downs to mask operating expenses, which results in overstated earnings.

• A company's earnings have been propped up through a series of acquisitions. Acquisitions can increase earnings if the acquiring company has a higher P/E ratio than the acquired firm, but such "growth" cannot be sustained over the long run.

• A company depreciates its assets more slowly than the industry average. Lower depreciation boosts current earnings, but again this cannot be sustained because eventually depreciation must be recognized.

• A company routinely has high earnings but low cash flow. As Tully points out, this warning sign would have exposed Enron's problems. In the second quarter of 2001 (a few months before its problems began to unfold), Enron reported earnings of $423 million versus a cash flow of minus $527 million.

Along similar lines, after consulting with various professionals, Ellen Simon of the *Newark Star Ledger* came up with her list of red flags:

• You wouldn't buy the stock at today's price.

• You don't really understand the company's financial statements.

• The company is in a business that lends itself to "creative accounting."

• The company keeps taking nonrecurring charges.

• Accounts receivable and inventory are increasing faster than sales revenues.

• The company's insiders are selling their stock.

• The company is making aggressive acquisitions, especially in unrelated fields.

There is some overlap between these two lists. Also, none of these items automatically means there is something wrong with the company—instead, the items should be viewed as warning signs that cause you to take a closer look at the company's performance before making an investment.

---

in interpreting ratios is bound to be weak at this point, but it will improve as you go through the remainder of the book.

## Self Test

List three types of users of ratio analysis. Would the different users emphasize the same or different types of ratios? Explain.

List several potential difficulties with ratio analysis.

## 4-11 Looking Beyond the Numbers

Working through this chapter should increase your ability to understand and interpret financial statements. This is critically important for anyone making business decisions or forecasting stock prices. However, sound financial analysis involves more than just numbers—good analysis requires that certain qualitative factors also be considered. These factors, as summarized by the American Association of Individual Investors (AAII), include the following:

*Students might want to refer to AAII's educational website at **aaii.com**. The site provides information on investing basics, financial planning, and portfolio management, so that individuals can manage their own assets more effectively.*

1. Are the company's revenues tied to one key customer? If so, the company's performance may decline dramatically if that customer goes elsewhere. On the other hand, if the customer has no alternative to the company's products, this might actually stabilize sales.

2. To what extent are the company's revenues tied to one key product? Firms that focus on a single product are often efficient, but a lack of diversification also increases risk because having revenues from several products stabilizes profits and cash flows in a volatile world.

3. To what extent does the company rely on a single supplier? Depending on a single supplier may lead to an unanticipated shortage and a hit to sales and profits.

4. What percentage of the company's business is generated overseas? Companies with a large percentage of overseas business are often able to realize higher growth and larger profit margins. However, overseas operations may expose the firm to political risks and exchange rate problems.

5. How much competition does the firm face? Increases in competition tend to lower prices and profit margins; so when forecasting future performance, it is important to assess the likely actions of current competitors and the entry of new ones.

6. Is it necessary for the company to continually invest in research and development? If so, its future prospects will depend critically on the success of new products in the pipeline. For example, investors in a pharmaceutical company want to know whether the company has a strong pipeline of potential blockbuster drugs and whether those products are doing well in the required tests.

7. Are changes in laws and regulations likely to have important implications for the firm? For example, when the future of electric utilities is forecasted, it is crucial to factor in the effects of proposed regulations affecting the use of coal, nuclear, and gas-fired plants.

As a good illustration of the need to look beyond the numbers, consider the recent rise of Netflix. In early 2013, its stock price was right around $100 a share. Two years later in late February 2015, its shares were trading at $483. Although Netflix's financial statements have improved over time, the rapid improvement in the company's stock price is mostly due to dramatic positive shifts in the market's expectations regarding its future prospects. Investors have been impressed with the company's ability to successfully take advantage of changing technology, as an increased number of households have used Netflix to access movies directly through streaming video. Netflix has also greatly benefited from the creation of its own content, most notably its *House of Cards* and *Orange Is the New Black* series; both have been incredibly well received. At the same time, Netflix's future success is far from guaranteed. The company continues to confront (and hopefully take advantage of) ever-changing technology and stiff competition from on-demand offerings from cable companies and from other sources, such as Apple's iTunes. It will be interesting for both consumers and Netflix's shareholders to see how this plays out in the years ahead.

## Self Test

What are some qualitative factors that analysts should consider when evaluating a company's likely future financial performance?

# TYING IT ALL TOGETHER

In the last chapter, we discussed the key financial statements; and in this one, we described how ratios are used to analyze the statements to identify weaknesses that need to be strengthened to maximize the stock price. Ratios are grouped into five categories:

- Liquidity
- Asset management
- Debt management
- Profitability
- Market value

The firm's ratios are compared with averages for its industry and with the leading firms in the industry (benchmarking), and these comparisons are used to help formulate policies that will lead to improved future performance. Similarly, the firm's own ratios can be analyzed over time to see if its financial situation is getting better or worse (trend analysis).

The single most important ratio over which management has control is the ROE—the other ratios are also important, but mainly because they affect the ROE. One tool used to show how ROE is determined is the DuPont equation: ROE = Profit margin × Total assets turnover × Equity multiplier. If the firm's ROE is below the industry average and that of the benchmark companies, a DuPont analysis can help identify problem areas that should be strengthened. In later chapters, we consider specific actions that can be taken to improve ROE and thus a firm's stock price. One closing note: Although ratio analysis is useful, it must be applied with care and good judgment. Actions taken to improve one ratio can have negative effects on other ratios. For example, it might be possible to improve the ROE by using more debt, but the risk of the additional debt may lead to a decrease in the P/E ratio and thus in the firm's stock price. Quantitative analysis such as ratio analysis can be useful, but thinking through the results is even more important.

## Self-Test Questions and Problems

(Solutions Appear in Appendix A)

ST-1    **KEY TERMS**   Define each of the following terms:
   a. Liquid asset
   b. Liquidity ratios: current ratio; quick (acid test) ratio
   c. Asset management ratios: inventory turnover ratio; days sales outstanding (DSO); fixed assets turnover ratio; total assets turnover ratio
   d. Debt management ratios: total debt to total capital; times-interest-earned (TIE) ratio
   e. Profitability ratios: operating margin; profit margin; return on total assets (ROA); return on common equity (ROE); return on invested capital (ROIC); basic earning power (BEP) ratio
   f. Market value ratios: price/earnings (P/E) ratio; market/book (M/B) ratio
   g. DuPont equation; benchmarking; trend analysis
   h. "Window dressing" techniques

ST-2    **TOTAL DEBT TO TOTAL CAPITAL**   Last year K. Billingsworth & Co. had earnings per share of $4 and dividends per share of $2. Total retained earnings increased by $12 million during the year, while book value per share at year-end was $40. Billingsworth has no preferred stock, and no new common stock was issued during the year. If its year-end total debt was $120 million, what was the company's year-end total debt to total capital ratio?

**ST-3**    **RATIO ANALYSIS**   The following data apply to A.L. Kaiser & Company (millions of dollars):

| | |
|---|---|
| Cash and equivalents | $ 100.00 |
| Fixed assets | 283.50 |
| Sales | 1,000.00 |
| Net income | 50.00 |
| Current liabilities | 105.50 |
| Notes payable to bank | 20.00 |
| Current ratio | 3.00× |
| DSO[a] | 40.55 days |
| ROE | 12.00% |

[a]This calculation is based on a 365-day year.

Kaiser has no preferred stock—only common equity, current liabilities, and long-term debt.

a.  Find Kaiser's (1) accounts receivable, (2) current assets, (3) total assets, (4) ROA, (5) common equity, (6) quick ratio, and (7) long-term debt.

b.  In part a, you should have found that Kaiser's accounts receivable (A/R) = $111.1 million. If Kaiser could reduce its DSO from 40.55 days to 30.4 days while holding other things constant, how much cash would it generate? If this cash were used to buy back common stock (at book value), thus reducing common equity, how would this affect (1) the ROE, (2) the ROA, and (3) the total debt/total capital ratio?

# Questions

**4-1**    Financial ratio analysis is conducted by three main groups of analysts: credit analysts, stock analysts, and managers. What is the primary emphasis of each group, and how would that emphasis affect the ratios on which they focus?

**4-2**    Why would the inventory turnover ratio be more important for someone analyzing a grocery store chain than an insurance company?

**4-3**    Over the past year, M.D. Ryngaert & Co. had an increase in its current ratio and a decline in its total assets turnover ratio. However, the company's sales, cash and equivalents, DSO, and fixed assets turnover ratio remained constant. What balance sheet accounts must have changed to produce the indicated changes?

**4-4**    Profit margins and turnover ratios vary from one industry to another. What differences would you expect to find between the turnover ratios, profit margins, and DuPont equations for a grocery chain and a steel company?

**4-5**    How does inflation distort ratio analysis comparisons for one company over time (trend analysis) and for different companies that are being compared? Are only balance sheet items or both balance sheet and income statement items affected?

**4-6**    If a firm's ROE is low and management wants to improve it, explain how using more debt might help.

**4-7**    Give some examples that illustrate how (a) seasonal factors and (b) different growth rates might distort a comparative ratio analysis. How might these problems be alleviated?

**4-8**    Why is it sometimes misleading to compare a company's financial ratios with those of other firms that operate in the same industry?

**4-9**    Suppose you were comparing a discount merchandiser with a high-end merchandiser. Suppose further that both companies had identical ROEs. If you applied the DuPont equation to both firms, would you expect the three components to be the same for each company? If not, explain what balance sheet and income statement items might lead to the component differences.

**4-10** Refer to an online finance source such as Yahoo! Finance or Google Finance to look up the P/E ratios for Verizon Communications and Walmart. Which company has the higher P/E ratio? What factors could explain this?

**4-11** Differentiate between ROE and ROIC.

**4-12** Indicate the effects of the transactions listed in the following table on total current assets, current ratio, and net income. Use (+) to indicate an increase, (−) to indicate a decrease, and (0) to indicate either no effect or an indeterminate effect. Be prepared to state any necessary assumptions and assume an initial current ratio of more than 1.0. (Note: A good accounting background is necessary to answer some of these questions; if yours is not strong, answer the questions you can.)

|  | | Total Current Assets | Current Ratio | Effect on Net Income |
|---|---|---|---|---|
| a. | Cash is acquired through issuance of additional common stock. | _____ | _____ | _____ |
| b. | Merchandise is sold for cash. | _____ | _____ | _____ |
| c. | Federal income tax due for the previous year is paid. | _____ | _____ | _____ |
| d. | A fixed asset is sold for less than book value. | _____ | _____ | _____ |
| e. | A fixed asset is sold for more than book value. | _____ | _____ | _____ |
| f. | Merchandise is sold on credit. | _____ | _____ | _____ |
| g. | Payment is made to trade creditors for previous purchases. | _____ | _____ | _____ |
| h. | A cash dividend is declared and paid. | _____ | _____ | _____ |
| i. | Cash is obtained through short-term bank loans. | _____ | _____ | _____ |
| j. | Short-term notes receivable are sold at a discount. | _____ | _____ | _____ |
| k. | Marketable securities are sold below cost. | _____ | _____ | _____ |
| l. | Advances are made to employees. | _____ | _____ | _____ |
| m. | Current operating expenses are paid. | _____ | _____ | _____ |
| n. | Short-term promissory notes are issued to trade creditors in exchange for past due accounts payable. | _____ | _____ | _____ |
| o. | 10-year notes are issued to pay off accounts payable. | _____ | _____ | _____ |
| p. | A fully depreciated asset is retired. | _____ | _____ | _____ |
| q. | Accounts receivable are collected. | _____ | _____ | _____ |
| r. | Equipment is purchased with short-term notes. | _____ | _____ | _____ |
| s. | Merchandise is purchased on credit. | _____ | _____ | _____ |
| t. | The estimated taxes payable are increased. | _____ | _____ | _____ |

# Problems

**Easy Problems 1–6**

**4-1** **DAYS SALES OUTSTANDING** Baxley Brothers has a DSO of 23 days, and its annual sales are $3,650,000. What is its accounts receivable balance? Assume that it uses a 365-day year.

**4-2** **DEBT TO CAPITAL RATIO** Kaye's Kitchenware has a market/book ratio equal to 1. Its stock price is $12 per share and it has 4.8 million shares outstanding. The firm's total capital is $110 million and it finances with only debt and common equity. What is its debt-to-capital ratio?

**4-3** **DuPONT ANALYSIS** Henderson's Hardware has an ROA of 11%, a 6% profit margin, and an ROE of 23%. What is its total assets turnover? What is its equity multiplier?

**4-4** **MARKET/BOOK RATIO** Edelman Engines has $17 billion in total assets. Its balance sheet shows $1.7 billion in current liabilities, $10.2 billion in long-term debt, and $5.1 billion in common equity. It has 300 million shares of common stock outstanding, and its stock price is $20 per share. What is Edelman's market/book ratio?

**4-5** **PRICE/EARNINGS RATIO** A company has an EPS of $2.40, a book value per share of $21.84, and a market/book ratio of 2.7×. What is its P/E ratio?

**4-6** **DuPONT AND ROE** A firm has a profit margin of 3% and an equity multiplier of 1.9. Its sales are $150 million, and it has total assets of $60 million. What is its ROE?

**4-7**   **ROE AND ROIC**   Baker Industries's net income is $24,000, its interest expense is $5,000, and its tax rate is 40%. Its notes payable equals $27,000, long-term debt equals $75,000, and common equity equals $250,000. The firm finances with only debt and common equity, so it has no preferred stock. What are the firm's ROE and ROIC?

**4-8**   **DuPONT AND NET INCOME**   Precious Metal Mining has $17 million in sales, its ROE is 17%, and its total assets turnover is 3.2×. Common equity on the firm's balance sheet is 50% of its total assets. What is its net income?

**4-9**   **BEP, ROE, AND ROIC**   Broward Manufacturing recently reported the following information:

| | |
|---|---|
| Net income | $615,000 |
| ROA | 10% |
| Interest expense | $202,950 |
| Accounts payable and accruals | $950,000 |

Broward's tax rate is 30%. Broward finances with only debt and common equity, so it has no preferred stock. 40% of its total invested capital is debt, and 60% of its total invested capital is common equity. Calculate its basic earning power (BEP), its return on equity (ROE), and its return on invested capital (ROIC).

**4-10**   **M/B AND SHARE PRICE**   You are given the following information: Stockholders' equity as reported on the firm's balance sheet = $6.5 billion, price/earnings ratio = 9, common shares outstanding = 180 million, and market/book ratio = 2.0. Calculate the price of a share of the company's common stock.

**4-11**   **RATIO CALCULATIONS**   Assume the following relationships for the Caulder Corp.:

| | |
|---|---|
| Sales/Total assets | 1.3× |
| Return on assets (ROA) | 4.0% |
| Return on equity (ROE) | 8.0% |

Calculate Caulder's profit margin and debt-to-capital ratio assuming the firm uses only debt and common equity, so total assets equal total invested capital.

**4-12**   **RATIO CALCULATIONS**   Thomson Trucking has $16 billion in assets, and its tax rate is 40%. Its basic earning power (BEP) ratio is 10%, and its return on assets (ROA) is 5%. What is its times-interest-earned (TIE) ratio?

**4-13**   **TIE AND ROIC RATIOS**   The W.C. Pruett Corp. has $600,000 of interest-bearing debt outstanding, and it pays an annual interest rate of 7%. In addition, it has $600,000 of common stock on its balance sheet. It finances with only debt and common equity, so it has no preferred stock. Its annual sales are $2.7 million, its average tax rate is 35%, and its profit margin is 7%. What are its TIE ratio and its return on invested capital (ROIC)?

**4-14**   **RETURN ON EQUITY**   Pacific Packaging's ROE last year was only 5%; but its management has developed a new operating plan that calls for a debt-to-capital ratio of 40%, which will result in annual interest charges of $561,000. The firm has no plans to use preferred stock and total assets equal total invested capital. Management projects an EBIT of $1,258,000 on sales of $17,000,000, and it expects to have a total assets turnover ratio of 2.1. Under these conditions, the tax rate will be 35%. If the changes are made, what will be the company's return on equity?

**4-15**   **RETURN ON EQUITY AND QUICK RATIO**   Lloyd Inc. has sales of $200,000, a net income of $15,000, and the following balance sheet:

| | | | |
|---|---|---|---|
| Cash | $ 10,000 | Accounts payable | $ 30,000 |
| Receivables | 50,000 | Notes payable to bank | 20,000 |
| Inventories | 150,000 | Total current liabilities | $ 50,000 |
| Total current assets | $210,000 | Long-term debt | 50,000 |
| Net fixed assets | 90,000 | Common equity | 200,000 |
| Total assets | $300,000 | Total liabilities and equity | $300,000 |

The new owner thinks that inventories are excessive and can be lowered to the point where the current ratio is equal to the industry average, 2.5×, without affecting sales or net income. If inventories are sold and not replaced (thus reducing the current ratio to 2.5×); if the funds generated are used to reduce common equity (stock can be repurchased at book value); and if no other changes occur, by how much will the ROE change? What will be the firm's new quick ratio?

**4-16** **RETURN ON EQUITY** Commonwealth Construction (CC) needs $3 million of assets to get started, and it expects to have a basic earning power ratio of 35%. CC will own no securities, so all of its income will be operating income. If it so chooses, CC can finance up to 30% of its assets with debt, which will have an 8% interest rate. If it chooses to use debt, the firm will finance using only debt and common equity, so no preferred stock will be used. Assuming a 40% tax rate on all taxable income, what is the *difference* between CC's expected ROE if it finances these assets with 30% debt versus its expected ROE if it finances these assets entirely with common stock?

**4-17** **CONCEPTUAL: RETURN ON EQUITY** Which of the following statements is most correct? (Hint: Work Problem 4-16 before answering 4-17, and consider the solution setup for 4-16 as you think about 4-17.)

a. If a firm's expected basic earning power (BEP) is constant for all of its assets and exceeds the interest rate on its debt, adding assets and financing them with debt will raise the firm's expected return on common equity (ROE).
b. The higher a firm's tax rate, the lower its BEP ratio, other things held constant.
c. The higher the interest rate on a firm's debt, the lower its BEP ratio, other things held constant.
d. The higher a firm's debt ratio, the lower its BEP ratio, other things held constant.
e. Statement a is false; but statements b, c, and d are true.

**4-18** **TIE RATIO** MPI Incorporated has $6 billion in assets, and its tax rate is 35%. Its basic earning power (BEP) ratio is 11%, and its return on assets (ROA) is 6%. What is MPI's times-interest-earned (TIE) ratio?

**4-19** **CURRENT RATIO** The Stewart Company has $2,392,500 in current assets and $1,076,625 in current liabilities. Its initial inventory level is $526,350, and it will raise funds as additional notes payable and use them to increase inventory. How much can its short-term debt (notes payable) increase without pushing its current ratio below 2.0?

**Challenging Problems 20–24**

**4-20** **DSO AND ACCOUNTS RECEIVABLE** Ingraham Inc. currently has $205,000 in accounts receivable, and its days sales outstanding (DSO) is 71 days. It wants to reduce its DSO to 20 days by pressuring more of its customers to pay their bills on time. If this policy is adopted, the company's average sales will fall by 15%. What will be the level of accounts receivable following the change? Assume a 365-day year.

**4-21** **P/E AND STOCK PRICE** Ferrell Inc. recently reported net income of $8 million. It has 540,000 shares of common stock, which currently trades at $21 a share. Ferrell continues to expand and anticipates that 1 year from now, its net income will be $13.2 million. Over the next year, it also anticipates issuing an additional 81,000 shares of stock so that 1 year from now it will have 621,000 shares of common stock. Assuming Ferrell's price/earnings ratio remains at its current level, what will be its stock price 1 year from now?

**4-22** **BALANCE SHEET ANALYSIS** Complete the balance sheet and sales information using the following financial data:

Total assets turnover: 1.5×

Days sales outstanding: 36.5 days[a]

Inventory turnover ratio: 5×

Fixed assets turnover: 3.0×

Current ratio: 2.0×

Gross profit margin on sales: (Sales − Cost of goods sold)/Sales = 25%

[a]Calculation is based on a 365-day year.

## Balance Sheet

| | | | |
|---|---|---|---|
| Cash | | Current liabilities | |
| Accounts receivable | | Long-term debt | 60,000 |
| Inventories | | Common stock | |
| Fixed assets | | Retained earnings | 97,500 |
| Total assets | $300,000 | Total liabilities and equity | |
| Sales | | Cost of goods sold | |

**4-23** **RATIO ANALYSIS** Data for Barry Computer Co. and its industry averages follow.

a. Calculate the indicated ratios for Barry.
b. Construct the DuPont equation for both Barry and the industry.
c. Outline Barry's strengths and weaknesses as revealed by your analysis.
d. Suppose Barry had doubled its sales as well as its inventories, accounts receivable, and common equity during 2016. How would that information affect the validity of your ratio analysis? (Hint: Think about averages and the effects of rapid growth on ratios if averages are not used. No calculations are needed.)

### Barry Computer Company:
### Balance Sheet as of December 31, 2016 (in Thousands)

| | | | |
|---|---|---|---|
| Cash | $ 77,500 | Accounts payable | $129,000 |
| Receivables | 336,000 | Other current liabilities | 117,000 |
| Inventories | 241,500 | Notes payable to bank | 84,000 |
| Total current assets | $655,000 | Total current liabilities | $330,000 |
| | | Long-term debt | 256,500 |
| Net fixed assets | 292,500 | Common equity | 361,000 |
| Total assets | $947,500 | Total liabilities and equity | $947,500 |

### Barry Computer Company: Income Statement for Year Ended
### December 31, 2016 (in Thousands)

| | | |
|---|---|---|
| Sales | | $1,607,500 |
| Cost of goods sold | | |
| Materials | $717,000 | |
| Labor | 453,000 | |
| Heat, light, and power | 68,000 | |
| Indirect labor | 113,000 | |
| Depreciation | 41,500 | 1,392,500 |
| Gross profit | | $ 215,000 |
| Selling expenses | | 115,000 |
| General and administrative expenses | | 30,000 |
| Earnings before interest and taxes (EBIT) | | $ 70,000 |
| Interest expense | | 24,500 |
| Earnings before taxes (EBT) | | $ 45,500 |
| Federal and state income taxes (40%) | | 18,200 |
| Net income | | $ 27,300 |

| Ratio | Barry | Industry Average |
|---|---|---|
| Current | _____ | 2.0× |
| Quick | _____ | 1.3× |
| Days sales outstanding[a] | _____ | 35 days |
| Inventory turnover | _____ | 6.7× |
| Total assets turnover | _____ | 3.0× |
| Profit margin | _____ | 1.2% |
| ROA | _____ | 3.6% |
| ROE | _____ | 9.0% |
| ROIC | _____ | 7.5% |
| TIE | _____ | 3.0× |
| Debt/Total capital | _____ | 47.0% |

[a]Calculation is based on a 365-day year.

4-24 **DuPONT ANALYSIS** A firm has been experiencing low profitability in recent years. Perform an analysis of the firm's financial position using the DuPont equation. The firm has no lease payments but has a $2 million sinking fund payment on its debt. The most recent industry average ratios and the firm's financial statements are as follows:

### Industry Average Ratios

| | | | |
|---|---|---|---|
| Current ratio | 3× | Fixed assets turnover | 6× |
| Debt-to-capital ratio | 20% | Total assets turnover | 3× |
| Times interest earned | 7× | Profit margin | 3% |
| EBITDA coverage | 9× | Return on total assets | 9% |
| Inventory turnover | 10× | Return on common equity | 12.86% |
| Days sales outstanding[a] | 24 days | Return on invested capital | 11.50% |

[a]Calculation is based on a 365-day year.

### Balance Sheet as of December 31, 2016 (Millions of Dollars)

| | | | |
|---|---|---|---|
| Cash and equivalents | $ 78 | Accounts payable | $ 45 |
| Accounts receivable | 66 | Other current liabilities | 11 |
| Inventories | 159 | Notes payable | 29 |
| Total current assets | $303 | Total current liabilities | $ 85 |
| | | Long-term debt | 50 |
| | | Total liabilities | $135 |
| Gross fixed assets | 225 | Common stock | 114 |
| Less depreciation | 78 | Retained earnings | 201 |
| Net fixed assets | $147 | Total stockholders' equity | $315 |
| Total assets | $450 | Total liabilities and equity | $450 |

### Income Statement for Year Ended December 31, 2016 (Millions of Dollars)

| | |
|---|---|
| Net sales | $795.0 |
| Cost of goods sold | 660.0 |
| Gross profit | $135.0 |
| Selling expenses | 73.5 |
| EBITDA | $ 61.5 |
| Depreciation expense | 12.0 |
| Earnings before interest and taxes (EBIT) | $ 49.5 |
| Interest expense | 4.5 |
| Earnings before taxes (EBT) | $ 45.0 |
| Taxes (40%) | 18.0 |
| Net income | $ 27.0 |

a. Calculate the ratios you think would be useful in this analysis.

b. Construct a DuPont equation, and compare the company's ratios to the industry average ratios.

c. Do the balance sheet accounts or the income statement figures seem to be primarily responsible for the low profits?

d. Which specific accounts seem to be most out of line relative to other firms in the industry?

e. If the firm had a pronounced seasonal sales pattern or if it grew rapidly during the year, how might that affect the validity of your ratio analysis? How might you correct for such potential problems?

# Comprehensive/Spreadsheet Problem

4-25    **RATIO ANALYSIS**  The Corrigan Corporation's 2015 and 2016 financial statements follow, along with some industry average ratios.

a. Assess Corrigan's liquidity position, and determine how it compares with peers and how the liquidity position has changed over time.

b. Assess Corrigan's asset management position, and determine how it compares with peers and how its asset management efficiency has changed over time.

c. Assess Corrigan's debt management position, and determine how it compares with peers and how its debt management has changed over time.

d. Assess Corrigan's profitability ratios, and determine how they compare with peers and how its profitability position has changed over time.

e. Assess Corrigan's market value ratios, and determine how its valuation compares with peers and how it has changed over time.

f. Calculate Corrigan's ROE as well as the industry average ROE, using the DuPont equation. From this analysis, how does Corrigan's financial position compare with the industry average numbers?

g. What do you think would happen to its ratios if the company initiated cost-cutting measures that allowed it to hold lower levels of inventory and substantially decreased the cost of goods sold? No calculations are necessary. Think about which ratios would be affected by changes in these two accounts.

### Corrigan Corporation: Balance Sheets as of December 31

|  | 2016 | 2015 |
|---|---|---|
| Cash | $    72,000 | $    65,000 |
| Accounts receivable | 439,000 | 328,000 |
| Inventories | 894,000 | 813,000 |
| Total current assets | $1,405,000 | $1,206,000 |
| Land and building | 238,000 | 271,000 |
| Machinery | 132,000 | 133,000 |
| Other fixed assets | 61,000 | 57,000 |
| Total assets | $1,836,000 | $1,667,000 |
|  |  |  |
| Accounts payable | $    80,000 | $    72,708 |
| Accrued liabilities | 45,010 | 40,880 |
| Notes payable | 476,990 | 457,912 |
| Total current liabilities | $  602,000 | $  571,500 |
| Long-term debt | 404,290 | 258,898 |
| Common stock | 575,000 | 575,000 |
| Retained earnings | 254,710 | 261,602 |
| Total liabilities and equity | $1,836,000 | $1,667,000 |

## Corrigan Corporation: Income Statements for Years Ending December 31

|  | 2016 | 2015 |
|---|---|---|
| Sales | $4,240,000 | $3,635,000 |
| Cost of goods sold | 3,680,000 | 2,980,000 |
| Gross operating profit | $ 560,000 | $ 655,000 |
| General administrative and selling expenses | 303,320 | 297,550 |
| Depreciation | 159,000 | 154,500 |
| EBIT | $ 97,680 | $ 202,950 |
| Interest | 67,000 | 43,000 |
| Earnings before taxes (EBT) | $ 30,680 | $ 159,950 |
| Taxes (40%) | 12,272 | 63,980 |
| Net income | $ 18,408 | $ 95,970 |

## Per-Share Data

|  | 2016 | 2015 |
|---|---|---|
| EPS | $ 0.80 | $ 4.17 |
| Cash dividends | $ 1.10 | $ 0.95 |
| Market price (average) | $12.34 | $23.57 |
| P/E ratio | 15.42× | 5.65× |
| Number of shares outstanding | 23,000 | 23,000 |

## Industry Financial Ratios[a]

|  | 2016 |
|---|---|
| Current ratio | 2.7× |
| Inventory turnover[b] | 7.0× |
| Days sales outstanding[c] | 32.0 days |
| Fixed assets turnover[b] | 13.0× |
| Total assets turnover[b] | 2.6× |
| Return on assets | 9.1% |
| Return on equity | 18.2% |
| Return on invested capital | 14.5% |
| Profit margin | 3.5% |
| Debt-to-capital ratio | 50.0% |
| P/E ratio | 6.0× |

[a]Industry average ratios have been constant for the past 4 years.
[b]Based on year-end balance sheet figures.
[c]Calculation is based on a 365-day year.

## INTEGRATED CASE

### D'LEON INC., PART II

**4-26**  **FINANCIAL STATEMENTS AND TAXES**  Part I of this case, presented in Chapter 3, discussed the situation of D'Leon Inc., a regional snack foods producer, after an expansion program. D'Leon had increased plant capacity and undertaken a major marketing campaign in an attempt to "go national." Thus far, sales have not been up to the forecasted level; costs have been higher than were projected; and a large loss occurred in 2016 rather than the expected profit. As a result, its managers, directors, and investors are concerned about the firm's survival.

Donna Jamison was brought in as assistant to Fred Campo, D'Leon's chairman, who had the task of getting the company back into a sound financial position. D'Leon's 2015 and 2016 balance sheets and income statements, together with projections for 2017, are given in Tables IC 4.1 and IC 4.2. In addition, Table IC 4.3 gives the company's 2015 and 2016 financial ratios, together with industry average data. The 2017 projected financial statement data represent Jamison's and Campo's best guess for 2017 results, assuming that some new financing is arranged to get the company "over the hump."

Jamison examined monthly data for 2016 (not given in the case), and she detected an improving pattern during the year. Monthly sales were rising, costs were falling, and large losses in the early months had turned to a small profit by December. Thus, the annual data look somewhat worse than final monthly data. Also, it appears to be taking longer for the advertising program to get the message out, for the new sales offices to generate sales, and for the new manufacturing facilities to operate efficiently. In other words, the lags between spending money and deriving benefits were longer than D'Leon's managers had anticipated. For these reasons, Jamison and Campo see hope for the company—provided it can survive in the short run.

Jamison must prepare an analysis of where the company is now, what it must do to regain its financial health, and what actions should be taken. Your assignment is to help her answer the following questions. Provide clear explanations, not yes or no answers.

a.  Why are ratios useful? What are the five major categories of ratios?

b.  Calculate D'Leon's 2017 current and quick ratios based on the projected balance sheet and income statement data. What can you say about the company's liquidity positions in 2015, in 2016, and as projected for 2017? We often think of ratios as being useful (1) to managers to help run the business, (2) to bankers for credit analysis, and (3) to stockholders for stock valuation. Would these different types of analysts have an equal interest in the company's liquidity ratios? Explain your answer.

c.  Calculate the 2017 inventory turnover, days sales outstanding (DSO), fixed assets turnover, and total assets turnover. How does D'Leon's utilization of assets stack up against other firms in the industry?

d.  Calculate the 2017 debt-to-capital and times-interest-earned ratios. How does D'Leon compare with the industry with respect to financial leverage? What can you conclude from these ratios?

e.  Calculate the 2017 operating margin, profit margin, basic earning power (BEP), return on assets (ROA), return on equity (ROE), and return on invested capital (ROIC). What can you say about these ratios?

f.  Calculate the 2017 price/earnings ratio and market/book ratio. Do these ratios indicate that investors are expected to have a high or low opinion of the company?

g.  Use the DuPont equation to provide a summary and overview of D'Leon's financial condition as projected for 2017. What are the firm's major strengths and weaknesses?

h.  Use the following simplified 2017 balance sheet to show, in general terms, how an improvement in the DSO would tend to affect the stock price. For example, if the company could improve its collection procedures and thereby lower its DSO from 45.6 days to the 32-day industry average without affecting sales, how would that change "ripple through" the financial statements (shown in thousands below) and influence the stock price?

| | | | |
|---|---|---|---|
| Accounts receivable | $ 878 | Current liabilities | $ 845 |
| Other current assets | 1,802 | Debt | 700 |
| Net fixed assets | 817 | Equity | 1,952 |
| Total assets | $3,497 | Liabilities plus equity | $3,497 |

i. Does it appear that inventories could be adjusted? If so, how should that adjustment affect D'Leon's profitability and stock price?

j. In 2016, the company paid its suppliers much later than the due dates; also, it was not maintaining financial ratios at levels called for in its bank loan agreements. Therefore, suppliers could cut the company off, and its bank could refuse to renew the loan when it comes due in 90 days. On the basis of data provided, would you, as a credit manager, continue to sell to D'Leon on credit? (You could demand cash on delivery—that is, sell on terms of COD—but that might cause D'Leon to stop buying from your company.) Similarly, if you were the bank loan officer, would you recommend renewing the loan or demanding its repayment? Would your actions be influenced if, in early 2017, D'Leon showed you its 2017 projections along with proof that it was going to raise more than $1.2 million of new equity?

k. In hindsight, what should D'Leon have done in 2015?

l. What are some potential problems and limitations of financial ratio analysis?

m. What are some qualitative factors that analysts should consider when evaluating a company's likely future financial performance?

**Balance Sheets**     **TABLE IC 4.1**

| | 2017E | 2016 | 2015 |
|---|---|---|---|
| **Assets** | | | |
| Cash | $ 85,632 | $ 7,282 | $ 57,600 |
| Accounts receivable | 878,000 | 632,160 | 351,200 |
| Inventories | 1,716,480 | 1,287,360 | 715,200 |
| Total current assets | $2,680,112 | $1,926,802 | $1,124,000 |
| Gross fixed assets | 1,197,160 | 1,202,950 | 491,000 |
| Less accumulated depreciation | 380,120 | 263,160 | 146,200 |
| Net fixed assets | $ 817,040 | $ 939,790 | $ 344,800 |
| Total assets | $3,497,152 | $2,866,592 | $1,468,800 |
| **Liabilities and Equity** | | | |
| Accounts payable | $ 436,800 | $ 524,160 | $ 145,600 |
| Accruals | 408,000 | 489,600 | 136,000 |
| Notes payable | 300,000 | 636,808 | 200,000 |
| Total current liabilities | $1,144,800 | $1,650,568 | $ 481,600 |
| Long-term debt | 400,000 | 723,432 | 323,432 |
| Common stock | 1,721,176 | 460,000 | 460,000 |
| Retained earnings | 231,176 | 32,592 | 203,768 |
| Total equity | $1,952,352 | $ 492,592 | $ 663,768 |
| Total liabilities and equity | $3,497,152 | $2,866,592 | $1,468,800 |

Note: E indicates estimated. The 2017 data are forecasts.

**TABLE IC 4.2**  Income Statements

|  | 2017E | 2016 | 2015 |
|---|---|---|---|
| Sales | $7,035,600 | $6,034,000 | $3,432,000 |
| Cost of goods sold | 5,875,992 | 5,528,000 | 2,864,000 |
| Other expenses | 550,000 | 519,988 | 358,672 |
| Total operating costs excluding depreciation and amortization | $6,425,992 | $ 6,047,988 | $3,222,672 |
| EBITDA | $ 609,608 | ($ 13,988) | $ 209,328 |
| Depreciation & amortization | 116,960 | 116,960 | 18,900 |
| EBIT | $ 492,648 | ($ 130,948) | $ 190,428 |
| Interest expense | 70,008 | 136,012 | 43,828 |
| EBT | $ 422,640 | ($ 266,960) | $ 146,600 |
| Taxes (40%) | 169,056 | (106,784)[a] | 58,640 |
| Net income | $ 253,584 | ($ 160,176) | $ 87,960 |
|  |  |  |  |
| EPS | $ 1.014 | ($ 1.602) | $ 0.880 |
| DPS | $ 0.220 | $ 0.110 | $ 0.220 |
| Book value per share | $ 7.809 | $ 4.926 | $ 6.638 |
| Stock price | $ 12.17 | $ 2.25 | $ 8.50 |
| Shares outstanding | 250,000 | 100,000 | 100,000 |
| Tax rate | 40.00% | 40.00% | 40.00% |
| Lease payments | $40,000 | $40,000 | $40,000 |
| Sinking fund payments | 0 | 0 | 0 |

Note: E indicates estimated. The 2017 data are forecasts.
[a]The firm had sufficient taxable income in 2014 and 2015 to obtain its full tax refund in 2016.

**TABLE IC 4.3**  Ratio Analysis

|  | 2017E | 2016 | 2015 | Industry Average |
|---|---|---|---|---|
| Current | | 1.2× | 2.3× | 2.7× |
| Quick | | 0.4× | 0.8× | 1.0× |
| Inventory turnover | | 4.7× | 4.8× | 6.1× |
| Days sales outstanding (DSO)[a] | | 38.2 | 37.4 | 32.0 |
| Fixed assets turnover | | 6.4× | 10.0× | 7.0× |
| Total assets turnover | | 2.1× | 2.3× | 2.6× |
| Debt-to-capital ratio | | 73.4% | 44.1% | 40.0% |
| TIE | | −1.0× | 4.3× | 6.2× |
| Operating margin | | −2.2% | 5.5% | 7.3% |
| Profit margin | | −2.7% | 2.6% | 3.5% |
| Basic earning power | | −4.6% | 13.0% | 19.1% |
| ROA | | −5.6% | 6.0% | 9.1% |
| ROE | | −32.5% | 13.3% | 18.2% |
| ROIC | | −4.2% | 9.6% | 14.5% |
| Price/earnings | | −1.4× | 9.7× | 14.2× |
| Market/book | | 0.5× | 1.3× | 2.4× |
| Book value per share | | $4.93 | $6.64 | n.a. |

Note: E indicates estimated. The 2017 data are forecasts.
[a]Calculation is based on a 365-day year.

# TAKING A CLOSER LOOK

## CONDUCTING A FINANCIAL RATIO ANALYSIS ON HEWLETT PACKARD CO.

*Use online resources to work on this chapter's questions. Please note that website information changes over time, and these changes may limit your ability to answer some of these questions.*

In Chapter 3, we looked at Whole Foods' financial statements. In this chapter, we will use financial Internet websites (specifically, www.morningstar.com and www.google.com/finance) to analyze Hewlett Packard Co. Once on either website, you simply enter Hewlett Packard's ticker symbol (HPQ) to obtain the financial information needed.

The text mentions that financial statement analysis has two major components: a trend analysis, where we evaluate changes in key ratios over time, and a peer analysis, where we compare financial ratios with firms that are in the same industry and/or line of business. We will do both of these types of analysis in this problem.

Through the Morningstar website, you can find the firm's financials (Income Statement, Balance Sheet, and Cash Flow) on an annual or quarterly basis for the 5 most recent time periods. In addition, the site contains Key Ratios (Profitability, Growth, Cash Flow, Financial Health, and Efficiency) for 10 years. We will use the Key Ratios on this site to conduct the firm's trend analysis. (At the bottom of the screen you will see that you can click "Glossary" to find definitions for the different ratios. For example, Morningstar's Financial Leverage ratio is the same as the Equity multiplier that we use in the textbook.)

On the Google Finance site, you can find the firm's financial statements for the 4 most recent years or the five most recent quarters and key financial data for related companies for the most recent year or quarter. We will use the related companies' annual data to conduct the firm's peer analysis. Notice that when you go to the "Related Companies" screen, you can "add or remove columns." Click on that phrase, and you can check which peer data items you'd like to show on the computer screen. Also, once you have chosen the data, you can click on a term, and the companies will be ranked in either ascending or descending order for the specific term selected.

## DISCUSSION QUESTIONS

1. Looking at Morningstar's Financial Health ratios, what has happened to Hewlett Packard's liquidity position over the past 10 years?

2. Looking at Morningstar's Financial Health ratios, what has happened to Hewlett Packard's financial leverage position over the past 10 years?

3. Looking at Morningstar's Profitability ratios, what has happened to Hewlett Packard's profit margin (net margin %) over the past 10 years? What has happened to its return on assets (ROA) and return on equity (ROE) over the past 10 years?

4. Identify Google Finance's list of related companies to Hewlett Packard. Which is the largest in terms of market capitalization? Which is the smallest? Where does Hewlett Packard rank (in terms of market capitalization)?

5. From the Google Finance site, look at Hewlett Packard's liquidity position (as measured by its current ratio). How does this ratio compare with those of its peers?

6. From the Google Finance site, look at Hewlett Packard's profitability ratios (as measured by its profit margin, ROA, and ROE). How do these ratios compare with those of its peers?

7. From the Google Finance site, use the DuPont analysis to determine the total assets turnover ratio for each of the peer companies. (Hint: ROA = Profit margin × Total assets turnover.) Once you've calculated each peer's total assets turnover ratio, then you can use the DuPont analysis to calculate each peer's equity multiplier.

8. From the information gained in question 7 and using the DuPont analysis, what are Hewlett Packard's strengths and weaknesses compared to those of its competitors?

# Solutions to Self-Test Questions and Problems

**ST-1** Refer to the marginal glossary definitions or relevant chapter sections to check your responses.

**ST-2** Billingsworth paid $2 in dividends and retained $2 per share. Because total retained earnings rose by $12 million, there must be 6 million shares outstanding. With a book value of $40 per share, total common equity must be $40(6 million) = $240 million. Because Billingsworth has $120 million of total debt, its total debt to total capital ratio must be 33.3%:

$$\frac{\text{Total debt}}{\text{Total debt} + \text{Equity}} = \frac{\$120 \text{ million}}{\$120 \text{ million} + \$240 \text{ million}}$$
$$= 0.333 = 33.3\%$$

**ST-3** a. In answering questions such as this, always begin by writing down the relevant definitional equations, and then start filling in numbers. Note that the extra zeros indicating millions have been deleted in the following calculations.

(1) $\text{DSO} = \dfrac{\text{Accounts receivable}}{\text{Sales}/365}$

$40.55 = \dfrac{\text{A/R}}{\text{Sales}/365}$

$\text{A/R} = 40.55(\$2.7397) = \$111.1 \text{ million}$

(2) $\text{Current ratio} = \dfrac{\text{Current assets}}{\text{Current liabilities}} = 3.0$

$= \dfrac{\text{Current assets}}{\$105.5} = 3.0$

$\text{Current assets} = 3.0(\$105.5) = \$316.50 \text{ million}$

(3) Total assets = Current assets + Fixed assets
$= \$316.5 + \$283.5 = \$600 \text{ million}$

(4) ROA = Profit margin × Total assets turnover

$= \dfrac{\text{Net income}}{\text{Sales}} \times \dfrac{\text{Sales}}{\text{Total assets}}$

$= \dfrac{\$50}{\$1,000} \times \dfrac{\$1,000}{\$600}$

$= 0.05 \times 1.667 = 0.083333 = 8.3333\%$

(5) $\text{ROE} = \text{ROA} \times \dfrac{\text{Assets}}{\text{Equity}}$

$12.0\% = 8.3333\% \times \dfrac{\$600}{\text{Equity}}$

$\text{Equity} = \dfrac{(8.3333\%)(\$600)}{12.0\%}$

$\text{Equity} = \$416.67 \text{ million}$

(6) Current assets = Cash and equivalents + Accounts receivable + Inventories
$\$316.5 = \$100.0 + \$111.1 + \text{Inventories}$
Inventories = $105.4 million

$\text{Quick ratio} = \dfrac{\text{Current assets} - \text{Inventories}}{\text{Current liabilities}}$

$= \dfrac{\$316.5 - \$105.4}{\$105.5} = 2.00$

(7) Total assets = Total claims = \$600 million

$$\text{Current liabilities} + \text{Long-term debt} + \text{Equity} = \$600 \text{ million}$$
$$\$105.5 + \text{Long-term debt} + \$416.67 = \$600 \text{ million}$$
$$\text{Long-term debt} = \$600 - \$105.5 - \$416.67 = \$77.83 \text{ million}$$

Note: We could have found equity as follows:

$$\text{ROE} = \frac{\text{Net income}}{\text{Equity}}$$

$$12.0\% = \frac{\$50}{\text{Equity}}$$

$$\text{Equity} = \$50/0.12$$
$$\text{Equity} = \$416.67 \text{ million}$$

Then we could have gone on to find long-term debt.

b. Kaiser's average sales per day were \$1,000/365 = \$2.74 million. Its DSO was 40.55, so A/R = 40.55(\$2.74) = \$111.1 million. Its new DSO of 30.4 would cause A/R = 30.4(\$2.74) = \$83.3 million. The reduction in receivables would be \$111.1 − \$83.3 = \$27.8 million, which would equal the amount of cash generated.

(1) New equity = Old equity − Stock bought back
= \$416.7 − \$27.8
= \$388.9 million

Thus,

$$\text{New ROE} = \frac{\text{Net income}}{\text{New equity}}$$

$$= \frac{\$50}{\$388.9}$$

$$= 12.86\% \text{ (versus old ROE of 12.0\%)}$$

(2) $$\text{New ROA} = \frac{\text{Net income}}{\text{Total assets} - \text{Reduction in A/R}}$$

$$= \frac{\$50}{\$600 - \$27.8}$$

$$= 8.74\% \text{ (versus old ROA of 8.33\%)}$$

(3) Total debt before the asset reduction is the same as total debt after the asset reduction. Neither notes payable nor long-term debt was impacted by the asset reduction. However, after the asset reduction equity has declined, so total capital has declined.

Total debt = Notes payable + Long-term debt
\$97.8 = \$20 + \$77.8

New total assets = Old total assets − Reduction in A/R
= \$600 − \$27.8
= \$572.2 million

*Before asset reduction:*

$$\begin{aligned}\text{Total capital} &= \text{Total debt} + \text{Old equity}\\ &= \$97.8 + \$416.7\\ &= \$514.5 \text{ million}\end{aligned}$$

*After asset reduction:*

$$\begin{aligned}\text{Total capital} &= \text{Total debt} + \text{New equity}\\ &= \$97.8 + \$388.9\\ &= \$486.7 \text{ million}\end{aligned}$$

Therefore,

$$\frac{\text{Total debt}}{\text{Old total capital}} = \frac{\$97.8}{\$514.5} = 19.0\%$$

and

$$\frac{\text{Total debt}}{\text{New total capital}} = \frac{\$97.8}{\$486.7} = 20.1\%$$

## Answers to Selected End-of-Chapter Problems

**4-2**  47.64%

**4-4**  M/B = 1.1765

**4-6**  ROE = 14.25%

**4-8**  NI = $451,562.50

**4-10**  $P_0$ = $72.22

**4-12**  TIE = 6.00×

**4-14**  ROE = 9.33%

**4-16**  ΔROE = +6.94%

**4-18**  TIE = 6.22×

**4-20**  Accounts receivable = $49,085

**4-22**  Sales = $450,000; AR = $45,000;
Inv = $90,000; FA = $150,000; CL = $75,000

**4-24**  a. Current ratio = 3.56×;
Debt to total capital = 20.05%;
DSO = 30.3 days; ROA = 6.00%;
ROIC = 7.54%

b. Firm: ROE = 3.4% × 1.77 × $450/$315
= 8.6%

Industry: ROE = 3.0% × 3 × ROE/ROA
= 3.0% × 3 × 12.86%/9.00%
= 12.86%

## Selected Equations and Tables

$$\text{Current ratio} = \frac{\text{Current assets}}{\text{Current liabilities}}$$

$$\text{Quick, or acid test, ratio} = \frac{\text{Current assets} - \text{Inventories}}{\text{Current liabilities}}$$

$$\text{Inventory turnover} = \frac{\text{Sales}}{\text{Inventories}}$$

$$\text{Days sales outstanding (DSO)} = \frac{\text{Receivables}}{\text{Average sales per day}} = \frac{\text{Receivables}}{\text{Annual sales}/365}$$

$$\text{Fixed assets turnover} = \frac{\text{Sales}}{\text{Net fixed assets}}$$

$$\text{Total assets turnover} = \frac{\text{Sales}}{\text{Total assets}}$$

$$\text{Total-debt-to-total-capital ratio} = \frac{\text{Total debt}}{\text{Total capital}} = \frac{\text{Total debt}}{\text{Total debt} + \text{Equity}}$$

$$\text{Total-liabilities-to-assets ratio} = \frac{\text{Total liabilities}}{\text{Total assets}}$$

$$\text{Debt-to-equity ratio} = \frac{\text{Total debt}}{\text{Equity}}$$

$$\text{Times-interest-earned (TIE)} = \frac{\text{EBIT}}{\text{Interest charges}}$$

$$\text{EBITDA coverage} = \frac{\text{EBITDA} + \text{Lease payments}}{\text{Interest} + \text{Principal payments} + \text{Lease payments}}$$

$$\text{Operating margin} = \frac{\text{EBIT}}{\text{Sales}}$$

$$\text{Profit margin} = \frac{\text{Net income}}{\text{Sales}}$$

$$\text{Return on total assets (ROA)} = \frac{\text{Net income}}{\text{Total assets}}$$

$$\text{Return on common equity (ROE)} = \frac{\text{Net income}}{\text{Common equity}}$$

$$\text{Return on invested capital (ROIC)} = \frac{\text{EBIT}(1 - T)}{\text{Total invested capital}} = \frac{\text{EBIT}(1 - T)}{\text{Debt} + \text{Equity}}$$

$$\text{Basic earning power (BEP)} = \frac{\text{EBIT}}{\text{Total assets}}$$

$$\text{Price/Earnings (P/E)} = \frac{\text{Price per share}}{\text{Earnings per share}}$$

$$\text{Book value per share} = \frac{\text{Common equity}}{\text{Shares outstanding}}$$

$$\text{Market/Book (M/B)} = \frac{\text{Market price per share}}{\text{Book value per share}}$$

$$\text{ROE} = \text{ROA} \times \text{Equity multiplier}$$

$$= \text{Profit margin} \times \text{Total assets turnover} \times \text{Equity multiplier}$$

$$= \frac{\text{Net income}}{\text{Sales}} \times \frac{\text{Sales}}{\text{Total assets}} \times \frac{\text{Total assets}}{\text{Total common equity}}$$

$$\text{EVA} = \text{Net income} - [\text{Equity} \times \text{Cost of equity}]$$

$$= (\text{Equity})[\text{Net income}/\text{Equity} - \text{Cost of equity}]$$

$$= (\text{Equity})(\text{ROE} - \text{Cost of equity})$$

# Chapter 5

# Time Value of Money

CHAPTER

Goodluz/Shutterstock.com

## Will You Be Able to Retire?

For an interesting website that looks at global savings rates, refer to **www.gfmag .com/global-data/economic-data/9161qg-household-saving-rates.**

Your reaction to that question is probably, "First things first! I'm worried about getting a job, not about retiring!" However, understanding the retirement situation can help you land a job because (1) this is an important issue today; (2) employers like to hire people who know what's happening in the real world; and (3) professors often test on the time value of money with problems related to saving for future purposes (including retirement).

A recent study by the Employee Benefit Research Institute suggests that many U.S. workers are not doing enough to prepare for retirement. The survey found that 60% of workers had less than $25,000 in savings and investments (not including the values of their homes and defined benefit plans). Equally concerning, 24% of those

surveyed said they had "no confidence" that they would be able to retire comfortably.[1] Unfortunately, there is no easy solution. In order to reach their retirement goals, many current workers will need to work longer, spend less and save more, and hopefully earn higher returns on their current savings.

Historically, many Americans have relied on Social Security as an important source of their retirement income. However, given current demographics, it is likely that this important program will need to be restructured down the road in order to maintain its viability. Although the average personal savings rate in the United States had edged up in recent years, in January 2015 it was still at a fairly low level of 5.5%.[2] In addition, the ratio of U.S. workers to

---

[1] Refer to Ruth Helman et al., "The 2015 Retirement Confidence Survey: Having a Retirement Savings Plan a Key Factor in Americans' Retirement Confidence," Employee Benefit Research Institute, no. 413, April 2015, ebri.org/pdf/briefspdf/EBRI_IB_413_Apr15_RCS-2015.pdf.

[2] Refer to the U.S. Department of Commerce: Bureau of Economic Analysis, *Personal Saving Rate: January 1, 1959–January 1, 2015,* research.stlouisfed.org/fred2/series/PSAVERT.

retirees has steadily declined over the past half century. In 1955, there were 8.6 workers supporting each retiree, but by 1975, that number had declined to 3.2 workers for every one retiree. From 1975 through 2013, the ratio remained between 2.8 and 3.4 workers for every retiree. Current projections show this ratio significantly declining in the years ahead—the forecast is for 2.1 workers per retiree in 2035 and 2.0 workers per retiree in 2090.[3] With so few people paying into the Social Security system and so many drawing funds out, Social Security is going to be in serious trouble. In fact, for the first time since its inception, in 2010 (and seven years ahead of schedule), Social Security was in the red—paying out more in benefits than it received in payroll tax revenues. Considering these facts, many people may have trouble maintaining a reasonable standard of living after they retire, and many of today's college students will have to support their parents.

This is an important issue for millions of Americans, but many don't know how to deal with it. Most Americans have been ignoring what is most certainly going to be a huge personal and social problem. However, if you study this chapter carefully, you can use the tools and techniques presented here to avoid the trap that has caught, and is likely to catch, so many people.

# PUTTING THINGS IN PERSPECTIVE

Time value analysis has many applications, including planning for retirement, valuing stocks and bonds, setting up loan payment schedules, and making corporate decisions regarding investing in new plants and equipment. *In fact, of all financial concepts, time value of money is the single most important concept. Indeed, time value analysis is used throughout the book; so it is vital that you understand this chapter before continuing.*

You need to understand basic time value concepts, but conceptual knowledge will do you little good if you can't do the required calculations. Therefore, this chapter is heavy on calculations. Most students studying finance have a financial or scientific calculator; some also own or have access to a computer. One of these tools is necessary to work many finance problems in a reasonable length of time. However, when students begin reading this chapter, many of them don't know how to use the time value functions on their calculator or computer. If you are in that situation, you will find yourself simultaneously studying concepts and trying to learn to use your calculator, and you will need more time to cover this chapter than you might expect.[4]

When you finish this chapter, you should be able to

- Explain how the time value of money works and discuss why it is such an important concept in finance.

- Calculate the present value and future value of lump sums.

- Identify the different types of annuities, calculate the present value and future value of both an ordinary annuity and an annuity due, and calculate the relevant annuity payments.

*Excellent retirement calculators are available at **money.msn.com/en-us /money/tools /retirementplanner**, ssa .gov, and **choosetosave .org/calculators**. These calculators allow you to input hypothetical retirement savings information; the program then shows if current retirement savings will be sufficient to meet retirement needs.*

---

[3]Refer to the U.S. Social Security Administration, *2014 Annual Report of the Board of Trustees of the Federal Old-Age and Survivors Insurance and Federal Disability Insurance Trust Funds*, Table IV.B2, p. 58.

[4]Calculator manuals tend to be long and complicated, partly because they cover a number of topics that aren't required in the basic finance course. We provide tutorials for the most commonly used calculators on the textbook website and you can access these by going to www.cengagebrain.com and searching ISBN 9781305635937. The tutorials are keyed to this chapter, and they show exactly how to do the required calculations. If you don't know how to use your calculator, go to the textbook's website, find the relevant tutorial, and work through it as you study the chapter.

- Calculate the present value and future value of an uneven cash flow stream. You will use this knowledge in later chapters that show how to value common stocks and corporate projects.

- Explain the difference between nominal, periodic, and effective interest rates. An understanding of these concepts is necessary when comparing rates of returns on alternative investments.

- Discuss the basics of loan amortization and develop a loan amortization schedule that you might use when considering an auto loan or home mortgage loan.

# 5-1 Time Lines

**Time Line**

An important tool used in time value analysis; it is a graphical representation used to show the timing of cash flows.

The first step in time value analysis is to set up a **time line**, which will help you visualize what's happening in a particular problem. As an illustration, consider the following diagram, where PV represents $100 that is on hand today, and FV is the value that will be in the account on a future date:

| Periods | 0 | | 1 | 2 | 3 |
|---------|---|---|---|---|---|
| | | 5% | | | |
| Cash | PV = $100 | | | | FV = ? |

The intervals from 0 to 1, 1 to 2, and 2 to 3 are time periods such as years or months. Time 0 is today, and it is the beginning of Period 1; Time 1 is one period from today, and it is both the end of Period 1 and the beginning of Period 2; and so forth. Although the periods are often years, periods can also be quarters or months or even days. Note that each tick mark corresponds to both the *end* of one period and the *beginning* of the next one. Thus, if the periods are years, the tick mark at Time 2 represents the *end* of Year 2 and the *beginning* of Year 3.

Cash flows are shown directly below the tick marks, and the relevant interest rate is shown just above the time line. Unknown cash flows, which you are trying to find, are indicated by question marks. Here the interest rate is 5%; a single cash outflow, $100, is invested at Time 0; and the Time 3 value is an unknown inflow. In this example, cash flows occur only at Times 0 and 3, with no flows at Times 1 or 2. Note that in our example, the interest rate is constant for all three years. That condition is generally true; but if it were not, we would show different interest rates for the different periods.

Time lines are essential when you are first learning time value concepts, but even experts use them to analyze complex finance problems; and we use them throughout the book. We begin each problem by setting up a time line to illustrate the situation, after which we provide an equation that must be solved to find the answer. Then we explain how to use a regular calculator, a financial calculator, and a spreadsheet to find the answer.

# SelfTest

Do time lines deal only with years, or can other time periods be used?

Set up a time line to illustrate the following situation: You currently have $2,000 in a 3-year certificate of deposit (CD) that pays a guaranteed 4% annually.

# 5-2 Future Values

A dollar in hand today is worth more than a dollar to be received in the future because if you had it now, you could invest it, earn interest, and own more than a dollar in the future. The process of going to **future value (FV)** from **present value (PV)** is called **compounding**. For an illustration, refer back to our 3-year time line, and assume that you plan to deposit $100 in a bank that pays a guaranteed 5% interest each year. How much would you have at the end of Year 3? We first define some terms, and then we set up a time line to show how the future value is calculated.

PV = Present value, or beginning amount. In our example, PV = $100.

$FV_N$ = Future value, or ending amount, of your account after N periods. Whereas PV is the value now, or the *present value*, $FV_N$ is the value N periods into the *future*, after the interest earned has been added to the account.

$CF_t$ = Cash flow. Cash flows can be positive or negative. The cash flow for a particular period is often given as a subscript, $CF_t$, where t is the period. Thus, $CF_0 = PV$ = the cash flow at Time 0, whereas $CF_3$ is the cash flow at the end of Period 3.

I = Interest rate earned per year. Sometimes a lowercase i is used. Interest earned is based on the balance at the beginning of each year, and we assume that it is paid at the end of the year. Here I = 5% or, expressed as a decimal, 0.05. Throughout this chapter, we designate the interest rate as I because that symbol (or I/YR, for interest rate per year) is used on most financial calculators. Note, though, that in later chapters, we use the symbol r to denote rates because r (for rate of return) is used more often in the finance literature. Note too that in this chapter we generally assume that interest payments are guaranteed by the U.S. government; hence, they are certain. In later chapters, we consider risky investments, where the interest rate earned might differ from its expected level.

INT = Dollars of interest earned during the year = Beginning amount × I. In our example, INT = $100(0.05) = $5.

N = Number of periods involved in the analysis. In our example, N = 3. Sometimes the number of periods is designated with a lowercase n, so both N and n indicate the number of periods involved.

**Future Value (FV)**
The amount to which a cash flow or series of cash flows will grow over a given period of time when compounded at a given interest rate.

**Present Value (PV)**
The value today of a future cash flow or series of cash flows.

**Compounding**
The arithmetic process of determining the final value of a cash flow or series of cash flows when compound interest is applied.

We can use four different procedures to solve time value problems.[5] These methods are described in the following sections.

## 5-2A STEP-BY-STEP APPROACH

The time line used to find the FV of $100 compounded for 3 years at 5%, along with some calculations, is shown. Multiply the initial amount and each succeeding amount by $(1 + I) = (1.05)$:

---

[5]A fifth procedure, using tables that show "interest factors," was used before financial calculators and computers became available. Now, though, calculators and spreadsheet applications such as Microsoft Excel are programmed to calculate the specific factor needed for a given problem and then to use it to find the FV. This is more efficient than using the tables. Moreover, calculators and spreadsheets can handle fractional periods and fractional interest rates, such as the FV of $100 after 3.75 years when the interest rate is 5.375%, whereas tables provide numbers only for whole periods and rates. For these reasons, tables are not used in business today; hence, we do not discuss them in the text.

| Time | 0 | | 1 | 2 | 3 |
|------|---|---|---|---|---|
| | | 5% | | | |
| Amount at beginning of period | $100.00 | ----➤ | $105.00 ----➤ | $110.25 ----➤ | $115.76 |

You start with $100 in the account—this is shown at t = 0:

- You earn $100(0.05) = $5 of interest during the first year, so the amount at the end of Year 1 (or t = 1) is $100 + $5 = $105.

- You begin the second year with $105, earn 0.05($105) = $5.25 on the now larger beginning-of-period amount, and end the year with $110.25. Interest during Year 2 is $5.25; and it is higher than the first year's interest, $5.00, because you earned $5(0.05) = $0.25 interest on the first year's interest. This is called compounding, and interest earned on interest is called compound interest.

- This process continues; and because the beginning balance is higher each successive year, the interest earned each year increases.

- The total interest earned, $15.76, is reflected in the final balance, $115.76.

The step-by-step approach is useful because it shows exactly what is happening. However, this approach is time consuming, especially when a number of years are involved; so streamlined procedures have been developed.

## 5-2B FORMULA APPROACH

In the step-by-step approach, we multiply the amount at the beginning of each period by $(1 + I) = (1.05)$. If $N = 3$, we multiply by $(1 + I)$ three different times, which is the same as multiplying the beginning amount by $(1 + I)^3$. This concept can be extended, and the result is this key equation:

**Compound Interest**
Occurs when interest is earned on prior periods' interest.

$$FV_N = PV(1 + I)^N$$

5.1

We can apply Equation 5.1 to find the FV in our example:

$$FV_3 = \$100(1.05)^3 = \$115.76$$

**Simple Interest**
Occurs when interest is not earned on interest.

Equation 5.1 can be used with any calculator that has an exponential function, making it easy to find FVs no matter how many years are involved.

## SIMPLE VERSUS COMPOUND INTEREST

Interest earned on the interest earned in prior periods, as was true in our example and is always true when we apply Equation 5.1, is called **compound interest**. If interest is not earned on interest, we have **simple interest**. The formula for FV with simple interest is $FV = PV + PV(I)(N)$; so in our example, FV would have been $100 + $100(0.05)(3) = $100 + $15 = $115 based on simple interest. Most financial contracts are based on compound interest; but in legal proceedings, the law often specifies that simple interest must be used. For example, Maris Distributing, a company founded by home-run king Roger Maris, won a lawsuit against Anheuser-Busch (A-B) because A-B had breached a contract and taken away Maris's franchise to sell Budweiser beer. The judge awarded Maris $50 million plus interest at 10% from 1997 (when A-B breached the contract) until the payment was actually made. The interest award was based on simple interest, which as of 2005 (when a settlement was reached between A-B and the Maris family) had raised the total from $50 million to $50 million + 0.10($50 million)(8 years) = $90 million. (No doubt the sheer size of this award and the impact of the interest, even simple interest, influenced A-B to settle.) If the law had allowed compound interest, the award would have totaled ($50 million)$(1.10)^8$ = $107.18 million, or $17.18 million more. This legal procedure dates back to the days before calculators and computers. The law moves slowly!

## 5-2C FINANCIAL CALCULATORS

Financial calculators are extremely helpful in working time value problems. Their manuals explain calculators in detail; and on the textbook's website, we provide summaries of the features needed to work the problems in this book for several popular calculators. Also see the box titled "Hints on Using Financial Calculators," on page 149, for suggestions that will help you avoid common mistakes. If you are not yet familiar with your calculator, we recommend that you work through the tutorial as you study this chapter.

First, note that financial calculators have five keys that correspond to the five variables in the basic time value equations. We show the inputs for our text example above the respective keys and the output, the FV, below its key. Because there are no periodic payments, we enter 0 for PMT. We describe the keys in more detail after this calculation.

| 3 | 5 | −100 | 0 | |
|---|---|---|---|---|
| N | I/YR | PV | PMT | FV |
| | | | | 115.76 |

Where:

N = Number of periods. Some calculators use n rather than N.

I/YR = Interest rate per period. Some calculators use i or I rather than I/YR.

PV = Present value. In our example, we begin by making a deposit, which is an outflow (the cash leaves our wallet and is deposited at one of many financial institutions); so the PV should be entered with a negative sign. On most calculators, you must enter the 100, then press the +/− key to switch from +100 to −100. If you enter −100 directly, 100 will be subtracted from the last number in the calculator, giving you an incorrect answer.

PMT = Payment. This key is used when we have a series of equal, or constant, payments. Because there are no such payments in our illustrative problem, we enter PMT = 0. We will use the PMT key when we discuss annuities later in this chapter.

FV = Future value. In this example, the FV is positive because we entered the PV as a negative number. If we had entered the 100 as a positive number, the FV would have been negative.

As noted in our example, you enter the known values (N, I/YR, PV, and PMT) and then press the FV key to get the answer, 115.76. Again, note that if you enter the PV as 100 without a minus sign, the FV will be shown on the calculator display as a negative number. The calculator *assumes* that either the PV or the FV is negative. This should not be confusing if you think about what you are doing. When PMT is zero, it doesn't matter what sign you enter for PV as your calculator will automatically assign the opposite sign to FV. We will discuss this point in greater detail later in the chapter when we cover annuities.

## 5-2D SPREADSHEETS[6]

Students generally use calculators for homework and exam problems; but in business, people generally use spreadsheets for problems that involve the time value of

---

[6]If you have never worked with spreadsheets, you may choose to skip this section. However, you might want to read through it and refer to this chapter's Excel model to get an idea of how spreadsheets work.

money (TVM). Spreadsheets show in detail what is happening, and they help reduce both conceptual and data-entry errors. The spreadsheet discussion can be skipped without loss of continuity, but if you understand the basics of Excel and have access to a computer, we recommend that you read through this section. Even if you aren't familiar with spreadsheets, the discussion will still give you an idea of how they operate.

We used Excel to create Table 5.1, which is part of the spreadsheet model that corresponds to this chapter. Table 5.1 summarizes the four methods of finding the FV and shows the spreadsheet formulas toward the bottom. Note that spreadsheets can be used to do calculations, but they can also be used like a word processor to create exhibits like Table 5.1, which includes text, drawings, and calculations. The letters across the top designate columns; the numbers to the left designate rows; and the rows and columns jointly designate cells. Thus, C14 is the cell in which we specify the −$100 investment; C15 shows the interest rate; and C16 shows the number of periods. We then created a time line on rows 17 to 19; and on row 21, we have Excel go through the step-by-step calculations, multiplying the beginning-of-year values by $(1 + I)$ to find the compounded value at the end of each period. Cell G21 shows the final result. Then on row 23, we illustrate the formula approach, using Excel to solve Equation 5.1 and find the FV, $115.76. Next, on rows 25 to 27, we show a picture of the calculator solution. Finally, on rows 30 and 31, we use Excel's built-in FV function to find the answers given in cells G30 and G31. The G30 answer is based on fixed inputs, while the G31 answer is based on cell references, which makes it easy to change inputs and see the effects on the output.

For example, if you want to quickly see how the future value changes if the interest rate is 7% instead of 5%, all you need to do is change cell C15 to 7%. Looking at cell G30, you will immediately see that the future value is now $122.50.

Students can download the Excel chapter models from the student companion site on the text's website. Once downloaded onto your computer, retrieve the Excel chapter model and follow along as you read this chapter.

---

**TABLE 5.1**　　　　　Summary of Future Value Calculations

| | A | B | C | D | E | F | G |
|---|---|---|---|---|---|---|---|
| 14 | Investment | = CF$_0$ = PV = | -$100.00 | | | | |
| 15 | Interest rate | = I = | 5.00% | | | | |
| 16 | No. of periods = | N = | 3 | | | | |
| 17 | | | Periods: | 0 | 1 | 2 | 3 |
| 18 | | | | | | | |
| 19 | | | Cash Flow Time Line: | -$100 | | | FV = ? |
| 20 | | | | | | | |
| 21 | Step-by-Step Approach: | | | $100 | $105.00 | $110.25 | $115.76 |
| 22 | | | | | | | |
| 23 | Formula Approach: $FV_N = PV(1 + I)^N$ | | | $FV_N =$ | $100(1.05)^3$ | = | $115.76 |
| 24 | | | | | | | |
| 25 | | | 3 | 5 | -$100.00 | $0 | |
| 26 | Calculator Approach: | | N | I/YR | PV | PMT | FV |
| 27 | | | | | | | $115.76 |
| 28 | | | | | | | |
| 29 | Excel Approach: | | FV function: | $FV_N =$ | =FV(rate,nper,pmt,pv,type) | | |
| 30 | | | Fixed inputs: | $FV_N =$ | =FV(0.05,3,0,-100)　= | | $115.76 |
| 31 | | | Cell references: | $FV_N =$ | =FV(C15,C16,0,C14) = | | $115.76 |
| 32 | In the Excel formula, the terms are entered in this sequence: interest, periods, 0 to indicate no intermediate cash flows, and then the PV. The data can be entered as fixed numbers or as cell references. | | | | | | |

## Hints on Using Financial Calculators

When using a financial calculator, make sure it is set up as indicated here. Refer to your calculator manual or to our calculator tutorial on the text's website for information on setting up your calculator.

- *One payment per period.* Many calculators "come out of the box," assuming that 12 payments are made per year; that is, monthly payments. However, in this book, we generally deal with problems in which only one payment is made each year. *Therefore, you should set your calculator at one payment per year and leave it there. See our tutorial or your calculator manual if you need assistance.*

- *End mode.* With most contracts, payments are made at the end of each period. However, some contracts call for payments at the beginning of each period. You can switch between "End Mode" and "Begin Mode," depending on the problem you are solving. *Because most of the problems in this book call for end-of-period payments, you should return your calculator to End Mode after you work a problem where payments are made at the beginning of periods.*

- *Negative sign for outflows.* Outflows must be entered as negative numbers. This generally means typing the outflow as a positive number and then pressing the +/− key to convert from + to − before hitting the enter key.

- *Decimal places.* With most calculators, you can specify from 0 to 11 decimal places. When working with dollars, we generally specify two decimal places. When dealing with interest rates, we generally specify two places after the decimal when the rate is expressed as a percentage (e.g., 5.25%), but we specify four decimal places when the rate is expressed as a decimal (e.g., 0.0525).

- *Interest rates.* For arithmetic operations with a nonfinancial calculator, 0.0525 must be used; but with a financial calculator and its TVM keys, you must enter 5.25, not 0.0525, because financial calculators assume that rates are stated as percentages.

If you are using Excel, there are a few things to keep in mind:

- When calculating time value of money problems in Excel, interest rates are entered as percentages or decimals (e.g., 5% or .05). However, when using the time value of money function on most financial calculators you generally enter the interest rate as a whole number (e.g., 5).

- When calculating time value of money problems in Excel, the abbreviation for the number of periods is nper, whereas for most financial calculators the abbreviation is simply N. Throughout the text, we will use these terms interchangeably.

- When calculating time value of money problems in Excel, you will often be prompted to enter Type. Type refers to whether the payments come at the end of the year (in which case Type = 0, or you can just omit it), or at the beginning of the year (in which case Type = 1). Most financial calculators have a BEGIN/END mode function that you toggle on or off to indicate whether the payments come at the beginning or at the end of the period.

Table 5.1 demonstrates that all four methods get the same result, but they use different calculating procedures. It also shows that with Excel, all inputs are shown in one place, which makes checking data entries relatively easy. Finally, it shows that Excel can be used to create exhibits, which are quite important in the real world. In business, it's often as important to explain what you are doing as it is to "get the right answer," because if decision makers don't understand your analysis, they may reject your recommendations.

## 5-2E GRAPHIC VIEW OF THE COMPOUNDING PROCESS

Figure 5.1 shows how a $1 investment grows over time at different interest rates. We made the curves by solving Equation 5.1 with different values for N and I. The interest rate is a growth rate: If a sum is deposited and earns 5% interest per year,

| FIGURE 5.1 | Growth of $1 at Various Interest Rates and Time Periods |
|---|---|

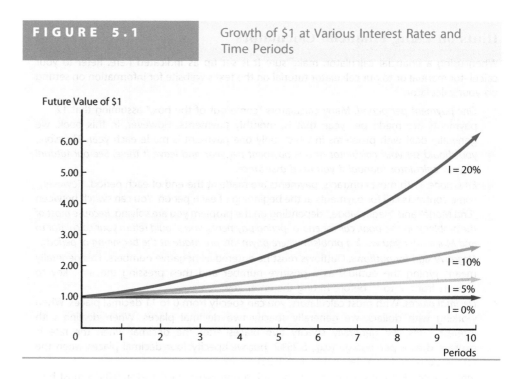

the funds on deposit will grow by 5% per year. Note also that time value concepts can be applied to anything that grows—sales, population, earnings per share, or future salary.

## quick question

### QUESTION:

At the beginning of your freshman year, your favorite aunt and uncle deposit $10,000 into a 4-year bank certificate of deposit (CD) that pays 5% annual interest. You will receive the money in the account (including the accumulated interest) if you graduate with honors in 4 years. How much will there be in the account after 4 years?

### ANSWER:

Using the formula approach, we know that $FV_N = PV(1 + I)^N$. In this case, you know that $N = 4$, $PV = \$10,000$, and $I = 0.05$. It follows that the future value after 4 years will be $FV_4 = \$10,000(1.05)^4 = \$12,155.06$. Alternatively, using the calculator approach we can set the problem up as follows:

| 4 | 5 | −10000 | 0 | |
|---|---|---|---|---|
| N | I/YR | PV | PMT | FV |
| | | | | 12,155.06 |

Finally, we can use Excel's FV function:

=FV(0.05,4,0,−10000)
FV(rate, nper, pmt, [pv], [type])

Here we find that the future value equals $12,155.06.

## SelfTest

Explain why this statement is true: A dollar in hand today is worth more than a dollar to be received next year.

What is compounding? What's the difference between simple interest and compound interest? What would the future value of $100 be after 5 years at 10% *compound* interest? At 10% *simple* interest? **($161.05, $150.00)**

Suppose you currently have $2,000 and plan to purchase a 3-year certificate of deposit (CD) that pays 4% interest compounded annually. How much will you have when the CD matures? How would your answer change if the interest rate were 5% or 6% or 20%? **($2,249.73, $2,315.25, $2,382.03, $3,456.00. Hint: With a calculator, enter N = 3, I/YR = 4, PV = −2000, and PMT = 0; then press FV to get 2,249.73. Enter I/YR = 5 to override the 4%, and press FV again to get the second answer. In general, you can change one input at a time to see how the output changes.)**

A company's sales in 2016 were $100 million. If sales grow at 8%, what will they be 10 years later, in 2026? **($215.89 million)**

How much would $1 growing at 5% per year be worth after 100 years? What would the FV be if the growth rate were 10%? **($131.50, $13,780.61)**

# 5-3 Present Values

Finding a present value is the reverse of finding a future value. Indeed, we simply solve Equation 5.1, the formula for the future value, for the PV to produce the basic present value formula, Equation 5.2:

$$\text{Future value} = FV_N = PV(1 + I)^N \qquad \blacktriangledown \quad 5.1$$

$$\text{Present value} = PV = \frac{FV_N}{(1 + I)^N} \qquad \blacktriangledown \quad 5.2$$

We illustrate PVs with the following example. A broker offers to sell you a Treasury bond that will pay $115.76 three years from now. Banks are currently offering a guaranteed 5% interest on 3-year certificates of deposit (CDs); and if you don't buy the bond, you will buy a CD. The 5% rate paid on the CDs is defined as your **opportunity cost**, or the rate of return you could earn on an alternative investment of similar risk. Given these conditions, what's the most you should pay for the bond? We answer this question using the four methods discussed in the last section—step-by-step, formula, calculator, and spreadsheet. Table 5.2 summarizes the results.

*Opportunity Cost*
The rate of return you could earn on an alternative investment of similar risk.

First, recall from the future value example in the last section that if you invested $100 at 5%, it would grow to $115.76 in 3 years. You would also have $115.76 after 3 years if you bought the T-bond. Therefore, the most you should pay for the bond is $100—this is its "fair price." If you could buy the bond for *less than* $100, you should buy it rather than invest in the CD. Conversely, if its price was *more than* $100, you should buy the CD. If the bond's price was exactly $100, you should be indifferent between the T-bond and the CD.

**TABLE 5.2**　　　　　Summary of Present Value Calculations

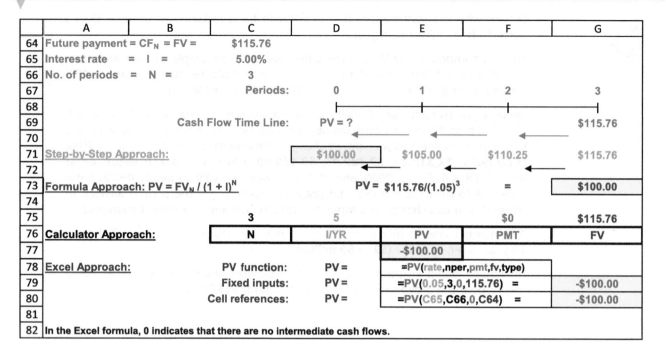

|  | A | B | C | D | E | F | G |
|---|---|---|---|---|---|---|---|
| 64 | Future payment = $CF_N$ = FV = | | $115.76 | | | | |
| 65 | Interest rate　　= I　= | | 5.00% | | | | |
| 66 | No. of periods　=　N　= | | 3 | | | | |
| 67 | | | Periods: | 0 | 1 | 2 | 3 |
| 68 | | | | | | | |
| 69 | | Cash Flow Time Line: | PV = ? | | | | $115.76 |
| 70 | | | | | | | |
| 71 | Step-by-Step Approach: | | | $100.00 | $105.00 | $110.25 | $115.76 |
| 72 | | | | | | | |
| 73 | Formula Approach: PV = $FV_N$ / $(1 + I)^N$ | | | | PV = $115.76/$(1.05)^3$ | = | $100.00 |
| 74 | | | | | | | |
| 75 | | | 3 | 5 | | $0 | $115.76 |
| 76 | Calculator Approach: | | N | I/YR | PV | PMT | FV |
| 77 | | | | | -$100.00 | | |
| 78 | Excel Approach: | | PV function: | PV = | =PV(rate,nper,pmt,fv,type) | | |
| 79 | | | Fixed inputs: | PV = | =PV(0.05,3,0,115.76) = | | -$100.00 |
| 80 | | | Cell references: | PV = | =PV(C65,C66,0,C64) = | | -$100.00 |
| 81 | | | | | | | |
| 82 | In the Excel formula, 0 indicates that there are no intermediate cash flows. | | | | | | |

The $100 is defined as the present value, or PV, of $115.76 due in 3 years when the appropriate interest rate is 5%. In general, *the present value of a cash flow due N years in the future is the amount which, if it were on hand today, would grow to equal the given future amount.* Because $100 would grow to $115.76 in 3 years at a 5% interest rate, $100 is the present value of $115.76 due in 3 years at a 5% rate. Finding present values is called **discounting**; and as noted above it is the reverse of compounding— if you know the PV, you can compound to find the FV, while if you know the FV, you can discount to find the PV.

**Discounting**

The process of finding the present value of a cash flow or a series of cash flows; discounting is the reverse of compounding.

The top section of Table 5.2 calculates the PV using the step-by-step approach. When we found the future value in the previous section, we worked from left to right, multiplying the initial amount and each subsequent amount by $(1 + I)$. To find present values, we work backward, or from right to left, dividing the future value and each subsequent amount by $(1 + I)$. This procedure shows exactly what's happening, which can be quite useful when you are working complex problems. However, it's inefficient, especially when you are dealing with a large number of years.

With the formula approach, we use Equation 5.2, simply dividing the future value by $(1 + I)^N$. This is more efficient than the step-by-step approach, and it gives the same result. Equation 5.2 is built into financial calculators; and as shown in Table 5.2, we can find the PV by entering values for N, I/YR, PMT, and FV and then pressing the PV key. Finally, Excel's PV function:

=PV(0.05,3,0,–115.76)

**PV**(rate, nper, pmt, [fv], [type])

can be used. It is essentially the same as the calculator and solves Equation 5.2.

The fundamental goal of financial management is to maximize the firm's value, and the value of a business (or any asset, including stocks and bonds) is the *present value* of its expected future cash flows. Because present value lies at the heart of the valuation process, we will have much more to say about it in the remainder of this chapter and throughout the book.

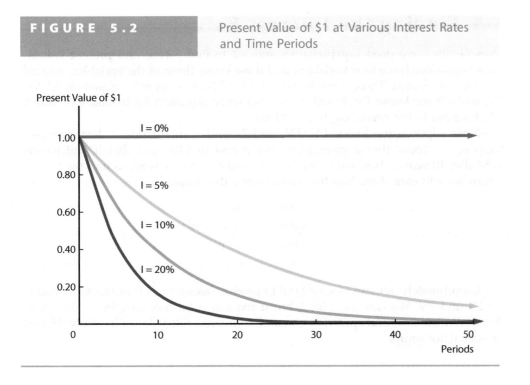

**FIGURE 5.2** Present Value of $1 at Various Interest Rates and Time Periods

## 5-3A GRAPHIC VIEW OF THE DISCOUNTING PROCESS

Figure 5.2 shows that the present value of a sum to be received in the future decreases and approaches zero as the payment date is extended further into the future and that the present value falls faster at higher interest rates. At relatively high rates, funds due in the future are worth very little today; and even at relatively low rates, present values of sums due in the very distant future are quite small. For example, at a 20% discount rate, $1 million due in 100 years would be worth only $0.0121 today. This is because $0.0121 would grow to $1 million in 100 years when compounded at 20%.

## SelfTest

What is discounting, and how is it related to compounding? How is the future value equation (5.1) related to the present value equation (5.2)?

How does the present value of a future payment change as the time to receipt is lengthened? As the interest rate increases?

Suppose a U.S. government bond promises to pay $2,249.73 three years from now. If the going interest rate on 3-year government bonds is 4%, how much is the bond worth today? How much is it worth today if the bond matured in 5 years rather than 3? How much is it worth today if the interest rate on the 5-year bond was 6% rather than 4%? **($2,000, $1,849.11, $1,681.13)**

How much would $1,000,000 due in 100 years be worth today if the discount rate was 5%? If the discount rate was 20%? **($7,604.49, $0.0121)**

## 5-4 Finding the Interest Rate, I

Thus far we have used Equations 5.1 and 5.2 to find future and present values. Those equations have four variables; and if we know three of the variables, we can solve for the fourth. Thus, if we know PV, I, and N, we can solve Equation 5.1 for FV, while if we know FV, I, and N, we can solve Equation 5.2 to find PV. That's what we did in the preceding two sections.

Now suppose we know PV, FV, and N and want to find I. For example, suppose we know that a given bond has a cost of $100 and that it will return $150 after 10 years. Thus, we know PV, FV, and N, and we want to find the rate of return we will earn if we buy the bond. Here's the situation:

$$FV = PV(1+I)^N$$
$$\$150 = \$100(1+I)^{10}$$
$$\$150/\$100 = (1+I)^{10}$$
$$1.5 = (1+I)^{10}$$

Unfortunately, we can't factor I out to produce as simple a formula as we could for FV and PV. We can solve for I, but it requires a bit more algebra.[7] However, financial calculators and spreadsheets can find interest rates almost instantly. Here's the calculator setup:

| 10 | | −100 | 0 | 150 |
|---|---|---|---|---|
| N | I/YR | PV | PMT | FV |
| | 4.14 | | | |

Enter N = 10, PV = −100, PMT = 0, because there are no payments until the security matures, and FV = 150. Then when you press the I/YR key, the calculator gives the answer, 4.14%. You would get this same answer using the RATE function in Excel:

=RATE(10,0,−100,150)
**RATE**(nper, pmt, pv, [fv], [type], [guess])

Here we find that the interest rate is equal to 4.14%.[8]

### SelfTest

The U.S. Treasury offers to sell you a bond for $585.43. No payments will be made until the bond matures 10 years from now, at which time it will be redeemed for $1,000. What interest rate would you earn if you bought this bond for $585.43? What rate would you earn if you could buy the bond for $550? For $600? **(5.5%, 6.16%, 5.24%)**

Microsoft earned $1.04 per share in 2004. Ten years later in 2014 it earned $2.63. What was the growth rate in Microsoft's earnings per share (EPS) over the 10-year period? If EPS in 2014 had been $2.15 rather than $2.63, what would the growth rate have been? **(9.72%, 7.53%)**

---

[7]Raise the left side of the equation, the 1.5, to the power $1/N = 1/10 = 0.1$, getting 1.0414. That number is 1 plus the interest rate, so the interest rate is $0.0414 = 4.14\%$.

[8]The RATE function prompts you to make a guess. In many cases, you can leave this blank, but if Excel is unable to find a solution to the problem, you should enter a reasonable guess, which will help the program converge to the correct solution.

# 5-5 Finding the Number of Years, N

We sometimes need to know how long it will take to accumulate a certain sum of money, given our beginning funds and the rate we will earn on those funds. For example, suppose we believe that we could retire comfortably if we had $1 million. We want to find how long it will take us to acquire $1 million, assuming we now have $500,000 invested at 4.5%. We cannot use a simple formula—the situation is like that with interest rates. We can set up a formula that uses logarithms, but calculators and spreadsheets find N very quickly. Here's the calculator setup:

| | 4.5 | −500000 | 0 | 1000000 |
|---|---|---|---|---|
| N | I/YR | PV | PMT | FV |
| 15.7473 | | | | |

Enter I/YR = 4.5, PV = −500000, PMT = 0, and FV = 1000000. Then when you press the N key, you get the answer, 15.7473 years. If you plug N = 15.7473 into the FV formula, you can prove that this is indeed the correct number of years:

$$FV = PV(1 + I)^N = \$500{,}000(1.045)^{15.7473} = \$1{,}000{,}000$$

You can also use Excel's NPER function:

=NPER(0.045,0,–500000,1000000)

**NPER**(rate, pmt, pv, [fv], [type])

Here we find that it will take 15.7473 years for $500,000 to double at a 4.5% interest rate.

## SelfTest

How long would it take $1,000 to double if it was invested in a bank that paid 6% per year? How long would it take if the rate was 10%? **(11.9 years, 7.27 years)**

Microsoft's 2014 earnings per share were $2.63, and its growth rate during the prior 10 years was 9.72% per year. If that growth rate was maintained, how long would it take for Microsoft's EPS to double? **(7.47 years)**

# 5-6 Annuities

Thus far we have dealt with single payments, or "lump sums." However, many assets provide a series of cash inflows over time; and many obligations, such as auto, student, and mortgage loans, require a series of payments. When the payments are equal and are made at fixed intervals, the series is an **annuity**. For example, $100 paid at the end of each of the next 3 years is a 3-year annuity. If the payments occur at the *end* of each year, the annuity is an **ordinary** (or **deferred**) **annuity**. If the payments are made at the *beginning* of each year, the annuity is an **annuity due**. Ordinary annuities are more common in finance; so when we use the term *annuity* in this book, assume that the payments occur at the ends of the periods unless otherwise noted.

*Annuity*
A series of equal payments at fixed intervals for a specified number of periods.

*Ordinary (Deferred) Annuity*
An annuity whose payments occur at the end of each period.

*Annuity Due*
An annuity whose payments occur at the beginning of each period.

Here are the time lines for a $100, 3-year, 5% ordinary annuity and for an annuity due. With the annuity due, each payment is shifted to the left by one year. A $100 deposit will be made each year, so we show the payments with minus signs:

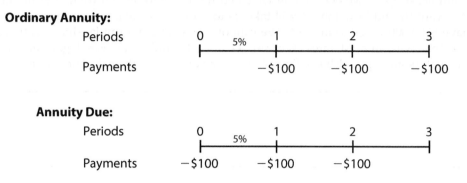

**Ordinary Annuity:**

Periods      0   5%   1     2     3

Payments      −$100    −$100    −$100

**Annuity Due:**

Periods      0   5%   1     2     3

Payments   −$100    −$100    −$100

As we demonstrate in the following sections, we can find an annuity's future and present values, the interest rate built into annuity contracts, and the length of time it takes to reach a financial goal using an annuity. Keep in mind that annuities must have *constant payments* at *fixed intervals* for a *specified number of periods*. If these conditions don't hold, then the payments do not constitute an annuity.

## SelfTest

What's the difference between an ordinary annuity and an annuity due?

Why would you prefer to receive an annuity due for $10,000 per year for 10 years than an otherwise similar ordinary annuity?

# 5-7 Future Value of an Ordinary Annuity

The future value of an annuity can be found using the step-by-step approach or using a formula, a financial calculator, or a spreadsheet. As an illustration, consider the ordinary annuity diagrammed earlier, where you deposit $100 at the end of each year for 3 years and earn 5% per year. How much will you have at the end of the third year? The answer, $315.25, is defined as the future value of the annuity, **FVA_N**; it is shown in Table 5.3.

**FVA_N**

The future value of an annuity over N periods.

As shown in the step-by-step section of the table, we compound each payment out to Time 3, then sum those compounded values to find the annuity's FV, $FVA_3 = \$315.25$. The first payment earns interest for two periods, the second payment earns interest for one period, and the third payment earns no interest at all because it is made at the end of the annuity's life. This approach is straightforward; but if the annuity extends out for many years, the approach is cumbersome and time consuming.

As you can see from the time line diagram, with the step-by-step approach, we apply the following equation, with N = 3 and I = 5%:

$$\begin{aligned} FVA_N &= PMT(1+I)^{N-1} + PMT(1+I)^{N-2} + PMT(1+I)^{N-3} \\ &= \$100(1.05)^2 + \$100(1.05)^1 + \$100(1.05)^0 \\ &= \$315.25 \end{aligned}$$

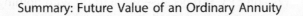

Summary: Future Value of an Ordinary Annuity      TABLE 5.3

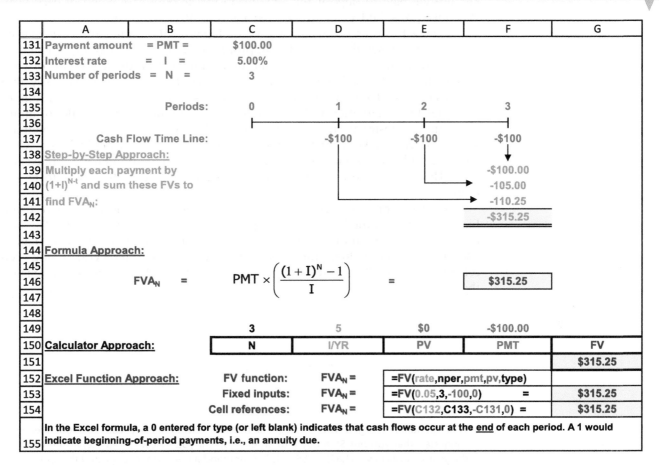

| | A | B | C | D | E | F | G |
|---|---|---|---|---|---|---|---|
| 131 | Payment amount | = PMT = | $100.00 | | | | |
| 132 | Interest rate | = I = | 5.00% | | | | |
| 133 | Number of periods | = N = | 3 | | | | |
| 134 | | | | | | | |
| 135 | | Periods: | 0 | 1 | 2 | 3 | |
| 136 | | | | | | | |
| 137 | | Cash Flow Time Line: | | -$100 | -$100 | -$100 | |
| 138 | **Step-by-Step Approach:** | | | | | | |
| 139 | Multiply each payment by | | | | | -$100.00 | |
| 140 | $(1+I)^{N-t}$ and sum these FVs to | | | | | -105.00 | |
| 141 | find FVA$_N$: | | | | | -110.25 | |
| 142 | | | | | | -$315.25 | |
| 143 | | | | | | | |
| 144 | **Formula Approach:** | | | | | | |
| 145 | | | | | | | |
| 146 | | FVA$_N$ = | | $PMT \times \left( \dfrac{(1+I)^N - 1}{I} \right)$ | | = | $315.25 | |
| 147 | | | | | | | |
| 148 | | | | | | | |
| 149 | | | 3 | 5 | $0 | -$100.00 | |
| 150 | **Calculator Approach:** | | N | I/YR | PV | PMT | FV |
| 151 | | | | | | | $315.25 |
| 152 | **Excel Function Approach:** | | FV function: | FVA$_N$ = | =FV(rate,nper,pmt,pv,type) | | |
| 153 | | | Fixed inputs: | FVA$_N$ = | =FV(0.05,3,-100,0)    = | | $315.25 |
| 154 | | | Cell references: | FVA$_N$ = | =FV(C132,C133,-C131,0) = | | $315.25 |
| 155 | In the Excel formula, a 0 entered for type (or left blank) indicates that cash flows occur at the <u>end</u> of each period. A 1 would indicate beginning-of-period payments, i.e., an annuity due. | | | | | | |

We can generalize and streamline the equation as follows:

$$FVA_N = PMT(1+I)^{N-1} + PMT(1+I)^{N-2} + PMT(1+I)^{N-3} + \ldots + PMT(1+I)^0$$

5.3

$$= PMT \left[ \frac{(1+I)^N - 1}{I} \right]$$

The first line shows the equation in its long form. It can be transformed to the second form on the last line, which can be used to solve annuity problems with a nonfinancial calculator.[9] This equation is also built into financial calculators and spreadsheets. With an annuity, we have recurring payments; hence, the PMT key is used. Here's the calculator setup for our illustrative annuity:

| 3 | 5 | 0 | −100 | **End Mode** |
|---|---|---|---|---|
| N | I/YR | PV | PMT | FV |
| | | | | 315.25 |

---

[9]The long form of the equation is a geometric progression that can be reduced to the second form.

We enter $PV = 0$ because we start off with nothing, and we enter $PMT = -100$ because we plan to deposit this amount in the account at the end of each year. When we press the FV key, we get the answer, $FVA_3 = 315.25$.

Because this is an ordinary annuity, with payments coming at the *end* of each year, we must set the calculator appropriately. As noted earlier, calculators "come out of the box" set to assume that payments occur at the end of each period, that is, to deal with ordinary annuities. However, there is a key that enables us to switch between ordinary annuities and annuities due. For ordinary annuities the designation is "End Mode" or something similar, while for annuities due the designation is "Begin" or "Begin Mode" or "Due" or something similar. If you make a mistake and set your calculator on Begin Mode when working with an ordinary annuity, each payment will earn interest for one extra year. That will cause the compounded amounts, and thus the FVA, to be too large.

The last approach in Table 5.3 shows the spreadsheet solution using Excel's built-in function. We can put in fixed values for N, I, PV, and PMT or set up an Input Section where we assign values to those variables, and then input values into the function as cell references. Using cell references makes it easy to change the inputs to see the effects of changes on the output.

## quick question

**QUESTION:**

Your grandfather urged you to begin a habit of saving money early in your life. He suggested that you put $5 a day into an envelope. If you follow his advice, at the end of the year you will have $1,825 ($365 \times \$5$). Your grandfather further suggested that you take that money at the end of the year and invest it in an online brokerage mutual fund account that has an annual expected return of 8%.

You are 18 years old. If you start following your grandfather's advice today, and continue saving in this way the rest of your life, how much do you expect to have in the brokerage account when you are 65 years old?

**ANSWER:**

This problem is asking you to calculate the future value of an ordinary annuity. More specifically, you are making 47 payments of $1,825, where the annual interest rate is 8%.

To quickly find the answer, enter the following inputs into a financial calculator: N = 47; I/YR = 8; PV = 0; and PMT = −1825. Then solve for the FV of the ordinary annuity by pressing the FV key, FV = **$826,542.78**.

In addition, we can use Excel's FV function:

Here we find that the future value is **$826,542.78**.

You can see your grandfather is right—it definitely pays to start saving early!

## SelfTest

For an ordinary annuity with five annual payments of $100 and a 10% interest rate, how many years will the first payment earn interest? What will this payment's value be at the end? Answer this same question for the fifth payment. **(4 years, $146.41, 0 years, $100)**

Assume that you plan to buy a condo 5 years from now, and you estimate that you can save $2,500 per year. You plan to deposit the money in a bank account that pays 4% interest, and you will make the first deposit at the end of the year. How much will you have after 5 years? How much will you have if the interest rate is increased to 6% or lowered to 3%? **($13,540.81, $14,092.73, $13,272.84)**

# 5-8 Future Value of an Annuity Due

Because each payment occurs one period earlier with an annuity due, all of the payments earn interest for one additional period. Therefore, the FV of an annuity due will be greater than that of a similar ordinary annuity. If you went through the step-by-step procedure, you would see that our illustrative annuity due has an FV of $331.01 versus $315.25 for the ordinary annuity.

With the formula approach, we first use Equation 5.3; but because each payment occurs one period earlier, we multiply the Equation 5.3 result by $(1 + I)$:

$$FVA_{due} = FVA_{ordinary}(1 + I) \qquad \qquad 5.4$$

Thus, for the annuity due, $FVA_{due} = \$315.25(1.05) = \$331.01$, which is the same result when the period-by-period approach is used. With a calculator, we input the variables just as we did with the ordinary annuity; but now we set the calculator to Begin Mode to get the answer, $331.01.

## SelfTest

Why does an annuity due always have a higher future value than an ordinary annuity?

If you calculated the value of an ordinary annuity, how could you find the value of the corresponding annuity due?

Assume that you plan to buy a condo 5 years from now, and you need to save for a down payment. You plan to save $2,500 per year (with the first deposit made *immediately*), and you will deposit the funds in a bank account that pays 4% interest. How much will you have after 5 years? How much will you have if you make the deposits at the end of each year? **($14,082.44, $13,540.81)**

# 5-9 Present Value of an Ordinary Annuity

**PVA_N**

The present value of an annuity of N periods.

The present value of an annuity, **PVA$_N$**, can be found using the step-by-step, formula, calculator, or spreadsheet method. Look back at Table 5.3. To find the FV of the annuity, we compounded the deposits. To find the PV, we discount them, dividing each payment by $(1 + I)^t$. The step-by-step procedure is diagrammed as follows:

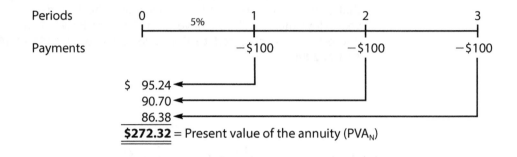

Equation 5.5 expresses the step-by-step procedure in a formula. The bracketed form of the equation can be used with a scientific calculator, and it is helpful if the annuity extends out for a number of years:

$$PVA_N = PMT/(1 + I)^1 + PMT/(1 + I)^2 + \dots + PMT/(1 + I)^N$$ 

▼ 5.5

$$= PMT \left[ \frac{1 - \dfrac{1}{(1 + I)^N}}{I} \right]$$

$$= \$100 \times [1 - 1/(1.05)^3]/0.05 = \$272.32$$

Calculators are programmed to solve Equation 5.5, so we merely input the variables and press the PV key, *making sure the calculator is set to End Mode.* The calculator setup follows for both an ordinary annuity and an annuity due. Note that the PV of the annuity due is larger because each payment is discounted back one less year. Note too that you can find the PV of the ordinary annuity and then multiply by $(1 + I) = 1.05$, calculating $\$272.32(1.05) = \$285.94$, the PV of the annuity due.

| N | I/YR | PV | PMT | FV | |
|---|------|-----|------|-----|---|
| 3 | 5 | | −100 | 0 | **End Mode** (Ordinary Annuity) |
| | | 272.32 | | | |

| N | I/YR | PV | PMT | FV | |
|---|------|-----|------|-----|---|
| 3 | 5 | | −100 | 0 | **Begin Mode** (Annuity Due) |
| | | 285.94 | | | |

## quick question

**QUESTION:**

You just won the Florida lottery. To receive your winnings, you must select one of the two following choices:

1. You can receive $1,000,000 a year at the end of each of the next 30 years; OR
2. You can receive a one-time payment of $15,000,000 today.

Assume that the current interest rate is 6%. Which option is most valuable?

**ANSWER:**

The most valuable option is the one with the largest present value. You know that the second option has a present value of $15,000,000, so we need to determine whether the present value of the $1,000,000 30-year ordinary annuity exceeds $15,000,000.

Using the formula approach, we see that the present value of the annuity is:

$$PVA_N = PMT \left[ \frac{1 - \frac{1}{(1+I)^N}}{I} \right]$$

$$= \$1,000,000 \left[ \frac{1 - \frac{1}{(1.06)^{30}}}{0.06} \right]$$

$$= \$13,764,831.15$$

Alternatively, using the calculator approach we can set up the problem as follows:

| 30 | 6 | | −1000000 | 0 |
|----|----|----|----|----|
| N | I/YR | PV | PMT | FV |
| | | 13,764,831.15 | | |

Finally, we can use Excel's PV function:

=PV(0.06,30,−1000000,0)

**PV**(rate, nper, pmt, [fv], [type])

Here we find that the present value is **$13,746,831.15**.

Because the present value of the 30-year annuity is less than $15,000,000, you should choose to receive your winnings as a one-time upfront payment.

## SelfTest

Why does an annuity due have a higher present value than a similar ordinary annuity?

If you know the present value of an ordinary annuity, how can you find the PV of the corresponding annuity due?

What is the PVA of an ordinary annuity with 10 payments of $100 if the appropriate interest rate is 10%? What would the PVA be if the interest rate was 4%? What if the interest rate was 0%? How much would the PVA values be if we were dealing with annuities due? **($614.46, $811.09, $1,000.00, $675.90, $843.53, $1,000.00)**

Assume that you are offered an annuity that pays $100 at the end of each year for 10 years. You could earn 8% on your money in other investments with equal risk. What is the most you should pay for the annuity? If the payments began immediately, how much would the annuity be worth? **($671.01, $724.69)**

# 5-10 Finding Annuity Payments, Periods, and Interest Rates

We can find payments, periods, and interest rates for annuities. Here five variables come into play: N, I, PMT, FV, and PV. If we know any four, we can find the fifth.

## 5-10A FINDING ANNUITY PAYMENTS, PMT

Suppose we need to accumulate $10,000 and have it available 5 years from now. Suppose further that we can earn a return of 6% on our savings, which are currently zero. Thus, we know that FV = 10,000, PV = 0, N = 5, and I/YR = 6. We can enter these values in a financial calculator and press the PMT key to find how large our deposits must be. The answer will, of course, depend on whether we make deposits at the end of each year (ordinary annuity) or at the beginning (annuity due). Here are the results for each type of annuity:

**Ordinary Annuity:**

| 5 | 6 | 0 | | 10000 | **End Mode** |
|---|---|---|---|---|---|
| N | I/YR | PV | PMT | FV | (Ordinary |
| | | | −1,773.96 | | Annuity) |

We can also use Excel's PMT function:

```
=PMT(0.06,5,0,10000
```
**PMT**(rate, nper, pv, [fv], [type])

Because the deposits are made at the end of the year, we can leave "type" blank. Here we find that an annual deposit of $1,773.96 is needed to reach your goal.

**Annuity Due:**

| 5 | 6 | 0 | | 10000 | Begin Mode |
|---|---|---|---|---|---|
| N | I/YR | PV | PMT | FV | (Annuity Due) |
| | | | −1,673.55 | | |

Alternatively, Excel's PMT function can be used to calculate the annual deposit for the annuity due:

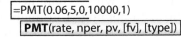

=PMT(0.06,5,0,10000,1)

**PMT**(rate, nper, pv, [fv], [type])

Because the deposits are now made at the beginning of the year, enter 1 for type. Here we find that an annual deposit of $1,673.55 is needed to reach your goal.

Thus, you must save $1,773.96 per year if you make deposits at the *end* of each year, but only $1,673.55 if the deposits begin *immediately*. Note that the required annual deposit for the annuity due can also be calculated as the ordinary annuity payment divided by $(1 + I)$: $1,773.96/1.06 = $1,673.55.

## 5-10B FINDING THE NUMBER OF PERIODS, N

Suppose you decide to make end-of-year deposits, but you can save only $1,200 per year. Again assuming that you would earn 6%, how long would it take to reach your $10,000 goal? Here is the calculator setup:

| | 6 | 0 | −1200 | 10000 | End Mode |
|---|---|---|---|---|---|
| N | I/YR | PV | PMT | FV | |
| 6.96 | | | | | |

With these smaller deposits, it would take 6.96 years to reach your $10,000 goal. If you began the deposits immediately, you would have an annuity due, and N would be a bit smaller, 6.63 years.

You can also use Excel's NPER function to arrive at both of these answers. If we assume end-of-year payments, Excel's NPER function looks like this:

=NPER(0.06,−1200,0,10000)

**NPER**(rate, pmt, pv, [fv], [type])

Here we find that it will take 6.96 years to reach your goal.

If we assume beginning-of-year payments, Excel's NPER function looks like this:

=NPER(0.06,−1200,0,10000,1)

**NPER**(rate, pmt, pv, [fv], [type])

Here we find that it will take only 6.63 years to reach your goal.

## 5-10C FINDING THE INTEREST RATE, I

Now suppose you can save only $1,200 annually, but you still need the $10,000 in 5 years. What rate of return would enable you to achieve your goal? Here is the calculator setup:

| 5 | | 0 | −1200 | 10000 | End Mode |
|---|---|---|---|---|---|
| N | I/YR | PV | PMT | FV | |
| | 25.78 | | | | |

Excel's RATE function will arrive at the same answer:

=RATE(5,–1200,0,10000)

**RATE**(nper, pmt, pv, [fv], [type], [guess])

Here we find that the interest rate is 25.78%.

You must earn a whopping 25.78% to reach your goal. About the only way to earn such a high return would be to invest in speculative stocks or head to the casinos in Las Vegas. Of course, investing in speculative stocks and gambling aren't like making deposits in a bank with a guaranteed rate of return, so there's a good chance you'd end up with nothing. You might consider changing your plans—save more, lower your $10,000 target, or extend your time horizon. It might be appropriate to seek a somewhat higher return, but trying to earn 25.78% in a 6% market would require taking on more risk than would be prudent.

It's easy to find rates of return using a financial calculator or a spreadsheet. However, to find rates of return without one of these tools, you would have to go through a trial-and-error process, which would be very time consuming if many years were involved.

## SelfTest

Suppose you inherited $100,000 and invested it at 7% per year. What is the most you could withdraw at the *end* of each of the next 10 years and have a zero balance at Year 10? How much could you withdraw if you made withdrawals at the *beginning* of each year? **($14,237.75, $13,306.31)**

If you had $100,000 that was invested at 7% and you wanted to withdraw $10,000 at the end of each year, how long would your funds last? How long would they last if you earned 0%? How long would they last if you earned the 7% but limited your withdrawals to $7,000 per year? **(17.8 years, 10 years, forever)**

Your uncle named you beneficiary of his life insurance policy. The insurance company gives you a choice of $100,000 today or a 12-year annuity of $12,000 at the end of each year. What rate of return is the insurance company offering? **(6.11%)**

Assume that you just inherited an annuity that will pay you $10,000 per year for 10 years, with the first payment being made today. A friend of your mother offers to give you $60,000 for the annuity. If you sell it, what rate of return would your mother's friend earn on his investment? If you think a "fair" return would be 6%, how much should you ask for the annuity? **(13.70%, $78,016.92)**

## 5-11 Perpetuities

**Perpetuity**
A stream of equal payments at fixed intervals expected to continue forever.

A **perpetuity** is simply an annuity with an extended life. Because the payments go on forever, you can't apply the step-by-step approach. However, it's easy to find the PV of a perpetuity with a formula found by solving Equation 5.5 with N set at infinity:[10]

---

[10]Equation 5.6 was found by letting N in Equation 5.5 approach infinity.

$$\text{PV of a perpetuity} = \frac{\text{PMT}}{\text{I}}$$

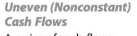 5.6

Let's say, for example, that you buy preferred stock in a company that pays you a fixed dividend of $2.50 each year the company is in business. If we assume that the company will go on indefinitely, the preferred stock can be valued as a perpetuity. If the discount rate on the preferred stock is 10%, the present value of the perpetuity, the preferred stock, is $25:

$$\text{PV of a perpetuity} = \frac{\$2.50}{0.10} = \$25$$

## Self Test

What's the present value of a perpetuity that pays $1,000 per year beginning 1 year from now, if the appropriate interest rate is 5%? What would the value be if payments on the annuity began immediately? **($20,000, $21,000. Hint: Just add the $1,000 to be received immediately to the value of the annuity.)**

# 5-12 Uneven Cash Flows

The definition of an annuity includes the words *constant payment*—in other words, annuities involve payments that are equal in every period. Although many financial decisions involve constant payments, many others involve **uneven**, or **nonconstant, cash flows**. For example, the dividends on common stocks typically increase over time, and investments in capital equipment almost always generate uneven cash flows. Throughout the book, we reserve the term **payment (PMT)** for annuities with their equal payments in each period and use the term **cash flow (CF$_t$)** to denote uneven cash flows, where t designates the period in which the cash flow occurs.

There are two important classes of uneven cash flows: (1) a stream that consists of a series of annuity payments plus an additional final lump sum and (2) all other uneven streams. Bonds represent the best example of the first type, while stocks and capital investments illustrate the second type. Here are numerical examples of the two types of flows:

*Uneven (Nonconstant) Cash Flows*
A series of cash flows where the amount varies from one period to the next.

*Payment (PMT)*
This term designates equal cash flows coming at regular intervals.

*Cash Flow (CF$_t$)*
This term designates a cash flow that's not part of an annuity.

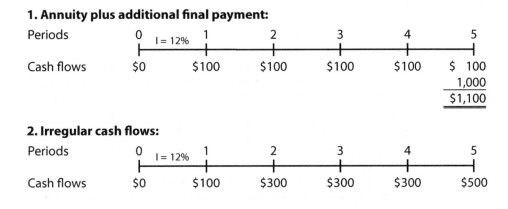

**1. Annuity plus additional final payment:**

| Periods | 0 | | 1 | 2 | 3 | 4 | 5 |
|---|---|---|---|---|---|---|---|
| | | I = 12% | | | | | |
| Cash flows | $0 | | $100 | $100 | $100 | $100 | $ 100 |
| | | | | | | | 1,000 |
| | | | | | | | $1,100 |

**2. Irregular cash flows:**

| Periods | 0 | | 1 | 2 | 3 | 4 | 5 |
|---|---|---|---|---|---|---|---|
| | | I = 12% | | | | | |
| Cash flows | $0 | | $100 | $300 | $300 | $300 | $500 |

We can find the PV of either stream by using Equation 5.7 and following the step-by-step procedure, where we discount each cash flow and then sum them to find the PV of the stream:

$$PV = \frac{CF_1}{(1+I)^1} + \frac{CF_2}{(1+I)^2} + \cdots + \frac{CF_N}{(1+I)^N} = \sum_{t=1}^{N} \frac{CF_t}{(1+I)^t} \qquad \blacktriangledown \quad 5.7$$

If we did this, we would find the PV of Stream 1 to be $927.90 and the PV of Stream 2 to be $1,016.35.

The step-by-step procedure is straightforward; but if we have a large number of cash flows, it is time consuming. However, financial calculators speed up the process considerably. First, consider Stream 1; notice that we have a 5-year, 12% ordinary annuity plus a final payment of $1,000. We could find the PV of the annuity, and then find the PV of the final payment and sum them to obtain the PV of the stream. Financial calculators do this in one simple step—use the five TVM keys; enter the data as shown below and press the PV key to obtain the answer, $927.90.

| 5 | 12 | | 100 | 1000 |
|---|---|---|---|---|
| N | I/YR | PV | PMT | FV |
| | | −927.90 | | |

The solution procedure is different for the second uneven stream. Here we must use the step-by-step approach, as shown in Figure 5.3. Even calculators and spreadsheets solve the problem using the step-by-step procedure, but they do it quickly and efficiently. First, you enter all of the cash flows and the interest rate; then the calculator or computer discounts each cash flow to find its present value and sums these PVs to produce the PV of the stream. You must enter each cash flow in the calculator's "cash flow register," enter the interest rate, and then press the NPV key to find the PV of the stream. NPV stands for "net present value." We cover the calculator mechanics in the calculator tutorial, and we discuss the process in more detail in Chapters 9 and 11, where we use the NPV calculation to analyze stocks and proposed capital budgeting projects. If you don't know how to do the calculation with your calculator, it would be worthwhile to review the tutorial or your calculator manual, learn the steps, and make sure you can do this calculation. Because you will have to learn to do it eventually, now is a good time to begin.

**FIGURE 5.3**    PV of an Uneven Cash Flow Stream

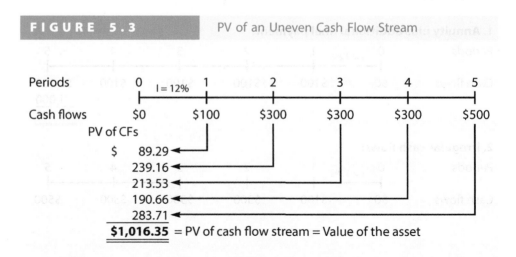

## SelfTest

How could you use Equation 5.2 to find the PV of an uneven stream of cash flows?

What's the present value of a 5-year ordinary annuity of $100 plus an additional $500 at the end of Year 5 if the interest rate is 6%? What is the PV if the $100 payments occur in Years 1 through 10 and the $500 comes at the end of Year 10? **($794.87; $1,015.21)**

What's the present value of the following uneven cash flow stream: $0 at Time 0, $100 in Year 1 (or at Time 1), $200 in Year 2, $0 in Year 3, and $400 in Year 4 if the interest rate is 8%? **($558.07)**

Would a typical common stock provide cash flows more like an annuity or more like an uneven cash flow stream? Explain.

# 5-13 Future Value of an Uneven Cash Flow Stream

We find the future value of uneven cash flow streams by compounding rather than discounting. Consider Cash Flow Stream 2 in the preceding section. We discounted those cash flows to find the PV, but we would compound them to find the FV. Figure 5.4 illustrates the procedure for finding the FV of the stream, using the step-by-step approach.

The values of all financial assets—stocks, bonds, and business capital investments—are found as the present values of their expected future cash flows. Therefore, we need to calculate present values very often, far more often than future values. As a result, all financial calculators provide automated functions for finding PVs, but they generally do not provide automated FV functions. On the relatively few occasions when we need to find the FV of an uneven cash flow stream, we generally use the step-by-step procedure shown in Figure 5.4. That approach works for all cash flow streams, even those for which some cash flows are zero or negative.[11]

---

**FIGURE 5.4**     FV of an Uneven Cash Flow Stream

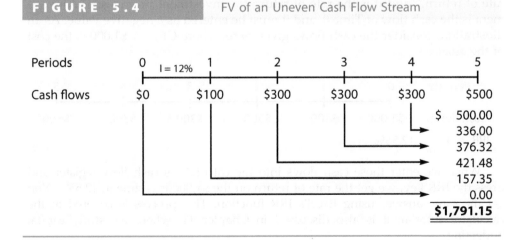

---

[11]The HP 10bII+ calculator provides a shortcut to finding the FV of a cash flow stream. Enter the cash flows into the cash flow register; input the interest rate; and calculate the net present value of the stream. Once the NPV of the stream is calculated, simply press SWAP, and the calculator will display the FV of the cash flow stream.

Why are we more likely to need to calculate the PV of cash flow streams than the FV of streams?

What is the future value of this cash flow stream: $100 at the end of 1 year, $150 due after 2 years, and $300 due after 3 years, if the appropriate interest rate is 15%? **($604.75)**

## 5-14 Solving for I with Uneven Cash Flows[12]

Before financial calculators and spreadsheets existed, it was *extremely difficult* to find I when the cash flows were uneven. With spreadsheets and financial calculators, however, it's relatively easy to find I. If you have an annuity plus a final lump sum, you can input values for N, PV, PMT, and FV into the calculator's TVM registers and then press the I/YR key. Here is the setup for Stream 1 from Section 5-12, assuming we must pay $927.90 to buy the asset. The rate of return on the $927.90 investment is 12%.

| 5 | | −927.90 | 100 | 1000 |
|---|---|---|---|---|
| N | I/YR | PV | PMT | FV |
| | 12.00 | | | |

Finding the interest rate for an uneven cash flow stream such as Stream 2 is a bit more complicated. First, note that there is no simple procedure—finding the rate requires a trial-and-error process, which means that a financial calculator or a spreadsheet is needed. With a calculator, we enter each CF into the cash flow register and then press the IRR key to get the answer. IRR stands for "internal rate of return," and it is the rate of return the investment provides. The investment is the cash flow at Time 0, and it must be entered as a negative value. As an illustration, consider the cash flows given here, where $CF_0 = -\$1,000$ is the cost of the asset.

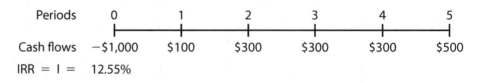

| Periods | 0 | 1 | 2 | 3 | 4 | 5 |
|---|---|---|---|---|---|---|
| Cash flows | −$1,000 | $100 | $300 | $300 | $300 | $500 |
| IRR = I = | 12.55% | | | | | |

When we enter those cash flows into the calculator's cash flow register and press the IRR key, we get the rate of return on the $1,000 investment, 12.55%. You get the same answer using Excel's IRR function. This process is covered in the calculator tutorial; it is also discussed in Chapter 11, where we study capital budgeting.

---

[12]This section is relatively technical. It can be deferred at this point, but the calculations will be required in Chapter 11.

## SelfTest

An investment costs $465 and is expected to produce cash flows of $100 at the end of each of the next 4 years, then an extra lump sum payment of $200 at the end of the fourth year. What is the expected rate of return on this investment? **(9.05%)**

An investment costs $465 and is expected to produce cash flows of $100 at the end of Year 1, $200 at the end of Year 2, and $300 at the end of Year 3. What is the expected rate of return on this investment? **(11.71%)**

# 5-15 Semiannual and Other Compounding Periods

In all of our examples thus far, we assumed that interest was compounded once a year, or annually. This is called **annual compounding**. Suppose, however, that you deposit $100 in a bank that pays a 5% annual interest rate but credits interest each 6 months. So in the second 6-month period, you earn interest on your original $100 plus interest on the interest earned during the first 6 months. This is called **semiannual compounding**. Note that banks generally pay interest more than once a year; virtually all bonds pay interest semiannually; and most mortgages, student loans, and auto loans require monthly payments. Therefore, it is important to understand how to deal with nonannual compounding.

For an illustration of semiannual compounding, assume that we deposit $100 in an account that pays 5% and leave it there for 10 years. First, consider again what the future value would be under *annual* compounding:

$$FV_N = PV(1 + I)^N = \$100(1.05)^{10} = \$162.89$$

We would, of course, get the same answer using a financial calculator or a spreadsheet.

How would things change in this example if interest was paid semiannually rather than annually? First, whenever payments occur more than once a year, you must make two conversions: (1) Convert the stated interest rate into a "periodic rate." (2) Convert the number of years into "number of periods." The conversions are done as follows, where I is the stated annual rate, M is the number of compounding periods per year, and N is the number of years:

$$\text{Periodic rate } (I_{PER}) = \frac{\text{Stated annual rate}}{\text{Number of payments per year}} = I/M \qquad \text{5.8}$$

With a stated annual rate of 5%, compounded semiannually, the periodic rate is 2.5%:

$$\text{Periodic rate} = 5\%/2 = 2.5\%$$

The number of compounding periods is found with Equation 5.9:

$$\text{Number of periods} = (\text{Number of years})(\text{Periods per year}) = NM \qquad \text{5.9}$$

With 10 years and semiannual compounding, there are 20 periods:

$$\text{Number of periods} = 10(2) = 20 \text{ periods}$$

**Annual Compounding**
The arithmetic process of determining the final value of a cash flow or series of cash flows when interest is added once a year.

**Semiannual Compounding**
The arithmetic process of determining the final value of a cash flow or series of cash flows when interest is added twice a year.

Under semiannual compounding, our $100 investment will earn 2.5% every 6 months for 20 semiannual periods, not 5% per year for 10 years. The periodic rate and number of periods, not the annual rate and number of years, must be shown on time lines and entered into the calculator or spreadsheet whenever you are working with nonannual compounding.[13]

With this background, we can find the value of $100 after 10 years if it is held in an account that pays a stated annual rate of 5.0%, but with semiannual compounding. Here's the time line and the future value:

Periods | 0 | | 1 | | 2 | | | 19 | | 20
Cash flows | −$100

$I = 2.5\%$

$\text{PV } (1 + I)^N = \$100(1.025)^{20} = FV_{20} = \$163.86$

With a financial calculator, we get the same result using the periodic rate and number of periods:

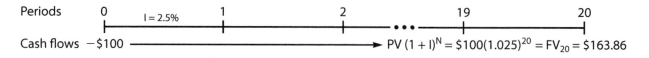

| 20 | 2.5 | −100 | 0 | |
|---|---|---|---|---|
| N | I/YR | PV | PMT | FV |
| | | | | 163.86 |

The future value under semiannual compounding, $163.86, exceeds the FV under annual compounding, $162.89, because interest starts accruing sooner; thus, you earn more interest on interest.

How would things change in our example if interest was compounded quarterly or monthly or daily? With quarterly compounding, there would be NM = 10(4) = 40 periods and the periodic rate would be I/M = 5%/4 = 1.25% per quarter. Using those values, we would find FV = $164.36. If we used monthly compounding, we would have 10(12) = 120 periods, the monthly rate would be 5%/12 = 0.416667%, and the FV would rise to $164.70. If we went to daily compounding, we would have 10(365) = 3,650 periods, the daily rate would be 5%/365 = 0.0136986% per day, and the FV would be $164.87 (based on a 365-day year).

The same logic applies when we find present values under semiannual compounding. Again, we use Equation 5.8 to convert the stated annual rate to the periodic (semiannual) rate and Equation 5.9 to find the number of semiannual periods. We then use the periodic rate and number of periods in the calculations. For example, we can find the PV of $100 due after 10 years when the stated annual rate is 5%, with semiannual compounding:

$$\text{Periodic rate} = 5\%/2 = 2.5\% \text{ per period}$$
$$\text{Number of periods} = 10(2) = 20 \text{ periods}$$
$$\text{PV of } \$100 = \$100/(1.025)^{20} = \$61.03$$

---

[13]With some financial calculators, you can enter the annual (nominal) rate and the number of compounding periods per year rather than make the conversions we recommend. We prefer the conversions because they must be used on time lines and because it is easy to forget to reset your calculator after you change its settings, which may lead to an error on your next calculations.

We would get this same result with a financial calculator:

| 20 | 2.5 | | 0 | −100 |
|---|---|---|---|---|
| N | I/YR | PV | PMT | FV |
| | | 61.03 | | |

If we increased the number of compounding periods from 2 (semiannual) to 12 (monthly), the PV would decline to $60.72; and if we went to daily compounding, the PV would fall to $60.66.

## Self*Test*

Would you rather invest in an account that pays 7% with annual compounding or 7% with monthly compounding? Would you rather borrow at 7% and make annual or monthly payments? Why?

What's the *future value* of $100 after 3 years if the appropriate interest rate is 8% compounded annually? Compounded monthly? **($125.97, $127.02)**

What's the *present value* of $100 due in 3 years if the appropriate interest rate is 8% compounded annually? Compounded monthly? **($79.38, $78.73)**

# 5-16 Comparing Interest Rates

Different compounding periods are used for different types of investments. For example, bank accounts generally pay interest daily; most bonds pay interest semiannually; stocks pay dividends quarterly; and mortgages, auto loans, and other instruments require monthly payments.[14] If we are to compare investments or loans with different compounding periods properly, we need to put them on a common basis. Here are some terms you need to understand:

- The **nominal interest rate** ($I_{NOM}$), also called the **annual percentage rate (APR)** (or **quoted** or **stated rate**), is the rate that credit card companies, student loan officers, auto dealers, and other lenders tell you they are charging on loans. Note that if two banks offer loans with a stated rate of 8%, but one requires monthly payments and the other quarterly payments, they are not charging the same "true" rate. The one that requires monthly payments is charging more than the one with quarterly payments because it will receive your money sooner. So to compare loans across lenders, or interest rates earned on different securities, you should calculate effective annual rates as described here.[15]

- The **effective annual rate**, abbreviated **EFF%**, is also called the **equivalent annual rate (EAR)**. This is the rate that would produce the same future value

*Nominal (Quoted or Stated) Interest Rate, $I_{NOM}$*
The contracted interest rate.

*Annual Percentage Rate (APR)*
The periodic rate times the number of periods per year.

*Effective (Equivalent) Annual Rate (EFF% or EAR)*
The annual rate of interest actually being earned, as opposed to the quoted rate.

---

[14]Some banks even pay interest compounded continuously. Continuous compounding is discussed in Web Appendix 5A.

[15]Note, though, that if you are comparing two bonds that both pay interest semiannually, it's okay to compare their nominal rates. Similarly, you can compare the nominal rates on two money funds that pay interest daily. But don't compare the nominal rate on a semiannual bond with the nominal rate on a money fund that compounds daily because that will make the money fund look worse than it really is.

under annual compounding as would more frequent compounding at a given nominal rate.

- If a loan or an investment uses annual compounding, its nominal rate is also its effective rate. However, if compounding occurs more than once a year, the EFF% is higher than $I_{NOM}$.

- To illustrate, a nominal rate of 10% with semiannual compounding is equivalent to a rate of 10.25% with annual compounding because both rates will cause $100 to grow to the same amount after 1 year. The top line in the following diagram shows that $100 will grow to $110.25 at a nominal rate of 10.25%. The lower line shows the situation if the nominal rate is 10% but semiannual compounding is used.

```
0                                                                    1
     Nom = EFF% = 10.25%

$100.00 - - - - - - - - - - - - - - - - - - - - - - - - - - - - - -→ $110.25


0                                                      1              2
     Nom = 10.00% semi; EFF% = 10.25%

$100.00 - - - - - - - - - - - -→ $105 ────────────────→ $110.25
```

Given the nominal rate and the number of compounding periods per year, we can find the effective annual rate with this equation:

$$\text{Effective annual rate (EFF\%)} = \left[1 + \frac{I_{NOM}}{M}\right]^M - 1.0 \qquad \blacktriangledown \quad 5.10$$

Here $I_{NOM}$ is the nominal rate expressed as a decimal and M is the number of compounding periods per year. In our example, the nominal rate is 10%; but with semiannual compounding, $I_{NOM} = 10\% = 0.10$ and $M = 2$. This results in EFF% = 10.25%:

$$\text{Effective annual rate (EFF\%)} = \left[1 + \frac{0.10}{2}\right]^2 - 1 = 0.1025 = 10.25\%$$

We can also use the EFFECT function in Excel to solve for the effective rate:

```
=EFFECT (0.1,2)
  EFFECT(nominal_rate, npery)
```

Here we find that the effective rate is 10.25%. NPERY refers to the number of payments per year. Likewise, if you know the effective rate and want to solve for the nominal rate, you can use the NOMINAL function in Excel.[16] Thus, if one investment promises to pay 10% with semiannual compounding, and an equally risky investment promises 10.25% with annual compounding, we would be indifferent between the two.

---

[16]Most financial calculators are programmed to find the EFF% or, given the EFF%, to find the nominal rate. This is called *interest rate conversion*. You enter the nominal rate and the number of compounding periods per year and then press the EFF% key to find the effective annual rate. However, we generally use Equation 5.10 because it's as easy to use as the interest rate conversion feature, and the equation reminds us of what we are really doing. If you use the interest rate conversion feature on your calculator, don't forget to reset your calculator settings. Interest rate conversion is discussed in the calculator tutorials.

quick question

QUESTION:

You just received your first credit card and decided to purchase a new Apple iPad. You charged the iPad's $500 purchase price on your new credit card. Assume that the nominal interest rate on the credit card is 18% and that interest is compounded monthly.

The minimum payment on the credit card is only $10 a month. If you pay the minimum and make no other charges, how long will it take you to fully pay off the credit card?

ANSWER:

Here we are given that the nominal interest rate is 18%. It follows that the monthly periodic rate is 1.5% (18%/12). Using a financial calculator, we can solve for the number of months that it takes to pay off the credit card.

| | 1.5 | 500 | −10 | 0 |
|---|---|---|---|---|
| N | I/YR | PV | PMT | FV |
| 93.11 | | | | |

We can also use Excel's NPER function:

=NPER(0.015,−10,500,0)

NPER(rate, pmt, pv, [fv], [type])

Here we find that it will take **93.11** months to pay off the credit card.

Note that it would take you almost 8 years to pay off your iPad purchase. Now, you see why you can quickly get into financial trouble if you don't manage your credit cards wisely!

## SelfTest

Define the terms *annual percentage rate (APR)*, *effective annual rate (EFF%)*, and *nominal interest rate* ($I_{NOM}$).

A bank pays 5% with daily compounding on its savings accounts. Should it advertise the nominal or effective rate if it is seeking to attract new deposits?

By law, credit card issuers must print their annual percentage rate on their monthly statements. A common APR is 18% with interest paid monthly. What is the EFF% on such a loan? [EFF% = $(1 + 0.18 / 12)^{12} - 1 = 0.1956 = 19.56\%$]

Some years ago banks didn't have to reveal the rates they charged on credit cards. Then Congress passed the Truth in Lending Act that required banks to publish their APRs. Is the APR really the most truthful rate, or would the EFF% be more truthful? Explain.

# 5-17 Fractional Time Periods

Thus far we have assumed that payments occur at the beginning or the end of periods but not *within* periods. However, we often encounter situations that require compounding or discounting over fractional periods. For example, suppose you deposited $100 in a bank that pays a nominal rate of 10% but adds interest daily, based on a 365-day year. How much would you have after 9 months? The answer is $107.79, found as follows:[17]

$$
\begin{aligned}
\text{Periodic rate} &= \text{I}_{PER} = 0.10/365 = 0.000273973 \text{ per day} \\
\text{Number of days} &= (9/12)(365) = 0.75(365) = 273.75, \text{ rounded to } 274 \\
\text{Ending amount} &= \$100(1.000273973)^{274} = \$107.79
\end{aligned}
$$

Now suppose you borrow $100 from a bank whose nominal rate is 10% per year simple interest, which means that interest is not earned on interest. If the loan is outstanding for 274 days, how much interest would you have to pay? Here we would calculate a daily interest rate, $\text{I}_{PER}$, as just shown, but multiply it by 274 rather than use the 274 as an exponent:

$$
\text{Interest owed} = \$100(0.000273973)(274) = \$7.51
$$

You would owe the bank a total of $107.51 after 274 days. This is the procedure that most banks use to calculate interest on loans, except that they require borrowers to pay the interest on a monthly basis rather than after 274 days.

## SelfTest

Suppose a company borrowed $1 million at a rate of 9% simple interest, with interest paid at the end of each month. The bank uses a 360-day year. How much interest would the firm have to pay in a 30-day month? What would the interest be if the bank used a 365-day year? **[(0.09/360) (30) ($1,000,000) = $7,500 interest for the month. For the 365-day year, (0.09/365)(30)($1,000,000) = $7,397.26 of interest. The use of a 360-day year raises the interest cost by $102.74, which is why banks like to use it on loans.]**

Suppose you deposited $1,000 in a credit union account that pays 7% with daily compounding and a 365-day year. What is the EFF%, and how much could you withdraw after seven months, assuming this is seven-twelfths of a year? **[EFF% = $(1 + 0.07/365)^{365} - 1 = 0.07250098 = 7.250098\%$. Thus, your account would grow from $1,000 to $1,000 $(1.07250098)^{0.583333} = \$1,041.67$, and you could withdraw that amount.]**

---

[17]Bank loan contracts specifically state whether they are based on a 360- or a 365-day year. If a 360-day year is used, the daily rate is higher, which means that the effective rate is also higher. Here we assumed a 365-day year. Also note that in real-world calculations, banks' computers have built-in calendars, so they can calculate the exact number of days, taking account of 30-day, 31-day, and 28- or 29-day months.

# 5-18 Amortized Loans[18]

An important application of compound interest involves loans that are paid off in installments over time. Included are automobile loans, home mortgage loans, student loans, and many business loans. A loan that is to be repaid in equal amounts on a monthly, quarterly, or annual basis is called an **amortized loan**.[19]

*Amortized Loan*
A loan that is repaid in equal payments over its life.

Table 5.4 illustrates the amortization process. A homeowner borrows $100,000 on a mortgage loan, and the loan is to be repaid in five equal payments at the end of each of the next 5 years.[20] The lender charges 6% on the balance at the beginning of each year. Our first task is to determine the payment the homeowner must make each year. Here's a picture of the situation:

The payments must be such that the sum of their PVs equals $100,000:

$$\$100,000 = \frac{PMT}{(1.06)^1} + \frac{PMT}{(1.06)^2} + \frac{PMT}{(1.06)^3} + \frac{PMT}{(1.06)^4} + \frac{PMT}{(1.06)^5} = \sum_{t=1}^{5} \frac{PMT}{(1.06)^t}$$

We could insert values into a calculator as shown on the next page to get the required payments, $23,739.64:[21]

**Loan Amortization Schedule, $100,000 at 6% for 5 Years**   **TABLE 5.4**

Amount borrowed: $100,000
Years: 5
Rate: 6%
PMT: −$23,739.64

| Year | Beginning Amount (1) | Payment (2) | Interest[a] (3) | Repayment of Principal[b] (4) | Ending Balance (5) |
|---|---|---|---|---|---|
| 1 | $100,000.00 | $23,739.64 | $6,000.00 | $17,739.64 | $82,260.36 |
| 2 | 82,260.36 | 23,739.64 | 4,935.62 | 18,804.02 | 63,456.34 |
| 3 | 63,456.34 | 23,739.64 | 3,807.38 | 19,932.26 | 43,524.08 |
| 4 | 43,524.08 | 23,739.64 | 2,611.44 | 21,128.20 | 22,395.89 |
| 5 | 22,395.89 | 23,739.,64 | 1,343.75 | 22,395.89 | 0.00 |

*Notes:*

[a]Interest in each period is calculated by multiplying the loan balance at the beginning of the year by the interest rate. Therefore, interest in Year 1 is $100,000(0.06) = $6,000; in Year 2, it is $4,935.62; and so forth.

[b]Repayment of principal is equal to the payment of $23,739.64 minus the interest charge for the year.

---

[18]Amortized loans are important, but this section can be omitted without loss of continuity.

[19]The word *amortized* comes from the Latin *mors,* meaning "death"; so an amortized loan is one that is "killed off" over time.

[20]Most mortgage loans call for monthly payments over 10 to 30 years, but we use a shorter period to reduce the calculations.

[21]You could also factor out the PMT term; find the value of the remaining summation term (4.212364); and divide it into the $100,000 to find the payment, $23,739.64.

**Amortization Schedule**
A table showing precisely how a loan will be repaid. It gives the required payment on each payment date and a breakdown of the payment, showing how much is interest and how much is repayment of principal.

| 5 | 6 | 100000 | | 0 |
|---|---|--------|---|---|
| N | I/YR | PV | PMT | FV |
| | | | −23,739.64 | |

Therefore, the borrower must pay the lender $23,739.64 per year for the next 5 years.

Each payment will consist of two parts—interest and repayment of principal. This breakdown is shown on an **amortization schedule**, such as the one in Table 5.4. The interest component is relatively high in the first year, but it declines as the loan balance decreases. For tax purposes, the borrower would deduct the interest component, and the lender would report the same amount as taxable income.

## Self Test

Suppose you borrowed $30,000 on a student loan at a rate of 8% and must repay it in three equal installments at the end of each of the next 3 years. How large would your payments be; how much of the first payment would represent interest, how much would be principal; and what would your ending balance be after the first year? **(PMT = $11,641.01; Interest = $2,400; Principal = $9,241.01; Balance at end of Year 1 = $20,758.99)**

# TYING IT ALL TOGETHER

In this chapter, we worked with single payments, ordinary annuities, annuities due, perpetuities, and uneven cash flow streams. One fundamental equation, Equation 5.1, is used to calculate the future value of a given amount. The equation can be transformed to Equation 5.2 and then used to find the present value of a given future amount. We used time lines to show when cash flows occur; and we saw that time value of money problems can be solved in a step-by-step manner when we work with individual cash flows, with formulas that streamline the approach, with financial calculators, and with spreadsheets.

As we noted at the outset, TVM is the single most important concept in finance, and the procedures developed in Chapter 5 are used throughout this book. Time value analysis is used to find the values of stocks, bonds, and capital budgeting projects. It is also used to analyze personal finance problems, such as the retirement issue set forth in the opening vignette. You will become more familiar with time value analysis as you go through the book, but we *strongly recommend* that you get a good handle on Chapter 5 before you continue.

## Self-Test Questions and Problems

(Solutions Appear in Appendix A)

ST-1 **KEY TERMS**  Define each of the following terms:

a. Time line
b. $FV_N$; PV; I; INT; N; $FVA_N$; PMT; $PVA_N$
c. Compounding; discounting
d. Simple interest; compound interest

    e. Opportunity cost

    f. Annuity; ordinary (deferred) annuity; annuity due; perpetuity

    g. Uneven (nonconstant) cash flow; payment (PMT); cash flow ($CF_t$)

    h. Annual compounding; semiannual compounding

    i. Nominal (quoted) interest rate; annual percentage rate (APR); effective (equivalent) annual rate (EAR or EFF%)

    j. Amortized loan; amortization schedule

**ST-2**   **FUTURE VALUE**   It is now January 1, 2016. Today you will deposit $1,000 into a savings account that pays 8%.

    a. If the bank compounds interest annually, how much will you have in your account on January 1, 2019?

    b. What will your January 1, 2019, balance be if the bank uses quarterly compounding?

    c. Suppose you deposit $1,000 in three payments of $333.333 each on January 1 of 2017, 2018, and 2019. How much will you have in your account on January 1, 2019, based on 8% annual compounding?

    d. How much will be in your account if the three payments begin on January 1, 2016?

    e. Suppose you deposit three equal payments into your account on January 1 of 2017, 2018, and 2019. Assuming an 8% interest rate, how large must your payments be to have the same ending balance as in part a?

**ST-3**   **TIME VALUE OF MONEY**   It is now January 1, 2016; and you will need $1,000 on January 1, 2020, in 4 years. Your bank compounds interest at an 8% annual rate.

    a. How much must you deposit today to have a balance of $1,000 on January 1, 2020?

    b. If you want to make four equal payments on each January 1 from 2017 through 2020 to accumulate the $1,000, how large must each payment be? (Note that the payments begin a year from today.)

    c. If your father offers to make the payments calculated in part b ($221.92) or to give you $750 on January 1, 2017 (a year from today), which would you choose? Explain.

    d. If you have only $750 on January 1, 2017, what interest rate, compounded annually for 3 years, must you earn to have $1,000 on January 1, 2020?

    e. Suppose you can deposit only $200 each January 1 from 2017 through 2020 (4 years). What interest rate, with annual compounding, must you earn to end up with $1,000 on January 1, 2020?

    f. Your father offers to give you $400 on January 1, 2017. You will then make six additional equal payments each 6 months from July 2017 through January 2020. If your bank pays 8% compounded semiannually, how large must each payment be for you to end up with $1,000 on January 1, 2020?

    g. What is the EAR, or EFF%, earned on the bank account in part f? What is the APR earned on the account?

**ST-4**   **EFFECTIVE ANNUAL RATES**   Bank A offers loans at an 8% nominal rate (its APR) but requires that interest be paid quarterly; that is, it uses quarterly compounding. Bank B wants to charge the same effective rate on its loans, but it wants to collect interest on a monthly basis, that is, to use monthly compounding. What nominal rate must Bank B set?

# Questions

5-1   What is an *opportunity cost?* How is this concept used in TVM analysis, and where is it shown on a time line? Is a single number used in all situations? Explain.

5-2   Explain whether the following statement is true or false: $100 a year for 10 years is an annuity; but $100 in Year 1, $200 in Year 2, and $400 in Years 3 through 10 does *not* constitute an annuity. However, the second series *contains* an annuity.

**5-3** If a firm's earnings per share grew from $1 to $2 over a 10-year period, the *total growth* would be 100%, but the *annual growth rate* would be *less than* 10%. True or false? Explain. (Hint: If you aren't sure, plug in some numbers and check it out.)

**5-4** Would you rather have a savings account that pays 5% interest compounded semiannually or one that pays 5% interest compounded daily? Explain.

**5-5** To find the present value of an uneven series of cash flows, you must find the PVs of the individual cash flows and then sum them. Annuity procedures can never be of use, even when some of the cash flows constitute an annuity, because the entire series is not an annuity. True or false? Explain.

**5-6** The present value of a perpetuity is equal to the payment on the annuity, PMT, divided by the interest rate, I: PV = PMT/I. What is the *future value* of a perpetuity of PMT dollars per year? (Hint: The answer is infinity, but explain why.)

**5-7** Banks and other lenders are required to disclose a rate called the APR. What is this rate? Why did Congress require that it be disclosed? Is it the same as the effective annual rate? If you were comparing the costs of loans from different lenders, could you use their APRs to determine the loan with the lowest effective interest rate? Explain.

**5-8** What is a loan amortization schedule, and what are some ways these schedules are used?

# Problems

**Easy Problems 1–8**

**5-1** **FUTURE VALUE** If you deposit $2,000 in a bank account that pays 6% interest annually, how much will be in your account after 5 years?

**5-2** **PRESENT VALUE** What is the present value of a security that will pay $29,000 in 20 years if securities of equal risk pay 5% annually?

**5-3** **FINDING THE REQUIRED INTEREST RATE** Your parents will retire in 19 years. They currently have $350,000 saved, and they think they will need $800,000 at retirement. What annual interest rate must they earn to reach their goal, assuming they don't save any additional funds?

**5-4** **TIME FOR A LUMP SUM TO DOUBLE** If you deposit money today in an account that pays 4% annual interest, how long will it take to double your money?

**5-5** **TIME TO REACH A FINANCIAL GOAL** You have $33,556.25 in a brokerage account, and you plan to deposit an additional $5,000 at the end of every future year until your account totals $220,000. You expect to earn 12% annually on the account. How many years will it take to reach your goal?

**5-6** **FUTURE VALUE: ANNUITY VERSUS ANNUITY DUE** What's the future value of a 5%, 5-year ordinary annuity that pays $800 each year? If this was an annuity due, what would its future value be?

**5-7** **PRESENT AND FUTURE VALUES OF A CASH FLOW STREAM** An investment will pay $150 at the end of each of the next 3 years, $250 at the end of Year 4, $300 at the end of Year 5, and $500 at the end of Year 6. If other investments of equal risk earn 11% annually, what is its present value? Its future value?

**5-8** **LOAN AMORTIZATION AND EAR** You want to buy a car, and a local bank will lend you $40,000. The loan will be fully amortized over 5 years (60 months), and the nominal interest rate will be 8% with interest paid monthly. What will be the monthly loan payment? What will be the loan's EAR?

**Intermediate Problems 9–26**

**5-9   PRESENT AND FUTURE VALUES FOR DIFFERENT PERIODS**   Find the following values *using the equations* and then a financial calculator. Compounding/discounting occurs annually.

a.  An initial $600 compounded for 1 year at 6%
b.  An initial $600 compounded for 2 years at 6%
c.  The present value of $600 due in 1 year at a discount rate of 6%
d.  The present value of $600 due in 2 years at a discount rate of 6%

**5-10   PRESENT AND FUTURE VALUES FOR DIFFERENT INTEREST RATES**   Find the following values. Compounding/discounting occurs annually.

a.  An initial $200 compounded for 10 years at 4%
b.  An initial $200 compounded for 10 years at 8%
c.  The present value of $200 due in 10 years at 4%
d.  The present value of $1,870 due in 10 years at 8% and at 4%
e.  Define *present value* and illustrate it using a time line with data from part d. How are present values affected by interest rates?

**5-11   GROWTH RATES**   Sawyer Corporation's 2015 sales were $5 million. Its 2010 sales were $2.5 million.

a.  At what rate have sales been growing?
b.  Suppose someone made this statement: "Sales doubled in 5 years. This represents a growth of 100% in 5 years; so dividing 100% by 5, we find the growth rate to be 20% per year." Is the statement correct?

**5-12   EFFECTIVE RATE OF INTEREST**   Find the interest rates earned on each of the following:

a.  You *borrow* $720 and promise to pay back $792 at the end of 1 year.
b.  You *lend* $720 and the borrower promises to pay you $792 at the end of 1 year.
c.  You *borrow* $65,000 and promise to pay back $98,319 at the end of 14 years.
d.  You *borrow* $15,000 and promise to make payments of $4,058.60 at the end of each year for 5 years.

**5-13   TIME FOR A LUMP SUM TO DOUBLE**   How long will it take $300 to double if it earns the following rates? Compounding occurs once a year.

a.  6%
b.  13%
c.  21%
d.  100%

**5-14   FUTURE VALUE OF AN ANNUITY**   Find the *future values* of these *ordinary annuities*. Compounding occurs once a year.

a.  $500 per year for 8 years at 14%
b.  $250 per year for 4 years at 7%
c.  $700 per year for 4 years at 0%
d.  Rework parts a, b, and c assuming they are *annuities due.*

**5-15   PRESENT VALUE OF AN ANNUITY**   Find the *present values* of these *ordinary annuities*. Discounting occurs once a year.

a.  $600 per year for 12 years at 8%
b.  $300 per year for 6 years at 4%
c.  $500 per year for 6 years at 0%
d.  Rework parts a, b, and c assuming they are *annuities due.*

**5-16   PRESENT VALUE OF A PERPETUITY**   What is the present value of a $600 perpetuity if the interest rate is 5%? If interest rates doubled to 10%, what would its present value be?

**5-17   EFFECTIVE INTEREST RATE**   You borrow $230,000; the annual loan payments are $20,430.31 for 30 years. What interest rate are you being charged?

**5-18    UNEVEN CASH FLOW STREAM**

a. Find the present values of the following cash flow streams at a 5% discount rate.

| | 0 | 1 | 2 | 3 | 4 | 5 |
|---|---|---|---|---|---|---|
| Stream A | $0 | $150 | $450 | $450 | $450 | $250 |
| Stream B | $0 | $250 | $450 | $450 | $450 | $150 |

b. What are the PVs of the streams at a 0% discount rate?

**5-19    FUTURE VALUE OF AN ANNUITY**   Your client is 26 years old. She wants to begin saving for retirement, with the first payment to come one year from now. She can save $8,000 per year, and you advise her to invest it in the stock market, which you expect to provide an average return of 10% in the future.

a. If she follows your advice, how much money will she have at 65?
b. How much will she have at 70?
c. She expects to live for 20 years if she retires at 65 and for 15 years if she retires at 70. If her investments continue to earn the same rate, how much will she be able to withdraw at the end of each year after retirement at each retirement age?

**5-20    PV OF A CASH FLOW STREAM**   A rookie quarterback is negotiating his first NFL contract. His opportunity cost is 7%. He has been offered three possible 4-year contracts. Payments are guaranteed, and they would be made at the end of each year. Terms of each contract are as follows:

| | 1 | 2 | 3 | 4 |
|---|---|---|---|---|
| Contract 1 | $3,000,000 | $3,000,000 | $3,000,000 | $3,000,000 |
| Contract 2 | $2,000,000 | $3,000,000 | $4,500,000 | $5,500,000 |
| Contract 3 | $7,000,000 | $1,000,000 | $1,000,000 | $1,000,000 |

As his adviser, which contract would you recommend that he accept?

**5-21    EVALUATING LUMP SUMS AND ANNUITIES**   Kristina just won the lottery, and she must choose among three award options. She can elect to receive a lump sum today of $62 million, to receive 10 end-of-year payments of $9.5 million, or to receive 30 end-of-year payments of $5.6 million.

a. If she thinks she can earn 7% annually, which should she choose?
b. If she expects to earn 8% annually, which is the best choice?
c. If she expects to earn 9% annually, which option would you recommend?
d. Explain how interest rates influence her choice.

**5-22    LOAN AMORTIZATION**   Jan sold her house on December 31 and took a $10,000 mortgage as part of the payment. The 10-year mortgage has a 10% nominal interest rate, but it calls for semiannual payments beginning next June 30. Next year Jan must report on Schedule B of her IRS Form 1040 the amount of interest that was included in the two payments she received during the year.

a. What is the dollar amount of each payment Jan receives?
b. How much interest was included in the first payment? How much repayment of principal was included? How do these values change for the second payment?
c. How much interest must Jan report on Schedule B for the first year? Will her interest income be the same next year?
d. If the payments are constant, why does the amount of interest income change over time?

**5-23    FUTURE VALUE FOR VARIOUS COMPOUNDING PERIODS**   Find the amount to which $500 will grow under each of these conditions:

a. 12% compounded annually for 5 years
b. 12% compounded semiannually for 5 years

    c. 12% compounded quarterly for 5 years

    d. 12% compounded monthly for 5 years

    e. 12% compounded daily for 5 years

    f. Why does the observed pattern of FVs occur?

**5-24**   **PRESENT VALUE FOR VARIOUS DISCOUNTING PERIODS**  Find the present value of $500 due in the future under each of these conditions:

    a. 12% nominal rate, semiannual compounding, discounted back 5 years

    b. 12% nominal rate, quarterly compounding, discounted back 5 years

    c. 12% nominal rate, monthly compounding, discounted back 1 year

    d. Why do the differences in the PVs occur?

**5-25**   **FUTURE VALUE OF AN ANNUITY**  Find the future values of the following ordinary annuities:

    a. FV of $400 paid each 6 months for 5 years at a nominal rate of 12% compounded semiannually

    b. FV of $200 paid each 3 months for 5 years at a nominal rate of 12% compounded quarterly

    c. These annuities receive the same amount of cash during the 5-year period and earn interest at the same nominal rate, yet the annuity in part b ends up larger than the one in part a. Why does this occur?

**5-26**   **PV AND LOAN ELIGIBILITY**  You have saved $4,000 for a down payment on a new car. The largest monthly payment you can afford is $350. The loan will have a 12% APR based on end-of-month payments. What is the most expensive car you can afford if you finance it for 48 months? For 60 months?

**Challenging Problems 27–40**

**5-27**   **EFFECTIVE VERSUS NOMINAL INTEREST RATES**  Bank A pays 2% interest compounded annually on deposits, while Bank B pays 1.75% compounded daily.

    a. Based on the EAR (or EFF%), which bank should you use?

    b. Could your choice of banks be influenced by the fact that you might want to withdraw your funds during the year as opposed to at the end of the year? Assume that your funds must be left on deposit during an entire compounding period in order to receive any interest.

**5-28**   **NOMINAL INTEREST RATE AND EXTENDING CREDIT**  As a jewelry store manager, you want to offer credit, with interest on outstanding balances paid monthly. To carry receivables, you must borrow funds from your bank at a nominal 9%, monthly compounding. To offset your overhead, you want to charge your customers an EAR (or EFF%) that is 3% more than the bank is charging you. What APR rate should you charge your customers?

**5-29**   **BUILDING CREDIT COST INTO PRICES**  Your firm sells for cash only, but it is thinking of offering credit, allowing customers 90 days to pay. Customers understand the time value of money, so they would all wait and pay on the 90th day. To carry these receivables, you would have to borrow funds from your bank at a nominal 9%, daily compounding based on a 360-day year. You want to increase your base prices by exactly enough to offset your bank interest cost. To the closest whole percentage point, by how much should you raise your product prices?

**5-30**   **REACHING A FINANCIAL GOAL**  Allison and Leslie, who are twins, just received $10,000 each for their 25th birthday. They both have aspirations to become millionaires. Each plans to make a $5,000 annual contribution to her "early retirement fund" on her birthday, beginning a year from today. Allison opened an account with the Safety First Bond Fund, a mutual fund that invests in high-quality bonds whose investors have earned 8% per year in the past. Leslie invested in the New Issue Bio-Tech Fund, which invests in small, newly issued bio-tech stocks and whose investors have earned an average of 13% per year in the fund's relatively short history.

    a. If the two women's funds earn the same returns in the future as in the past, how old will each be when she becomes a millionaire?

    b. How large would Allison's annual contributions have to be for her to become a millionaire at the same age as Leslie, assuming their expected returns are realized?

    c. Is it rational or irrational for Allison to invest in the bond fund rather than in stocks?

**5-31**   **REQUIRED LUMP SUM PAYMENT**  Starting next year, you will need $5,000 annually for 4 years to complete your education. (One year from today you will withdraw the first

$5,000.) Your uncle deposits an amount *today* in a bank paying 6% annual interest, which will provide the needed $5,000 payments.

a. How large must the deposit be?

b. How much will be in the account immediately after you make the first withdrawal?

**5-32  REACHING A FINANCIAL GOAL**  Six years from today you need $10,000. You plan to deposit $1,500 annually, with the first payment to be made a year from today, in an account that pays a 5% effective annual rate. Your last deposit, which will occur at the end of Year 6, will be for less than $1,500 if less is needed to reach $10,000. How large will your last payment be?

**5-33  FV OF UNEVEN CASH FLOW**  You want to buy a house within 3 years, and you are currently saving for the down payment. You plan to save $9,000 at the end of the first year, and you anticipate that your annual savings will increase by 5% annually thereafter. Your expected annual return is 8%. How much will you have for a down payment at the end of Year 3?

**5-34  AMORTIZATION SCHEDULE**

a. Set up an amortization schedule for a $19,000 loan to be repaid in equal installments at the end of each of the next 3 years. The interest rate is 8% compounded annually.

b. What percentage of the payment represents interest and what percentage represents principal for each of the 3 years? Why do these percentages change over time?

**5-35  AMORTIZATION SCHEDULE WITH A BALLOON PAYMENT**  You want to buy a house that costs $140,000. You have $14,000 for a down payment, but your credit is such that mortgage companies will not lend you the required $126,000. However, the realtor persuades the seller to take a $126,000 mortgage (called a seller take-back mortgage) at a rate of 5%, provided the loan is paid off in full in 3 years. You expect to inherit $140,000 in 3 years; but right now all you have is $14,000, and you can afford to make payments of no more than $22,000 per year given your salary. (The loan would call for monthly payments, but assume end-of-year annual payments to simplify things.)

a. If the loan was amortized over 3 years, how large would each annual payment be? Could you afford those payments?

b. If the loan was amortized over 30 years, what would each payment be? Could you afford those payments?

c. To satisfy the seller, the 30-year mortgage loan would be written as a balloon note, which means that at the end of the third year, you would have to make the regular payment plus the remaining balance on the loan. What would the loan balance be at the end of Year 3, and what would the balloon payment be?

**5-36  NONANNUAL COMPOUNDING**

a. You plan to make five deposits of $1,000 each, one every 6 months, with the first payment being made in 6 months. You will then make no more deposits. If the bank pays 6% nominal interest, compounded semiannually, how much will be in your account after 3 years?

b. One year from today you must make a payment of $4,000. To prepare for this payment, you plan to make two equal quarterly deposits (at the end of Quarters 1 and 2) in a bank that pays 6% nominal interest compounded quarterly. How large must each of the two payments be?

**5-37  PAYING OFF CREDIT CARDS**  Simon recently received a credit card with an 18% nominal interest rate. With the card, he purchased an Apple iPhone 6 for $372.71. The minimum payment on the card is only $10 per month.

a. If Simon makes the minimum monthly payment and makes no other charges, how many months will it be before he pays off the card? Round to the nearest month.

b. If Simon makes monthly payments of $35, how many months will it be before he pays off the debt? Round to the nearest month.

c. How much more in total payments will Simon make under the $10-a-month plan than under the $35-a-month plan? Make sure you use three decimal places for N.

**5-38  PV AND A LAWSUIT SETTLEMENT**  It is now December 31, 2015 (t = 0), and a jury just found in favor of a woman who sued the city for injuries sustained in a January 2014 accident. She requested recovery of lost wages plus $300,000 for pain and suffering plus $60,000 for legal expenses. Her doctor testified that she has been unable to work since the accident and that she will not be able to work in the future. She is now 62, and the jury decided that she would have worked for another three years. She was scheduled to have earned $36,000 in 2014. (To simplify this problem, assume that the entire annual salary amount would have been received on December 31, 2014.) Her employer testified that she probably would have received raises of 3% per year. The actual payment for the jury award will be made on December 31, 2016. The judge stipulated that all dollar amounts are to be adjusted to a present value basis on December 31, 2016, using an 8% annual interest rate and using compound, not simple, interest. Furthermore, he stipulated that the pain and suffering and legal expenses should be based on a December 31, 2015, date. How large a check must the city write on December 31, 2016?

**5-39**  **REQUIRED ANNUITY PAYMENTS**  Your father is 50 years old and will retire in 10 years. He expects to live for 25 years after he retires, until he is 85. He wants a fixed retirement income that has the same purchasing power at the time he retires as $50,000 has today. (The real value of his retirement income will decline annually after he retires.) His *retirement income will begin the day he retires*, 10 years from today, at which time he will receive 24 additional annual payments. Annual inflation is expected to be 4%. He currently has $90,000 saved, and he expects to earn 8% annually on his savings. How much must he save during each of the next 10 years (end-of-year deposits) to meet his retirement goal?

**5-40**  **REQUIRED ANNUITY PAYMENTS**  A father is now planning a savings program to put his daughter through college. She is 13, plans to enroll at the university in 5 years, and should graduate 4 years later. Currently, the annual cost (for everything—food, clothing, tuition, books, transportation, and so forth) is $12,000, but these costs are expected to increase by 6% annually. The college requires total payment at the start of the year. She now has $10,000 in a college savings account that pays 9% annually. Her father will make six equal annual deposits into her account; the first deposit today and the sixth on the day she starts college. How large must each of the six payments be? (Hint: Calculate the cost (inflated at 6%) for each year of college and find the total present value of those costs, discounted at 9%, as of the day she enters college. Then find the compounded value of her initial $10,000 on that same day. The difference between the PV of costs and the amount that would be in the savings account must be made up by the father's deposits, so find the six equal payments that will compound to the required amount.)

# Comprehensive/Spreadsheet Problem

**5-41**  **TIME VALUE OF MONEY**  Answer the following questions:

a. Assuming a rate of 10% annually, find the FV of $1,000 after 5 years.
b. What is the investment's FV at rates of 0%, 5%, and 20% after 0, 1, 2, 3, 4, and 5 years?
c. Find the PV of $1,000 due in 5 years if the discount rate is 10%.
d. What is the rate of return on a security that costs $1,000 and returns $2,000 after 5 years?
e. Suppose California's population is 36.5 million people and its population is expected to grow by 2% annually. How long will it take for the population to double?
f. Find the PV of an ordinary annuity that pays $1,000 each of the next 5 years if the interest rate is 15%. What is the annuity's FV?
g. How will the PV and FV of the annuity in part f change if it is an annuity due?
h. What will the FV and the PV be for $1,000 due in 5 years if the interest rate is 10%, semiannual compounding?
i. What will the annual payments be for an ordinary annuity for 10 years with a PV of $1,000 if the interest rate is 8%? What will the payments be if this is an annuity due?

j. Find the PV and the FV of an investment that pays 8% annually and makes the following end-of-year payments:

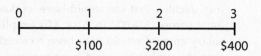

k. Five banks offer nominal rates of 6% on deposits; but A pays interest annually; B pays semiannually; C pays quarterly; D pays monthly; and E pays daily.

1. What effective annual rate does each bank pay? If you deposit $5,000 in each bank today, how much will you have in each bank at the end of 1 year? 2 years?

2. If all of the banks are insured by the government (the FDIC) and thus are equally risky, will they be equally able to attract funds? If not (and the TVM is the only consideration), what nominal rate will cause all of the banks to provide the same effective annual rate as Bank A?

3. Suppose you don't have the $5,000 but need it at the end of 1 year. You plan to make a series of deposits—annually for A, semiannually for B, quarterly for C, monthly for D, and daily for E—with payments beginning today. How large must the payments be to each bank?

4. Even if the five banks provided the same effective annual rate, would a rational investor be indifferent between the banks? Explain.

l. Suppose you borrow $15,000. The loan's annual interest rate is 8%, and it requires four equal end-of-year payments. Set up an amortization schedule that shows the annual payments, interest payments, principal repayments, and beginning and ending loan balances.

## INTEGRATED CASE

**5-42**    **TIME VALUE OF MONEY ANALYSIS**   You have applied for a job with a local bank. As part of its evaluation process, you must take an examination on time value of money analysis covering the following questions:

a. Draw time lines for (1) a $100 lump sum cash flow at the end of Year 2; (2) an ordinary annuity of $100 per year for 3 years; and (3) an uneven cash flow stream of −$50, $100, $75, and $50 at the end of Years 0 through 3.

b. 1. What's the future value of $100 after 3 years if it earns 4%, annual compounding?

2. What's the present value of $100 to be received in 3 years if the interest rate is 4%, annual compounding?

c. What annual interest rate would cause $100 to grow to $119.10 in 3 years?

d. If a company's sales are growing at a rate of 10% annually, how long will it take sales to double?

e. What's the difference between an ordinary annuity and an annuity due? What type of annuity is shown here? How would you change it to the other type of annuity?

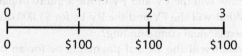

f.  1. What is the future value of a 3-year, $100 ordinary annuity if the annual interest rate is 4%?

   2. What is its present value?

   3. What would the future and present values be if it was an annuity due?

g.  A 5-year $100 ordinary annuity has an annual interest rate of 4%.
   1. What is its present value?

   2. What would the present value be if it was a 10-year annuity?

   3. What would the present value be if it was a 25-year annuity?

   4. What would the present value be if this was a perpetuity?

h.  A 20-year-old student wants to save $5 a day for her retirement. Every day she places $5 in a drawer. At the end of each year, she invests the accumulated savings ($1,825) in a brokerage account with an expected annual return of 8%.

   1. If she keeps saving in this manner, how much will she have accumulated at age 65?

   2. If a 40-year-old investor began saving in this manner, how much would he have at age 65?

   3. How much would the 40-year-old investor have to save each year to accumulate the same amount at 65 as the 20-year-old investor?

i.  What is the present value of the following uneven cash flow stream? The annual interest rate is 4%.

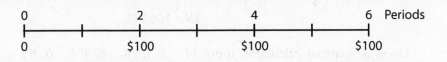

j.  1. Will the future value be larger or smaller if we compound an initial amount more often than annually (e.g., semiannually, holding the stated (nominal) rate constant)? Why?

   2. Define (a) the stated (or quoted or nominal) rate, (b) the periodic rate, and (c) the effective annual rate (EAR or EFF%).

   3. What is the EAR corresponding to a nominal rate of 4% compounded semiannually? Compounded quarterly? Compounded daily?

   4. What is the future value of $100 after 3 years under 4% semiannual compounding? Quarterly compounding?

k.  When will the EAR equal the nominal (quoted) rate?

l.  1. What is the value at the end of Year 3 of the following cash flow stream if interest is 4% compounded semiannually? (Hint: You can use the EAR and treat the cash flows as an ordinary annuity or use the periodic rate and compound the cash flows individually.)

```
0                2                4                6   Periods
├────────┼────────┼────────┼────────┼────────┼
0              $100             $100             $100
```

   2. What is the PV?

   3. What would be wrong with your answer to parts l(1) and l(2) if you used the nominal rate, 4%, rather than the EAR or the periodic rate, $I_{NOM}/2 = 4\%/2 = 2\%$, to solve the problems?

m.  1. Construct an amortization schedule for a $1,000, 4% annual interest loan with three equal installments.

   2. What is the annual interest expense for the borrower and the annual interest income for the lender during Year 2?

## Solutions to Self-Test Questions and Problems

**ST-1** Refer to the marginal glossary definitions or relevant chapter sections to check your responses.

**ST-2** a.
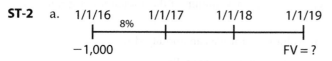

1/1/16    8%    1/1/17    1/1/18    1/1/19

−1,000                      FV = ?

$1,000 is being compounded for 3 years, so your balance on January 1, 2019, is $1,259.71:

$$FV_N = PV(1 + I)^N = \$1,000(1 + 0.08)^3 = \$1,259.71$$

Alternatively, using a financial calculator, input $N = 3$, $I/YR = 8$, $PV = -1000$, $PMT = 0$, and $FV = ?$ Solve for $FV = \$1,259.71$.

b.

1/1/16   2%   1/1/17    1/1/18    1/1/19

−1,000                      FV = ?

$$FV_N = PV\left(1 + \frac{I_{NOM}}{M}\right)^{MN} = FV_{12} = \$1,000(1.02)^{12} = \$1,268.24$$

Alternatively, using a financial calculator, input $N = 12$, $I/YR = 2$, $PV = -1000$, $PMT = 0$, and $FV = ?$ Solve for $FV = \$1,268.24$.

c.

1/1/16    8%    1/1/17    1/1/18    1/1/19

          −333.333    −333.333   −333.333

Using a financial calculator, input $N = 3$, $I/YR = 8$, $PV = 0$, $PMT = -333.333$, and $FV = ?$ Solve for $FV = \$1,082.13$.

d.

1/1/16    8%    1/1/17    1/1/18    1/1/19

−333.333    −333.333    −333.333    FV = ?

Using a financial calculator in begin mode, input $N = 3$, $I/YR = 8$, $PV = 0$, $PMT = -333.333$, and $FV = ?$ Solve for $FV = \$1,168.70$.

e.

1/1/16    8%    1/1/17    1/1/18    1/1/19

             ?       ?       ?

                       FV = 1,259.71

Using a financial calculator, input $N = 3$, $I/YR = 8$, $PV = 0$, $FV = 1259.71$, and $PMT = ?$ Solve for $PMT = -\$388.03$. Therefore, you would have to make three payments of $388.03 beginning on January 1, 2017.

**ST-3** a. Set up a time line like the one in the preceding problem:

1/1/16   8%   1/1/17    1/1/18    1/1/19    1/1/20

PV = ?                        FV = 1,000

Note that your deposit will grow for 4 years at 8%. The deposit on January 1, 2016, is the PV, and the FV is $1,000. Using a financial calculator, input $N = 4$, $I/YR = 8$, $PMT = 0$, $FV = 1000$, and $PV = ?$ Solve for $PV = -\$735.03$.

$$PV = \frac{FV_N}{(1 + I)^N} = \frac{\$1,000}{(1.08)^4} = \$735.03$$

b.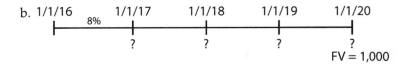

Here, we are dealing with a 4-year annuity whose first payment occurs 1 year from today, on January 1, 2017, and whose future value must equal $1,000. You should modify the time line to help visualize the situation. Using a financial calculator, input N = 4, I/YR = 8, PV = 0, FV = 1000, and PMT = ? Solve for PMT = −$221.92.

c. This problem can be approached in several ways. Perhaps the simplest is to ask this question: "If I received $750 on January 1, 2017, and deposited it to earn 8%, would I have the required $1,000 on January 1, 2020?" The answer is no.

1/1/16        1/1/17        1/1/18        1/1/19        1/1/20

      8%

          −750                                        FV = ?

$$FV_3 = \$750(1.08)(1.08)(1.08) = \$944.78$$

This indicates that you should let your father make the payments of $221.92 rather than accept the lump sum of $750 on January 1, 2017.

You could also compare the $750 with the PV of the payments, as shown below:

1/1/16        1/1/17        1/1/18        1/1/19        1/1/20

      8%

          −221.92    −221.92    −221.92    −221.92

          PV = ?

Using a financial calculator, input N = 4, I/YR = 8, PMT = −221.92, FV = 0, and PV = ? Solve for PV = $735.03.

This is less than the $750 lump sum offer, so your initial reaction might be to accept the lump sum of $750. However, this would be a mistake. The problem is that when you found the $735.03 PV of the annuity, you were finding the value of the annuity *today*, on January 1, 2016. You were comparing $735.03 today with the lump sum of $750 one year from now. This is, of course, not correct. What you should have done was take the $735.03, recognize that this is the PV of an annuity as of January 1, 2016, multiply $735.03 by 1.08 to get $793.83, and compare $793.83 with the lump sum of $750. You would then take your father's offer to make the payments of $221.92 rather than take the lump sum on January 1, 2017.

d.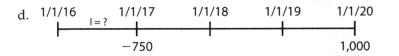

Using a financial calculator, input N = 3, PV = −750, PMT = 0, FV = 1000, and I/YR = ? Solve for I/YR = 10.0642%.

e.

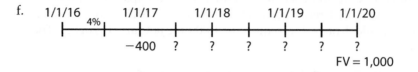

Using a financial calculator, input N = 4, PV = 0, PMT = −200, FV = 1000, and I/YR = ? Solve for I/YR = 15.09%.

You might be able to find a borrower willing to offer you a 15% interest rate, but there would be some risk involved—he or she might not actually pay you the $1,000!

f.

$$
\begin{array}{cccccc}
1/1/16 & 1/1/17 & 1/1/18 & 1/1/19 & 1/1/20 \\
\end{array}
$$

Find the future value of the original $400 deposit:

$$FV_6 = PV(1.04)^6 = \$400(1.2653) = \$506.13$$

This means that on January 1, 2020, you need an additional sum of $493.87:

$$\$1,000.00 - \$506.13 = \$493.87$$

This will be accumulated by making 6 equal payments that earn 8% compounded semiannually, or 4% each 6 months. Using a financial calculator, input N = 6, I/YR = 4, PV = 0, FV = 493.87, and PMT = ? Solve for PMT = −$74.46.

Alternatively, input N = 6, I/YR = 4, PV = −400, FV = 1000, and PMT = ? Solve for PMT = −$74.46. Note that the sign on the PV amount entered in the calculator was negative because the initial deposit will offset the total amount needed. If the signs on both the FV and PV amounts had been the same, you would have calculated a larger payment than was necessary.

g. **Effective annual rate** $= \left(1 + \dfrac{I_{NOM}}{M}\right)^{M} - 1.0$

$$= \left(1 + \dfrac{0.08}{2}\right)^{2} - 1 = (1.04)^{2} - 1$$

$$= 1.0816 - 1 = 0.0816 = 8.16\%$$

$$APR = I_{PER} \times M$$

$$= 0.04 \times 2 = 0.08 = 8\%$$

**ST-4**  Bank A's effective annual rate is 8.24%:

**Effective annual rate** $= \left(1 + \dfrac{0.08}{4}\right)^{4} - 1.0$

$$= (1.02)^{4} - 1$$

$$= 1.0824 - 1$$

$$= 0.0824 = 8.24\%$$

Now Bank B must have the same effective annual rate:

$$\left(1 + \frac{I_{NOM}}{12}\right)^{12} - 1.0 = 0.0824$$

$$\left(1 + \frac{I_{NOM}}{12}\right)^{12} = 1.0824$$

$$1 + \frac{I_{NOM}}{12} = (1.0824)^{1/12}$$

$$1 + \frac{I_{NOM}}{12} = 1.00662$$

$$\frac{I_{NOM}}{12} = 0.00662$$

$$I_{NOM} = 0.07944 = 7.94\%$$

Thus, the two banks have different quoted rates—Bank A's quoted rate is 8%, while Bank B's quoted rate is 7.94%; however, both banks have the same effective annual rate of 8.24%. The difference in their quoted rates is due to the difference in compounding frequency.

## Answers to Selected End-of-Chapter Problems

**5-2**  PV = $10,929.80

**5-4**  N = 17.67 yrs.

**5-6**  $FVA_5 = \$4,420.51$; $FVA_{5\,Due} = \$4,641.53$

**5-8**  PMT = $811.06; EAR = 8.30%

**5-10**  a. $296.05
  b. $431.78
  c. $135.11
  d. $866.17; $1,263.30

**5-12**  a. 10%
  b. 10%
  c. 3%
  d. 11%

**5-14**  a. $6,616.38
  b. $1,109.99
  c. $2,800.00
  d(l). $7,542.67
  d(2). $1,187.68
  d(3). $2,800.00

**5-16**  $PV_{5\%} = \$12,000$; $PV_{10\%} = \$6,000$

**5-18**  a. Stream A: $1,505.84;
    Stream B: $1,522.73
  b. Stream A and Stream B: $1,750

**5-20**  Contract 2: PV = $12,358,739.18

**5-22**  a. $802.43
  b. Pymt 1: Int = $500; Princ = $302.43;
    Pymt 2: Int = $484.88; Princ = $317.55
  c. $984.88

**5-24**  a. $279.20
  b. $276.84
  c. $443.72

**5-26**  $17,290.89; $19,734.26

**5-28**  $I_{NOM} = 11.729145\% \approx 11.73\%$

**5-30**  a. A = 59.89 yrs.; L = 50.08 yrs.
  b. $12,649.64

**5-32**  $1,297.13

**5-34**  a. PMT = $7,372.64
  b. Yr.1: Int/Pymt = 20.62%; Princ/Pymt
      = 79.38%;
    Yr.2: Int/Pymt = 14.27%; Princ/Pymt
      = 85.73%;
    Yr.3: Int/Pymt = 7.41%; Princ/Pymt
      = 92.59%

**5-36**  a. $5,468.41
  b. $1,926.87

**5-38**  $580,191

**5-40**  $6,147

## Selected Equations and Tables

**Future value** $= FV_N = PV(1+I)^N$

**Present value** $= PV = \dfrac{FV_N}{(1+I)^N}$

$FVA_N = PMT(1+I)^{N-1} + PMT(1+I)^{N-2} + PMT(1+I)^{N-3} + \cdots + PMT(1+I)^0$

$\qquad = PMT\left[\dfrac{(1+I)^N - 1}{I}\right]$

$FVA_{due} = FVA_{ordinary}(1+I)$

$PVA_N = PMT/(1+I)^1 + PMT/(1+I)^2 + \cdots + PMT/(1+I)^N$

$\qquad = PMT\left[\dfrac{1 - \dfrac{1}{(1+I)^N}}{I}\right]$

$PVA_{due} = PVA_{ordinary}(1+I)$

**PV of a perpetuity** $= \dfrac{PMT}{I}$

$PV = \dfrac{CF_1}{(1+I)^1} + \dfrac{CF_2}{(1+I)^2} + \cdots + \dfrac{CF_N}{(1+I)^N}$

$\quad = \displaystyle\sum_{t=1}^{N} \dfrac{CF_t}{(1+I)^t}$

**Periodic rate** $(I_{PER}) = \dfrac{\text{Stated annual rate}}{\text{Number of payments per year}} = I/M$

**Number of periods** $= (\text{Number of years})(\text{Periods per year}) = NM$

**Effective annual rate (EFF%)** $= \left(1 + \dfrac{I_{NOM}}{M}\right)^M - 1.0$

# Interest Rates

CHAPTER

Drew Angerer/Bloomberg/Getty Images

## The Fed Contemplates an Increase in Interest Rates as the U.S. Economy Shows Signs of a Strong Rebound

To keep the economy afloat after the financial crisis of 2008–2009, the Federal Reserve established extremely low interest rates. The hope was that the lower cost of capital would encourage business investment, help repair a damaged housing market, and prop up stock and bond markets, all of which would help stimulate the overall economy. Looking back, after the crisis, it appears that policymakers have successfully kept the economy from immediately collapsing, but the economy was still weak, and unemployment remained stubbornly high.

In response to the economy's continued sluggishness, the Federal Reserve redoubled its efforts to strengthen the economy with its policy of "quantitative easing." Through this policy, the Fed has systematically purchased large amounts of longer-term financial assets from leading financial institutions. The Fed pays for these assets by injecting new funds into the economy, which helps put downward pressure on interest rates. In December 2012, the Federal Reserve announced that it would maintain this policy until the unemployment rate fell below 6.5% or the inflation rate rose above 2.5%. As a result of their actions, the 10-year Treasury rate was pushed below 2%, and shorter-term Treasury rates were close to zero. Six months later, as the economy began to show limited signs of life, there were concerns that the Federal Reserve's stimulative policies would eventually trigger a rise in inflation. Trying to maintain a delicate balance, the Fed reaffirmed its policy of quantitative easing. However, the Federal Reserve also suggested that in the months ahead it might "taper" its aggressive bond-buying program.

More recently in early 2014, Janet Yellen succeeded Ben Bernanke as Chair of the Federal Reserve, and immediately supported the Fed's balancing act. In her first major set of speeches, Yellen indicated that the Fed would continue to slowly taper its bond purchases. But she also indicated that, given the economy's continued lack of robustness, the Fed would be in no hurry to take any active steps to raise interest rates until the economy had shown signs of steady improvement.

By March 2015, those signs were beginning to emerge. The Labor Department reported that the U.S. economy had created 295,000 jobs in February. A front-page article in *The Wall Street Journal* put these numbers in a broader perspective: "That marked the 12th straight month the economy added more than 200,000 jobs, the best streak since 1995. The unemployment rate fell to 5.5%, the lowest level since May 2008." Responding to the news, stock and bond markets fell sharply as many investors feared that the Fed would accelerate its timetable for raising rates. As we will see in subsequent chapters, all else equal, higher rates work to reduce both stock and bond prices. That said, many argue that the economy is still fragile, and that it has failed to yet produce strong improvement in wage growth—and they have urged the Fed to resist the urge to raise rates.

Although the Federal Reserve has a tremendous influence on interest rates, other factors have helped keep interest rates low. Most notably, inflation remains low (particularly after the recent sharp drop in oil prices), and foreign investors have maintained a strong willingness to purchase U.S. securities. Looking ahead, there is a concern that some of these forces may start working in reverse. Although the Federal Reserve has kept interest rates low for the time being, there are fears that we will pay the price later in the form of higher inflation, which could also lead to a drop in the value of the U.S. dollar. At the same time, federal budget deficits also put upward pressure on interest rates. To the extent that deficits and inflation fears combine with a weakening dollar, foreign investors may sell U.S. bonds, which would put even more upward pressure on rates.

Because corporations and individuals are greatly affected by interest rates, this chapter takes a closer look at the major factors that determine those rates. As we will see, there is no single interest rate—various factors determine the rate that each borrower pays—and in some cases, rates on different types of debt move in different directions. With these issues in mind, we will also consider the various factors influencing the spreads between long- and short-term interest rates and between Treasury and corporate bonds.

Sources: John Hilsenrath and Victoria McGrane, "Yellen Stakes Out a Flexible Policy Path," *The Wall Street Journal* (online.wsj.com), April 16, 2014; Jeff Cox, "Fed to Keep Easing, Sets Target for Rates," www.cnbc.com, December 12, 2012; and Eric Morath, "Brisk Jobs Growth Puts Fed on Notice," *The Wall Street Journal Weekend*, March 7–8, 2015, pp. A1–A2.

# PUTTING THINGS IN PERSPECTIVE

**Companies raise capital in two main forms: debt and equity. In a free economy, capital, like other items, is allocated through a market system, where funds are transferred and prices are established. The interest rate is the price that lenders receive and borrowers pay for debt capital. Similarly, equity investors expect to receive dividends and capital gains, the sum of which represents the cost of equity. We take up the cost of equity in a later chapter, but our focus in this chapter is on the cost of debt. We begin by examining the factors that affect the supply of and demand for capital, which in turn affects the cost of money. We will see that there is no single interest rate—interest rates on different types of debt vary depending on the borrower's risk, the use of the funds borrowed, the type of collateral used to back the loan, and the length of time the money is needed. In this chapter, we concentrate mainly on how these various factors affect the cost of debt for individuals; but in later chapters, we delve into the cost of debt for a business and its role in investment decisions. As you will see in Chapters 7 and 9, the cost of debt is a key determinant of bond and stock prices; it is also an important component of the cost of corporate capital, which we cover in Chapter 10.**

**When you finish this chapter, you should be able to:**

- **List the various factors that influence the cost of money.**

- **Discuss how market interest rates are affected by borrowers' need for capital, expected inflation, different securities' risks, and securities' liquidity.**

- **Explain what the yield curve is, what determines its shape, and how you can use the yield curve to help forecast future interest rates.**

# 6-1  The Cost of Money

*Production Opportunities*

The investment opportunities in productive (cash-generating) assets.

*Time Preferences for Consumption*

The preferences of consumers for current consumption as opposed to saving for future consumption.

*Risk*

In a financial market context, the chance that an investment will provide a low or negative return.

*Inflation*

The amount by which prices increase over time.

The four most fundamental factors affecting the cost of money are (1) **production opportunities**, (2) **time preferences for consumption**, (3) **risk**, and (4) **inflation**. To see how these factors operate, visualize an isolated island community where people live on fish. They have a stock of fishing gear that permits them to survive reasonably well, but they would like to have more fish. Now suppose one of the island's inhabitants, Mr. Crusoe, had a bright idea for a new type of fishnet that would enable him to double his daily catch. However, it would take him a year to perfect the design, build the net, and learn to use it efficiently. Mr. Crusoe would probably starve before he could put his new net into operation. Therefore, he might suggest to Ms. Robinson, Mr. Friday, and several others that if they would give him one fish each day for a year, he would return two fish a day the next year. If someone accepted the offer, the fish that Ms. Robinson and the others gave to Mr. Crusoe would constitute *savings*, these savings would be *invested* in the fishnet, and the extra fish the net produced would constitute a *return on the investment.*

Obviously, the more productive Mr. Crusoe thought the new fishnet would be, the more he could afford to offer potential investors for their savings. In this example, we assume that Mr. Crusoe thought he would be able to pay (and thus he offered) a 100% rate of return—he offered to give back two fish for every one he received. He might have tried to attract savings for less—for example, he might have offered only 1.5 fish per day next year for every one he received this year, which would represent a 50% rate of return to Ms. Robinson and the other potential savers.

How attractive Mr. Crusoe's offer appeared to a potential saver would depend in large part on the saver's *time preference for consumption.* For example, Ms. Robinson might be thinking of retirement, and she might be willing to trade fish today for fish in the future on a one-for-one basis. On the other hand, Mr. Friday might have a wife and several young children and need his current fish; so he might be unwilling to "lend" a fish today for anything less than three fish next year. Mr. Friday would be said to have a high time preference for current consumption, and Ms. Robinson, a low time preference. Note also that if the entire population were living right at the subsistence level, time preferences for current consumption would necessarily be high; aggregate savings would be low; interest rates would be high; and capital formation would be difficult.

The *risk* inherent in the fishnet project (and thus in Mr. Crusoe's ability to repay the loan) also affects the return that investors require: The higher the perceived risk, the higher the required rate of return. Also, in a more complex society, there are many businesses like Mr. Crusoe's, many goods other than fish, and many savers like Ms. Robinson and Mr. Friday. Therefore, people use money as a medium of exchange rather than barter with fish. When money is used, its value in the future, which is affected by *inflation,* comes into play: The higher the expected rate of inflation, the larger the required dollar return. We discuss this point in detail later in the chapter.

*Thus, we see that the interest rate paid to savers depends (1) on the rate of return that producers expect to earn on invested capital, (2) on savers' time preferences for current versus future consumption, (3) on the riskiness of the loan, and (4) on the expected future rate of inflation.* Producers' expected returns on their business investments set an upper limit to how much they can pay for savings, while consumers' time preferences for consumption establish how much consumption they are willing to defer and hence how much they will save at different interest rates.[1] Higher risk and higher inflation also lead to higher interest rates.

---

[1]The term *producers* in this example is too narrow. A better word might be *borrowers*, which would include corporations, home purchasers, people borrowing to go to college, and even people borrowing to buy autos or to pay for vacations. Also, the wealth of a society and its demographics influence its people's ability to save and thus their time preferences for current versus future consumption.

## SelfTest

What is the price paid to borrow debt capital called?

What are the two items whose sum is the cost of equity?

What four fundamental factors affect the cost of money?

Which factor sets an upper limit on how much can be paid for savings?

Which factor determines how much will be saved at different interest rates?

How do risk and inflation impact interest rates in the economy?

# 6-2 Interest Rate Levels

Borrowers bid for the available supply of debt capital using interest rates: The firms with the most profitable investment opportunities are willing and able to pay the most for capital, so they tend to attract it away from inefficient firms and firms whose products are not in demand. At the same time, government policy can also influence the allocation of capital and the level of interest rates. For example, the federal government has agencies that help designated individuals or groups obtain credit on favorable terms. Among those eligible for this kind of assistance are small businesses, certain minorities, and firms willing to build plants in areas with high unemployment. Still, most capital in the United States is allocated through the price system, where the interest rate is the price.

Figure 6.1 shows how supply and demand interact to determine interest rates in two capital markets. Markets L and H represent two of the many capital markets in existence. The supply curve in each market is upward sloping, which indicates that investors are willing to supply more capital the higher the interest rate they receive on their capital. Likewise, the downward-sloping demand curve indicates that borrowers will borrow more if interest rates are lower. The interest rate in each market is the point where the supply and demand curves intersect. The going interest rate, designated as r, is initially 5% for the low-risk securities in

| **FIGURE 6.1** | Interest Rates as a Function of Supply and Demand for Funds |
| --- | --- |

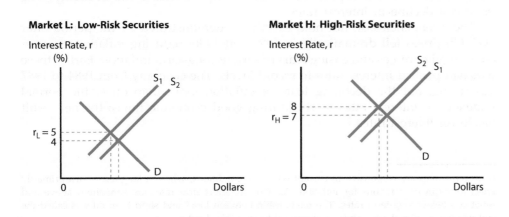

Market L. Borrowers whose credit is strong enough to participate in this market can obtain funds at a cost of 5%, and investors who want to put their money to work without much risk can obtain a 5% return. Riskier borrowers must obtain higher-cost funds in Market H, where investors who are more willing to take risks expect to earn a 7% return but also realize that they might receive much less. In this scenario, investors are willing to accept the higher risk in Market H in exchange for a *risk premium* of $7\% - 5\% = 2\%$.

Now let's assume that because of changing market forces, investors perceive that Market H has become relatively more risky. This changing perception will induce many investors to shift toward safer investments—referred to as a "flight to quality." As investors move their money from Market H to Market L, the supply of funds is increased in Market L from $S_1$ to $S_2$; and the increased availability of capital will push down interest rates in this market from 5% to 4%. At the same time, as investors move their money out of Market H, there will be a decreased supply of funds in that market; and tighter credit in that market will force interest rates up from 7% to 8%. In this new environment, money is transferred from Market H to Market L and the risk premium rises from 2% to $8\% - 4\% = 4\%$.

There are many capital markets in the United States, and Figure 6.1 highlights the fact that they are interconnected. U.S. firms also invest and raise capital throughout the world, and foreigners both borrow and lend in the United States. There are markets for home loans; farm loans; business loans; federal, state, and local government loans; and consumer loans. Within each category, there are regional markets as well as different types of submarkets. For example, in real estate, there are separate markets for first and second mortgages and for loans on single-family homes, apartments, office buildings, shopping centers, and vacant land. And, of course, there are separate markets for prime and subprime mortgage loans. Within the business sector, there are dozens of types of debt securities and there are several different markets for common stocks.

There is a price for each type of capital, and these prices change over time as supply and demand conditions change. Figure 6.2 shows how long- and short-term interest rates to business borrowers have varied since the early 1970s. Notice that short-term interest rates are especially volatile, rising rapidly during booms and falling equally rapidly during recessions. (The shaded areas of the chart indicate recessions.) In particular, note the dramatic drop in short-term interest rates during the recent recession. When the economy is expanding, firms need capital; and this demand pushes rates up. Inflationary pressures are strongest during business booms, also exerting upward pressure on rates. Conditions are reversed during recessions: Slack business reduces the demand for credit, inflation falls, and the Federal Reserve increases the supply of funds to help stimulate the economy. The result is a decline in interest rates.

These tendencies do not hold exactly, as demonstrated by the period after 1984. Oil prices fell dramatically in 1985 and 1986, reducing inflationary pressures on other prices and easing fears of serious long-term inflation. Earlier these fears had pushed interest rates to record levels. The economy from 1984 to 1987 was strong, but the declining fears of inflation more than offset the normal tendency for interest rates to rise during good economic times; the net result was lower interest rates.[2]

---

[2]Short-term rates are responsive to current economic conditions, whereas long-term rates primarily reflect long-run expectations for inflation. As a result, short-term rates are sometimes above and sometimes below long-term rates. The relationship between long- and short-term rates is called the *term structure of interest rates*, and it is discussed later in this chapter.

**FIGURE 6.2**  Long- and Short-Term Interest Rates, 1972–2015

Source: St. Louis Federal Reserve, FRED database, research.stlouisfed.org/fred2.

*Notes:*

1. The shaded areas designate business recessions.

2. Short-term rates are measured by 3- to 6-month loans to very large, strong corporations; long-term rates are measured by AAA corporate bonds.

The relationship between inflation and long-term interest rates is highlighted in Figure 6.3, which plots inflation over time along with long-term interest rates. In the early 1960s, inflation averaged 1% per year and interest rates on high-quality long-term bonds averaged 4%. Then the Vietnam War heated up, leading to an increase in inflation; and interest rates began an upward climb. When the war ended in the early 1970s, inflation dipped a bit; but then the 1973 Arab oil embargo led to rising oil prices, much higher inflation rates, and sharply higher interest rates.

Inflation peaked at about 13% in 1980. But interest rates continued to increase into 1981 and 1982, and they remained quite high until 1985 because people feared another increase in inflation. Thus, the "inflationary psychology" created during the 1970s persisted until the mid-1980s. People gradually realized that the Federal Reserve was serious about keeping inflation down, that global competition was keeping U.S. auto producers and other corporations from raising prices as they had in the past, and that constraints on corporate price increases were diminishing labor unions' ability to push through cost-increasing wage hikes. As these realizations set in, interest rates declined.

The current interest rate minus the current inflation rate (which is also the gap between the inflation bars and the interest rate curve in Figure 6.3) is defined as the "current real rate of interest." It is called a "real rate" because it shows how much investors really earned after the effects of inflation are removed. The real rate was extremely high during the mid-1980s, but it has generally been in the range of 1% to 4% since 1987.[3]

In recent years, inflation has been quite low, averaging about 2% a year, and it was even negative in 2009, as prices fell in the midst of the deep recession.

---

[3]Refer to Carmen M. Reinhart and Kenneth S. Rogoff, *This Time Is Different: Eight Centuries of Financial Folly* (Princeton, New Jersey: Princeton University Press, 2009).

**FIGURE 6.3** Relationship between Annual Inflation Rates and Long-Term Interest Rates, 1972–2015

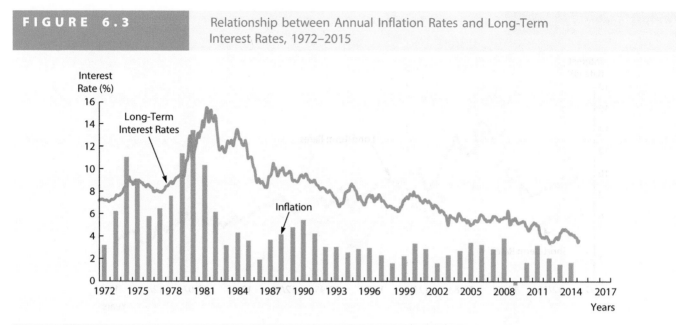

Source: St. Louis Federal Reserve, FRED database, research.stlouisfed.org/fred2.

*Notes:*

1. Interest rates are rates on AAA long-term corporate bonds.

2. Inflation is measured as the annual rate of change in the consumer price index (CPI).

However, long-term interest rates have been volatile because investors are not sure if inflation is truly under control or is about to jump back to the higher levels of the 1980s. In the years ahead, we can be sure of two things: (1) Interest rates will vary. (2) They will increase if inflation appears to be headed higher or decrease if inflation is expected to decline.

## Self*Test*

What role do interest rates play in allocating capital to different potential borrowers?

What happens to market-clearing, or equilibrium, interest rates in a capital market when the supply of funds declines? What happens when expected inflation increases or decreases?

How does the price of capital tend to change during a boom? During a recession?

How does risk affect interest rates?

If inflation during the last 12 months was 2% and the interest rate during that period was 5%, what was the real rate of interest? If inflation is expected to average 4% during the next year and the real rate is 3%, what should the current interest rate be? **(3%; 7%)**

# 6-3 The Determinants of Market Interest Rates

In general, the quoted (or nominal) interest rate on a debt security, r, is composed of a real risk-free rate, $r^*$, plus several premiums that reflect inflation, the security's risk, its liquidity (or marketability), and the years to its maturity. This relationship can be expressed as follows:

$$\text{Quoted interest rate} = r = r^* + IP + DRP + LP + MRP \qquad \blacktriangledown \quad 6.1$$

Where:

$r$ = the quoted, or nominal, rate of interest on a given security.[4]

$r^*$ = the real risk-free rate of interest, $r^*$ is pronounced "r-star," and it is the rate that would exist on a riskless security in a world where no inflation was expected.

$r_{RF}$ = $r^* + IP$. It is the quoted rate on a risk-free security such as a U.S. Treasury bill, which is very liquid and is free of most types of risk. Note that the premium for expected inflation, IP, is included in $r_{RF}$.

$IP$ = inflation premium. IP is equal to the average expected rate of inflation over the life of the security. The expected future inflation rate is not necessarily equal to the current inflation rate, so IP is not necessarily equal to current inflation, as shown in Figure 6.3.

$DRP$ = default risk premium. This premium reflects the possibility that the issuer will not pay the promised interest or principal at the stated time. DRP is zero for U.S. Treasury securities, but it rises as the riskiness of the issuer increases.

$LP$ = liquidity (or marketability) premium. This is a premium charged by lenders to reflect the fact that some securities cannot be converted to cash on short notice at a "reasonable" price. LP is very low for Treasury securities and for securities issued by large, strong firms; but it is relatively high on securities issued by small, privately held firms.

$MRP$ = maturity risk premium. As we will explain later, longer-term bonds, even Treasury bonds, are exposed to a significant risk of price declines due to increases in inflation and interest rates; and a maturity risk premium is charged by lenders to reflect this risk.

Because $r_{RF} = r^* + IP$, we can rewrite Equation 6.1 as follows:

$$\text{Nominal, or quoted, rate} = r = r_{RF} + DRP + LP + MRP$$

We discuss the components whose sum makes up the quoted, or nominal, rate on a given security in the following sections.

## 6-3A THE REAL RISK-FREE RATE OF INTEREST, r*

The **real risk-free rate of interest, $r^*$**, is the interest rate that would exist on a riskless security if no inflation were expected. It may be thought of as the rate of interest on short-term U.S. Treasury securities in an inflation-free world. The real

*Real Risk-Free Rate of Interest, r**
The rate of interest that would exist on default-free U.S. Treasury securities if no inflation were expected.

---

[4]The term *nominal* as it is used here means the *stated* rate as opposed to the *real* rate, where the real rate is adjusted to remove inflation's effects. If you had bought a 30-year Treasury bond in March 2015, the quoted, or nominal, rate would have been about 2.5%; but if inflation averages 2.0% over the next 30 years, the real rate would turn out to be about 2.5% − 2.0% = 0.5%. Also note that in later chapters, when we discuss both debt and equity, we use the subscripts $d$ and $s$ to designate returns on debt and stock, that is, $r_d$ and $r_s$.

# GLOBAL PERSPECTIVES

## *European Banks Confront the Reality of Negative Interest Rates*

In the text, we point out that in recent years there have been times when expected real interest rates have appeared to be negative. These negative real rates occur when nominal interest rates are below expected inflation. While real rates can be negative, many economists have long thought that nominal rates can't be negative. After all, why would investors ever accept a negative interest rate if they could simply earn a zero return by holding cash?

But as a recent article in *The Economist* highlights, there have indeed been some high profile examples of negative nominal rates in key European markets. For example, banks that deposit money in the European Central Bank (ECB) receive negative returns. *The Economist* also points out that negative nominal rates exist in Denmark, Sweden, and Switzerland, and that there is also evidence that this practice is beginning to extend to bank customers. In effect, negative nominal rates mean that you are paying the bank to hold your money. Although to many this practice seems crazy, it is not hard to see scenarios where you might actually prefer to have your money in a well-respected bank than under the mattress. Moreover, apart from storage there are other benefits to having your money in a bank account; for example, you can easily transfer funds throughout the world or move money from one account to another. If these benefits are large enough, then a rational investor may actually be willing to pay a bank to hold his or her funds in an account.

This phenomenon is part of a larger global movement toward lower interest rates in the face of the types of policy actions taken by global central bankers that are described in the opening vignette to this chapter. *The Economist* article argues that one consequence of negative interest rates is that it may lead to reduced bank profitability, because banks receive lower/negative returns on the excess reserves they hold with the ECB, and they are then unable to reduce the amount they pay on their consumer deposits by the same amount. If this occurs, these low rates may, instead of stimulating the economy, paradoxically lead banks to curtail lending.

Source: Refer to "Free Exchange: Worse Than Nothing," *The Economist* (www.economist.com), February 21, 2015.

risk-free rate is not static—it changes over time, depending on economic conditions, especially on (1) the rate of return that corporations and other borrowers expect to earn on productive assets and (2) people's time preferences for current versus future consumption. Borrowers' expected returns on real assets set an upper limit on how much borrowers can afford to pay for funds, whereas savers' time preferences for consumption establish how much consumption savers will defer—hence, the amount of money they will lend at different interest rates.

It is difficult to measure the real rate precisely, but most experts believe that $r^*$ typically fluctuates in the range of 1% to 3%.[5] Perhaps the best estimate of $r^*$ is the rate of return on indexed Treasury bonds, which are discussed later in the chapter. It is interesting to note that between 2011 and 2015, the rate on indexed Treasury bonds has often been negative. These negative real rates of interest have arisen largely because of Federal Reserve policies that have pushed interest rates on Treasury securities below the rate of expected inflation.

---

[5]The real rate of interest as discussed here is different from the *current* real rate as discussed in connection with Figure 6.3. The current real rate is the current interest rate minus the current (or latest past) inflation rate, while the real rate (without the word *current*) is the current interest rate minus the *expected future* inflation rate over the life of the security. For example, suppose the current quoted rate for a one-year Treasury bill is 2.0%, inflation during the latest year was 1.0%, and inflation expected for the coming year is 1.5%. The *current* real rate would be 2.0% − 1.0% = 1.0%, but the *expected* real rate would be 2.0% − 1.5% = 0.5%. The rate on a 10-year bond would be related to the average expected inflation rate over the next 10 years, and so on. In the press, the term *real rate* generally means the current real rate; but in economics and finance (hence, in this book unless otherwise noted), the real rate means the one based on *expected* inflation rates.

## 6-3B THE NOMINAL, OR QUOTED, RISK-FREE RATE OF INTEREST, $r_{RF} = r^* + IP$

The **nominal, or quoted, risk-free rate, $r_{RF}$,** is the real risk-free rate plus a premium for expected inflation: $r_{RF} = r^* + IP$. To be strictly correct, the risk-free rate should be the interest rate on a totally risk-free security—one that has no default risk, no maturity risk, no liquidity risk, no risk of loss if inflation increases, and no risk of any other type. However, as the recent downgrade of U.S. Treasuries illustrates, there is no such security; hence, there is no observable truly risk-free rate. However, one security is free of most risks—a Treasury Inflation Protected Security (TIPS), whose value increases with inflation. Short-term TIPS are free of default, maturity, and liquidity risks and of risk due to changes in the general level of interest rates. However, they are not free of changes in the real rate.[6]

If the term *risk-free rate* is used without the modifiers *real* or *nominal*, people generally mean the quoted (or nominal) rate; and we follow that convention in this book. Therefore, when we use the term *risk-free rate, $r_{RF}$*, we mean the nominal risk-free rate, which includes an inflation premium equal to the average expected inflation rate over the remaining life of the security. In general, we use the T-bill rate to approximate the short-term risk-free rate and the T-bond rate to approximate the long-term risk-free rate. So whenever you see the term *risk-free rate*, assume that we are referring to the quoted U.S. T-bill rate or to the quoted T-bond rate. Our definition of the risk-free rate assumes that, despite the recent downgrade, Treasury securities have no meaningful default risk. And for convenience, we will assume in our subsequent problems and examples that Treasury securities have no default risk.

*Nominal (Quoted) Risk-Free Rate, $r_{RF}$*
The rate of interest on a security that is free of all risk; $r_{RF}$ is proxied by the T-bill rate or the T-bond rate; $r_{RF}$ includes an inflation premium.

## 6-3C INFLATION PREMIUM (IP)

Inflation has a major impact on interest rates because it erodes the real value of what you receive from the investment. To illustrate, suppose you have saved $10,000 to purchase a car. Rather than buying a car today, you could invest the money with the hope of buying a better car one year from now. If you decide to invest in a one-year Treasury bill that pays a 1% interest rate, you will have a little bit more money ($10,100—your original money plus $100 in interest) at the end of the year. Now suppose that the overall inflation rate increased by 3% that year. In this case, a similar version of the $10,000 car that you would have purchased at the beginning of the year would cost 3% more ($10,300) at the end of the year. Notice, in this case, the additional interest that you earn on the Treasury bill is not enough to compensate for the expected increase in the price of the car. In real terms you are worse off because the nominal interest rate is less than the expected inflation rate.

Investors are well aware of all this; so when they lend money, they build an **inflation premium (IP)** equal to the average expected inflation rate over the life of the security into the rate they charge. As discussed previously, the actual interest rate on a short-term default-free U.S. Treasury bill, $r_{T-bill}$, would be the real risk-free rate, $r^*$, plus the inflation premium (IP):

$$r_{T-bill} = r_{RF} = r^* + IP$$

*Inflation Premium (IP)*
A premium equal to expected inflation that investors add to the real risk-free rate of return.

[6]Indexed Treasury securities are the closest thing we have to a riskless security, but even they are not totally riskless because $r^*$ can change and cause a decline in the prices of these securities. For example, between its issue date in April 1998 and January 14, 2000, the price of the TIPS that matures on April 15, 2028, declined because during this time period the real rate on long-term securities *increased*. Conversely, between January 14, 2000, and March 19, 2015, the real rate on this security has *decreased*. As a result, the bond's price during this time increased approximately 34%.

Therefore, if the real risk-free rate was $r^* = 1.7\%$ and if inflation was expected to be 1.5% (and hence IP = 1.5%) during the next year, the quoted rate of interest on one-year T-bills would be 1.7% + 1.5% = 3.2%.

It is important to note that the inflation rate built into interest rates is the *inflation rate expected in the future,* not the rate experienced in the past. Thus, the latest reported figures might show an annual inflation rate of 3% over the past 12 months, but that is for the *past* year. If people, on average, expect a 4% inflation rate in the future, 4% would be built into the current interest rate. Note also that the inflation rate reflected in the quoted interest rate on any security is the *average inflation rate expected over the security's life.* Thus, the inflation rate built into a 1-year bond is the expected inflation rate for the next year, but the inflation rate built into a 30-year bond is the average inflation rate expected over the next 30 years.[7]

Expectations for future inflation are closely, but not perfectly, correlated with past inflation rates. Therefore, if the inflation rate reported for last month increased, people would tend to raise their expectations for future inflation; and this change in expectations would increase current rates. Also, consumer prices change with a lag following changes at the producer level. Thus, if the price of oil increases this month, gasoline prices are likely to increase in the coming months. This lagged situation between final product and producer goods prices exists throughout the economy.

*Students should go to **Bloomberg.com/markets/ rates-bonds** to find current interest rates in the United States as well as in Great Britain and Japan.*

Note that Switzerland has, over the past several years, had lower inflation rates than the United States; hence, its interest rates have generally been lower than those of the United States. The United Kingdom, Australia, and most South American countries have experienced higher inflation, so their rates have been higher than those of the United States. For example, in March 2015, Brazil's inflation rate was around 7.7%, above its Central Bank's 6.5% target range ceiling. On the other hand, the U.S. inflation rate was much lower (1.6%) and the Fed's targeted interest rate was 0.25%.

## 6-3D DEFAULT RISK PREMIUM (DRP)

*Students should go to **tradingeconomics.com** for information on a number of economic indicators such as interest rates, inflation, and GDP.*

**Default Risk Premium (DRP)**

The difference between the interest rate on a U.S. Treasury bond and a corporate bond of equal maturity and marketability.

The risk that a borrower will *default,* which means the borrower will not make scheduled interest or principal payments, also affects the market interest rate on a bond: The greater the bond's risk of default, the higher the market rate. Once again, we are assuming that Treasury securities have no default risk; hence, they carry the lowest interest rates on taxable securities in the United States. For corporate bonds, bond ratings are often used to measure default risk. The higher the bond's rating, the lower its default risk and, consequently, the lower its interest rate.[8] The difference between the quoted interest rate on a T-bond and that on a corporate bond with similar maturity, liquidity, and other features is the **default risk premium (DRP)**. The average default risk premiums vary over time, and tend to get larger when the economy is weaker and borrowers are more likely to have a hard time paying off their debts.

---

[7]To be theoretically precise, we should use a *geometric average.* Also, because millions of investors are active in the market, it is impossible to determine exactly the consensus-expected inflation rate. Survey data are available, however, that give us a reasonably good idea of what investors expect over the next few years. For example, in 1980, the University of Michigan's Survey Research Center reported that people expected inflation during the next year to be 11.9% and that the average rate of inflation expected over the next 5 to 10 years was 10.5%. Those expectations led to record-high interest rates. However, the economy cooled thereafter; and as Figure 6.3 showed, actual inflation dropped sharply. This led to a gradual reduction in the *expected future* inflation rate; and as inflationary expectations dropped, so did quoted market interest rates.

[8]Bond ratings and bonds' riskiness in general are discussed in detail in Chapter 7. For now, merely note that bonds rated AAA are judged to have less default risk than bonds rated AA; AA bonds are less risky than A bonds; and so forth. Ratings are designated AAA or Aaa, AA or Aa, and so forth, depending on the rating agency. In this book, the designations are used interchangeably.

## 6-3E LIQUIDITY PREMIUM (LP)

A "liquid" asset can be converted to cash quickly at a "fair market value." Real assets are generally less liquid than financial assets, but different financial assets vary in their liquidity. Because they prefer assets that are more liquid, investors include a **liquidity premium (LP)** in the rates charged on different debt securities. Although it is difficult to measure liquidity premiums accurately, we can get some sense of an asset's liquidity by looking at its trading volume. Assets with higher trading volume are generally easier to sell and are therefore more liquid. The average liquidity premiums also vary over time. During the recent financial crisis, the liquidity premiums on many assets soared. The market for many assets that were once highly liquid suddenly dried up as everyone rushed to sell them at the same time. The liquidity of real assets also varies over time. For example, at the height of the housing boom, many homes in "hot" real estate markets were often sold the first day they were listed. After the bubble burst, homes in these same markets often sat unsold for months.

*Liquidity Premium (LP)*
A premium added to the equilibrium interest rate on a security if that security cannot be converted to cash on short notice and at close to its "fair market value."

## 6-3F INTEREST RATE RISK AND THE MATURITY RISK PREMIUM (MRP)

Despite a few recent concerns about the Treasury's long-run ability to service its growing debt, we generally assume that U.S. Treasury securities are free of default risk in the sense that one can be virtually certain that the federal government will pay interest on its bonds and pay them off when they mature. Therefore, we assume that the default risk premium on Treasury securities is zero. Further, active markets exist for Treasury securities, so we assume that their liquidity premium is also zero.[9] Thus, as a first approximation, the rate of interest on a Treasury security should be the risk-free rate, $r_{RF}$, which is the real risk-free rate plus an inflation premium, $r_{RF} = r^* + IP$. However, the prices of long-term bonds decline whenever interest rates rise; and because interest rates can and do occasionally rise, all long-term bonds, even Treasury bonds, have an element of risk called **interest rate risk**. As a general rule, the bonds of any organization have more interest rate risk the longer the maturity of the bond.[10] Therefore, a **maturity risk premium (MRP)**, which is higher the greater the years to maturity, is included in the required interest rate.

*Interest Rate Risk*
The risk of capital losses to which investors are exposed because of changing interest rates.

The effect of maturity risk premiums is to raise interest rates on long-term bonds relative to those on short-term bonds. This premium, like the others, is difficult to measure, but (1) it varies somewhat over time, rising when interest rates are more volatile and uncertain, and then falling when interest rates are more stable. (2) In recent years, the maturity risk premium on 20-year T-bonds has generally been in the range of one to two percentage points.[11]

*Maturity Risk Premium (MRP)*
A premium that reflects interest rate risk.

We should also note that although long-term bonds are heavily exposed to interest rate risk, short-term bills are heavily exposed to **reinvestment rate risk**. When short-term bills mature and the principal must be reinvested, or "rolled over," a decline in interest rates would necessitate reinvestment at a lower rate,

*Reinvestment Rate Risk*
The risk that a decline in interest rates will lead to lower income when bonds mature and funds are reinvested.

---

[9]Although it is a reasonable approximation to assume that the liquidity premium is zero for Treasury securities, in reality some Treasury securities are more liquid than others. In particular, bonds tend to be less liquid if it has been a long time since the bonds were originally issued.

[10]For example, if someone had bought a 20-year Treasury bond for $1,000 in October 1998, when the long-term interest rate was 5.3%, and sold it in May 2002, when long-term T-bond rates were about 5.8%, the value of the bond would have declined to about $942. That would represent a loss of 5.8%; and it demonstrates that long-term bonds, even U.S. Treasury bonds, are not riskless. However, had the investor purchased short-term T-bills in 1998 and subsequently reinvested the principal each time the bills matured, he or she would still have had the original $1,000. This point is discussed in detail in Chapter 7.

[11]The MRP for long-term bonds has averaged 1.6% over the last 89 years. See *Ibbotson Stocks, Bonds, Bills, and Inflation: 2015 Classic Yearbook* (Chicago: Morningstar, Inc., 2015).

# AN ALMOST RISKLESS TREASURY BOND

Investors who purchase bonds must constantly worry about inflation. If inflation turns out to be greater than expected, bonds will provide a lower-than-expected real return. To protect themselves against expected increases in inflation, investors build an inflation risk premium into their required rate of return. This raises borrowers' costs.

To provide investors with an inflation-protected bond and to reduce the cost of debt to the government, the U.S. Treasury issues Treasury Inflation Protected Securities (TIPS), which are bonds that are indexed to inflation. For example, in 2009, the Treasury issued 10-year TIPS with a $2\frac{1}{8}\%$ coupon. These bonds pay an interest rate of $2\frac{1}{8}\%$ plus an additional amount that is just sufficient to offset inflation. At the end of each 6-month period, the principal (originally set at par or $1,000) is adjusted by the inflation rate. To understand how TIPS work, consider that during the first 6-month interest period, inflation (as measured by the CPI) declined by 0.55% (1/15/09 CPI = 214.69971 and 7/15/09 CPI = 213.51819). The inflation-adjusted principal was then calculated as $1,000 $(1 - 0.0055) = \$1,000 \times 0.9945 = \$994.50$. So on July 15, 2009, each bond paid interest of $(0.02125/2) \times \$994.50 = \$10.57$. Note that the interest rate is divided by 2 because interest on Treasury (and most other) bonds is paid twice a year. This same adjustment process will continue each year until the bonds mature on January 15, 2019, at which time they will pay the adjusted maturity value. On January 15, 2015, the change in the CPI from when the bonds were originally issued was 10.3187%. The inflation-adjusted principal was calculated as $1,000 \times 1.103187 = \$1,103.19$. So on January 15, 2015 each bond paid interest of $(0.02125/2) \times \$1,103.19 = \$11.72$. Thus,

the cash income provided by the bonds rises and falls by exactly enough to cover inflation or a decline in inflation, producing a real inflation-adjusted rate of $2\frac{1}{8}\%$ for those who hold the bond from its original issue date until its maturity. Further, because the principal also rises and falls by the inflation rate or its decline, it too is protected from inflation.

Both the annual interest received and the increase in principal are taxed each year as interest income, even though cash from the appreciation will not be received until the bond matures. Therefore, these bonds are not good for accounts subject to current income taxes; but they are excellent for individual retirement accounts (IRAs) and 401(k) plans, which are not taxed until funds are withdrawn.

The Treasury regularly conducts auctions to issue indexed bonds. The $2\frac{1}{8}\%$ coupon rate was based on the relative supply and demand for the issue, and it will remain fixed over the life of the bond. However, after the bonds are issued, they continue to trade in the open market; and their price will vary as investors' perceptions of the real rate of interest changes. The following graph shows that real rates steadily declined during 2009–2012, but they began to increase after the early part of 2013. Confirming the point we made earlier, the graph also shows that real rates have been negative in recent years. Finally, as we see in the graph, the real rate of interest has varied quite a bit since this TIPS was issued; and as the real rate changes, so does the price of the bond. Thus, despite their protection against inflation, indexed bonds are not completely riskless. The real rate can change; and if $r^*$ rises, the prices of indexed bonds will decline. This confirms again that there is no such thing as a free lunch or a riskless security.

**10-Year $2\frac{1}{8}$ % Treasury Inflation-Indexed Note, Due 1/15/2019©**

Shaded areas indicate US recessions-2015 research.stlouisfed.org

Sources: Dow Jones & Company, Haver Analytics, and St. Louis Federal Reserve, FRED database, research.stlouisfed.org/fred2.

which would result in a decline in interest income. To illustrate, suppose you had $100,000 invested in T-bills and you lived on the income. In 1981, short-term Treasury rates were about 15%, so your income would have been about $15,000. However, your income would have declined to about $9,000 by 1983 and to just $240 by March 2015. Had you invested your money in long-term T-bonds, your income (but not the value of the principal) would have been stable.[12] Thus, although "investing short" preserves one's principal, the interest income provided by short-term T-bills is less stable than that on long-term bonds.

### quick question

QUESTION:

An analyst evaluating securities has obtained the following information. The real rate of interest is 2% and is expected to remain constant for the next 3 years. Inflation is expected to be 3% next year, 3.5% the following year, and 4% the third year. The maturity risk premium is estimated to be $0.1 \times (t - 1)\%$, where $t = $ number of years to maturity. The liquidity premium on relevant 3-year securities is 0.25% and the default risk premium on relevant 3-year securities is 0.6%.

a. What is the yield on a 1-year T-bill?
b. What is the yield on a 3-year T-bond?
c. What is the yield on a 3-year corporate bond?

ANSWER:

a. A Treasury security has no default risk premium or liquidity risk premium. Therefore,

$r_{T1} = r^* + IP_1 + MRP_1$
$r_{T1} = 2\% + 3\% + 0.1(1 - 1)\%$
$r_{T1} = $ **5%**.

b. A Treasury security has no default risk premium or liquidity risk premium. Therefore,

$r_{T3} = r^* + IP_3 + MRP_3$
$r_{T3} = 2\% + [(3\% + 3.5\% + 4\%)/3] + 0.1(3 - 1)\%$
$r_{T3} = 2\% + 3.5\% + 0.2\%$
$r_{T3} = $ **5.7%**.

c. Unlike Treasury securities, corporate bonds have both a default risk premium and a liquidity risk premium.

$r_{C3} = r^* + IP_3 + MRP_3 + DRP + LP$.

Realize that the first three terms in this equation are identical to the terms in the part b equation. So we can rewrite this equation as follows:

$r_{C3} = r_{T3} + DRP + LP$.

Now, we can insert the known values for these variables.

$r_{C3} = 5.7\% + 0.6\% + 0.25\%$
$r_{C3} = $ **6.55%**.

---

[12]Most long-term bonds also have some reinvestment rate risk. If a person is saving and investing for some future purpose (say, to buy a house or to retire), to actually earn the quoted rate on a long-term bond, each interest payment must be reinvested at the quoted rate. However, if interest rates fall, the interest payments would be reinvested at a lower rate; so the realized return would be less than the quoted rate. Note, though, that reinvestment rate risk is lower on long-term bonds than on short-term bonds because only the interest payments (rather than interest plus principal) on a long-term bond are exposed to reinvestment rate risk. Noncallable zero coupon bonds, which are discussed in Chapter 7, are completely free of reinvestment rate risk during their lifetime.

## SelfTest

Write an equation for the nominal interest rate on any security.

Distinguish between the *real* risk-free rate of interest, $r^*$, and the *nominal,* or *quoted,* risk-free rate of interest, $r_{RF}$.

How do investors deal with inflation when they determine interest rates in the financial markets?

Does the interest rate on a T-bond include a default risk premium? Explain.

Distinguish between liquid and illiquid assets, and list some assets that are liquid and some that are illiquid.

Briefly explain the following statement: Although long-term bonds are heavily exposed to interest rate risk, short-term T-bills are heavily exposed to reinvestment rate risk. The maturity risk premium reflects the net effects of those two opposing forces.

Assume that the real risk-free rate is $r^* = 2\%$ and the average expected inflation rate is 3% for each future year. The DRP and LP for Bond X are each 1%, and the applicable MRP is 2%. What is Bond X's interest rate? Is Bond X (1) a Treasury bond or a corporate bond and (2) more likely to have a 3-month or a 20-year maturity? **(9%, corporate, 20-year)**

# 6-4 The Term Structure of Interest Rates

**Term Structure of Interest Rates**

The relationship between bond yields and maturities.

The **term structure of interest rates** describes the relationship between long- and short-term rates. The term structure is important to corporate treasurers deciding whether to borrow by issuing long- or short-term debt and to investors who are deciding whether to buy long- or short-term bonds. Therefore, both borrowers and lenders should understand (1) how long- and short-term rates relate to each other and (2) what causes shifts in their relative levels.

Interest rates for bonds with different maturities can be found in a variety of publications, including *The Wall Street Journal* and *the Federal Reserve Bulletin,* and on a number of websites, including those of Bloomberg, Yahoo!, CNN Money, and the Federal Reserve Board. Using interest rate data from these sources, we can determine the term structure at any given point in time. For example, the table section of Figure 6.4 presents interest rates for different maturities on three different dates. The set of data for a given date, when plotted on a graph such as Figure 6.4, is called the **yield curve** for that date.

**Yield Curve**

A graph showing the relationship between bond yields and maturities.

As the figure shows, the yield curve changes in position and in slope over time. In March 1980, all rates were quite high because high inflation was expected. However, the rate of inflation was expected to decline; so short-term rates were higher than long-term rates, and the yield curve was thus *downward sloping.* By February 2000, inflation had indeed declined; thus, all rates were lower, and the yield curve had become *humped*—intermediate-term rates were higher than either short- or long-term rates. By March 2015, all rates had fallen below the 2000 levels; and because short-term rates had dropped below long-term rates, the yield curve was *upward sloping.*

Figure 6.4 shows yield curves for U.S. Treasury securities; but we could have constructed curves for bonds issued by GE, IBM, Delta Air Lines, or any other company that borrows money over a range of maturities. Had we constructed such corporate yield curves and plotted them on Figure 6.4, they would have been above those for Treasury securities because corporate yields include default risk premiums and somewhat higher liquidity premiums. Even so, the corporate yield curves would have had the same general shape as the Treasury curves. Also, the riskier the corporation, the higher its yield curve. For example, in March 2015, Cisco Systems, Inc.'s bonds with a six-year maturity were rated AA by Fitch and yielded 2.157%, whereas Toys R Us, Inc. had six-year bonds outstanding that were rated CCC and had a yield of 14.90%. At the same point in time, six-year Treasury securities had an interest rate of 1.615%.

# FIGURE 6.4 U.S. Treasury Bond Interest Rates on Different Dates

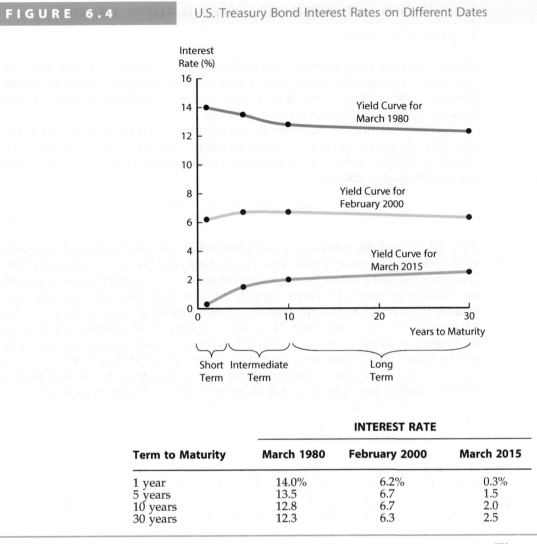

| | INTEREST RATE | | |
|---|---|---|---|
| **Term to Maturity** | **March 1980** | **February 2000** | **March 2015** |
| 1 year | 14.0% | 6.2% | 0.3% |
| 5 years | 13.5 | 6.7 | 1.5 |
| 10 years | 12.8 | 6.7 | 2.0 |
| 30 years | 12.3 | 6.3 | 2.5 |

Historically, long-term rates are generally above short-term rates because of the maturity risk premium; so all yield curves usually slope upward. For this reason, people often call an upward-sloping yield curve a **"normal" yield curve** and a yield curve that slopes downward an **inverted or "abnormal" yield curve**. Thus, in Figure 6.4, the yield curve for March 1980 was inverted, while the one for March 2015 was normal. However, the February 2000 curve is humped—a **humped yield curve**—which means that interest rates on intermediate-term maturities were higher than rates on both short- and long-term maturities. We will explain in detail why an upward slope is the normal situation. Briefly, however, the reason is that short-term securities have less interest rate risk than longer-term securities; hence, they have smaller MRPs. So short-term rates are normally lower than long-term rates.

**"Normal" Yield Curve**
An upward-sloping yield curve.

**Inverted ("Abnormal") Yield Curve**
A downward-sloping yield curve.

**Humped Yield Curve**
A yield curve where interest rates on intermediate-term maturities are higher than rates on both short- and long-term maturities.

## Self Test

What is a yield curve, and what information would you need to draw this curve?

Distinguish among the shapes of a "normal" yield curve, an "abnormal" curve, and a "humped" curve.

If the interest rates on 1-, 5-, 10-, and 30-year bonds are 4%, 5%, 6%, and 7%, respectively, how would you describe the yield curve? If the rates were reversed, how would you describe it?

# 6-5 What Determines the Shape of the Yield Curve?

Because maturity risk premiums are positive, if other things were held constant, long-term bonds would always have higher interest rates than short-term bonds. However, market interest rates also depend on expected inflation, default risk, and liquidity, each of which can vary with maturity.

Expected inflation has an especially important effect on the yield curve's shape, especially the curve for U.S. Treasury securities. Treasuries have essentially no default or liquidity risk, so the yield on a Treasury bond that matures in t years can be expressed as follows:

$$\text{T-bond yield} = r_t^* + IP_t + MRP_t$$

▼ 6.2

Although the real risk-free rate, $r^*$, varies somewhat over time because of changes in the economy and demographics, these changes are random rather than predictable. Therefore, the best forecast for the future value of $r^*$ is its current value. However, the inflation premium, IP, varies significantly over time and in a somewhat predictable manner. Recall that the inflation premium is the average level of expected inflation over the life of the bond. Thus, if the market expects inflation to increase in the future (say, from 3% to 4% to 5% over the next 3 years), the inflation premium will be higher on a 3-year bond than on a 1-year bond. On the other hand, if the market expects inflation to decline in the future, long-term bonds will have a smaller inflation premium than will short-term bonds. Finally, because investors consider long-term bonds to be riskier than short-term bonds because of interest rate risk, the maturity risk premium always increases with maturity.

Figure 6.5 shows two illustrative yield curves—one where inflation is expected to increase over time and another where inflation is expected to decrease. Note that these hypothetical interest rates are similar to historical rates, but they are much higher than current interest rates. Panel a shows the Treasury yield curve when inflation is expected to increase. Here long-term bonds have higher yields for two reasons: (1) Inflation is expected to be higher in the future. (2) There is a positive maturity risk premium. Panel b shows the yield curve when inflation is expected to decline. Such a downward-sloping yield curve often foreshadows an economic downturn because weaker economic conditions generally lead to declining inflation, which in turn results in lower long-term rates.[13]

Now let's consider the yield curve for corporate bonds. Recall that corporate bonds include a default risk premium (DRP) and a liquidity premium (LP).

Therefore, the yield on a corporate bond that matures in t years can be expressed as follows:

$$\text{Corporate bond yield} = r_t^* + IP_t + MRP_t + DRP_t + LP_t$$

▼ 6.3

Comparing the Treasury bond yield in Equation 6.2 and the corporate bond yield in Equation 6.3, we can calculate the corporate bond yield spread:

$$\text{Corporate bond yield spread} = \text{Corporate bond yield} - \text{Treasury bond yield} = DRP_t + LP_t$$

---

[13]Note that yield curves tend to rise or fall relatively sharply over the first 5 to 10 years and then flatten out. One reason this occurs is that when forecasting future interest rates, people often predict relatively high or low inflation for the next few years, after which they assume an average long-run inflation rate. Consequently, the short end of the yield curve tends to have more curvature, and the long end of the yield curve tends to be more stable.

**FIGURE 6.5**     Illustrative Treasury Yield Curves

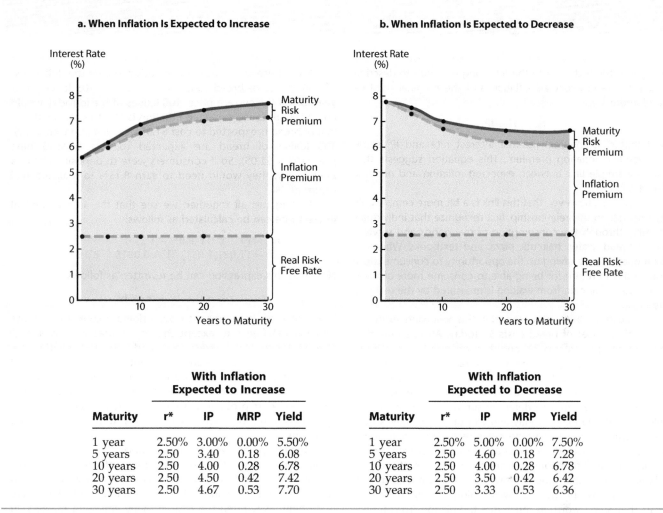

| Maturity | With Inflation Expected to Increase | | | | | Maturity | With Inflation Expected to Decrease | | | |
|---|---|---|---|---|---|---|---|---|---|---|
| | r* | IP | MRP | Yield | | | r* | IP | MRP | Yield |
| 1 year | 2.50% | 3.00% | 0.00% | 5.50% | | 1 year | 2.50% | 5.00% | 0.00% | 7.50% |
| 5 years | 2.50 | 3.40 | 0.18 | 6.08 | | 5 years | 2.50 | 4.60 | 0.18 | 7.28 |
| 10 years | 2.50 | 4.00 | 0.28 | 6.78 | | 10 years | 2.50 | 4.00 | 0.28 | 6.78 |
| 20 years | 2.50 | 4.50 | 0.42 | 7.42 | | 20 years | 2.50 | 3.50 | 0.42 | 6.42 |
| 30 years | 2.50 | 4.67 | 0.53 | 7.70 | | 30 years | 2.50 | 3.33 | 0.53 | 6.36 |

One recent study estimates that both the default risk premium and liquidity premium vary over time, and that the majority of the corporate bond yield spread can be attributed to default risk.[14] Corporate bonds' default and liquidity risks are affected by their maturities. For example, the default risk on Coca-Cola's short-term debt is very small because there is almost no chance that Coca-Cola will go bankrupt over the next few years. However, Coke has some bonds that have a maturity of almost 100 years; and although the odds of Coke defaulting on those bonds might not be very high, there is still a higher probability of default risk on Coke's long-term bonds than on its short-term bonds.

Longer-term corporate bonds also tend to be less liquid than shorter-term bonds. Because short-term debt has less default risk, someone can buy a short-term bond without doing as much credit checking as would be necessary for a long-term bond. Thus, people can move in and out of short-term corporate

---

[14]Refer to Francis A. Longstaff, Sanjay Mithal, and Eric Neis, "Corporate Yield Spreads: Default Risk or Liquidity? New Evidence from the Credit Default Swap Market," *Journal of Finance*, vol. 60, no. 5 (October 2005), pp. 2213–2253.

# THE LINKS BETWEEN EXPECTED INFLATION AND INTEREST RATES: A CLOSER LOOK

Throughout the text, we use the following equation to describe the link between expected inflation and the nominal risk-free rate of interest, $r_{RF}$:

$$r_{RF} = r^* + IP$$

Recall that $r^*$ is the real risk-free interest rate and IP is the corresponding inflation premium. This equation suggests that there is a simple link between expected inflation and nominal interest rates.

It turns out, however, that this link is a bit more complex. To fully understand this relationship, first recognize that individuals get utility through the consumption of real goods and services such as bread, water, haircuts, pizza, and textbooks. When we save money, we are giving up the opportunity to consume these goods today in return for being able to consume more of them in the future. Our gain from waiting is measured by the real rate of interest, $r^*$.

To illustrate this point, consider the following example. Assume that a loaf of bread costs $1 today. Also assume that the real rate of interest is 3% and that inflation is expected to be 5% over the next year. The 3% real rate indicates that the average consumer is willing to trade 100 loaves of bread today for 103 loaves next year. If a "bread bank" were available, consumers who wanted to defer consumption until next year could deposit 100 loaves today and withdraw 103 loaves next year. In practice, most of us do not directly trade real goods such as bread—instead, we purchase these goods with money because in a well-functioning economy, it is more efficient to exchange money than goods. However, when we lend money over time, we worry that borrowers might pay us back with dollars that aren't worth as much due to inflation. To compensate for this risk, lenders build in a premium for expected inflation.

With these concerns in mind, let's compare the dollar cost of 100 loaves of bread today to the cost of 103 loaves next year. Given the current price, 100 loaves of bread today would cost $100. Because expected inflation is 5%, this means that a loaf of bread is expected to cost $1.05 next year. Consequently, 103 loaves of bread are expected to cost $108.15 next year (103 × $1.05). So if consumers were to deposit $100 in a bank today, they would need to earn 8.15% to realize a real return of 3%.

Putting this all together, we see that the 1-year nominal interest rate can be calculated as follows:

$$r_{RF} = (1 + r^*)(1 + IP) - 1$$
$$= (1.03)(1.05) - 1 = 0.0815 = 8.15\%$$

Note that this expression can be rewritten as follows:

$$r_{RF} = r^* + IP + (r^* \times IP)$$

That equation is identical to our original expression for the nominal risk-free rate except that it includes a "cross-term," $r^* \times IP$. When real interest rates and expected inflation are relatively low, the cross-term turns out to be quite small and thus is often ignored. Because it is normally insignificant, we disregard the cross-term in the text unless stated otherwise. (When working problems, we will tell you when to include the cross-term; otherwise, ignore this term when solving problems.)

One last point—you should recognize that while it may be reasonable to ignore the cross-term when interest rates are low (as they are in the United States today), it is a mistake to do so when investing in a market where interest rates and inflation are quite high, as is often the case in many emerging markets. In these markets, the cross-term can be significant and thus should not be disregarded.

debt relatively rapidly. As a result, a corporation's short-term bonds are typically more liquid and thus have lower liquidity premiums than its long-term bonds.

Figure 6.6 shows yield curves for two hypothetical corporate bonds—an AA-rated bond with minimal default risk and a BBB-rated bond with more default risk—along with the yield curve for Treasury securities taken from panel a of Figure 6.5. Here we assume that inflation is expected to increase, so the Treasury yield curve is upward sloping. Because of their additional default and liquidity risk, corporate bonds yield more than Treasury bonds with the same maturity and BBB-rated bonds yield more than AA-rated bonds. Finally, note that the yield spread between corporate and Treasury bonds is larger the longer the maturity. This occurs because longer-term corporate bonds have more default and liquidity risk than shorter-term bonds, and both of these premiums are absent in Treasury bonds.

## FIGURE 6.6  Illustrative Corporate and Treasury Yield Curves

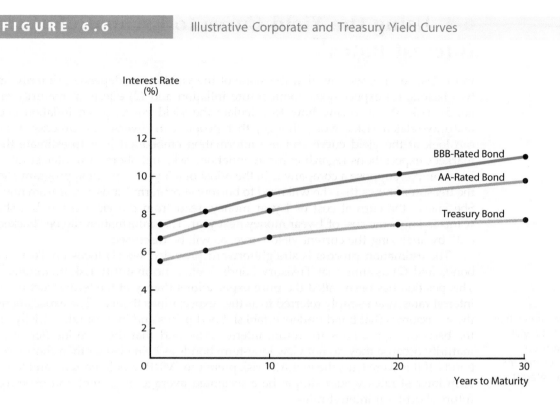

|  | Interest Rate | | |
| --- | --- | --- | --- |
|  | **Treasury Bond** | **AA-Rated Bond** | **BBB-Rated Bond** |
| 1 year | 5.5% | 6.7% | 7.4% |
| 5 years | 6.1 | 7.4 | 8.1 |
| 10 years | 6.8 | 8.2 | 9.1 |
| 20 years | 7.4 | 9.2 | 10.2 |
| 30 years | 7.7 | 9.8 | 11.1 |

## SelfTest

How do maturity risk premiums affect the yield curve?

If the inflation rate is expected to increase, would this increase or decrease the slope of the yield curve?

If the inflation rate is expected to remain constant at the current level in the future, would the yield curve slope up, slope down, or be horizontal? Consider all factors that affect the yield curve, not just inflation.

Explain why corporate bonds' default and liquidity premiums are likely to increase with their maturity.

Explain why corporate bonds always yield more than Treasury bonds and why BBB-rated bonds always yield more than AA-rated bonds.

# 6-6 Using the Yield Curve to Estimate Future Interest Rates[15]

In the last section, we saw that the slope of the yield curve depends primarily on two factors: (1) expectations about future inflation and (2) effects of maturity on bonds' risk. We also saw how to calculate the yield curve, given inflation and maturity-related risks. Note, though, that people can reverse the process: They can look at the yield curve and use information embedded in it to estimate the market's expectations regarding future inflation, risk, and short-term interest rates. For example, suppose a company is in the midst of a 5-year expansion program and the treasurer knows that she will need to borrow short-term funds a year from now. She knows the current cost of 1-year money, read from the yield curve, but she wants to know the cost of 1-year money next year. That information can be "backed out" by analyzing the current yield curve, as will be discussed.

The estimation process is straightforward provided we (1) focus on Treasury bonds and (2) assume that Treasury bonds contain no maturity risk premiums.[16] This position has been called the **pure expectations theory** of the term structure of interest rates, often simply referred to as the "expectations theory." The expectations theory assumes that bond traders establish bond prices and interest rates strictly on the basis of expectations for future interest rates and that they are indifferent to maturity because they do not view long-term bonds as being riskier than short-term bonds. If this were true, the maturity risk premium (MRP) would be zero, and long-term interest rates would simply be a weighted average of current and expected future short-term interest rates.

*Pure Expectations Theory*

A theory that states that the shape of the yield curve depends on investors' expectations about future interest rates.

To illustrate the pure expectations theory, assume that a 1-year Treasury bond currently yields 5.00%, and a 2-year bond yields 5.50%. Investors who want to invest for a 2-year horizon have two primary options:

**Option 1:** *Buy a two-year security and hold it for 2 years.*

**Option 2:** *Buy a 1-year security; hold it for 1 year; and then at the end of the year, reinvest the proceeds in another 1-year security.*

If they select Option 1, for every dollar they invest today, they will have accumulated $1.113025 by the end of Year 2:

$$\text{Funds at end of Year 2} = \$1 \times (1.055)^2 = \$1.113025$$

If they select Option 2, they should end up with the same amount; but this equation is used to find the ending amount:

$$\text{Funds at end of Year 2} = \$1 \times (1.05) \times (1 + X)$$

Here X is the expected interest rate on a 1-year Treasury security 1 year from now.

If the expectations theory is correct, each option must provide the same amount of cash at the end of 2 years, which implies the following:

$$(1.05)(1 + X) = (1.055)^2$$

---

[15]This section is relatively technical, but instructors can omit it without loss of continuity.

[16]Although most evidence suggests that there is a positive maturity risk premium, some academics and practitioners contend that this second assumption is reasonable, at least as an approximation. They argue that the market is dominated by large bond traders who buy and sell securities of different maturities each day, that these traders focus only on short-term returns, and that they are not concerned with maturity risk. According to this view, a bond trader is just as willing to buy a 20-year bond to pick up a short-term profit as he or she is to buy a 3-month security. Proponents of this view argue that the shape of the Treasury yield curve is therefore determined only by market expectations about future interest rates. Later in this section, we show what happens when we include the effects of maturity risk premiums.

We can rearrange this equation and then solve for X:

$$1 + X = (1.055)^2 / 1.05$$
$$= (1.055)^2 / 1.05 - 1 = 0.0600238 = 6.00238\%$$

Therefore, X, the 1-year rate 1 year from today, must be 6.00238%; otherwise, one option will be better than the other, and the market will not be in equilibrium. However, if the market is not in equilibrium, buying and selling will quickly bring about equilibrium. For example, suppose investors expect the 1-year Treasury rate to be 6.00238% a year from now but a 2-year bond now yields 5.25%, not the 5.50% rate required for equilibrium. Bond traders could earn a profit by adopting the following strategy:

1. Borrow money for 2 years at the 2-year rate, 5.25% per year.

2. Invest the money in a series of 1-year securities, expecting to earn 5.00% this year and 6.00238% next year, for an overall expected return over the 2 years of $[1.05 \times 1.0600238]^{1/2} - 1 = 5.50\%$.

Borrowing at 5.25% and investing to earn 5.50% is a good deal, so bond traders would rush to borrow money (demand funds) in the 2-year market and invest (or supply funds) in the 1-year market.

Recall from Figure 6.1 that a decline in the supply of funds raises interest rates, while an increase in the supply lowers rates. Likewise, an increase in the demand for funds raises rates, while a decline in demand lowers rates. Therefore, bond traders would push up the 2-year yield and simultaneously lower the yield on 1-year bonds. This buying and selling would cease when the 2-year rate becomes a weighted average of expected future 1-year rates.[17]

Let's suppose that the yield curve looks as follows:

1-year T-bond: 5.00%

2-year T-bond: 5.50%

4-year T-bond: 6.25%

An investor would like to purchase a 1-year T-bond today and then to invest in a 3-year T-bond one year from now. What yield would this investor expect to earn on the 3-year T-bond one year from now? You have enough information from the yield curve above to determine the expected yield on the 3-year T-bond one year from today. Here's the equation setup:

$$(1.0625)^4 = (1.05) \times (1 + X)^3$$
$$(1.0625)^4 / 1.05 = (1 + X)^3$$
$$1.213742 = (1 + X)^3$$
$$(1.213742)^{1/3} = 1 + X$$
$$1.0667 = 1 + X, \text{ so } X = 6.67\%.$$

To eliminate the exponent, each side of the equation is raised to the 1/3 power.

The investor would expect to earn one year from today a yield of 6.67% for three years on the 3-year T-bond. Note that the investor would expect to earn the same yield investing in a 4-year T-bond today as he would investing in a 1-year T-bond today and then investing in a 3-year T-bond one year from now.

The preceding analysis was based on the assumption that the maturity risk premium is zero. However, most evidence suggests that a positive maturity risk

---

[17]In our calculations, we used the geometric average of the current and expected 1-year rates: $[1.05 \times 1.0600238]^{1/2} - 1 = 0.055$ or 5.50%. The arithmetic average of the two rates is $(5\% + 6.00238\%)/2 = 5.50119\%$. The geometric average is theoretically correct, but the difference is only 0.00119%. With interest rates at the levels they have been in the United States and most other nations in recent years, the geometric and arithmetic averages are so close that many people use the arithmetic average, especially given the other assumptions that underlie the estimation of future 1-year rates.

premium exists. For example, assume once again that 1- and 2-year maturities yield 5.00% and 5.50%, respectively; so we have a rising yield curve. However, now assume that the maturity risk premium on the 2-year bond is 0.20% versus zero for the 1-year bond. This premium means that in equilibrium, the expected annual return on a 2-year bond (5.50%) must be 0.20% higher than the expected return on a series of two 1-year bonds (5.00% and X%). Therefore, the expected return on the series must be $5.50\% - 0.20\% = 5.30\%$:

$$\text{Expected return on 2-year series} = \text{Rate on two-year bond} - \text{MRP}$$
$$= 0.055 - 0.002 = 0.053 = 5.30\%$$

Now recall that the annual expected return from the series of two 1-year bonds can be expressed as follows, where X is the 1-year rate next year:

$$(1.05)(1 + X) = (1 + \text{Expected return on 2-year series})^2 = (1.053)^2$$

$$1.05X = (1.053)^2 - 1.05$$

$$X = \frac{0.0588090}{1.05} = 0.0560086 = 5.60086\%.$$

Under these conditions, equilibrium requires that market participants expect the 1-year rate next year to be 5.60086%.

Note that the rate read from the yield curve rises by 0.50% when the years to maturity increase from one to two: $5.50\% - 5.00\% = 0.50\%$. Of this 0.50% increase, 0.20% is attributable to the MRP, and the remaining 0.30% is due to the increase in expected 1-year rates next year.

Putting all of this together, we see that one can use the yield curve to estimate what the market expects the short-term rate to be next year. However, this requires an estimate of the maturity risk premium; and if our estimated MRP is incorrect, then so will our yield-curve-based interest rate forecast. Thus, though the yield curve can be used to obtain insights into what the market thinks future interest rates will be, the calculations above (although they appear to be precise) will only approximate these expectations unless the pure expectations theory holds or we know with certainty the exact maturity risk premium. Because neither of these conditions holds, it is difficult to know for sure what the market is forecasting.

Note too that even if we could determine the market's consensus forecast for future rates, the market is not always right. So a forecast of next year's rate based on the yield curve could be wrong. Therefore, obtaining an accurate forecast of rates for next year—or even for next month—is extremely difficult.

## SelfTest

What key assumption underlies the pure expectations theory?

Assuming that the pure expectations theory is correct, how are expected short-term rates used to calculate expected long-term rates?

According to the pure expectations theory, what would happen if long-term rates were not an average of expected short-term rates?

Most evidence suggests that a positive maturity risk premium exists. How would this affect your calculations when determining interest rates?

Assume that the interest rate on a 1-year T-bond is currently 7% and the rate on a 2-year bond is 9%. If the maturity risk premium is zero, what is a reasonable forecast of the rate on a 1-year bond next year? What would the forecast be if the maturity risk premium on the 2-year bond was 0.5% versus zero for the 1-year bond? **(11.04%; 10.02%)**

# 6-7 Macroeconomic Factors That Influence Interest Rate Levels

We described how key components such as expected inflation, default risk, maturity risk, and liquidity concerns influence the level of interest rates over time and across different markets. On a day-to-day basis, a variety of macroeconomic factors may influence one or more of these components; hence, macroeconomic factors have an important effect on both the general level of interest rates and the shape of the yield curve. The primary factors are (1) Federal Reserve policy; (2) the federal budget deficit or surplus; (3) international factors, including the foreign trade balance and interest rates in other countries; and (4) the level of business activity.

*The home page for the Board of Governors of the Federal Reserve System can be found at **federalreserve.gov**. You can access general information about the Federal Reserve, including press releases, speeches, and monetary policy.*

## 6-7A FEDERAL RESERVE POLICY

As you probably learned in your economics courses, (1) the money supply has a significant effect on the level of economic activity, inflation, and interest rates. (2) In the United States, the Federal Reserve Board controls the money supply. If the Fed wants to stimulate the economy, it increases the money supply. The Fed buys and sells short-term securities, so the initial effect of a monetary easing would be to cause short-term rates to decline. However, a larger money supply might lead to an increase in expected future inflation, which would cause long-term rates to rise even as short-term rates fell. The reverse holds if the Fed tightens the money supply. The Fed's job is to promote economic growth while keeping inflation at bay. This is a delicate balancing act.

As you can see from Figure 6.2, interest rates in recent years have been relatively low, with short-term rates especially low during the last 5 years shown (January 2010 through March 2015). Economists anticipate that rates will remain low for the foreseeable future; however, some worry that the Fed might be increasing the risk of inflation down the road.

During the last several years, the Fed has been trying to increase business investment to generate growth in our economy. In addition to lower interest rates, the Fed through its program of "Quantitative Easing" has pumped trillions of dollars into the economy by purchasing mortgage-backed securities and long-term Treasury securities and through special lending programs. The Fed stopped purchasing mortgage-backed securities on October 29, 2014, and the housing market is improving slowly. However, now there is concern that interest rates will rise, which may limit any further improvements in the housing market. But if the Fed anticipates inflation returning, it could be forced to raise rates or to reduce the money supply. Likewise, the stock market has been skittish due to anticipation of the Fed increasing rates. However, as of this writing (March 2015) no hike has been announced. In fact, the European Central Bank has started its own quantitative easing policy recently, and it appears to be putting downward pressure on longer-term rates in the U.S.[18]

Actions that lower short-term rates won't necessarily lower long-term rates. Lower rates could cause foreigners to sell their holdings of U.S. bonds. These investors would be paid with dollars, which they would then sell to buy their own currencies. The sale of dollars and the purchase of other currencies would lower the value of the dollar relative to other currencies, which would make U.S. goods less expensive, which would help manufacturers and thus lower the trade deficit. Note also that during periods when the Fed is actively intervening in the markets, the yield curve may be temporarily distorted. Short-term rates may be driven below the long-run equilibrium level if the Fed is easing credit and above the equilibrium rate if the Fed is tightening credit. Long-term rates are not affected as much by Fed intervention.

---

[18]Refer to Myles Udland, "Fed's Fischer: We'll Probably Raise Rates This Year," *Business Insider* (www.businessinsider.com), March 23, 2015.

## 6-7B FEDERAL BUDGET DEFICITS OR SURPLUSES

If the federal government spends more than it takes in as taxes, it runs a deficit; and that deficit must be covered by additional borrowing (selling more Treasury bonds) or by printing money. If the government borrows, this increases the demand for funds and thus pushes up interest rates. If the government prints money, investors recognize that with "more money chasing a given amount of goods," the result will be increased inflation, which will also increase interest rates. So the larger the federal deficit, other things held constant, the higher the level of interest rates.

Over the past several decades, the federal government has generally run large budget deficits. There were some surpluses in the late 1990s; but the September 11, 2001, terrorist attacks; the subsequent recession; and the Iraq war all boosted government spending and caused the deficits to return.

## 6-7C INTERNATIONAL FACTORS

**Foreign Trade Deficit**
The situation that exists when a country imports more than it exports.

Businesses and individuals in the United States buy from and sell to people and firms all around the globe. If they buy more than they sell (that is, if there are more imports than exports), they are said to be running a **foreign trade deficit**. When trade deficits occur, they must be financed, and this generally means borrowing from nations with export surpluses. Thus, if the United States imported $200 billion of goods but exported only $100 billion, it would run a trade deficit of $100 billion, and other countries would have a $100 billion trade surplus. The United States would probably borrow the $100 billion from the surplus nations.[19] At any rate, the larger the trade deficit, the higher the tendency to borrow. Note that foreigners will hold U.S. debt if and only if the rates on U.S. securities are competitive with rates in other countries. This causes U.S. interest rates to be highly dependent on rates in other parts of the world.

All this interdependency limits the ability of the Federal Reserve to use monetary policy to control economic activity in the United States. For example, if the Fed attempts to lower U.S. interest rates and this causes rates to fall below rates abroad, foreigners will begin selling U.S. bonds. Those sales will depress bond prices, which will push up rates in the United States. Thus, the large U.S. trade deficit (and foreigners' holdings of U.S. debt that resulted from many years of deficits) hinders the Fed's ability to combat a recession by lowering interest rates.

For about 25 years following World War II, the United States ran large trade surpluses, and the rest of the world owed it many billions of dollars. However, the situation changed, and the United States has been running trade deficits since the mid-1970s. (The U.S. annual 2014 international trade deficit for goods and services was $505 billion, which was up 6% from the prior year.) The cumulative effect of these deficits has been to change the United States from being the largest creditor nation to being the largest debtor nation of all time. As a result, interest rates are very much influenced by interest rates in other countries—higher or lower rates abroad lead to higher or lower U.S. rates. Because of all of this, U.S. corporate treasurers and everyone else who is affected by interest rates should keep up with developments in the world economy.

## 6-7D BUSINESS ACTIVITY

You can examine Figure 6.2 to see how business conditions influence interest rates. Here are the key points revealed by the graph:

1. Because inflation increased from 1972 to 1981, the general tendency during that period was toward higher interest rates. However, since the 1981 peak, the trend has generally been downward.

---

[19]The deficit could also be financed by selling assets, including gold, corporate stocks, entire companies, and real estate. The United States has financed its massive trade deficits by all of these means in recent years. Although the primary method has been by borrowing from foreigners, in recent years, there has been a sharp increase in foreign purchases of U.S. assets, especially oil exporters' purchases of U.S. businesses.

2. The shaded areas in the graph represent recessions, during which (a) the demand for money and the rate of inflation tended to fall and (b) the Federal Reserve tended to increase the money supply in an effort to stimulate the economy. As a result, there is a tendency for interest rates to decline during recessions. For example, the economy began to slow down in 2000, and the country entered a mild recession in 2001. In response, the Federal Reserve cut interest rates. In 2004, the economy began to rebound; so the Fed began to raise rates. However, the subprime debacle hit in 2007; so the Fed began lowering rates in September 2007. By February 2008, the Fed's target rate had fallen from 5.25% to 3.00%. In March 2015, the Federal Reserve target rate ranged from 0% to 0.25%.

3. During recessions, short-term rates decline more sharply than long-term rates. This occurs for two reasons: (a) The Fed operates mainly in the short-term sector, so its intervention has the strongest effect there. (b) Long-term rates reflect the average expected inflation rate over the next 20 to 30 years; and this expectation generally does not change much, even when the current inflation rate is low because of a recession or high because of a boom. So short-term rates are more volatile than long-term rates. Taking another look at Figure 6.2, we see that short-term rates did decline recently by much more than long-term rates.

## SelfTest

Identify some macroeconomic factors that influence interest rates and explain the effects of each.

How does the Fed stimulate the economy? How does the Fed affect interest rates?

Does the Fed have complete control over U.S. interest rates? That is, can it set rates at any level it chooses? Why or why not?

# 6-8 Interest Rates and Business Decisions

As you might expect, companies look carefully at the level of interest rates and the shape of the yield curve when making important business decisions. For example, assume that Leading Edge Co. is considering building a new plant with a 30-year life that will cost $1 million, and it plans to raise the $1 million by borrowing rather than by issuing new stock. At the time of its decision in March 2015, the company faces an upward-sloping yield curve. If it borrows on a short-term basis from a bank—say for 1 year—its annual interest cost would be only 0.5%, or $5,000. On the other hand, if it issued long-term bonds, then its annual cost would be 3.6%, or $36,000. Therefore, at first glance, it would seem that Leading Edge should use short-term debt.

However, this could prove to be a horrible mistake. If it used short-term debt, it will have to renew its loan every year; and the rate charged on each new loan will reflect the then-current short-term rate. Interest rates could dramatically increase, in which case the company's interest payments would soar over time. Those high interest payments would cut into and perhaps eliminate its profits. Even more concerning, if at some point in time the company's lenders refused to renew the loan and demanded its repayment, as they would have every right to do, Leading Edge might have to sell assets at a loss, which could result in bankruptcy. On the other hand, if the company used long-term financing in 2015, its interest costs would remain constant at $36,000 per year; so it would not be directly hurt if interest rates in the economy increased over time.

Does all of this suggest that firms should avoid short-term debt? Not at all. If inflation falls over the next few years, so will interest rates. If Leading Edge had borrowed on a long-term basis in March 2015, it would be at a disadvantage if it was locked into 3.6% debt while its competitors (who used short-term debt in 2015) had a borrowing cost of only 0.5%.

Financing decisions would be easy if we could make accurate forecasts of future interest rates. Unfortunately, predicting interest rates with consistent accuracy is nearly impossible. However, although it is difficult to predict future interest rate *levels,* it is easy to predict that interest rates will *fluctuate*—they always have, and they always will. That being the case, sound financial policy calls for using a mix of long- and short-term debt as well as equity to position the firm so that it can survive in any interest rate environment. Further, the optimal financial policy depends in an important way on the nature of the firm's assets—the easier it is to sell assets to generate cash, the more feasible it is to use more short-term debt. This makes it logical for a firm to finance current assets such as inventories and receivables with short-term debt and to finance fixed assets such as buildings and equipment with long-term debt. We return to this issue later in the book when we discuss capital structure and financing policy.

Changes in interest rates also have implications for savers. For example, if you had a 401(k) plan—and someday most of you will—you would probably want to invest some of your money in a bond mutual fund. You could choose a fund that had an average maturity of 25 years, 20 years, or on down to only a few months (a money market fund). How would your choice affect your investment results and hence your retirement income? First, your decision would affect your annual interest income. For example, if the yield curve was upward sloping, as it normally is, you would earn more interest if you chose a fund that held long-term bonds. Note, though, that if you chose a long-term fund and interest rates then rose, the market value of your fund would decline. For example, as we will see in Chapter 7, if you had $100,000 in a fund whose average bond had a maturity of 25 years and a coupon rate of 6%, and if interest rates then rose from 6% to 10%, the market value of your fund would decline from $100,000 to about $63,500. On the other hand, if rates declined, your fund would increase in value. If you invested in a short-term fund, its value would be more stable, but it would probably provide less interest income per year. In any event, your choice of maturity would have a major effect on your investment performance and therefore on your future income.

## Self Test

If short-term interest rates are lower than long-term rates, why might a borrower still choose to finance with long-term debt?

Explain the following statement: The optimal financial policy depends in an important way on the nature of the firm's assets.

# TYING IT ALL TOGETHER

In this chapter, we discussed the way interest rates are determined, the term structure of interest rates, and some of the ways interest rates affect business decisions. We saw that the interest rate on a given bond, r, is based on this equation:

$$r = r^* + IP + DRP + LP + MRP$$

Here r* is the real risk-free rate, IP is the premium for expected inflation, DRP is the premium for potential default risk, LP is the premium for lack of liquidity, and MRP is the premium to compensate for the risk inherent in bonds with long maturities. Both r* and the various premiums can and do change over time, depending on economic conditions, Federal Reserve actions, and the like. Because changes in these factors are difficult to predict, it is hard to forecast the future direction of interest rates.

The yield curve, which relates bonds' interest rates to their maturities, usually has an upward slope; but it can slope up or down, and both its slope and level change over time. The main determinants of the slope of the curve are expectations for future inflation and the MRP. We can analyze yield curve data to estimate what market participants think future interest rates are likely to be. We will use the insights gained from this chapter in later chapters when we analyze the values of bonds and stocks and examine various corporate investment and financing decisions.

## Self-Test Questions and Problems

(Solutions Appear in Appendix A)

**ST-1** **KEY TERMS**  Define each of the following terms:

a. Production opportunities; time preferences for consumption; risk; inflation

b. Real risk-free rate of interest, $r^*$; nominal (quoted) risk-free rate of interest, $r_{RF}$

c. Inflation premium (IP)

d. Default risk premium (DRP)

e. Liquidity premium (LP); maturity risk premium (MRP)

f. Interest rate risk; reinvestment rate risk

g. Term structure of interest rates; yield curve

h. "Normal" yield curve; inverted ("abnormal") yield curve; humped yield curve

i. Pure expectations theory

j. Foreign trade deficit

**ST-2** **INFLATION AND INTEREST RATES**  The real risk-free rate of interest, $r^*$, is 3%; and it is expected to remain constant over time. Inflation is expected to be 2% per year for the next 3 years and 4% per year for the next 5 years. The maturity risk premium is equal to $0.1 \times (t - 1)$%, where $t$ = the bond's maturity. The default risk premium for a BBB-rated bond is 1.3%.

a. What is the average expected inflation rate over the next 4 years?

b. What is the yield on a 4-year Treasury bond?

c. What is the yield on a 4-year BBB-rated corporate bond with a liquidity premium of 0.5%?

d. What is the yield on an 8-year Treasury bond?

e. What is the yield on an 8-year BBB-rated corporate bond with a liquidity premium of 0.5%?

f. If the yield on a 9-year Treasury bond is 7.3%, what does that imply about expected inflation in 9 years?

**ST-3** **PURE EXPECTATIONS THEORY**  The yield on 1-year Treasury securities is 6%, 2-year securities yield 6.2%, 3-year securities yield 6.3%, and 4-year securities yield 6.5%. There is no maturity risk premium. Using expectations theory and geometric averages, forecast the yields on the following securities:

a. A 1-year security, 1 year from now

b. A 1-year security, 2 years from now

c. A 2-year security, 1 year from now

d. A 3-year security, 1 year from now

## Questions

**6-1**  Suppose interest rates on residential mortgages of equal risk are 5.5% in California and 7.0% in New York. Could this differential persist? What forces might tend to equalize rates? Would differentials in borrowing costs for businesses of equal risk located in California and New York be more or less likely to exist than differentials in residential mortgage rates? Would differentials in the cost of money for New York and California firms be more likely to exist if the firms being compared were very large or if they were very small? What are the implications of all of this with respect to nationwide branching?

6-2    Which fluctuate more—long-term or short-term interest rates? Why?

6-3    Suppose you believe that the economy is just entering a recession. Your firm must raise capital immediately, and debt will be used. Should you borrow on a long-term or a short-term basis? Why?

6-4    Suppose the population of Area Y is relatively young, and the population of Area O is relatively old, but everything else about the two areas is the same.

   a.  Would interest rates likely be the same or different in the two areas? Explain.
   b.  Would a trend toward nationwide branching by banks and the development of nationwide diversified financial corporations affect your answer to part a? Explain.

6-5    Suppose a new process was developed that could be used to make oil out of seawater. The equipment required is quite expensive; but it would in time lead to low prices for gasoline, electricity, and other types of energy. What effect would this have on interest rates?

6-6    Suppose a new and more liberal Congress and administration are elected. Their first order of business is to take away the independence of the Federal Reserve System and to force the Fed to greatly expand the money supply. What effect will this have:

   a.  On the level and slope of the yield curve immediately after the announcement?
   b.  On the level and slope of the yield curve that would exist two or three years in the future?

6-7    It is a fact that the federal government (1) encouraged the development of the savings and loan industry, (2) virtually forced the industry to make long-term fixed-interest-rate mortgages, and (3) forced the savings and loans to obtain most of their capital as deposits that were withdrawable on demand.

   a.  Would the savings and loans have higher profits in a world with a "normal" or an inverted yield curve? Explain your answer.
   b.  Would the savings and loan industry be better off if the individual institutions sold their mortgages to federal agencies and then collected servicing fees or if the institutions held the mortgages that they originated?

6-8    Suppose interest rates on Treasury bonds rose from 5% to 9% as a result of higher interest rates in Europe. What effect would this have on the price of an average company's common stock?

6-9    What does it mean when it is said that the United States is running a trade deficit? What impact will a trade deficit have on interest rates?

6-10   Suppose you have noticed that the slope of the corporate yield curve has become steeper over the past few months. What factors might explain the change in the slope?

# Problems

**Easy Problems 1–7**

6-1    **YIELD CURVES**   Assume that yields on U.S. Treasury securities were as follows:

| Term | Rate |
| --- | --- |
| 6 months | 4.69% |
| 1 year | 5.49 |
| 2 years | 5.66 |
| 3 years | 5.71 |
| 4 years | 5.89 |
| 5 years | 6.05 |
| 10 years | 6.12 |
| 20 years | 6.64 |
| 30 years | 6.76 |

a. Plot a yield curve based on these data.

b. What type of yield curve is shown?

c. What information does this graph tell you?

d. Based on this yield curve, if you needed to borrow money for longer than 1 year, would it make sense for you to borrow short term and renew the loan or borrow long term? Explain.

**6-2** **REAL RISK-FREE RATE** You read in *The Wall Street Journal* that 30-day T-bills are currently yielding 5.8%. Your brother-in-law, a broker at Safe and Sound Securities, has given you the following estimates of current interest rate premiums:

- Inflation premium = 3.25%
- Liquidity premium = 0.6%
- Maturity risk premium = 1.85%
- Default risk premium = 2.15%

On the basis of these data, what is the real risk-free rate of return?

**6-3** **EXPECTED INTEREST RATE** The real risk-free rate is 2.25%. Inflation is expected to be 2.5% this year and 4.25% during the next 2 years. Assume that the maturity risk premium is zero. What is the yield on 2-year Treasury securities? What is the yield on 3-year Treasury securities?

**6-4** **DEFAULT RISK PREMIUM** A Treasury bond that matures in 10 years has a yield of 5.75%. A 10-year corporate bond has a yield of 8.75%. Assume that the liquidity premium on the corporate bond is 0.35%. What is the default risk premium on the corporate bond?

**6-5** **MATURITY RISK PREMIUM** The real risk-free rate is 2.5% and inflation is expected to be 2.75% for the next 2 years. A 2-year Treasury security yields 5.55%. What is the maturity risk premium for the 2-year security?

**6-6** **INFLATION CROSS-PRODUCT** An analyst is evaluating securities in a developing nation where the inflation rate is very high. As a result, the analyst has been warned not to ignore the cross-product between the real rate and inflation. If the real risk-free rate is 5% and inflation is expected to be 18% each of the next 4 years, what is the yield on a 4-year security with no maturity, default, or liquidity risk? (Hint: Refer to "The Links between Expected Inflation and Interest Rates: A Closer Look" on page 206.)

**6-7** **EXPECTATIONS THEORY** One-year Treasury securities yield 4.85%. The market anticipates that 1 year from now, 1-year Treasury securities will yield 5.2%. If the pure expectations theory is correct, what is the yield today for 2-year Treasury securities? Calculate the yield using a geometric average.

**Intermediate Problems 8–16**

**6-8** **EXPECTATIONS THEORY** Interest rates on 4-year Treasury securities are currently 6.7%, while 6-year Treasury securities yield 7.25%. If the pure expectations theory is correct, what does the market believe that 2-year securities will be yielding 4 years from now? Calculate the yield using a geometric average.

**6-9** **EXPECTED INTEREST RATE** The real risk-free rate is 2.05%. Inflation is expected to be 3.05% this year, 4.75% next year, and 2.3% thereafter. The maturity risk premium is estimated to be $0.05 \times (t - 1)\%$, where t = number of years to maturity. What is the yield on a 7-year Treasury note?

**6-10** **INFLATION** Due to a recession, expected inflation this year is only 3.25%. However, the inflation rate in Year 2 and thereafter is expected to be constant at some level above 3.25%. Assume that the expectations theory holds and the real risk-free rate (r*) is 2.5%. If the yield on 3-year Treasury bonds equals the 1-year yield plus 1.5%, what inflation rate is expected after Year 1?

**6-11** **DEFAULT RISK PREMIUM** A company's 5-year bonds are yielding 7% per year. Treasury bonds with the same maturity are yielding 5.2% per year, and the real risk-free rate (r*) is

2.75%. The average inflation premium is 2.05%; and the maturity risk premium is estimated to be $0.1 \times (t - 1)\%$, where t = number of years to maturity. If the liquidity premium is 0.7%, what is the default risk premium on the corporate bonds?

**6-12    MATURITY RISK PREMIUM**   An investor in Treasury securities expects inflation to be 2.1% in Year 1, 2.7% in Year 2, and 3.65% each year thereafter. Assume that the real risk-free rate is 1.95% and that this rate will remain constant. Three-year Treasury securities yield 5.20%, while 5-year Treasury securities yield 6.00%. What is the difference in the maturity risk premiums (MRPs) on the two securities; that is, what is $MRP_5 - MRP_3$?

**6-13    DEFAULT RISK PREMIUM**   The real risk-free rate, $r^*$, is 1.7%. Inflation is expected to average 1.5% a year for the next 4 years, after which time inflation is expected to average 4.8% a year. Assume that there is no maturity risk premium. An 11-year corporate bond has a yield of 8.7%, which includes a liquidity premium of 0.3%. What is its default risk premium?

**6-14    EXPECTATIONS THEORY AND INFLATION**   Suppose 2-year Treasury bonds yield 4.1%, while 1-year bonds yield 3.2%. $r^*$ is 1%, and the maturity risk premium is zero.

a.  Using the expectations theory, what is the yield on a 1-year bond 1 year from now? Calculate the yield using a geometric average.

b.  What is the expected inflation rate in Year 1? Year 2?

**6-15    EXPECTATIONS THEORY**   Assume that the real risk-free rate is 2% and that the maturity risk premium is zero. If a 1-year Treasury bond yield is 5% and a 2-year Treasury bond yields 7%, what is the 1-year interest rate that is expected for Year 2? Calculate this yield using a geometric average. What inflation rate is expected during Year 2? Comment on why the average interest rate during the 2-year period differs from the 1-year interest rate expected for Year 2.

**6-16    INFLATION CROSS-PRODUCT**   An analyst is evaluating securities in a developing nation where the inflation rate is very high. As a result, the analyst has been warned not to ignore the cross-product between the real rate and inflation. A 6-year security with no maturity, default, or liquidity risk has a yield of 20.84%. If the real risk-free rate is 6%, what average rate of inflation is expected in this country over the next 6 years? (Hint: Refer to "The Links between Expected Inflation and Interest Rates: A Closer Look" on page 206.)

**Challenging Problems 17–19**

**6-17    INTEREST RATE PREMIUMS**   A 5-year Treasury bond has a 5.2% yield. A 10-year Treasury bond yields 6.4%, and a 10-year corporate bond yields 8.4%. The market expects that inflation will average 2.5% over the next 10 years ($IP_{10} = 2.5\%$). Assume that there is no maturity risk premium (MRP = 0) and that the annual real risk-free rate, $r^*$, will remain constant over the next 10 years. (Hint: Remember that the default risk premium and the liquidity premium are zero for Treasury securities: DRP = LP = 0.) A 5-year corporate bond has the same default risk premium and liquidity premium as the 10-year corporate bond described. What is the yield on this 5-year corporate bond?

**6-18    YIELD CURVES**   Suppose the inflation rate is expected to be 7% next year, 5% the following year, and 3% thereafter. Assume that the real risk-free rate, $r^*$, will remain at 2% and that maturity risk premiums on Treasury securities rise from zero on very short-term bonds (those that mature in a few days) to 0.2% for 1-year securities. Furthermore, maturity risk premiums increase 0.2% for each year to maturity, up to a limit of 1.0% on 5-year or longer-term T-bonds.

a.  Calculate the interest rate on 1-, 2-, 3-, 4-, 5-, 10-, and 20-year Treasury securities and plot the yield curve.

b.  Suppose a AAA-rated company (which is the highest bond rating a firm can have) had bonds with the same maturities as the Treasury bonds. Estimate and plot what you believe a AAA-rated company's yield curve would look like on the same graph with the

Treasury bond yield curve. (Hint: Think about the default risk premium on its long-term versus its short-term bonds.)

c. On the same graph, plot the approximate yield curve of a much riskier lower-rated company with a much higher risk of defaulting on its bonds.

6-19 **INFLATION AND INTEREST RATES** In late 1980, the U.S. Commerce Department released new data showing inflation was 15%. At the time, the prime rate of interest was 21%, a record high. However, many investors expected the new Reagan administration to be more effective in controlling inflation than the Carter administration had been. Moreover, many observers believed that the extremely high interest rates and generally tight credit, which resulted from the Federal Reserve System's attempts to curb the inflation rate, would lead to a recession, which, in turn, would lead to a decline in inflation and interest rates. Assume that, at the beginning of 1981, the expected inflation rate for 1981 was 13%; for 1982, 9%; for 1983, 7%; and for 1984 and thereafter, 6%.

a. What was the average expected inflation rate over the 5-year period 1981–1985? (Use the arithmetic average.)

b. Over the 5-year period, what average *nominal* interest rate would be expected to produce a 2% real risk-free return on 5-year Treasury securities? Assume MRP = 0.

c. Assuming a real risk-free rate of 2% and a maturity risk premium that equals $0.1 \times (t)\%$, where t is the number of years to maturity, estimate the interest rate in January 1981 on bonds that mature in 1, 2, 5, 10, and 20 years. Draw a yield curve based on these data.

d. Describe the general economic conditions that could lead to an upward-sloping yield curve.

e. If investors in early 1981 expected the inflation rate for every future year to be 10% (i.e., $I_t = I_{t+1} = 10\%$ for $t = 1$ to $\infty$), what would the yield curve have looked like? Consider all the factors that are likely to affect the curve. Does your answer here make you question the yield curve you drew in part c?

## Comprehensive/Spreadsheet Problem

6-20 **INTEREST RATE DETERMINATION AND YIELD CURVES**

a. What effect would each of the following events likely have on the level of nominal interest rates?
   1. Households dramatically increase their savings rate.
   2. Corporations increase their demand for funds following an increase in investment opportunities.
   3. The government runs a larger-than-expected budget deficit.
   4. There is an increase in expected inflation.

b. Suppose you are considering two possible investment opportunities: a 12-year Treasury bond and a 7-year, A-rated corporate bond. The current real risk-free rate is 4%; and inflation is expected to be 2% for the next 2 years, 3% for the following 4 years, and 4% thereafter. The maturity risk premium is estimated by this formula: MRP = 0.02(t − 1)%. The liquidity premium (LP) for the corporate bond is estimated to be 0.3%. You may determine the default risk premium (DRP), given the company's bond rating, from the table below. Remember to subtract the bond's LP from the corporate spread given in the table to arrive at the bond's DRP. What yield would you predict for each of these two investments?

| | Rate | Corporate Bond Yield Spread = DRP + LP |
|---|---|---|
| U.S. Treasury | 0.83% | |
| AAA corporate | 0.93 | 0.10% |
| AA corporate | 1.29 | 0.46 |
| A corporate | 1.67 | 0.84 |

c. Given the following Treasury bond yield information, construct a graph of the yield curve.

| Maturity | Yield |
| --- | --- |
| 1 year | 5.37% |
| 2 years | 5.47 |
| 3 years | 5.65 |
| 4 years | 5.71 |
| 5 years | 5.64 |
| 10 years | 5.75 |
| 20 years | 6.33 |
| 30 years | 5.94 |

d. Based on the information about the corporate bond provided in part b, calculate yields and then construct a new yield curve graph that shows both the Treasury and the corporate bonds.
e. Which part of the yield curve (the left side or right side) is likely to be most volatile over time?
f. Using the Treasury yield information in part c, calculate the following rates using geometric averages:
   1. The 1-year rate 1 year from now
   2. The 5-year rate 5 years from now
   3. The 10-year rate 10 years from now
   4. The 10-year rate 20 years from now

# INTEGRATED CASE

## MORTON HANDLEY & COMPANY

**6-21** **INTEREST RATE DETERMINATION** Maria Juarez is a professional tennis player, and your firm manages her money. She has asked you to give her information about what determines the level of various interest rates. Your boss has prepared some questions for you to consider.

a. What are the four most fundamental factors that affect the cost of money, or the general level of interest rates, in the economy?
b. What is the real risk-free rate of interest ($r^*$) and the nominal risk-free rate ($r_{RF}$)? How are these two rates measured?
c. Define the terms *inflation premium (IP)*, *default risk premium (DRP)*, *liquidity premium (LP)*, and *maturity risk premium (MRP)*. Which of these premiums is included in determining the interest rate on (1) short-term U.S. Treasury securities, (2) long-term U.S. Treasury securities, (3) short-term corporate securities, and (4) long-term corporate securities? Explain how the premiums would vary over time and among the different securities listed.
d. What is the term structure of interest rates? What is a yield curve?
e. Suppose most investors expect the inflation rate to be 5% next year, 6% the following year, and 8% thereafter. The real risk-free rate is 3%. The maturity risk premium is zero for bonds that mature in 1 year or less and 0.1% for 2-year bonds; then the MRP increases by 0.1% per year thereafter for 20 years, after which it is stable. What is the interest rate on 1-, 10-, and 20-year Treasury bonds? Draw a yield curve with these data. What factors can explain why this constructed yield curve is upward sloping?
f. At any given time, how would the yield curve facing a AAA-rated company compare with the yield curve for U.S. Treasury securities? At any given time, how would the yield curve facing a BB-rated company compare with the yield curve for U.S. Treasury securities? Draw a graph to illustrate your answer.

g. What is the pure expectations theory? What does the pure expectations theory imply about the term structure of interest rates?

h. Suppose you observe the following term structure for Treasury securities:

| Maturity | Yield |
|---|---|
| 1 year | 6.0% |
| 2 years | 6.2 |
| 3 years | 6.4 |
| 4 years | 6.5 |
| 5 years | 6.5 |

Assume that the pure expectations theory of the term structure is correct. (This implies that you can use the yield curve provided to "back out" the market's expectations about future interest rates.) What does the market expect will be the interest rate on 1-year securities 1 year from now? What does the market expect will be the interest rate on 3-year securities 2 years from now? Calculate these yields using geometric averages.

i. Describe how macroeconomic factors affect the level of interest rates. How do these factors explain why interest rates have been lower in recent years?

# TAKING A CLOSER LOOK

## Using Yahoo! Finance's Bonds Center to Understand Interest Rates

*Use online resources to work on this chapter's questions. Please note that website information changes over time, and these changes may limit your ability to answer some of these questions.*

In Chapter 6, we looked at the determinants of market interest rates. The questions provided below are designed to aid with your understanding of interest rates. Here, we will access the Internet website Yahoo! Finance Bonds Center (finance.yahoo.com /bonds) to answer these questions.

1. Once you've accessed the Yahoo! Finance Bonds Center screen, click the "Composite Bond Rates" tab. Plot a yield curve for Treasury and corporate bonds. Compare the yield curves today and one month ago. Has the shape of the Treasury yield curve changed meaningfully over the past month? If so, what recent events could possibly explain this shift?

2. Has the spread between corporate and Treasury bonds changed meaningfully over the past month? If so, what factors could possibly explain this shift?

3. In today's market does the spread between corporate and Treasury bonds vary depending on bond maturity? If so, what factors could possibly explain these differences?

# Solutions to Self-Test Questions and Problems

**ST-1** Refer to the marginal glossary definitions or relevant chapter sections to check your responses.

**ST-2**  a. Average inflation over 4 years $= (2\% + 2\% + 2\% + 4\%)/4 = 2.5\%$

b. $T_4 = r_{RF} + MRP_4$
$= r^* + IP_4 + MRP_4$
$= 3\% + 2.5\% + (0.1)3\%$
$= 5.8\%$

c. $C_{4,BBB} = r^* + IP_4 + MRP_4 + DRP + LP$
$= 3\% + 2.5\% + 0.3\% + 1.3\% + 0.5\%$
$= 7.6\%$

d. $T_8 = r^* + IP_8 + MRP_8$
$= 3\% + (3 \times 2\% + 5 \times 4\%)/8 + 0.7\%$
$= 3\% + 3.25\% + 0.7\%$
$= 6.95\%$

e. $C_{8,BB} = r^* + IP_8 + MRP_8 + DRP + LP$
$= 3\% + 3.25\% + 0.7\% + 1.3\% + 0.5\%$
$= 8.75\%$

f.  $T_9 = r^* + IP_9 + MRP_9$
$7.3\% = 3\% + IP_9 + 0.8\%$
$IP_9 = 3.5\%$
$3.5\% = (3 \times 2\% + 5 \times 4\% + X)/9$
$31.5\% = 6\% + 20\% + X$
$5.5\% = X$

$X =$ Inflation in Year 9 $= 5.5\%$

**ST-3**  $T_1 = 6\%$; $T_2 = 6.2\%$; $T_3 = 6.3\%$; $T_4 = 6.5\%$; $MRP = 0$

a. Yield of 1-year security, 1 year from now, is calculated as follows:

$$(1.062)^2 = (1.06)(1 + X)$$

$$\frac{(1.062)^2}{1.06} = 1 + X$$

$$1.064 = 1 + X$$

$$6.4\% = X$$

b. Yield of 1-year security, 2 years from now, is calculated as follows:

$$(1.063)^3 = (1.06)^2(1 + X)$$

$$\frac{(1.063)^3}{(1.062)^2} = 1 + X$$

$$1.065 = 1 + X$$

$$6.5\% = X$$

c. Yield of 2-year security, 1 year from now, is calculated as follows:

$$(1.063)^3 = (1.06)(1+X)^2$$

$$\frac{(1.063)^3}{1.06} = (1+X)^2$$

$$1.13317 = (1+X)^2$$

$$(1.13317)^{1/2} = 1+X$$

$$6.45\% = X$$

d. Yield of 3-year security, 1 year from now, is calculated as follows:

$$(1.065)^4 = (1.06)(1+X)^3$$

$$\frac{(1.065)^4}{1.06} = (1+X)^3$$

$$1.213648 = (1+X)^3$$

$$(1.213648)^{1/3} = 1+X$$

$$6.67\% = X$$

## Answers to Selected End-of-Chapter Problems

**6-2**  2.55%

**6-4**  2.65%

**6-6**  23.9%

**6-8**  8.36%

**6-10**  5.5%

**6-12**  0.47%

**6-14**  a. $r_1$ in Yr. 2 = 5%

  b. $I_1 = 2.2\%$; $I_2 = 4\%$

**6-16**  14%

**6-18**  a. $r_{T1} = 9.20\%$; $r_{T2} = 8.40\%$; $r_{T3} = 7.60\%$; $r_{T4} = 7.30\%$; $r_{T5} = 7.20\%$; $r_{T10} = 6.60\%$; $r_{T20} = 6.30\%$

## Selected Equations and Tables

$$\text{Quoted interest rate } (r) = r^* + IP + DRP + LP + MRP$$
$$= r_{RF} + DRP + LP + MRP$$

$$r_{T\text{-bill}} = r_{RF} = r^* + IP$$
$$r_{T\text{-bond}} = r_t^* + IP_t + MRP_t$$
$$r_{C\text{-bond}} = r_t^* + IP_t + MRP_t + DRP_t + LP_t$$
$$r_{RF} \text{ with cross-product term} = r^* + IP + (r^* \times IP)$$

# Chapter 7

# Bonds and Their Valuation

## Sizing Up Risk in the Bond Market

Many people view Treasury securities as a lackluster but ultrasafe investment. From a default standpoint, Treasuries are indeed our safest investments, but their prices can still decline in any given year if interest rates increase. This is especially true for long-term Treasury bonds, which lost nearly 15% in 2009. However, bonds can also perform well—Treasury bonds earned a return of nearly 26% in 2008, and they out-gained stocks in 8 of the 15 years between 2000 and 2014.

Not all bonds are alike, and they don't always move in the same direction. For example, corporate bonds are often callable, and issuers can default on them, whereas Treasury bonds are not exposed to these risks. To compensate investors for these additional risks, corporate bonds typically have higher yields. When the economy is strong, corporate bonds generally produce higher returns than Treasuries because their promised returns are higher, and most make their

promised payments because few go into default. However, when the economy weakens, concerns about defaults rise, which lead to declines in corporate bond prices. Furthermore, at any point in time, there are widespread differences among corporate bonds. For example, in March 2015, outstanding bonds issued by Johnson & Johnson, with an AAA credit rating, maturing in 2037, were trading at a yield to maturity of 3.511%. At the same point in time, bonds issued by J.C. Penney Corp., with a CCC credit rating, maturing in 2036, were trading at a yield to maturity of 9.279%.

A 2009 article in *The Wall Street Journal* highlighted the concerns that bond investors face in today's environment. The article offers what it refers to as "five key pointers":

1. *Watch Out for Defaults.* Investors should be wary of low-rated corporate bonds on the edge of default. The article cautions

investors about increased default risk in the municipal market as state and local governments struggle to balance their budgets.

2. *Limit Your Rate Risk.* Rates are likely to increase over time as the economy hopefully continues to recover. As we see in this chapter, increasing interest rates reduce the value of bonds, and this effect is particularly important for investors of long-term bonds. For this reason, *The Wall Street Journal* writer suggests that some bond investors may want to gradually shift away from longer-maturity bonds.

3. *Consider a Passive Strategy.* This advice is directed specifically to investors in bond mutual funds. Rather than investing in actively managed funds, where the portfolio manager is constantly moving in and out of different bonds, the author suggests that investors invest in index funds or exchange-traded funds (ETFs) that track a broad index of bonds.

4. *Have an Inflation Hedge.* Many analysts worry that down the road, higher government spending and a relaxed monetary policy will ultimately lead to higher levels of inflation. As we will see in this chapter, one way to hedge against rising inflation is to invest in Treasury securities that are indexed to inflation.

5. *Don't Try to Time the Market.* As we have seen in recent years, bond prices can move quickly and dramatically, which makes it difficult to effectively bet on where the market is heading next. Rather than trying to time the next move in the market, the article urges investors to adopt a more steady long-term strategy when it comes to bonds.

Although these pointers are relevant in today's market, in many ways the advice is timeless. In the face of similar risks in 2001, a *BusinessWeek Online* article gave investors the following similar advice, which is still applicable today:

*Take the same diversified approach to bonds as you do with stocks. Blend in U.S. government, corporate—both high-quality and high-yield—and perhaps even some foreign government debt. If you're investing taxable dollars, consider tax-exempt municipal bonds. And it doesn't hurt to layer in some inflation-indexed bonds.*

Sources: Michael A. Pollack, "The New Bond Equation," *The Wall Street Journal* (online.wsj.com), August 3, 2009; Scott Patterson, "Ahead of the Tape: Junk Yields Flashing Back to '01 Slump," *The Wall Street Journal*, January 30, 2008, p. C1; *Ibbotson Stocks, Bonds, Bills, and Inflation: 2015 Classic Yearbook* (Chicago: Morningstar, Inc., 2015); and Susan Scherreik, "Getting the Most Bang Out of Your Bonds," *BusinessWeek Online* (businessweek.com), November 12, 2001.

# PUTTING THINGS IN PERSPECTIVE

In previous chapters, we noted that companies raise capital in two main forms: debt and equity. In this chapter, we examine the characteristics of bonds and discuss the various factors that influence bond prices. In Chapter 9, we will turn our attention to stocks and their valuation.

If you skim through *The Wall Street Journal*, you will see references to a wide variety of bonds. This variety may seem confusing; but in actuality, only a few characteristics distinguish the various types of bonds.

When you finish this chapter, you should be able to:

- Identify the different features of corporate and government bonds.

- Discuss how bond prices are determined in the market, what the relationship is between interest rates and bond prices, and how a bond's price changes over time as it approaches maturity.

- Calculate a bond's yield to maturity and yield to call if it is callable, and determine the "true" yield.

- Explain the different types of risk that bond investors and issuers face, and discuss how a bond's terms and collateral can be changed to affect its interest rate.

# 7-1 Who Issues Bonds?

**Bond**
A long-term debt instrument.

A **bond** is a long-term contract under which a borrower agrees to make payments of interest and principal on specific dates to the holders of the bond. Bonds are issued by corporations and government agencies that are looking for long-term debt capital. For example, on January 4, 2016, Allied Food Products borrowed $170 million by issuing $170 million of bonds. For convenience, we assume that Allied sold 170,000 individual bonds for $1,000 each. Actually, it could have sold one $170 million bond, 17 bonds each with a $10 million face value, or any other combination that totaled $170 million. In any event, Allied received the $170 million; and in exchange, it promised to make annual interest payments and to repay the $170 million on a specified maturity date.

Until the 1970s, most bonds were beautifully engraved pieces of paper and their key terms, including their face values, were spelled out on the bonds. Today, though, virtually all bonds are represented by electronic data stored in secure computers, much like the "money" in a bank checking account.

Bonds are grouped in several ways. One grouping is based on the issuer: the U.S. Treasury, corporations, state and local governments, and foreigners. Each bond differs with respect to risk and consequently its expected return.

**Treasury Bonds**
Bonds issued by the federal government, sometimes referred to as government bonds.

**Treasury bonds**, generally called Treasuries and sometimes referred to as government bonds, are issued by the federal government.[1] It is reasonable to assume that the U.S. government will make good on its promised payments, so Treasuries have no default risk. However, these bonds' prices do decline when interest rates rise; so they are not completely riskless.

**Corporate Bonds**
Bonds issued by corporations.

**Corporate bonds** are issued by business firms. Unlike Treasuries, corporates are exposed to default risk—if the issuing company gets into trouble, it may be unable to make the promised interest and principal payments and bondholders may suffer losses. Corporate bonds have different levels of default risk depending on the issuing company's characteristics and the terms of the specific bond. Default risk is often referred to as "credit risk"; and as we saw in Chapter 6, the larger this risk, the higher the interest rate investors demand.

**Municipal Bonds**
Bonds issued by state and local governments.

**Municipal bonds**, or munis, is the term given to bonds issued by state and local governments. Like corporates, munis are exposed to some default risk, but they have one major advantage over all other bonds: As we discussed in Chapter 3, the interest earned on most munis is exempt from federal taxes and from state taxes if the holder is a resident of the issuing state. Consequently, the market interest rate on a muni is considerably lower than on a corporate bond of equivalent risk.

**Foreign Bonds**
Bonds issued by foreign governments or by foreign corporations.

**Foreign bonds** are issued by a foreign government or a foreign corporation. All foreign corporate bonds are exposed to default risk, as are some foreign government bonds. Indeed, recently, concerns have risen about possible defaults in many countries including Greece, Ireland, Portugal, and Spain. An additional risk exists when the bonds are denominated in a currency other than that of the investor's home currency. Consider, for example, a U.S. investor who purchases a corporate bond denominated in Japanese yen. At some point, the investor will want to close out his investment and convert the yen back to U.S. dollars. If the Japanese yen unexpectedly falls relative to the dollar, the investor will have fewer dollars than he originally expected to receive. Consequently, the investor could still lose money even if the bond does not default.

---

[1]The U.S. Treasury actually calls its debt "bills," "notes," or "bonds." T-bills generally have maturities of 1 year or less at the time of issue, notes generally have original maturities of 2 to 7 years, and bonds originally mature in 8 to 30 years. There are technical differences between bills, notes, and bonds; but they are not important for our purposes. So we generally call all Treasury securities "bonds." Note too that a 30-year T-bond at the time of issue becomes a 29-year bond the next year, and it is a 1-year bond after 29 years.

## SelfTest

What is a bond?

What are the four main issuers of bonds?

Why are U.S. Treasury bonds not completely riskless?

In addition to default risk, what key risk do investors in foreign bonds face? Explain.

# 7-2 Key Characteristics of Bonds

Although all bonds have some common characteristics, different types of bonds can have different contractual features. For example, most corporate bonds have provisions that allow the issuer to pay them off early ("call" features), but the specific call provisions vary widely among different bonds. Similarly, some bonds are backed by specific assets that must be turned over to the bondholders if the issuer defaults, while other bonds have no such collateral backup. Differences in contractual provisions (and in the fundamental underlying financial strength of the companies backing the bonds) lead to differences in bonds' risks, prices, and expected returns. To understand bonds, it is essential that you understand the following terms.

*An excellent website on bonds is **finance.yahoo.com/bonds**. Yahoo's Bonds Center provides educational information as well as current information on treasury, municipal, and corporate bonds. In addition, it provides a bond screener that allows you to search for bonds with specified criteria.*

## 7-2A PAR VALUE

The **par value** is the stated face value of the bond; for illustrative purposes, we generally assume a par value of $1,000, although any multiple of $1,000 (e.g., $10,000 or $10 million) can be used. The par value generally represents the amount of money the firm borrows and promises to repay on the maturity date.

*Par Value*
The face value of a bond.

## 7-2B COUPON INTEREST RATE

Allied Food Products's bonds require the company to pay a fixed number of dollars of interest each year. This payment, generally referred to as the **coupon payment**, is set at the time the bond is issued and remains in force during the bond's life.[2] Typically, at the time a bond is issued, its coupon payment is set at a level that will induce investors to buy the bond at or near its par value. Most of the examples and problems throughout this text focus on bonds with fixed coupon rates.

When this annual coupon payment is divided by the par value, the result is the **coupon interest rate**. For example, Allied's bonds have a $1,000 par value, and they pay $100 in interest each year. The bond's coupon payment is $100, so its coupon interest rate is $100/$1,000 = 10%. In this regard, the $100 is the annual income that an investor receives when he or she invests in the bond.

*Coupon Payment*
The specified number of dollars of interest paid each year.

*Coupon Interest Rate*
The stated annual interest rate on a bond.

---

[2]Back when bonds were engraved pieces of paper rather than electronic information stored on a computer, each bond had a number of small (1/2- by 2 inch) dated coupons attached to them. On each interest payment date, the owner would "clip the coupon" for that date, send it to the company's paying agent, and receive a check for the interest. A 30-year semiannual bond would start with 60 coupons, whereas a 5-year annual payment bond would start with only 5 coupons. Today no physical coupons are involved, and interest checks are mailed or deposited automatically to the bonds' registered owners on the payment date. Even so, people continue to use the terms *coupon* and *coupon interest rate* when discussing bonds. You can think of the coupon interest rate as the *promised rate*.

**Fixed-Rate Bonds**
Bonds whose interest rate is fixed for their entire life.

**Floating-Rate Bonds**
Bonds whose interest rate fluctuates with shifts in the general level of interest rates.

**Zero Coupon Bonds**
Bonds that pay no annual interest but are sold at a discount below par, thus compensating investors in the form of capital appreciation.

**Original Issue Discount (OID) Bond**
Any bond originally offered at a price below its par value.

**Maturity Date**
A specified date on which the par value of a bond must be repaid.

**Original Maturity**
The number of years to maturity at the time a bond is issued.

**Call Provision**
A provision in a bond contract that gives the issuer the right to redeem the bonds under specified terms prior to the normal maturity date.

Allied's bonds are **fixed-rate bonds** because the coupon rate is fixed for the life of the bond. In some cases, however, a bond's coupon payment is allowed to vary over time. These **floating-rate bonds** work as follows: The coupon rate is set for an initial period, often 6 months, after which it is adjusted every 6 months based on some open market rate. For example, the bond's rate may be adjusted so as to equal the 10-year Treasury bond rate plus a "spread" of 1.5 percentage points. Other provisions can be included in corporate bonds. For example, some can be converted at the holders' option into fixed-rate debt, and some floaters have upper limits (caps) and lower limits (floors) on how high or low the rate can go.

Some bonds pay no coupons at all but are offered at a discount below their par values and hence provide capital appreciation rather than interest income. These securities are called **zero coupon bonds** (*zeros*). Other bonds pay some coupon interest, but not enough to induce investors to buy them at par. In general, any bond originally offered at a price significantly below its par value is called an **original issue discount (OID) bond**. Some of the details associated with issuing or investing in zero coupon bonds are discussed more fully in Web Appendix 7A.

## 7-2C MATURITY DATE

Bonds generally have a specified **maturity date** on which the par value must be repaid. Allied's bonds, which were issued on January 4, 2016, will mature on January 3, 2031; thus, they had a 15-year maturity at the time they were issued. Most bonds have an **original maturity** (the maturity at the time the bond is issued) ranging from 10 to 40 years, but any maturity is legally permissible.[3] Of course, the effective maturity of a bond declines each year after it has been issued. Thus, Allied's bonds had a 15-year original maturity. But in 2017, a year later, they will have a 14-year maturity; a year after that, they will have a 13-year maturity; and so on.

## 7-2D CALL PROVISIONS

Many corporate and municipal bonds contain a **call provision** that gives the issuer the right to call the bonds for redemption. The call provision generally states that the issuer must pay the bondholders an amount greater than the par value if they are called. The additional sum, which is termed a *call premium*, is often equal to one year's interest. For example, the call premium on a 10-year bond with a 10% annual coupon and a par value of $1,000 might be $100, which means that the issuer would have to pay investors $1,100 (the par value plus the call premium) if it wanted to call the bonds. In most cases, the provisions in the bond contract are set so that the call premium declines over time as the bonds approach maturity. Also, although some bonds are immediately callable, in most cases, bonds are often not callable until several years after issue, generally 5 to 10 years. This is known as a *deferred call*, and such bonds are said to have *call protection*.

Companies are not likely to call bonds unless interest rates have declined significantly since the bonds were issued. Suppose a company sold bonds when

---

[3]In July 1993, The Walt Disney Company, attempting to lock in a low interest rate, stretched the meaning of "long-term bond" by issuing the first 100-year bonds sold by any borrower in modern times. Soon after, Coca-Cola became the second company to sell 100-year bonds. Other companies that have issued 100-year bonds include Columbia/HCA Healthcare Corporation, BellSouth Telecommunications, Wisconsin Electric Power Company, and IBM.

interest rates were relatively high. Provided the issue is callable, the company could sell a new issue of low-yielding securities if and when interest rates drop, use the proceeds of the new issue to retire the high-rate issue, and thus reduce its interest expense. This process is called a *refunding operation*. Thus, the call privilege is valuable to the firm but detrimental to long-term investors, who will need to reinvest the funds they receive at the new and lower rates. Accordingly, the interest rate on a new issue of callable bonds will exceed that on the company's new noncallable bonds. For example, on April 28, 2016, Pacific Timber Company sold a bond issue yielding 6% that was callable immediately. On the same day, Northwest Milling Company sold an issue with similar risk and maturity that yielded only 5.5%; but its bonds were noncallable for 10 years. Investors were willing to accept a 0.5% lower coupon interest rate on Northwest's bonds for the assurance that the 5.5% interest rate would be earned for at least 10 years. Pacific, on the other hand, had to incur a 0.5% higher annual interest rate for the option of calling the bonds in the event of a decline in rates.

Note that the refunding operation is similar to a homeowner refinancing his or her home mortgage after a decline in interest rates. Consider, for example, a homeowner with an outstanding mortgage at 7%. If mortgage rates fall to 4%, the homeowner will probably find it beneficial to refinance the mortgage. There may be some fees involved in the refinancing, but the lower rate may be more than enough to offset those fees. The analysis required is essentially the same for homeowners and corporations.

## 7-2E SINKING FUNDS

Some bonds include a **sinking fund provision** that facilitates the orderly retirement of the bond issue. Years ago firms were required to deposit money with a trustee that invested the funds and then used the accumulated sum to retire the bonds when they matured. Today, though, sinking fund provisions require the issuer to buy back a specified percentage of the issue each year. A failure to meet the sinking fund requirement constitutes a default, which may throw the company into bankruptcy. Therefore, a sinking fund is a mandatory payment.

**Sinking Fund Provision**
A provision in a bond contract that requires the issuer to retire a portion of the bond issue each year.

Suppose a company issued $100 million of 20-year bonds and it is required to call 5% of the issue, or $5 million of bonds, each year. In most cases, the issuer can handle the sinking fund requirement in either of two ways:

1. It can call in for redemption, at par value, the required $5 million of bonds. The bonds are numbered serially, and those called for redemption would be determined by a lottery administered by the trustee.

2. The company can buy the required number of bonds on the open market.

The firm will choose the least-cost method. If interest rates have fallen since the bond was issued, the bond will sell for more than its par value. In this case, the firm will use the call option. However, if interest rates have risen, the bonds will sell at a price below par; so the firm can and will buy $5 million par value of bonds in the open market for less than $5 million. Note that a call for sinking fund purposes is generally different from a refunding call because most sinking fund calls require no call premium. However, only a small percentage of the issue is normally callable in a given year.

Although sinking funds are designed to protect investors by ensuring that the bonds are retired in an orderly fashion, these funds work to the detriment of bondholders if the bond's coupon rate is higher than the current market rate. For example, suppose the bond has a 10% coupon, but similar bonds now yield only 7.5%. A sinking fund call at par would require a long-term investor to give up a bond that pays $100 of interest and then to reinvest in a bond that pays only $75 per year. This is an obvious disadvantage to those bondholders whose bonds are called. On balance, however, bonds that have a sinking fund are regarded as being safer than those without such a provision; so at the time they are issued, sinking fund bonds have lower coupon rates than otherwise similar bonds without sinking funds.

## 7-2F OTHER FEATURES

**Convertible Bonds**
Bonds that are exchangeable at the option of the holder for the issuing firm's common stock.

**Warrants**
Long-term options to buy a stated number of shares of common stock at a specified price.

**Putable Bonds**
Bonds with a provision that allows investors to sell them back to the company prior to maturity at a prearranged price.

**Income Bond**
A bond that pays interest only if it is earned.

**Indexed (Purchasing Power) Bond**
A bond that has interest payments based on an inflation index so as to protect the holder from inflation.

Several other types of bonds are used sufficiently often to warrant mention.[4] First, **convertible bonds** are bonds that are exchangeable into shares of common stock at a fixed price at the option of the bondholder. Convertibles offer investors the chance for capital gains if the stock price increases, but that feature enables the issuing company to set a lower coupon rate than on nonconvertible debt with similar credit risk. Bonds issued with **warrants** are similar to convertibles; but instead of giving the investor an option to exchange the bonds for stock, warrants give the holder an option to buy stock for a stated price, thereby providing a capital gain if the stock's price rises. Because of this factor, bonds issued with warrants, like convertibles, carry lower coupon rates than otherwise similar nonconvertible bonds.

Whereas callable bonds give the *issuer* the right to retire the debt prior to maturity, **putable bonds** allow *investors* to require the company to pay in advance. If interest rates rise, investors will put the bonds back to the company and reinvest in higher coupon bonds. Yet another type of bond is the **income bond**, which pays interest only if the issuer has earned enough money to pay the interest. Thus, income bonds cannot bankrupt a company; but from an investor's standpoint, they are riskier than "regular" bonds. Yet another bond is the **indexed**, or **purchasing power, bond**. The interest rate is based on an inflation index such as the consumer price index (CPI), so the interest paid rises automatically when the inflation rate rises, thus protecting bondholders against inflation. As we mentioned in Chapter 6, the U.S. Treasury is the main issuer of indexed bonds.

## SelfTest

Define floating-rate bonds, zero coupon bonds, callable bonds, putable bonds, income bonds, convertible bonds, and inflation-indexed bonds (TIPS).

Which is riskier to an investor, other things held constant—a callable bond or a putable bond? Explain.

In general, how is the rate on a floating-rate bond determined?

What are the two ways sinking funds can be handled? Which alternative will be used if interest rates have risen? If interest rates have fallen?

---

[4]An article by John D. Finnerty and Douglas R. Emery reviews new types of debt (and other) securities that have been created in recent years. See "Corporate Securities Innovations: An Update," *Journal of Applied Finance: Theory, Practice, Education*, vol. 12, no. 1 (Spring–Summer 2002), pp. 21–47.

## 7-3 Bond Valuation

The value of any financial asset—a stock, a bond, a lease, or even a physical asset such as an apartment building or a piece of machinery—is the present value of the cash flows the asset is expected to produce. The cash flows for a standard coupon-bearing bond, like those of Allied Food, consist of interest payments during the bond's 15-year life plus the amount borrowed (generally the par value) when the bond matures. In the case of a floating-rate bond, the interest payments vary over time. For zero coupon bonds, there are no interest payments, so the only cash flow is the face amount when the bond matures. For a "regular" bond with a fixed coupon, like Allied's, here is the situation:

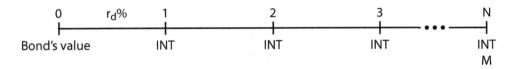

Where:

$r_d$ = the market rate of interest on the bond, 10%. This is the discount rate used to calculate the present value of the cash flows, which is also the bond's price. In Chapter 6, we discussed in detail the various factors that determine market interest rates. Note that $r_d$ is *not* the coupon interest rate. However, $r_d$ is equal to the coupon rate at times, especially the day the bond is issued; and when the two rates are equal, as in this case, the bond sells at par.

N = the number of years before the bond matures = 15. N declines over time after the bond has been issued, so a bond that had a maturity of 15 years when it was issued (original maturity = 15) will have N = 14 after 1 year, N = 13 after 2 years, and so forth. At this point, we assume that the bond pays interest once a year, or annually; so N is measured in years. Later on we will analyze semiannual payment bonds, which pay interest every 6 months.

INT = dollars of interest paid each year = Coupon rate × Par value = 0.10($1,000) = $100. In calculator terminology, INT = PMT = 100. If the bond had been a semiannual payment bond, the payment would have been $50 every 6 months. The payment would have been zero if Allied had issued zero coupon bonds, and it would have varied over time if the bond had been a "floater."

M = the par, or maturity, value of the bond = $1,000. This amount must be paid at maturity. Back in the 1970s and before, when paper bonds with paper coupons were used, most bonds had a $1,000 value. Now with computer-entry bonds, the par amount purchased can vary, but in the text we use $1,000 for simplicity.

We can now redraw the time line to show the numerical values for all variables except the bond's value (and price, assuming an equilibrium exists), $V_B$:

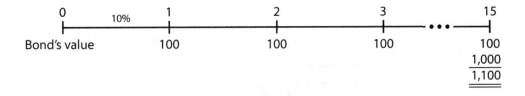

The following general equation can be solved to find the value of any bond:

$$\text{Bond's value} = V_B = \frac{INT}{(1+r_d)^1} + \frac{INT}{(1+r_d)^2} + \cdots + \frac{INT}{(1+r_d)^N} + \frac{M}{(1+r_d)^N}$$

$$= \sum_{t=1}^{N} \frac{INT}{(1+r_d)^t} + \frac{M}{(1+r_d)^N}$$

▼ 7.1

Inserting values for the Allied bond, we have:

$$V_B = \sum_{t=1}^{15} \frac{\$100}{(1.10)^t} + \frac{\$1,000}{(1.10)^{15}}$$

The cash flows consist of an annuity of N years plus a lump sum payment at the end of Year N, and this fact is reflected in Equation 7.1.

We could simply discount each cash flow back to the present and sum those PVs to find the bond's value; see Figure 7.1 for an example. However, this procedure is not very efficient, especially when the bond has many years to maturity. Therefore, we use a financial calculator to solve the problem. Here is the setup:

| 15 | 10 | | 100 | 1000 |
|---|---|---|---|---|
| N | I/YR | PV | PMT | FV |
| | | = −1,000 | | |

Simply input $N = 15$, $r_d = I/YR = 10$, $INT = PMT = 100$, and $M = FV = 1000$; then press the PV key to find the bond's value, $1,000.[5] Because the PV is an outflow to the investor, it is shown with a negative sign. The calculator is programmed to solve Equation 7.1. It finds the PV of an annuity of $100 per year for 15 years discounted at 10%; then it finds the PV of the $1,000 maturity value; then it adds those two PVs to find the bond's value. In this Allied example, the bond is selling at a price equal to its par value.

Whenever the bond's market, or going, rate, $r_d$, is equal to its coupon rate, a *fixed-rate* bond will sell at its par value. Normally, the coupon rate is set at the going rate in the market the day a bond is issued, causing it to sell at par initially.

The coupon rate remains fixed after the bond is issued, but interest rates in the market move up and down. Looking at Equation 7.1, we see that an *increase* in the market interest rate ($r_d$) causes the price of an outstanding bond to *fall*, whereas a *decrease* in the rate causes the bond's price to *rise*. For example, if the market interest rate on Allied's bond increased to 15% immediately after it was issued, we would recalculate the price with the new market interest rate as follows:

| 15 | 15 | | 100 | 1000 |
|---|---|---|---|---|
| N | I/YR | PV | PMT | FV |
| | | = −707.63 | | |

---

[5]Spreadsheets can also be used to solve for the bond's value. The PV of this bond can be calculated using Excel's PV function:

= PV(0.1,15,100,1000)

PV(rate, nper, pmt, [fv], [type])

This gives the bond's value as $1,000. Note that type is left blank because cash flows occur at year-end.

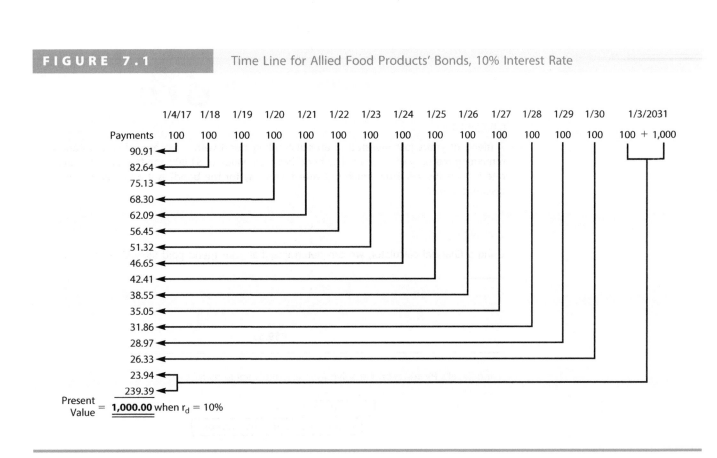

**FIGURE 7.1**    Time Line for Allied Food Products' Bonds, 10% Interest Rate

The bond's price would fall to $707.63, well below par, as a result of the increase in interest rates. Whenever the going rate of interest *rises above* the coupon rate, a fixed-rate bond's price will fall *below* its par value; this type of bond is called a **discount bond**.

On the other hand, bond prices rise when market interest rates fall. For example, if the market interest rate on Allied's bond decreased to 5% immediately after it was issued, we would once again recalculate its price as follows:

*Discount Bond*

A bond that sells below its par value; occurs whenever the going rate of interest is above the coupon rate.

| 15 | 5 | | 100 | 1000 |
|----|---|---|-----|------|
| N | I/YR | PV | PMT | FV |
| | | = −1,518.98 | | |

In this case, the price rises to $1,518.98. In general, whenever the going interest rate *falls below* the coupon rate, a fixed-rate bond's price will rise *above* its par value; this type of bond is called a **premium bond**.

To summarize, here is the situation:

$r_d$ = coupon rate, fixed-rate bond sells at par; hence, it is a *par bond*.
$r_d$ > coupon rate, fixed-rate bond sells below par; hence, it is a *discount bond*.
$r_d$ < coupon rate, fixed-rate bond sells above par; hence, it is a *premium bond*.

*Premium Bond*

A bond that sells above its par value; occurs whenever the going rate of interest is below the coupon rate.

**quick question**

QUESTION:

A friend of yours just invested in an outstanding bond with a 5% annual coupon and a remaining maturity of 10 years. The bond has a par value of $1,000 and the market interest rate is currently 7%. How much did your friend pay for the bond? Is it a par, premium, or discount bond?

ANSWER:

Using a financial calculator, we can determine that your friend paid **$859.53** for the bond.

| 10 | 7 | | 50 | 1000 |
|:---:|:---:|:---:|:---:|:---:|
| N | I/YR | PV | PMT | FV |
| | | = −859.53 | | |

Using Excel's PV function we solve for the bond's value as follows:

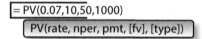

= PV(0.07,10,50,1000)

PV(rate, nper, pmt, [fv], [type])

Here we find that the bond's value is equal to **$859.53**.

Because the bond's coupon rate (5%) is less than the current market interest rate (7%), the bond is a discount bond—reflecting that interest rates have increased since this bond was originally issued.

## SelfTest

A bond that matures in 8 years has a par value of $1,000 and an annual coupon payment of $70; its market interest rate is 9%. What is its price? **($889.30)**

A bond that matures in 12 years has a par value of $1,000 and an annual coupon rate of 10%; the market interest rate is 8%. What is its price? **($1,150.72)**

Which of those two bonds is a discount bond, and which is a premium bond? Explain.

## 7-4 Bond Yields

If you examine the bond market table of *The Wall Street Journal* or a price sheet put out by a bond dealer, you will typically see information regarding each bond's maturity date, price, and coupon interest rate. You will also see a reported yield. Unlike the coupon interest rate, which is fixed, the bond's yield varies from day to day, depending on current market conditions.

To be most useful, the bond's yield should give us an estimate of the rate of return we would earn if we purchased the bond today and held it over its remaining life. If the bond is not callable, its remaining life is its years to maturity. If it is callable, its remaining life is the years to maturity if it is not called or the years to the call if it is called. In the following sections, we explain how to calculate those two possible yields and which one is likely to be earned by an investor.

## 7-4A YIELD TO MATURITY

Suppose you were offered a 14-year, 10% annual coupon, $1,000 par value bond at a price of $1,494.93. What rate of interest would you earn on your investment if you bought the bond, held it to maturity, and received the promised interest payments and maturity value? This rate is called the bond's **yield to maturity (YTM)**, and it is the interest rate generally discussed by investors when they talk about rates of return and the rate reported by *The Wall Street Journal* and other publications. To find the YTM, all you need to do is solve Equation 7.1 for $r_d$ as follows:

*Yield to Maturity (YTM)*
The rate of return earned on a bond if it is held to maturity.

$$V_B = \frac{INT}{(1+r_d)^1} + \frac{INT}{(1+r_d)^2} + \cdots + \frac{INT}{(1+r_d)^N} + \frac{M}{(1+r_d)^N}$$

$$\$1,494.93 = \frac{\$100}{(1+r_d)^1} + \cdots + \frac{\$100}{(1+r_d)^{14}} + \frac{\$1,000}{(1+r_d)^{14}}$$

You can substitute values for $r_d$ until you find a value that "works" and force the sum of the PVs in the equation to equal $1,494.93. However, finding $r_d$ = YTM by trial and error would be a tedious, time-consuming process. However, as you might guess, the calculation is easy with a financial calculator.[6] Here is the setup:

| 14 | | −1494.93 | 100 | 1000 |
|---|---|---|---|---|
| N | I/YR | PV | PMT | FV |
| | 5 | | | |

Simply enter N = 14, PV = −1494.93, PMT = 100, and FV = 1000; then press the I/YR key. The answer, 5%, will appear.

### quick question Q A

**QUESTION:**

You have just purchased an outstanding 15-year bond with a par value of $1,000 for $1,145.68. Its annual coupon payment is $75. What is the bond's yield to maturity?

**ANSWER:**

Using a financial calculator, we can determine that the bond's YTM is 6%.

| 15 | | −1145.68 | 75 | 1000 |
|---|---|---|---|---|
| N | I/YR | PV | PMT | FV |
| | 6 | | | |

---

[6]You can also find the YTM with a spreadsheet. In Excel, you use the RATE function:

= RATE(14,100,−1494.93,1000)

RATE(nper, pmt, pv, [fv], [type], [guess])

This gives the YTM as 5%. Note that we didn't need to specify a value for type (because the cash flows occur at the end of the year) or guess.

Using Excel's RATE function we solve for the bond's YTM as follows:

= RATE(15,75,–1145.68,1000)
RATE(nper, pmt, pv, [fv], [type], [guess])

Here we find the bond's YTM is equal to **6%**.

Because the bond's coupon rate ($75/$1,000 = 7.5%) is greater than its YTM (6%), the bond is a premium bond—indicating that interest rates have declined since the bond was originally issued.

The yield to maturity can also be viewed as the bond's *promised rate of return*, which is the return that investors will receive if all of the promised payments are made. However, the yield to maturity equals the *expected rate of return* only when (1) the probability of default is zero. (2) The bond cannot be called. If there is some default risk or the bond may be called, there is some chance that the promised payments to maturity will not be received, in which case the calculated yield to maturity will exceed the expected return.

Note also that a bond's calculated yield to maturity changes whenever interest rates in the economy change, which is almost daily. An investor who purchases a bond and holds it until it matures will receive the YTM that existed on the purchase date, but the bond's calculated YTM will change frequently between the purchase date and the maturity date.

## 7-4B YIELD TO CALL

If you purchase a bond that is callable and the company calls it, you do not have the option of holding it to maturity. Therefore, the yield to maturity would not be earned. For example, if Allied's 10% coupon bonds were callable and if interest rates fell from 10% to 5%, the company could call in the 10% bonds, replace them with 5% bonds, and save $100 − $50 = $50 interest per bond per year. This would be beneficial to the company, but not to its bondholders.

If current interest rates are well below an outstanding bond's coupon rate, a callable bond is likely to be called, and investors will estimate its most likely rate of return as the **yield to call (YTC)** rather than the yield to maturity. To calculate the YTC, we modify Equation 7.1, using years to call as N and the call price rather than the maturity value as the ending payment. Here's the modified equation:

*Yield to Call (YTC)*

The rate of return earned on a bond when it is called before its maturity date.

$$\text{Price of bond} = \sum_{t=1}^{N} \frac{\text{INT}}{(1+r_d)^t} + \frac{\text{Call price}}{(1+r_d)^N} \qquad \blacktriangledown \quad 7.2$$

Here N is the number of years until the company can call the bond; call price is the price the company must pay in order to call the bond (it is often set equal to the par value plus one year's interest); and $r_d$ is the YTC.

To illustrate, suppose Allied's bonds had a deferred call provision that permitted the company, if it desired, to call them 10 years after their issue date at a price of $1,100. Suppose further that interest rates had fallen and that 1 year after issuance, the going interest rate had declined, causing their price to rise to $1,494.93. Here is the time line and the setup for finding the bonds' YTC with a financial calculator:

| 0 | | 1 | | 2 | | 8 | | 9 |
|---|---|---|---|---|---|---|---|---|
| | YTC = ? | | | | ••• | | | |
| −1,494.93 | | 100 | | 100 | | 100 | | 100 |
| | | | | | | | | 1,100 |

| N | I/YR | PV | PMT | FV |
|---|------|-----|-----|-----|
| 9 |      | –1494.93 | 100 | 1100 |
|   | 4.21 |     |     |     |

The YTC is 4.21%—this is the return you would earn if you bought an Allied bond at a price of $1,494.93 and it was called 9 years from today. (It could not be called until 10 years after issuance because of its deferred call provision. One year has gone by, so there are 9 years left until the first call date.)

A company is more likely to call its bonds if they are able to replace their current high-coupon debt with less expensive financing. Broadly speaking, a bond is more likely to be called if its price is above par—because a price above par means that the going market interest rate (the yield to maturity) is less than the coupon rate. So, do you think Allied *will* call its 10% bonds when they become callable? Allied's action will depend on what the going interest rate is when they become callable. If the going rate remains at $r_d = 5\%$, Allied could save 10% − 5% = 5%, or $50 per bond per year; so it would call the 10% bonds and replace them with a new 5% issue. There would be some cost to the company to refund the bonds; but because the interest savings would most likely be worth the cost, Allied would probably refund them. Therefore, you should expect to earn the YTC = 4.21% rather than the YTM = 5% if you purchased the bond under the indicated conditions.

## quick question

**QUESTION:**

You have just purchased an outstanding 15-year bond with a par value of $1,000 for $1,145.68. Its annual coupon payment is $75. We calculated the YTM of this bond (6%) in the Quick Question box on page 233. Now, assume that this bond is callable in 7 years at a price of $1,075. What is the bond's YTC? If the yield curve remains flat at its current level during this time period, would you expect to earn the YTM or YTC?

**ANSWER:**

Using a financial calculator, we can determine that the bond's YTC is **5.81%**.

| N | I/YR | PV | PMT | FV |
|---|------|-----|-----|-----|
| 7 |      | –1145.68 | 75 | 1075 |
|   | 5.81 |     |     |     |

Using Excel's RATE function, we solve for the bond's YTC as follows:

```
=RATE(7,75,–1145.68,1075)
    RATE(nper, pmt, pv, [fv], [type], [guess])
```

Here we find the bond's YTC is equal to **5.81%**.

This bond sells at a premium so interest rates have declined since the bond was originally issued. If the yield curve remained flat at this current level during the next 7 years, you would expect the firm to call the bond and issue bonds at the lower 6% interest rate, assuming the cost of doing so was lower than the $75 − $60 = $15 savings per bond.

In the balance of this chapter, we assume that bonds are not callable unless otherwise noted. However, some of the end-of-chapter problems deal with yield to call.[7]

## SelfTest

Explain the difference between yield to maturity (YTM) and yield to call (YTC).

Halley Enterprises's bonds currently sell for $975. They have a 7-year maturity, an annual coupon of $90, and a par value of $1,000. What is their yield to maturity? **(9.51%)**

The Henderson Company's bonds currently sell for $1,275. They pay a $120 annual coupon, have a 20-year maturity, and a par value of $1,000, but they can be called in 5 years at $1,120. What are their YTM and their YTC, and if the yield curve remained flat, which rate would investors expect to earn? **(8.99%, 7.31%; YTC)**

## 7-5 Changes in Bond Values over Time

When a coupon bond is issued, the coupon is generally set at a level that causes the bond's market price to equal its par value. If a lower coupon were set, investors would not be willing to pay $1,000 for the bond; but if a higher coupon were set, investors would clamor for it and bid its price up over $1,000. Investment bankers can judge quite precisely the coupon rate that will cause a bond to sell at its $1,000 par value.

A bond that has just been issued is known as a *new issue*. Once it has been issued, it is an *outstanding bond*, also called a *seasoned issue*. Newly issued bonds generally sell at prices very close to par, but the prices of outstanding bonds can vary widely from par. Except for floating-rate bonds, coupon payments are constant; so when economic conditions change, a bond with a $100 coupon that sold at its $1,000 par value when it was issued will sell for more or less than $1,000 thereafter.

Among its outstanding bonds, Allied currently has three equally risky issues that will mature in 15 years:

- Allied's just-issued 15-year bonds have a 10% annual coupon. They were issued at par, which means that the market interest rate on their issue date was also 10%. Because the coupon rate equals the market interest rate, these bonds are trading at par, or $1,000.

- Five years ago Allied issued 20-year bonds with a 7% annual coupon. These bonds currently have 15 years remaining until maturity. They were originally issued at par, which means that 5 years ago the market interest rate was 7%.

---

[7]Brokerage houses occasionally report a bond's *current yield*, defined as the annual interest payment divided by the current price. For example, if Allied's 10% coupon bonds were selling for $985, the current yield would be $100/$985 = 10.15%. Unlike the YTM or YTC, the current yield *does not* represent the actual return that investors should expect because it does not account for the capital gain or loss that will be realized if the bond is held until it matures or is called. The current yield was popular before calculators and computers came along because it was easy to calculate. However, it can be misleading, and now it's easy enough to calculate the YTM and YTC.

Currently, this bond's coupon rate is less than the 10% market rate, so they sell at a discount. Using a financial calculator or spreadsheet, we can quickly find that they have a price of $771.82. (Set N = 15, I/YR = 10, PMT = 70, and FV = 1000, and solve for the PV to calculate the price.)

- Ten years ago Allied issued 25-year bonds with a 13% annual coupon. These bonds currently have 15 years remaining until maturity. They were originally issued at par, which means that 10 years ago the market interest rate must have been 13%. Because their coupon rate is greater than the current market rate, they sell at a premium. Using a financial calculator or spreadsheet, we can find that their price is $1,228.18. (Set N = 15, I/YR = 10, PMT = 130, and FV = 1000, and solve for the PV to determine the price.)

Each of these three bonds has a 15-year maturity; each has the same credit risk; and thus each has the same market interest rate, 10%. However, the bonds have different prices because of their different coupon rates.

Now let's consider what would happen to the prices of these three bonds over the 15 years until they mature, assuming that market interest rates remain constant at 10% and Allied does not default on its payments. Table 7.1 demonstrates how the prices of each of these bonds will change over time if market interest rates remain at 10%. One year from now each bond will have a maturity of 14 years—that is, N = 14. With a financial calculator, override N = 15 with N = 14, and press the PV key; that gives you the value of each bond 1 year from now. Continuing, set N = 13, N = 12, and so forth, to see how the prices change over time.

Table 7.1 also shows the current yield (which is the coupon interest divided by the bond's price), the capital gains yield, and the total return over time. For any given year, the *capital gains yield* is calculated as the bond's annual change in price divided by the beginning-of-year price. For example, if a bond was selling for $1,000 at the beginning of the year and $1,035 at the end of the year, its capital gains yield for the year would be $35/$1,000 = 3.5%. (If the bond was selling at a premium, its price would decline over time. Then the capital gains yield would be negative, but it would be offset by a high current yield.) A bond's total return is equal to the current yield plus the capital gains yield. In the absence of default risk and assuming market equilibrium, the total return is also equal to YTM and the market interest rate, which in our example is 10%.

Figure 7.2 plots the three bonds' predicted prices as calculated in Table 7.1. Notice that the bonds have very different price paths over time but that at maturity, all three will sell at their par value of $1,000. Here are some points about the prices of the bonds over time:

- The price of the 10% coupon bond trading at par will remain at $1,000 if the market interest rate remains at 10%. Therefore, its current yield will remain at 10%, and its capital gains yield will be zero each year.
- The 7% bond trades at a discount; but at maturity, it must sell at par because that is the amount the company will pay its bondholders. Therefore, its price must rise over time.
- The 13% coupon bond trades at a premium. However, its price must be equal to its par value at maturity; so the price must decline over time.

Although the prices of the 7% and 13% coupon bonds move in opposite directions over time, each bond provides investors with the same total return, 10%, which is also the total return on the 10% coupon par value bond. The discount bond has a low coupon rate (and therefore a low current yield), but it

**TABLE 7.1** Calculation of Current Yields, Capital Gains Yields, and Total Returns for 7%, 10%, and 13% Coupon Bonds When the Market Rate Remains Constant at 10%

| Number of Years Until Maturity | 7% Coupon Bond | | | | 10% Coupon Bond | | | | 13% Coupon Bond | | | |
|---|---|---|---|---|---|---|---|---|---|---|---|---|
| | Price[a] | Expected Current Yield[b] | Expected Capital Gains Yield[c] | Expected Total Return[d] | Price[a] | Expected Current Yield[b] | Expected Capital Gains Yield[c] | Expected Total Return[d] | Price[a] | Expected Current Yield[b] | Expected Capital Gains Yield[c] | Expected Total Return[d] |
| 15 | $ 771.82 | 9.1% | 0.9% | 10.0% | $1,000.00 | 10.0% | 0.0% | 10.0% | $1,228.18 | 10.6% | −0.6% | 10.0% |
| 14 | 779.00 | 9.0 | 1.0 | 10.0 | 1,000.00 | 10.0 | 0.0 | 10.0 | 1,221.00 | 10.6 | −0.6 | 10.0 |
| 13 | 786.90 | 8.9 | 1.1 | 10.0 | 1,000.00 | 10.0 | 0.0 | 10.0 | 1,213.10 | 10.7 | −0.7 | 10.0 |
| 12 | 795.59 | 8.8 | 1.2 | 10.0 | 1,000.00 | 10.0 | 0.0 | 10.0 | 1,204.41 | 10.8 | −0.8 | 10.0 |
| 11 | 805.15 | 8.7 | 1.3 | 10.0 | 1,000.00 | 10.0 | 0.0 | 10.0 | 1,194.85 | 10.9 | −0.9 | 10.0 |
| 10 | 815.66 | 8.6 | 1.4 | 10.0 | 1,000.00 | 10.0 | 0.0 | 10.0 | 1,184.34 | 11.0 | −1.0 | 10.0 |
| 9 | 827.23 | 8.5 | 1.5 | 10.0 | 1,000.00 | 10.0 | 0.0 | 10.0 | 1,172.77 | 11.1 | −1.1 | 10.0 |
| 8 | 839.95 | 8.3 | 1.7 | 10.0 | 1,000.00 | 10.0 | 0.0 | 10.0 | 1,160.05 | 11.2 | −1.2 | 10.0 |
| 7 | 853.95 | 8.2 | 1.8 | 10.0 | 1,000.00 | 10.0 | 0.0 | 10.0 | 1,146.05 | 11.3 | −1.3 | 10.0 |
| 6 | 869.34 | 8.1 | 1.9 | 10.0 | 1,000.00 | 10.0 | 0.0 | 10.0 | 1,130.66 | 11.5 | −1.5 | 10.0 |
| 5 | 886.28 | 7.9 | 2.1 | 10.0 | 1,000.00 | 10.0 | 0.0 | 10.0 | 1,113.72 | 11.7 | −1.7 | 10.0 |
| 4 | 904.90 | 7.7 | 2.3 | 10.0 | 1,000.00 | 10.0 | 0.0 | 10.0 | 1,095.10 | 11.9 | −1.9 | 10.0 |
| 3 | 925.39 | 7.6 | 2.4 | 10.0 | 1,000.00 | 10.0 | 0.0 | 10.0 | 1,074.61 | 12.1 | −2.1 | 10.0 |
| 2 | 947.93 | 7.4 | 2.6 | 10.0 | 1,000.00 | 10.0 | 0.0 | 10.0 | 1,052.07 | 12.4 | −2.4 | 10.0 |
| 1 | 972.73 | 7.2 | 2.8 | 10.0 | 1,000.00 | 10.0 | 0.0 | 10.0 | 1,027.27 | 12.7 | −2.7 | 10.0 |
| 0 | 1,000.00 | | | | 1,000.00 | | | | 1,000.00 | | | |

Notes:
[a] Using a financial calculator, the price of each bond is calculated by entering the data for N, I/YR, PMT, and FV, then solving for PV = the bond's value.
[b] The expected current yield is calculated as the annual interest divided by the price of the bond.
[c] The expected capital gains yield is calculated as the difference between the end-of-year bond price and the beginning-of-year bond price divided by the beginning-of-year bond price.
[d] The expected total return is the sum of the expected current yield and the expected capital gains yield.

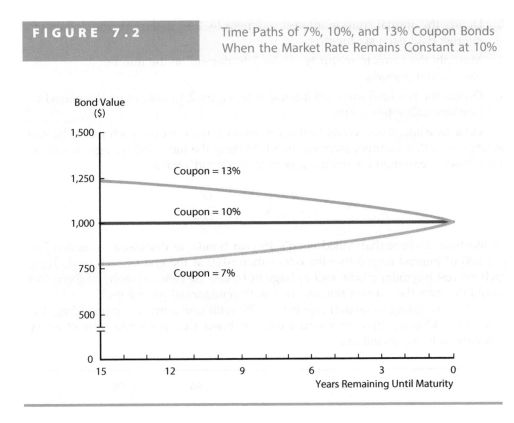

**FIGURE 7.2** Time Paths of 7%, 10%, and 13% Coupon Bonds When the Market Rate Remains Constant at 10%

provides a capital gain each year. In contrast, the premium bond has a high current yield, but it has an expected capital loss each year.[8]

## SelfTest

What is meant by the terms *new issue* and *seasoned issue*?

Last year a firm issued 20-year, 8% annual coupon bonds at a par value of $1,000.

a. Suppose that one year later the going market interest rate drops to 6%. What is the new price of the bonds, assuming they now have 19 years to maturity? **($1,223.16)**

b. Suppose that one year after issue, the going market interest rate is 10% (rather than 6%). What would the price have been? **($832.70)**

Why do the prices of fixed-rate bonds fall if expectations for inflation rise?

## 7-6 Bonds with Semiannual Coupons

Although some bonds pay interest annually, the vast majority actually make payments semiannually. To evaluate semiannual bonds, we must modify the valuation model (Equation 7.1) as follows:

---

[8]In this example (and throughout the text), we ignore the tax effects associated with purchasing different types of bonds. For coupon bonds, under the current Tax Code (March 2015), coupon payments are taxed as ordinary income, whereas long-term capital gains are taxed at the long-term capital gains tax rate. As we mentioned in Chapter 3, for most investors, the long-term capital gains tax rate is lower than the personal tax rate. Moreover, although coupon payments are taxed each year, capital gains taxes are deferred until the bond is sold or matures. Consequently, all else equal, investors end up paying lower taxes on discount bonds because a greater percentage of their total return comes in the form of capital gains. For details on the tax treatment of zero coupon bonds, see Web Appendix 7A.

1. Divide the annual coupon interest payment by 2 to determine the dollars of interest paid each six months.
2. Multiply the years to maturity, N, by 2 to determine the number of semiannual periods.
3. Divide the nominal (quoted) interest rate, $r_d$, by 2 to determine the periodic (semiannual) interest rate.

On a time line, there would be twice as many payments, but each would be half as large as with an annual payment bond. Making the indicated changes results in the following equation for finding a semiannual bond's value:

$$V_B = \sum_{t=1}^{2N} \frac{INT/2}{(1+r_d/2)^t} + \frac{M}{(1+r_d/2)^{2N}} \qquad \text{7.1a}$$

To illustrate, assume that Allied Food's 15-year bonds, as discussed in Section 7-3, pay $50 of interest each 6 months rather than $100 at the end of each year. Thus, each interest payment is only half as large but there are twice as many of them. We would describe the coupon rate as "10% with semiannual payments."[9]

When the going (nominal) rate is $r_d = 5\%$ with semiannual compounding, the value of a 15-year, 10% semiannual coupon bond that pays $50 interest every 6 months is found as follows:

| 30 | 2.5 | | 50 | 1000 |
|---|---|---|---|---|
| N | I/YR | PV | PMT | FV |
| | | = −1,523.26 | | |

Enter N = 30, $r_d$ = I/YR = 2.5, PMT = 50, and FV = 1000; then press the PV key to obtain the bond's value, $1,523.26. The value with semiannual interest payments is slightly larger than $1,518.98, the value when interest is paid annually as we calculated in Section 7-3. This higher value occurs because each interest payment is received somewhat faster under semiannual compounding.

Alternatively, when we know the price of a semiannual bond, we can easily back out the bond's nominal yield to maturity. In the previous example, if you were told that a 15-year bond with a 10% semiannual coupon was selling for $1,523.26, you could solve for the bond's periodic interest rate as follows:

| 30 | | −1523.26 | 50 | 1000 |
|---|---|---|---|---|
| N | I/YR | PV | PMT | FV |
| | 2.5 | | | |

---

[9]In this situation, the coupon rate of "10% paid semiannually" is the rate that bond dealers, corporate treasurers, and investors generally discuss. Of course, if this bond were issued at par, its *effective annual rate* would be higher than 10%.

$$EAR = EFF\% = \left(1 + \frac{r_{NOM}}{M}\right)^M - 1 = \left(1 + \frac{0.10}{2}\right)^2 - 1 = (1.05)^2 - 1 = 10.25\%$$

Because 10% with annual payments is quite different from 10% with semiannual payments, we have assumed a change in effective rates in this section from the situation in Section 7-3, where we assumed 10% with annual payments.

In this case, enter N = 30, PV = −1523.26, PMT = 50, and FV = 1000; then press the I/YR key to obtain the interest rate per semiannual period, 2.5%. Multiplying by 2, we calculate the bond's nominal yield to maturity to be 5%.[10]

### quick question

**QUESTION:**

You have just purchased an outstanding noncallable, 15-year bond with a par value of $1,000. Assume that this bond pays interest of 7.5%, with semiannual compounding. If the going (nominal) annual rate is 6%, what price did you pay for this bond? How does the price compare to the price of the annual coupon bond?

**ANSWER:**

Using a financial calculator, we can determine that the bond's price is **$1,147.00**.

| 30 | 3 | | 37.50 | 1000 |
|---|---|---|---|---|
| N | I/YR | PV | PMT | FV |

$$= -1{,}147.00$$

Using Excel's PV function we solve for the semiannual bond's price as follows:

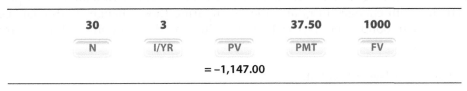

```
= PV(0.03,30,37.5,1000)
  PV(rate, nper, pmt, [fv], [type])
```

Here we find that the bond's value is equal to **$1,147.00**.

In the Quick Question box on page 233 we calculated the YTM on this annual bond whose price was $1,145.68. Notice that the semiannual bond's price is $1,147.00 − $1,145.68 = $1.32 greater due to the interest payments being received semiannually rather than on an annual basis.

## Self*Test*

Describe how the annual payment bond valuation formula is changed to evaluate semiannual coupon bonds, and write the revised formula.

Hartwell Corporation's bonds have a 20-year maturity, an 8% semiannual coupon, and a face value of $1,000. The going nominal annual interest rate ($r_d$) is 7%. What is the bond's price? **($1,106.78)**

## 7-7 Assessing a Bond's Riskiness

In this section, we identify and explain the two key factors that impact a bond's riskiness. Once those factors are identified, we differentiate between them and discuss how you can minimize these risks.

---

[10]We can use a similar process to calculate the nominal yield to call for a semiannual bond. The only difference would be that N should represent the number of semiannual periods until the bond is callable, and FV should be the bond's call price rather than its par value.

## 7-7A PRICE RISK

*Price (Interest Rate) Risk*

The risk of a decline in a bond's price due to an increase in interest rates.

As we saw in Chapter 6, interest rates fluctuate over time, and when they rise, the value of outstanding bonds decline. This risk of a decline in bond values due to an increase in interest rates is called **price risk** (or **interest rate risk**). To illustrate, refer back to Allied's bonds; assume once more that they have a 10% annual coupon; and assume that you bought one of these bonds at its par value, $1,000. Shortly after your purchase, the going interest rate rises from 10% to 15%.[11] As we saw in Section 7-3, this interest rate increase would cause the bond's price to fall from $1,000 to $707.63, so you would have a loss of $292.37 on the bond.[12] Because interest rates can and do rise, rising rates cause losses to bondholders; people or firms who invest in bonds are exposed to risk from increasing interest rates.

Price risk is higher on bonds that have long maturities than on bonds that will mature in the near future.[13] This follows because the longer the maturity, the longer before the bond will be paid off and the bondholder can replace it with another bond with a higher coupon. This point can be demonstrated by showing how the value of a 1-year bond with a 10% annual coupon fluctuates with changes in $r_d$ and then comparing those changes with changes on a 15-year bond. The 1-year bond's values at different interest rates are shown below.

Value of a 1-year bond at:

| $r_d = 5\%$: | 1 | 5 | | 100 | 1000 |
|---|---|---|---|---|---|
| | N | I/YR | PV | PMT | FV |
| | | | = −1,047.62 | | |

| $r_d = 10\%$: | 1 | 10 | | 100 | 1000 |
|---|---|---|---|---|---|
| | N | I/YR | PV | PMT | FV |
| | | | = −1,000.00 | | |

| $r_d = 15\%$: | 1 | 15 | | 100 | 1000 |
|---|---|---|---|---|---|
| | N | I/YR | PV | PMT | FV |
| | | | = −956.52 | | |

---

[11]An immediate increase in rates from 10% to 15% would be quite unusual, and it would occur only if something quite bad were revealed about the company or happened in the economy. Smaller but still significant rate increases that adversely affect bondholders do occur fairly often.

[12]You would have an accounting (and tax) loss only if you sold the bond; if you held it to maturity, you would not have such a loss. However, even if you did not sell, you would still have suffered a real economic loss in an opportunity cost sense because you would have lost the opportunity to invest at 15% and would be stuck with a 10% bond in a 15% market. In an economic sense, "paper losses" are just as bad as realized accounting losses.

[13]Actually, a bond's maturity and coupon rate both affect price risk. Low coupons mean that most of the bond's return will come from repayment of principal, whereas on a high-coupon bond with the same maturity, more of the cash flows will come in during the early years due to the relatively large coupon payments.

You would obtain the first value with a financial calculator by entering N = 1, I/YR = 5, PMT = 100, and FV = 1000 and then pressing PV to get $1,047.62. With all the data still in your calculator, enter I/YR = 10 to override the old I/YR = 5 and press PV to find the bond's value at a 10% rate; it drops to $1,000. Then enter I/YR = 15, and press the PV key to find the last bond value, $956.52.

The effects of increasing rates on the 15-year bond value as found earlier in Section 7-3 can be compared with the just-calculated effects for the 1-year bond. This comparison is shown in Figure 7.3, where we show bond prices at several rates and then plot those prices on the graph. Compared to the 1-year bond, the 15-year bond is far more sensitive to changes in rates. At a 10% interest rate, both the 15-year and 1-year bonds are valued at $1,000. When rates rise to 15%, the 15-year bond falls to $707.63, but the 1-year bond falls only to $956.52. The price decline for the 1-year bond is only 4.35%, while that for the 15-year bond is 29.24%.

*For bonds with similar coupons, this differential interest rate sensitivity always holds true—the longer a bond's maturity, the more its price changes in response to a given change in interest rates.* Thus, even if the risk of default on two bonds is exactly the same, the one with the longer maturity is typically exposed to more risk from a rise in interest rates.[14]

The logical explanation for this difference in price risk is simple. Suppose you bought a 15-year bond that yielded 10%, or $100 a year. Now suppose interest rates on comparable-risk bonds rose to 15%. You would be stuck receiving only $100 of interest for the next 15 years. On the other hand, had you bought a 1-year bond, you would have earned a low return for only 1 year. At the end of the year, you would have received your $1,000 back; then you could have reinvested it and earned 15%, or $150 per year, for the next 14 years.

## 7-7B REINVESTMENT RISK

As we saw in the preceding section, an *increase* in interest rates hurts bondholders because it leads to a decline in the current value of a bond portfolio. But can a *decrease* in interest rates also hurt bondholders? The answer is yes because if interest rates fall, long-term investors will suffer a reduction in income. For example, consider a retiree who has a bond portfolio and lives off the income it produces. The bonds in the portfolio, on average, have coupon rates of 10%. Now suppose interest rates decline to 5%. Many of the bonds will mature or be called; as this occurs, the bondholder will have to replace 10% bonds with 5% bonds. Thus, the retiree will suffer a reduction of income.[15]

The risk of an income decline due to a drop in interest rates is called **reinvestment risk**, and its importance has been demonstrated to all bondholders in recent years as a result of the sharp drop in rates since the mid-1980s. Reinvestment risk is obviously high on callable bonds. It is also high on short-term bonds because the shorter the bond's maturity, the fewer the years before the relatively high old-coupon bonds will be replaced with the new low-coupon issues. Thus, retirees whose primary holdings are short-term bonds or other debt securities will be hurt badly by a decline in rates, but holders of noncallable long-term bonds will continue to enjoy the old high rates.

*Reinvestment Risk*
The risk that a decline in interest rates will lead to a decline in income from a bond portfolio.

---

[14]If a 10-year bond were plotted on the graph in Figure 7.3, its curve would lie between those of the 15-year and the 1-year bonds. The curve of a 1-month bond would be almost horizontal, indicating that its price would change very little in response to an interest rate change; but a 100-year bond would have a very steep slope, and the slope of a perpetuity would be even steeper. Also, a zero coupon bond's price is quite sensitive to interest rate changes; and the longer its maturity, the greater its price sensitivity. Therefore, a 30-year zero coupon bond would have a huge amount of price risk.

[15]Charles Schwab makes this point in a recent opinion piece in *The Wall Street Journal*, where he argues that continued low interest rates have had a devastating effect on many senior citizens who live off of the interest generated from their investments. For additional information, refer to Charles Schwab, "Low Interest Rates Are Squeezing Seniors," *The Wall Street Journal* (online.wsj.com), March 30, 2010.

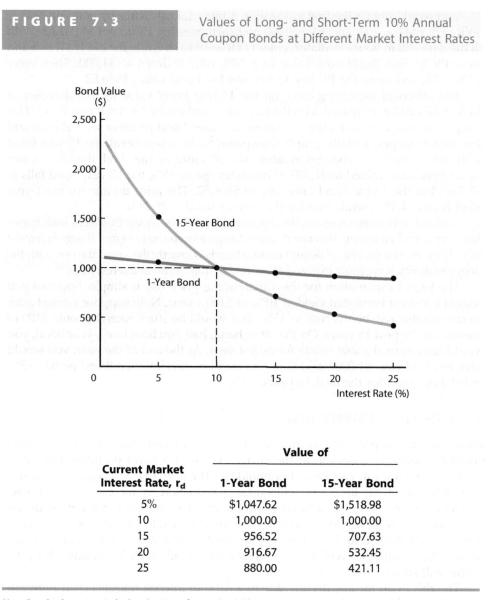

**FIGURE 7.3** Values of Long- and Short-Term 10% Annual Coupon Bonds at Different Market Interest Rates

| Current Market Interest Rate, $r_d$ | Value of | |
|---|---|---|
| | **1-Year Bond** | **15-Year Bond** |
| 5% | $1,047.62 | $1,518.98 |
| 10 | 1,000.00 | 1,000.00 |
| 15 | 956.52 | 707.63 |
| 20 | 916.67 | 532.45 |
| 25 | 880.00 | 421.11 |

*Note:* Bond values were calculated using a financial calculator assuming annual, or once-a-year, compounding.

## 7-7C COMPARING PRICE RISK AND REINVESTMENT RISK

Note that price risk relates to the *current market value* of the bond portfolio, while reinvestment risk relates to the *income* the portfolio produces. If you hold long-term bonds, you will face significant price risk because the value of your portfolio will decline if interest rates rise, but you will not face much reinvestment risk because your income will be stable. On the other hand, if you hold short-term bonds, you will not be exposed to much price risk, but you will be exposed to significant reinvestment risk. Table 7.2 summarizes how a bond's maturity and coupon rate affect its price risk and reinvestment risk. For example, a long-term zero coupon bond will have a very high level of price risk and relatively little reinvestment risk. In contrast, a short-term bond with a high coupon rate will have low price risk but considerable reinvestment risk.

*Investment Horizon*

The period of time an investor plans to hold a particular investment.

Which type of risk is "more relevant" to a given investor depends on how long the investor plans to hold the bonds—this is often referred to as his or her **investment horizon**. To illustrate, consider an investor who has a relatively

Comparing Price Risk and Reinvestment Risk TABLE 7.2

| Bond | Level of Price Risk | Level of Reinvestment Risk |
|------|---------------------|----------------------------|
| Longer maturity bonds | High | Low |
| Higher coupon bonds | Low | High |

short 1-year investment horizon—say, the investor plans to go to graduate school a year from now and needs money for tuition and expenses. Reinvestment risk is of minimal concern to this investor because there is little time to reinvest. The investor could eliminate price risk by buying a 1-year Treasury security because he would be assured of receiving the face value of the bond 1 year from now (the investment horizon). However, if this investor were to buy a long-term Treasury security, he would bear a considerable amount of price risk because, as we have seen, long-term bond prices decline when interest rates rise. Consequently, investors with shorter investment horizons should view long-term bonds as being more risky than short-term bonds.

By contrast, the reinvestment risk inherent in short-term bonds is especially relevant to investors with longer investment horizons. Consider a retiree who is living on income from her portfolio. If this investor buys 1-year bonds, she will have to "roll them over" every year; and if rates fall, her income in subsequent years will likewise decline. A younger couple saving for their retirement or their children's college costs, for example, would be affected similarly because if they buy short-term bonds, they too will have to roll over their portfolio at possibly much lower rates. Because of the uncertainty today about the rates that will be earned on these reinvested cash flows, long-term investors should be especially concerned about the reinvestment risk inherent in short-term bonds.

To account for the effects related to both a bond's maturity and coupon, many analysts focus on a measure called **duration**. A bond's duration is the weighted average of the time it takes to receive each of the bond's cash flows. It follows that a zero coupon bond whose only cash flow is paid at maturity has a duration equal to its maturity. On the other hand, a coupon bond will have a duration that is less than its maturity. You can use Excel's DURATION function to calculate a bond's duration. We discuss duration in greater detail in Web Appendix 7B.

*Duration*
The weighted average of the time it takes to receive each of the bond's cash flows.

One way to manage both price and reinvestment risk is to buy a zero coupon Treasury bond with a duration equal to the investor's investment horizon. A very simple way to do this is to buy a zero coupon bond with a maturity that matches the investment horizon. For example, assume your investment horizon is 10 years. If you buy a 10-year zero, you will receive a guaranteed payment in 10 years equal to the bond's face value.[16] Moreover, as there are no coupons to reinvest, there is no reinvestment risk. This explains why investors with specific goals often invest in zero coupon bonds.[17]

---

[16]Note that in this example, the 10-year zero technically has a considerable amount of price risk because its *current* price is highly sensitive to changes in interest rates. However, the year-to-year movements in price should not be of great concern to an investor with a 10-year investment horizon because the investor knows that, regardless of what happens to interest rates, the bond's price will still be $1,000 when it matures.

[17]Two words of caution about zeros are in order. First, as we show in Web Appendix 7A, investors in zeros must pay taxes each year on their accrued gain in value, even though the bonds don't pay any cash until they mature. Second, buying a zero coupon bond with a maturity equal to your investment horizon enables you to lock in a nominal cash payoff, but the *real* value of that payment still depends on what happens to inflation during your investment horizon.

Recall from Chapter 6 that maturity risk premiums are generally positive.[18] Moreover, a positive maturity risk premium implies that investors, on average, regard longer-term bonds as being riskier than shorter-term bonds. That, in turn, suggests that the average investor is more concerned with price risk. Still, it is appropriate for each investor to consider his or her own situation, to recognize the risks inherent in bonds with different maturities, and to construct a portfolio that deals best with the investor's most relevant risk.

## SelfTest

Differentiate between price risk and reinvestment risk.

To which type of risk are holders of long-term bonds more exposed? Short-term bondholders?

What type of security can be used to minimize both price risk and reinvestment risk for an investor with a fixed investment horizon? Does this security protect the real payoff? Explain.

# 7-8 Default Risk

Potential default is another important risk that bondholders face. If the issuer defaults, investors will receive less than the promised return. Recall from Chapter 6 that the quoted interest rate includes a default risk premium—the higher the probability of default, the higher the premium and thus the yield to maturity. Default risk on Treasuries is zero, but this risk is substantial for lower-grade corporate and municipal bonds.

To illustrate, suppose two bonds have the same promised cash flows—their coupon rates, maturities, liquidity, and inflation exposures are identical—but one has more default risk than the other. Investors will naturally pay more for the one with less chance of default. As a result, bonds with higher default risk have higher market rates: $r_d = r^* + IP + DRP + LP + MRP$. If a bond's default risk changes, $r_d$ and thus the price will be affected. Thus, if the default risk on Allied's bonds increases, their price will fall and the yield to maturity ($YTM = r_d$) will increase.

## 7-8A VARIOUS TYPES OF CORPORATE BONDS

Default risk is influenced by the financial strength of the issuer and the terms of the bond contract, including whether collateral has been pledged to secure the bond. The characteristics of some key types of bonds are described in this section.

### Mortgage Bonds

*Mortgage Bond*
A bond backed by fixed assets. First mortgage bonds are senior in priority to claims of second mortgage bonds.

Under a **mortgage bond**, the corporation pledges specific assets as security for the bond. To illustrate, in 2016, Billingham Corporation needed $10 million to build a regional distribution center. Bonds in the amount of $4 million, secured by *a first mortgage* on the property, were issued. (The remaining $6 million was financed with equity capital.) If Billingham defaults on the bonds, the bondholders can foreclose on the property and sell it to satisfy their claims.

---

[18]The fact that maturity risk premiums are positive suggests that most investors have relatively short investment horizons, or at least worry about short-term changes in their net worth. See *Ibbotson Stocks, Bonds, Bills, and Inflation: 2015 Classic Yearbook* (Chicago: Morningstar, Inc., 2015), which finds that the maturity risk premium for long-term bonds has averaged 1.6% over the past 89 years.

If Billingham had chosen to, it could have issued *second mortgage bonds* secured by the same $10 million of assets. In the event of liquidation, the holders of the second mortgage bonds would have a claim against the property, but only after the first mortgage bondholders had been paid in full. Thus, second mortgages are sometimes called *junior mortgages* because they are junior in priority to the claims of *senior mortgages*, or *first mortgage bonds*.

All mortgage bonds are subject to an **indenture**, which is a legal document that spells out in detail the rights of the bondholders and the corporation. The indentures of many major corporations were written 20, 30, 40, or more years ago. These indentures are generally "open ended," meaning that new bonds can be issued from time to time under the same indenture. However, the amount of new bonds that can be issued is usually limited to a specified percentage of the firm's total "bondable property," which generally includes all land, plant, and equipment. And, of course, the coupon interest rate on newly issued bonds changes over time, along with the market rate on the older bonds.

**Indenture**
A formal agreement between the issuer and the bondholders.

## Debentures

A **debenture** is an unsecured bond, and as such, it provides no specific collateral as security for the obligation. Therefore, debenture holders are general creditors whose claims are protected by property not otherwise pledged. In practice, the use of debentures depends on the nature of the firm's assets and on its general credit strength. Extremely strong companies such as General Electric and Exxon Mobil can use debentures because they do not need to put up property as security for their debt. Debentures are also issued by weak companies that have already pledged most of their assets as collateral for mortgage loans. In this case, the debentures are quite risky, and that risk will be reflected in their interest rates.

**Debenture**
A long-term bond that is not secured by a mortgage on specific property.

## Subordinated Debentures

The term *subordinate* means "below" or "inferior to," and in the event of bankruptcy, subordinated debt has a claim on assets only after senior debt has been paid in full. **Subordinated debentures** may be subordinated to designated notes payable (usually bank loans) or to all other debt. In the event of liquidation or reorganization, holders of subordinated debentures receive nothing until all senior debt, as named in the debentures' indenture, has been paid. Precisely how subordination works and how it strengthens the position of senior debtholders are explained in detail in Web Appendix 7C.

**Subordinated Debentures**
Bonds having a claim on assets only after the senior debt has been paid in full in the event of liquidation.

## 7-8B BOND RATINGS

Since the early 1900s, bonds have been assigned quality ratings that reflect their probability of going into default. The three major rating agencies are Moody's Investors Service (Moody's), Standard & Poor's Corporation (S&P), and Fitch Investors Service. Moody's and S&P's rating designations are shown in Table 7.3.[19] The triple- and double-A bonds are extremely safe. Single-A and triple-B bonds are also strong enough to be called **investment-grade bonds**, and they are the lowest-rated bonds that many banks and other institutional investors are permitted by law to hold. Double-B and lower bonds are speculative, or **junk bonds**; and they have a significant probability of going into default.

**Investment-Grade Bonds**
Bonds rated triple-B or higher; many banks and other institutional investors are permitted by law to hold only investment-grade bonds.

## Bond Rating Criteria

The framework used by rating agencies examines both qualitative and quantitative factors. Quantitative factors relate to financial risk—examining a firm's financial ratios, such as those discussed in Chapter 4. Published ratios are, of course,

**Junk Bonds**
High-risk, high-yield bonds.

---

[19]In the discussion to follow, reference to the S&P rating is intended to imply the Moody's and Fitch's ratings as well. Thus, triple-B bonds mean both BBB and Baa bonds; double-B bonds mean both BB and Ba bonds; and so forth.

**TABLE 7.3**       Moody's and S&P Bond Ratings

| | Investment Grade | | | | | Junk | | | |
|---|---|---|---|---|---|---|---|---|---|
| Moody's | Aaa | Aa | A | Baa | | Ba | B | Caa | C |
| S&P | AAA | AA | A | BBB | | BB | B | CCC | C |

*Note:* Both Moody's and S&P use "modifiers" for bonds rated below triple A. S&P uses a plus and minus system. Thus, A+ designates the strongest A-rated bonds; A–, the weakest. Moody's uses a 1, 2, or 3 designation, with 1 denoting the strongest and 3 denoting the weakest; thus, within the double-A category, Aa1 is the best, Aa2 is average, and Aa3 is the weakest.

historical—they show the firm's condition in the past, whereas bond investors are more interested in the firm's condition in the future. Qualitative factors considered include an analysis of a firm's business risk, such as its competitiveness within its industry and the quality of its management. Determinants of bond ratings include the following:

1. *Financial Ratios.* All of the ratios are potentially important, but those related to financial risk are key. The rating agencies' analysts perform a financial analysis along the lines discussed in Chapter 4 and forecast future ratios along the lines described in Chapter 16.

2. *Qualitative Factors: Bond Contract Terms.* Every bond is covered by a contract, often called an indenture, between the issuer and the bondholders. The indenture spells out all the terms related to the bond. Included in the indenture are the maturity, the coupon interest rate, a statement of whether the bond is secured by a mortgage on specific assets, any sinking fund provisions, and a statement of whether the bond is guaranteed by some other party with a high credit ranking. Other provisions might include *restrictive covenants* such as requirements that the firm not let its debt ratio exceed a stated level and that it keep its times-interest-earned ratio at or above a given level. Some bond indentures are hundreds of pages long, while others are quite short and cover just the terms of the loan.

3. *Miscellaneous Qualitative Factors.* Included here are issues like the sensitivity of the firm's earnings to the strength of the economy, the way it is affected by inflation, a statement of whether it is having or likely to have labor problems, the extent of its international operations (including the stability of the countries in which it operates), potential environmental problems, and potential antitrust problems. Today the most important factor is exposure to subprime loans, including the difficulty to determine the extent of this exposure as a result of the complexity of the assets backed by such loans.

We see that bond ratings are determined by a great many factors, some quantitative and some qualitative (or subjective). Also, the rating process is dynamic—at times, one factor is of primary importance; at other times, some other factor is key. Table 7.4 provides a summary of the criteria a rating agency examines when rating a company's bonds. Panel a shows how business and financial risk determine the "anchor" for establishing the underlying bond rating. Panel b further illustrates how this anchor is combined with a comprehensive set of other factors to determine the issuer's final credit rating.

## Importance of Bond Ratings

Bond ratings are important to both firms and investors. First, because a bond's rating is an indicator of its default risk, the rating has a direct, measurable influence on the bond's interest rate and the firm's cost of debt. Second, most bonds are purchased by institutional investors rather than individuals, and many institutions

**Panel a: Combining the Business and Financial Risk Profiles to Determine the Anchor**

| Business Risk Profile | Financial Risk Profile | | | | | |
|---|---|---|---|---|---|---|
| | Minimal | Modest | Intermediate | Significant | Aggressive | Highly Leveraged |
| Excellent | AAA/AA+ | AA | A+/A | A− | BBB | BBB−/BB+ |
| Strong | AA/AA− | A+/A | A−/BBB+ | BBB | BB+ | BB |
| Satisfactory | A/A− | BBB+ | BBB/BBB− | BBB−/BB+ | BB | B+ |
| Fair | BBB/BBB− | BBB− | BB+ | BB | BB− | B |
| Weak | BB+ | BB+ | BB | BB− | B+ | B/B− |
| Vulnerable | BB− | BB− | BB−/B+ | B+ | B | B− |

**Panel b: Issuer Credit Rating**

Issuer Credit Rating

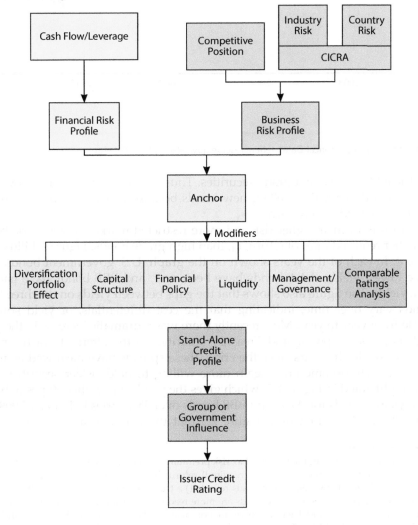

Source: "How Standard & Poor's Rates Nonfinancial Corporate Entities," *S&P Capital IQ*, February 24, 2014.

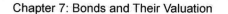

**FIGURE 7.4** Yields on Selected Long-Term Bonds, 1994–2015

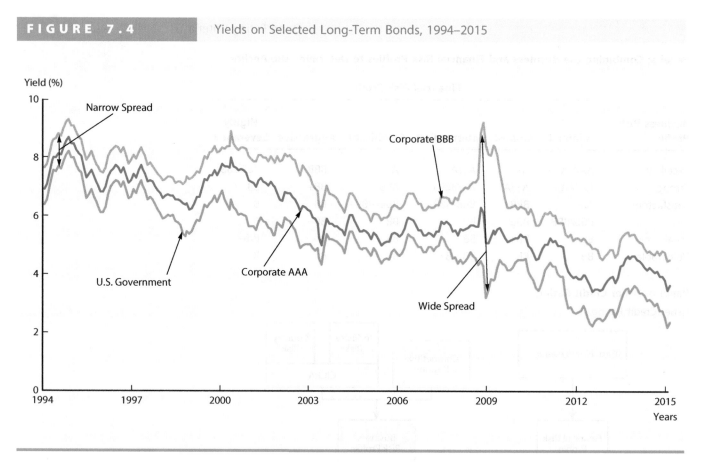

Source: *Federal Reserve Statistical Release*, Selected Interest Rates (Historical Data), federalreserve.gov/releases/H15/data.htm.

are restricted to investment-grade securities. Thus, if a firm's bonds fall below BBB, it will have a difficult time selling new bonds because many potential purchasers will not be allowed to buy them.

As a result of their higher risk and more restricted market, lower-grade bonds have higher required rates of return, $r_d$, than high-grade bonds. Figure 7.4 illustrates this point. In each of the years shown on the graph, U.S. government bonds have had the lowest yields, AAA bonds have been next, and BBB bonds have had the highest yields. The figure also shows that the gaps between yields on the three types of bonds vary over time, indicating that the cost differentials, or yield spreads, fluctuate from year to year. Most recently there was a dramatic increase in the yield spreads between corporate and Treasury securities in the aftermath of the recent financial crisis. In the years since the crisis, these spreads have narrowed as investors have slowly become once again more willing to hold riskier securities. This point is highlighted in Figure 7.5, which gives the yields on the three types of bonds and the yield spreads for AAA and BBB bonds over Treasuries in January 2009 and January 2015.[20] Note first from Figure 7.5 that the risk-free rate, or vertical axis

---

[20]A yield spread is related to, but not identical to, risk premiums on corporate bonds. The true *risk premium* reflects only the difference in expected (and required) returns between two securities that results from differences in their risk. However, yield spreads reflect (1) a true risk premium; (2) a liquidity premium, which reflects the fact that U.S. Treasury bonds are more readily marketable than most corporate bonds; (3) a call premium because most Treasury bonds are not callable, whereas corporate bonds are; and (4) an expected loss differential, which reflects the probability of loss on the corporate bonds. As an example of the last point, suppose the yield to maturity on a BBB bond was 6.0% versus 4.8% on government bonds, but there was a 5% probability of total default loss on the corporate bond. In this case, the *expected* return on the BBB bond would be 0.95(6.0%) + 0.05(0%) = 5.7% and the yield spread would be 0.9%, not the full 1.2 percentage points difference in "promised" yields to maturity.

| FIGURE 7.5 | Relationship between Bond Ratings and Bond Yields, 2009 and 2015 |
|---|---|

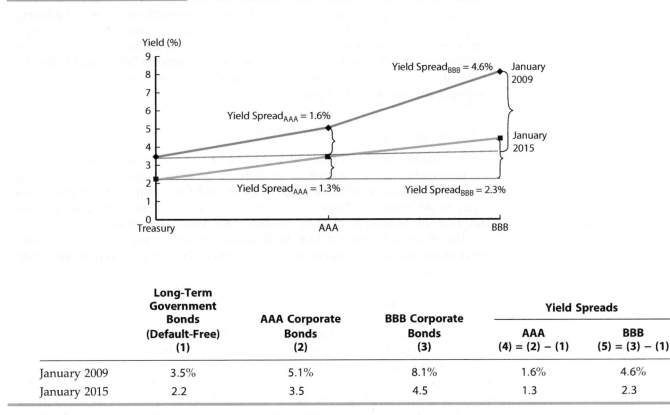

| | Long-Term Government Bonds (Default-Free) (1) | AAA Corporate Bonds (2) | BBB Corporate Bonds (3) | Yield Spreads | |
|---|---|---|---|---|---|
| | | | | AAA (4) = (2) − (1) | BBB (5) = (3) − (1) |
| January 2009 | 3.5% | 5.1% | 8.1% | 1.6% | 4.6% |
| January 2015 | 2.2 | 3.5 | 4.5 | 1.3 | 2.3 |

Source: *Federal Reserve Statistical Release*, Selected Interest Rates (Historical Data), federalreserve.gov/releases/H15/data.htm.

intercept, was lower in January 2015 than it was in January 2009. Second, the slope of the line has decreased. In the crisis period of 2009, investors were both pessimistic and risk-averse, so spreads were quite high. As noted above, these spreads have subsequently fallen as economic conditions have slowly improved.

## Changes in Ratings

Changes in a firm's bond rating affect its ability to borrow funds and its cost of that capital. Rating agencies review outstanding bonds on a periodic basis, occasionally upgrading or downgrading a bond as a result of its issuer's changed circumstances. For example, on March 20, 2015, S&P raised the corporate credit rating of Apartment Investment and Management Co. (AIMCO), one of the largest owners and operators of apartment communities in the United States, from BB+ to BBB−. S&P's decision to upgrade the firm's credit rating was due to its well-diversified apartment portfolio both in terms of geography and price, the expectations of modest rent increases, and a modest decline in its debt levels. At the same time, S&P lowered the corporate credit rating of Sprint Corp., a telecommunications and wireless network company, from BB− to B+. S&P's decision to downgrade the company's credit rating reflected expectations of aggressive price competition in the industry, network performance issues, and the company's high cost structure.

Over the long run, rating agencies have done a reasonably good job of measuring the average credit risk of bonds and of changing ratings whenever there is a significant change in credit quality. However, it is important to understand that ratings do not adjust immediately to changes in credit quality, and in some cases, there can be a considerable lag between a change in credit quality and a change in rating. For example, Enron's bonds still carried an investment-grade rating on a

Friday in December 2001, but the company declared bankruptcy two days later, on Sunday. More recently, the rating agencies have come under considerable fire for significantly underestimating the risks of many of the securities that were backed by subprime mortgages. Many worry that rating agencies don't have the proper incentives to measure risk because they are paid by the issuing firms. In response to these concerns, the Dodd-Frank Act, which was enacted in 2010, directed the SEC to put in place stronger oversight of the rating agencies. The exact nature of this oversight remains a work in progress.[21]

## 7-8C BANKRUPTCY AND REORGANIZATION

When a business becomes *insolvent*, it doesn't have enough cash to meet its interest and principal payments. A decision must then be made whether to dissolve the firm through *liquidation* or to permit it to *reorganize* and thus continue to operate. These issues are addressed in Chapter 7 and Chapter 11 of the federal bankruptcy statutes, and the final decision is made by a federal bankruptcy court judge.

The decision to force a firm to liquidate versus permitting it to reorganize depends on whether the value of the reorganized business is likely to be greater than the value of its assets if they were sold off piecemeal. In a reorganization, the firm's creditors negotiate with management on the terms of a potential reorganization. The reorganization plan may call for *restructuring* the debt, in which case the interest rate may be reduced; the term to maturity, lengthened; or some of the debt may be exchanged for equity. The point of the restructuring is to reduce the financial charges to a level that is supportable by the firm's projected cash flows. Of course, the common stockholders also have to "take a haircut"—they generally see their position diluted as a result of additional shares being given to debtholders in exchange for accepting a reduced amount of debt principal and interest. A trustee may be appointed by the court to oversee the reorganization, but the existing management generally is allowed to retain control.

Liquidation occurs if the company is deemed to be worth more "dead" than "alive." If the bankruptcy court orders a liquidation, assets are auctioned off and the cash obtained is distributed as specified in Chapter 7 of the Bankruptcy Act. Web Appendix 7C provides an illustration of how a firm's assets are distributed after liquidation. For now, you should know that (1) the federal bankruptcy statutes govern reorganization and liquidation. (2) Bankruptcies occur frequently. (3) A priority of the specified claims must be followed when the assets of a liquidated firm are distributed. (4) Bondholders' treatment depends on the terms of the bond. (5) Stockholders generally receive little in reorganizations and nothing in liquidations because the assets are usually worth less than the amount of debt outstanding.

## Self Test

Differentiate between mortgage bonds and debentures.

Name the major rating agencies, and list some factors that affect bond ratings.

Why are bond ratings important to firms and investors?

Do bond ratings adjust immediately to changes in credit quality? Explain.

Differentiate between Chapter 7 liquidations and Chapter 11 reorganizations. In general, when should each be used?

[21]For a recent overview of the SEC's current policy, see the SEC's website www.sec.gov/spotlight /dodd-frank.shtml. Relatedly, a recent *New York Times* article discusses the difficulties involved in drafting these new regulations. Refer to Gretchen Morgenson, "The Stone Unturned: Credit Ratings," *The New York Times* (www.nytimes.com), March 22, 2014.

## 7-9 Bond Markets

Corporate bonds are traded primarily in the over-the-counter market. Most bonds are owned by and traded among large financial institutions (e.g., life insurance companies, mutual funds, hedge funds, and pension funds, all of which deal in very large blocks of securities), and it is relatively easy for over-the-counter bond dealers to arrange the transfer of large blocks of bonds among the relatively few holders of the bonds. It would be more difficult to conduct similar operations in the stock market among the literally millions of large and small stockholders, so a higher percentage of stock trades occur on the exchanges.

A number of leading business publications and websites routinely report key developments in the Treasury, corporate, and municipal bond markets. For example, *The Wall Street Journal* provides a list of bonds whose yield spreads (relative to Treasury securities) widened and narrowed the most in the previous day. Table 7.5 reprints a portion of this data for a given day in March 2015. The table also reports the company's previous day's stock performance, which enables an investor to easily see how recent news has affected both the company's stock price and the interest rate on its debt. As part of its reported data, *The Wall Street Journal* also includes interesting data regarding a

### ACCRUED INTEREST AND THE PRICING OF COUPON BONDS

In this chapter, we have demonstrated the various factors that influence bond prices. But in practice, how much you are willing to pay for a bond also depends on when the next coupon payment is due. Clearly, all else equal, you would be willing to pay more for a bond the day before a coupon is paid, than you would the day after it has been paid. So, if you purchase a bond between coupon payments, you also have to pay what is called *accrued interest*. Accrued interest represents the amount of interest that has accumulated between coupon payments, and it can be calculated as follows:

$$\text{Accrued interest} = \text{Coupon payment} \times \frac{\text{Number of days since the last coupon payment}}{\text{Number of days in the coupon period}}$$

Let's consider, for example, a corporate bond that was issued on March 21, 2015. The bond has an 8% semiannual coupon and a par value of $1,000—which means six months later, on September 21, 2015, the bond will pay its first $40 coupon, and on March 21, 2016, it will pay its second $40 coupon. If you buy the bond on June 8, 2015 (79 days since the bond's last coupon payment on March 21), you will have to pay the seller $17.56 in accrued interest:[22]

$$\text{Accrued interest} = \$40 \times (79/180) = \$17.56$$

In most cases, bonds are quoted net of accrued interest—in what is often referred to as a *clean price*. The actual invoice price you pay (often referred to as the *dirty price*) is the clean price plus accrued interest. In the case of the above bond, let's assume that the bond's nominal yield to maturity is the same as it was when the bond was issued (8%), which means that excluding accrued interest the bond continues to trade at par. It follows that:

$$\text{Clean price (quoted price)} = \$1,000$$
$$\text{Accrued interest} = \$17.56$$
$$\text{Dirty price (invoice price)} = \text{Clean price} + \text{Accrued interest}$$
$$= \$1,017.56$$

You can also use the Accrued Interest function in Excel (ACCRINT) to easily calculate a bond's accrued interest.[23] As a final point, in the examples we use in the text, when we refer to a bond's price we are referring to the bond's quoted, or clean, price. But you should keep in mind that if you buy or sell a bond, the actual price paid or received is the dirty price, which includes accrued interest.

---

[22]If you look up accrued interest in Yahoo! Finance's glossary, you will see more details regarding the payment of accrued interest. Most notably, it points out that accrued interest is calculated slightly differently for corporate and Treasury bonds:

Interest on most bonds and fixed-income securities is paid twice a year. On corporate and municipal bonds, interest is calculated on 30-day months and a 360-day year. For government bonds, interest is calculated on actual days and a 365-day year.

[23]Refer to the Accrued Interest tab on the Chapter 7 Excel Model. In the ACCRINT Excel function for this example, we used Actual days/360 as the day count basis, which is entered as 2.

**TABLE 7.5** *The Wall Street Journal* Corporate Debt Section, March 23, 2015

# Corporate Debt

Price moves by a company's debt in the credit markets sometimes mirror and sometimes anticipate moves in that same company's share price. Here's a look at both for two companies in the news.

## Investment-grade spreads that tightened the most...

| Issuer | Symbol | Coupon (%) | Maturity | SPREAD*, in basis points — Current | One-day change | Last week | STOCK PERFORMANCE Close ($) | %chg |
|---|---|---|---|---|---|---|---|---|
| Nram | NRKLN | 5.625 | June 22, '17 | 81 | −30 | n.a. | ... | ... |
| Toronto-Dominion Bank* | TD | 2.625 | Sept. 10, '18 | 67 | −26 | 56 | 43.29 | 0.53 |
| Commonwealth Bank of Australia | CBAAU | 2.000 | June 18, '19 | 34 | −19 | n.a. | ... | ... |
| ADT | ADT | 6.250 | Oct.15, '21 | 373 | −17 | 374 | 41.63 | 3.17 |
| Johnson & Johnson | JNJ | 5.550 | Aug. 15, '17 | 22 | −15 | 21 | 102.98 | 0.57 |
| Kinder Morgan | KMI | 3.050 | Dec. 1, '19 | 154 | −13 | 142 | 42.15 | 0.07 |
| Zimmer Holdings | ZMH | 3.150 | April 1, '22 | 128 | −13 | 129 | 118.47 | −0.24 |
| Freeport-McMoran | FCX | 3.100 | March 15, '20 | 250 | −10 | 275 | 19.33 | 5.00 |

## ...And spreads that widened the most

| Issuer | Symbol | Coupon (%) | Maturity | Current | One-day change | Last week | Close ($) | %chg |
|---|---|---|---|---|---|---|---|---|
| Pfizer | PFE | 2.100 | May 15, '19 | 48 | 25 | n.a. | 35.05 | 2.34 |
| Imperial Tobacco Finance | IMTLN | 2.050 | Feb. 11, '18 | 95 | 19 | n.a. | ... | ... |
| JPMorgan Chase Bank NA | JPM | 6.000 | Oct. 1, '17 | 102 | 12 | n.a. | ... | ... |
| UBS AG | UBS | 7.625 | Aug 17, '22 | 233 | 12 | n.a. | 19.04 | 1.82 |
| American Honda Finance | HNDA | 1.500 | March 13, '18 | 44 | 11 | 45 | ... | ... |
| Wyndham Worldwide | WYN | 4.250 | March 1, '22 | 163 | 11 | 148 | 91.41 | −0.77 |
| Credit Agricole S.A. | ACAFP | 4.375 | March 17, '25 | 226 | 10 | 228 | ... | ... |
| HSBC Holdings | HSBC | 5.100 | April 5, '21 | 117 | 9 | n.a. | 43.21 | −0.80 |

## High-yield issues with the biggest price increases...

| Issuer | Symbol | Coupon (%) | Maturity | BOND PRICE as % of face value — Current | One-day change | Last week | STOCK PERFORMANCE Close ($) | % chg |
|---|---|---|---|---|---|---|---|---|
| Comstock Resources | CRK | 9.500 | June 15, '20 | 44.250 | 4.50 | 45.000 | 3.33 | 1.52 |
| Swift Energy | SFY | 8.875 | Jan. 15, '20 | 42.000 | 2.00 | 47.000 | 2.17 | 2.36 |
| International Lease Finance | AER | 3.875 | April 15, '18 | 102.500 | 1.25 | 101.000 | ... | ... |
| First Quantum Minerals | FMCN | 7.250 | May 15, '22 | 91.000 | 1.25 | 91.000 | ... | ... |
| Guitar Center | GTRC | 9.625 | April 15, '20 | 72.750 | 1.25 | n.a. | ... | ... |
| JC Penney | JCP | 6.375 | Oct. 15, '36 | 73.500 | 1.13 | 72.625 | 8.02 | 4.16 |
| Linn Energy | LINE | 6.500 | May 15, '19 | 81.750 | 1.13 | 79.500 | 11.31 | 0.62 |
| Beazer Homes USA | BZH | 7.250 | Feb.1, '23 | 95.750 | 1.00 | n.a. | 17.21 | 0.17 |

## ...And with the biggest price decreases

| Issuer | Symbol | Coupon (%) | Maturity | Current | One-day change | Last week | Close ($) | % chg |
|---|---|---|---|---|---|---|---|---|
| Dcp Midstream | DCPMID | 8.125 | Aug. 16, '30 | 103.178 | −1.32 | 104.500 | ... | ... |
| Hexion U.S. Finance | HXN | 9.000 | Nov. 15, '20 | 68.250 | −1.13 | 66.500 | ... | ... |
| General Motors Financial | GM | 4.375 | Sept. 25, '21 | 106.210 | −0.76 | 105.708 | ... | ... |
| Peabody Energy | BTU | 6.250 | Nov. 15, '21 | 67.250 | −0.75 | 67.625 | 6.38 | 3.91 |
| Endeavor Energy Resources | ENDENR | 7.000 | Aug. 15, '21 | 96.000 | −0.75 | 97.000 | ... | ... |
| KB Home* | KBH | 7.000 | Dec. 15, '21 | 101.750 | −0.75 | 100.468 | 14.99 | −1.77 |
| United States Steel | X | 7.375 | April 1, '20 | 100.250 | −0.75 | 102.500 | 24.19 | 4.36 |
| Virgin Media Finance | VMED | 5.750 | Jan. 15, '25 | 102.790 | −0.71 | 104.750 | ... | ... |

*Estimated spread over 2-year, 3-year, 5-year, 10-year or 30-year hot-run Treasury; 100 basis points = one percentage pt; change in spread shown is for Z-spread. Note: Data are for the most active issue of bonds with maturities of two years or more

Sources: MarketAxess Corporate BondTicker; WSJ Market Data Group;
Corporate Debt Section, *The Wall Street Journal* (online.wsj.com), March 24, 2015, p. C8.

number of bond indices and a snapshot of government bond rates in different countries. Other helpful sources include the bond sections of Yahoo! Finance, Google Finance, and Morningstar.com.

## Self*Test*

Why do most bond trades occur in the over-the-counter market?

How is accrued interest calculated?

What is meant by the terms *clean price* and *dirty price*?

# TYING IT ALL TOGETHER

This chapter described the different types of bonds governments and corporations issue, explained how bond prices are established, and discussed how investors estimate rates of return on bonds. It also discussed various types of risks that investors face when they purchase bonds.

When an investor purchases a company's bonds, the investor is providing the company with capital. Moreover, when a firm issues bonds, *the return that investors require on the bonds represents the cost of debt capital to the firm*. This point is extended in Chapter 10, where the ideas developed in this chapter are used to help determine a company's overall cost of capital, which is a basic component of the capital budgeting process.

In recent years, many companies have used zero coupon bonds to raise billions of dollars, and bankruptcy is an important consideration for companies that issue debt and for investors. These two related issues are discussed in detail in Web Appendixes 7A and 7C. Duration, a measurement involving a weighted average of the bond's cash flows, is discussed in Web Appendix 7B. These appendixes can be accessed through the textbook's website.

## Self-Test Questions and Problems

(Solutions Appear in Appendix A)

**ST-1  KEY TERMS**  Define each of the following terms:

    a.  Bond; treasury bond; corporate bond; municipal bond; foreign bond
    b.  Par value; maturity date; original maturity
    c.  Coupon payment; coupon interest rate
    d.  Fixed-rate bond; floating-rate bond; zero coupon bond; original issue discount (OID) bond
    e.  Call provision; sinking fund provision
    f.  Convertible bond; warrant; putable bond; income bond; indexed, or purchasing power, bond
    g.  Discount bond; premium bond
    h.  Yield to maturity (YTM); yield to call (YTC)

i.   Current yield; capital gains yield; total return
j.   Price risk; reinvestment risk; investment horizon; default risk; duration
k.   Mortgage bond; indenture; debenture; subordinated debenture
l.   Investment-grade bond; junk bond

**ST-2**   **BOND VALUATION**   The Pennington Corporation issued a new series of bonds on January 1, 1992. The bonds were sold at par ($1,000); had a 12% coupon; and mature in 30 years, on December 31, 2021. Coupon payments are made semiannually (on June 30 and December 31).

a.   What was the YTM on January 1, 1992?
b.   What was the price of the bonds on January 1, 1997, 5 years later, assuming that interest rates had fallen to 10%?
c.   Find the current yield, capital gains yield, and total return on January 1, 1997, given the price as determined in part b.
d.   On July 1, 2015, 6½ years before maturity, Pennington's bonds sold for $916.42. What were the YTM, the current yield, the capital gains yield, and the total return at that time?
e.   Now assume that you plan to purchase an outstanding Pennington bond on March 1, 2015, when the going rate of interest given its risk was 15.5%. How large a check must you write to complete the transaction? (This is a difficult question.)

**ST-3**   **SINKING FUND**   The Vancouver Development Company (VDC) is planning to sell a $100 million, 10-year, 12%, semiannual payment bond issue. Provisions for a sinking fund to retire the issue over its life will be included in the indenture. Sinking fund payments will be made at the end of each year, and each payment must be sufficient to retire 10% of the original amount of the issue. The last sinking fund payment will retire the last of the bonds. The bonds to be retired each period can be purchased on the open market or obtained by calling up to 5% of the original issue at par, at VDC's option.

a.   How large must each sinking fund payment be if the company (1) uses the option to call bonds at par or (2) decides to buy bonds on the open market? For part (2), you can only answer in words.
b.   What will happen to debt service requirements per year associated with this issue over its 10-year life?
c.   Now consider an alternative plan where VDC sets up its sinking fund so that *equal annual amounts* are paid into a sinking fund trust held by a bank, with the proceeds being used to buy government bonds that are expected to pay 7% annual interest. The payments, plus accumulated interest, must total $100 million at the end of 10 years, when the proceeds will be used to retire the issue. How large must the annual sinking fund payments be? Is this amount known with certainty, or might it be higher or lower?
d.   What are the annual cash requirements for covering bond service costs under the trusteeship arrangement described in part c? (*Note:* Interest must be paid on Vancouver's outstanding bonds but not on bonds that have been retired.) Assume level interest rates for purposes of answering this question.
e.   What would have to happen to interest rates to cause the company to buy bonds on the open market rather than call them under the plan where some bonds are retired each year?

# Questions

7-1   A sinking fund can be set up in one of two ways:

- The corporation makes annual payments to the trustee, who invests the proceeds in securities (frequently government bonds) and uses the accumulated total to retire the bond issue at maturity.
- The trustee uses the annual payments to retire a portion of the issue each year, calling a given percentage of the issue by a lottery and paying a specified price per bond or buying bonds on the open market, whichever is cheaper.

What are the advantages and disadvantages of each procedure from the viewpoint of the firm and the bondholders?

7-2  Can the following equation be used to find the value of a bond with N years to maturity that pays interest once a year? Assume that the bond was issued several years ago.

$$V_B = \sum_{t=1}^{N} \frac{\text{Annual interest}}{(1 + r_d)^t} + \frac{\text{Par value}}{(1 + r_d)^N}$$

7-3  The values of outstanding bonds change whenever the going rate of interest changes. In general, short-term interest rates are more volatile than long-term interest rates. Therefore, short-term bond prices are more sensitive to interest rate changes than are long-term bond prices. Is that statement true or false? Explain. (Hint: Make up a "reasonable" example based on a 1-year and a 20-year bond to help answer the question.)

7-4  If interest rates rise after a bond issue, what will happen to the bond's price and YTM? Does the time to maturity affect the extent to which interest rate changes affect the bond's price? (Again, an example might help you answer this question.)

7-5  Discuss the following statement: A bond's yield to maturity is the bond's promised rate of return, which equals its expected rate of return.

7-6  If you buy a *callable* bond and interest rates decline, will the value of your bond rise by as much as it would have risen if the bond had not been callable? Explain.

7-7  Assume that you have a short investment horizon (less than 1 year). You are considering two investments: a 1-year Treasury security and a 20-year Treasury security. Which of the two investments would you view as being riskier? Explain.

7-8  Indicate whether each of the following actions will increase or decrease a bond's yield to maturity:
a.  The bond's price increases.
b.  The bond is downgraded by the rating agencies.
c.  A change in the bankruptcy code makes it more difficult for bondholders to receive payments in the event the firm declares bankruptcy.
d.  The economy seems to be shifting from a boom to a recession. Discuss the effects of the firm's credit strength in your answer.
e.  Investors learn that the bonds are subordinated to another debt issue.

7-9  Why is a call provision advantageous to a bond issuer? When would the issuer be likely to initiate a refunding call?

7-10  Are securities that provide for a sinking fund more or less risky from the bondholder's perspective than those without this type of provision? Explain.

7-11  What's the difference between a call for sinking fund purposes and a refunding call?

7-12  Why are convertibles and bonds with warrants typically offered with lower coupons than similarly rated straight bonds?

7-13  Explain whether the following statement is true or false: Only weak companies issue debentures.

7-14  Would the yield spread on a corporate bond over a Treasury bond with the same maturity tend to become wider or narrower if the economy appeared to be heading toward a recession? Would the change in the spread for a given company be affected by the firm's credit strength? Explain.

7-15  A bond's expected return is sometimes estimated by its YTM and sometimes by its YTC. Under what conditions would the YTM provide a better estimate, and when would the YTC be better?

7-16  Which of the following bonds has the most price risk? Explain your answer. (Hint: Refer to Table 7.2.)
a.  7-year bonds with a 5% coupon.
b.  1-year bonds with a 12% coupon.
c.  3-year bonds with a 5% coupon.
d.  15-year zero coupon bonds.
e.  15-year bonds with a 10% coupon.

7-17 Which of the bonds has the most reinvestment risk? Explain your answer. (Hint: Refer to Table 7.2.)

    a. 7-year bonds with a 5% coupon.

    b. 1-year bonds with a 12% coupon.

    c. 3-year bonds with a 5% coupon.

    d. 15-year zero coupon bonds.

    e. 15-year bonds with a 10% coupon.

# Problems

**Easy Problems 1–4**

**7-1**   **BOND VALUATION**  Madsen Motors's bonds have 23 years remaining to maturity. Interest is paid annually; they have a $1,000 par value; the coupon interest rate is 9%; and the yield to maturity is 11%. What is the bond's current market price?

**7-2**   **YIELD TO MATURITY AND FUTURE PRICE**  A bond has a $1,000 par value, 12 years to maturity, and an 8% annual coupon and sells for $980.

    a. What is its yield to maturity (YTM)?

    b. Assume that the yield to maturity remains constant for the next three years. What will the price be 3 years from today?

**7-3**   **BOND VALUATION**  Nesmith Corporation's outstanding bonds have a $1,000 par value, an 8% semiannual coupon, 14 years to maturity, and an 11% YTM. What is the bond's price?

**7-4**   **YIELD TO MATURITY**  A firm's bonds have a maturity of 8 years with a $1,000 face value, have an 11% semiannual coupon, are callable in 4 years at $1,154, and currently sell at a price of $1,283.09. What are their nominal yield to maturity and their nominal yield to call? What return should investors expect to earn on these bonds?

**Intermediate Problems 5–14**

**7-5**   **BOND VALUATION**  An investor has two bonds in his portfolio that have a face value of $1,000 and pay an 11% annual coupon. Bond L matures in 12 years, while Bond S matures in 1 year.

    a. What will the value of each bond be if the going interest rate is 6%, 8%, and 12%? Assume that only one more interest payment is to be made on Bond S at its maturity and that 12 more payments are to be made on Bond L.

    b. Why does the longer-term bond's price vary more than the price of the shorter-term bond when interest rates change?

**7-6**   **BOND VALUATION**  An investor has two bonds in her portfolio, Bond C and Bond Z. Each bond matures in 4 years, has a face value of $1,000, and has a yield to maturity of 8.2%. Bond C pays an 11.5% annual coupon, while Bond Z is a zero coupon bond.

    a. Assuming that the yield to maturity of each bond remains at 8.2% over the next 4 years, calculate the price of the bonds at each of the following years to maturity:

| Years to Maturity | Price of Bond C | Price of Bond Z |
|---|---|---|
| 4 | | |
| 3 | | |
| 2 | | |
| 1 | | |
| 0 | | |

    b. Plot the time path of prices for each bond.

**7-7**   **INTEREST RATE SENSITIVITY**  An investor purchased the following 5 bonds. Each bond had a par value of $1,000 and an 8% yield to maturity on the purchase day. Immediately after the investor purchased them, interest rates fell, and each then had a new YTM of 7%. What is the percentage change in price for each bond after the decline in interest rates? Fill in the following table:

| Bond | Price @8% | Price @7% | Percentage Change |
|---|---|---|---|
| 10-year, 10% annual coupon | _____ | _____ | _____ |
| 10-year zero | _____ | _____ | _____ |
| 5-year zero | _____ | _____ | _____ |
| 30-year zero | _____ | _____ | _____ |
| $100 perpetuity | _____ | _____ | _____ |

**7-8** **YIELD TO CALL** Seven years ago the Templeton Company issued 20-year bonds with an 11% annual coupon rate at their $1,000 par value. The bonds had a 7.5% call premium, with 5 years of call protection. Today Templeton called the bonds. Compute the realized rate of return for an investor who purchased the bonds when they were issued and held them until they were called. Explain why the investor should or should not be happy that Templeton called them.

**7-9** **YIELD TO MATURITY** Harrimon Industries bonds have 6 years left to maturity. Interest is paid annually, and the bonds have a $1,000 par value and a coupon rate of 10%.

a. What is the yield to maturity at a current market price of (1) $865 and (2) $1,166?
b. Would you pay $865 for each bond if you thought that a "fair" market interest rate for such bonds was 12%—that is, if $r_d = 12\%$? Explain your answer.

**7-10** **CURRENT YIELD, CAPITAL GAINS YIELD, AND YIELD TO MATURITY** Pelzer Printing Inc. has bonds outstanding with 9 years left to maturity. The bonds have a 9% annual coupon rate and were issued 1 year ago at their par value of $1,000. However, due to changes in interest rates, the bond's market price has fallen to $910.30. The capital gains yield last year was −8.97%.

a. What is the yield to maturity?
b. For the coming year, what are the expected current and capital gains yields? (Hint: Refer to footnote 7 for the definition of the current yield and to Table 7.1.)
c. Will the actual realized yields be equal to the expected yields if interest rates change? If not, how will they differ?

**7-11** **BOND YIELDS** Last year Carson Industries issued a 10-year, 13% semiannual coupon bond at its par value of $1,000. Currently, the bond can be called in 6 years at a price of $1,065 and it sells for $1,200.

a. What are the bond's nominal yield to maturity and its nominal yield to call? Would an investor be more likely to earn the YTM or the YTC?
b. What is the current yield? Is this yield affected by whether the bond is likely to be called? (Hint: Refer to footnote 7 for the definition of the current yield and to Table 7.1.)
c. What is the expected capital gains (or loss) yield for the coming year? Is this yield dependent on whether the bond is expected to be called? Explain your answer.

**7-12** **YIELD TO CALL** It is now January 1, 2016, and you are considering the purchase of an outstanding bond that was issued on January 1, 2014. It has an 8% annual coupon and had a 30-year original maturity. (It matures on December 31, 2043.) There is 5 years of call protection (until December 31, 2018), after which time it can be called at 108—that is, at 108% of par, or $1,080. Interest rates have declined since it was issued, and it is now selling at 119.12% of par, or $1,191.20.

a. What is the yield to maturity? What is the yield to call?
b. If you bought this bond, which return would you actually earn? Explain your reasoning.
c. Suppose the bond had been selling at a discount rather than a premium. Would the yield to maturity have been the most likely return, or would the yield to call have been most likely?

**7-13** **PRICE AND YIELD** A 7% semiannual coupon bond matures in 4 years. The bond has a face value of $1,000 and a current yield of 7.5401%. What are the bond's price and YTM? (Hint: Refer to footnote 7 for the definition of the current yield and to Table 7.1.)

**7-14  EXPECTED INTEREST RATE**   Lourdes Corporation's 12% coupon rate, semiannual payment, $1,000 par value bonds, which mature in 25 years, are callable 6 years from today at $1,025. They sell at a price of $1,278.56, and the yield curve is flat. Assume that interest rates are expected to remain at their current level.

a.  What is the best estimate of these bonds' remaining life?
b.  If Lourdes plans to raise additional capital and wants to use debt financing, what coupon rate would it have to set in order to issue new bonds at par?

**Challenging Problems 15–18**

**7-15  BOND VALUATION**   Bond X is noncallable and has 20 years to maturity, an 8% annual coupon, and a $1,000 par value. Your required return on Bond X is 9%; if you buy it, you plan to hold it for 5 years. You (and the market) have expectations that in 5 years, the yield to maturity on a 15-year bond with similar risk will be 7.5%. How much should you be willing to pay for Bond X today? (Hint: You will need to know how much the bond will be worth at the end of 5 years.)

**7-16  BOND VALUATION**   You are considering a 10-year, $1,000 par value bond. Its coupon rate is 8%, and interest is paid semiannually. If you require an "effective" annual interest rate (not a nominal rate) of 7.1225%, how much should you be willing to pay for the bond?

**7-17  BOND RETURNS**   Last year Janet purchased a $1,000 face value corporate bond with an 8% annual coupon rate and a 15-year maturity. At the time of the purchase, it had an expected yield to maturity of 10.45%. If Janet sold the bond today for $820.17, what rate of return would she have earned for the past year?

**7-18  YIELD TO MATURITY AND YIELD TO CALL**   Kempton Enterprises has bonds outstanding with a $1,000 face value and 10 years left until maturity. They have an 11% annual coupon payment, and their current price is $1,185. The bonds may be called in 5 years at 109% of face value (Call price = $1,090).

a.  What is the yield to maturity?
b.  What is the yield to call if they are called in 5 years?
c.  Which yield might investors expect to earn on these bonds? Why?
d.  The bond's indenture indicates that the call provision gives the firm the right to call the bonds at the end of each year beginning in Year 5. In Year 5, the bonds may be called at 109% of face value; but in each of the next 4 years, the call percentage will decline by 1%. Thus, in Year 6, they may be called at 108% of face value; in Year 7, they may be called at 107% of face value; and so forth. If the yield curve is horizontal and interest rates remain at their current level, when is the latest that investors might expect the firm to call the bonds?

## Comprehensive/Spreadsheet Problem

**7-19  BOND VALUATION**   Clifford Clark is a recent retiree who is interested in investing some of his savings in corporate bonds. His financial planner has suggested the following bonds:

- Bond A has a 7% annual coupon, matures in 12 years, and has a $1,000 face value.
- Bond B has a 9% annual coupon, matures in 12 years, and has a $1,000 face value.
- Bond C has an 11% annual coupon, matures in 12 years, and has a $1,000 face value.

Each bond has a yield to maturity of 9%.

a.  Before calculating the prices of the bonds, indicate whether each bond is trading at a premium, at a discount, or at par.
b.  Calculate the price of each of the three bonds.
c.  Calculate the current yield for each of the three bonds. (Hint: Refer to footnote 7 for the definition of the current yield and to Table 7.1.)
d.  If the yield to maturity for each bond remains at 9%, what will be the price of each bond 1 year from now? What is the expected capital gains yield for each bond? What is the expected total return for each bond?

e. Mr. Clark is considering another bond, Bond D. It has an 8% semiannual coupon and a $1,000 face value (i.e., it pays a $40 coupon every 6 months). Bond D is scheduled to mature in 9 years and has a price of $1,150. It is also callable in 5 years at a call price of $1,040.

   1. What is the bond's nominal yield to maturity?

   2. What is the bond's nominal yield to call?

   3. If Mr. Clark were to purchase this bond, would he be more likely to receive the yield to maturity or yield to call? Explain your answer.

f. Explain briefly the difference between price risk and reinvestment risk. Which of the following bonds has the most price risk? Which has the most reinvestment risk?

   - A 1-year bond with a 9% annual coupon
   - A 5-year bond with a 9% annual coupon
   - A 5-year bond with a zero coupon
   - A 10-year bond with a 9% annual coupon
   - A 10-year bond with a zero coupon

g. Only do this part if you are using a spreadsheet. Calculate the price of each bond (A, B, and C) at the end of each year until maturity, assuming interest rates remain constant. Create a graph showing the time path of each bond's value, similar to that shown in Figure 7.2.

   1. What is the expected interest yield for each bond in each year?

   2. What is the expected capital gains yield for each bond in each year?

   3. What is the total return for each bond in each year?

## INTEGRATED CASE

**WESTERN MONEY MANAGEMENT INC.**

**7-20    BOND VALUATION**   Robert Black and Carol Alvarez are vice presidents of Western Money Management and codirectors of the company's pension fund management division. A major new client, the California League of Cities, has requested that Western present an investment seminar to the mayors of the represented cities. Black and Alvarez, who will make the presentation, have asked you to help them by answering the following questions.

a. What are a bond's key features?

b. What are call provisions and sinking fund provisions? Do these provisions make bonds more or less risky?

c. How is the value of any asset whose value is based on expected future cash flows determined?

d. How is a bond's value determined? What is the value of a 10-year, $1,000 par value bond with a 10% annual coupon if its required return is 10%?

e. 1. What is the value of a 13% coupon bond that is otherwise identical to the bond described in part d? Would we now have a discount or a premium bond?

   2. What is the value of a 7% coupon bond with these characteristics? Would we now have a discount or premium bond?

   3. What would happen to the values of the 7%, 10%, and 13% coupon bonds over time if the required return remained at 10%? (Hint: With a financial calculator, enter PMT, I/YR, FV, and N; then change (override) N to see what happens to the PV as it approaches maturity.)

f. 1. What is the yield to maturity on a 10-year, 9% annual coupon, $1,000 par value bond that sells for $887.00? That sells for $1,134.20? What does the fact that it sells at a discount or at a premium tell you about the relationship between $r_d$ and the coupon rate?

   2. What are the total return, the current yield, and the capital gains yield for the discount bond? Assume that it is held to maturity, and the company does not default on it. (Hint: Refer to footnote 7 for the definition of the current yield and to Table 7.1.)

g. What is *price risk*? Which has more price risk, an annual payment 1-year bond or a 10-year bond? Why?

h. What is *reinvestment risk*? Which has more reinvestment risk, a 1-year bond or a 10-year bond?

i. How does the equation for valuing a bond change if semiannual payments are made? Find the value of a 10-year, semiannual payment, 10% coupon bond if nominal $r_d = 13\%$.

j. Suppose for $1,000 you could buy a 10%, 10-year, annual payment bond or a 10%, 10-year, semiannual payment bond. They are equally risky. Which would you prefer? If $1,000 is the proper price for the semiannual bond, what is the equilibrium price for the annual payment bond?

k. Suppose a 10-year, 10% semiannual coupon bond with a par value of $1,000 is currently selling for $1,135.90, producing a nominal yield to maturity of 8%. However, it can be called after 4 years for $1,050.

    1. What is the bond's *nominal yield to call (YTC)*?

    2. If you bought this bond, would you be more likely to earn the YTM or the YTC? Why?

l. Does the yield to maturity represent the promised or expected return on the bond? Explain.

m. These bonds were rated AA– by S&P. Would you consider them investment-grade or junk bonds?

n. What factors determine a company's bond rating?

o. If this firm were to default on the bonds, would the company be immediately liquidated? Would the bondholders be assured of receiving all of their promised payments? Explain.

# TAKING A CLOSER LOOK

## USING YAHOO! FINANCE'S BONDS CENTER TO UNDERSTAND THE IMPACT OF INTEREST RATES ON BOND VALUATION

*Use online resources to work on this chapter's questions. Please note that website information changes over time, and these changes may limit your ability to answer some of these questions.*

In Chapter 7, we looked at how interest rates impact bond valuation. The questions provided below are designed to help you understand how bond values are affected by different interest rate levels. Here, we will access the Internet website Yahoo! Finance Bonds Center (finance.yahoo.com/bonds) to answer these questions.

1. Once you've accessed the Yahoo! Finance Bonds Center screen, click the "Bond Screener" tab. Run a quick screen where you select corporate bonds with a 10-year maturity. Looking at this set of bonds, controlling for other factors, describe briefly how the yields to maturity of the bonds vary according to bond rating and whether the bonds are callable.

2. Click the name of any selected bond. Note the date that the bond was issued, its coupon rate, current price, yield to maturity, current yield, and whether it is callable. Based on this information, has the bond's yield to maturity increased, decreased, or stayed the same since it was issued? Is the bond currently selling at a discount, at par, or at a premium?

3. Looking at the bond issue selected, why are the current yield and yield to maturity numbers different? Briefly explain in words the difference between these two terms.

## Solutions to Self-Test Questions and Problems

**ST-1**   Refer to the marginal glossary definitions or relevant chapter sections to check your responses.

**ST-2**   a. Pennington's bonds were sold at par; therefore, the original YTM equaled the coupon rate of 12%.

b. $$V_B = \sum_{t=1}^{50} \frac{\$120/2}{\left(1 + \frac{0.10}{2}\right)^t} + \frac{\$1,000}{\left(1 + \frac{0.10}{2}\right)^{50}}$$

With a financial calculator, input the following: N = 50, I/YR = 5, PMT = 60, FV = 1000, and PV = ? Solve for PV = $1,182.56.

c. **Current yield = Annual coupon payment/Price**
   $$= \$120/\$1,182.56$$
   $$= 0.1015 = 10.15\%$$

   **Capital gains yield = Total yield − Current yield**
   $$= 10\% - 10.15\% = -0.15\%$$

   **Total return = YTM = 10%**

d. With a financial calculator, input the following: N = 13, PV = −916.42, PMT = 60, FV = 1000, and $r_d/2$ = I/YR =? Calculator solution = $r_d/2$ = 7.00%; therefore, $r_d$ = YTM = 14.00%.

   **Current yield = $120/$916.42 = 13.09%**
   **Capital gains yield = 14% − 13.09% = 0.91%**
   **Total return = YTM = 14.00%**

e. The following time line illustrates the years to maturity of the bond:

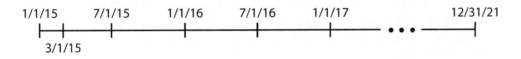

Thus, on March 1, 2015, there were 13 2/3 periods left before the bond matured. Bond traders actually use the following procedure to determine the price of the bond:

(1) Find the price of the bond on the next coupon date, July 1, 2015. Using a financial calculator, input N = 13, I/YR = 7.75, PMT = 60, FV = 1000, and PV = ? Solve for PV = $859.76.

(2) Add the coupon, $60, to the bond price to get the total value of the bond on the next interest payment date: $859.76 + $60.00 = $919.76.

(3) Discount this total value back to the purchase date (March 1, 2015). Using a financial calculator, input N = 4/6, I/YR = 7.75, PMT = 0, FV = 919.76, and PV = ? Solve for PV = $875.11.

(4) Therefore, you would have written a check for $875.11 to complete the transaction. Of this amount, $20 = (1/3)($60) would represent accrued interest and $855.11 would represent the bond's basic value. This breakdown would affect both your taxes and those of the seller.

(5) This problem could be solved *very* easily using a spreadsheet or a financial calculator with a bond valuation function, such as the HP-12C or the HP-17BII. This is explained in the calculator manual under the heading, "Bond Calculations."

**ST-3** a. (1) $100,000,000/10 = $10,000,000 per year, or $5 million each 6 months.

(2) VDC will purchase bonds on the open market if they're selling at less than par. So, the sinking fund payment will be less than $5,000,000 each period.

b. The debt service requirements will decline. As the amount of bonds outstanding declines, so will the interest requirements (amounts given in millions of dollars). If the bonds are called at par, the total bond service payments are calculated as follows:

| Semiannual Payment Period (1) | Sinking Fund Payment (2) | Outstanding Bonds on which Interest Is Paid (3) | Interest Payment[a] (4) | Total Debt Service (2) + (4) = (5) |
|---|---|---|---|---|
| 1 | $5 | $100 | $6.0 | $11.0 |
| 2 | 5 | 95 | 5.7 | 10.7 |
| 3 | 5 | 90 | 5.4 | 10.4 |
| ⋮ | ⋮ | ⋮ | ⋮ | ⋮ |
| 20 | 5 | 5 | 0.3 | 5.3 |

[a]Interest is calculated as (0.5)(0.12)(column 3); for example, Interest in Period 2 = (0.5)(0.12)($95) = $5.7.

The company's total cash bond service requirement will be $21.7 million per year for the first year. For both options, interest will decline by 0.12($10,000,000) = $1,200,000 per year for the remaining years. The total debt service requirement for the open market purchases cannot be precisely determined, but the amounts would be less than what's shown in column 5 of the table above.

c. Here we have a 10-year 7% annuity whose compound value is $100 million, and we are seeking the annual payment, PMT. The solution can be obtained with a financial calculator. Input $N = 10$, $I/YR = 7$, $PV = 0$, and $FV = 100000000$, and press the PMT key to obtain $7,237,750. This amount is not known with certainty as interest rates over time will change, so the amount could be higher (if interest rates fall) or lower (if interest rates rise).

d. Annual debt service costs will be $100,000,000(0.12) + $7,237,750 = $19,237,750.

e. If interest rates rose, causing the bond's price to fall, the company would use open market purchases. This would reduce its debt service requirements.

## Answers to Selected End-of-Chapter Problems

**7-2** a. 8.27%
b. $983.38

**7-4** YTM = $6.42%; YTC = 6.32%; most likely yield = 6.32%

**7-6** a. Bond C: $1,108.82; $1,084.74; $1,058.69; $1,030.50; $1,000.00
Bond Z: $729.61; $789.44; $854.17; $924.21; $1,000.00

**7-8** 11.75%

**7-10** a. YTM = 10.595%
b. CY = 9.887%; CGY = 0.708%

**7-12** a. YTM = 6.50%; YTC = 3.72%

**7-14** a. 6 yrs.
b. YTC = 6.64%

**7-16** $1,071.06

**7-18** a. YTM = 8.22%
b. YTC = 7.91%
c. YTC = 7.91%
d. Yr. 7; YTC = 8.20%

## Selected Equations and Tables

$$\text{Bond's value} = V_B = \frac{INT}{(1 + r_d)^1} + \frac{INT}{(1 + r_d)^2} + \cdots + \frac{INT}{(1 + r_d)^N} + \frac{M}{(1 + r_d)^N}$$

$$= \sum_{t=1}^{N} \frac{INT}{(1 + r_d)^t} + \frac{M}{(1 + r_d)^N}$$

$$\text{Price of callable bond} = \sum_{t=1}^{N} \frac{INT}{(1 + r_d)^t} + \frac{\text{Call price}}{(1 + r_d)^N}$$

$$V_B = \sum_{t=1}^{2N} \frac{INT/2}{(1 + r_d/2)^t} + \frac{M}{(1 + r_d/2)^{2N}}$$

$$\text{Accrued interest} = \text{Coupon payment} \times \left( \frac{\begin{array}{c}\text{Number of days since} \\ \text{last coupon payment}\end{array}}{\begin{array}{c}\text{Number of days} \\ \text{in coupon period}\end{array}} \right)$$

$$\text{Dirty price} = \text{Clean price} + \text{Accrued interest}$$
$$\text{Invoice price} = \text{Quoted price} + \text{Accrued interest}$$

# Chapter 8

# Risk and Rates of Return

CHAPTER

rry Vine/Blend Images/Alamy

## Managing Risk in Difficult Times

Over the past few decades, the U.S. stock market has seen more than its share of ups and downs. To give you a quick sense of the market's recent performance, consider that in April 1993, the S&P 500 index had a value around 440. In the following seven years, the market roared to a high of 1,516. Slightly more than two years later—following the 2001 terrorist attacks and the resulting recession—the index had lost nearly half of its value. Five bumpy years later, in September 2007, the market finally recovered back to where it was trading near its old highs above 1,500. But then the housing market collapsed and the financial crisis began, and by March 2009, the S&P 500 plunged to a level below 700. A little more than six years later, in March 2015, the market stood at a new record high above 2,100.

In many cases, the returns on individual stocks have been even more volatile than the S&P 500 index. For example, in a recent two-year

period, Netflix Inc.'s stock rose more than 600%—from a price below $40 per share in July 2009 to more than $290 per share in July 2011. But following this incredible run-up, the stock's price subsequently plummeted to $54 per share just a little over a year later in August 2012. Afterwards, the stock took off once again, and by early 2015, Netflix's stock was trading above $480 per share.

As we see in this chapter, one way to reduce the risk of investing is to hold a diversified portfolio of stocks. One approach is to invest in mutual funds or exchange traded funds (ETFs) that track the overall market. An even broader diversification strategy is to invest in a wide range of global assets including stocks, bonds, commodities, and real estate. Although many U.S. investors are reluctant to invest in foreign stocks and bonds, many foreign markets have performed well, and their performance has not been perfectly correlated with U.S. markets. Therefore, global diversification offers U.S. investors an opportunity to increase returns and at the same time reduce risk. To be sure, however, these other investments can also be quite risky at times.

Although many investors are trained to expect some risk, the huge and dramatic swings we have seen in recent years have been unnerving to many. Consequently, there has been increased interest in understanding these extreme price swings. In his bestselling book, *The Black Swan,* Professor Nassim Taleb defines a Black Swan event as:

> … a highly improbable event with three principal characteristics. It is unpredictable, it carries a massive impact, and after the fact, we concoct an explanation that makes it appear less random, and more predictable than it was.

Over the past decade, we have had a series of what could be characterized as Black Swan events—for example, the rise of Google, the terrorist attacks in 2001, the financial crisis, and the tsunami disaster in Japan. Arguably, these events have contributed largely to the high levels of volatility in the overall stock market.

Although diversification is important, the events of the past decade show all too well that even fully diversified investors can suffer large losses in short periods of time. As a result, many have become more conservative with their money and are holding larger amounts of cash and other safe assets in their portfolios. Many are convinced that these investors won't return to the market unless they are reasonably assured that the expected returns are enough to justify the risks of stocks and other more speculative investments.

In this chapter, we explore these ideas in more detail, and specifically consider the different types of risk that investors face, the benefits of diversification, and the fundamental trade-off between risk and return. After studying the concepts in this chapter, you should be able to avoid some of the investing pitfalls that a number of investors have faced recently in their quest for wealth.

Source: Nassim Nicholas Taleb, *The Black Swan: The Impact of the Highly Improbable* (New York: Random House, 2007).

# PUTTING THINGS IN PERSPECTIVE

We start this chapter from the basic premise that investors like returns and dislike risk; hence, they will invest in risky assets only if those assets offer higher expected returns. We define what risk means as it relates to investments, examine procedures that are used to measure risk, and discuss the relationship between risk and return. Investors should understand these concepts, as should corporate managers as they develop the plans that will shape their firms' futures.

Risk can be measured in different ways, and different conclusions about an asset's riskiness can be reached depending on the measure used. Risk analysis can be confusing, but it will help if you keep the following points in mind:

1. All business assets are expected to produce *cash flows,* and the riskiness of an asset is based on the riskiness of its cash flows. The riskier the cash flows, the riskier the asset.

2. Assets can be categorized as *financial assets,* especially stocks and bonds, and as *real assets,* such as trucks, machines, and whole businesses. In theory, risk analysis for all types of assets is similar, and the same fundamental concepts apply to all assets. However, in practice, differences in the types of available data lead to different procedures for stocks, bonds, and real assets. Our focus in this chapter is on financial assets, especially stocks. We considered bonds in Chapter 7, and we take up real assets in the capital budgeting chapters, especially Chapter 12.

3. A stock's risk can be considered in two ways: (a) on a *stand-alone, or single-stock, basis,* or (b) in a *portfolio context,* where a number of stocks are

combined and their consolidated cash flows are analyzed.[1] There is an important difference between stand-alone and portfolio risk, and a stock that has a great deal of risk held by itself may be much less risky when held as part of a larger portfolio.

4. In a portfolio context, a stock's risk can be divided into two components: (a) *diversifiable risk,* which can be diversified away and is thus of little concern to diversified investors, and (b) *market risk,* which reflects the risk of a general stock market decline and cannot be eliminated by diversification (hence, does concern investors). Only market risk is *relevant* to rational investors because diversifiable risk can and will be eliminated.

5. A stock with high market risk must offer a relatively high expected rate of return to attract investors. Investors in general are *averse to risk,* so they will not buy risky assets unless they are compensated with high expected returns.

6. If investors, on average, think a stock's expected return is too low to compensate for its risk, they will start selling it, driving down its price and boosting its expected return. Conversely, if the expected return on a stock is more than enough to compensate for the risk, people will start buying it, raising its price and thus lowering its expected return. The stock will be in equilibrium, with neither buying nor selling pressure, when its expected return is exactly sufficient to compensate for its risk.

7. Stand-alone risk, the topic of Section 8-2, is important in stock analysis primarily as a lead-in to portfolio risk analysis. However, stand-alone risk is extremely important when analyzing real assets such as capital budgeting projects.

When you finish this chapter, you should be able to:

- Explain the difference between stand-alone risk and risk in a portfolio context.
- Describe how risk aversion affects a stock's required rate of return.
- Discuss the difference between diversifiable risk and market risk, and explain how each type of risk affects well-diversified investors.
- Describe what the CAPM is, and illustrate how it can be used to estimate a stock's required rate of return.
- Discuss how changes in the general stock and bond markets could lead to changes in the required rate of return on a firm's stock.
- Discuss how changes in a firm's operations might lead to changes in the required rate of return on the firm's stock.

## 8-1 The Risk-Return Trade-Off

As we mention above, we start from a very simple premise that investors like returns and they dislike risk. This premise suggests that there is a fundamental trade-off between risk and return: to entice investors to take on more risk, you have to provide them with higher expected returns. This trade-off is illustrated in Figure 8.1.

The slope of the risk-return line in panel a of Figure 8.1 indicates how much additional return an individual investor requires in order to take on a higher level

---

[1]A *portfolio* is a collection of investment securities. If you owned stock in General Motors, Exxon Mobil, and IBM, you would be holding a three-stock portfolio. Because diversification lowers risk without sacrificing much, if any, expected return, most stocks are held in portfolios.

**FIGURE 8.1**     The Trade-Off between Risk and Return

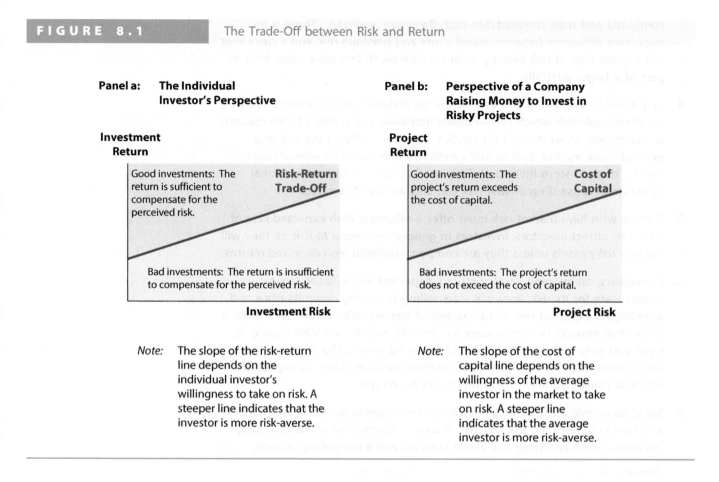

*Note:* The slope of the risk-return line depends on the individual investor's willingness to take on risk. A steeper line indicates that the investor is more risk-averse.

*Note:* The slope of the cost of capital line depends on the willingness of the average investor in the market to take on risk. A steeper line indicates that the average investor is more risk-averse.

of risk. A steeper line suggests that an investor is very averse to taking on risk, whereas a flatter line would suggest that the investor is more comfortable bearing risk. Not surprisingly, investors who are less comfortable bearing risk tend to gravitate toward lower-risk investments, while investors with a greater-risk appetite tend to put more of their money into higher-risk, higher-return investments. The average investor's willingness to take on risk also varies over time. For example, prior to the recent financial crisis, an increasing number of investors were putting their money into riskier investments that included high-growth stocks, junk bonds, and emerging market funds. In the aftermath of the crisis, there was a tremendous "flight to quality" where investors rapidly moved away from riskier investments and instead flocked toward safer investments such as Treasury securities and money market funds. At any point in time, an investor's goal should be to earn returns that are more than sufficient to compensate for the perceived risk of the investment—in other words, getting above the risk-return trade-off line illustrated in panel a of Figure 8.1.

The trade-off between risk and return is also an important concept for companies trying to create value for their shareholders. Panel b of Figure 8.1 suggests that if a company is investing in riskier projects, it must offer its investors (both bond-holders and stockholders) higher expected returns. As we showed in Chapter 7, higher-risk companies must pay higher yields on their bonds to compensate bondholders for the additional default risk. Likewise, as we will see in this chapter, riskier companies trying to increase their stock price must generate higher returns to compensate their stockholders for the additional risk. It is important to understand that the returns that companies have to pay their investors represent the companies' costs of obtaining capital. Thus from a company's perspective, the risk-return line in panel b of Figure 8.1 represents its cost of obtaining capital, and the slope of the risk-return line reflects the average investor's current willingness to take on risk. As we will see in Chapters 10 through 12, companies create value by investing in projects where the returns on the investments exceed their costs of capital. Once again, this translates into operating above the risk-return trade-off line.

Throughout the rest of this chapter, we discuss these simple ideas in greater detail. We begin by discussing the concept of risk. Later we discuss returns, and we provide a model for estimating the trade-off between risk and return.

## Self Test

Briefly explain the fundamental trade-off between risk and return.

What do the slopes of the risk-return lines illustrated in Figure 8.1 indicate?

Does the average investor's willingness to take on risk vary over time? Explain.

What do you think the average investor's risk perception is now? In what types of investments do you think the average investor is investing currently?

Should companies completely avoid high-risk projects? Explain.

# 8-2 Stand-Alone Risk

**Risk** is defined by *Webster's Dictionary* as "a hazard; a peril; exposure to loss or injury." Thus, risk refers to the chance that some unfavorable event will occur. If you engage in skydiving, you are taking a chance with your life—skydiving is risky. If you bet on the horses, you are risking your money.

As we saw in previous chapters, individuals and firms invest funds today with the expectation of receiving additional funds in the future. Bonds offer relatively low returns, but with relatively little risk—at least if you stick to Treasury and high-grade corporate bonds. Stocks offer the chance of higher returns, but stocks are generally riskier than bonds. If you invest in speculative stocks (or, really, *any* stock), you are taking a significant risk in the hope of making an appreciable return.

An asset's risk can be analyzed in two ways: (1) on a stand-alone basis, where the asset is considered by itself, and (2) on a portfolio basis, where the asset is held as one of a number of assets in a portfolio. Thus, an asset's **stand-alone risk** is the risk an investor would face if he or she held only this one asset. Most financial assets, and stocks in particular, are held in portfolios; but it is necessary to understand stand-alone risk to understand risk in a portfolio context.

To illustrate stand-alone risk, suppose an investor buys $100,000 of short-term Treasury bills with an expected return of 5%. In this case, the investment's return, 5%, can be estimated quite precisely; and the investment is defined as being essentially *risk-free*. This same investor could also invest the $100,000 in the stock of a company just being organized to prospect for oil in the mid-Atlantic. Returns on the stock would be much harder to predict. In the worst case, the company would go bankrupt, and the investor would lose all of his or her money, in which case the return would be −100%. In the best-case scenario, the company would discover huge amounts of oil, and the investor would receive a 1,000% return. When evaluating this investment, the investor might analyze the situation and conclude that the *expected* rate of return, in a statistical sense, is 20%; but the *actual* rate of return could range from, say, +1,000% to −100%. Because there is a significant danger of earning much less than the expected return, such a stock would be relatively risky.

*No investment should be undertaken unless the expected rate of return is high enough to compensate for the perceived risk.* In our example, it is clear that few if any investors would be willing to buy the oil exploration stock if its expected return didn't exceed that of the T-bill. This is an extreme example. Generally, things are much less

**Risk**
The chance that some unfavorable event will occur.

**Stand-Alone Risk**
The risk an investor would face if he or she held only one asset.

obvious, and we need to measure risk in order to decide whether a potential investment should be undertaken. Therefore, we need to define risk more precisely.

As you will see, the risk of an asset is different when the asset is held by itself versus when it is held as a part of a group, or portfolio, of assets. We look at stand-alone risk in this section, and then at portfolio risk in later sections. It's necessary to know something about stand-alone risk in order to understand portfolio risk. Also, stand-alone risk is important to the owners of small businesses and in our examination of physical assets in the capital budgeting chapters. For stocks and most financial assets, though, it is portfolio risk that is most important. Still, you need to understand the key elements of both types of risk.

## 8-2A STATISTICAL MEASURES OF STAND-ALONE RISK

This is not a statistics book, and we won't spend a great deal of time on statistics. However, you do need an intuitive understanding of the relatively simple statistics presented in this section. All of the calculations can be done easily with a calculator or with Excel; and though we show pictures of the Excel setup, Excel is not needed for the calculations.

Here are the five key items that are covered:

- Probability distributions
- Expected rates of return, $\hat{r}$ ("r hat")
- Historical, or past realized, rates of return, $\bar{r}$ ("r bar")
- Standard deviation, $\sigma$ (sigma)
- Coefficient of variation (CV)

**Probability Distributions**

Listings of possible outcomes or events with a probability (chance of occurrence) assigned to each outcome.

Table 8.1 gives the **probability distributions** for Martin Products, which makes engines for long-haul trucks (18-wheelers), and for U.S. Water, which supplies an essential product and thus has very stable sales and profits. Three possible states of the economy are shown in column 1; and the probabilities of these outcomes, expressed as decimals rather than percentages, are given in column 2 and then repeated in column 5. There is a 30% chance of a strong economy and thus strong demand, a 40% probability of normal demand, and a 30% probability of weak demand.

Columns 3 and 6 show the returns for the two companies under each state of the economy. Returns are relatively high when demand is strong and low when demand is weak. Notice, though, that Martin's rate of return could vary far more widely than U.S. Water's. Indeed, there is a fairly high probability that Martin's stock will suffer a 60% loss, though at worst, U.S. Water should have a 5% return.[2]

**TABLE 8.1**      Probability Distributions and Expected Returns

| | A | B | C | D | E | F | G | H |
|---|---|---|---|---|---|---|---|---|
| 16 | | Martin Products | | | | | U.S. Water | |
| 17 | | | Rate of | | | | Rate of | |
| 18 | Economy, | Probability | Return | | | Probability | Return | |
| 19 | Which | of This | if This | | | of This | if This | |
| 20 | Affects | Demand | Demand | Product | | Demand | Demand | Product |
| 21 | Demand | Occurring | Occurs | (2) × (3) | | Occurring | Occurs | (5) × (6) |
| 22 | (1) | (2) | (3) | (4) | | (5) | (6) | (7) |
| 23 | Strong | 0.30 | 80% | 24% | | 0.30 | 15% | 4.5% |
| 24 | Normal | 0.40 | 10% | 4% | | 0.40 | 10% | 4.0% |
| 25 | Weak | 0.30 | −60% | −18% | | 0.30 | 5% | 1.5% |
| 26 | | 1.00 | Expected return = | 10% | | 1.00 | Expected return = | 10.0% |
| 27 | | | | | | | | |

[2]Although this example is illustrative, it is also somewhat unrealistic. In reality, most stocks have at least some chance of producing a negative return.

Columns 4 and 7 show the products of the probabilities times the returns under the different demand levels. When we sum these products, we obtain the **expected rate of return, r̂** ("r-hat"), for each stock. Both stocks have an expected return of 10%.[3]

We can graph the data in Table 8.1 as shown in Figure 8.2. The height of each bar indicates the probability that a given outcome will occur. The range of possible returns for Martin is from −60% to +80%, and the expected return is 10%. The expected return for U.S. Water is also 10%, but its possible range (and thus maximum loss) is much narrower.

In Figure 8.2, we assumed that only three economic states could occur: strong, normal, and weak. Actually, the economy can range from a deep depression to a fantastic boom; and there are an unlimited number of possibilities in between. Suppose we had the time and patience to assign a probability to each possible level of demand (with the sum of the probabilities still equaling 1.0) and to assign a rate of return to each stock for each level of demand. We would have a table similar to Table 8.1 except that it would have many more demand levels. This table could be

*Expected Rate of Return, r̂*

The rate of return expected to be realized from an investment; the weighted average of the probability distribution of possible results.

### FIGURE 8.2     Probability Distributions of Martin Products's and U.S. Water's Rates of Return

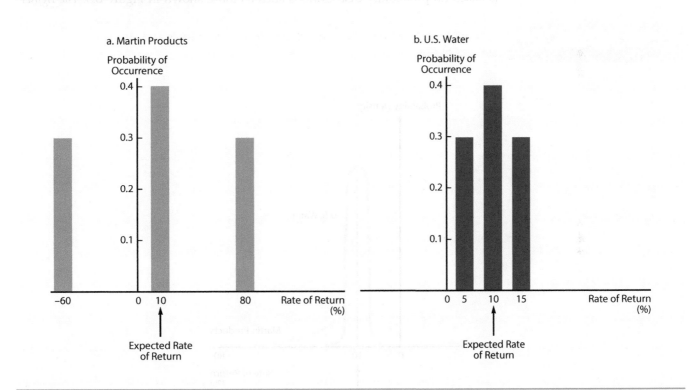

[3]The expected return can also be calculated with an equation that does the same thing as the table:

$$\text{Expected rate of return} = \hat{r} = P_1r_1 + P_2r_2 + \cdots + P_Nr_N \qquad \text{8.1}$$

$$= \sum_{i=1}^{N} P_i r_i$$

The second form of the equation is a shorthand expression in which sigma ($\sum$) means "sum up," or add, the values of N factors. If $i = 1$, then $P_i r_i = P_1 r_1$; if $i = 2$, then $P_i r_i = P_2 r_2$; and so forth, until $i = N$, the last possible outcome. The symbol $\sum_{i=1}^{N}$ simply says, "Go through the following process: First, let $i = 1$ and find the first product; then let $i = 2$ and find the second product; then continue until each individual product up to N has been found. Add these individual products to find the expected rate of return."

used to calculate expected rates of return as shown previously, and the probabilities and outcomes could be represented by continuous curves such as those shown in Figure 8.3. Here we changed the assumptions so that there is essentially no chance that Martin's return will be less than −60% or more than 80% or that U.S. Water's return will be less than 5% or more than 15%. However, virtually any return within these limits is possible.

The tighter (or more peaked) the probability distributions, the more likely the actual outcome will be close to the expected value and, consequently, the less likely the actual return will end up far below the expected return. *Thus, the tighter the probability distribution, the lower the risk.* As shown in Figure 8.3, because U.S. Water has a relatively tight distribution, its actual return is likely to be closer to its 10% expected return than is true for Martin; so U.S. Water is less risky.[4]

## 8-2B MEASURING STAND-ALONE RISK: THE STANDARD DEVIATION[5]

It is useful to measure risk for comparative purposes, but risk can be defined and measured in several ways. A common definition that is satisfactory for our purpose is based on probability distributions such as those shown in Figure 8.3: *The tighter*

| **FIGURE 8.3** | Continuous Probability Distributions of Martin Products's and U.S. Water's Rates of Return |

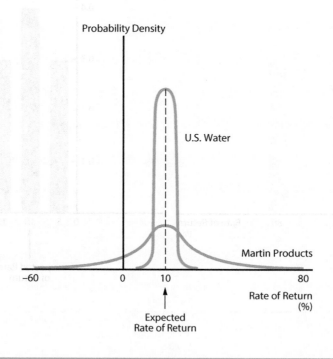

*Note*: The assumptions regarding the probabilities of various outcomes have been changed from those in Figure 8.2. There the probability of obtaining exactly 10% was 40%; here it is *much smaller* because there are many possible outcomes instead of just three. With continuous distributions, it is more appropriate to ask what the probability is of obtaining at least some specified rate of return than to ask what the probability is of obtaining exactly that rate. This topic is covered in detail in statistics courses.

---

[4]In this example, we implicitly assume that the state of the economy is the only factor that affects returns. In reality, many factors, including labor, materials, and development costs, influence returns. This is discussed at greater length in the chapters on capital budgeting.

[5]This section is relatively technical, but it can be omitted without loss of continuity.

*the probability distribution of expected future returns, the smaller the risk of a given investment.* According to this definition, U.S. Water is less risky than Martin Products because there is a smaller chance that the actual return of U.S. Water will end up far below its expected return.

We can use the standard deviation ($\sigma$, pronounced "sigma") to quantify the tightness of the probability distribution.[6] The smaller the standard deviation, the tighter the probability distribution and, accordingly, the lower the risk. We calculate Martin's $\sigma$ in Table 8.2. We picked up columns 1, 2, and 3 from Table 8.1. Then in column 4, we find the deviation of the return in each demand state from the expected return: Actual return – Expected 10% return. The deviations are squared and shown in column 5. Each squared deviation is then multiplied by the relevant probability and shown in column 6. The sum of the products in column 6 is the *variance* of the distribution. Finally, we find the square root of the variance—this is the *standard deviation,* and it is shown at the bottom of column 6 both as a fraction and a percentage.[7]

The **standard deviation, $\sigma$,** is a measure of how far the actual return is likely to deviate from the expected return. Martin's standard deviation is 54.22%, so its actual return is likely to be quite different from the expected 10%.[8] U.S. Water's standard deviation is 3.87%, so its actual return should be much closer to the expected return of 10%. The average publicly traded firm's $\sigma$ has been in the range of 20% to 30% in recent years; so Martin is more risky than most stocks, and U.S. Water is less risky.

*Standard Deviation, $\sigma$*
A statistical measure of the variability of a set of observations.

Calculating Martin Products's Standard Deviation

TABLE 8.2

| | A | B | C | D | E | F | G | H |
|---|---|---|---|---|---|---|---|---|
| 33 | | | Rate of | Deviation: | | | | |
| 34 | Economy, | Probability | Return | Actual – | | | | |
| 35 | Which | of This | if This | 10% | | | Squared | |
| 36 | Affects | Demand | Demand | Expected | | Deviation | Deviation | |
| 37 | Demand | Occurring | Occurs | Return | | Squared | × Prob. | |
| 38 | (1) | (2) | (3) | (4) | | (5) | (6) | |
| 39 | Strong | 0.30 | 80% | 70% | | 0.4900 | 0.1470 | |
| 40 | Normal | 0.40 | 10% | 0% | | 0.0000 | 0.0000 | |
| 41 | Weak | 0.30 | −60% | −70% | | 0.4900 | 0.1470 | |
| 42 | | 1.00 | | | | Σ = Variance: | 0.2940 | |
| 43 | | | Standard deviation = square root of variance: $\sigma$ = | | | | 0.5422 | |
| 44 | | | Standard deviation expressed as a percentage: $\sigma$ = | | | | 54.22% | |

---

[6]There are actually two types of standard deviations, one for complete distributions and one for situations that involve only a sample. Different formulas and notations are used. Also, the standard deviation should be modified if the distribution is not normal, or bell-shaped. Because our purpose is simply to get the general idea across, we leave the refinements to advanced finance and statistics courses.

[7]This formula summarizes what we did in Table 8.2:

$$\text{Standard deviation} = \sigma = \sqrt{\sum_{i=1}^{N} (r_i - \hat{r})^2 P_i}$$

8.2

[8]With a normal (bell-shaped) distribution, the actual return should be within one $\sigma$ about 68% of the time.

## 8-2C USING HISTORICAL DATA TO MEASURE RISK[9]

In the last section, we found the mean and standard deviation based on a subjective probability distribution. If we had actual historical data instead, the standard deviation of returns could be found as shown in Table 8.3.[10] Because past results are often repeated in the future, the historical σ is often used as an estimate of future risk.[11] A key question that arises when historical data is used to forecast the future is how far back in time we should go. Unfortunately, there is no simple answer. Using a longer historical time series has the benefit of giving more information, but some of that information may be misleading if you believe that the level of risk in the future is likely to be very different from the level of risk in the past.

All financial calculators (and Excel) have easy-to-use functions for finding σ based on historical data.[12] Simply enter the rates of return and press the key marked S (or $S_x$) to obtain the standard deviation. However, neither calculators nor Excel have a built-in formula for finding σ where probabilistic data are involved. In those cases, you must go through the process outlined in Table 8.2.

**TABLE 8.3**          Finding σ Based on Historical Data

| | A | B | C | D | E | F | G | H |
|---|---|---|---|---|---|---|---|---|
| 73 | | | | Deviation | | | | |
| 74 | | | | from | | | Squared | |
| 75 | Year | Return | | Average | | | Deviation | |
| 76 | (1) | (2) | | (3) | | | (4) | |
| 77 | 2013 | 30.0% | | 19.8% | | | 0.0390 | |
| 78 | 2014 | –10.0% | | –20.3% | | | 0.0410 | |
| 79 | 2015 | –19.0% | | –29.3% | | | 0.0856 | |
| 80 | 2016 | 40.0% | | 29.8% | | | 0.0885 | |
| 81 | Average | 10.3% | | Sum of Squared Devs (SSDevs): | | | 0.2541 | |
| 82 | | | | SSDevs/(N – 1) = SSDevs/3: | | | 0.0847 | |
| 83 | | | Standard deviation = Square root of SSDevs/3: σ = | | | | 29.10% | |
| 84 | | | Excel Function: STDEV(B77:B80)   σ = | | | | 29.10% | |

---

[9] Again, this section is relatively technical, but it can be omitted without loss of continuity.

[10] The four years of historical data are considered to be a "sample" of the full (but unknown) set of data, and the procedure used to find the standard deviation is different from the one used for probabilistic data. Here is the equation for sample data, and it is the basis for Table 8.3:

$$\text{Estimated } \sigma = \sqrt{\frac{\sum_{t=1}^{N} (\bar{r}_t - \bar{r}_{Avg})^2}{N - 1}}$$

8.2a

Here $\bar{r}_t$ ("r bar t") denotes the past realized rate of return in period t, and $\bar{r}_{Avg}$ is the average annual return earned over the last N years.

[11] The average return for the past period (10.3% in our example) may also be used as an estimate of future returns, but this is problematic because the average historical return varies widely depending on the period examined. In our example, if we went from 2013 to 2015, we would get a different average from the 10.3%. The average historical return stabilizes with more years of data, but that brings into question whether data from many years ago are still relevant today.

[12] See our tutorials on the text's website or your calculator manual for instructions on calculating historical standard deviations.

## 8-2D  MEASURING STAND-ALONE RISK: THE COEFFICIENT OF VARIATION

If a choice has to be made between two investments that have the same expected returns but different standard deviations, most people would choose the one with the lower standard deviation and therefore the lower risk. Similarly, given a choice between two investments with the same risk (standard deviation) but different expected returns, investors would generally prefer the investment with the higher expected return. To most people, this is common sense—return is "good" and risk is "bad"; consequently, investors want as much return and as little risk as possible. But how do we choose between two investments if one has the higher expected return but the other has the lower standard deviation? To help answer that question, we use another measure of risk, the **coefficient of variation (CV)**, which is the standard deviation divided by the expected return:

$$\text{Coefficient of variation} = CV = \frac{\sigma}{\hat{r}} \qquad \blacktriangledown \quad 8.3$$

*Coefficient of Variation (CV)*
The standardized measure of the risk per unit of return; calculated as the standard deviation divided by the expected return.

*The coefficient of variation shows the risk per unit of return, and it provides a more meaningful risk measure when the expected returns on two alternatives are not the same.* Because U.S. Water and Martin Products have the same expected return, the coefficient of variation is not necessary in this case. In this example, the firm with the larger standard deviation, Martin, must also have the larger coefficient of variation. In fact, the coefficient of variation for Martin is $54.22/10 = 5.42$, and the coefficient of variation for U.S. Water is $3.87/10 = 0.39$. Thus, Martin is about 14 times riskier than U.S. Water on the basis of this criterion.

## 8-2E  RISK AVERSION AND REQUIRED RETURNS

Suppose you inherited \$1 million, which you plan to invest and then retire on the income. You can buy a 5% U.S. Treasury bill, and you will be sure of earning \$50,000 interest. Alternatively, you can buy stock in R&D Enterprises. If R&D's research programs are successful, your stock will increase to \$2.1 million. However, if the research is a failure, the value of your stock will be zero, and you will be penniless. You regard R&D's chances of success or failure as 50–50, so the expected value of the stock a year from now is $0.5(\$0) + 0.5(\$2,100,000) = \$1,050,000$. Subtracting the \$1 million cost leaves an expected \$50,000 profit and a 5% rate of return, the same as for the T-bill:

$$
\begin{aligned}
\text{Expected rate of return} &= \frac{\text{Expected ending value} - \text{Cost}}{\text{Cost}} \\
&= \frac{\$1,050,000 - \$1,000,000}{\$1,000,000} \\
&= \frac{\$50,000}{\$1,000,000} = 5\%
\end{aligned}
$$

Given the choice of the sure \$50,000 profit (and 5% rate of return) and the risky expected \$50,000 profit and 5% return, which one would you choose? *If you choose the less risky investment, you are risk-averse. Most investors are risk-averse, and certainly the average investor is with regard to his or her "serious money." Because this is a well-documented fact, we assume* **risk aversion** *in our discussions throughout the remainder of the book.*

*Risk Aversion*
Risk-averse investors dislike risk and require higher rates of return as an inducement to buy riskier securities.

What are the implications of risk aversion for security prices and rates of return? *The answer is that, other things held constant, the higher a security's risk, the higher its required return; and if this situation does not hold, prices will change to bring about the required condition.* To illustrate this point, look back at Figure 8.3 and consider again the U.S. Water and Martin Products stocks. Suppose each stock sells

# THE HISTORICAL TRADE-OFF BETWEEN RISK AND RETURN

The table accompanying this box summarizes the historical trade-off between risk and return for different classes of investments from 1926 through 2014. As the table shows, those assets that produced the highest average returns also had the highest standard deviations and the widest ranges of returns. For example, small-cap stocks had the highest average annual return, 16.7%, but the standard deviation of their returns, 32.1%, was also the highest. By contrast, U.S. Treasury bills had the lowest standard deviation, 3.1%, but they also had the lowest average return, 3.5%. Although there is no guarantee that history will repeat itself, the returns and standard deviations observed in the past are often used as a starting point for estimating future returns.

### Selected Realized Returns, 1926–2014

|  | Average Return | Standard Deviation |
| --- | --- | --- |
| Small–cap stocks | 16.7% | 32.1% |
| Large–cap stocks | 12.1 | 20.1 |
| Long-term corporate bonds | 6.4 | 8.4 |
| Long-term government bonds | 6.1 | 10.0 |
| U.S. Treasury bills | 3.5 | 3.1 |
| Portfolios: |  |  |
| 90% stocks/10% bonds | 11.4% | 18.1% |
| 70% stocks/30% bonds | 10.2 | 14.3 |

Source: Based on *Ibbotson Stocks, Bonds, Bills, and Inflation: 2015 Classic Yearbook* (Chicago: Morningstar, Inc., 2015), pp. 40, 50.

for $100 per share and each has an expected rate of return of 10%. Investors are averse to risk; so under those conditions, there would be a general preference for U.S. Water. People with money to invest would bid for U.S. Water, and Martin's stockholders would want to sell and use the money to buy U.S. Water. Buying pressure would quickly drive U.S. Water's stock price up, and selling pressure would simultaneously cause Martin's price to fall.

These price changes, in turn, would change the expected returns of the two securities. Suppose, for example, that U.S. Water's stock price was bid up from $100 to $125 and Martin's stock price declined from $100 to $77. These price changes would cause U.S. Water's expected return to fall to 8% and Martin's return to rise to 13%.[13] The difference in returns, 13% − 8% = 5%, would be a **risk premium (RP)**, which represents the additional compensation investors require for bearing Martin's higher risk.

This example demonstrates a very important principle: *In a market dominated by risk-averse investors, riskier securities compared to less risky securities must have higher expected returns as estimated by the marginal investor. If this situation does not exist, buying and selling will occur until it does exist.* Later in the chapter we will consider the question of how much higher the returns on risky securities must be, after we see how diversification affects the way risk should be measured.

*Risk Premium (RP)*

The difference between the expected rate of return on a given risky asset and that on a less risky asset.

---

[13]We assume that each stock is expected to pay shareholders $10 a year in perpetuity. The price of this perpetuity can be found by dividing the annual cash flow by the stock's return. Thus, if the stock's expected return is 10%, the price must be $10/0.10 = $100. Likewise, an 8% expected return would be consistent with a $125 stock price ($10/0.08 = $125) and a 13% return with a $77 stock price ($10/0.13 = $77).

## SelfTest

What does *investment risk* mean?

Set up an illustrative probability distribution table for an investment with probabilities for different conditions, returns under those conditions, and the expected return.

Which of the two stocks graphed in Figure 8.3 is less risky? Why?

Explain why you agree or disagree with this statement: Most investors are risk-averse.

How does risk aversion affect rates of return?

An investment has a 50% chance of producing a 20% return, a 25% chance of producing an 8% return, and a 25% chance of producing a –12% return. What is its expected return? **(9%)**

# 8-3 Risk in a Portfolio Context: The CAPM

In this section, we discuss the risk of stocks when they are held in portfolios rather than as stand-alone assets. Our discussion is based on an extremely important theory, the **capital asset pricing model,** or **CAPM**, that was developed in the 1960s.[14] We do not attempt to cover the CAPM in detail—rather, we simply use its intuition to explain how risk should be considered in a world where stocks and other assets are held in portfolios. If you go on to take a course in investments, you will cover the CAPM in detail.

Thus far in the chapter we have considered the riskiness of assets when they are held in isolation. This is generally appropriate for small businesses, many real estate investments, and capital budgeting projects. However, the risk of a stock held in a portfolio is typically lower than the stock's risk when it is held alone. Because investors dislike risk and because risk can be reduced by holding portfolios, most stocks are held in portfolios. Banks, pension funds, insurance companies, mutual funds, and other financial institutions are required by law to hold diversified portfolios. Most individual investors—at least those whose security holdings constitute a significant part of their total wealth—also hold portfolios. Therefore, the fact that one particular stock's price increases or decreases is not important—*what is important is the return on the portfolio and the portfolio's risk. Logically, then, the risk and return of an individual stock should be analyzed in terms of how the security affects the risk and return of the portfolio in which it is held.*

To illustrate, Pay Up Inc. is a collection agency that operates nationwide through 37 offices. The company is not well known; its stock is not very liquid; and its earnings have experienced sharp fluctuations in the past. This suggests that Pay Up is risky and that its required rate of return, r, should be relatively high. However, Pay Up's required return in 2016 (and all other years) was quite low in comparison to most other companies. This indicates that investors think Pay Up is a low-risk company in spite of its uncertain profits. *This counterintuitive finding has to do with diversification and its effect on risk.* Pay Up's earnings rise during recessions, whereas most other companies' earnings decline when the economy slumps. Thus, Pay Up's stock is like insurance—it pays off when other investments go bad—so adding Pay Up to a portfolio of "regular" stocks stabilizes the portfolio's returns and makes it less risky.

*Capital Asset Pricing Model (CAPM)*
A model based on the proposition that any stock's required rate of return is equal to the risk-free rate of return plus a risk premium that reflects only the risk remaining after diversification.

---

[14]The CAPM was originated by Professor William F. Sharpe in his article "Capital Asset Prices: A Theory of Market Equilibrium under Conditions of Risk," *Journal of Finance*, vol. 19, no. 3 (1964), pp. 425–442. Literally thousands of articles exploring various aspects of the CAPM have been published subsequently, and it is very widely used in investment analysis.

## 8-3A EXPECTED PORTFOLIO RETURNS, $\hat{r}_p$

**Expected Return on a Portfolio, $\hat{r}_p$**
The weighted average of the expected returns on the assets held in the portfolio.

The **expected return on a portfolio, $\hat{r}_p$,** is the weighted average of the expected returns of the individual assets in the portfolio, with the weights being the percentage of the total portfolio invested in each asset:

$$\hat{r}_p = w_1\hat{r}_1 + w_2\hat{r}_2 + \cdots + w_N\hat{r}_N$$

$$= \sum_{i=1}^{N} w_i\hat{r}_i$$

▼ 8.4

Here $\hat{r}_i$ is the expected return on the $i$th stock; the $w_i$'s are the stocks' weights, or the percentage of the total value of the portfolio invested in each stock; and N is the number of stocks in the portfolio.

Table 8.4 can be used to implement the equation. Here we assume that an analyst estimated returns on the four stocks shown in column 1 for the coming year, as shown in column 2. Suppose further that you had $100,000 and you planned to invest $25,000, or 25% of the total, in each stock. You could multiply each stock's percentage weight as shown in column 4 by its expected return; obtain the product terms in column 5; and then sum column 5 to calculate the expected portfolio return, 7.875%.

If you added a fifth stock with a higher expected return, the portfolio's expected return would increase, and vice versa if you added a stock with a lower expected return. *The key point to remember is that the expected return on a portfolio is a weighted average of expected returns on the stocks in the portfolio.*

Several additional points should be made:

1. The expected returns in column 2 would be based on a study of some type, but they would still be essentially subjective and judgmental because different analysts could look at the same data and reach different conclusions. Therefore, this type of analysis must be viewed with a critical eye. Nevertheless, it is useful, indeed necessary, if one is to make intelligent investment decisions.

**Realized Rates of Return, $\bar{r}$**
Returns that were actually earned during some past period. Actual returns ($\bar{r}$) usually turn out to be different from expected returns ($\hat{r}$) except for riskless assets.

2. If we added companies such as U.S. Steel Corp. and GM, which are generally considered to be relatively risky, their expected returns as estimated by the marginal investor would be relatively high; otherwise, investors would sell them, drive down their prices, and force the expected returns above the returns on safer stocks.

3. After the fact and a year later, the actual **realized rates of return, $\bar{r}_i$** on the individual stocks—the $\bar{r}_i$, or "r-bar," values—would almost certainly be different from the initial expected values. That would cause the portfolio's

▼ **TABLE 8.4**     Hypothetical Illustration: Expected Return on a Portfolio, $\hat{r}_p$

|  | A | B | C | D | E | F | G | H |
|---|---|---|---|---|---|---|---|---|
| 101 |  | Expected | Dollars | Percent of |  | Product: |  |  |
| 102 | Stock | Return | Invested | Total ($w_i$) |  | (2) × (4) |  |  |
| 103 | (1) | (2) | (3) | (4) |  | (5) |  |  |
| 104 | Microsoft | 7.75% | $25,000 | 25.0% |  | 1.9375% |  |  |
| 105 | IBM | 7.25% | $25,000 | 25.0% |  | 1.8125% |  |  |
| 106 | GE | 8.75% | $25,000 | 25.0% |  | 2.1875% |  |  |
| 107 | Exxon Mobil | 7.75% | $25,000 | 25.0% |  | 1.9375% |  |  |
| 108 |  | 7.875% | $100,000 | 100.0% |  | 7.875% = Expected $r_p$ |  |  |
| 109 |  |  |  |  |  |  |  |  |

actual return, $\bar{r}_p$, to differ from the expected return, $\hat{r}_p = 7.875\%$. For example, Microsoft's price might double and thus provide a return of $+100\%$, whereas IBM might have a terrible year, fall sharply, and have a return of $-75\%$. Note, though, that those two events would be offsetting; so the portfolio's return still might be close to its expected return even though the returns on the individual stocks were far from their expected values.

## 8-3B PORTFOLIO RISK

Although the expected return on a portfolio is simply the weighted average of the expected returns on its individual stocks, the portfolio's risk, $\sigma_p$, is *not* the weighted average of the individual stocks' standard deviations. The portfolio's risk is generally *smaller* than the average of the stocks' $\sigma$s because diversification lowers the portfolio's risk.

To illustrate this point, consider the situation in Figure 8.4. The bottom section gives data on Stocks W and M individually and data on a portfolio with 50% in each stock. The left graph plots the data in a time series format, and it shows that the returns on the individual stocks vary widely from year to year. Therefore, the individual stocks are risky. However, the portfolio's returns are constant at 15%, indicating that it is not risky at all. The probability distribution graphs to the right show the same thing—the two stocks would be quite risky if

**FIGURE 8.4**    Returns with Perfect Negative Correlation, $\rho = -1.0$

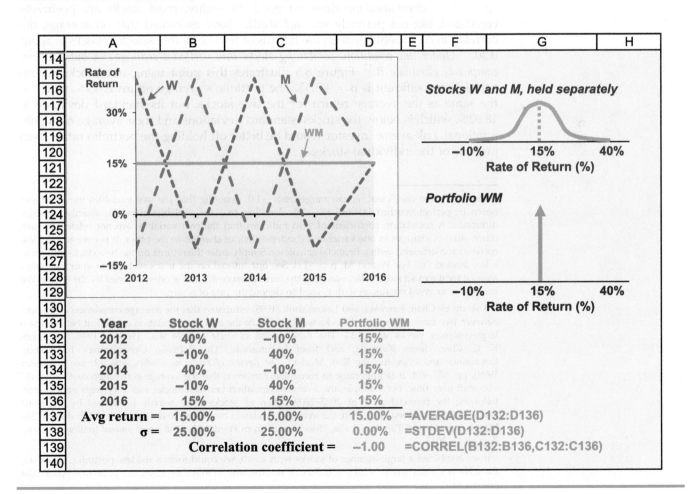

| Year | Stock W | Stock M | Portfolio WM | |
|---|---|---|---|---|
| 2012 | 40% | −10% | 15% | |
| 2013 | −10% | 40% | 15% | |
| 2014 | 40% | −10% | 15% | |
| 2015 | −10% | 40% | 15% | |
| 2016 | 15% | 15% | 15% | |
| Avg return = | 15.00% | 15.00% | 15.00% | =AVERAGE(D132:D136) |
| σ = | 25.00% | 25.00% | 0.00% | =STDEV(D132:D136) |
| Correlation coefficient = | | | −1.00 | =CORREL(B132:B136,C132:C136) |

they were held in isolation, but when they are combined to form Portfolio WM, they have no risk whatsoever.

If you invested all of your money in Stock W, you would have an expected return of 15%, but you would face a great deal of risk. The same thing would hold if you invested entirely in Stock M. However, if you invested 50% in each stock, you would have the same expected return of 15%, but with no risk whatsoever. Being rational and averse to risk, you and all other rational investors would choose to hold the portfolio, not the stocks individually.

Stocks W and M can be combined to form a riskless portfolio because their returns move countercyclically to each other—when W's fall, M's rise, and vice versa. The tendency of two variables to move together is called **correlation**, and the **correlation coefficient, ρ** (pronounced "rho"), measures this tendency.[15] In statistical terms, we say that the returns on Stocks W and M are *perfectly negatively correlated*, with ρ = −1.0. The opposite of perfect negative correlation is *perfect positive correlation*, with ρ = +1.0. If returns are not related to one another at all, they are said to be *independent* and ρ = 0.

The returns on two perfectly positively correlated stocks with the same expected return would move up and down together, and a portfolio consisting of these stocks would be exactly as risky as the individual stocks. If we drew a graph like Figure 8.4, we would see just one line because the two stocks and the portfolio would have the same return at each point in time. *Thus, diversification is completely useless for reducing risk if the stocks in the portfolio are perfectly positively correlated.*

We see then that when stocks are perfectly negatively correlated (ρ = −1.0), all risk can be diversified away; but when stocks are perfectly positively correlated (ρ = +1.0), diversification does no good. In reality, most stocks are positively correlated, but not perfectly so. Past studies have estimated that on average, the correlation coefficient between the returns of two randomly selected stocks is about 0.30.[16] *Under this condition, combining stocks into portfolios reduces risk but does not completely eliminate it.*[17] Figure 8.5 illustrates this point using two stocks whose correlation coefficient is ρ = +0.35. The portfolio's average return is 15%, which is the same as the average return for the two stocks; but its standard deviation is 18.62%, which is below the stocks' standard deviations and their average σ. Again, a rational, risk-averse investor would be better off holding the portfolio rather than just one of the individual stocks.

**Correlation**

The tendency of two variables to move together.

**Correlation Coefficient, ρ**

A measure of the degree of relationship between two variables.

---

[15]The correlation coefficient, ρ, can range from +1.0, denoting that the two variables move up and down in perfect synchronization, to −1.0, denoting that the variables move in exactly opposite directions. A correlation coefficient of zero indicates that the two variables are not related to each other—that is, changes in one variable are independent of changes in the other. It is easy to calculate correlation coefficients with a financial calculator. Simply enter the returns on the two stocks and press a key labeled "r." For W and M, ρ = −1.0. See our tutorial on the text's website or your calculator manual for the exact steps. Also, note that the correlation coefficient is often denoted by the term r. We use ρ here to avoid confusion with r, used to denote the rate of return.

[16]A study by Chan, Karceski, and Lakonishok (1999) estimated that the average correlation coefficient between two randomly selected stocks was 0.28, while the average correlation coefficient between two large-company stocks was 0.33. The time period of their sample was 1968 to 1998. See Louis K. C. Chan, Jason Karceski, and Josef Lakonishok, "On Portfolio Optimization: Forecasting Covariance and Choosing the Risk Model," *The Review of Financial Studies*, vol. 12, no. 5 (Winter 1999), pp. 937–974. It is important to recognize, however, that the average correlation coefficient will also shift over time. For example, the average correlation between stocks was very high immediately following the financial crisis of 2007–2009, when all stocks were heavily influenced by the same macroeconomic factors. Since then, the average correlation has begun to once again steadily decline. See Matt Jarzemsky and Tom Lauricella, "Stock Break from Herd," *The Wall Street Journal* (online.wsj.com), August 18, 2013.

[17]If we combined a large number of stocks with ρ = 0, we could form a riskless portfolio. However, there are not many stocks with ρ = 0. Stocks' returns tend to move together, not to be independent of one another.

**FIGURE 8.5** Returns with Partial Correlation, $\rho = +0.35$

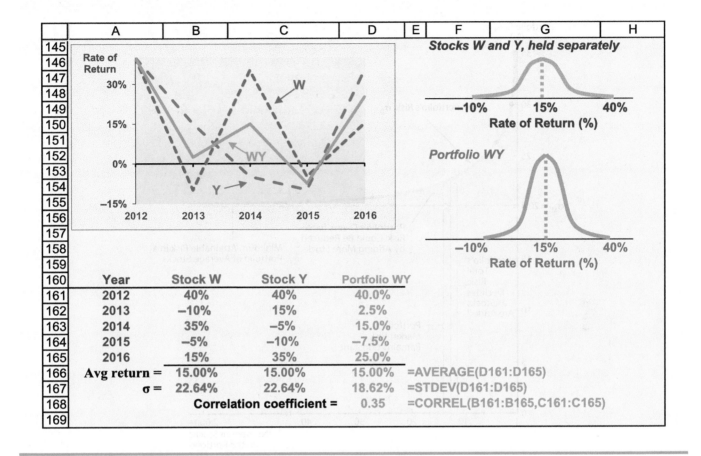

| | Year | Stock W | Stock Y | Portfolio WY | |
|---|---|---|---|---|---|
| 160 | Year | Stock W | Stock Y | Portfolio WY | |
| 161 | 2012 | 40% | 40% | 40.0% | |
| 162 | 2013 | −10% | 15% | 2.5% | |
| 163 | 2014 | 35% | −5% | 15.0% | |
| 164 | 2015 | −5% | −10% | −7.5% | |
| 165 | 2016 | 15% | 35% | 25.0% | |
| 166 | Avg return = | 15.00% | 15.00% | 15.00% | =AVERAGE(D161:D165) |
| 167 | σ = | 22.64% | 22.64% | 18.62% | =STDEV(D161:D165) |
| 168 | | Correlation coefficient = | | 0.35 | =CORREL(B161:B165,C161:C165) |

In our examples, we considered portfolios with only two stocks. What would happen if we increased the number of stocks in the portfolio? *As a rule, on average, portfolio risk declines as the number of stocks in a portfolio increases.*

If we added enough partially correlated stocks, could we completely eliminate risk? In general, the answer is no. For an illustration, see Figure 8.6, which shows that a portfolio's risk declines as stocks are added. Here are some points to keep in mind about the figure:

1. The portfolio's risk declines as stocks are added, but at a decreasing rate; and once 40 to 50 stocks are in the portfolio, additional stocks do little to reduce risk.

2. The portfolio's total risk can be divided into two parts, **diversifiable risk** and **market risk**. Diversifiable risk is the risk that is eliminated by adding stocks. Market risk is the risk that remains even if the portfolio holds every stock in the market.

3. Diversifiable risk is caused by such random, unsystematic events as lawsuits, strikes, successful and unsuccessful marketing and R&D programs, the winning or losing of a major contract, and other events that are unique to the particular firm. Because these events are random, their effects on a portfolio can be eliminated by diversification—bad events for one firm will be offset by good events for another. Market risk, on the other hand, stems from factors that systematically affect most firms: war, inflation, recessions, high interest rates, and other macro factors. Because most stocks are affected by macro factors, market risk cannot be eliminated by diversification.

*Diversifiable Risk*

That part of a security's risk associated with random events; it can be eliminated by proper diversification. This risk is also known as company-specific, or unsystematic, risk.

*Market Risk*

The risk that remains in a portfolio after diversification has eliminated all company-specific risk. This risk is also known as nondiversifiable or systematic or beta risk.

**FIGURE 8.6**     Effects of Portfolio Size on Risk for a Portfolio of Randomly Selected Stocks

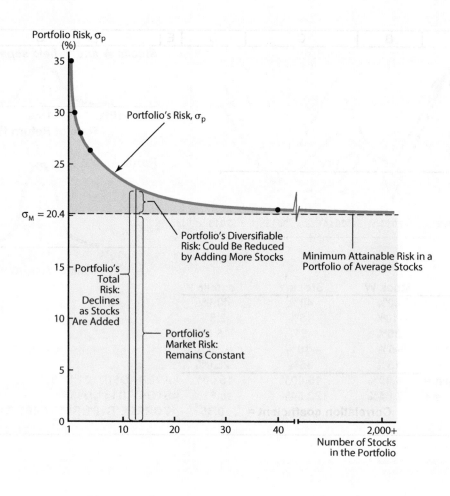

*Note*: This graph assumes that stocks in the portfolio are randomly selected from the universe of large, publicly traded stocks listed on the NYSE.

4.  If we carefully selected the stocks included in the portfolio rather than adding them randomly, the graph would change. In particular, if we chose stocks with low correlations with one another and with low stand-alone risk, the portfolio's risk would decline faster than if random stocks were added. The reverse would hold if we added stocks with high correlations and high $\sigma$s.

5.  Most investors are rational in the sense that they dislike risk, other things held constant. That being the case, why would an investor ever hold one (or a few) stocks? Why not hold a **market portfolio** consisting of all stocks? There are several reasons. First, high administrative costs and commissions would more than offset the benefits for individual investors. Second, index funds can be used by investors for diversification, and many individuals can and do get broad diversification through these funds. Third, some people think they can pick stocks that will "beat the market," so they buy them rather than the broad market. And fourth, some people can, through superior analysis, beat the market; so they find and buy undervalued stocks and sell overvalued ones and, in the process, cause most stocks to be properly valued, with their expected returns consistent with their risks.

*Market Portfolio*

A portfolio consisting of all stocks.

# ADDING MORE STOCKS DOESN'T ALWAYS REDUCE THE RISK OF YOUR PORTFOLIO

Although Figure 8.6 illustrates the importance of diversification, it is important to realize that in some cases adding more stocks to your portfolio does not always reduce risk. In fact, in some cases, it can even increase risk. To understand why this is so, assume that the first stock you randomly select for your portfolio is a very safe utility firm, but the second stock you randomly select for your portfolio is a very risky biotechnology firm. In this case, your two-stock portfolio is likely to have more risk, even though you are realizing some benefits from diversification.

A recent article in *The Wall Street Journal* sheds more light on this issue. The article discusses some recent research by Professor Don Chance of Louisiana State University. Professor Chance conducted a classroom study where he asked students to first select a stock for their portfolio, and then to keep adding stocks until they had a portfolio of 30 stocks. Here's a summary of his findings:

> Prof. Chance wanted to prove to his students that diversification works. On average, for the group as a whole, diversifying from 1 stock to 20 cut the riskiness of portfolios by roughly 40%, just as the research predicted. "It was like a magic trick," says Prof. Chance. "The classes produced the exact same graph that's in their textbook."
>
> But then Prof. Chance went back and analyzed the results, student by student, and found that diversification failed remarkably often. As they broadened their holdings from a single stock to a basket of 30, many of the students raised their risk instead of lowering it. One in nine times, they ended up with 30-stock portfolios that were riskier than the single company they had started with. For 23%, the final 30-stock basket fluctuated more than it had with only five stocks in it.
>
> The lesson: For any given investor, the averages mightn't apply. "We send this message out that you don't need that

many stocks to diversify," says Prof. Chance, "but that's just not true." What accounts for these odd results?

Leave it to a professor called Chance to show that even a random process produces seemingly unlikely outliers. Thirteen percent of the time, a 20-stock portfolio generated by computer will be riskier than a one-stock portfolio.

Also note that if instead of randomly adding stocks to your portfolio, you keep adding the same types of stocks (e.g., all technology stocks or all financial stocks) to your portfolio, then the benefits of diversification will be considerably less dramatic. Keep in mind, however, the larger point. On average, you will have a hard time reducing risk if you only hold a small number of stocks in your portfolio. With this point in mind, many analysts recommend that individual investors invest in index funds that provide extensive diversification with low transactions costs. Echoing this argument, *The Wall Street Journal* article concludes by offering the following observation and recommendation:

> According to the Federal Reserve's Survey of Consumer Finances, 84% of households that own shares directly have no more than nine stocks; 36% hold shares in only a single company.
>
> That's way too few. But 30 or 40 isn't enough either. If you want to pick stocks directly, put 90% to 95% of your money in a total stock-market index fund, which will give you a stake in thousands of companies at low cost. Put the rest in three to five stocks, at most, that you can follow closely and hold patiently. Beyond a handful, more companies may well leave you less diversified.

You should note that Figure 8.6 shows what happens *on average* if you *randomly* add more stocks to your portfolio. But although the picture shows what happens on average, there is certainly no guarantee that every time you add stocks to your portfolio the portfolio's risk will decline.

Source: Jason Zweig, "More Stocks May Not Make a Portfolio Safer," *The Wall Street Journal* (online.wsj.com), November 26, 2009.

6. One key question remains: How should the risk of an individual stock be measured? The standard deviation of expected returns, $\sigma$, is not appropriate because it includes risk that can be eliminated by holding the stock in a portfolio. How then should we measure a stock's risk in a world where most people hold portfolios? That's the subject of the next section.

## 8-3C RISK IN A PORTFOLIO CONTEXT: THE BETA COEFFICIENT

When a stock is held by itself, its risk can be measured by the standard deviation of its expected returns. However, $\sigma$ is not appropriate when the stock is held in a portfolio, as stocks generally are. So how do we measure a stock's **relevant risk** in a portfolio context?

**Relevant Risk**
The risk that remains once a stock is in a diversified portfolio is its contribution to the portfolio's market risk. It is measured by the extent to which the stock moves up or down with the market.

First, note that all risk except that related to broad market movements can and will be diversified away by most investors—rational investors will hold enough stocks to move down the risk curve in Figure 8.6 to the point where only market risk remains in their portfolios.

*The risk that remains once a stock is in a diversified portfolio is its contribution to the portfolio's market risk, and that risk can be measured by the extent to which the stock moves up or down with the market.*

**Beta Coefficient, b**
A metric that shows the extent to which a given stock's returns move up and down with the stock market. Beta measures market risk.

The tendency of a stock to move with the market is measured by its **beta coefficient, b**. Ideally, when estimating a stock's beta, we would like to have a crystal ball that tells us how the stock is going to move relative to the overall stock market in the future. But because we can't look into the future, we often use historical data and assume that the stock's historical beta will give us a reasonable estimate of how the stock will move relative to the market in the future.

To illustrate the use of historical data, consider Figure 8.7, which shows the historical returns on three stocks and a market index. In Year 1, "the market," as defined by a portfolio containing all stocks, had a total return (dividend yield plus capital gains yield) of 10%, as did the three individual stocks. In Year 2, the market went up sharply, and its return was 20%. Stock H (for high) soared to 30%; A (for average) returned 20%, the same as the market; and L (for low) returned 15%. In Year 3, the market dropped sharply; its return was −10%. The three stocks' returns also fell—H's return was −30%, A's was −10%, and L broke even with a 0% return. In Years 4 and 5, the market returned 0% and 5%, respectively, and the three stocks' returns were as shown in the figure.

A plot of the data shows that the three stocks moved up or down with the market but that H was twice as volatile as the market, A was exactly as volatile as the market, and L had only half the market's volatility. It is apparent that the steeper the line, the greater the stock's volatility and thus the larger its loss in a down market. *The slopes of the lines are the stocks' beta coefficients.* We see in the figure that the slope coefficient for H is 2.0; for A, it is 1.0; and for L, it is 0.5.[18] Thus, beta measures a given stock's volatility relative to the market, and an **average stock's beta, $b_A$ = 1.0.**

**Average Stock's Beta, $b_A$**
By definition, $b_A = 1$ because an average-risk stock is one that tends to move up and down in step with the general market.

Stock A is defined as an *average-risk stock* because it has a beta of b = 1.0 and thus moves up and down in step with the general market. Thus, an average stock will, in general, move up by 10% when the market moves up by 10% and fall by 10% when the market falls by 10%. A large portfolio of such b = 1.0 stocks would (1) have all of its diversifiable risk removed but (2) still move up and down with the broad market averages and thus have a degree of risk.

Stock H, which has b = 2.0, is twice as volatile as an average stock, which means that it is twice as risky. The value of a portfolio consisting of b = 2.0 stocks could double—or halve—in a short time; and if you held such a portfolio, you could quickly go from being a millionaire to being a pauper. Stock L, on the other hand, with b = 0.5, is only half as volatile as the average stock, and a portfolio of such stocks would rise and fall only half as rapidly as the market. Thus, its risk would be half that of an average-risk portfolio with b = 1.0.

Betas for literally thousands of companies are calculated and published by Value Line, Yahoo!, Google, and numerous other organizations, and the beta coefficients of some well-known companies are shown in Table 8.5. Most

---

[18]For more on calculating betas, see Brigham and Daves, *Intermediate Financial Management*, 12th edition (Mason, OH: Cengage Learning, 2016), Chapters 2 and 3.

**FIGURE 8.7** Betas: Relative Volatility of Stocks H, A, and L

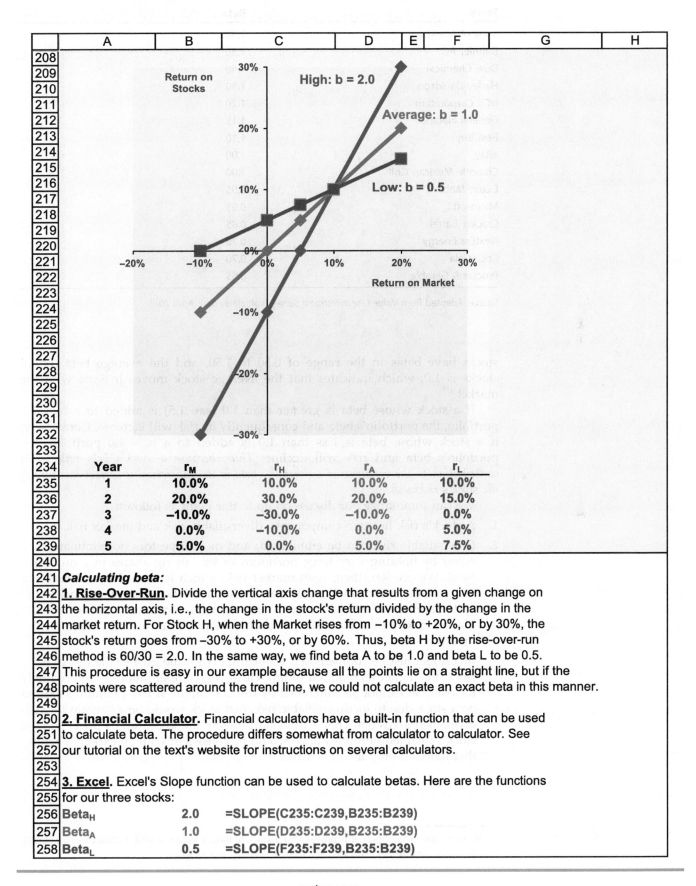

| | Year | $r_M$ | $r_H$ | $r_A$ | $r_L$ |
|---|---|---|---|---|---|
| 235 | 1 | 10.0% | 10.0% | 10.0% | 10.0% |
| 236 | 2 | 20.0% | 30.0% | 20.0% | 15.0% |
| 237 | 3 | −10.0% | −30.0% | −10.0% | 0.0% |
| 238 | 4 | 0.0% | −10.0% | 0.0% | 5.0% |
| 239 | 5 | 5.0% | 0.0% | 5.0% | 7.5% |

*Calculating beta:*

**1. Rise-Over-Run.** Divide the vertical axis change that results from a given change on the horizontal axis, i.e., the change in the stock's return divided by the change in the market return. For Stock H, when the Market rises from −10% to +20%, or by 30%, the stock's return goes from −30% to +30%, or by 60%. Thus, beta H by the rise-over-run method is 60/30 = 2.0. In the same way, we find beta A to be 1.0 and beta L to be 0.5. This procedure is easy in our example because all the points lie on a straight line, but if the points were scattered around the trend line, we could not calculate an exact beta in this manner.

**2. Financial Calculator.** Financial calculators have a built-in function that can be used to calculate beta. The procedure differs somewhat from calculator to calculator. See our tutorial on the text's website for instructions on several calculators.

**3. Excel.** Excel's Slope function can be used to calculate betas. Here are the functions for our three stocks:

| | | | |
|---|---|---|---|
| Beta$_H$ | 2.0 | =SLOPE(C235:C239,B235:B239) |
| Beta$_A$ | 1.0 | =SLOPE(D235:D239,B235:B239) |
| Beta$_L$ | 0.5 | =SLOPE(F235:F239,B235:B239) |

▼ **TABLE 8.5**     List of Selected Company Beta Coefficients

| Stock | Beta |
| --- | --- |
| Bank of America | 1.50 |
| Daimler AG | 1.50 |
| Dow Chemical | 1.40 |
| Harley-Davidson | 1.30 |
| NCR Corporation | 1.20 |
| General Electric | 1.15 |
| Best Buy | 1.10 |
| eBay | 1.00 |
| Chipotle Mexican Grill | 1.00 |
| Exxon Mobil | 0.95 |
| Microsoft | 0.95 |
| Cracker Barrel | 0.85 |
| NextEra Energy | 0.70 |
| Coca-Cola | 0.70 |
| Procter & Gamble | 0.65 |

Source: Adapted from *Value Line Investment Survey* (valueline.com), April 2015.

stocks have betas in the range of 0.50 to 1.50, and the average beta for all stocks is 1.0, which indicates that the average stock moves in sync with the market.[19]

If a stock whose beta is greater than 1.0 (say 1.5) is added to a $b_p = 1.0$ portfolio, the portfolio's beta and consequently its risk will increase. Conversely, if a stock whose beta is less than 1.0 is added to a $b_p = 1.0$ portfolio, the portfolio's beta and risk will decline. *Thus, because a stock's beta reflects its contribution to the riskiness of a portfolio, beta is the theoretically correct measure of the stock's riskiness.*

We can summarize our discussion up to this point as follows:

1.  A stock's risk has two components, diversifiable risk and market risk.

2.  Diversifiable risk can be eliminated; and most investors do eliminate it, either by holding very large portfolios or by buying shares in a mutual fund. We are left, then, with market risk, which is caused by general movements in the stock market and reflects the fact that most stocks are systematically affected by events such as wars, recessions, and inflation. Market risk is the only risk that should matter to a rational, diversified investor.

3.  Investors must be compensated for bearing risk—the greater the risk of a stock, the higher its required return. However, compensation is required only for risk that cannot be eliminated by diversification. If risk premiums existed on a stock due to its diversifiable risk, that stock would be a bargain to well-diversified investors. They would start buying it and bid up its price, and the stock's final (equilibrium) price would be consistent with an expected return that reflected only its market risk.

---

[19]Although fairly uncommon, it is possible for a stock to have a negative beta. In that case, the stock's returns would tend to rise whenever the returns on other stocks fell.

To illustrate this point, suppose half of Stock B's risk is market risk (it occurs because the stock moves up and down with the market), and the other half is diversifiable. You are thinking of buying Stock B and holding it in a one-stock portfolio, so you would be exposed to all of its risk. As compensation for bearing so much risk, you want a risk premium of 8% over the 3% T-bond rate; so your required return is $r_B = 3\% + 8\% = 11\%$. But other investors, including your professor, are well diversified. They are also looking at Stock B, but they would hold it in diversified portfolios, eliminate its diversifiable risk, and thus be exposed to only half as much risk as you are. Therefore, their required risk premium would be half as large as yours, and their required rate of return would be $r_B = 3\% + 4\% = 7\%$.

If the stock was priced to yield the 11% you require, those diversified investors, including your professor, would buy it, push its price up and its yield down, and prevent you from purchasing the stock at a price low enough to provide the 11% return. In the end, you would have to accept a 7% return or keep your money in the bank.

4. The market risk of a stock is measured by its beta coefficient, which is an index of the stock's relative volatility. Here are some benchmark betas:

   $b = 0.5$: Stock is only half as volatile, or risky, as an average stock.
   $b = 1.0$: Stock is of average risk.
   $b = 2.0$: Stock is twice as risky as an average stock.

5. A portfolio consisting of low-beta stocks will also have a low beta because the beta of a portfolio is a weighted average of its individual securities' betas, found using this equation:

$$b_p = w_1 b_1 + w_2 b_2 + \cdots + w_N b_N$$

$$= \sum_{i=1}^{N} w_i b_i$$

8.5

Here $b_p$ is the beta of the portfolio, and it shows how volatile the portfolio is relative to the market; $w_i$ is the fraction of the portfolio invested in the $i$th stock; and $b_i$ is the beta coefficient of the $i$th stock. To illustrate, if an investor holds a $100,000 portfolio consisting of $33,333.33 invested in each of three stocks and if each of the stocks has a beta of 0.70, the portfolio's beta will be $b_p = 0.70$:

$$b_p = 0.333(0.70) + 0.333(0.70) + 0.333(0.70) = 0.70$$

Such a portfolio would be less risky than the market, so it should experience relatively narrow price swings and have relatively small rate-of-return fluctuations. In terms of Figure 8.7, the slope of its regression line would be 0.70, which is less than that for a portfolio of average stocks.

Now suppose one of the existing stocks is sold and replaced by a stock with $b_i = 2.00$. This action will increase the portfolio's beta from $b_{p1} = 0.70$ to $b_{p2} = 1.13$:

$$b_{p2} = 0.333(0.70) + 0.333(0.70) + 0.333(2.00) = 1.13$$

Had a stock with $b_i = 0.20$ been added, the portfolio's beta would have declined from 0.70 to 0.53. Adding a low-beta stock would therefore reduce the portfolio's riskiness. Consequently, changing the stocks in a portfolio can change the riskiness of that portfolio.

6. Because a stock's beta coefficient determines how the stock affects the riskiness of a diversified portfolio, beta is, in theory, the most relevant measure of a stock's risk.

## quick question

**QUESTION:**

Portfolio P consists of two stocks: 50% is invested in Stock A and 50% is invested in Stock B. Stock A has a standard deviation of 25% and a beta of 1.2, and Stock B has a standard deviation of 35% and a beta of 0.80. The correlation between these stocks is 0.4.

a. What is the standard deviation of Portfolio P?
1. Less than 30%
2. 30%
3. More than 30%
b. What is the beta of Portfolio P?
c. Which stock is riskier to a diversified investor?

**ANSWER:**

a. No calculation is needed to answer this question. Remember that the standard deviation of a portfolio of two stocks is less than the weighted average of the individual stocks' standard deviations, as long as the correlation between the stocks is less than 1.0. So, in this case because the correlation is 0.4, we know that the standard deviation of Portfolio P is **less than 30%.**

b. $b_p = 0.5(1.2) + 0.5(0.8)$
$b_p = $ **1.0**

The beta of a portfolio is equal to the weighted average of the individual stocks' betas.

c. The relevant measure of risk to a diversified investor is beta. It follows that a diversified investor would view the higher beta stock **(Stock A)** as being more risky.

## GLOBAL PERSPECTIVES

### *The Benefits of Diversifying Overseas*

The increasing availability of international securities is making it possible to achieve a better risk-return trade-off than could be obtained by investing only in U.S. securities. So investing overseas might result in a portfolio with less risk but a higher expected return. This result occurs because of low correlations between the returns on U.S. and international securities, along with potentially high returns on overseas stocks.

Figure 8.6, presented earlier, demonstrated that an investor can reduce the risk of his or her portfolio by holding a number of stocks. The figure below suggests that investors may be able to reduce risk even further by holding a portfolio of stocks from all around the world, given the fact that the returns on domestic and international stocks are not perfectly correlated.

Even though foreign stocks represent roughly 60% of the worldwide equity market and despite the apparent benefits from investing overseas, the typical U.S. investor still puts less than 10% of his or her money in foreign stocks. One possible explanation for this reluctance to invest overseas is that investors prefer domestic stocks because of lower transactions costs. However, this explanation is questionable because recent studies reveal that investors buy and sell overseas stocks more frequently than they trade their domestic stocks.

Other explanations for the domestic bias include the additional risks from investing overseas (e.g., exchange rate risk) and the fact that the typical U.S. investor is uninformed about international investments and/or thinks that international investments are extremely risky. It has been argued that world capital markets have become more integrated, causing the correlation of returns between different countries to increase, which reduces the benefits from international diversification. In addition, U.S. corporations are investing more internationally, providing U.S. investors with international diversification even if they purchase only U.S. stocks.

Given the benefits of global diversification, many analysts recommend that U.S. investors hold a significant percentage of foreign assets in their portfolio. A recent report in *The Wall Street Journal* asked a team of top investment advisors their thoughts regarding the optimal allocation of foreign assets. As you might expect, their opinions varied—but there seemed to be a fairly broad consensus that the average U.S. investor should hold somewhere between 30% and 40% of foreign assets in his or her portfolio. The analysts also pointed out that the optimal target varies over time and across individuals.

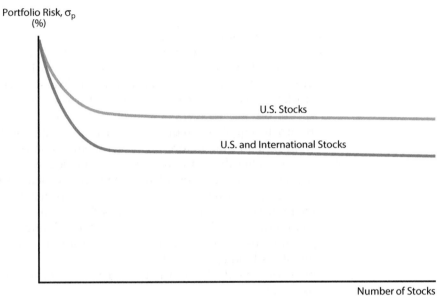

Portfolio Risk, $\sigma_p$ (%)

U.S. Stocks

U.S. and International Stocks

Number of Stocks in the Portfolio

Sources: "The Experts: How Much Should You Invest Abroad?" *The Wall Street Journal* (online.wsj.com), June 10, 2013; and Kenneth Kasa, "Measuring the Gains from International Portfolio Diversification," *Federal Reserve Bank of San Francisco Weekly Letter*, no. 94–14, April 8, 1994.

## SelfTest

Explain the following statement: An asset held as part of a portfolio is generally less risky than the same asset held in isolation.

What is meant by *perfect positive correlation, perfect negative correlation,* and *zero correlation*?

In general, can the riskiness of a portfolio be reduced to zero by increasing the number of stocks in the portfolio? Explain.

What is an average-risk stock? What is the beta of such a stock?

Why is it argued that beta is the best measure of a stock's risk?

An investor has a two-stock portfolio with $25,000 invested in Stock X and $50,000 invested in Stock Y. X's beta is 1.50, and Y's beta is 0.60. What is the beta of the investor's portfolio? **(0.90)**

# 8-4 The Relationship between Risk and Rates of Return

The preceding section demonstrated that under the CAPM theory, beta is the most appropriate measure of a stock's relevant risk. The next issue is this: For a given level of risk as measured by beta, what rate of return is required to compensate investors for bearing that risk? To begin, let us define the following terms:

$\hat{r}_i$ = *expected* rate of return on the $i$th stock.

$r_i$ = *required* rate of return on the $i$th stock. Note that if $\hat{r}_i$ is less than $r_i$, the typical investor will not purchase this stock or will sell it if he or she owns it. If $\hat{r}_i$ is greater than $r_i$, the investor will purchase the stock because it looks like a bargain. Investors will be indifferent if $\hat{r}_i = r_i$. Buying and selling by investors tends to force the expected return to equal the required return, although the two can differ from time to time before the adjustment is completed.

$\bar{r}_i$ = realized, after-the-fact return. A person obviously does not know $\bar{r}_i$ at the time he or she is considering the purchase of a stock.

$r_{RF}$ = risk-free rate of return. In this context, $r_{RF}$ is generally measured by the return on U.S. Treasury securities. Some analysts recommend that short-term T-bills be used; others recommend long-term T-bonds. We generally use T-bonds because their maturity is closer to the average investor's holding period for stocks.

$b_i$ = beta coefficient of the $i$th stock. The beta of an average stock is $b_A = 1.0$.

$r_M$ = required rate of return on a portfolio consisting of all stocks, which is called the *market portfolio*. $r_M$ is also the required rate of return on an average ($b_A = 1.0$) stock.

$RP_M = (r_M - r_{RF})$ = risk premium on "the market" and the premium on an average stock. This is the additional return over the risk-free rate required to compensate an average investor for assuming an average amount of risk. Average risk means a stock where $b_i = b_A = 1.0$.

$RP_i = (r_M - r_{RF})b_i = (RP_M)b_i$ = risk premium on the $i$th stock. A stock's risk premium will be less than, equal to, or greater than the premium on an average stock, $RP_M$, depending on whether its beta is less than, equal to, or greater than 1.0. If $b_i = b_A = 1.0$, then $RP_i = RP_M$.

**Market Risk Premium, $RP_M$**

The additional return over the risk-free rate needed to compensate investors for assuming an average amount of risk.

The **market risk premium, $RP_M$**, shows the premium that investors require for bearing the risk of an average stock. The size of this premium depends on how risky investors think the stock market is and on their degree of risk aversion. Let us assume that at the current time, Treasury bonds yield $r_{RF} = 3\%$, and an average share of stock has a required rate of return of $r_M = 8\%$. Therefore, the market risk premium is 5%, calculated as follows:

$$RP_M = r_M - r_{RF} = 8\% - 3\% = 5\%$$

It should be noted that the risk premium of an average stock, $r_M - r_{RF}$, is hard to measure because it is impossible to obtain a precise estimate of the expected future return of the market, $r_M$.[20] Given the difficulty of estimating future market returns, analysts often look to historical data to estimate the

---

[20]This concept, as well as other aspects of the CAPM, is discussed in more detail in Chapter 3 of Eugene F. Brigham and Phillip R. Daves, *Intermediate Financial Management*, 12th edition (Mason, OH: Cengage Learning, 2016). That chapter also discusses the assumptions embodied in the CAPM framework. Some of those assumptions are unrealistic; and because of this, the theory does not hold exactly.

market risk premium. Historical data suggest that the market risk premium varies somewhat from year to year due to changes in investors' risk aversion but that it has generally ranged from 4% to 8%.

Although historical estimates might be a good starting point for estimating the market risk premium, those estimates would be misleading if investors' attitudes toward risk changed considerably over time. (See "Estimating the Market Risk Premium" box on page 290.) Indeed, many analysts have argued that the market risk premium has fallen in recent years. If this claim is correct, the market risk premium is considerably lower than one based on historical data.

The risk premium on individual stocks varies in a systematic manner from the market risk premium. For example, if one stock is twice as risky as another stock as measured by their beta coefficients, its risk premium should be twice as high. Therefore, if we know the market risk premium, $RP_M$, and the stock's beta, $b_i$, we can find its risk premium as the product $(RP_M)b_i$. For example, if beta for Stock L = 0.5 and $RP_M$ = 5%, $RP_L$ will be 2.5%:

$$\text{Risk premium for Stock L} = RP_L = (RP_M)b_L$$
$$= (5\%)(0.5)$$
$$= 2.5\%$$

▼ 8.6

As the discussion in Chapter 6 implied, the required return for any stock can be found as follows:

**Required return on a stock = Risk-free return + Premium for the stock's risk**

Here the risk-free return includes a premium for expected inflation; and if we assume that the stocks under consideration have similar maturities and liquidity, the required return on Stock L can be found using the **security market line (SML) equation**:

$$\frac{\text{Required return}}{\text{on Stock L}} = \frac{\text{Risk-free}}{\text{return}} + \left(\begin{array}{c}\text{Market risk}\\\text{premium}\end{array}\right)\left(\begin{array}{c}\text{Stock L's}\\\text{beta}\end{array}\right)$$

▼ 8.7

$$r_L = r_{RF} + (r_M - r_{RF})b_L$$
$$= r_{RF} + (RP_M)b_L$$
$$= 3\% + (8\% - 3\%)(0.5)$$
$$= 3\% + 2.5\%$$
$$= 5.5\%$$

*Security Market Line (SML) Equation*
An equation that shows the relationship between risk as measured by beta and the required rates of return on individual securities.

Stock H had $b_H$ = 2.0, so its required rate of return is 13%:

$$r_H = 3\% + (5\%)2.0 = 13\%$$

An average stock, with b = 1.0, would have a required return of 8%, the same as the market return:

$$r_A = 3\% + (5\%)1.0 = 8\% = r_M$$

The SML equation is plotted in Figure 8.8 using the data shown below the graph on Stocks L, A, and H and assuming that $r_{RF}$ = 3% and $r_M$ = 8%. Note the following points:

1. Required rates of return are shown on the vertical axis, and risk as measured by beta is shown on the horizontal axis. This graph is quite different from the one shown in Figure 8.7, where we calculated betas. In the earlier graph, the returns on individual stocks were plotted on the vertical axis, and returns on the market index were shown on the horizontal axis. The betas found in Figure 8.7 were then plotted as points on the horizontal axis of Figure 8.8.

# ESTIMATING THE MARKET RISK PREMIUM

The capital asset pricing model (CAPM) is more than a theory describing the trade-off between risk and return—it is also widely used in practice. As we will see later, investors use the CAPM to determine the discount rate for valuing stocks, and corporate managers use it to estimate the cost of equity capital.

The market risk premium is a key component of the CAPM, and it should be the difference between the *expected future return on the overall stock market and the expected future return on a riskless investment.* However, we cannot obtain investors' expectations; instead, academicians and practitioners often use a historical risk premium as a proxy for the expected risk premium. The historical premium is found by taking the difference between the actual return on the overall stock market and the risk-free rate during a number of different years and then averaging the annual results. Morningstar (through its recent purchase of Ibbotson Associates) may provide the most comprehensive estimates of historical risk premiums. It reports that the annual premiums have averaged 7% over the past 89 years.

There are three potential problems with historical risk premiums. First, what is the proper number of years over which to compute the average? Morningstar goes back to 1926, when good data first became available; but that is an arbitrary choice, and the starting and ending points make a major difference in the calculated premium.

Second, historical premiums are likely to be misleading at times when the market risk premium is changing. To illustrate, the stock market was very strong from 1995 through 1999, *in part because investors were becoming less risk-averse, which means that they applied a lower risk premium when they valued stocks.* The strong market resulted in stock returns of about 30% per year; and when bond yields were subtracted from the high stock returns, the calculated risk premiums averaged 22.3% a year. When those high numbers were added to data from prior years, they caused the long-run historical risk premium as reported by Morningstar to increase. Thus, a declining "true" risk premium led to very high stock returns, which in turn led to an increase in the calculated historical risk premium. That's a worrisome result, to say the least.

The third concern is that historical estimates may be biased upward because they include only the returns of firms that have survived—they do not reflect the losses incurred on investments in failed firms. Stephen Brown, William Goetzmann, and Stephen Ross discussed the implications of this *survivorship bias* in a 1995 *Journal of Finance* article. Putting these ideas into practice, Tim Koller, Marc Goedhart, and David Wessels recently suggested that survivorship bias increases historical returns by 1% to 2% a year. Therefore, they suggest that practitioners subtract 1% to 2% from the historical estimates to obtain the risk premium for use in the CAPM.

A 2015 survey of more than 5,056 academics, analysts, and practitioners in 41 countries provides further insights into the required market risk premium. For the United States, responses from academics, analysts, and practitioners indicated an average required market risk premium of 5.5%. Respondents from Argentina indicated an average required market risk premium of 22.9%, and respondents from the United Kingdom indicated an average required market risk premium of only 5.2%.

Sources: *Ibbotson Stocks, Bonds, Bills, and Inflation: 2015 Classic Yearbook* (Chicago: Morningstar, Inc., 2015), p.91; Pablo Fernandez, Pablo Linares, and Isabel Fernando Acín, "Discount Rate (Risk-Free Rate and Market Risk Premium) Used for 41 Countries in 2015: A Survey," *Social Science Research Network*, April 23, 2015, ssrn.com/abstract=2598104; John R. Graham and Campbell R. Harvey, "The Equity Risk Premium in 2013," *Social Science Research Network*, January 28, 2013, ssrn.com/abstract=2206538; Stephen J. Brown, William N. Goetzmann, and Stephen A. Ross, "Survival," *Journal of Finance*, vol. 50, no. 3 (July 1995), pp. 853–873; and Tim Koller, Marc Goedhart, and David Wessels, *Valuation: Measuring and Managing the Value of Companies*, 5th edition (New York: McKinsey & Company, 2010).

2. Riskless securities have $b_i = 0$; so the return on the riskless asset, $r_{RF} = 3\%$, is shown as the vertical axis intercept in Figure 8.8.

3. The slope of the SML in Figure 8.8 can be found using the rise-over-run procedure. When beta goes from 0 to 1.0, the required return goes from 3% to 8%, or 5%; so the slope is 5%/1.0 = 5%. Thus, a 1-unit increase in beta causes a 5% increase in the required rate of return.

4. The slope of the SML reflects the degree of risk aversion in the economy—the greater the average investor's risk aversion, (a) the steeper the slope of the line and (b) the greater the risk premium for all stocks—hence, the higher the required rate of return on all stocks.

Both the SML and a company's position on it change over time due to changes in interest rates, investors' risk aversion, and individual companies' betas. Such changes are discussed in the following sections.

**FIGURE 8.8** The Security Market Line (SML)

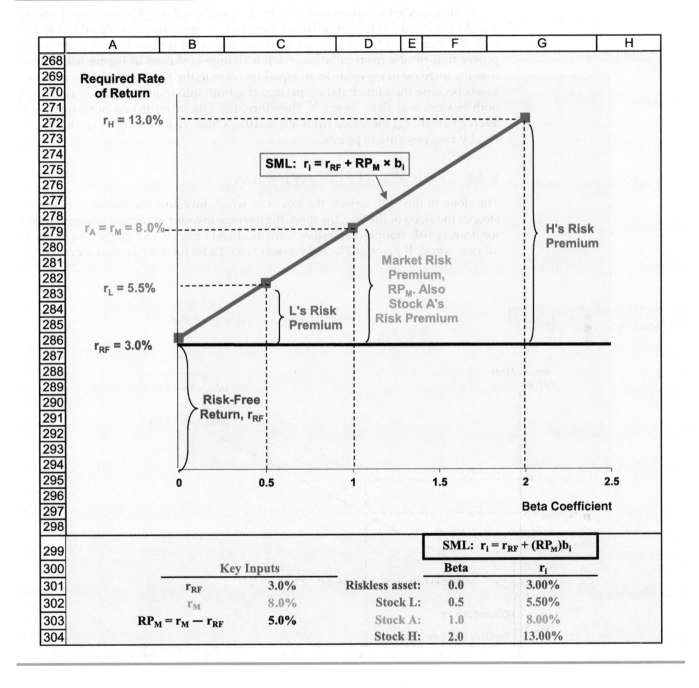

| | Key Inputs | | | Beta | $r_i$ |
|---|---|---|---|---|---|
| | $r_{RF}$ | 3.0% | Riskless asset: | 0.0 | 3.00% |
| | $r_M$ | 8.0% | Stock L: | 0.5 | 5.50% |
| $RP_M = r_M - r_{RF}$ | | 5.0% | Stock A: | 1.0 | 8.00% |
| | | | Stock H: | 2.0 | 13.00% |

SML: $r_i = r_{RF} + (RP_M)b_i$

## 8-4A THE IMPACT OF EXPECTED INFLATION

As we discussed in Chapter 6, interest amounts to "rent" on borrowed money, or the price of money. Thus, $r_{RF}$ is the price of money to a riskless borrower. We also saw that the risk-free rate as measured by the rate on U.S. Treasury securities is called the *nominal, or quoted, rate,* and it consists of two elements: (1) a *real inflation-free rate of return, r\**, and (2) an *inflation premium, IP*, equal to the anticipated rate of inflation.[21] Thus, $r_{RF} = r^* + IP$. Therefore, the 3% $r_{RF}$ shown in Figure 8.8 might be

---

[21]Long-term Treasury bonds also contain a maturity risk premium, MRP. We include the MRP in r* to simplify the discussion.

thought of as consisting of a 1% real risk-free rate of return plus a 2% inflation premium: $r_{RF} = r^* + IP = 1\% + 2\% = 3\%$.

If the expected inflation rate rose by 2%, to $2\% + 2\% = 4\%$, $r_{RF}$ would rise to 5%. As the expected rate of inflation increases, a premium must be added to the real risk-free rate of return to compensate investors for the loss of purchasing power that results from inflation. Such a change is shown in Figure 8.9. Notice that the increase in $r_{RF}$ leads to an equal increase in the rates of return on all risky assets because the same inflation premium is built into required rates of return on both riskless and risky assets.[22] Therefore, the rate of return on our illustrative average stock, $r_A$, increases from 8% to 10%. Other risky securities' returns also rise by two percentage points.

## 8-4B CHANGES IN RISK AVERSION

The slope of the SML reflects the extent to which investors are averse to risk—the steeper the slope of the line, the more the average investor requires as compensation for bearing risk. Suppose investors were indifferent to risk; that is, they were not at all risk-averse. If $r_{RF}$ was 3%, risky assets would also have a required return of 3%

---

**FIGURE 8.9**    Shift in the SML Caused by an Increase in Expected Inflation

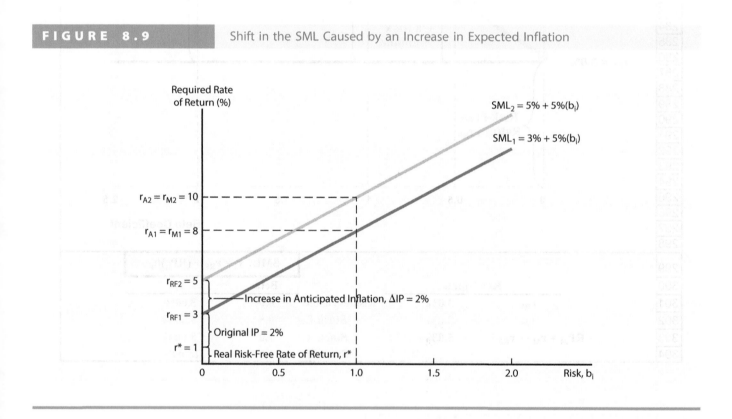

---

[22]Recall that the inflation premium for any asset is the average expected rate of inflation over the asset's life. Thus, in this analysis, we must assume that all securities plotted on the SML graph have the same life or that the expected rate of future inflation is constant.

It should also be noted that r in a CAPM analysis can be proxied by either a long-term rate (the T-bond rate) or a short-term rate (the T-bill rate). Traditionally, the T-bill rate was used; but in recent years, there has been a movement toward use of the T-bond rate because there is a closer relationship between T-bond yields and stocks' returns than between T-bill yields and stocks' returns. See *Ibbotson Stocks, Bonds, Bills, and Inflation: 2013 Valuation Yearbook* (Chicago: Morningstar, Inc., 2013), p. 44, for a discussion.

FIGURE 8.10 Shift in the SML Caused by Increased Risk Aversion

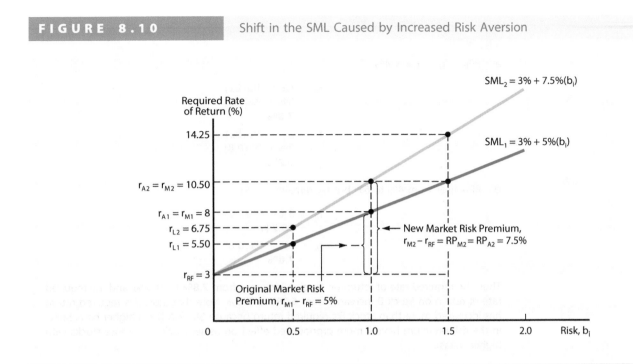

because if there were no risk aversion, there would be no risk premium. In that case, the SML would plot as a horizontal line. However, because investors are risk-averse, there is a risk premium; and the greater the risk aversion, the steeper the slope of the SML.

Figure 8.10 illustrates an increase in risk aversion. The market risk premium rises from 5% to 7.5%, causing $r_M$ to rise from $r_{M1} = 8\%$ to $r_{M2} = 10.5\%$. The returns on other risky assets also rise, and the effect of this shift in risk aversion is more pronounced on riskier securities. For example, the required return on Stock L with $b = 0.5$ increases by only 1.25 percentage points, from 5.5% to 6.75%, whereas the required return on a stock with a beta of 1.5 increases by 3.75 percentage points, from 10.5% to 14.25%.

quick question

QUESTION:

The risk-free rate is 3%, and the market risk premium $(r_M - r_{RF})$ is 4%. Stock A has a beta of 1.2, and Stock B has a beta of 0.8.

a. What is the required rate of return on each stock?
b. Assume that investors become less willing to take on risk (i.e., they become more risk averse), so the market risk premium rises from 4% to 6%. Assume that the risk-free rate remains constant. What effect will this have on the required rates of return on the two stocks?

ANSWER:

a.   $RP_M = r_M - r_{RF} = 4\%$

$$r_A = r_{RF} + RP_M(b_A)$$
$$= 3\% + 4\%(1.2)$$
$$= \textbf{7.8\%}$$

$$r_B = r_{RF} + RP_M(b_B)$$
$$= 3\% + 4\%(0.8)$$
$$= \textbf{6.2\%}$$

b.   $RP_M$ rises from 4% to 6% but $r_{RF}$ remains at 3%.

$$r_A = 3\% + 6\%(1.2)$$
$$= \textbf{10.2\%}$$

$$r_B = 3\% + 6\%(0.8)$$
$$= \textbf{7.8\%}$$

Thus, the required rate of return on Stock A increases from **7.8%** to **10.2%**, and the required rate of return on Stock B increases from **6.2%** to **7.8%**. Note that Stock A's required return has increased more than Stock B's required return because Stock A has a higher beta. Shifts in the risk premium have a more pronounced effect on riskier stocks (i.e., those stocks with higher betas).

## 8-4C CHANGES IN A STOCK'S BETA COEFFICIENT

As we see later in the book, a firm can influence its market risk (hence, its beta) through changes in the composition of its assets and through changes in the amount of debt it uses. A company's beta can also change as a result of external factors such as increased competition in its industry and expiration of basic patents. When such changes occur, the firm's required rate of return also changes; and as we see in Chapter 9, this change will affect its stock price. For example, consider Keller Medical Products, with a beta of 1.20. Now suppose some action occurred that caused Keller's beta to increase from 1.2 to 2.0. If the conditions depicted in Figure 8.8 held, Keller's required rate of return would increase from 9% to 13%:

$$r_1 = r_{RF} + (r_M - r_{RF})b_i$$
$$= 3\% + (8\% - 3\%)1.20$$
$$= 9\%$$

to

$$r_2 = 3\% + (8\% - 3\%)2.0$$
$$= 13\%$$

As we will see in Chapter 9, increases in beta have a negative effect on a firm's stock price.[23]

---

[23]The concepts covered in this chapter are obviously important to investors, but they are also important for managers in two key ways. First, as we see in the next chapter, the risk of a stock affects the required rate of return on equity capital, and that feeds directly into the important subject of capital budgeting. Second, and also related to capital budgeting, the "true" risk of individual projects is impacted by their correlation with the firm's other projects and with other assets that the firm's stockholders might hold. We discuss these topics in later chapters.

## SelfTest

Differentiate between a stock's expected rate of return ($\hat{r}$); required rate of return (r); and realized, after-the-fact historical return ($\bar{r}$). Which would have to be larger to induce you to buy the stock, $\hat{r}$ or r? At a given point in time, would $\hat{r}$, r, and $\bar{r}$ typically be the same or different? Explain.

What are the differences between the relative volatility graph (Figure 8.7), where "betas are made," and the SML graph (Figure 8.8), where "betas are used"? Explain how both graphs are constructed and what information they convey.

What would happen to the SML graph in Figure 8.8 if expected inflation increased or decreased?

What happens to the SML graph when risk aversion increases or decreases?

What would the SML look like if investors were indifferent to risk, that is, if they had zero risk aversion?

How can a firm influence the size of its beta?

A stock has a beta of 1.2. Assume that the risk-free rate is 4.5%, and the market risk premium is 5%. What is the stock's required rate of return? **(10.5%)**

# 8-5 Some Concerns about Beta and the CAPM[24]

The capital asset pricing model (CAPM) is more than just an abstract theory described in textbooks—it has great intuitive appeal and is widely used by analysts, investors, and corporations. However, a number of recent studies have raised concerns about its validity. For example, a study by Eugene Fama of the University of Chicago and Kenneth French of Dartmouth found no historical relationship between stocks' returns and their market betas, confirming a position long held by some professors and stock market analysts.[25]

As an alternative to the traditional CAPM, researchers and practitioners are developing models with more explanatory variables than just beta. These multivariable models represent an attractive generalization of the traditional CAPM model's insight that market risk—risk that cannot be diversified away—underlies the pricing of assets. In the multivariable models, risk is assumed to be caused by a number of different factors, whereas the CAPM gauges risk only relative to returns on the market portfolio. These multivariable models represent a potentially important step forward in finance theory; however, they also have some deficiencies when applied in practice. As a result, the basic CAPM is still the most widely used method for estimating required rates of return on stocks.

*Kenneth French's website, mba.tuck.dartmouth.edu /pages/faculty/ken.french /index.html, is an excellent resource for information regarding factors related to stock returns.*

---

[24]This section presents a brief overview regarding alternative models to the CAPM. For a more detailed discussion on this topic refer to Eugene F. Brigham and Phillip R. Daves, *Intermediate Financial Management*, 12th edition (Mason, OH: Cengage Learning, 2016), Chapter 3.

[25]See Eugene F. Fama and Kenneth R. French, "The Cross-Section of Expected Stock Returns," *Journal of Finance*, vol. 47, no. 2 (June 1992), pp. 427–465; and Eugene F. Fama and Kenneth R. French, "Common Risk Factors in the Returns on Stocks and Bonds," *Journal of Financial Economics*, vol. 33, no. 1 (February 1993), pp. 3–56. They found that stock returns are related to firm size and market/book ratios. Small firms and firms with low market/book ratios had higher returns; however, they found no relationship between returns and beta.

**Self Test**

Have there been any studies that question the validity of the CAPM? Explain.

## 8-6 Some Concluding Thoughts: Implications for Corporate Managers and Investors

The connection between risk and return is an important concept, and it has numerous implications for both corporate managers and investors. As we will see in later chapters, corporate managers spend a great deal of time assessing the risk and returns on individual projects. Indeed, given their concerns about the risk of individual projects, it might be fair to ask why we spend so much time discussing the riskiness of stocks. Why not begin by looking at the riskiness of such business assets as plant and equipment? *The reason is that for management whose primary goal is stock price maximization, the overriding consideration is the riskiness of the firm's stock, and the relevant risk of any physical asset must be measured in terms of its effect on the stock's risk as seen by investors.* For example, suppose Goodyear, the tire company, is considering a major investment in a new product, recapped tires. Sales of recaps (hence, earnings on the new operation) are highly uncertain; so on a stand-alone basis, the new venture appears to be quite risky. However, suppose returns in the recap business are negatively correlated with Goodyear's other operations—when times are good and people have plenty of money, they buy new cars with new tires; but when times are bad, they tend to keep their old cars and buy recaps for them. Therefore, returns would be high on regular operations and low on the recap division during good times, but the opposite would be true during recessions. The result might be a pattern like that shown earlier in Figure 8.4 for Stocks W and M. Thus, what appears to be a risky investment when viewed on a stand-alone basis might not be very risky when viewed within the context of the company as a whole.

This analysis can be extended to the corporation's stockholders. Because Goodyear's stock is owned by diversified stockholders, the real issue each time management makes an investment decision is this: How will this investment affect the risk of our stockholders? Again, the stand-alone risk of an individual project may look quite high; however, viewed in the context of the project's effect on stockholder risk, it may not be very large. We address this issue again in Chapter 12, where we examine the effects of capital budgeting on companies' beta coefficients and thus on stockholders' risks.

Although these concepts are obviously important for individual investors, they are also important for corporate managers. We summarize some key ideas that all investors should consider:

1. There is a trade-off between risk and return. The average investor likes higher returns but dislikes risk. It follows that higher-risk investments need to offer investors higher expected returns. Put another way—if you are seeking higher returns, you must be willing to assume higher risks.

2. Diversification is crucial. By diversifying wisely, investors can dramatically reduce risk without reducing their expected returns. Don't put all of your money in one or two stocks or in one or two industries. A huge mistake that many people make is to invest a high percentage of their funds in their employer's stock. If the company goes bankrupt, they not only lose their job but also their invested capital. Although no stock is completely riskless, you can smooth out the bumps by holding a well-diversified portfolio.

3. Real returns are what matters. All investors should understand the difference between nominal and real returns. When assessing performance, the real return (what remains after inflation) is what matters. It follows that as expected inflation increases, investors need to receive higher nominal returns.

4. The risk of an investment often depends on how long you plan to hold the investment. Common stocks, for example, can be extremely risky for short-term investors. However, over the long haul, the bumps tend to even out; thus, stocks are less risky when held as part of a long-term portfolio. Indeed, in his best-selling book *Stocks for the Long Run,* Jeremy Siegel of the University of Pennsylvania concludes that "[t]he safest long-term investment for the preservation of purchasing power has clearly been stocks, not bonds."

5. Although the past gives us insights into the risk and returns on various investments, there is no guarantee that the future will repeat the past. Stocks that have performed well in recent years might tumble, while stocks that have struggled may rebound. The same thing may hold true for the stock market as a whole. Even Jeremy Siegel, who has preached that stocks have historically been good long-term investments, also has argued that there is no assurance that returns in the future will be as strong as they have been in the past. More importantly, when purchasing a stock, you always need to ask, "Is this stock fairly valued, or is it currently priced too high?" We discuss this issue more completely in the next chapter.

## Self*Test*

Explain the following statement: The stand-alone risk of an individual corporate project may be quite high, but viewed in the context of its effect on stockholders' risk, the project's true risk may not be very large.

How does the correlation between returns on a project and returns on the firm's other assets affect the project's risk?

What are some important concepts for individual investors to consider when evaluating the risk and returns of various investments?

## TYING IT ALL TOGETHER

In this chapter, we described the relationship between risk and return. We discussed how to calculate risk and return for individual assets and for portfolios. In particular, we differentiated between stand-alone risk and risk in a portfolio context, and we explained the benefits of diversification. We also discussed the CAPM, which describes how risk should be measured and how risk affects rates of return. In the chapters that follow, we give you the tools needed to estimate the required rates of return on a firm's common stock and explain how that return and the yield on its bonds are used to develop the firm's cost of capital. As you will see, the cost of capital is a key element in the capital budgeting process.

# Self-Test Questions and Problems

(Solutions Appear in Appendix A)

**ST-1**   **KEY TERMS**   Define each of the following terms using graphs or equations to illustrate your answers whenever feasible:

a. Risk; stand-alone risk; probability distribution
b. Expected rate of return, $\hat{r}$
c. Standard deviation, $\sigma$; coefficient of variation (CV)
d. Risk aversion; risk premium (RP); realized rate of return, $\bar{r}$
e. Risk premium for Stock i, $RP_i$; market risk premium, $RP_M$
f. Expected return on a portfolio, $\hat{r}_p$; market portfolio
g. Correlation; correlation coefficient $\rho$
h. Market risk; diversifiable risk; relevant risk
i. Capital asset pricing model (CAPM)
j. Beta coefficient, b; average stock's beta, $b_A$
k. Security market line (SML) equation

**ST-2**   **REALIZED RATES OF RETURN**   Stocks A and B have the following historical returns:

| Year | Stock A's Returns, $r_A$ | Stock B's Returns, $r_B$ |
|------|------|------|
| 2011 | (24.25%) | 5.50% |
| 2012 | 18.50 | 26.73 |
| 2013 | 38.67 | 48.25 |
| 2014 | 14.33 | (4.50) |
| 2015 | 39.13 | 43.86 |

a. Calculate the average rate of return for each stock during the period 2011 through 2015. Assume that someone held a portfolio consisting of 50% of Stock A and 50% of Stock B. What would the realized rate of return on the portfolio have been in each year from 2011 through 2015? What would the average return on the portfolio have been during that period?

b. Calculate the standard deviation of returns for each stock and for the portfolio. Use Equation 8.2a.

c. Looking at the annual returns on the two stocks, would you guess that the correlation coefficient between the two stocks is closer to +0.8 or to −0.8?

d. If more randomly selected stocks had been included in the portfolio, which of the following is the most accurate statement of what would have happened to $\sigma_p$?
1. $\sigma_p$ would have remained constant.
2. $\sigma_p$ would have been in the vicinity of 20%.
3. $\sigma_p$ would have declined to zero if enough stocks had been included.

**ST-3**   **BETA AND THE REQUIRED RATE OF RETURN**   ECRI Corporation is a holding company with four main subsidiaries. The percentage of its capital invested in each of the subsidiaries (and their respective betas) are as follows:

| Subsidiary | Percentage of Capital | Beta |
|------|------|------|
| Electric utility | 60% | 0.70 |
| Cable company | 25 | 0.90 |
| Real estate development | 10 | 1.30 |
| International/special projects | 5 | 1.50 |

a. What is the holding company's beta?

b. If the risk-free rate is 4% and the market risk premium is 5%, what is the holding company's required rate of return?

c. ECRI is considering a change in its strategic focus; it will reduce its reliance on the electric utility subsidiary, so the percentage of its capital in this subsidiary will be reduced to 50%. At the same time, it will increase its reliance on the international/special projects division, so the percentage of its capital in that subsidiary will rise to 15%. What will the company's required rate of return be after these changes?

## Questions

8-1 Suppose you owned a portfolio consisting of $250,000 of long-term U.S. government bonds.

a. Would your portfolio be riskless? Explain.

b. Now suppose the portfolio consists of $250,000 of 30-day Treasury bills. Every 30 days your bills mature, and you will reinvest the principal ($250,000) in a new batch of bills. You plan to live on the investment income from your portfolio, and you want to maintain a constant standard of living. Is the T-bill portfolio truly riskless? Explain.

c. What is the least risky security you can think of? Explain.

8-2 The probability distribution of a less risky expected return is more peaked than that of a riskier return. What shape would the probability distribution be for (a) completely certain returns and (b) completely uncertain returns?

8-3 A life insurance policy is a financial asset, with the premiums paid representing the investment's cost.

a. How would you calculate the expected return on a 1-year life insurance policy?

b. Suppose the owner of a life insurance policy has no other financial assets—the person's only other asset is "human capital," or earnings capacity. What is the correlation coefficient between the return on the insurance policy and the return on the human capital?

c. Life insurance companies must pay administrative costs and sales representatives' commissions; hence, the expected rate of return on insurance premiums is generally low or even negative. Use portfolio concepts to explain why people buy life insurance in spite of low expected returns.

8-4 Is it possible to construct a portfolio of real-world stocks that has a required return equal to the risk-free rate? Explain.

8-5 Stock A has an expected return of 7%, a standard deviation of expected returns of 35%, a correlation coefficient with the market of −0.3, and a beta coefficient of −0.5. Stock B has an expected return of 12%, a standard deviation of returns of 10%, a 0.7 correlation with the market, and a beta coefficient of 1.0. Which security is riskier? Why?

8-6 A stock had a 12% return last year, a year when the overall stock market declined. Does this mean that the stock has a negative beta and thus very little risk if held in a portfolio? Explain.

8-7 If investors' aversion to risk increased, would the risk premium on a high-beta stock increase by more or less than that on a low-beta stock? Explain.

8-8 If a company's beta were to double, would its required return also double?

8-9 In Chapter 7, we saw that if the market interest rate, $r_d$, for a given bond increased, the price of the bond would decline. Applying this same logic to stocks, explain (a) how a decrease in risk aversion would affect stocks' prices and earned rates of return, (b) how this would affect risk premiums as measured by the historical difference between returns on stocks and returns on bonds, and (c) what the implications of this would be for the use of historical risk premiums when applying the SML equation.

# Problems

**Easy Problems 1–5**

**8-1**   **EXPECTED RETURN**   A stock's returns have the following distribution:

| Demand for the Company's Products | Probability of This Demand Occurring | Rate of Return if This Demand Occurs |
|---|---|---|
| Weak | 0.1 | (30%) |
| Below average | 0.1 | (14) |
| Average | 0.3 | 11 |
| Above average | 0.3 | 20 |
| Strong | 0.2 | 45 |
| | 1.0 | |

Calculate the stock's expected return, standard deviation, and coefficient of variation.

**8-2**   **PORTFOLIO BETA**   An individual has $20,000 invested in a stock with a beta of 0.6 and another $75,000 invested in a stock with a beta of 2.5. If these are the only two investments in her portfolio, what is her portfolio's beta?

**8-3**   **REQUIRED RATE OF RETURN**   Assume that the risk-free rate is 5.5% and the required return on the market is 12%. What is the required rate of return on a stock with a beta of 2?

**8-4**   **EXPECTED AND REQUIRED RATES OF RETURN**   Assume that the risk-free rate is 3.5% and the market risk premium is 4%. What is the required return for the overall stock market? What is the required rate of return on a stock with a beta of 0.8?

**8-5**   **BETA AND REQUIRED RATE OF RETURN**   A stock has a required return of 9%, the risk-free rate is 4.5%, and the market risk premium is 3%.

a. What is the stock's beta?

b. If the market risk premium increased to 5%, what would happen to the stock's required rate of return? Assume that the risk-free rate and the beta remain unchanged.

**Intermediate Problems 6–12**

**8-6**   **EXPECTED RETURNS**   Stocks A and B have the following probability distributions of expected future returns:

| Probability | A | B |
|---|---|---|
| 0.1 | (10%) | (35%) |
| 0.2 | 2 | 0 |
| 0.4 | 12 | 20 |
| 0.2 | 20 | 25 |
| 0.1 | 38 | 45 |

a. Calculate the expected rate of return, $\hat{r}_B$, for Stock B ($\hat{r}_A = 12\%$).

b. Calculate the standard deviation of expected returns, $\sigma_A$, for Stock A ($\sigma_B = 20.35\%$). Now calculate the coefficient of variation for Stock B. Is it possible that most investors will regard Stock B as being less risky than Stock A? Explain.

**8-7**   **PORTFOLIO REQUIRED RETURN**   Suppose you are the money manager of a $4.82 million investment fund. The fund consists of four stocks with the following investments and betas:

| Stock | Investment | Beta |
|---|---|---|
| A | $ 460,000 | 1.50 |
| B | 500,000 | (0.50) |
| C | 1,260,000 | 1.25 |
| D | 2,600,000 | 0.75 |

If the market's required rate of return is 8% and the risk-free rate is 4%, what is the fund's required rate of return?

**8-8**  **BETA COEFFICIENT**  Given the following information, determine the beta coefficient for Stock L that is consistent with equilibrium: $\hat{r}_L = 10.5\%$; $r_{RF} = 3.5\%$; $r_M = 9.5\%$.

**8-9**  **REQUIRED RATE OF RETURN**  Stock R has a beta of 2.0, Stock S has a beta of 0.45, the required return on an average stock is 10%, and the risk-free rate of return is 5%. By how much does the required return on the riskier stock exceed the required return on the less risky stock?

**8-10**  **CAPM AND REQUIRED RETURN**  Beale Manufacturing Company has a beta of 1.1, and Foley Industries has a beta of 0.30. The required return on an index fund that holds the entire stock market is 11%. The risk-free rate of interest is 4.5%. By how much does Beale's required return exceed Foley's required return?

**8-11**  **CAPM AND REQUIRED RETURN**  Calculate the required rate of return for Mudd Enterprises assuming that investors expect a 3.6% rate of inflation in the future. The real risk-free rate is 1.0%, and the market risk premium is 6.0%. Mudd has a beta of 1.5, and its realized rate of return has averaged 8.5% over the past 5 years.

**8-12**  **REQUIRED RATE OF RETURN**  Suppose $r_{RF} = 4\%$, $r_M = 10\%$, and $b_i = 1.4$.

   a. What is $r_i$, the required rate of return on Stock i?
   b. Now suppose that $r_{RF}$ (1) increases to 5% or (2) decreases to 3%. The slope of the SML remains constant. How would this affect $r_M$ and $r_i$?
   c. Now assume that $r_{RF}$ remains at 4%, but $r_M$ (1) increases to 12% or (2) falls to 9%. The slope of the SML does not remain constant. How would these changes affect $r_i$?

**Challenging Problems 13–21**

**8-13**  **CAPM, PORTFOLIO RISK, AND RETURN**  Consider the following information for Stocks A, B, and C. The returns on the three stocks are positively correlated, but they are not perfectly correlated. (That is, each of the correlation coefficients is between 0 and 1.)

| Stock | Expected Return | Standard Deviation | Beta |
|-------|-----------------|--------------------|------|
| A | 9.55% | 15% | 0.9 |
| B | 10.45 | 15 | 1.1 |
| C | 12.70 | 15 | 1.6 |

Fund P has one-third of its funds invested in each of the three stocks. The risk-free rate is 5.5%, and the market is in equilibrium. (That is, required returns equal expected returns.)

   a. What is the market risk premium $(r_M - r_{RF})$?
   b. What is the beta of Fund P?
   c. What is the required return of Fund P?
   d. Would you expect the standard deviation of Fund P to be less than 15%, equal to 15%, or greater than 15%? Explain.

**8-14**  **PORTFOLIO BETA**  Suppose you held a diversified portfolio consisting of a $7,500 investment in each of 20 different common stocks. The portfolio's beta is 1.25. Now suppose you decided to sell one of the stocks in your portfolio with a beta of 1.0 for $7,500 and use the proceeds to buy another stock with a beta of 0.80. What would your portfolio's new beta be?

**8-15**  **CAPM AND REQUIRED RETURN**  HR Industries (HRI) has a beta of 1.6; LR Industries's (LRI) beta is 0.8. The risk-free rate is 6%, and the required rate of return on an average stock is 13%. The expected rate of inflation built into $r_{RF}$ falls by 1.5 percentage points; the real risk-free rate remains constant; the required return on the market falls to 10.5%; and all betas remain constant. After all of these changes, what will be the difference in the required returns for HRI and LRI?

**8-16**  **CAPM AND PORTFOLIO RETURN**  You have been managing a $5 million portfolio that has a beta of 1.15 and a required rate of return of 11.475%. The current risk-free rate is 4%. Assume that you receive another $500,000. If you invest the money in a stock with a beta of 0.85, what will be the required return on your $5.5 million portfolio?

8-17 **PORTFOLIO BETA** A mutual fund manager has a $20 million portfolio with a beta of 1.7. The risk-free rate is 4.5%, and the market risk premium is 7%. The manager expects to receive an additional $5 million, which she plans to invest in a number of stocks. After investing the additional funds, she wants the fund's required return to be 15%. What should be the average beta of the new stocks added to the portfolio?

8-18 **EXPECTED RETURNS** Suppose you won the lottery and had two options: (1) receiving $0.5 million or (2) taking a gamble in which, at the flip of a coin, you receive $1 million if a head comes up but receive zero if a tail comes up.

a. What is the expected value of the gamble?
b. Would you take the sure $0.5 million or the gamble?
c. If you chose the sure $0.5 million, would that indicate that you are a risk averter or a risk seeker?
d. Suppose the payoff was actually $0.5 million—that was the only choice. You now face the choice of investing it in a U.S. Treasury bond that will return $537,500 at the end of a year or a common stock that has a 50–50 chance of being worthless or worth $1,150,000 at the end of the year.
   1. The expected profit on the T-bond investment is $37,500. What is the expected dollar profit on the stock investment?
   2. The expected rate of return on the T-bond investment is 7.5%. What is the expected rate of return on the stock investment?
   3. Would you invest in the bond or the stock? Why?
   4. Exactly how large would the expected profit (or the expected rate of return) have to be on the stock investment to make you invest in the stock, given the 7.5% return on the bond?
   5. How might your decision be affected if, rather than buying one stock for $0.5 million, you could construct a portfolio consisting of 100 stocks with $5,000 invested in each? Each of these stocks has the same return characteristics as the one stock—that is, a 50–50 chance of being worth zero or $11,500 at year-end. Would the correlation between returns on these stocks matter? Explain.

8-19 **EVALUATING RISK AND RETURN** Stock X has a 10% expected return, a beta coefficient of 0.9, and a 35% standard deviation of expected returns. Stock Y has a 12.5% expected return, a beta coefficient of 1.2, and a 25% standard deviation. The risk-free rate is 6%, and the market risk premium is 5%.

a. Calculate each stock's coefficient of variation.
b. Which stock is riskier for a diversified investor?
c. Calculate each stock's required rate of return.
d. On the basis of the two stocks' expected and required returns, which stock would be more attractive to a diversified investor?
e. Calculate the required return of a portfolio that has $7,500 invested in Stock X and $2,500 invested in Stock Y.
f. If the market risk premium increased to 6%, which of the two stocks would have the larger increase in its required return?

8-20 **REALIZED RATES OF RETURN** Stocks A and B have the following historical returns:

| Year | Stock A's Returns, $r_A$ | Stock B's Returns, $r_B$ |
|------|------|------|
| 2011 | (18.00%) | (14.50%) |
| 2012 | 33.00 | 21.80 |
| 2013 | 15.00 | 30.50 |
| 2014 | (0.50) | (7.60) |
| 2015 | 27.00 | 26.30 |

a. Calculate the average rate of return for each stock during the period 2011 through 2015.
b. Assume that someone held a portfolio consisting of 50% of Stock A and 50% of Stock B. What would the realized rate of return on the portfolio have been each year? What would the average return on the portfolio have been during this period?

c. Calculate the standard deviation of returns for each stock and for the portfolio.

d. Calculate the coefficient of variation for each stock and for the portfolio.

e. Assuming you are a risk-averse investor, would you prefer to hold Stock A, Stock B, or the portfolio? Why?

**8-21    SECURITY MARKET LINE**   You plan to invest in the Kish Hedge Fund, which has total capital of $500 million invested in five stocks:

| Stock | Investment | Stock's Beta Coefficient |
|-------|------------|--------------------------|
| A | $160 million | 0.5 |
| B | 120 million | 1.2 |
| C | 80 million | 1.8 |
| D | 80 million | 1.0 |
| E | 60 million | 1.6 |

Kish's beta coefficient can be found as a weighted average of its stocks' betas. The risk-free rate is 6%, and you believe the following probability distribution for future market returns is realistic:

| Probability | Market Return |
|-------------|---------------|
| 0.1 | −28% |
| 0.2 | 0 |
| 0.4 | 12 |
| 0.2 | 30 |
| 0.1 | 50 |

a. What is the equation for the security market line (SML)? (Hint: First, determine the expected market return.)

b. Calculate Kish's required rate of return.

c. Suppose Rick Kish, the president, receives a proposal from a company seeking new capital. The amount needed to take a position in the stock is $50 million, it has an expected return of 15%, and its estimated beta is 1.5. Should Kish invest in the new company? At what expected rate of return should Kish be indifferent to purchasing the stock?

# Comprehensive/Spreadsheet Problem

**8-22    EVALUATING RISK AND RETURN**   Bartman Industries's and Reynolds Inc.'s stock prices and dividends, along with the Winslow 5000 Index, are shown here for the period 2010–2015. The Winslow 5000 data are adjusted to include dividends.

| | Bartman Industries | | Reynolds Inc. | | Winslow 5000 |
|------|-------------|----------|-------------|----------|-------------------|
| Year | Stock Price | Dividend | Stock Price | Dividend | Includes Dividends |
| 2015 | $17.25 | $1.15 | $48.75 | $3.00 | $11,663.98 |
| 2014 | 14.75 | 1.06 | 52.30 | 2.90 | 8,785.70 |
| 2013 | 16.50 | 1.00 | 48.75 | 2.75 | 8,679.98 |
| 2012 | 10.75 | 0.95 | 57.25 | 2.50 | 6,434.03 |
| 2011 | 11.37 | 0.90 | 60.00 | 2.25 | 5,602.28 |
| 2010 | 7.62 | 0.85 | 55.75 | 2.00 | 4,705.97 |

a. Use the data to calculate annual rates of return for Bartman, Reynolds, and the Winslow 5000 Index. Then calculate each entity's average return over the 5-year period. (Hint: Remember, returns are calculated by subtracting the beginning price from the ending price to get the capital gain or loss, adding the dividend to the capital gain or loss, and dividing the result by the beginning price. Assume that dividends are already included in the index. Also, you cannot calculate the rate of return for 2010 because you do not have 2009 data.)

b. Calculate the standard deviations of the returns for Bartman, Reynolds, and the Winslow 5000. (Hint: Use the sample standard deviation formula, Equation 8.2a in this chapter, which corresponds to the STDEV function in Excel.)

c. Calculate the coefficients of variation for Bartman, Reynolds, and the Winslow 5000.

d. Construct a scatter diagram that shows Bartman's and Reynolds's returns on the vertical axis and the Winslow 5000 Index's returns on the horizontal axis.

e. Estimate Bartman's and Reynolds's betas by running regressions of their returns against the index's returns. (Hint: Refer to Web Appendix 8A.) Are these betas consistent with your graph?

f. Assume that the risk-free rate on long-term Treasury bonds is 4.5%. Assume also that the average annual return on the Winslow 5000 is *not* a good estimate of the market's required return—it is too high. So use 10% as the expected return on the market. Use the SML equation to calculate the two companies' required returns.

g. If you formed a portfolio that consisted of 50% Bartman and 50% Reynolds, what would the portfolio's beta and required return be?

h. Suppose an investor wants to include Bartman Industries's stock in his portfolio. Stocks A, B, and C are currently in the portfolio; and their betas are 0.769, 0.985, and 1.423, respectively. Calculate the new portfolio's required return if it consists of 25% of Bartman, 15% of Stock A, 40% of Stock B, and 20% of Stock C.

# INTEGRATED CASE

## MERRILL FINCH INC.

**8-23** **RISK AND RETURN** Assume that you recently graduated with a major in finance. You just landed a job as a financial planner with Merrill Finch Inc., a large financial services corporation. Your first assignment is to invest $100,000 for a client. Because the funds are to be invested in a business at the end of 1 year, you have been instructed to plan for a 1-year holding period. Further, your boss has restricted you to the investment alternatives in the following table, shown with their probabilities and associated outcomes. (For now, disregard the items at the bottom of the data; you will fill in the blanks later.)

|  |  |  | Returns on Alternative Investments | | | | |
|  |  |  | Estimated Rate of Return | | | | |
| State of the Economy | Probability | T-Bills | High Tech | Collections | U.S. Rubber | Market Portfolio | Two-Stock Portfolio |
| --- | --- | --- | --- | --- | --- | --- | --- |
| Recession | 0.1 | 3.0% | (29.5%) | 24.5% | 3.5%[a] | (19.5%) | (2.5%) |
| Below average | 0.2 | 3.0 | (9.5) | 10.5 | (16.5) | (5.5) |  |
| Average | 0.4 | 3.0 | 12.5 | (1.0) | 0.5 | 7.5 | 5.8 |
| Above average | 0.2 | 3.0 | 27.5 | (5.0) | 38.5 | 22.5 |  |
| Boom | 0.1 | 3.0 | 42.5 | (20.0) | 23.5 | 35.5 | 11.3 |
| $\hat{r}$ |  |  | 1.2% | 7.3% | 8.0% |  |  |
| $\sigma$ |  | 0.0 | 11.2 | 18.8 | 15.2 | 4.6 |  |
| CV |  |  | 9.8 | 2.6 | 1.9 | 0.8 |  |
| b |  |  | −0.50 | 0.88 |  |  |  |

*Note:*

[a]The estimated returns of U.S. Rubber do not always move in the same direction as the overall economy. For example, when the economy is below average, consumers purchase fewer tires than they would if the economy was stronger. However, if the economy is in a flat-out recession, a large number of consumers who were planning to purchase a new car may choose to wait and instead purchase new tires for the car they currently own. Under these circumstances, we would expect U.S. Rubber's stock price to be higher if there is a recession than if the economy is just below average.

Merrill Finch's economic forecasting staff has developed probability estimates for the state of the economy, and its security analysts developed a sophisticated computer program to estimate the rate of return on each alternative under each state of the economy. High Tech Inc. is an electronics firm; Collections Inc. collects past-due debts; and U.S. Rubber manufactures tires and various other rubber and plastics products. Merrill Finch also maintains a "market portfolio" that owns a market-weighted fraction of all publicly traded stocks; you can invest in that portfolio and thus obtain average stock market results. Given the situation described, answer the following questions:

a. 1. Why is the T-bill's return independent of the state of the economy? Do T-bills promise a completely risk-free return? Explain.
   2. Why are High Tech's returns expected to move with the economy, whereas Collections's are expected to move counter to the economy?

b. Calculate the expected rate of return on each alternative, and fill in the blanks on the row for $\hat{r}$ in the previous table.

c. You should recognize that basing a decision solely on expected returns is appropriate only for risk-neutral individuals. Because your client, like most people, is risk-averse, the riskiness of each alternative is an important aspect of the decision. One possible measure of risk is the standard deviation of returns.
   1. Calculate this value for each alternative and fill in the blank on the row for $\sigma$ in the table.
   2. What type of risk is measured by the standard deviation?
   3. Draw a graph that shows *roughly* the shape of the probability distributions for High Tech, U.S. Rubber, and T-bills.

d. Suppose you suddenly remembered that the coefficient of variation (CV) is generally regarded as being a better measure of stand-alone risk than the standard deviation when the alternatives being considered have widely differing expected returns. Calculate the missing CVs, and fill in the blanks on the row for CV in the table. Does the CV produce the same risk rankings as the standard deviation? Explain.

e. Suppose you created a two-stock portfolio by investing $50,000 in High Tech and $50,000 in Collections.
   1. Calculate the expected return ($\hat{r}_p$), the standard deviation ($\sigma_p$), and the coefficient of variation ($CV_P$) for this portfolio, and fill in the appropriate blanks in the table.
   2. How does the riskiness of this two-stock portfolio compare with the riskiness of the individual stocks if they were held in isolation?

f. Suppose an investor starts with a portfolio consisting of one randomly selected stock.
   1. What would happen to the riskiness and to the expected return of the portfolio as more randomly selected stocks were added to the portfolio?
   2. What is the implication for investors? Draw a graph of the two portfolios to illustrate your answer.

g. 1. Should the effects of a portfolio impact the way investors think about the riskiness of individual stocks?
   2. If you decided to hold a one-stock portfolio (and consequently were exposed to more risk than diversified investors), could you expect to be compensated for all of your risk; that is, could you earn a risk premium on the part of your risk that you could have eliminated by diversifying?

h. The expected rates of return and the beta coefficients of the alternatives supplied by an independent analyst are as follows:

| Security | Return, $\hat{r}$ | Risk (Beta) |
|---|---|---|
| High Tech | 9.9% | 1.31 |
| Market | 8.0 | 1.00 |
| U.S. Rubber | 7.3 | 0.88 |
| T-bills | 3.0 | 0.00 |
| Collections | 1.2 | (0.50) |

   1. What is a beta coefficient, and how are betas used in risk analysis?
   2. Do the expected returns appear to be related to each alternative's market risk?
   3. Is it possible to choose among the alternatives on the basis of the information developed thus far? Use the data given at the start of the problem to construct a graph that shows how the T-bill's, High Tech's, and the market's beta coefficients are calculated. Then discuss what betas measure and how they are used in risk analysis.

   i. The yield curve is currently flat; that is, long-term Treasury bonds also have a 3.0% yield. Consequently, Merrill Finch assumes that the risk-free rate is 3.0%.

     1. Write out the security market line (SML) equation; use it to calculate the required rate of return on each alternative; and graph the relationship between the expected and required rates of return.

     2. How do the expected rates of return compare with the required rates of return?

     3. Does the fact that Collections has an expected return that is less than the T-bill rate make any sense? Explain.

     4. What would be the market risk and the required return of a 50–50 portfolio of High Tech and Collections? Of High Tech and U.S. Rubber?

   j. 1. Suppose investors raised their inflation expectations by 3 percentage points over current estimates as reflected in the 3.0% risk-free rate. What effect would higher inflation have on the SML and on the returns required on high- and low-risk securities?

     2. Suppose instead that investors' risk aversion increased enough to cause the market risk premium to increase by 3 percentage points. (Inflation remains constant.) What effect would this have on the SML and on returns of high- and low-risk securities?

# TAKING A CLOSER LOOK

## USING PAST INFORMATION TO ESTIMATE REQUIRED RETURNS

*Use online resources to work on this chapter's questions. Please note that website information changes over time, and these changes may limit your ability to answer some of these questions.*

Chapter 8 discussed the basic trade-off between risk and return. In the capital asset pricing model (CAPM) discussion, beta was identified as the correct measure of risk for diversified shareholders. Recall that beta measures the extent to which the returns of a given stock move with the stock market. When using the CAPM to estimate required returns, we would like to know how the stock will move with the market in the future; but because we don't have a crystal ball, we generally use historical data to estimate this relationship with beta.

As mentioned in Web Appendix 8A, beta can be estimated by regressing the individual stock's returns against the returns of the overall market. As an alternative to running our own regressions, we can rely on reported betas from a variety of sources. These published sources make it easy for us to readily obtain beta estimates for most large publicly traded corporations. However, a word of caution is in order. Beta estimates can often be quite sensitive to the time period in which the data are estimated, the market index used, and the frequency of the data used. Therefore, it is not uncommon to find a wide range of beta estimates among the various Internet websites.

## DISCUSSION QUESTIONS

1. Begin by looking at the historical performance of the overall stock market. Typically, on most of the financial websites you can enter S&P 500 and go right to the index's summary page. You will see a quick summary of the market's performance over the past 24 hours and 12 months. How has the market performed over the past year?

2. On the summary screen, you should see an interactive chart. Typically, you can chart performance over the last 24 hours, 1 month, three months, six months—up to 10 years, or even longer. Select different time periods and watch how the graph changes. On this screen you should also see a menu to select historical prices. Some websites will not only show daily activity but also weekly or monthly activity. In addition, some websites will allow you to download the data into an Excel spreadsheet.

3. Now let's take a closer look at the stocks of four companies: Colgate Palmolive (Ticker = CL), Campbell Soup (CPB), Motorola Solutions (MSI), and Tiffany & Co (TIF). Before looking at the data, which of these companies would you expect to have a relatively high beta (greater than 1.0) and which of these companies would you expect to have a relatively low beta (less than 1.0)?

4. Select one of the four stocks listed in Question 3 by entering the company's ticker symbol on the financial website you have chosen. On the screen you should see the interactive chart. Select the six-month time period and select the S&P 500, so the stock's performance will be compared to the S&P 500's performance on the graph. Has the stock outperformed or underperformed the overall market during this time period?

5. Go back to the summary page to see an estimate of the company's beta. What is the company's beta? What was the source of the estimated beta? Realize that if you go to another website, the beta shown could be different due to measurement differences.

6. What is the company's current dividend yield? What has been its total return to investors over the past year? Over the past 3 years? (Remember that total return includes the dividend yield plus any capital gains or losses.) You will have to go to more than one website to find this information. MSN Money gives DPS information over the past five years on the detailed Income Statement Financials page. You can use the price information to calculate dividend yield and capital gains yield. Yahoo! Finance provides historical price information.

7. Assume that the risk-free rate is 4% and the market risk premium is 5%. What is the required return on the company's stock?

8. Repeat the same exercise for each of the three remaining companies. Do the reported betas confirm your earlier intuition? In general, do you find that the higher-beta stocks tend to do better in up markets and worse in down markets? Explain.

## Solutions to Self-Test Questions and Problems

**ST-1**   Refer to the marginal glossary definitions or relevant chapter sections to check your responses.

**ST-2**   a. The average rate of return for each stock is calculated simply by averaging the returns over the 5-year period. The average return for Stock A is:

$$r_{Avg\ A} = (-24.25\% + 18.50\% + 38.67\% + 14.33\% + 39.13\%)/5$$
$$= 17.28\%$$

The average return for Stock B is:

$$r_{Avg\ B} = (5.50\% + 26.73\% + 48.25\% + -4.50\% + 43.86\%)/5$$
$$= 23.97\%$$

The realized rate of return on a portfolio made up of Stock A and Stock B would be calculated by finding the average return in each year as $r_A$(% of Stock A) + $r_B$(% of Stock B) and then averaging these annual returns:

| Year | Portfolio AB's Return, $r_{AB}$ |
|------|------|
| 2011 | (9.38%) |
| 2012 | 22.62 |
| 2013 | 43.46 |
| 2014 | 4.92 |
| 2015 | 41.50 |
| | $r_{Avg}$ = 20.62% |

b. The standard deviation of returns is estimated, using Equation 8.2a, as follows:

$$\text{Estimated } \sigma = \sqrt{\frac{\sum_{t=1}^{N}(\bar{r}_t - \bar{r}_{Avg})^2}{N-1}}$$

For Stock A, the estimated $\sigma$ is 25.84%:

$$\sigma_A = \sqrt{\frac{\begin{array}{c}(-24.25\% - 17.28\%)^2 + (18.50\% - 17.28\%)^2 + (38.67\% - 17.28\%)^2 + \\ (14.33\% - 17.28\%)^2 + (39.13\% - 17.28\%)^2\end{array}}{5-1}}$$

$$= 25.84\%$$

The standard deviations of returns for Stock B and for the portfolio are similarly determined, and they are as follows:

|  | Stock A | Stock B | Portfolio AB |
|---|---|---|---|
| Standard deviation | 25.84% | 23.15% | 22.96% |

c. Because the risk reduction from diversification is small ($\sigma_{AB}$ falls only to 22.96%), the most likely value of the correlation coefficient is 0.8. If the correlation coefficient were −0.8, the risk reduction would be much larger. In fact, the correlation coefficient between Stocks A and B is 0.76.

d. If more randomly selected stocks were added to a portfolio, $\sigma_p$ would decline to somewhere in the vicinity of 20% (see Figure 8.6); $\sigma_p$ would remain constant only if the correlation coefficient were +1.0, which is most unlikely. $\sigma_p$ would decline to zero only if the correlation coefficient, $\rho$, were equal to zero and a large number of stocks were added to the portfolio, or if the proper proportions were held in a two-stock portfolio with $\rho = -1.0$.

**ST-3**  a.  $b = (0.6)(0.70) + (0.25)(0.90) + (0.1)(1.30) + (0.05)(1.50)$
$= 0.42 + 0.225 + 0.13 + 0.075 = 0.85$

b.  $r_{RF} = 4\%$; $RP_M = 5\%$; $b = 0.85$ (calculated in part a)
$r_p = 4\% + (5\%)(0.85)$
$= 8.25\%$

c.  $b_N = (0.5)(0.70) + (0.25)(0.90) + (0.1)(1.30) + (0.15)(1.50)$
$= 0.35 + 0.225 + 0.13 + 0.225$
$= 0.93$

$r = 4\% + (5\%)(0.93)$
$= 8.65\%$

# Answers to Selected End-of-Chapter Problems

**8-2**   $b_p = 2.10$
**8-4**   $r_M = 7.5\%$; $r = 6.7\%$
**8-6**   a. $\hat{r}_B = 14\%$
          b. $\sigma_A = 12.20\%$; $CV_B = 1.45$
**8-8**   $b = 1.1667$
**8-10**  5.2%
**8-12**  a. $r_i = 12.4\%$
          b(1). $r_M = 11\%$; $r_i = 13.4\%$
          b(2). $r_M = 9\%$; $r_i = 11.4\%$
          c(1). $r_i = 15.2\%$
          c(2). $r_i = 11.0\%$

**8-14**  $b_N = 1.24$
**8-16**  $r_p = 11.30\%$
**8-18**  a. \$0.5 million
          d(l). \$75,000
          d(2). 15%
**8-20**  a. $r_A = 11.30\%$; $r_B = 11.30\%$
          b. $r_{p\ Avg} = 11.30\%$
          c. $\sigma_A = 20.8\%$; $\sigma_B = 20.8\%$; $\sigma_p = 20.1\%$
          d. $CV_A = CV_B = 1.84$; $CV_p = 1.78$

# Selected Equations and Tables

**Expected rate of return** $= \hat{r} = P_1 r_1 + P_2 r_2 + \cdots + P_N r_N$

$$= \sum_{i=1}^{N} P_i r_i$$

**Standard deviation** $= \sigma = \sqrt{\sum_{i=1}^{N} (r_i - \hat{r})^2 P_i}$

**Estimated** $\sigma = \sqrt{\dfrac{\sum_{t=1}^{N} (\bar{r}_t - \bar{r}_{Avg})^2}{N - 1}}$

**Coefficient of variation** $= CV = \dfrac{\sigma}{\hat{r}}$

$$\hat{r}_p = w_1 \hat{r}_1 + w_2 \hat{r}_2 + \cdots + w_N \hat{r}_N$$

$$= \sum_{i=1}^{N} w_i \hat{r}_i$$

$$b_p = w_1 b_1 + w_2 b_2 + \cdots + w_N b_N$$

$$= \sum_{i=1}^{N} w_i b_i$$

$$RP_M = r_M - r_{RF}$$

$$RP_i = (RP_M) b_i$$

$$r_i = r_{RF} + (r_M - r_{RF}) b_i$$

# Chapter 9

# Stocks and Their Valuation

CHAPTER

© newphotoservice/Shutterstock.com

## Searching for the Right Stock

Over the long run, returns in the U.S. stock market have been quite strong, averaging approximately 12% per year. However, these returns are far from certain, and there is considerable variation in the market's performance from year to year. Indeed, as the chart below indicates, the S&P 500 index has been on a real roller coaster ride since early 2000, where there have been a series of sharp peaks and valleys. Most notably, we see the dramatic collapse of the market in 2008 and early 2009. Since then, the S&P 500 has dramatically rebounded from a value of 811 in April 2009 to 2,100.44 in July 2015.

As we discussed in Chapter 8, the returns of individual stocks are even more volatile than the returns of the overall market. For example, in 2014, Allergan Inc.'s stock price rose 91.4%; Southwest Airlines' stock price increased 124.6%; and, most impressively, Radius Health's stock price soared 385.8%. Even with the S&P 500 up more than 11% in 2014, not all stocks fared well. On the down side, North Atlantic Drilling's stock price dropped 80.9%; Sprint's stock price declined 61.4%; and HH Gregg's stock price declined 45.8%. This wide range in individual stocks' performance shows, first, that diversification is important and, second, that when it comes to picking stocks, it is not enough to simply pick a good company—the stock must also be "fairly" priced.

To determine whether a stock is fairly priced, you first need to estimate the stock's true value, or "intrinsic value," a concept first discussed in Chapter 1. With this objective in mind, in this chapter we describe some models that analysts have used to estimate intrinsic values. As you will see, though it is difficult to predict stock prices, we are not completely in the dark. Indeed, after studying this chapter, you should have a reasonably good understanding of the factors that influence stock prices; and with that knowledge—plus a little luck—you should be able to successfully navigate the market's often treacherous ups and downs.

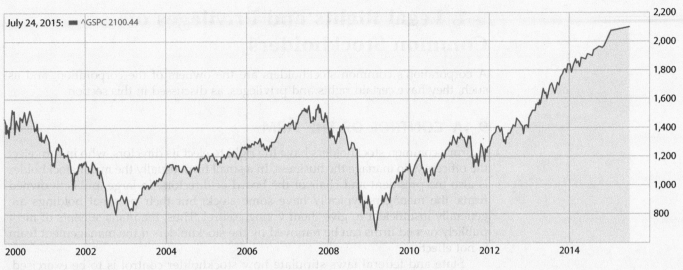

July 24, 2015: ■ ^GSPC 2100.44

Source: Finance.yahoo.com, July 24, 2015.

Source: Allan Sloan, "The Incredible Shrinking Bull," *Fortune*, March 17, 2008, p. 24.

# PUTTING THINGS IN PERSPECTIVE

In Chapter 7, we examined bonds and their valuation. We now turn to stocks, both common and preferred. Because the cash flows provided by bonds are set by contract, it is generally easy to predict their cash flows. Preferred stock dividends are also set by contract, which makes them similar to bonds; and they are valued in much the same way. However, common stock dividends are not contractual—they depend on the firm's earnings, which in turn depend on many random factors, making their valuation more difficult. Two fairly straightforward models are used to estimate stocks' intrinsic (or "true") values: (1) the discounted dividend model and (2) the corporate valuation model. A stock should, of course, be bought if its price is less than its estimated intrinsic value and sold if its price exceeds its intrinsic value.

By the time you finish this chapter, you should be able to:

• **Discuss the legal rights of stockholders.**

• **Explain the distinction between a stock's price and its intrinsic value.**

• **Identify the two models that can be used to estimate a stock's intrinsic value: the discounted dividend model and the corporate valuation model.**

• **List the key characteristics of preferred stock, and describe how to estimate the value of preferred stock.**

Stock valuation is interesting in its own right, but you also need to understand valuation when estimating a firm's cost of capital for use in its capital budgeting analysis, which is probably a firm's most important task.

*Key trends in the securities industry are listed and explained at **sifma.org /research/statistics.aspx**.*

# 9-1 Legal Rights and Privileges of Common Stockholders

A corporation's common stockholders are the owners of the corporation, and as such, they have certain rights and privileges, as discussed in this section.

## 9-1A CONTROL OF THE FIRM

A firm's common stockholders have the right to elect its directors, who in turn elect the officers who manage the business. In a small firm, usually the major stockholder is also the president and chair of the board of directors. In large, publicly owned firms, the managers typically have some stock, but their personal holdings are generally insufficient to give them voting control. Thus, the managements of most publicly owned firms can be removed by the stockholders if the management team is not effective.

State and federal laws stipulate how stockholder control is to be exercised. First, corporations must hold elections of directors periodically, usually once a year, with the vote taken at the annual meeting. Each share of stock has one vote; thus, the owner of 1,000 shares has 1,000 votes for each director.[1] Stockholders can appear at the annual meeting and vote in person, but typically they transfer their right to vote to another person by means of a **proxy**. Management always solicits stockholders' proxies and usually receives them. However, if earnings are poor and stockholders are dissatisfied, an outside group may solicit the proxies in an effort to overthrow management and take control of the business. This is known as a **proxy fight**.

The question of control has become a central issue in finance in recent years. The frequency of proxy fights has increased, as have attempts by one corporation to take over another by purchasing a majority of the outstanding stock. These actions are called **takeovers**. Some well-known examples of takeover battles in past years include KKR's acquisition of RJR Nabisco, Chevron's acquisition of Gulf Oil, and the QVC/Viacom fight to take over Paramount. More recently, in November 2009, Kraft Foods made a hostile takeover bid of $16.7 billion for Cadbury, the British chocolate and gum manufacturer. On January 19, 2010, Cadbury's management accepted Kraft's revised $21.8 billion buyout offer and agreed to recommend the offer to its shareholders. Interestingly, Kraft continued its deal-making in March 2015, when it announced plans to merge with Heinz, in a deal that was partially financed by the Brazilian private equity firm 3G Capital and Warren Buffett's Berkshire Hathaway.

Managers without more than 50% of their firms' stock are very concerned about proxy fights and takeovers, and many of them have attempted to obtain stockholder approval for changes in their corporate charters that would make takeovers more difficult. For example, a number of companies have persuaded their stockholders to agree (1) to elect only one-third of the directors each year (rather than electing all directors each year), (2) to require 75% of the stockholders (rather than 50%) to approve a merger, and (3) to vote in a "poison pill" provision that would allow the stockholders of a firm that is taken over by another firm to buy shares in the second firm at a reduced price. The poison pill makes the acquisition unattractive and thus helps ward off hostile takeover attempts. Managers seeking such changes generally cite a fear that

**Proxy**

A document giving one person the authority to act for another, typically the power to vote shares of common stock.

**Proxy Fight**

An attempt by a person or group to gain control of a firm by getting its stockholders to grant that person or group the authority to vote its shares to replace the current management.

**Takeover**

An action whereby a person or group succeeds in ousting a firm's management and taking control of the company.

---

[1]In the situation described, a 1,000-share stockholder could cast 1,000 votes for each of three directors if there were three contested seats on the board. An alternative procedure that may be prescribed in the corporate charter calls for *cumulative voting*. There the 1,000-share stockholder would get 3,000 votes if there were three vacancies, and he or she could cast all of them for one director. Cumulative voting helps small groups obtain representation on the board.

the firm will be picked up at a bargain price, but it often appears that the managers' concern about their own positions is the primary consideration.

Managers' moves to make takeovers more difficult have been countered by stockholders, especially large institutional stockholders, who do not like barriers erected to protect incompetent managers. To illustrate, the California Public Employees Retirement System (CalPERS), which is one of the largest institutional investors, has led proxy fights with several corporations whose financial performances were poor in CalPERS's judgment. CalPERS wants companies to increase outside (nonmanagement) directors' ability to force managers to be more responsive to stockholder complaints.

Managers' pay is another contentious issue. It has been asserted that in some cases CEOs receive excessive compensation because they are too closely aligned with the company's board of directors. At the same time, enlightened boards want to reward CEOs when they act in shareholders' interests, but also hold them accountable for poor performance. CalPERS and other institutional investors have further encouraged firms to make their compensation packages more transparent and aligned with shareholders' interests. Similarly, the Dodd-Frank bill imposed a Say-on-Pay provision, which provides shareholders the ability to vote on executive compensation. Although this provision is nonbinding it imposes some pressure on managers who don't want to see shareholders voting to disapprove of their pay package. For example, in 2014, Coca-Cola adjusted the compensation package of its senior executives after receiving negative feedback from Warren Buffett and other shareholders.[2]

For many years, SEC rules prohibited large investors such as CalPERS from getting together to force corporate managers to institute policy changes. However, the SEC began changing its rules in 1993, and now large investors can work together to force management changes. These rulings have helped keep managers focused on stockholder concerns.

## 9-1B THE PREEMPTIVE RIGHT

Common stockholders often have the right, called the **preemptive right**, to purchase on a pro rata basis any additional shares sold by the firm. In some states, the preemptive right is automatically included in every corporate charter; in other states, it must be specifically inserted into the charter.

The purpose of the preemptive right is twofold. First, it prevents the management of a corporation from issuing a large number of additional shares and purchasing those shares itself. Management could use this tactic to seize control of the corporation and frustrate the will of the current stockholders. The second, and far more important, reason for the preemptive right is to protect stockholders from a dilution of value. For example, suppose 1,000 shares of common stock, each with a price of $100, were outstanding, making the total market value of the firm $100,000. If an additional 1,000 shares were sold at $50 a share, or for $50,000, this would raise the firm's total market value to $150,000. When the new total market value is divided by the 2,000 total shares now outstanding, a value of $75 a share is obtained. The old stockholders would thus lose $25 per share, and the new stockholders would have an instant profit of $25 per share. Thus, selling common stock at a price below the market value would dilute a firm's price and transfer wealth from its present stockholders to those who were allowed to purchase the new shares. The preemptive right prevents this.

*Preemptive Right*
A provision in the corporate charter or bylaws that gives common stockholders the right to purchase on a pro rata basis new issues of common stock (or convertible securities).

---

[2]For a discussion about this, refer to Anupreeta Das, Mike Esterl, and Joann S. Lublin, "Buffett Pressures Coca-Cola over Executive Pay," *The Wall Street Journal* (online.wsj.com), April 30, 2014; and Mark Melin, "Coca-Cola Changes Pay Plan, Warren Buffett Influence Credited," *ValueWalk* (www.valuewalk.com), October 1, 2014.

## Self*Test*

Identify some actions that companies have taken to make takeovers more difficult.

What is the preemptive right, and what are the two primary reasons for its existence?

## 9-2 Types of Common Stock

**Classified Stock**

Common stock that is given a special designation such as Class A or Class B to meet special needs of the company.

**Founders' Shares**

Stock owned by the firm's founders that enables them to maintain control over the company without having to own a majority of stock.

Although most firms have only one type of common stock, in some instances, **classified stock** is used to meet special needs. Generally, when special classifications are used, one type is designated *Class A,* another *Class B,* and so forth. Small, new companies seeking funds from outside sources frequently use different types of common stock. For example, when Google went public, it sold Class A stock to the public while its Class B stock was retained by the company's insiders. The key difference is that the Class B stock has 10 votes per share while the Class A stock has 1 vote per share. Google's Class B shares are predominantly held by the company's two founders and its current CEO. The use of classified stock thus enables the company's founders to maintain control over the company without having to own a majority of the common stock. For this reason, Class B stock of this type is sometimes called **founders' shares**. Because *dual-class* share structures of this type give special voting privileges to key insiders, these structures are sometimes criticized because they may enable insiders to make decisions that are counter to the interests of the majority of stockholders.

Note that "Class A," "Class B," and so forth, have no standard meanings. Most firms have no classified shares, but a firm that does could designate its Class B shares as founders' shares and its Class A shares as those sold to the public, while another could reverse those designations. Still other firms could use stock classifications for entirely different purposes. For example, when General Motors acquired Hughes Aircraft for $5 billion, it paid in part with a new Class H common, GMH, which had limited voting rights and whose dividends were tied to Hughes's performance as a GM subsidiary. The reasons for the new stock were that (1) GM wanted to limit voting privileges on the new classified stock because of management's concern about a possible takeover. (2) Hughes's employees wanted to be rewarded more directly on Hughes's own performance than would have been possible through regular GM stock. These Class H shares disappeared in 2003 when GM decided to sell off the Hughes unit.

## Self*Test*

What are some reasons a company might use classified stock?

## 9-3 Stock Price versus Intrinsic Value

We saw in Chapter 1 that a manager should seek to maximize the value of his or her firm's stock. In that chapter, we also emphasized the difference between stock price and intrinsic value. The stock price is simply the current market price, and it is

## ARE "SMART BETA" FUNDS A SMART IDEA?

In Chapter 8, we demonstrated the benefits of diversification. These benefits lead many experts to recommend that investors regularly hold some portion of their wealth in well-diversified index funds. These index funds have the benefit of providing diversification with low transactions costs. For example, a Vanguard fund that tracks the S&P 500 has total transactions costs that are less than 0.20% of the total amount invested.

In effect, these funds are holding a portfolio of S&P 500 stocks, where each stock's weight in the portfolio is determined by its current market capitalization (which is its stock price multiplied by the number of shares outstanding). So, for example, if a stock's market capitalization equals 1% of the total market capitalization of the S&P 500, then an S&P 500 index fund or exchange traded fund would have 1% invested in that stock.

While generally applauded, some analysts have expressed concern that index funds may typically overinvest in "overvalued" stocks. Here's the idea: As stocks become overvalued, their market capitalization rises (to levels above what should be given their intrinsic value), and this increase automatically results in an index fund holding a larger percentage of the overvalued stock. To address these concerns, fund investments have arisen that use portfolio weights that are based on approaches other than market capitalization. Oftentimes these alternatives are characterized as "smart beta" or "strategic beta" funds.

These funds typically use a variety of different approaches for weighting the index. For example, some use an equal weighted approach where each stock in the index has the same weight regardless of market capitalization. Others weight the stocks according to some "fundamentals" such as dividends or earnings that are believed to be correlated with intrinsic value. In a recent article on CNBC.com, a Morningstar analyst summarized these funds in the following way:

*"What investors are getting here is an active bet, and no two products are the same even if they have the same strategy," said Morningstar analyst Alex Bryan. "Fees are usually considerably lower than [those associated with] actively managed funds, but more than with traditional index funds."*

The article also points out that these funds have become quite popular in recent years. Using data from Morningstar, they report in 2015 that mutual funds and exchange-traded funds in this category have grown more than 170% in the previous five years, and they now have total invested assets of more than $540 billion.

As you might expect, not all analysts think that smart beta is a smart idea. Some point out that you are still paying higher fees to try to outguess the market, something which has been notoriously hard to do for many funds. Perhaps not surprisingly, Jack Bogle, Vanguard's founder and a long-time champion of index funds, has characterized smart beta investing as "stupid."

Source: "Do 'Smart Beta' Funds Outperform Index Funds?" finance.yahoo.com, March 16, 2015.

easily observed for publicly traded companies. By contrast, intrinsic value, which represents the "true" value of the company's stock, cannot be directly observed and must instead be estimated. Figure 9.1 illustrates once again the connection between stock price and intrinsic value.

As the figure suggests, market equilibrium occurs when the stock's price equals its intrinsic value. If the stock market is reasonably efficient, gaps between the stock price and intrinsic value should not be very large, and they should not persist for very long. However, in some cases, an individual company's stock price may be much higher or lower than its intrinsic value. During several years leading up to the credit crunch of 2007–2008, most of the large investment banks were reporting record profits and selling at record prices. However, much of those earnings were illusory because they did not reflect the huge risks that existed in the mortgage-backed securities that these firms were purchasing. So with hindsight, we now know that the market prices of most financial firms' stocks exceeded their intrinsic values just prior to 2007. Then when the market realized what was happening, those stock prices crashed. Citigroup, Merrill Lynch, and others lost more than 60% of their value in a few short months; and Bear Stearns, at that time the fifth-largest investment bank, saw its stock price drop from $171 in 2007 to $2 just before its ultimate collapse in mid-March 2008. It clearly pays to question market prices at times!

**FIGURE 9.1** Determinants of Intrinsic Values and Stock Prices

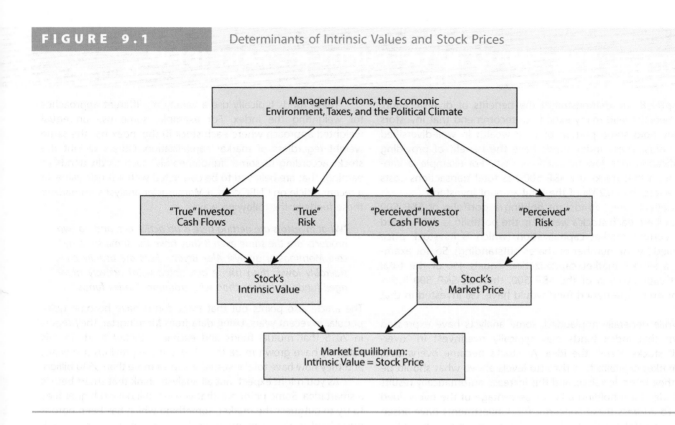

## 9-3A WHY DO INVESTORS AND COMPANIES CARE ABOUT INTRINSIC VALUE?

The remainder of this chapter focuses primarily on different approaches for estimating a stock's intrinsic value. Before these approaches are described, it is worth asking why it is important for investors and companies to understand how to calculate intrinsic value.

When investing in common stocks, one's goal is to purchase stocks that are undervalued (i.e., the price is below the stock's intrinsic value) and avoid stocks that are overvalued. Consequently, Wall Street analysts, institutional investors who control mutual funds and pension funds, and many individual investors are interested in finding reliable models that help predict a stock's intrinsic value.

Investors obviously care about intrinsic value, but managers also need to understand how intrinsic value is estimated. First, managers need to know how alternative actions are likely to affect stock prices; the models of intrinsic value that we cover help demonstrate the connection between managerial decisions and firm value. Second, managers should consider whether their stock is significantly undervalued or overvalued before making certain decisions. For example, firms should consider carefully the decision to issue new shares if they believe their stock is undervalued; an estimate of their stock's intrinsic value is the key to such decisions.

Two basic models are used to estimate intrinsic values: the *discounted dividend model* and the *corporate valuation model*. The dividend model focuses on dividends, while the corporate model goes beyond dividends and focuses on sales, costs, and free cash flows. In the following sections, we describe these approaches in more detail.

## SelfTest

What is the difference between a stock's price and its intrinsic value?

Why do investors and managers need to understand how to estimate a firm's intrinsic value?

What are two commonly used approaches for estimating a stock's intrinsic value? How do they differ in their focus?

# 9-4 The Discounted Dividend Model

The value of a share of common stock depends on the cash flows it is expected to provide, and those flows consist of two elements: (1) the dividends the investor receives each year while he or she holds the stock and (2) the price received when the stock is sold. The final price includes the original price paid plus an expected capital gain. Keep in mind that there are many different investors in the market and thus many different sets of expectations. Therefore, investors will have different opinions about a stock's true intrinsic value and thus its proper price. The analysis as performed by the **marginal investor**, whose actions actually determine the equilibrium stock price, is critical; but every investor, marginal or not, implicitly goes through the same type of analysis.

The following terms are used in our analysis:[3]

**Marginal Investor**
A representative investor whose actions reflect the beliefs of those people who are currently trading a stock. It is the marginal investor who determines a stock's price.

$D_t$ = the dividend a stockholder expects to receive at the end of each Year t. $D_0$ is the last dividend the company paid. Because it has already been paid, a buyer of the stock will not receive $D_0$. The first dividend a new buyer will receive is $D_1$, which is paid at the end of Year 1. $D_2$ is the dividend expected at the end of Year 2; $D_3$, at the end of Year 3; and so forth. $D_0$ is known with certainty; but $D_1$, $D_2$, and all other future dividends are *expected values*; and different investors can have different expectations.[4] Our primary concern is with $D_t$ as forecasted by the *marginal investor*.

$P_0$ = actual **market price** of the stock today. $P_0$ is known with certainty, but predicted future prices are subject to uncertainty.

$\hat{P}_t$ = both the expected price and the expected intrinsic value of the stock at the end of each Year t (pronounced

**Market Price, $P_0$**
The price at which a stock sells in the market.

---

[3]Many terms are described here, and students sometimes get concerned about having to memorize all of them. We tell our students that we will provide formula sheets for use on exams, so they don't have to try to memorize everything. With their minds thus eased, they end up learning what the terms actually mean rather than memorizing formulas.

[4]Stocks generally pay dividends quarterly, so theoretically we should evaluate them on a quarterly basis. However, most analysts actually work with annual data because forecasted stock data are not precise enough to warrant the use of a quarterly model. For additional information on the quarterly model, see Charles M. Linke and J. Kenton Zumwalt, "Estimation Biases in Discounted Cash Flow Analysis of Equity Capital Costs in Rate Regulation," *Financial Management*, vol. 13, no. 3 (Autumn 1984), pp. 15–21.

**Growth Rate, g**

The expected rate of growth in dividends per share.

**Required Rate of Return, $r_s$**

The minimum rate of return on a common stock that a stockholder considers acceptable.

**Expected Rate of Return, $\hat{r}_s$**

The rate of return on a common stock that a stockholder expects to receive in the future.

**Actual (Realized) Rate of Return, $\bar{r}_s$**

The rate of return on a common stock actually received by stockholders in some past period; $\bar{r}_s$ may be greater or less than $\hat{r}_s$ and/or $r_s$.

**Dividend Yield**

The expected dividend divided by the current price of a share of stock.

**Capital Gains Yield**

The capital gain during a given year divided by the beginning price.

**Expected Total Return**

The sum of the expected dividend yield and the expected capital gains yield.

"P hat t") as seen by the investor doing the analysis. $\hat{P}_t$ is based on the investor's estimates of the dividend stream and the riskiness of that stream. There are many investors in the market, so there can be many estimates for $\hat{P}_t$. However, for the marginal investor, $P_0$ must equal $\hat{P}_0$. Otherwise, a disequilibrium would exist, and buying and selling in the market would soon result in $P_0$ equaling $\hat{P}_0$ as seen by the marginal investor.

$g$ = expected **growth rate g** in dividends as predicted by an investor. If dividends are expected to grow at a constant rate, g should also equal the expected growth rate in earnings and the stock's price. Different investors use different g's to evaluate a firm's stock; but the market price, $P_0$, is based on g as estimated by the marginal investor.

$r_s$ = **required**, or minimum acceptable, **rate of return** on the stock considering its riskiness and the returns available on other investments. Different investors typically have different opinions, but the key is again the marginal investor. The determinants of $r_s$ include factors discussed in Chapter 8, including the real rate of return, expected inflation, and risk.

$\hat{r}_s$ = **expected rate of return** (pronounced "r hat s") that an investor believes the stock will provide in the future. The expected return can be above or below the required return; but a rational investor will buy the stock if $\hat{r}_s$ exceeds $r_s$, sell the stock if $\hat{r}_s$ is less than $r_s$, and simply hold the stock if these returns are equal. Again, the key is the marginal investor, whose views determine the actual stock price.

$\bar{r}_s$ = **actual**, or **realized**, *after-the-fact* **rate of return**, pronounced "r bar s." You can *expect* to obtain a return of $\bar{r}_s = 10\%$ if you buy a stock today; but if the market declines, you may earn an actual realized return that is much lower, perhaps even negative.

$D_1/P_0$ = **dividend yield** expected during the coming year. If Company X's stock is expected to pay a dividend of $D_1 = \$1$ during the next 12 months and if X's current price is $P_0 = \$20$, the expected dividend yield will be $\$1/\$20 = 0.05 = 5\%$. Different investors could have different expectations for $D_1$; but again, the marginal investor is the key.

$(\hat{P}_1 - P_0)/P_0$ = expected **capital gains yield** on the stock during the coming year. If the stock sells for $20.00 today and if it is expected to rise to $21.00 by the end of the year, the expected capital gain will be $\hat{P}_1 - P_0 = \$21.00 - \$20.00 = \$1.00$ and the expected capital gains yield will be $\$1.00/\$20.00 = 0.05 = 5\%$. Different investors can have different expectations for $\hat{P}_1$, but the marginal investor is key.

Expected total return = $\hat{r}_s$ = expected dividend yield $(D_1/P_0)$ plus expected capital gains yield $[(\hat{P}_1 - P_0)/P_0]$. In our example, the **expected total return** = $5\% + 5\% = 10\%$.

All active investors hope to achieve better-than-average returns—they hope to identify stocks whose intrinsic values exceed their current prices and whose expected returns (expected by this investor) exceed their required rates of return. Note, though, that about half of all investors are likely to be disappointed. A good understanding of the points made in this chapter can help you avoid being disappointed.

## 9-4A EXPECTED DIVIDENDS AS THE BASIS FOR STOCK VALUES

In our discussion of bonds, we used Equation 7.1 to find the value of a bond; the equation is the present value of interest payments over the bond's life plus the present value of its maturity (or par) value:

$$V_B = \frac{INT}{(1 + r_d)^1} + \frac{INT}{(1 + r_d)^2} + \cdots + \frac{INT}{(1 + r_d)^N} + \frac{M}{(1 + r_d)^N}$$

Stock prices are likewise determined as the present value of a stream of cash flows, and the basic stock valuation equation is similar to the one for bonds. What are the cash flows that a corporation will provide to its stockholders? To answer that question, think of yourself as an investor who purchases the stock of a company that is expected to exist indefinitely (e.g., GE). You intend to hold it (in your family) forever. In this case, all you (and your heirs) will receive is a stream of dividends; and the value of the stock today can be calculated as the present value of an infinite stream of dividends:

$$\text{Value of stock} = \hat{P}_0 = \text{PV of expected future dividends}$$

$$= \frac{D_1}{(1 + r_s)^1} + \frac{D_2}{(1 + r_s)^2} + \cdots + \frac{D_\infty}{(1 + r_s)^\infty}$$

$$= \sum_{t=1}^{\infty} \frac{D_t}{(1 + r_s)^t}$$

9.1

What about the more typical case, where you expect to hold the stock for a finite period and then sell it—what will be the value of $\hat{P}_0$ in this case? Unless the company is likely to be liquidated or sold and thus disappears, *the value of the stock is again determined by Equation 9.1*. To see this, recognize that for any individual investor, the expected cash flows consist of expected dividends plus the expected sale price of the stock. However, the sale price to the current investor depends on the dividends some future investor expects, and that investor's expected sale price is also dependent on some future dividends, and so forth. Therefore, for all present and future investors in total, expected cash flows must be based on expected future dividends. Put another way, unless a firm is liquidated or sold to another concern, the cash flows it provides to its stockholders will consist only of a stream of dividends. Therefore, the value of a share of stock must be established as the present value of the stock's expected dividend stream.[5]

---

[5]The general validity of Equation 9.1 can also be confirmed by asking yourself the following question: Suppose I buy a stock and expect to hold it for one year. I will receive dividends during the year plus the value $\hat{P}_1$ when I sell it at the end of the year. But what will determine the value of $\hat{P}_1$? The answer is that it will be determined as the present value of the dividends expected during Year 2 plus the stock price at the end of that year, which in turn will be determined as the present value of another set of future dividends and an even more distant stock price. This process can be continued ad infinitum, and the ultimate result is Equation 9.1.

We should note that investors periodically lose sight of the long-run nature of stocks as investments and forget that in order to sell a stock at a profit, one must find a buyer who will pay the higher price. If you analyze a stock's value in accordance with Equation 9.1, conclude that the stock's market price exceeds a reasonable value, and buy the stock anyway, you would be following the *"bigger fool" theory of investment*—you think you may be a fool to buy the stock at its excessive price; but you also believe that when you get ready to sell it, you can find someone who is an even bigger fool. The bigger fool theory was widely followed in the summer of 2000, just before the stock market crashed.

## Self Test

Explain the following statement: Whereas a bond contains a promise to pay interest, a share of common stock typically provides an expectation of, but no promise of, dividends plus capital gains.

What are the two parts of most stocks' expected total return?

If $D_1 = \$2.00$, $g = 6\%$, and $P_0 = \$40.00$, what are the stock's expected dividend yield, capital gains yield, and total expected return for the coming year? **(5%, 6%, 11%)**

Is it necessary for all investors to have the same expectations regarding a stock for the stock to be in equilibrium?

What would happen to a stock's price if the "marginal investor" examined a stock and concluded that its intrinsic value was greater than its current market price?

## 9-5 Constant Growth Stocks

Equation 9.1 is a generalized stock valuation model in the sense that the time pattern of $D_t$ can be anything: $D_t$ can be rising, falling, or fluctuating randomly; or it can be zero for several years. Equation 9.1 can be applied in any of these situations; and with a computer spreadsheet, we can easily use the equation to find a stock's intrinsic value—provided we have an estimate of the future dividends. However, it is not easy to obtain accurate estimates of future dividends.

Still, for many companies it is reasonable to predict that dividends will grow at a constant rate. In this case, Equation 9.1 may be rewritten as follows:

$$\hat{P}_0 = \frac{D_0(1+g)^1}{(1+r_s)^1} + \frac{D_0(1+g)^2}{(1+r_s)^2} + \cdots + \frac{D_0(1+g)^\infty}{(1+r_s)^\infty}$$

$$= \frac{D_0(1+g)}{r_s - g} = \frac{D_1}{r_s - g}$$

9.2

**Constant Growth (Gordon) Model**
Used to find the value of a constant growth stock.

The last term of Equation 9.2 is the **constant growth**, or **Gordon, model**, named after Myron J. Gordon, who did much to develop and popularize it.[6]

The term $r_s$ in Equation 9.2 is the *required rate of return,* which is a riskless rate plus a risk premium. However, we know that if the stock is in equilibrium, the required rate of return must equal the expected rate of return, which is the expected dividend yield plus an expected capital gains yield. So we can solve Equation 9.2 for $r_s$, but now using the hat to indicate that we are dealing with an expected rate of return:[7]

$$
\begin{array}{ccccc}
\text{Expected rate} & = & \text{Expected} & + & \text{Expected growth rate, or} \\
\text{of return} & & \text{dividend yield} & & \text{capital gains yield} \\
\hat{r}_s & = & \dfrac{D_1}{P_0} & + & g
\end{array}
$$

9.3

We illustrate Equations 9.2 and 9.3 in the following section.

---

[6]The last term in Equation 9.2 is derived in the Web Extension of Chapter 8 of Eugene F. Brigham and Phillip R. Daves, *Intermediate Financial Management,* 12th edition (Mason, OH: Cengage Learning, 2016). In essence, Equation 9.2 is the sum of a geometric progression, and the final result is the solution value of the progression.

[7]The $r_s$ value in Eqaution 9.2 is a *required* rate of return; but when we transform Equation 9.2 to obtain Equation 9.3, we are finding an *expected* rate of return. Obviously, the transformation requires that $r_s = \hat{r}_s$. This equality must hold if the stock is in equilibrium, as most normally are.

## 9-5A ILLUSTRATION OF A CONSTANT GROWTH STOCK

Table 9.1 presents an analysis of Keller Medical Products's stock as performed by a security analyst after a meeting for analysts and other investors presided over by Keller's CFO. The table looks complicated, but it is really quite straightforward.[8] Part I, in the upper left corner, provides some basic data. The last dividend, which was just paid, was $1.00; the stock's last closing price was $20.80; and it is in equilibrium. Based on an analysis of Keller's history and likely future, the analyst forecasts that earnings and dividends will grow at a constant rate of 4% per year

Analysis of a Constant Growth stock  **TABLE 9.1**

| | A | B | C | D | E | F | G | H | I |
|---|---|---|---|---|---|---|---|---|---|
| 3 | | | | | | | | | |
| 4 | **I. Basic Information:** | | | | **II. Formulas Used in the Analysis:** | | | | |
| 5 | $D_0$ = | $1.00 | | Dividend in Year t, $D_t$, in column 2 | | | | $D_{t-1}(1 + g)$ | |
| 6 | $P_0$ = | $20.80 | | Intrinsic value (and price) in Year t, $P_t$, in column 3 | | | | $D_{t+1} / (r_s - g)$ | |
| 7 | g = | 4.00% | | Dividend yield (constant) in column 4 | | | | $D_t / P_{t-1}$ | |
| 8 | $r_s$ = | 9.00% | | Capital gains yield (constant) in column 5 | | | | $(P_t - P_{t-1}) / P_{t-1}$ | |
| 9 | | | | Total return (constant) in column 6 | | | | Div. yield + CG yield | |
| 10 | | | | PV of dividends discounted at 9% in column 7 | | | | $D_t / (1 + r_s)^t$ | |
| 11 | **III. Examples:** | | | | | | | | |
| 12 | | column 2 | | $D_1 = \$1.00(1.04)$ | | | | $1.04 | |
| 13 | | column 3 | | $P_0 = \$1.04 / (0.09 - 0.04)$ | | | | $20.80 | |
| 14 | | column 4 | | Dividend yield, Year 1: $1.04 / $20.80 | | | | 5.0% | |
| 15 | | column 5 | | Cap gains yield, Year 1: ($21.63 - $20.80) / $20.80 | | | | 4.0% | |
| 16 | | column 6 | | Total return, Year 1: 5.0% + 4.0% | | | | 9.0% | |
| 17 | | column 7 | | PV of $D_1$ discounted at 9.0% | | | | $0.95 | |
| 18 | | | | | | | | | |
| 19 | **IV. Forecasted Results over Time:** | | | | | | PV of | | |
| 20 | At end | | | Dividend | Capital | Total | dividend | | |
| 21 | of year: | Dividend | Price * | yield | gains yield | return | at 9.0% | | |
| 22 | (1) | (2) | (3) | (4) | (5) | (6) | (7) | | |
| 23 | 2016 | $1.00 | $20.80 | | | | | | |
| 24 | 2017 | $1.04 | $21.63 | 5.0% | 4.0% | 9.0% | $0.95 | | |
| 25 | 2018 | $1.08 | $22.50 | 5.0% | 4.0% | 9.0% | $0.91 | | |
| 26 | 2019 | $1.12 | $23.40 | 5.0% | 4.0% | 9.0% | $0.87 | | |
| 27 | 2020 | $1.17 | $24.33 | 5.0% | 4.0% | 9.0% | $0.83 | | |
| 28 | 2021 | $1.22 | $25.31 | 5.0% | 4.0% | 9.0% | $0.79 | | |
| 29 | 2022 | $1.27 | $26.32 | 5.0% | 4.0% | 9.0% | $0.75 | | |
| 30 | 2023 | $1.32 | $27.37 | 5.0% | 4.0% | 9.0% | $0.72 | | |
| 31 | 2024 | $1.37 | $28.47 | 5.0% | 4.0% | 9.0% | $0.69 | | |
| 32 | 2025 | $1.42 | $29.60 | 5.0% | 4.0% | 9.0% | $0.66 | | |
| 33 | 2026 | $1.48 | $30.79 | 5.0% | 4.0% | 9.0% | $0.63 | | |
| 34 | ↓ | | | | | | ↓ | | |
| 35 | ∞ | | | Sum of PVs from 1 to ∞ = $P_0$ = | | | $20.80 | = Value on 1/1/2017 | |
| 36 | | | | | | | | | |
| 37 | * Because this is a constant growth stock, we could have found the value for $P_t$ as $P_{t-1}(1 + g)$. For example, $P_1 = \$20.80(1.04) = \$21.63$. | | | | | | | | |

[8]You may notice some minor "errors" in the table. These are not errors—they are simply differences caused by rounding.

and that the stock's price will grow at this same rate. Moreover, the analyst believes that the most appropriate required rate of return is 9%. Different analysts might use different inputs, but we assume for now that because this analyst is widely followed, her results represent those of the marginal investor.

Look at part IV, where we show the predicted stream of dividends and stock prices along with annual values for the dividend yield, the capital gains yield, and the expected total return. Notice that the total return shown in column 6 is equal to the required rate of return shown in part I. This indicates that the stock analyst thinks that the stock is fairly priced; hence, it is in equilibrium. She forecasted data for 10 years, but she could have forecasted out to infinity.

Part II shows the formulas used to calculate the data in part IV, and part III gives examples of the calculations. For example, $D_1$, the first dividend a purchaser would receive, is forecasted to be $D_1 = \$1.00(1.04) = \$1.04$, and the other forecasted dividends in column 2 were calculated similarly. The estimated intrinsic values shown in column 3 are based on Equation 9.2, the constant growth model: $P_0 = D_1/(r_s - g) = \$1.04/(0.09 - 0.04) = \$20.80$, $\hat{P}_1 = \$21.63$, and so forth.

Column 4 shows the dividend yield, which for 2017 is $D_1/P_0 = 5.0\%$, and this number is constant thereafter. The capital gain expected during 2017 is $\hat{P}_1 - P_0 = \$21.63 - \$20.80 = \$0.83$, which when divided by $P_0$ gives the expected capital gains yield, $\$0.83/\$20.80 = 4.0\%$. The total return is found as the dividend yield plus the capital gains yield, 9.0%; and it is both constant and equal to the required rate of return given in part I.

Finally, look at column 7 in the table. Here we find the present value of each of the dividends shown in column 2, discounted at the required rate of return. For example, the PV of $D_1 = \$1.04/(1.09)^1 = \$0.95$, the PV of $D_2 = \$1.08/(1.09)^2 = \$0.91$, and so forth. If you extended the table out to about 170 years (with Excel, this is easy), then summed the PVs of the dividends, you would obtain the same value as that found using Equation 9.2, $\$20.80$.[9] Figure 9.2 shows graphically what's happening. We extended the table out 20 years and then plotted dividends from column 2 in the upper step function curve and the PV of those dividends in the lower curve. The sum of the PVs is an estimate of the stock's forecasted intrinsic value.

Note that in Table 9.1, the forecasted intrinsic value is equal to the current stock price, and the expected total return is equal to the required rate of return. In this situation, the analyst would call the stock a "Hold" and would recommend that investors not buy or sell it. However, if the analyst were somewhat more optimistic and thought the growth rate would be 5.0% rather than 4.0%, the forecasted intrinsic value would be (by Equation 9.2) $26.25 and the analyst would call it a "Buy." At $g = 3.0\%$, the intrinsic value would be $17.17 and the stock would be a "Sell." Changes in the required rate of return would produce similar changes in the forecasted intrinsic value and thus the equilibrium current price.

## 9-5B DIVIDENDS VERSUS GROWTH

The discounted dividend model as expressed in Equation 9.2 shows that, other things held constant, a higher value for $D_1$ increases a stock's price. However, Equation 9.2 shows that a higher growth rate also increases the stock's price. But now recognize the following:

- Dividends are paid out of earnings.

- Therefore, growth in dividends requires growth in earnings.

---

[9]The dividends get quite large, but the discount rate exceeds the growth rate; so the PVs of the dividends become quite small. In theory, you would have to go out to infinity to find the exact price of a constant growth stock, but the difference between the Equation 9.2 value and the sum of the PVs can't be seen out to two decimal places if you extend the analysis to 170 periods.

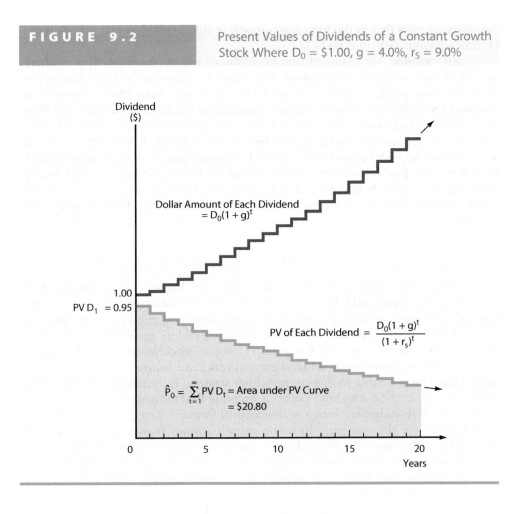

**FIGURE 9.2** Present Values of Dividends of a Constant Growth Stock Where $D_0 = \$1.00$, $g = 4.0\%$, $r_s = 9.0\%$

Dividend ($)

Dollar Amount of Each Dividend $= D_0(1 + g)^t$

1.00
PV $D_1$ = 0.95

PV of Each Dividend $= \dfrac{D_0(1 + g)^t}{(1 + r_s)^t}$

$\hat{P}_0 = \displaystyle\sum_{t=1}^{\infty} PV\ D_t$ = Area under PV Curve
$= \$20.80$

0    5    10    15    20

Years

- Earnings growth in the long run occurs primarily because firms retain earnings and reinvest them in the business.
- Therefore, the higher the percentage of earnings retained, the higher the growth rate.

To illustrate this, suppose you inherit a business that has $1,000,000 of assets and no debt, thus $1,000,000 of equity. The expected return on equity (ROE) equals 10.0%, so its expected earnings for the coming year are $(0.10)(\$1,000,000) = \$100,000$. You could take out the entire $100,000 of earnings in dividends, or you could reinvest some or all of the $100,000 in the business. If you pay out all the earnings, you will have $100,000 of dividend income this year, but dividends will not grow because assets, and therefore earnings, will not grow.

However, suppose you decide to have the firm pay out 60% and retain 40%. Now your dividend income in Year 1 will be $60,000; but assets will rise by $40,000, and earnings and dividends will likewise increase:

$$\begin{aligned}
\text{Next year's earnings} &= \text{Prior earnings} + \text{ROE}(\text{Retained earnings}) \\
&= \$100,000 + 0.1(\$40,000) \\
&= \$104,000 \\
\text{Next year's dividends} &= 0.6(\$104,000) = \$62,400
\end{aligned}$$

Moreover, your dividend income will continue to grow by 4% per year thereafter:

$$\begin{aligned}
\text{Growth rate} &= (1 - \text{Payout ratio})\,\text{ROE} \\
&= (1 - 0.6)10.0\% \\
&= 0.4(10.0\%) = 4.0\%
\end{aligned}$$

9.4

This demonstrates that in the long run, growth in dividends depends primarily on the firm's payout ratio and its ROE.

In our example, we assumed that other things remain constant. This is often, but not always, a logical assumption. For example, suppose the firm develops a successful new product, hires a better CEO, or makes some other change that increased the ROE. Any of these actions could cause the ROE to increase and thus the growth rate to increase. Also note that the earnings of new firms are often low or even negative for several years, and then begin to rise rapidly. Finally, growth levels off as the firm approaches maturity. Such a firm might pay no dividends for its first few years, then pay a low initial dividend but let it increase rapidly, and finally make regular payments that grow at a constant rate once earnings have stabilized. In any such situation, the nonconstant model, as discussed in a later section, must be used.

## 9-5C WHICH IS BETTER: CURRENT DIVIDENDS OR GROWTH?

We saw in the preceding section that a firm can pay a higher current dividend by increasing its payout ratio, but that will lower its dividend growth rate. So the firm can provide a relatively high current dividend or a high growth rate, but not both. This being the case, which would stockholders prefer? The answer is not clear. As we will see in Chapter 14, some stockholders prefer current dividends while others prefer a lower payout ratio and future growth. Empirical studies have been unable to determine which strategy is optimal for maximizing a firm's stock price. So dividend policy is an issue that management must decide on the basis of its judgment, not a mathematical formula. Logically, shareholders should prefer for the company to retain more earnings (hence pay less current dividends) if the firm has exceptionally good investment opportunities; however, shareholders should prefer a high payout if investment opportunities are poor. In spite of this, taxes and other factors complicate the situation. We will discuss all this in detail in Chapter 14; but for now, just assume that the firm's management has decided on a payout policy and uses that policy to determine the actual dividend.

## 9-5D REQUIRED CONDITIONS FOR THE CONSTANT GROWTH MODEL

Several conditions are necessary for Equation 9.2 to be used. First, the required rate of return, $r_s$, must be greater than the long-run growth rate, g. *If the equation is used in situations where g is greater than $r_s$, the results will be wrong, meaningless, and misleading.* For example, if the forecasted growth rate in our example were 10% and thus exceeded the 9.0% required rate of return, stock price as calculated by Equation 9.2 would be a *negative* $110.00. That would be nonsense—stocks can't have negative prices. Moreover, in Table 9.1, the PV of each future dividend would exceed that of the prior year. If this situation were graphed in Figure 9.2, the step-function curve for the PV of dividends would be increasing, not decreasing; so the sum would be infinitely high, which would indicate an infinitely high stock price. Obviously, stock prices cannot be either infinite or negative, so Equation 9.2 cannot be used unless $r_s > g$.

Second, the constant growth model as expressed in Equation 9.2 is not appropriate unless a company's growth rate is expected to remain constant in the future. This condition almost never holds for new start-up firms, but it does exist for many mature companies. Indeed, mature firms such as Keller, Allied, and GE are generally expected to grow at about the same rate as nominal gross domestic product (i.e., real GDP plus inflation). On this basis, one might expect the dividends of an average, or "normal," company to grow at a rate of 3% to 6% a year.

Note too that Equation 9.2 is sufficiently general to handle the case of a **zero growth stock**, where the dividend is expected to remain constant over time. If $g = 0$, Equation 9.2 reduces to Equation 9.5:

$$\hat{P}_0 = \frac{D}{r_s} \qquad \blacktriangledown \quad 9.5$$

**Zero Growth Stock**
A common stock whose future dividends are not expected to grow at all; that is, $g = 0$.

This is the same equation as the one we developed in Chapter 5 for a perpetuity, and it is simply the current dividend divided by the required rate of return.

Finally, as we discuss later in the chapter, most firms, even rapidly growing start-ups and others that pay no dividends at present, can be expected to pay dividends at some point in the future, at which time the constant growth model will be appropriate. For such firms, Equation 9.2 is used as one part of a more complicated valuation equation that we discuss next.

## Self Test

✔

Write out and explain the valuation formula for a constant growth stock.

Describe how the formula for a zero growth stock can be derived from the formula for a normal constant growth stock.

Firm A is expected to pay a dividend of $1.00 at the end of the year. The required rate of return is $r_s = 11\%$. Other things held constant, what would the stock's price be if the growth rate was 5%? What if g was 0%? **($16.67, $9.09)**

Firm B has a 12% ROE. Other things held constant, what would its expected growth rate be if it paid out 25% of its earnings as dividends? 75%? **(9%, 3%)**

If Firm B had a 75% payout ratio but then lowered it to 25%, causing its growth rate to rise from 3% to 9%, would that action necessarily increase the price of its stock? Why or why not?

## 9-6 Valuing Nonconstant Growth Stocks

For many companies, it is not appropriate to assume that dividends will grow at a constant rate. Indeed, most firms go through *life cycles* where they experience different growth rates during different parts of the cycle. In their early years, most firms grow much faster than the economy as a whole; then they match the economy's growth; and finally they grow at a slower rate than the economy.[10] Automobile manufacturers in the 1920s, computer software firms such as Microsoft in the 1990s, and Google in the 2000s are examples of firms in the early part of their cycle. These firms are defined as **supernormal**, or **nonconstant, growth**, firms.

**Supernormal (Nonconstant) Growth**
The part of the firm's life cycle in which it grows much faster than the economy as a whole.

[10]The concept of life cycles could be broadened to *product cycle*, which would include both small start-up companies and large companies such as Microsoft and Procter & Gamble, which periodically introduce new products that give sales and earnings a boost. We should also mention *business cycles*, which alternately depress and boost sales and profits. The growth rate just after a major new product has been introduced (or just after a firm emerges from the depths of a recession) is likely to be much higher than the "expected long-run average growth rate," which is the proper number for use in the discounted dividend model.

Figure 9.3 illustrates nonconstant growth and compares it with normal growth, zero growth, and negative (or declining) growth.[11]

In the figure, the dividends of the supernormal growth firm are expected to grow at a 30% rate for three years, after which the growth rate is expected to fall to 4%, the assumed average for the economy. The value of this firm's stock, like any other asset, is the present value of its expected future dividends as determined by Equation 9.1. When $D_t$ is growing at a constant rate, we can simplify Equation 9.1 to Equation 9.2, $\hat{P}_0 = D_1/(r_s - g)$. In the supernormal case, however, the expected growth rate is not a constant. In our example, there are two distinctly different rates.

Because Equation 9.2 requires a constant growth rate, we obviously cannot use it to value stocks that are not growing at a constant rate. However, assuming that a company currently enjoying supernormal growth will eventually slow down and become a constant growth stock, we can combine Equations 9.1 and 9.2 to construct a new formula, Equation 9.6, for valuing the stock.

First, we assume that the dividend will grow at a nonconstant rate (generally a relatively high rate) for N periods, after which it will grow at a constant rate, g. N is often called the **horizon,** or **terminal, date.** Second, we can use the constant growth formula, Equation 9.2, to determine what the stock's **horizon,** or **continuing, value** will be N periods from today:

**Horizon (Terminal) Date**

The date when the growth rate becomes constant. At this date, it is no longer necessary to forecast the individual dividends.

**Horizon (Continuing) Value**

The value at the horizon date of all dividends expected thereafter.

$$\text{Horizon value} = \hat{P}_N = \frac{D_{N+1}}{r_s - g}$$

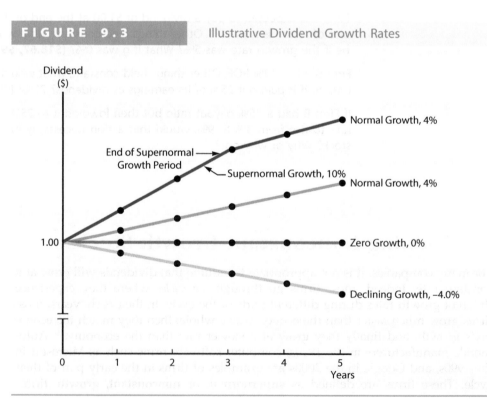

**FIGURE 9.3** Illustrative Dividend Growth Rates

Dividend ($)

- Normal Growth, 4%
- End of Supernormal Growth Period
- Supernormal Growth, 10%
- Normal Growth, 4%
- Zero Growth, 0%
- Declining Growth, −4.0%

1.00

Years: 0  1  2  3  4  5

---

[11]A negative growth rate indicates a declining company. A mining company whose profits are falling because of a declining ore body is an example. Someone purchasing stock in such a company would expect its earnings (and consequently its dividends and stock price) to decline each year, which would lead to capital losses rather than capital gains. Obviously, a declining-growth company's stock price is relatively low, and its dividend yield must be high enough to offset the expected capital loss and still produce a competitive total return. Students sometimes argue that they would never be willing to buy a stock whose price was expected to decline. However, if the present value of the expected dividends exceeds the stock price, the stock is still a good investment that would provide a good return.

The stock's intrinsic value today, $\hat{P}_0$, is the present value of the dividends during the nonconstant growth period plus the present value of the horizon value:

$$\hat{P}_0 = \underbrace{\frac{D_1}{(1+r_s)^1} + \frac{D_2}{(1+r_s)^2} + \cdots + \frac{D_N}{(1+r_s)^N}}_{\substack{\text{PV of dividends during the} \\ \text{nonconstant growth} \\ \text{period, } t = 1, \cdots N}} + \underbrace{\frac{D_{N+1}}{(1+r_s)^{N+1}} + \cdots + \frac{D_\infty}{(1+r_s)^\infty}}_{\substack{\text{Horizon value} = \text{PV of dividends} \\ \text{during the constant growth} \\ \text{period, } t = N+1, \cdots \infty}}$$

$$\hat{P}_0 = \underbrace{\frac{D_1}{(1+r_s)^1} + \frac{D_2}{(1+r_s)^2} + \cdots + \frac{D_N}{(1+r_s)^N}}_{\substack{\text{PV of dividends during the} \\ \text{nonconstant growth period} \\ t = 1, \cdots N}} + \underbrace{\frac{\hat{P}_N}{(1+r_s)^N}}_{\substack{\text{PV of horizon} \\ \text{value, } \hat{P}_N: \\ \frac{[(D_{N+1})/(r_s - g)]}{(1+r_s)^N}}}$$

9.6

To implement Equation 9.6, we go through the following three steps:

1. Find the PV of each dividend during the period of nonconstant growth and sum them.

2. Find the expected stock price at the end of the nonconstant growth period. At this point it has become a constant growth stock, so it can be valued with the constant growth model. Discount this price back to the present.

3. Add these two components to find the stock's intrinsic value, $\hat{P}_0$.

Figure 9.4 illustrates the process for valuing nonconstant growth stocks. Here we use a new company, Firm M, and we assume the following information:

$r_s$ = stockholders' required rate of return = 9.0%. This rate is used to discount the cash flows.

$N$ = years of nonconstant growth = 3.

$g_s$ = rate of growth in both earnings and dividends during the nonconstant growth period = 10%. This rate is shown directly on the time line. (*Note:* The growth rate during the nonconstant growth period could vary from year to year. Also, there could be several different nonconstant growth periods—e.g., 10% for three years, 8% for the next three years, and a constant 4% thereafter.)

$g_n$ = rate of normal, constant growth after the nonconstant period = 4.0%. This rate is also shown on the time line, after Year 3, when it is in effect.

$D_0$ = last dividend the company paid = $1.00.

The valuation process diagrammed in Figure 9.4 is explained in the steps set forth below the time line. The value of the nonconstant growth stock is calculated as $24.43.

Note that in this example, we assumed a relatively short 3-year horizon to keep things simple. When evaluating stocks, most analysts use a longer horizon (e.g., 10 years) to estimate intrinsic values. This requires a few more calculations, but because analysts use spreadsheets, the arithmetic is not a problem. In practice, the real limitation is obtaining reliable forecasts for future growth.

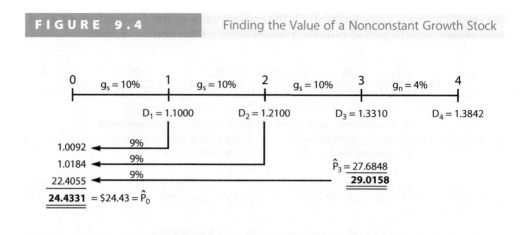

**FIGURE 9.4** Finding the Value of a Nonconstant Growth Stock

*Notes:*

Step 1. Calculate the dividends expected at the end of each year during the nonconstant growth period. Calculate the first dividend, $D_1 = D_0(1 + g_s) = \$1.00(1.10) = \$1.1000$. Here $g_s$ is the growth rate during the 3-year nonconstant growth period, 10%. Show the $1.1000 on the time line as the cash flow at Time 1. Calculate $D_2 = D_1(1 + g_s) = \$1.1000(1.10) = \$1.2100$, then $D_3 = D_2(1 + g_s) = \$1.2100(1.10) = \$1.3310$. Show these values on the time line as the cash flows at Time 2 and Time 3. Note that $D_0$ is used only to calculate $D_1$.

Step 2. The price of the stock is the PV of dividends from Time 1 to infinity; so in theory, we could project each future dividend, with the normal growth rate, $g_n = 4\%$, used to calculate $D_4$ and subsequent dividends. However, we know that after $D_3$ has been paid at Time 3, the stock becomes a constant growth stock. Therefore, we can use the constant growth formula to find $\hat{P}_3$, which is the PV of the dividends from Time 4 to infinity as evaluated at Time 3.

First, we determine $D_4 = \$1.3310(1.04) = \$1.3842$ for use in the formula; then we calculate $\hat{P}_3$ as follows:

$$\hat{P}_3 = \frac{D_4}{r_s - g_n} = \frac{\$1.3842}{0.09 - 0.04} = \$27.6848$$

We show this $27.6848 on the time line as a second cash flow at Time 3. The $27.6848 is a Time 3 cash flow in the sense that the stockholder could sell the stock for $27.6848 at Time 3 and in the sense that $27.6848 is the present value of the dividend cash flows from Time 4 to infinity. Note that the total cash flow at Time 3 consists of the sum of $D_3 + \hat{P}_3 = \$1.3310 + \$27.6848 = \$29.0158$.

Step 3. Now that the cash flows have been placed on the time line, we can discount each cash flow at the required rate of return, $r_s = 9.0\%$. We could discount each cash flow by dividing by $(1.09)^t$, where $t = 1$ for Time 1, $t = 2$ for Time 2, and $t = 3$ for Time 3. This produces the PVs shown to the left below the time line; and the sum of the PVs is the value of the nonconstant growth stock, $24.43.

With a financial calculator, you can find the PV of the cash flows as shown on the time line with the cash flow (CFLO) register of your calculator. Enter 0 for $CF_0$ because you receive no cash flow at Time 0, $CF_1 = 1.10$, $CF_2 = 1.21$, and $CF_3 = 1.3310 + 27.6848 = 29.0158$. Then enter I/YR = 9.0 and press the NPV key to find the value of the stock, $24.43.

## SelfTest

Explain how one would find the value of a nonconstant growth stock.

Explain what is meant by horizon (terminal) date and horizon (continuing) value.

# EVALUATING STOCKS THAT DON'T PAY DIVIDENDS

The discounted dividend model assumes that the firm is currently paying a dividend. However, many firms, even highly profitable ones, including Google and Dell, have never paid a dividend. If a firm is expected to begin paying dividends in the future, we can modify the equations presented in the chapter and use them to determine the value of the stock.

A new business often expects to have low sales during its first few years of operation as it develops its product. Then if the product catches on, sales will grow rapidly for several years. Sales growth brings with it the need for additional assets—a firm cannot increase sales without also increasing its assets, and asset growth requires an increase in liability and/or equity accounts. Small firms can generally obtain some bank credit, but they must maintain a reasonable balance between debt and equity. Thus, additional bank borrowings require increases in equity, and getting the equity capital needed to support growth can be difficult for small firms. They have limited access to the capital markets, and even when they can sell common stock, their owners are reluctant to do so for fear of losing voting control. Therefore, the best source of equity for most small businesses is retained earnings; for this reason most small firms pay no dividends during their rapid growth years. Eventually, though, successful small firms do pay dividends, and those dividends generally grow rapidly at first, but slow down to a sustainable constant rate once the firm reaches maturity.

If a firm currently pays no dividends but is expected to pay future dividends, the value of its stock can be found as follows:

1. Estimate at what point dividends will be paid, the amount of the first dividend, the growth rate during the supernormal growth period, the length of the supernormal period, the long-run (constant) growth rate, and the rate of return required by investors.

2. Use the constant growth model to determine the stock price after the firm reaches a stable growth situation.

3. Set out on a time line the cash flows (dividends during the supernormal growth period and the stock price once the constant growth state is reached); then find the present value of these cash flows. That present value represents the value of the stock today.

To illustrate this process, consider the situation for Marvel-Lure Inc., a company that was set up in 2015 to produce and market a new high-tech fishing lure. Marvel-Lure's sales are currently growing at a rate of 200% per year. The company expects to experience a high but declining rate of growth in sales and earnings during the next 10 years, after which analysts estimate that it will grow at a steady 10% per year. The firm's management has announced that it will pay no dividends for 5 years but that if earnings materialize as forecasted, it will pay a dividend of $0.20 per share at the end of Year 6, $0.30 in Year 7, $0.40 in Year 8, $0.45 in Year 9, and $0.50 in Year 10. After Year 10, current plans are to increase dividends by 10% per year.

Marvel-Lure's investment bankers estimate that investors require a 15% return on similar stocks. Therefore, we find the value of a share of Marvel-Lure's stock as follows:

$$\hat{P}_0 = \frac{\$0}{(1.15)^1} + \cdots + \frac{\$0}{(1.15)^5} + \frac{\$0.20}{(1.15)^6} + \frac{\$0.30}{(1.15)^7} + \frac{\$0.40}{(1.15)^8}$$

$$+ \frac{\$0.45}{(1.15)^9} + \frac{\$0.50}{(1.15)^{10}} + \left(\frac{\$0.50(1.10)}{0.15 - 0.10}\right)\left(\frac{1}{(1.15)^{10}}\right)$$

$$= \$3.30$$

The last term finds the expected stock price in Year 10 and then finds the present value of that price. Thus, we see that the discounted dividend model can be applied to firms that currently pay no dividends, provided we can estimate future dividends with a fair degree of confidence. However, in many cases, we can have more confidence in the forecasts of free cash flows, and in these situations, it is better to use the corporate valuation model.

# 9-7 Enterprise-Based Approach to Valuation[12]

Thus far we have discussed the discounted dividend model for valuing a firm's common stock. This procedure is widely used, but it is based on the assumption that the analyst can forecast future dividends reasonably well. This is often true for mature companies that have a history of steadily growing dividends. However, dividends are dependent on earnings; so a reliable dividend forecast must be based on an underlying forecast of the firm's future sales, costs, and capital requirements.

---

[12]The corporate valuation model presented in this section is widely used by analysts, and it is in many respects superior to the discounted dividend model. However, it is rather involved as it requires the estimation of future sales, costs, and cash flows before the discounting process is begun. Therefore, in the introductory course, some instructors may prefer to omit Section 9-7 and skip to Section 9-8.

**Corporate Valuation Model**

A valuation model used as an alternative to the discounted dividend model to determine a firm's value, especially one with no history of dividends, or the value of a division of a larger firm. The corporate model first calculates the firm's free cash flows, then finds their present values to determine the firm's value.

This recognition has led to an alternative stock valuation approach, the **corporate valuation model**.

Rather than starting with a forecast of dividends, the corporate valuation model focuses on the firm's future free cash flows. We discussed free cash flow (FCF) in Chapter 3, where we developed the following equation:

$$FCF = \left[ EBIT(1 - T) + \begin{array}{c} \text{Depreciation} \\ \text{and amortization} \end{array} \right] - \left[ \begin{array}{c} \text{Capital} \\ \text{expenditures} \end{array} + \begin{array}{c} \Delta\text{Net operating} \\ \text{working capital} \end{array} \right]$$

EBIT is earnings before interest and taxes, and free cash flow represents the cash generated from current operations less the cash that must be spent on investments in fixed assets and working capital to support future growth.

Consider the case of Home Depot (HD). The first term in brackets in the preceding equation represents the amount of cash that HD is generating from its existing stores. The second term represents the amount of cash the company plans to spend this period to construct new stores. To open a new store, HD must spend cash to purchase the land and construct the building—these are the capital expenditures, and they lead to a corresponding increase in the firm's fixed assets, as shown on the balance sheet. But HD also needs to increase its working capital, especially inventory. Putting everything together, HD generates positive free cash flow for its investors if and only if the money from its existing stores exceeds the money required to build and equip its new stores.

## 9-7A THE CORPORATE VALUATION MODEL

In Chapter 3, we explained that a firm's value is determined by its ability to generate cash flow both now and in the future. Therefore, its market value can be expressed as follows:

$$\begin{array}{c} \text{Market value} \\ \text{of company} \end{array} = V_{Company} = \text{PV of expected future free cash flows}$$

$$= \frac{FCF_1}{(1 + WACC)^1} + \frac{FCF_2}{(1 + WACC)^2} + \cdots + \frac{FCF_\infty}{(1 + WACC)^\infty} \qquad 9.7$$

Here $FCF_t$ is the free cash flow in Year t; and the discount rate, the WACC, is the weighted average cost of all the firm's capital. When thinking about the WACC, note these two points:

1. The firm finances with debt, preferred stock, and common equity. The WACC is the weighted average of these three types of capital, and we discuss it in detail in Chapter 10.

2. Free cash flow is the cash generated *before any payments are made to any investors; so it must be used to compensate common stockholders, preferred stockholders, and bondholders.* Moreover, each type of investor has a required rate of return; and the weighted average of those returns is the WACC, which is used to discount the free cash flows.

Free cash flows are generally forecasted for 5 to 10 years, after which it is assumed that the final explicitly forecasted FCF will grow at some long-run constant rate. Once the company reaches its horizon date, when cash flows begin to grow at a constant rate, we can use the following formula to calculate the market value of the company as of that date:

$$\text{Horizon value} = V_{Company\ at\ t\ =\ N} = FCF_{N\ +\ 1}/(WACC - g_{FCF}) \qquad 9.8$$

The corporate model is applied internally by the firm's financial staff and by outside security analysts. For illustrative purposes, we discuss Allied's free cash flow valuation analysis conducted by Susan Buskirk, senior food analyst for the investment banking firm Morton Staley and Company. Her analysis is summarized in Table 9.2, which was reproduced from the chapter Excel model.

Analysis of a Constant Growth stock          **TABLE 9.2**

| | A | B | C | D | E | F | G | H | I |
|---|---|---|---|---|---|---|---|---|---|
| 135 | Part 1. Key Inputs | | | Forecasted Years | | | | | |
| 136 | | | | 2017 | 2018 | 2019 | 2020 | 2021 | |
| 137 | Sales growth rate | | | 10.0% | 9.0% | 9.0% | 9.0% | 8.0% | |
| 138 | Operating costs as a % of sales | | | 87.0% | 87.0% | 86.0% | 85.0% | 85.0% | |
| 139 | Growth in net fixed assets | | | 8.0% | 8.0% | 8.0% | 8.0% | 8.0% | |
| 140 | Growth in NOWC | | | 8.0% | 8.0% | 8.0% | 8.0% | 8.0% | |
| 141 | Depr'n as a % of operating capital | | | 6.0% | 8.0% | 7.0% | 7.0% | 7.0% | |
| 142 | Tax rate | | | 40% | | | | | |
| 143 | WACC | | | 10% | | | | | |
| 144 | Long-run FCF growth, $g_{FCF}$ | | | 6.0% | | | | | |
| 145 | | | | | | | | | |
| 146 | Part 2. Forecast of Cash Flows During Period of Nonconstant Growth | | | | | | | | |
| 147 | | | Historical | Forecasted Years | | | | | |
| 148 | | | 2016 | 2017 | 2018 | 2019 | 2020 | 2021 | |
| 149 | | | | | | | | | |
| 150 | Sales | | $3,000.0 | $3,300.0 | $3,597.0 | $3,920.7 | $4,273.6 | $4,615.5 | |
| 151 | Operating costs | | 2,616.2 | 2,871.0 | 3,129.4 | 3,371.8 | 3,632.6 | 3,923.2 | |
| 152 | DEP = Depreciation | | 100.0 | 116.6 | 168.0 | 158.7 | 171.4 | 185.1 | |
| 153 | EBIT | | $283.8 | $312.4 | $299.6 | $390.2 | $469.6 | $507.2 | |
| 154 | EBIT x (1 − T) | | 170.3 | 187.4 | 179.8 | 234.1 | 281.8 | 304.3 | |
| 155 | EBIT x (1 − T) + DEP | | 270.3 | 304.1 | 347.8 | 392.8 | 453.2 | 489.4 | |
| 156 | | | | | | | | | |
| 157 | Net fixed assets | | $1,000.0 | $1,080.0 | $1,166.4 | $1,259.7 | $1,360.5 | $1,469.3 | |
| 158 | Net oper. working capital (NOWC) | | 800.0 | 864.0 | 933.1 | 1,007.8 | 1,088.4 | 1,175.5 | |
| 159 | Total operating capital | | $1,800.0 | $1,944.0 | $2,099.5 | $2,267.5 | $2,448.9 | $2,644.8 | |
| 160 | Net CAPEX = Change in net fixed assets | | 130.0 | 80.0 | 86.4 | 93.3 | 100.8 | 108.8 | |
| 161 | CAPEX = Gross capital expenditures = Net CAPEX + DEP | | 230.0 | 196.6 | 254.4 | 252.0 | 272.2 | 294.0 | |
| 162 | ΔNOWC | | 150.0 | 64.0 | 69.1 | 74.6 | 80.6 | 87.1 | |
| 163 | | | | | | | | | |
| 164 | Free Cash Flow, FCF = EBIT(1 − T) + DEP − CAPEX − ΔNOWC | | −$109.7 | $43.4 | $24.3 | $66.1 | $100.4 | $108.4 | |
| 165 | PV of FCFs | | N.A. | $39.5 | $20.1 | $49.7 | $68.6 | $67.3 | |
| 166 | | | | | | | | | |
| 167 | Part 3. Horizon Value and Intrinsic Value Estimation | | | | | | | | |
| 168 | Estimated Value at the Horizon, 2021 | | | | | | | | |
| 169 | Free Cash Flow (2022) | | | $114.9 | | | | | |
| 170 | Horizon Value at 2021, $HV_{2021}$ | | | $2,872.7 | | | | | |
| 171 | PV of $HV_{2021}$ | | | $1,783.7 | | | | | |
| 172 | | | | | | | | | |
| 173 | Calculation of Firm's Intrinsic Value | | | | | | | | |
| 174 | Sum of PVs of FCFs, 2017–2021 | | | $245.1 | | | | | |
| 175 | PV of $HV_{2021}$ | | | 1,783.7 | | | | | |
| 176 | Total corporate value | | | $2,028.8 | | | | | |
| 177 | Less: market value of debt and preferred | | | 860.0 | | | | | |
| 178 | Intrinsic value of common equity | | | $1,168.8 | | | | | |
| 179 | Shares outstanding (millions) | | | 50.0 | | | | | |
| 180 | | | | | | | | | |
| 181 | Intrinsic Value Per Share | | | $23.38 | | | | | |

Part 3 formulas:

$FCF_{2021}(1+g_{FCF})$

$HV_{2021} = \dfrac{FCF_{2022}}{WACC - g_{FCF}}$

$HV_{2021} / (1+WACC)^N$

- Based on Allied's history and Buskirk's knowledge of the firm's business plan, she estimated sales, costs, and cash flows on an annual basis for 5 years. Growth will vary during those years, but she assumes that things will stabilize, and growth will be constant after the fifth year. She would have made explicit forecasts for more years if she thought it would take longer to reach a steady-state, constant growth situation.

- For each of the first five years, Buskirk paid particular attention to the key variables that influence free cash flow. Specifically, she focused on EBIT, required capital expenditures, and the anticipated changes in net operating working capital (NOWC).

- Buskirk next calculated the expected free cash flows (FCFs) for each of the 5 nonconstant growth years, and she found the PV of those cash flows discounted at the WACC.

- After Year 5, she assumed that FCF growth would be constant; hence, the constant growth model could be used to find Allied's total market value at Year 5. This "horizon, or continuing, value" is the sum of the PVs of the FCFs from Year 6 on out into the future, discounted back to Year 5 at the WACC. It follows that: Horizon Value$_{t=5}$ = FCF$_6$/(WACC$-$g$_{FCF}$), where g$_{FCF}$ represents the long-run growth rate of the free cash flow.

- Next, she discounted the Year 5 horizon value back to the present to find its PV at Year 0.

- She then summed all the PVs, the annual cash flows during the nonconstant period plus the PV of the horizon value, to find the firm's estimated total market value.

- Then she subtracted the current market value of the debt and preferred stock to find the value of Allied's common equity.

Finally, she divided the equity value by the number of shares outstanding, and the result was her estimate of Allied's intrinsic value per share. This value was quite close to the stock's market price, so she concluded that Allied's stock is priced at its equilibrium level. Consequently, she issued a "Hold" recommendation on the stock. If the estimated intrinsic value had been significantly below the market price, she would have issued a "Sell" recommendation; if the estimated intrinsic value had been well above the market price, she would have called the stock a "Buy."

In practice, the corporate valuation model can be further extended to take into account a variety of other factors. For example, if a company has significant non-operating assets that are not captured in the estimated free cash flows, then they should be included as part of the company's total corporate value. Examples may include large holdings of excess cash, real estate holdings outside of its main operations, or a company's minority stake in another business. Alternatively, an analyst may also need to account for significant non-operating liabilities such as an underfunded pension liability or contingencies related to future litigation. Finally, another example is executive stock options—to the extent these options are valuable, it means that the company's executive will receive some portion of the company's future gains. For some companies, these other factors can be quite important, and often quite complicated. Consequently, we will leave a more detailed discussion of these issues to more advanced finance courses that focus more specifically on valuation.

## 9-7B COMPARING THE CORPORATE VALUATION AND DISCOUNTED DIVIDEND MODELS

Analysts use both the discounted dividend model and the corporate valuation model when valuing mature, dividend-paying firms; and they generally use the corporate model when valuing divisions and firms that do not pay dividends. In principle, we should find the same intrinsic value using either model, but differences are often observed. When a conflict exists, the assumptions embedded

# OTHER APPROACHES TO VALUING COMMON STOCKS

Although the dividend growth and the corporate valuation models presented in this chapter are the most widely used methods for valuing common stocks, they are by no means the only approaches. Analysts often use a number of different techniques to value stocks. Two of these alternative approaches are described here.

## The P/E Multiple Approach

Investors have long looked for simple rules of thumb to determine whether a stock is fairly valued. One such approach is to look at the stock's price-to-earnings (P/E) ratio. Recall from Chapter 4 that a company's P/E ratio shows how much investors are willing to pay for each dollar of reported earnings. As a starting point, you might conclude that stocks with low P/E ratios are undervalued because their price is "low" given current earnings, whereas stocks with high P/E ratios are overvalued.

Unfortunately, however, valuing stocks is not that simple. We should not expect all companies to have the same P/E ratio. P/E ratios are affected by risk—investors discount the earnings of riskier stocks at a higher rate. Thus, all else equal, riskier stocks should have lower P/E ratios. In addition, when you buy a stock, you have a claim not only on current earnings but also on all future earnings. All else equal, companies with stronger growth opportunities will generate larger future earnings and thus should trade at higher P/E ratios. Therefore, Chipotle Mexican Grill is not necessarily overvalued just because its P/E ratio is 46.7 at a time when the median firm in its industry has a P/E of 31.3. Investors believe that Chipotle's growth potential is well above average. Whether the stock's future prospects justify its P/E ratio remains to be seen; but in and of itself, a high P/E ratio does not mean that a stock is overvalued.

Nevertheless, P/E ratios can provide a useful starting point in stock valuation. If a stock's P/E ratio is well above its industry average and if the stock's growth potential and risk are similar to other firms in the industry, the stock's price may be too high. Likewise, if a company's P/E ratio falls well below its historical average, the stock may be undervalued—particularly if the company's growth prospects and risk are unchanged and if the overall P/E for the market has remained constant or increased.

One obvious drawback of the P/E approach is that it depends on reported accounting earnings. For this reason, some analysts choose to rely on other multiples to value stocks. For example, some analysts look at a company's price-to-cash-flow ratio, whereas others look at the price-to-sales ratio.

## The EVA Approach

In recent years, analysts have looked for more rigorous alternatives to the discounted dividend model. More than a quarter of all stocks listed on the NYSE pay no dividends. This proportion is even higher on NASDAQ. Although the discounted dividend model can still be used for these stocks (see "Evaluating Stocks That Don't Pay Dividends"), this approach requires that analysts forecast when the stock will begin paying dividends, what the dividend will be once it is established, and what the future dividend growth rate will be. In many cases, these forecasts contain considerable errors.

An alternative approach is based on the concept of Economic Value Added (EVA), which we discussed in Chapter 3 and in the Chapter 4 box "Economic Value Added (EVA) versus Net Income," that can be written as follows:

**EVA = (Equity capital)(ROE − Cost of equity capital)**

This equation suggests that companies can increase their EVA by investing in projects that provide shareholders with returns that are above their cost of equity capital, which is the return they could expect to earn on alternative investments with the same level of risk. When you purchase stock in a company, you receive more than just the book value of equity—you also receive a claim on all future value that is created by the firm's managers (the present value of all future EVAs). It follows that a company's market value of equity can be written as follows:

**Market value of equity = Book value + PV of all future EVAs**

We can find the "fundamental" value of the stock, $P_0$, by simply dividing the preceding expression by the number of shares outstanding.

As is the case with the discounted dividend model, we can simplify the expression by assuming that at some point in time, annual EVA becomes a perpetuity, or grows at some constant rate over time. Presented here is a simplified version of what is often referred to as the Edwards-Bell-Ohlson (EBO) model. For a more complete description of this technique and an excellent summary of how it can be used in practice, read the article "Measuring Wealth," by Charles M. C. Lee, in CA Magazine, April 1996, pp. 32–37.

in the corporate model can be reexamined; and once the analyst is convinced they are reasonable, the results of that model are used.

In practice, intrinsic value estimates based on the two models normally deviate from one another and from actual stock prices, leading different analysts to reach different conclusions about the attractiveness of a given stock. The better the analyst, the more often his or her valuations turn out to be correct; but no one can make perfect predictions because too many things can change randomly and unpredictably in the future. Given all this, does it matter whether you use the corporate model or the dividend model to value stocks? We would argue that it does. If we had to value, for example, 100 mature companies whose dividends were expected to grow steadily in the future, we would probably use the discounted dividend model. Here we would estimate only the growth rate in dividends, not the entire set of pro forma financial statements; hence, it would be more feasible to use the dividend model.

However, if we were studying just one company or a few companies, especially companies still in the high-growth stage of their life cycles, we would want to project future financial statements before estimating future dividends. Because we would already have projected future financial statements, we would go ahead and apply the corporate model. Intel, which pays a dividend of $0.90 versus earnings of about $2.33, is an example of a company where either model could be used; but we believe the corporate model is better.

Now suppose you were trying to estimate the value of a company such as eBay that, to date (April 2015), has never paid a dividend or a new firm that is about to go public. In either situation, you would be better off using the corporate valuation model. Actually, even if a company is paying steady dividends, much can be learned from the corporate model; so analysts today use it for all types of valuations. The process of projecting future financial statements can reveal a great deal about a company's operations and financing needs. Also, such an analysis can provide insights into actions that might be taken to increase the company's value; and for this reason, it is integral to the planning and forecasting process, as we discuss in a later chapter.

## Self Test

Write out the equation for free cash flows and explain it.

Why might someone use the corporate valuation model for companies that have a history of paying dividends?

What steps are taken to find a stock price using the corporate model?

Why might the calculated intrinsic value differ from the stock's current market price? Which would be "correct," and what does "correct" mean?

## 9-8 Preferred Stock[13]

Preferred stock is a *hybrid*—it is similar to a bond in some respects and to common stock in others. This hybrid nature becomes apparent when we try to classify preferred stock in relation to bonds and common stock. Like bonds, preferred stock has a par value and a fixed dividend that must be paid before dividends can be paid on the common stock. However, the directors can omit (or "pass") the preferred dividend without throwing the company into bankruptcy. So although preferred stock calls for a fixed payment like bonds, skipping the payment will not lead to bankruptcy.

As noted earlier, a preferred stock entitles its owners to regular, fixed dividend payments. If the payments last forever, the issue is a *perpetuity* whose value, $V_p$, is found as follows:

$$V_p = \frac{D_p}{r_p}$$

9.9

---

[13]Preferred stock is discussed in more detail in Chapter 20 of Brigham and Daves, *Intermediate Financial Management*, 12th edition (Mason, OH: Cengage Learning, 2016).

$V_p$ is the value of the preferred stock, $D_p$ is the preferred dividend, and $r_p$ is the required rate of return on the preferred. Allied Food has no preferred outstanding, but discussions about such an issue suggested that its preferred should pay a dividend of $10 per year. If its required return was 10.3%, the preferred's value would be $97.09, found as follows:

$$V_p = \frac{\$10.00}{0.103} = \$97.09$$

In equilibrium, the expected return, $\hat{r}_p$, must be equal to the required return, $r_p$. Thus, if we know the preferred's current price and dividend, we can solve for the expected rate of return as follows:

$$\hat{r}_p = \frac{D_p}{V_p} \qquad\qquad 9.9a$$

Some preferreds have a stated maturity, often 50 years. Assume that our illustrative preferred matured in 50 years, paid a $10 annual dividend, and had a required return of 8%. We could then find its price as follows: Enter $N = 50$, $I/YR = 8$, $PMT = 10$, and $FV = 100$. Then press PV to find the price, $V_p = \$124.47$. If $r_p$ rose to 10%, you would change $I/YR$ to 10, in which case $V_p = PV = \$100$. If you know the price of a share of preferred stock, you can solve for $I/YR$ to find the expected rate of return, $\hat{r}_p$.

## SelfTest

Explain the following statement: Preferred stock is a hybrid security.

Is the equation used to value preferred stock more like the one used to value a bond or the one used to value a "normal" constant growth common stock? Explain.

# TYING IT ALL TOGETHER

Corporate decisions should be analyzed in terms of how alternative courses of action are likely to affect a firm's value. However, it is necessary to know how stock prices are established before attempting to measure how a given decision will affect a specific firm's value. This chapter discussed the rights and privileges of common stockholders, showed how stock values are determined, and explained how investors estimate stocks' intrinsic values and expected rates of return.

Two types of stock valuation models were discussed: the discounted dividend model and the corporate valuation model. The discounted dividend model is useful for mature, stable companies. It is easier to use, but the corporate valuation model is more flexible and better for use with companies that do not pay dividends or whose dividends would be especially hard to predict.

We also discussed preferred stock, which is a hybrid security that has some characteristics of a common stock and some of a bond. Preferreds are valued using models similar to those for perpetual and "regular" bonds.

# Self-Test Questions and Problems

(Solutions Appear in Appendix A)

**ST-1  KEY TERMS**  Define the following terms:

a. Proxy; proxy fight; takeover
b. Preemptive right
c. Classified stock; founders' shares
d. Marginal investor; intrinsic value ($\hat{P}_0$); market price ($P_0$)
e. Required rate of return, $r_s$; expected rate of return, $\hat{r}_s$; actual (realized) rate of return, $\bar{r}_s$
f. Capital gains yield; dividend yield; expected total return; growth rate, g
g. Zero growth stock
h. Constant growth (Gordon) model; supernormal (nonconstant) growth
i. Corporate valuation model
j. Horizon (terminal) date; horizon (continuing) value
k. Preferred stock

**ST-2  STOCK GROWTH RATES AND VALUATION**  You are considering buying the stocks of two companies that operate in the same industry. They have very similar characteristics except for their dividend payout policies. Both companies are expected to earn $3 per share this year; but Company D (for "dividend") is expected to pay out all of its earnings as dividends, while Company G (for "growth") is expected to pay out only one-third of its earnings, or $1 per share. D's stock price is $25. G and D are equally risky. Which of the following statements is most likely to be true?

a. Company G will have a faster growth rate than Company D. Therefore, G's stock price should be greater than $25.
b. Although G's growth rate should exceed D's, D's current dividend exceeds that of G, which should cause D's price to exceed G's.
c. A long-term investor in Stock D will get his or her money back faster because D pays out more of its earnings as dividends. Thus, in a sense, D is like a short-term bond and G is like a long-term bond. Therefore, if economic shifts cause $r_d$ and $r_s$ to increase, and if the expected dividend streams from D and G remain constant, both Stocks D and G will decline, but D's price should decline further.
d. D's expected and required rate of return is $\hat{r}_s = r_s = 12\%$. G's expected return will be higher because of its higher expected growth rate.
e. If we observe that G's price is also $25, the best estimate of G's growth rate is 8%.

**ST-3  CONSTANT GROWTH STOCK VALUATION**  Fletcher Company's current stock price is $36.00, its last dividend was $2.40, and its required rate of return is 12%. If dividends are expected to grow at a constant rate, g, in the future, and if $r_s$ is expected to remain at 12%, what is Fletcher's expected stock price 5 years from now?

**ST-4  NONCONSTANT GROWTH STOCK VALUATION**  Snyder Computers Inc. is experiencing rapid growth. Earnings and dividends are expected to grow at a rate of 15% during the next 2 years, at 13% the following year, and at a constant rate of 6% during Year 4 and thereafter. Its last dividend was $1.15, and its required rate of return is 12%.

a. Calculate the value of the stock today.
b. Calculate $\hat{P}_1$ and $\hat{P}_2$.
c. Calculate the dividend and capital gains yields for Years 1, 2, and 3.

# Questions

**9-1** It is frequently stated that the one purpose of the preemptive right is to allow individuals to maintain their proportionate share of the ownership and control of a corporation.

    a. How important do you suppose control is for the average stockholder of a firm whose shares are traded on the New York Stock Exchange?

    b. Is the control issue likely to be of more importance to stockholders of publicly owned or closely held (private) firms? Explain.

**9-2** Is the following equation correct for finding the value of a constant growth stock? Explain.

$$\hat{P}_0 = \frac{D_0}{r_s + g}$$

**9-3** If you bought a share of common stock, you would probably expect to receive dividends plus an eventual capital gain. Would the distribution between the dividend yield and the capital gains yield be influenced by the firm's decision to pay more dividends rather than to retain and reinvest more of its earnings? Explain.

**9-4** Two investors are evaluating GE's stock for possible purchase. They agree on the expected value of $D_1$ and on the expected future dividend growth rate. Further, they agree on the riskiness of the stock. However, one investor normally holds stocks for 2 years, while the other holds stocks for 10 years. On the basis of the type of analysis done in this chapter, should they both be willing to pay the same price for GE's stock? Explain.

**9-5** A bond that pays interest forever and has no maturity is a perpetual bond. In what respect is a perpetual bond similar to a no-growth common stock? Are there preferred stocks that are evaluated similarly to perpetual bonds and other preferred issues that are more like bonds with finite lives? Explain.

**9-6** Discuss the similarities and differences between the discounted dividend and corporate valuation models.

**9-7** This chapter discusses the discounted dividend and corporate valuation models for valuing common stocks. Two alternative approaches, the P/E multiple and EVA approaches, were presented. Explain each approach and how you might use each one to value a common stock.

# Problems

**Easy Problems 1–6**

**9-1** **DPS CALCULATION** Weston Corporation just paid a dividend of $1.00 a share (i.e., $D_0 = \$1.00$). The dividend is expected to grow 12% a year for the next 3 years and then at 5% a year thereafter. What is the expected dividend per share for each of the next 5 years?

**9-2** **CONSTANT GROWTH VALUATION** Tresnan Brothers is expected to pay a $1.80 per share dividend at the end of the year (i.e., $D_1 = \$1.80$). The dividend is expected to grow at a constant rate of 4% a year. The required rate of return on the stock, $r_s$, is 10%. What is the stock's current value per share?

**9-3** **CONSTANT GROWTH VALUATION** Holtzman Clothiers's stock currently sells for $38.00 a share. It just paid a dividend of $2.00 a share (i.e., $D_0 = \$2.00$). The dividend is expected to grow at a constant rate of 5% a year. What stock price is expected 1 year from now? What is the required rate of return?

**9-4** **NONCONSTANT GROWTH VALUATION** Holt Enterprises recently paid a dividend, $D_0$, of $2.75. It expects to have nonconstant growth of 18% for 2 years followed by a constant rate of 6% thereafter. The firm's required return is 12%.

    a. How far away is the horizon date?

    b. What is the firm's horizon, or continuing, value?

    c. What is the firm's intrinsic value today, $\hat{P}_0$?

**9-5**  **CORPORATE VALUATION**  Scampini Technologies is expected to generate $25 million in free cash flow next year, and FCF is expected to grow at a constant rate of 4% per year indefinitely. Scampini has no debt or preferred stock, and its WACC is 10%. If Scampini has 40 million shares of stock outstanding, what is the stock's value per share?

**9-6**  **PREFERRED STOCK VALUATION**  Farley Inc. has perpetual preferred stock outstanding that sells for $30 a share and pays a dividend of $2.75 at the end of each year. What is the required rate of return?

**Intermediate Problems 7–15**

**9-7**  **PREFERRED STOCK RATE OF RETURN**  What will be the nominal rate of return on a perpetual preferred stock with a $100 par value, a stated dividend of 10% of par, and a current market price of (a) $61, (b) $90, (c) $100, and (d) $138?

**9-8**  **PREFERRED STOCK VALUATION**  Earley Corporation issued perpetual preferred stock with an 8% annual dividend. The stock currently yields 7%, and its par value is $100.

   a. What is the stock's value?

   b. Suppose interest rates rise and pull the preferred stock's yield up to 9%. What is its new market value?

**9-9**  **PREFERRED STOCK RETURNS**  Avondale Aeronautics has perpetual preferred stock outstanding with a par value of $100. The stock pays a quarterly dividend of $1.00 and its current price is $45.

   a. What is its nominal annual rate of return?

   b. What is its effective annual rate of return?

**9-10**  **VALUATION OF A DECLINING GROWTH STOCK**  Maxwell Mining Company's ore reserves are being depleted, so its sales are falling. Also, because its pit is getting deeper each year, its costs are rising. As a result, the company's earnings and dividends are declining at the constant rate of 6% per year. If $D_0 = \$3$ and $r_s = 10\%$, what is the value of Maxwell Mining's stock?

**9-11**  **VALUATION OF A CONSTANT GROWTH STOCK**  A stock is expected to pay a dividend of $2.75 at the end of the year (i.e., $D_1 = 2.75$), and it should continue to grow at a constant rate of 5% a year. If its required return is 15%, what is the stock's expected price 4 years from today?

**9-12**  **VALUATION OF A CONSTANT GROWTH STOCK**  Investors require an 8% rate of return on Mather Company's stock (i.e., $r_s = 8\%$).

   a. What is its value if the previous dividend was $D_0 = \$1.25$ and investors expect dividends to grow at a constant annual rate of (1) –2%, (2) 0%, (3) 3%, or (4) 5%?

   b. Using data from part a, what would the Gordon (constant growth) model value be if the required rate of return was 8% and the expected growth rate was (1) 8% or (2) 12%? Are these reasonable results? Explain.

   c. Is it reasonable to think that a constant growth stock could have $g > r_s$? Why or why not?

**9-13**  **CONSTANT GROWTH**  You are considering an investment in Justus Corporation's stock, which is expected to pay a dividend of $2.25 a share at the end of the year ($D_1 = \$2.25$) and has a beta of 0.9. The risk-free rate is 4.9%, and the market risk premium is 5%. Justus currently sells for $46.00 a share, and its dividend is expected to grow at some constant rate, g. Assuming the market is in equilibrium, what does the market believe will be the stock price at the end of 3 years? (That is, what is $\hat{P}_3$?)

**9-14**  **NONCONSTANT GROWTH**  Computech Corporation is expanding rapidly and currently needs to retain all of its earnings; hence, it does not pay dividends. However, investors expect Computech to begin paying dividends, beginning with a dividend of $0.50 coming 3 years from today. The dividend should grow rapidly—at a rate of 35% per year—during Years 4 and 5; but after Year 5, growth should be a constant 7% per year. If the required return on Computech is 13%, what is the value of the stock today?

**9-15** **CORPORATE VALUATION** Dantzler Corporation is a fast-growing supplier of office products. Analysts project the following free cash flows (FCFs) during the next 3 years, after which FCF is expected to grow at a constant 5% rate. Dantzler's WACC is 11%.

| Year | 0 | 1 | 2 | 3 |
|------|---|---|---|---|
| FCF ($ millions) | | −$11 | $17 | $45 |

a. What is Dantzler's horizon, or continuing, value? (Hint: Find the value of all free cash flows beyond Year 3 discounted back to Year 3.)

b. What is the firm's value today?

c. Suppose Dantzler has $112.60 million of debt and 25 million shares of stock outstanding. What is your estimate of the current price per share?

**Challenging Problems 16–21**

**9-16** **NONCONSTANT GROWTH** Carnes Cosmetics Co.'s stock price is $30, and it recently paid a $1.00 dividend. This dividend is expected to grow by 30% for the next 3 years, then grow forever at a constant rate, g; and $r_s = 9\%$. At what constant rate is the stock expected to grow after Year 3?

**9-17** **CONSTANT GROWTH** Your broker offers to sell you some shares of Bahnsen & Co. common stock that paid a dividend of $2.00 *yesterday*. Bahnsen's dividend is expected to grow at 5% per year for the next 3 years. If you buy the stock, you plan to hold it for 3 years and then sell it. The appropriate discount rate is 12%.

a. Find the expected dividend for each of the next 3 years; that is, calculate $D_1$, $D_2$, and $D_3$. Note that $D_0 = \$2.00$.

b. Given that the first dividend payment will occur 1 year from now, find the present value of the dividend stream; that is, calculate the PVs of $D_1$, $D_2$, and $D_3$, and then sum these PVs.

c. You expect the price of the stock 3 years from now to be $34.73; that is, you expect $\hat{P}_3$ to equal $34.73. Discounted at a 12% rate, what is the present value of this expected future stock price? In other words, calculate the PV of $34.73.

d. If you plan to buy the stock, hold it for 3 years, and then sell it for $34.73, what is the most you should pay for it today?

e. Use Equation 9.2 to calculate the present value of this stock. Assume that $g = 5\%$ and that it is constant.

f. Is the value of this stock dependent upon how long you plan to hold it? In other words, if your planned holding period was 2 years or 5 years rather than 3 years, would this affect the value of the stock today, $\hat{P}_0$? Explain.

**9-18** **NONCONSTANT GROWTH STOCK VALUATION** Taussig Technologies Corporation (TTC) has been growing at a rate of 20% per year in recent years. This same growth rate is expected to last for another 2 years, then decline to $g_n = 6\%$.

a. If $D_0 = \$1.60$ and $r_s = 10\%$, what is TTC's stock worth today? What are its expected dividend, and capital gains yields at this time, that is, during Year 1?

b. Now assume that TTC's period of supernormal growth is to last for 5 years rather than 2 years. How would this affect the price, dividend yield, and capital gains yield? Answer in words only.

c. What will TTC's dividend and capital gains yields be once its period of supernormal growth ends? (Hint: These values will be the same regardless of whether you examine the case of 2 or 5 years of supernormal growth; the calculations are very easy.)

d. Explain why investors are interested in the changing relationship between dividend and capital gains yields over time.

**9-19** **CORPORATE VALUATION** Brandtly Industries invests a large sum of money in R&D; as a result, it retains and reinvests all of its earnings. In other words, Brandtly does not pay any dividends, and it has no plans to pay dividends in the near future. A major pension fund is interested in purchasing Brandtly's stock. The pension fund manager has estimated Brandtly's free cash flows for the next 4 years as follows: $3 million, $6 million, $8 million, and $16 million. After the fourth year, free cash flow is projected to grow at a constant 3%.

Brandtly's WACC is 9%, the market value of its debt and preferred stock totals $75 million; and it has 7.5 million shares of common stock outstanding.

a. What is the present value of the free cash flows projected during the next 4 years?
b. What is the firm's horizon, or continuing, value?
c. What is the firm's total value today?
d. What is an estimate of Brandtly's price per share?

**9-20** **CORPORATE VALUE MODEL** Assume that today is December 31, 2016, and that the following information applies to Abner Airlines:

- After-tax operating income [EBIT(1 − T)] for 2017 is expected to be $400 million.
- The depreciation expense for 2017 is expected to be $140 million.
- The capital expenditures for 2017 are expected to be $225 million.
- No change is expected in net operating working capital.
- The free cash flow is expected to grow at a constant rate of 6% per year.
- The required return on equity is 14%.
- The WACC is 10%.
- The market value of the company's debt is $3.875 billion.
- 200 million shares of stock are outstanding.

Using the corporate valuation model approach, what should be the company's stock price today?

**9-21** **NONCONSTANT GROWTH** Assume that it is now January 1, 2017. Wayne-Martin Electric Inc. (WME) has developed a solar panel capable of generating 200% more electricity than any other solar panel currently on the market. As a result, WME is expected to experience a 15% annual growth rate for the next 5 years. Other firms will have developed comparable technology by the end of 5 years, and WME's growth rate will slow to 5% per year indefinitely. Stockholders require a return of 12% on WME's stock. The most recent annual dividend ($D_0$), which was paid yesterday, was $1.75 per share.

a. Calculate WME's expected dividends for 2017, 2018, 2019, 2020, and 2021.
b. Calculate the value of the stock today, $\hat{P}_0$. Proceed by finding the present value of the dividends expected at the end of 2017, 2018, 2019, 2020, and 2021 plus the present value of the stock price that should exist at the end of 2021. The year end 2021 stock price can be found by using the constant growth equation. Notice that to find the December 31, 2021, price, you must use the dividend expected in 2022, which is 5% greater than the 2021 dividend.
c. Calculate the expected dividend yield ($D_1/P_0$), capital gains yield, and total return (dividend yield plus capital gains yield) expected for 2017. (Assume that $\hat{P}_0 = P_0$ and recognize that the capital gains yield is equal to the total return minus the dividend yield.) Then calculate these same three yields for 2022.
d. How might an investor's tax situation affect his or her decision to purchase stocks of companies in the early stages of their lives, when they are growing rapidly, versus stocks of older, more mature firms? When does WME's stock become "mature" for purposes of this question?
e. Suppose your boss tells you she believes that WME's annual growth rate will be only 12% during the next 5 years and that the firm's long-run growth rate will be only 4%. Without doing any calculations, what general effect would these growth rate changes have on the price of WME's stock?
f. Suppose your boss also tells you that she regards WME as being quite risky and that she believes the required rate of return should be 14%, not 12%. Without doing any calculations, determine how the higher required rate of return would affect the price of the stock, the capital gains yield, and the dividend yield. Again, assume that the long-run growth rate is 4%.

## Comprehensive/Spreadsheet Problem

**9-22    NONCONSTANT GROWTH AND CORPORATE VALUATION**    Rework problem 9-18, parts a, b, and c, using a spreadsheet model. For part b, calculate the price, dividend yield, and capital gains yield as called for in the problem. After completing parts a through c, answer the following additional question, using the spreadsheet model.

d. TTC recently introduced a new line of products that has been wildly successful. On the basis of this success and anticipated future success, the following free cash flows were projected:

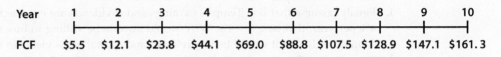

| Year | 1 | 2 | 3 | 4 | 5 | 6 | 7 | 8 | 9 | 10 |
|------|------|-------|-------|-------|-------|-------|--------|--------|--------|--------|
| FCF  | $5.5 | $12.1 | $23.8 | $44.1 | $69.0 | $88.8 | $107.5 | $128.9 | $147.1 | $161.3 |

After the tenth year, TTC's financial planners anticipate that its free cash flow will grow at a constant rate of 6%. Also, the firm concluded that the new product caused the WACC to fall to 9%. The market value of TTC's debt is $1,200 million; it uses no preferred stock; and there are 20 million shares of common stock outstanding. Use the corporate valuation model to value the stock.

## INTEGRATED CASE

### MUTUAL OF CHICAGO INSURANCE COMPANY

**9-23    STOCK VALUATION**    Robert Balik and Carol Kiefer are senior vice presidents of the Mutual of Chicago Insurance Company. They are codirectors of the company's pension fund management division, with Balik having responsibility for fixed-income securities (primarily bonds) and Kiefer being responsible for equity investments. A major new client, the California League of Cities, has requested that Mutual of Chicago present an investment seminar to the mayors of the represented cities; and Balik and Kiefer, who will make the actual presentation, have asked you to help them.

To illustrate the common stock valuation process, Balik and Kiefer have asked you to analyze the Bon Temps Company, an employment agency that supplies word-processor operators and computer programmers to businesses with temporarily heavy workloads. You are to answer the following questions:

a. Describe briefly the legal rights and privileges of common stockholders.

b. 1. Write a formula that can be used to value any stock, regardless of its dividend pattern.

   2. What is a constant growth stock? How are constant growth stocks valued?

   3. What are the implications if a company forecasts a constant g that exceeds its $r_s$? Will many stocks have expected g > $r_s$ in the short run (i.e., for the next few years)? In the long run (i.e., forever)?

c. Assume that Bon Temps has a beta coefficient of 1.2, that the risk-free rate (the yield on T-bonds) is 3%, and that the required rate of return on the market is 8%. What is Bon Temps's required rate of return?

d. Assume that Bon Temps is a constant growth company whose last dividend ($D_0$, which was paid yesterday) was $2.00 and whose dividend is expected to grow indefinitely at a 4% rate.

   1. What is the firm's expected dividend stream over the next 3 years?

   2. What is its current stock price?

3. What is the stock's expected value 1 year from now?

4. What are the expected dividend yield, capital gains yield, and total return during the first year?

e. Now assume that the stock is currently selling at $40.00. What is its expected rate of return?

f. What would the stock price be if its dividends were expected to have zero growth?

g. Now assume that Bon Temps's dividend is expected to grow 30% the first year, 20% the second year, 10% the third year, and return to its long-run constant growth rate of 4%. What is the stock's value under these conditions? What are its expected dividend and capital gains yields in Year 1? Year 4?

h. Suppose Bon Temps is expected to experience zero growth during the first 3 years and then resume its steady-state growth of 4% in the fourth year. What would be its value then? What would be its expected dividend and capital gains yields in Year 1? In Year 4?

i. Finally, assume that Bon Temps's earnings and dividends are expected to decline at a constant rate of 4% per year, that is, g = −4%. Why would anyone be willing to buy such a stock, and at what price should it sell? What would be its dividend and capital gains yields in each year?

j. Suppose Bon Temps embarked on an aggressive expansion that requires additional capital. Management decided to finance the expansion by borrowing $40 million and by halting dividend payments to increase retained earnings. Its WACC is now 7%, and the projected free cash flows for the next three years are −$5 million, $10 million, and $20 million. After Year 3, free cash flow is projected to grow at a constant 5%. What is Bon Temps's total value? If it has 10 million shares of stock and $40 million of debt and preferred stock combined, what is the price per share?

k. Suppose Bon Temps decided to issue preferred stock that would pay an annual dividend of $5.00 and that the issue price was $100.00 per share. What would be the stock's expected return? Would the expected rate of return be the same if the preferred was a perpetual issue or if it had a 20-year maturity?

# TAKING A CLOSER LOOK

## ESTIMATING EXXON MOBIL CORPORATION'S INTRINSIC STOCK VALUE

*Use online resources to work on this chapter's questions. Please note that website information changes over time, and these changes may limit your ability to answer some of these questions.*

In this chapter, we described the various factors that influence stock prices and the approaches that analysts use to estimate a stock's intrinsic value. By comparing these intrinsic value estimates to the current price, an investor can assess whether it makes sense to buy or sell a particular stock. Stocks trading at a price far below their estimated intrinsic values may be good candidates for purchase, whereas stocks trading at prices far in excess of their intrinsic value may be good stocks to avoid or sell. Although estimating a stock's intrinsic value is a complex exercise that requires reliable data and good judgment, we can use the Internet to find financial data in order to arrive at a quick "back-of-the-envelope" calculation of intrinsic value.

## DISCUSSION QUESTIONS

1. For purposes of this exercise, let's take a closer look at the stock of Exxon Mobil Corporation (XOM). Use websites such as Yahoo! Finance, Google Finance, MSN Money, and Morningstar to find the company's current stock price and see its performance relative to the overall market in recent months. What is Exxon Mobil's current stock price? How has the stock performed relative to the market over the past few months?

2. Check recent headlines on the website to see the company's recent news stories. Have there been any recent events impacting the company's stock price, or have things been relatively quiet?

3. To provide a starting point for gauging a company's relative valuation, analysts often look at a company's price-to-earnings (P/E) ratio. Go to the website's summary quote or key statistics screen to see XOM's forward P/E ratio, which uses XOM's next 12-month estimate of earnings in the calculation, and to see its current P/E ratio. What are the firm's forward and current P/E ratios?

4. To put XOM's P/E ratio in perspective, it is useful to see how this ratio has varied over time. (If you go to Morningstar and click on the valuation tab, you should see the 10-year summary of its P/E ratio. In addition, it shows a 10-year summary for the S&P 500 P/E ratio as well as Exxon Mobil's 5-year average.) Is XOM's current P/E ratio well above or well below its 5-year average? Explain why the current P/E deviates from its historical trend. On the basis of this information, does XOM's current P/E suggest that the stock is undervalued or overvalued? Explain.

5. To put the firm's current P/E ratio in perspective, it is useful to compare this ratio with that of other companies in the same industry. To see how XOM's P/E ratio stacks up to its peers, refer to Google Finance's Related Companies screen. (If you click "Add or remove columns," you will find that you can obtain comparisons of a number of key statistics for either the most recent year or quarter.) For the most part, is XOM's P/E ratio above or below that of its peers? In Chapter 4, we discussed the various factors that may influence P/E ratios. Can any of these factors explain why XOM's P/E ratio differs from its peers? Explain.

6. In the text, we discussed using the discounted dividend model to estimate a stock's intrinsic value. To keep things as simple as possible, let's assume at first that XOM's dividend is expected to grow at a constant rate of 5% annually over time. So, g = 5%. If so, the intrinsic value equals $D_1/(r_s - g)$, where $D_1$ is the expected annual dividend 1 year from now, $r_s$ is the stock's required rate of return, and g is the dividend's constant growth rate. Go back to the summary (overview) screen and find XOM's current dividend. Multiply this dividend by $1 + g$ to arrive at an estimate of $D_1$.

7. The required return on equity, $r_s$, is the final input needed to estimate intrinsic value. For our purposes, you can assume a number (say, 9% or 10%) or you can use the CAPM to calculate an estimate of the cost of equity, using the data available on the Internet. (For more details, look at the Taking a Closer Look exercise for Chapter 8.) Having decided on your best estimates for $D_1$, $r_s$, and g, you can calculate XOM's intrinsic value. Be careful to make sure that the long-run growth rate is less than the required rate of return. How does this estimate compare with the current stock price? Does your preliminary analysis suggest that XOM is undervalued or overvalued? Explain.

8. It is often useful to perform a sensitivity analysis, where you show how your estimate of intrinsic value varies according to different estimates of $D_1$, $r_s$, and g. To do so, recalculate your intrinsic value estimate for a range of different estimates for each of these key inputs. One convenient way to do this is to set up a simple data table in Excel. Refer to the Excel tutorial accessed through the student companion website for instructions on data tables. On the basis of this analysis, what inputs justify the current stock price?

9. Until now, we have assumed that XOM's dividend will grow at a long-run constant rate of 5%. To gauge whether this is a reasonable assumption, it's helpful to look at XOM's dividend history. If you go to the MSN Money website and go to the detailed annual income statement financials screen, you should see the firm's annual dividend over the past five years. On the basis of this information, what has been the average annual dividend growth rate?

   On the basis of the dividend history and your assessment of XOM's future dividend payout policies, do you think it is reasonable to assume that the constant growth model is a good proxy for intrinsic value? If not, how would you use the available data on the Internet to estimate intrinsic value using the nonconstant growth model?

10. Finally, you can also use the information on the Internet to value the entire corporation. This approach requires that you estimate XOM's annual free cash flows. Once you estimate the value of the entire corporation, you subtract the value of debt and preferred stock to arrive at an estimate of the company's equity value. By dividing this value by the number of shares of common stock outstanding, you calculate an alternative estimate of the stock's intrinsic value. Although this approach may take additional time and involves more judgment concerning forecasts of future free cash flows, you can use the financial statements and growth forecasts on the Internet as useful starting points.

   If you go to the detailed annual cash flow statement financials screen, you will find historical annual free cash flow values. Although these numbers are useful as a starting point to arrive at an estimate for the next year, MSN's definition of free cash flow subtracts out dividends. Therefore, to make it comparable to the measure in this text, you must add back dividends. To see MSN's definition of free cash flow (or any term), enter onlinehelp. microsoft.com/en-us/msn/azinvestglossary.aspx. On the next screen you will see an alphabetic index; just click the first letter of the term for the definition you're interested in.

# Appendix

## Stock Market Equilibrium

Recall that $r_X$, the required return on Stock X, can be found using the security market line (SML) equation from the capital asset pricing model (CAPM), as discussed in Chapter 8:

$$r_X = r_{RF} + (r_M - r_{RF})b_X = r_{RF} + (RP_M)b_X$$

If the risk-free rate is 3%, the market risk premium is 5%, and Stock X has a beta of 2, the marginal investor will require a return of 13% on the stock:

$$r_X = 3\% + (5\%)2.0$$
$$= 13\%$$

This 13% required return is shown as the point on the SML in Figure 9A.1 associated with beta = 2.0. A marginal investor will purchase Stock X if its expected return is more than 13%, will sell it if the expected return is less than 13%, and will be indifferent (will hold it, but not buy or sell it) if the expected return is exactly 13%.

## 9A-1 An Illustration

Now suppose the investor's portfolio contains Stock X; he or she analyzes its prospects and concludes that its earnings, dividends, and price can be expected to grow at a constant rate of 4% per year. The last dividend was $D_0 = \$1.9231$, so the next expected dividend is as follows:

$$D_1 = \$1.9231(1.04) = \$2.00$$

The investor observes that the stock price, $P_0$, is $25. Should he or she buy more of Stock X, sell the stock, or maintain the present position?

The investor can calculate Stock X's *expected rate of return* as follows:

$$\hat{r}_X = \frac{D_1}{P_0} + g = \frac{\$2}{\$25} + 4\% = 12\%$$

**FIGURE 9A.1**     Expected and Required Returns on Stock X

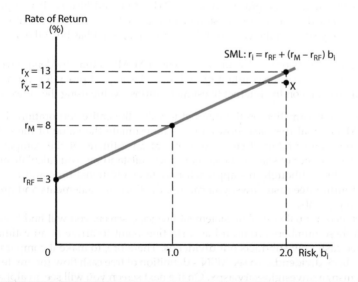

This value is plotted on Figure 9A.1 as point X, which is below the SML. Because the expected rate of return is less than the required return, he or she (and many other investors) would want to sell the stock. However, few people would want to buy at the $25 price, so the present owners would be unable to find buyers unless they cut the stock price. Thus, the price would decline, and the decline would continue until the price hit $22.22. At that point, the stock would be in **equilibrium**, defined as the price at which the expected rate of return, 13%, is equal to the required rate of return:

$$\hat{r}_X = \frac{\$2.00}{\$22.22} + 4\% = 9\% + 4\% = 13\% = r_X$$

*Equilibrium*
The condition under which the expected return on a security is just equal to its required return, $\hat{r}_i = r_i$. Also, $P_0 = \hat{P}_0$, and the price is stable.

Had the stock initially sold for less than $22.22 (say, $20), events would have been reversed. Investors would have wanted to purchase the stock because its expected rate of return would have exceeded its required rate of return; buy orders would have come in; and the stock's price would have been driven up to $22.22.

To summarize, in equilibrium, two related conditions must hold:

1. A stock's expected rate of return as seen by the marginal investor must equal its required rate of return: $\hat{r}_i = r_i$.

2. The actual market price of the stock must equal its intrinsic value as estimated by the marginal investor: $P_0 = \hat{P}_0$.

Of course, some individual investors may believe that $\hat{r}_i > r_i$ and $\hat{P}_0 > P_0$ (hence, they would invest most of their funds in the stock), while other investors might have an opposite view and sell all of their shares. However, investors at the margin establish the actual market price; and for these investors, we must have $\hat{r}_i = r_i$ and $\hat{P}_0 = P_0$. If these conditions do not hold, trading will occur until they do.

# 9B-2 Changes in Equilibrium Stock Prices

Stock prices are not constant—they undergo violent changes at times. For example, during the week of October 6, 2008, through October 10, 2008, the Dow Jones Industrial Average fell more than 1,874 points, representing an 18% decline. On October 27, 1997, the Dow Jones Industrials fell 554 points, a 7.18% drop in value. Even worse, on October 19, 1987, the Dow lost 508 points, causing an average stock to lose 23% of its value on that one day, and some individual stocks lost more than 70%. More recently, on August 8, 2011, the Dow lost 634 points, representing a 5.55% drop in value.

To see what could cause such changes to occur, assume that Stock X is in equilibrium, selling at a price of $22.22 per share. If all expectations were met exactly, during the next year the price would gradually rise to $23.11, or by 4%. However, suppose conditions changed as indicated in the second column of the following table:

| | Variable Value | |
|---|---|---|
| | Original | New |
| Risk-free rate, $r_{RF}$ | 3% | 2% |
| Market risk premium, $r_M - r_{RF}$ | 5% | 4% |
| Stock X's beta coefficient, $b_x$ | 2.0 | 1.25 |
| Stock X's expected growth rate, $g_x$ | 4% | 5% |
| $D_0$ | $1.9231 | $1.9231 |
| Price of Stock X | $22.22 | ? |

Now give yourself a test: How would the change in each variable, by itself, affect the price, and what new price would result?

Every change, taken alone, would lead to an *increase* in the price. The first three changes together lower $r_X$, which declines from 13% to 7%:

$$\text{Original } r_X = 3\% + 5\%(2.0) = 13\%$$

$$\text{New } r_X = 2\% + 4\%(1.25) = 7\%$$

Using these values, together with the new g, we find that $\hat{P}_0$ rises from $22.22 to $100.96, or by approximately 354%:[1]

$$\text{Original } \hat{P}_0 = \frac{\$1.9231(1.04)}{0.13 - 0.04} = \frac{\$2.00}{0.09} = \$22.22$$

$$\text{New } \hat{P}_0 = \frac{\$1.9231(1.05)}{0.07 - 0.05} = \frac{\$2.0193}{0.02} = \$100.96$$

Note too that at the new price, the expected and required rates of return will be equal:[2]

$$\hat{r}_X = \frac{\$2.0193}{\$100.96} + 5\% = 7\% = r_X$$

Evidence suggests that stocks, especially those of large companies, adjust rapidly when their fundamental positions change. Such stocks are followed closely by a number of security analysts; so as soon as things change, so does the stock price. Consequently, equilibrium ordinarily exists for any given stock, and required and expected returns are generally close to equal. Stock prices certainly change, sometimes violently and rapidly, but this simply reflects changing conditions and expectations. There are, of course, times when a stock will continue to react for several months to unfolding favorable or unfavorable developments. However, this does not signify a long adjustment period; it simply indicates that as more new information about the situation becomes available, the market adjusts to it.

## Questions

**9A-1**  For a stock to be in equilibrium, what two conditions must hold?

**9A-2**  If a stock is not in equilibrium, explain how financial markets adjust to bring it into equilibrium.

## Problems

**9A-1**  **RATES OF RETURN AND EQUILIBRIUM** Stock C's beta coefficient is $b_C = 0.4$, and Stock D's is $b_D = -0.5$. (Stock D's beta is negative, indicating that its return rises when returns on most other stocks fall. There are very few negative beta stocks, although collection agency stocks are sometimes cited as an example.)

   a. If the risk-free rate is 7% and the required rate of return on an average stock is 11%, what are the required rates of return on Stocks C and D?

---

[1] A price change of this magnitude is by no means rare. The prices of *many* stocks double or halve during a year. For example, in 2014, Radius Health's stock price increased by 385.8%. On the other hand, North Atlantic Drilling's stock price declined by 80.9%.

[2] It should be obvious by now that actual realized rates of return are not necessarily equal to expected and required returns. Thus, an investor might have expected to receive a return of 12% if he or she had purchased Radius Health's or North Atlantic Drilling's stock in 2014; but after the fact, the realized return on Radius Health was far above 12%, whereas the return on North Atlantic Drilling was far below 12%.

b. For Stock C, suppose the current price, $P_0$, is $25.00; the next expected dividend, $D_1$ is $1.50; and the stock's expected constant growth rate is 4%. Is the stock in equilibrium? Explain and describe what will happen if the stock is not in equilibrium.

**9A-2** **EQUILIBRIUM STOCK PRICE** The risk-free rate of return, $r_{RF}$, is 6%; the required rate of return on the market, $r_M$, is 10%; and Upton Company's stock has a beta coefficient of 1.5.

a. If the dividend expected during the coming year, $D_1$, is $2.25 and if g = a constant 5%, at what price should Upton's stock sell?

b. Now suppose the Federal Reserve Board increases the money supply, causing the risk-free rate to drop to 5% and $r_M$ to fall to 9%. What would happen to Upton's price?

c. In addition to the change in part b, suppose investors' risk aversion declines and this, combined with the decline in $r_{RF}$, causes $r_M$ to fall to 8%. Now what is Upton's price?

d. Suppose Upton has a change in management. The new group institutes policies that increase the expected constant growth rate from 5% to 6%. Also, the new management smoothes out fluctuations in sales and profits, causing beta to decline from 1.5 to 1.3. Assume that $r_{RF}$ and $r_M$ are equal to the values in part c. After all these changes, what is its new equilibrium price? (*Note:* $D_1$ is now $2.27.)

**9A-3** **BETA COEFFICIENTS** Suppose Chance Chemical Company's management conducted a study and concluded that if it expands its consumer products division (which is less risky than its primary business, industrial chemicals), its beta will decline from 1.2 to 0.9. However, consumer products have a somewhat lower profit margin, and this would cause its constant growth rate in earnings and dividends to fall from 6% to 4%. The following also apply: $r_M = 9\%$, $r_{RF} = 6\%$, and $D_0 = \$2.00$.

a. Should management expand the consumer products division? Explain.

b. Assume all the facts given except the change in the beta coefficient. How low would the beta have to fall to cause the expansion to be a good one? (Hint: Set $\hat{P}_0$ under the new policy equal to $\hat{P}_0$ under the old one, and find the new beta that will produce this equality.)

## Solutions to Self-Test Questions and Problems

**ST-1** Refer to the marginal glossary definitions or relevant chapter sections to check your responses.

**ST-2** a. This is not necessarily true. Because G plows back two-thirds of its earnings, its growth rate should exceed that of D, but D pays higher dividends ($3 versus $1). We cannot say which stock should have the higher price.

b. Again, we just do not know which price would be higher.

c. This is false. The changes in $r_d$ and $r_s$ would have a greater effect on G; its price would decline more.

d. The total expected return for D is $\hat{r}_D = D_1/P_0 + g = 12\% + 0\% = 12\%$. The total expected return for G will have $D_1/P_0$ less than 12% and g greater than 0%, but $\hat{r}_G$ should be neither greater nor smaller than D's total expected return, 12%, because the two stocks are stated to be equally risky.

e. We have eliminated a, b, c, and d, so e should be correct. On the basis of the available information, D and G should sell at about the same price, $25; thus, $\hat{r}_s = 12\%$ for both D and G. G's current dividend yield is $1/\$25 = 4\%$. Therefore, $g = 12\% - 4\% = 8\%$.

**ST-3** The first step is to solve for g, the unknown variable, in the constant growth equation. Because $D_1$ is unknown, but $D_0$ is known, substitute $D_0(1 + g)$ for $D_1$ as follows:

$$\hat{P}_0 = P_0 = \frac{D_1}{r_s - g} = \frac{D_0(1 + g)}{r_s - g}$$

$$\$36 = \frac{\$2.40(1 + g)}{0.12 - g}$$

Solving for g, we find the growth rate to be 5%:

$$\$4.32 - \$36g = \$2.40 + \$2.40g$$
$$\$38.4g = \$1.92$$
$$g = 0.05 = 5\%$$

The next step is to use the growth rate to project the stock price 5 years hence:

$$\hat{P}_5 = \frac{D_0(1 + g)^6}{r_s - g}$$

$$= \frac{\$2.40(1.05)^6}{0.12 - 0.05}$$

$$= \$45.95$$

(Alternatively, $\hat{P}_5 = \$36(1.05)^5 = \$45.95$)

Therefore, the firm's expected stock price 5 years from now, $\hat{P}_5$, is $45.95.

**ST-4**   a.   (1)   Calculate the PV of the dividends paid during the supernormal growth period:

$$D_1 = \$1.1500(1.15) = \$1.3225$$
$$D_2 = \$1.3225(1.15) = \$1.5209$$
$$D_3 = \$1.5209(1.13) = \$1.7186$$

$$\text{PV D} = \frac{\$1.3225}{1.12} + \frac{\$1.5209}{(1.12)^2} + \frac{\$1.7186}{(1.12)^3}$$

$$= \$1.1808 + \$1.2125 + \$1.2233$$

$$= \$3.6166 \approx \$3.62$$

(2)   Find the PV of the firm's stock price at the end of Year 3:

$$\hat{P}_3 = \frac{D_4}{r_s - g} = \frac{D_3(1 + g)}{r_s - g}$$
$$= \frac{\$1.7186(1.06)}{0.12 - 0.06}$$
$$= \$30.36$$

$$\text{PV } \hat{P}_3 = \frac{\$30.36}{(1.12)^3} = \$21.61$$

(3)   Sum the two components to find the value of the stock today:

$$\hat{P}_0 = \$3.62 + \$21.61 = \$25.23$$

Alternatively, the cash flows can be placed on a time line as follows:

Enter the cash flows into the cash flow register (remembering that $CF_0 = 0$) and $I/YR = 12$, and press the NPV key to obtain $P_0 = \$25.23$.

b.

$$\hat{P}_1 = \frac{\$1.5209}{1.12} + \frac{\$1.7186}{(1.12)^2} + \frac{\$30.36}{(1.12)^2}$$

$$= \$1.3579 + \$1.3701 + \$24.2028$$

$$= \$26.9308 \approx \$26.93$$

(Calculator solution: $26.93)

$$\hat{P}_2 = \frac{\$1.7186}{1.12} + \frac{\$30.36}{1.12}$$

$$= \$1.5345 + \$27.1071$$

$$= \$28.6416 \approx \$28.64$$

(Calculator solution: $28.64)

c.

| Year | Dividend Yield | + | Capital Gains Yield | = | Total Return |
|---|---|---|---|---|---|
| 1 | $\dfrac{\$1.3225}{\$25.23} \approx 5.24\%$ | | $\dfrac{\$26.93 - \$25.23}{\$25.23} \approx 6.74\%$ | | $\approx 12\%$ |
| 2 | $\dfrac{\$1.5209}{\$26.93} \approx 5.65\%$ | | $\dfrac{\$28.64 - \$26.93}{\$26.93} \approx 6.35\%$ | | $\approx 12\%$ |
| 3 | $\dfrac{\$1.7186}{\$28.64} \approx 6.00\%$ | | $\dfrac{\$30.36 - \$28.64}{\$28.64} \approx 6.00\%$ | | $\approx 12\%$ |

## Answers to Selected End-of-Chapter Problems

**9-2** $\hat{P}_0 = \$30.00$

**9-4** a. End of Yr. 2
b. $67.65
c. $59.88

**9-6** $r_p = 9.17\%$

**9-8** a. $114.29
b. $88.89

**9-10** $17.63

**9-12** a(1). $12.25
a(2). $15.63
a(3). $25.75

a(4). $43.75
b(1). Undefined
b(2). −$35.00, which is nonsense

**9-14** $P_0 = \$10.08$

**9-16** 2.25%

**9-18** a. $P_0 = \$54.11$; $D_1/P_0 = 3.55\%$; CGY $= 6.45\%$

**9-20** $20.00

**9A-2** a. $P_0 = \$32.14$
b. $P_0 = \$37.50$
c. $P_0 = \$50.00$
d. $P_0 = \$78.28$

## Selected Equations and Tables

**Value of stock** $= \hat{P}_0 =$ PV of expected future dividends

$$= \frac{D_1}{(1+r_s)^1} + \frac{D_2}{(1+r_s)^2} + \cdots + \frac{D_\infty}{(1+r_s)^\infty}$$

$$= \sum_{t=1}^{\infty} \frac{D_t}{(1+r_s)^t}$$

**Constant growth stock:** $\hat{P}_0 = \dfrac{D_0(1+g)^1}{(1+r_s)^1} + \dfrac{D_0(1+g)^2}{(1+r_s)^2} + \cdots + \dfrac{D_0(1+g)^\infty}{(1+r_s)^\infty}$

$$= \frac{D_0(1+g)}{r_s - g} = \frac{D_1}{r_s - g}$$

$$\text{Expected rate of return} = \text{Expected dividend yield} + \text{Expected growth rate, or capital gains yield}$$

$$\hat{r}_s = \frac{D_1}{P_0} + g$$

**Growth rate** $= (1 - \text{Payout ratio})\ \text{ROE}$

**Zero growth stock:** $\hat{P}_0 = \dfrac{D}{r_s}$

**Horizon value** $= \hat{P}_N = \dfrac{D_{N+1}}{r_s - g}$

Nonconstant growth stock: $\hat{P}_0 = \dfrac{D_1}{(1+r_s)^1} + \dfrac{D_2}{(1+r_s)^2} + \cdots + \dfrac{D_N}{(1+r_s)^N}$

$$+ \dfrac{D_{N+1}}{(1+r_s)^{N+1}} + \cdots + \dfrac{D_\infty}{(1+r_s)^\infty}$$

$$= \dfrac{D_1}{(1+r_s)^1} + \dfrac{D_2}{(1+r_s)^2} + \cdots + \dfrac{D_N}{(1+r_s)^N} + \dfrac{\hat{P}_N}{(1+r_s)^N}$$

$$= \text{PV of nonconstant dividends} + \text{PV of horizon value, } \hat{P}_N$$

PV of horizon value, $\hat{P}_N = \dfrac{D_{N+1}/(r_s - g)}{(1+r_s)^N}$

Market value of company $= V_{company} = \text{PV of expected future free cash flows}$

$$= \dfrac{FCF_1}{(1+WACC)^1} + \dfrac{FCF_2}{(1+WACC)^2} + \cdots + \dfrac{FCF_\infty}{(1+WACC)^\infty}$$

Horizon value $= V_{Company\ at\ t=N} = FCF_{N+1}/(WACC - g_{FCF})$

Market value of equity $=$ Book value $+$ PV of all future EVAs

$V_p = \dfrac{D_p}{r_p}$

$\hat{r}_p = \dfrac{D_p}{V_p}$

# Chapter 10

# The Cost of Capital

Carl Skepper/Alamy

## Creating Value at Disney

Walt Disney Co. (DIS) is one of the world's most successful companies. Despite a tough economic environment over the past few years, Disney's managers have worked hard to create value for shareholders by investing in assets that earn more than the cost of the capital used to acquire them. For example, if a project earns 20%, but the capital invested in it costs only 10%, taking on the project will increase the firm's value and thus its stock price.

Capital is obtained in three primary forms: debt, preferred stock, and common equity, with equity acquired by retaining earnings and issuing new stock. The investors who provide capital to Disney expect to earn at least their required rate of return on that capital, and the

required return represents the firm's cost of capital.[1] A variety of factors influence the cost of capital. Some—including interest rates, state and federal tax policies, and general economic conditions—are outside the firm's control. However, the firm's decisions regarding how it raises capital and how it invests those funds also have a profound effect on its cost of capital.

Estimating the cost of capital for a company such as Disney is conceptually straightforward. Disney's capital comes from debt plus common equity, so its cost of capital depends largely on the level of interest rates in the economy and the marginal stockholder's required rate of return on equity. However, Disney operates many different divisions throughout the

---

[1]Recall from earlier chapters that expected and required returns as seen by the marginal investor must be equal; otherwise, the security will not be in equilibrium. Therefore, buying and selling will force this equality to hold, except for short periods immediately following the release of new information. Because expected and required returns are normally equal, we use the two terms interchangeably.

world, so the corporation is similar to a portfolio that contains a number of different stocks, each with a different risk. Recall that portfolio risk is a weighted average of the relevant risks of the different stocks in the portfolio.

Similarly, each of Disney's divisions has its own level of risk and hence its own cost of capital. Therefore, Disney's overall cost of capital is a weighted average of its divisions' costs. For example, Disney's Media Networks's segment (which includes ABC and ESPN) probably has a different cost of capital than its

Parks and Resorts unit (which includes Disney World Resort, Disneyland, and the Disney Cruise Line, and Disney Vacation Club); and even projects within divisions have different costs because some projects are riskier than others. Moreover, its overseas projects may have different risks and thus different costs of capital than similar domestic projects. As we will see in this chapter, the cost of capital is an essential element in a firm's capital budgeting process. This process is the primary determinant of the firm's long-run stock price.

# PUTTING THINGS IN PERSPECTIVE

In the last four chapters, we explained how risk influences prices and required rates of return on bonds and stocks. A firm's primary objective is to maximize its shareholders' value. The principal way value is increased is by investing in projects that earn more than their cost of capital. In the next two chapters, we will see that a project's future cash flows can be forecasted and that those cash flows can be discounted to find their present value. Then if the PV of the future cash flows exceeds the project's cost, the firm's value will increase if the project is accepted. However, we need a discount rate to find the PV of these future cash flows, and that discount rate is the firm's cost of capital. Finding the cost of the capital required to take on new projects is the primary focus of this chapter.[2]

Most formulas used in this chapter were developed earlier, when we examined the required rates of return on bonds and stocks in Chapters 7 and 9. *Indeed, the rates of return that investors require on bonds and stocks represent the costs of those securities to the firm.* As we shall see, companies estimate the required returns on their securities, calculate a weighted average of the costs of their different types of capital, and use this average cost for capital budgeting purposes.

When you finish this chapter, you should be able to:

- Explain why the weighted average cost of capital (WACC) is used in capital budgeting.

- Estimate the costs of different capital components—debt, preferred stock, retained earnings, and common stock.

- Combine the different component costs to determine the firm's WACC.

These concepts are necessary to understand the firm's capital budgeting process.

---

[2]If projects differ in risk, risk-adjusted costs of capital should be used, not one single corporate cost of capital. We discuss this point later in Section 10-9.

# 10-1 An Overview of the Weighted Average Cost of Capital (WACC)

Table 10.1 shows Allied Food Products's balance sheet as presented in Chapter 3, with three additions: (1) the actual capital supplied by investors (banks, bond-holders, and stockholders), calculated using the accounting-based book values; (2) the market values of the investor-supplied capital; and (3) the target capital structure that Allied plans to use in the future.

When calculating the WACC, our concern is with capital that must be provided by *investors*—interest-bearing debt, preferred stock, and common equity. Accounts payable and accruals, which arise spontaneously when capital budgeting projects are undertaken, are not included as part of investor-supplied capital because they do not come directly from investors. Looking at column 1 of Table 10.1, we see that using the accounting-based book values, Allied's capital consists of 47.8% debt and 52.2% equity.

Although these accounting-based measures are important, Allied's investors are more concerned about the current market value of the company's debt and equity, which are shown in column 2 of Table 10.1. To keep things relatively simple, we assume that the market value of Allied's debt is equal to its book value (i.e., we assume that its average outstanding debt is trading at its par value).[3] The market

**TABLE 10.1**    Allied Food Products: Capital Structure Used to Calculate the WACC (Dollars in Millions)

| Assets and Claims Against Assets at Book Value on 12/31/16 | | | | | Investor-Supplied Capital: Payables and Accruals Are Excluded Because They Come from Operations, Not from Investors | | | | |
|---|---|---|---|---|---|---|---|---|---|
| Assets | | Claims | | | Book Value (1) | | Market Value (2) | | Target (3) |
| Cash | $ 10 | Accounts payable | $ 60 | 3.0% | | | | | |
| Receivables | 375 | Accruals | 140 | 7.0% | | | | | |
| Inventories | 615 | Notes payable | 110 | 5.5% | $ 110 | | $ 110 | | |
| Total C.A. | $1,000 | Total C.L. | $ 310 | 15.5% | | | | | |
| | | | | | | | | | |
| Net fixed assets | $1,000 | Long-term debt | 750 | 37.5% | 750 | | 750 | | |
| | | Total liabilities | $1,060 | 53.0% | $ 860 | 47.8% | $ 860 | 42.7% | 45.0% |
| | | Preferred stock | - | 0.0% | - | 0.0% | - | 0.0% | 2.0% |
| | | Common stock | 130 | 6.5% | 130 | | | | |
| | | Retained earnings | 810 | 40.5% | 810 | | | | |
| | | Total common equity | $ 940 | 47.0% | $ 940 | 52.2% | $1,153 | 57.3% | 53.0% |
| Total | $2,000 | Total | $2,000 | 100.0% | $1,800 | 100.0% | $2,013 | 100.0% | 100.0% |

Notes:

1. The market value calculations assume that the company's debt is trading at par, so the market value of debt equals the book value of debt.

2. The market value of equity is the share price of common stock multiplied by the number of shares outstanding. At 12/31/16, the firm has 50 million shares outstanding, and its stock sold for $23.06 per share.

---

[3]In practice, the market value of debt may be somewhat higher or lower than its book value, depending on whether the outstanding bonds are trading at a premium or at a discount. Again, to keep things simple, for our purposes we will generally assume that the market value of debt equals the book value of debt when calculating the WACC.

value of equity is the number of shares of stock outstanding multiplied by the current stock price. Recall from Chapter 3 that Allied has 50 million shares of common stock outstanding, and the company's stock currently trades at $23.06 per share, which means that the market value of its equity is $1.153 billion. Because the market value of its equity exceeds the book value of its equity, we see that Allied's market-based capital structure has a higher percentage of equity (57.3%) than the capital structure that was calculated using its accounting-based book values (52.2%).

Although these market-based numbers are a useful starting point, what ultimately matters is the **target capital structure**, which refers to how Allied plans to raise capital to fund its future projects. In Chapter 13, we explore in more detail how companies determine their target capital structure. As we will see, there is an optimal capital structure—one where the percentages of debt, preferred stock, and common equity maximize the firm's value. As shown in column 3 of Table 10.1, Allied Food has concluded that its target capital structure should include 45% debt, 2% preferred stock, and 53% common equity; and in the future it plans to raise capital in those proportions. Therefore, we use those target weights when we calculate Allied's weighted average cost of capital. It follows that Allied's overall cost of capital is a weighted average of the costs of the various types of capital it uses, where the weights correspond to the company's target capital structure.

*Target Capital Structure*
The mix of debt, preferred stock, and common equity the firm plans to raise to fund its future projects.

## SelfTest

When calculating WACC, what capital is excluded and why?

When calculating a company's WACC, should book value, market value, or target weights be used? Explain.

Why might the weights of capital be different depending on whether book values, market values, or target values are used?

## 10-2 Basic Definitions

The investor-supplied items—debt, preferred stock, and common equity—are called **capital components**. Increases in assets must be financed by increases in these capital components. The cost of each component is called its *component cost*; for example, Allied can borrow money at 10%, so its component cost of debt is 10%.[4] These costs are then combined to form a weighted average cost of capital, which is used in the firm's capital budgeting analysis. Throughout this chapter, we concentrate on the three major capital components. The following symbols identify the cost and weight of each:

*Capital Components*
One of the types of capital used by firms to raise funds.

$r_d$ = interest rate on the firm's new debt = before-tax component cost of debt. It can be found in several ways, including calculating the yield to maturity on the firm's currently outstanding bonds.

---

[4]We will see shortly that there is a before-tax and an after-tax cost of debt; for now, it is sufficient to know that 10% is the before-tax component cost of debt. Also, for simplicity, we assume that long- and short-term debt have the same cost; hence, we deal with just one type of debt. Finally, realize that Allied's cost of each capital component is meant to be illustrative. As we see in real-world examples, Allied's numbers are higher than current real-world numbers but closer in line with long-run averages.

$r_d(1-T)$ = after-tax component cost of debt, where T is the firm's marginal tax rate. *$r_d(1-T)$ is the debt cost used to calculate the weighted average cost of capital.* As we shall see, the after-tax cost of debt is lower than its before-tax cost because interest is tax deductible.

$r_p$ = component cost of preferred stock, found as the yield investors expect to earn on the preferred stock. Preferred dividends are not tax deductible; hence, the before- and after-tax costs of preferred are equal.

$r_s$ = component cost of common equity raised by retaining earnings, or *internal equity*. It is the $r_s$ developed in Chapters 8 and 9 and defined there as the rate of return that investors require on a firm's common stock. Most firms, once they have become well established, obtain all of their new equity as retained earnings; hence, $r_s$ is their cost of all new equity.

$r_e$ = component cost of *external equity*, or common equity raised by issuing new stock. As we will see, $r_e$ is equal to $r_s$ plus a factor that reflects the cost of issuing new stock. Note, though, that established firms such as Allied Food rarely issue new stock; hence, $r_e$ is rarely a relevant consideration except for very young, rapidly growing firms.

$w_d, w_p, w_c$ = target weights of debt, preferred stock, and common equity (which includes retained earnings, internal equity, and new common stock, external equity). The weights are the percentages of the different types of capital the firm plans to use when it raises capital in the future. Target weights may differ from actual current weights.[5]

WACC = the firm's weighted average, or overall, cost of capital.

The target proportions of debt ($w_d$), preferred stock ($w_p$), and common equity ($w_c$), along with the costs of those components, are used to calculate the firm's **weighted average cost of capital, WACC**. We assume at this point that all new common equity is raised as retained earnings, as is true for most companies; hence, the cost of common equity is $r_s$:

**Weighted Average Cost of Capital (WACC)**

A weighted average of the component costs of debt, preferred stock, and common equity.

$$\text{WACC} = \begin{pmatrix} \% \\ \text{of} \\ \text{debt} \end{pmatrix} \begin{pmatrix} \text{After-tax} \\ \text{cost of} \\ \text{debt} \end{pmatrix} + \begin{pmatrix} \% \text{ of} \\ \text{preferred} \\ \text{stock} \end{pmatrix} \begin{pmatrix} \text{Cost of} \\ \text{preferred} \\ \text{stock} \end{pmatrix} + \begin{pmatrix} \% \text{ of} \\ \text{common} \\ \text{equity} \end{pmatrix} \begin{pmatrix} \text{Cost of} \\ \text{common} \\ \text{equity} \end{pmatrix}$$

$$= \quad w_d r_d(1-T) \quad + \quad w_p r_p \quad + \quad w_c r_s \qquad \text{10.1}$$

Note that only debt has a tax adjustment factor, $(1-T)$. As discussed in the next section, this is because interest on debt is tax deductible, but preferred dividends and the returns on common stock (dividends and capital gains) are not.

These definitions and concepts are discussed in the remainder of the chapter, using Allied Food for illustrative purposes. Later in Chapter 13, we extend the discussion to show how the optimal mix of securities minimizes the firm's cost of capital and maximizes its value.

---

[5]In Chapter 13, we will discuss in more detail how firms determine their target weights of debt, preferred stock, and common equity. As we indicate in the text, these target weights may differ from actual current weights. The current weights can be estimated using either book or market values. Book values follow directly from the company's balance sheet, whereas market values depend on current market prices for the company's debt, preferred stock, and common equity. For example, the market value of equity equals the number of shares outstanding multiplied by the current stock price. From a theoretical perspective, most analysts believe that market value provides a better assessment of the company's current capital structure. However, bond rating agencies and security analysts will sometimes also consider the company's book weights when assessing the company's position.

## SelfTest

Identify the firm's three major capital structure components, and give their respective component cost and weight symbols.

Why might there be two different component costs for common equity? Which one is generally relevant, and for what type of firm is the second one likely to be relevant?

If a firm now has a debt ratio of 50% but plans to finance with only 40% debt in the future, what should it use as $w_d$ when it calculates its WACC? Explain.

# 10-3 Cost of Debt, $r_d(1-T)$

The interest rate a firm must pay on its *new* debt is defined as its **before-tax cost of debt, $r_d$**. Firms can estimate $r_d$ by asking their bankers what it will cost to borrow or by finding the yield to maturity on their currently outstanding debt (as we illustrated in Chapter 7). *However, the* **after-tax cost of debt, $r_d(1-T)$**, *should be used to calculate the weighted average cost of capital.* This is the interest rate on new debt, $r_d$, less the tax savings that result because interest is tax deductible:[6]

$$\text{After-tax cost of debt} = \text{Interest rate on new debt} - \text{Tax savings}$$
$$= r_d - r_d T$$
$$= r_d(1 - T)$$

10.2

In effect, the government pays part of the cost of debt because interest is tax deductible. Therefore, if Allied can borrow at an interest rate of 10%, and its marginal federal-plus-state tax rate is 40%, its after-tax cost of debt will be 6%:[7]

$$\text{After-tax cost of debt} = r_d(1 - T) = 10\%(1.0 - 0.4)$$
$$= 10\%(0.6)$$
$$= 6.0\%$$

We use the after-tax cost of debt in calculating the WACC because we are interested in maximizing the value of the firm's stock, and the stock price depends on *after-tax* cash flows. Because we are concerned with after-tax cash flows and because cash flows and rates of return should be calculated on a comparable basis, we adjust the interest rate downward due to debt's preferential tax treatment.[8]

It is important to emphasize that the cost of debt is the interest rate on *new* debt, not outstanding debt. We are interested in the cost of new debt because our primary

**Before-Tax Cost of Debt, $r_d$**
The interest rate the firm must pay on new debt.

**After-Tax Cost of Debt, $r_d(1-T)$**
The relevant cost of new debt, taking into account the tax deductibility of interest; used to calculate the WACC.

---

[6]If Allied borrowed $100,000 at 10%, it would have to write a check for $10,000 to pay annual interest charges. However, that $10,000 would be a tax deduction, which at a 40% tax rate would save $4,000 annually in taxes. The tax rate is *zero* for a firm with losses. Therefore, for a company that does not pay taxes, the cost of debt is not reduced. In Equation 10.2, if the tax rate is zero, the after-tax cost of debt is not reduced and is simply equal to the before-tax cost of debt.

[7]Note that in 2015, the federal tax rate for most large corporations is 35%. However, most corporations are also subject to state income taxes, so for illustrative purposes, we assume that the effective federal-plus-state tax rate on marginal income is 40%.

[8]Strictly speaking, the after-tax cost of debt should reflect the *expected* cost of debt. Although Allied's bonds have a promised return of 10%, there is some chance of default, so its bondholders' expected return (and consequently Allied's cost) is a bit less than 10%. For a relatively strong company such as Allied, this difference is quite small. As we discuss later in the chapter, Allied must also incur flotation costs when it issues debt, but like the difference between the promised and the expected rates of return, flotation costs for debt are generally small. Finally, note that these two factors tend to offset one another—not including the possibility of default leads to an overstatement of the cost of debt, but not including flotation costs leads to an understatement. For all these reasons, $r_d$ is generally a good approximation of the before-tax cost of debt capital and $r_d(1-T)$ of the after-tax cost.

concern with the cost of capital is its use in capital budgeting decisions. For example, would a new machine earn a return greater than the cost of the capital needed to acquire the machine? The rate at which the firm has borrowed in the past is irrelevant when answering this question because we need to know the cost of *new capital. For these reasons, the yield to maturity on outstanding debt (which reflects current market conditions) is a better measure of the cost of debt than the coupon rate.* Note that if the yield curve is upward or downward sloping, the cost of long- and short-term debt will differ. In these cases, the yield to maturity on the company's long-term debt is generally used to calculate the cost of debt because, more often than not, the capital is being raised to fund long-term projects.[9] However, as we see in Chapter 15, some companies regularly use a mix of short-term and long-term debt to finance their projects. When calculating their costs of debt, these companies may choose to calculate an average of their debt costs based on the proportion of long- and short-term debt that they plan to use.

## SelfTest

Why is the after-tax cost of debt rather than the before-tax cost used to calculate the WACC?

Why is the relevant cost of debt the interest rate on *new* debt, not that on already outstanding, or *old*, debt?

How can the yield to maturity on a firm's outstanding debt be used to estimate its before-tax cost of debt?

A company has outstanding 20-year noncallable bonds with a face value of $1,000, an 11% annual coupon, and a market price of $1,294.54. If the company was to issue new debt, what would be a reasonable estimate of the interest rate on that debt? If the company's tax rate is 40%, what is its after-tax cost of debt? **(8.0%, 4.8%)**

## 10-4 Cost of Preferred Stock, $r_p$

**Cost of Preferred Stock, $r_p$**
The rate of return investors require on the firm's preferred stock; $r_p$ is calculated as the preferred dividend, $D_p$, divided by the current price, $P_p$.

The component **cost of preferred stock, $r_p$,** used to calculate the weighted average cost of capital is the preferred dividend, $D_p$, divided by the current price of the preferred stock, $P_p$:

$$\text{Component cost of preferred stock} = r_p = \frac{D_p}{P_p}$$

10.3

Allied does not have any preferred stock outstanding, but the company plans to issue some in the future and therefore has included it in its target capital structure. Allied would sell this stock to a few large hedge funds, the stock would have a $10.00 dividend per share, and it would be priced at $97.50 a share. Therefore, Allied's cost of preferred stock would be 10.3%:[10]

$$r_p = \$10.00/\$97.50 = 10.3\%$$

---

[9]To get a true measure of the cost of debt, you should use the yield to maturity on outstanding debt that is noncallable and not convertible to common stock.

[10]This preferred stock would be sold directly to a group of hedge funds, so no flotation costs would be incurred. If significant flotation costs were involved, the cost of the preferred should be adjusted upward, as we explain in a later section.

As we can see from Equation 10.3, calculating the cost of preferred stock is easy. This is particularly true for traditional "plain vanilla" preferred that pays a fixed dividend in perpetuity. However, in Chapter 9, we noted that some preferred issues have a specified maturity date and we described how to calculate the expected return on these issues. Also, preferred stock may include an option to convert to common stock, which adds another layer of complexity. We leave these more complicated situations for advanced classes. Finally, note that no tax adjustments are made when calculating $r_p$ because preferred dividends, unlike interest on debt, are *not* tax deductible, so no tax savings are associated with preferred stock.

## Self*Test*

Is a tax adjustment made to the cost of preferred stock? Why or why not?

A company's preferred stock currently trades at $80 per share and pays a $6 annual dividend per share. Ignoring flotation costs, what is the firm's cost of preferred stock? **(7.50%)**

# 10-5 Cost of Retained Earnings, $r_s$

The costs of debt and preferred stock are based on the returns that investors require on these securities. Similarly, the cost of common equity is based on the rate of return that investors require on the company's common stock. Note, though, that new common equity is raised in two ways: (1) by retaining some of the current year's earnings and (2) by issuing new common stock.[11] We use the symbol $r_s$ to designate the **cost of retained earnings** and $r_e$ to designate the **cost of new common stock**, or external equity. Equity raised by issuing stock has a higher cost than equity from retained earnings due to the flotation costs required to sell new common stock. Therefore, once firms get beyond the start-up stage, they normally obtain all of their new equity by retaining earnings.

Some have argued that retained earnings should be "free" because they represent money that is "left over" after dividends are paid. Although it is true that no direct costs are associated with retained earnings, this capital still has a cost, an *opportunity cost*. The firm's after-tax earnings belong to its stockholders. Bondholders are compensated by interest payments; preferred stockholders, by preferred dividends. But the net earnings remaining after paying interest and preferred dividends belong to the common stockholders, and these earnings serve to compensate them for the use of their capital. The managers, who work for the stockholders, can either pay out earnings in the form of dividends or retain earnings for reinvestment in the business. When managers make this decision, they should recognize that there is an opportunity cost involved—stockholders could have received the earnings as

*Cost of Retained Earnings, $r_s$*
The rate of return required by stockholders on a firm's common stock.

*Cost of New Common Stock, $r_e$*
The cost of external equity; based on the cost of retained earnings, but increased for flotation costs necessary to issue new common stock.

---

[11]The term *retained earnings* can be interpreted to mean the balance sheet account *retained earnings*, consisting of all the earnings retained in the business throughout its history or the income statement item *addition to retained earnings*. The income statement item is relevant in this chapter. For our purpose, *retained earnings* refers to that part of the current year's earnings not paid as dividends (hence, available for reinvestment in the business this year). If this is not clear, look back at Allied's balance sheet shown in Table 3.1 and note that at the end of 2015, Allied had $750 million of retained earnings; but that figure rose to $810 million by the end of 2016. Then look at the 2016 income statement, where you will see that Allied retained $60 million of its 2016 income. This $60 million was the new equity from retained earnings that was used, along with some additional debt, to fund the 2016 capital budgeting projects. Also, you can see from the 2015 and 2016 balance sheets that Allied had $130 million of common stock at the end of both years. This indicates that it did not issue (sell) any new common stock to raise capital during 2016.

dividends and invested this money in other stocks, in bonds, in real estate, or in anything else. *Therefore, the firm needs to earn at least as much on any earnings retained as the stockholders could earn on alternative investments of comparable risk.*

What rate of return can stockholders expect to earn on equivalent-risk investments? First, recall from Chapter 9 that stocks are normally in equilibrium, with expected and required rates of return equal: $\hat{r}_s = r_s$. Thus, Allied's stockholders expect to be able to earn $r_s$ on their money. *Therefore, if the firm cannot invest retained earnings to earn at least $r_s$, it should pay those funds to its stockholders and let them invest directly in stocks or other assets that will provide that return.*

Whereas debt and preferred stocks are contractual obligations whose costs are clearly stated within the contracts, stocks have no comparable stated cost rate. That makes it difficult to measure $r_s$. However, we can employ the techniques developed in Chapters 8 and 9 to produce reasonably good estimates of the cost of equity from retained earnings. To begin, recall that if a stock is in equilibrium, its *required rate of return*, $r_s$, must be equal to its *expected rate of return*, $\hat{r}_s$. Further, its *required return* is equal to a risk-free rate, $r_{RF}$, plus a risk premium, RP, whereas the *expected return* on the stock is its expected dividend yield, $D_1/P_0$, plus its expected growth rate, g. Thus, we can write the following equation and estimate $r_s$ using the left term, the right term, or both terms:

$$\text{Required rate of return} = \text{Expected rate of return}$$
$$r_s = r_{RF} + RP = D_1/P_0 + g = \hat{r}_s$$

10.4

The left term is based on the capital asset pricing model (CAPM) as discussed in Chapter 8, and the right term is based on the discounted dividend model as developed in Chapter 9. We discuss these two procedures, in addition to one based on the firm's own cost of debt, in the following sections.

## 10-5A CAPM APPROACH

The most widely used method for estimating the cost of common equity is the capital asset pricing model (CAPM) as developed in Chapter 8.[12] Here are the steps used to find $r_s$:

**Step 1:** Estimate the risk-free rate, $r_{RF}$. We generally use the 10-year Treasury bond rate as the measure of the risk-free rate, but some analysts use the short-term Treasury bill rate.

**Step 2:** Estimate the stock's beta coefficient, $b_i$, and use it as an index of the stock's risk. The *i* signifies the *i*th company's beta.

**Step 3:** Estimate the market risk premium. Recall that the market risk premium is the difference between the return that investors require on an average stock and the risk-free rate.[13]

---

[12]A recent survey by John Graham and Campbell Harvey indicates that the CAPM approach is most often used to estimate the cost of equity. More than 70% of the surveyed firms used the CAPM approach. In some cases, they used beta from the CAPM as one determinant of $r_s$, but they also added other factors thought to improve the estimate. For more details, see John R. Graham and Campbell R. Harvey, "The Theory and Practice of Corporate Finance: Evidence from the Field," *Journal of Financial Economics*, vol. 60, nos. 2 and 3 (May–June 2001), pp. 187–243. For further survey evidence regarding techniques that companies use to estimate their costs of capital, refer to: W. Todd Brotherson, Kenneth Eades, Robert Harris, and Robert Higgins, "'Best Practices' in Estimating the Cost of Capital: An Update," *Journal of Applied Finance: Theory, Practice, Education*, vol. 23, no. 1 (2013), pp. 15–33.

[13]It is important to be consistent in the use of a long-term versus a short-term rate for $r_{RF}$ and for the market risk premium. The market risk premium ($RP_M = r_M - r_{RF}$) depends on the measure used for the risk-free rate. The yield curve is normally upward-sloping, so the 10-year Treasury bond rate normally exceeds the short-term Treasury bill rate. In this case, it follows that one will obtain a lower estimate of the market risk premium if the higher longer-term bond rate is used as the risk-free rate. At any rate, the $r_{RF}$ used to find the market risk premium should be the same as the $r_{RF}$ used as the first term in the CAPM equation.

**Step 4:** Substitute the preceding values in the CAPM equation to estimate the required rate of return on the stock in question:

$$r_s = r_{RF} + (RP_M)b_i$$
$$= r_{RF} + (r_M - r_{RF})b_i$$

10.5

Thus, the CAPM estimate of $r_s$ is equal to the risk-free rate, $r_{RF}$, plus a risk premium that is equal to the risk premium on an average stock, $(r_M - r_{RF})$, scaled up or down to reflect the particular stock's risk as measured by its beta coefficient, $b_i$.

Assume that in today's market, $r_{RF} = 5.6\%$, the market risk premium is $RP_M = 5.0\%$, and Allied's beta is 1.48. Using the CAPM approach, Allied's cost of equity is estimated to be 13.0%:

$$r_s = 5.6\% + (5.0\%)(1.48)$$
$$= 13.0\%$$

Although the CAPM appears to produce an accurate, precise estimate of $r_s$, several potential problems exist. First, as we saw in Chapter 8, if a firm's stockholders are not well diversified, they may be concerned with *stand-alone risk* rather than just market risk. In that case, the firm's true investment risk would not be measured by its beta and the CAPM estimate would understate the correct value of $r_s$. Further, even if the CAPM theory is valid, it is hard to obtain accurate estimates of the required inputs because (1) there is controversy about whether to use long-term or short-term Treasury yields for $r_{RF}$. (2) It is hard to estimate the beta that investors expect the company to have in the future. (3) It is difficult to estimate the proper market risk premium. As we indicated earlier, the CAPM approach is used most often; but because of the just-noted problems, analysts also estimate the cost of equity using the other approaches discussed in the following sections.

## 10-5B BOND-YIELD-PLUS-RISK-PREMIUM APPROACH

In situations where reliable inputs for the CAPM approach are not available, as would be true for a closely held company, analysts often use a somewhat subjective procedure to estimate the cost of equity. Empirical studies suggest that the risk premium on a firm's stock over its own bonds generally ranges from 3 to 5 percentage points.[14] Based on this evidence, one might simply add a judgmental risk premium of 3% to 5% to the interest rate on the firm's own long-term debt to estimate its cost of equity. Firms with risky, low-rated, and consequently high-interest-rate debt also have risky, high-cost equity; and the procedure of basing the cost of equity on the firm's own readily observable debt cost utilizes this logic. For example, given that Allied's bonds yield 10%, its cost of equity might be estimated as follows:

$$r_s = \text{Bond yield} + \text{Risk premium} = 10.0\% + 4.0\% = 14.0\%$$

The bonds of a riskier company might have a higher yield, 12%, in which case the estimated cost of equity would be 16%:

$$r_s = 12.0\% + 4.0\% = 16.0\%$$

---

[14]Ibbotson Associates, a well-known research firm, has calculated the historical returns on common stocks and on corporate bonds and used the differential as an estimate of the *historical risk premium* of stocks over corporate bonds. Historical risk premiums vary from year to year, but a range of 3% to 5% is common. Also, analysts have calculated the CAPM-required return on equity for publicly traded firms in a given industry, averaged them, subtracted those firms' average bond yield, and used the differential as an *expected risk premium*. Again, these risk premium estimates are often generally in the 3% to 5% range.

Because the 4% risk premium is an estimate based on judgment, the estimated value of $r_s$ is also judgmental. Therefore, one might use a range of 3% to 5% for the risk premium and obtain a range of 13% to 15% for Allied. Although this method does not produce a precise cost of equity, it should "get us in the right ballpark."

## 10-5C DIVIDEND-YIELD-PLUS-GROWTH-RATE, OR DISCOUNTED CASH FLOW (DCF), APPROACH

In Chapter 9, we saw that both the price and the expected rate of return on a share of common stock depend, ultimately, on the stock's expected cash flows. For companies that are expected to remain in business indefinitely, the cash flows are the dividends; on the other hand, if investors expect the firm to be acquired by some other company or to be liquidated, the cash flows will be dividends for some number of years plus a price at the horizon date when the firm is expected to be acquired or liquidated. Like most firms, Allied is expected to continue indefinitely, in which case the following equation applies:

$$P_0 = \frac{D_1}{(1 + r_s)^1} + \frac{D_2}{(1 + r_s)^2} + \cdots + \frac{D_\infty}{(1 + r_s)^\infty}$$

$$= \sum_{t=1}^{\infty} \frac{D_t}{(1 + r_s)^t}$$

▼ 10.6

Here $P_0$ is the current stock price, $D_t$ is the dividend expected to be paid at the end of Year t, and $r_s$ is the required rate of return. If dividends are expected to grow at a constant rate, as we saw in Chapter 9, Equation 10.6 reduces to this important formula:[15]

$$P_0 = \frac{D_1}{r_s - g}$$

▼ 10.7

We can solve for $r_s$ to obtain the required rate of return on common equity, which for the marginal investor is also equal to the expected rate of return:

$$r_s = \hat{r}_s = \frac{D_1}{P_0} + \text{Expected g}$$

▼ 10.8

Thus, investors expect to receive a dividend yield, $D_1/P_0$, plus a capital gain, g, for a total expected return of $\hat{r}_s$; and in equilibrium, this expected return is also equal to the required return, $r_s$. This method of estimating the cost of equity is called the *discounted cash flow*, or *DCF, method*. Henceforth, we will assume that equilibrium exists, which permits us to use the terms $r_s$ and $\hat{r}_s$ interchangeably.

It is easy to calculate the dividend yield; but because stock prices fluctuate, the yield varies from day to day, which leads to fluctuations in the DCF cost of equity. Also, it is difficult to determine the proper growth rate. If past growth rates in earnings and dividends have been relatively stable, and if investors expect a continuation of past trends, g may be based on the firm's historic growth rate. *However, if the company's past growth has been abnormally high or low due to a unique situation or because of general economic fluctuations, investors will not project historical growth rates into the future.* In this case, which applies to Allied, g must be obtained in some other manner.

Security analysts regularly forecast growth rates for earnings and dividends, looking at such factors as projected sales, profit margins, and competition. For example, *Value Line Investment Survey*, which is available in most libraries, provides

---

[15] If the growth rate is not expected to be constant, the DCF procedure can still be used to estimate $r_s$, but in this case, it is necessary to calculate an average growth rate using the procedures described in this chapter's Excel model.

growth rate forecasts for 1,700 companies; Citigroup, UBS, Credit Suisse, Morgan Stanley, and other organizations make similar forecasts. Averages of these forecasts are available on Yahoo! Finance and other websites. Therefore, someone estimating a firm's cost of equity can obtain analysts' forecasts and use them as a proxy for the growth expectations of investors in general. Then he or she can combine this g with the current dividend yield to estimate $\hat{r}_s$:

$$\hat{r}_s = \frac{D_1}{P_0} + \text{Growth rate as projected by security analysts}$$

Again, note that this estimate of $\hat{r}_s$ is based on the assumption that g is expected to remain constant in the future. Otherwise, we must use an average of expected future rates.[16]

To illustrate the DCF approach, Allied's stock sells for \$23.06; its next expected dividend is \$1.25; and analysts expect its growth rate to be 8.3%. Thus, Allied's expected and required rates of return (hence, its cost of retained earnings) are estimated to be 13.7%:

$$\hat{r}_s = r_s = \frac{\$1.25}{\$23.06} + 8.3\%$$
$$= 5.4\% + 8.3\%$$
$$= 13.7\%$$

Based on the DCF method, 13.7% is the minimum rate of return that should be earned on retained earnings to justify plowing earnings back into the business rather than paying them out to shareholders as dividends. Put another way, because investors are thought to have an *opportunity* to earn 13.7% if earnings are paid out as dividends, the *opportunity cost* of equity from retained earnings is 13.7%.

## 10-5D AVERAGING THE ALTERNATIVE ESTIMATES

In our examples, Allied's estimated cost of equity was 13.0% by the CAPM, 14.0% by the bond-yield-plus-risk premium method, and 13.7% by the DCF method. Which method should the firm use? If management has confidence in one method, it would probably use that method's estimate alone. Otherwise, it might use some weighted average of the three methods.

As consultants, we have estimated companies' costs of capital on numerous occasions. We generally take into account all three methods, but we rely most heavily on the method that seems best under the circumstances. Judgment is important and comes into play here, as is true for most decisions in finance. Also, we recognize that our final estimate will almost certainly be incorrect to some extent.[17] Therefore, we always provide a range and state that in our judgment, the cost of equity is within that range. For Allied, we used a range of 13% to 14%;

---

[16]Analysts' growth rate forecasts are usually for 5 years into the future, and the rates provided represent the average growth rate over that 5-year horizon. Studies have shown that analysts' forecasts represent the best source of growth rate data for DCF cost of capital estimates. See Robert Harris, "Using Analysts' Growth Rate Forecasts to Estimate Shareholder Required Rates of Return," *Financial Management* (Spring 1986), pp. 58–67.

[17]Investment bankers are generally regarded as experts on concepts such as the cost of capital, and they are paid big salaries for their analyses. But those investment bankers aren't always accurate. To illustrate, the stock price of the fifth-largest investment bank at that time, Bear Stearns, closed on Friday, March 14, 2008, at \$30. Its employees owned 33% of the stock. On Sunday, in a special meeting, its board of directors agreed to sell the company to JPMorgan for \$2 per share. Bear Stearns was eventually sold to JPMorgan for \$10 per share in 2008, and it has since discontinued the use of the Bear Stearns name. As you can see, even investment bankers don't always get it right, so don't expect precision unless you are given a set of numbers and told to do some relatively simple calculations.

the company then used 13.5% as the estimate of its cost of retained earnings when it calculated its WACC:

Final estimate of $r_s$ used to calculate Allied's WACC: 13.5%

## SelfTest

Why must a cost be assigned to retained earnings?

What three approaches are used to estimate the cost of common equity? Which approach is most commonly used in practice?

Identify some potential problems with the CAPM.

Which of the two components of the DCF formula, the dividend yield or the growth rate, do you think is more difficult to estimate? Why?

What's the logic behind the bond-yield-plus-risk-premium approach?

Suppose you are an analyst with the following data: $r_{RF} = 5.5\%$, $r_M - r_{RF} = 6\%$, $b = 0.8$, $D_1 = \$1.00$, $P_0 = \$25.00$, $g = 6\%$, and $r_d$ = firm's bond yield = 6.5%. What is this firm's cost of equity using the CAPM, DCF, and bond-yield-plus-risk-premium approaches? Use the midrange of the judgmental risk premium for the bond-yield-plus-risk-premium approach. **(CAPM = 10.3%, DCF = 10%, Bond yield + RP = 10.5%)**

## 10-6 Cost of New Common Stock, $r_e$

Companies generally use an investment banker when they issue new common stock and sometimes when they issue preferred stock or bonds. In return for a fee, investment bankers help the company structure the terms, set a price for the issue, and sell the issue to investors. The bankers' fees are called *flotation costs*, and the total cost of the capital raised is the investors' required return plus the flotation cost.

For most firms at most times, equity flotation costs are not an issue because most equity comes from retained earnings. Therefore, in our discussion to this point, we have ignored flotation costs. However, flotation costs can often be substantial. So if a firm does plan to issue new stock, these costs should not be ignored. When firms use investment bankers to raise capital, two approaches can be used to account for flotation costs.[18] We describe them in the next two sections.

### 10-6A ADD FLOTATION COSTS TO A PROJECT'S COST

In the next chapter, we show that capital budgeting projects typically involve an initial cash outlay followed by a series of cash inflows. One approach to handling flotation costs, found as the sum of the flotation costs for the debt, preferred, and common stock used to finance the project, is to add this sum to the initial investment cost. Because the investment cost is increased, the project's expected rate of return is reduced. For example, consider a 1-year project with an initial cost (not including flotation costs) of $100 million. After 1 year, the project is expected to produce an inflow of $115 million. Therefore, its expected rate of return is $\$115/\$100 - 1 = 0.15 = 15.0\%$. However, if the project requires the company to

---

[18]A more complete discussion of flotation cost adjustments can be found in Chapter 11 of Brigham and Daves, *Intermediate Financial Management*, 12th edition (Mason, OH: Cengage Learning, 2016), and other advanced texts.

raise $100 million of new capital and incur $2 million of flotation costs, the total upfront cost will rise to $102 million, which will lower the expected rate of return to $115/$102 − 1 = 0.1275 = 12.75%.

## 10-6B INCREASE THE COST OF CAPITAL

The second approach involves adjusting the cost of capital rather than increasing the project's investment cost. If the firm plans to continue using the capital in the future, as is generally true for equity, this second approach theoretically will be better. The adjustment process is based on the following logic. If there are flotation costs, the issuing firm receives only a portion of the capital provided by investors, with the remainder going to the underwriter. To provide investors with their required rate of return on the capital they contributed, each dollar the firm actually receives must "work harder"; that is, each dollar must earn a higher rate of return than the investors' required rate of return. For example, suppose investors require a 13.7% return on their investment, but flotation costs represent 10% of the funds raised. Therefore, the firm actually keeps and invests only 90% of the amount that investors supplied. In that case, the firm must earn about 14.3% on the available funds in order to provide investors with a 13.7% return on their investment. This higher rate of return is the flotation-adjusted cost of equity.

The DCF approach can be used to estimate the effects of flotation costs. Here is the equation for the *cost of new common stock*, $r_e$:

$$\text{Cost of equity from new stock} = r_e = \frac{D_1}{P_0(1 - F)} + g \qquad \text{10.9}$$

*Flotation Cost, F*
The percentage cost of issuing new common stock.

Here **F** is the percentage **flotation cost** required to sell the new stock, so $P_0(1 - F)$ is the net price per share received by the company.

Assuming that Allied has a flotation cost of 10%, its cost of new common equity, $r_e$, would be calculated as follows:

$$r_e = \frac{\$1.25}{\$23.06(1 - 0.10)} + 8.3\%$$

$$= \frac{\$1.25}{\$20.75} + 8.3\%$$

$$= 6.0\% + 8.3\% = 14.3\%$$

This is 0.6% higher than the previously estimated 13.7% DCF cost of equity, so the **flotation cost adjustment** is 0.6%:

*Flotation Cost Adjustment*
The amount that must be added to $r_s$ to account for flotation costs to find $r_e$.

$$\frac{\text{Flotation cost}}{\text{adjustment}} = \frac{\text{Adjusted}}{\text{DCF cost}} - \frac{\text{Pure}}{\text{DCF cost}} = 14.3\% - 13.7\% = 0.6\%$$

The 0.6% flotation cost adjustment can be added to the previously estimated $r_s = 13.5\%$ (Allied management's estimate of its cost of equity considering all three approaches), resulting in a cost of equity from new common stock, or external equity, of 14.1%:

$$\frac{\text{Cost of}}{\text{external equity}} = r_s + \frac{\text{Flotation cost}}{\text{adjustment}} = 13.5\% + 0.6\% = 14.1\%$$

If Allied earns 14.1% on funds obtained from selling new stock, the investors who purchased that stock will end up earning 13.5%, their required rate of return, on the money they invested. If Allied earns more than 14.1%, its stock price should rise; but the price should fall if Allied earns less than 14.1%.[19]

---

[19]Flotation costs for preferred stock and bonds are handled similarly to common stock. In both cases, the dollars of flotation costs are deducted from the price of the security, $P_p$ for preferred stock and $1,000 for bonds issued at par. Then for preferred, the cost is found using Equation 10.9 with $g = 0$. For bonds, we find the YTM based on the net proceeds received, $1,000 − Flotation costs, e.g., the net proceeds would be $970 if flotation costs are 3% of the issue price.

## 10-6C WHEN MUST EXTERNAL EQUITY BE USED?

Because of flotation costs, dollars raised by selling new stock must "work harder" than dollars raised by retaining earnings. Moreover, because no flotation costs are involved, retained earnings cost less than new stock. Therefore, firms should utilize retained earnings to the greatest extent possible. However, if a firm has more good investment opportunities than can be financed with retained earnings plus the debt and preferred stock supported by those retained earnings, it may need to issue new common stock. The total amount of capital that can be raised before new stock must be issued is defined as the **retained earnings breakpoint**, and it can be calculated as follows:

*Retained Earnings Breakpoint*

The amount of capital raised beyond which new common stock must be issued.

$$\text{Retained earnings breakpoint} = \frac{\text{Addition to retained earnings for the year}}{\text{Equity fraction}} \qquad 10.10$$

Allied's addition to retained earnings in 2017 is expected to be $66 million (as we will see later in Chapter 16); and its target capital structure consists of 45% debt, 2% preferred, and 53% equity. Therefore, its retained earnings breakpoint for 2017 is as follows:

$$\text{Retained earnings breakpoint} = \$66/0.53 = \$124.5 \text{ million}$$

To prove that this is correct, note that a capital budget of $124.5 million could be financed as 0.45($124.5) = $56 million of debt, 0.02($124.5) = $2.5 million of preferred stock, and 0.53($124.5) = $66 million of equity raised from retained earnings. Up to a total of $124.5 million of new capital raised for the capital budget will not exhaust the addition to retained earnings, so equity would have a cost of $r_s = 13.5\%$. However, if the capital budget exceeded $124.5 million, the addition to retained earnings would be exhausted, and Allied would have to obtain equity by issuing new common stock at a cost of $r_e = 14.1\%$.[20]

## Self Test

What are the two approaches that can be used to adjust for flotation costs?

Would a firm that has many good investment opportunities be likely to have a higher or a lower dividend payout ratio than a firm with few good investment opportunities? Explain.

A firm's common stock has $D_1 = \$1.50$, $P_0 = \$30.00$, $g = 5\%$, and $F = 4\%$. If the firm must issue new stock, what is its cost of new external equity? **(10.21%)**

Suppose Firm A plans to retain $100 million of earnings for the year. It wants to finance its capital budget using a target capital structure of 46% debt, 3% preferred, and 51% common equity. How large could its capital budget be before it must issue new common stock? **($196.08 million)**

---

[20]This breakpoint is only suggested—it is not written in stone. For example, rather than issuing new common stock, the company could use more debt (hence, increase its debt ratio) or it could increase its addition to retained earnings by reducing its dividend payout ratio. Both actions would change the retained earnings breakpoint. Also, breakpoints could occur due to increases in the costs of debt and preferred. Indeed, a number of changes could occur, and the end result would be a large number of potential breakpoints.

# 10-7 Composite, or Weighted Average, Cost of Capital, WACC

Allied's target capital structure calls for 45% debt, 2% preferred stock, and 53% common equity. Earlier we saw that its before-tax cost of debt is 10.0%; its after-tax cost of debt is $r_d(1 - T) = 10\%(0.6) = 6.0\%$; its cost of preferred stock is 10.3%; its cost of common equity from retained earnings is 13.5%; and its marginal tax rate is 40%. Equation 10.1, presented earlier, can be used to calculate its WACC when all of the new common equity comes from retained earnings:

$$\text{WACC} = w_d r_d(1 - T) \quad + \quad w_p r_p \quad + w_c r_s$$
$$= 0.45(10\%)(0.6) + 0.02(10.3\%) + 0.53(13.5\%)$$
$$= 10.1\% \text{ if equity comes from retained earnings}$$

Under these conditions, every dollar of new capital that Allied raises would consist of 45 cents of debt with an after-tax cost of 6%, 2 cents of preferred stock with a cost of 10.3%, and 53 cents of common equity from additions to retained earnings with a cost of 13.5%. The average cost of each whole dollar, or the WACC, would be 10.1%.

This estimate of Allied's WACC assumes that common equity comes exclusively from retained earnings. If, instead, Allied had to issue new common stock, its WACC would be slightly higher because of the additional flotation costs:

$$\text{WACC} = w_d r_d(1 - T) \quad + w_p r_p \quad + w_c r_e$$
$$= 0.45(10\%)(0.6) + 0.02(10.3\%) + 0.53(14.1\%)$$
$$= 10.4\% \text{ with equity raised by selling new stock}$$

In Web Appendix 10A, we discuss in more detail the connection between the firm's WACC and the costs of issuing new common stock.

## SelfTest

Write the equation for the WACC.

Firm A has the following data: Target capital structure of 46% debt, 3% preferred, and 51% common equity; Tax rate = 40%; $r_d = 7\%$; $r_p = 7.5\%$; $r_s = 11.5\%$; and $r_e = 12.5\%$. What is the firm's WACC if it does not issue any new stock? **(8.02%)**

What is Firm A's WACC if it issues new common stock? **(8.53%)**

Firm A has 11 equally risky capital budgeting projects, each costing $19,608 million and each having an expected rate of return of 8.25%. Firm A's retained earnings breakpoint is $196.08 million. The firm's WACC using retained earnings is 8.0% but increases to 8.5% if new equity must be issued. The company invests in projects where the expected return exceeds the cost of capital. How much capital should Firm A raise and invest? Why? **($196.08 million; the 11th project would have a higher WACC than its expected rate of return.)**

# 10-8 Factors That Affect the WACC

The cost of capital is affected by a number of factors. Some are beyond the firm's control, but others can be influenced by its financing and investment decisions.

## 10-8A FACTORS THE FIRM CANNOT CONTROL

The three most important factors that the firm cannot directly control are *interest rates in the economy, the general level of stock prices,* and *tax rates.* If interest rates in the economy rise, the cost of debt increases because the firm must pay bondholders more when it borrows. Similarly, if stock prices in general decline, pulling the firm's stock price down, its cost of equity will rise. Also, because tax rates are used in the calculation of the component cost of debt, they have an important effect on the firm's cost of capital. Taxes also affect the cost of capital in other less apparent ways. For example, when tax rates on dividends and capital gains were lowered relative to rates on interest income, stocks became relatively more attractive than debt; consequently, the cost of equity and WACC declined.

# SOME REAL-WORLD ESTIMATES OF THE WACC

In the table below, we have summarized quick estimates (done in May 2015) of the WACC for some leading companies. Our calculations were based on the following assumptions:

1. We did not have access to the company's internal target capital structure forecasts, so we used the current market-value weights for debt and equity as the capital structure weights. For simplicity, we assumed that the market value of the company's debt equaled the book value of debt (as estimated by *Value Line Investment Survey*). The market value of equity is the company's stock price multiplied by the number of shares outstanding. The market equity weight and the market debt weight are the percentage of capital (on a market basis) coming from equity and debt, respectively. Note that the firms in this table do not use preferred stock, so we can eliminate the preferred stock term in the WACC equation.

2. The yield to maturity of the company's debt was compiled from Standard & Poor's, Morningstar, or Yahoo! Finance Bonds Center. Where available, we selected an outstanding bond issue with a maturity of 10 years or more. The income tax rate was obtained from *Value Line Investment Survey*. The after-tax cost of debt is the yield to maturity multiplied by one minus the company's tax rate.

3. The risk-free rate approximates the yield to maturity on 10-year government debt. We assumed a market risk premium of 6.0%, and we used the CAPM to estimate the cost of equity. The stock's betas were obtained from *Value Line Investment Survey*.

4. The WACC was calculated as follows:

WACC = (Market debt weight) × (After-tax cost of debt)
　　　 + (Market equity weight) × (CAPM cost of equity)

As expected, companies in more stable businesses (Campbell Soup, Walmart, and Coca-Cola) have the lowest WACC estimates, whereas companies in riskier industries (Exxon Mobil, Disney, Boeing, and Southwest Airlines) have higher WACC estimates. Although these quick estimates can give you a broad sense of the WACC for each of these companies, you should recognize that these calculations are very sensitive to changes in the underlying assumptions. For example, if we assume a higher or lower market risk premium, or use a different source to estimate betas, we can often arrive at significantly different estimates for these WACCs.

| Company | Market Equity Weight | Market Debt Weight | Yield to Maturity on Existing Debt | Income Tax Rate | After-Tax Cost of Debt | Risk-Free Rate | Market Risk Premium | Value Line Beta | CAPM Cost of Equity | WACC |
|---|---|---|---|---|---|---|---|---|---|---|
| Campbell Soup | 78.83% | 21.17% | 3.19% | 31.7% | 2.18% | 2.14% | 6.00% | 0.60 | 5.74% | 4.99% |
| Walmart | 84.13 | 15.87 | 2.53 | 31.8 | 1.73 | 2.14 | 6.00 | 0.60 | 5.74 | 5.10 |
| Coca-Cola | 80.90 | 19.10 | 2.66 | 22.5 | 2.06 | 2.14 | 6.00 | 0.70 | 6.34 | 5.52 |
| Merck & Co. | 88.55 | 11.45 | 2.94 | 24.3 | 2.23 | 2.14 | 6.00 | 0.75 | 6.64 | 6.13 |
| Wyndham Worldwide | 67.33 | 32.67 | 3.88 | 36.3 | 2.47 | 2.14 | 6.00 | 1.20 | 9.34 | 7.10 |
| Home Depot | 89.85 | 10.15 | 2.59 | 36.4 | 1.65 | 2.14 | 6.00 | 0.95 | 7.84 | 7.21 |
| Apple Inc. | 95.30 | 4.70 | 2.77 | 26.1 | 2.04 | 2.14 | 6.00 | 0.90 | 7.54 | 7.28 |
| Microsoft Corp. | 92.34 | 7.66 | 2.30 | 20.7 | 1.83 | 2.14 | 6.00 | 0.95 | 7.84 | 7.38 |
| Exxon Mobil Corp. | 94.55 | 5.45 | 2.66 | 34.9 | 1.73 | 2.14 | 6.00 | 0.95 | 7.84 | 7.51 |
| Disney (Walt) | 91.87 | 8.13 | 2.40 | 34.6 | 1.57 | 2.14 | 6.00 | 1.05 | 8.44 | 7.88 |
| Boeing | 92.36 | 7.64 | 2.52 | 23.7 | 1.92 | 2.14 | 6.00 | 1.05 | 8.44 | 7.94 |
| Southwest Airlines | 91.45 | 8.55 | 3.96 | 37.4 | 2.48 | 2.14 | 6.00 | 1.10 | 8.74 | 8.20 |

## 10-8B FACTORS THE FIRM CAN CONTROL

A firm can directly affect its cost of capital in three primary ways: (1) by changing its *capital structure,* (2) by changing its *dividend payout ratio,* and (3) by *altering its capital budgeting decision rules* to accept projects with more or less risk than projects previously undertaken.

Capital structure impacts a firm's cost of capital. So far we have assumed that Allied has a given target capital structure, and we used the target weights to calculate its WACC. However, if the firm changes its target capital structure, the weights used to calculate the WACC will change. Other things held constant, an increase in the target debt ratio tends to lower the WACC (and vice versa if the debt ratio is lowered) because the after-tax cost of debt is lower than the cost of equity. However, other things are not likely to remain constant. An increase in the use of debt will increase the riskiness of both the debt and the equity, and these increases in component costs might more than offset the effects of the changes in the weights and raise the WACC. In Chapter 13, we discuss how a firm can try to balance these effects to reach its optimal capital structure.

Dividend policy affects the amount of retained earnings available to the firm and thus the need to sell new stock and incur flotation costs. This suggests that the higher the dividend payout ratio, the smaller the addition to retained earnings, the higher the cost of equity, and therefore the higher the firm's WACC will be. However, investors may prefer dividends to retained earnings, in which case reducing dividends might lead to an increase in both $r_s$ and $r_e$. As we will see in Chapter 14, the optimal dividend policy is a complicated issue, but one that can have an important effect on the cost of capital.

The firm's capital budgeting decisions can also affect its cost of capital. When we estimate the firm's cost of capital, we use as the starting point the required rates of return on its outstanding stock and bonds. These cost rates reflect the riskiness of the firm's existing assets. Therefore, we have been implicitly assuming that new capital will be invested in assets that have the same risk as existing assets. This assumption is generally correct, as most firms do invest in assets similar to ones they currently operate. However, if the firm decides to invest in an entirely new and risky line of business, its component costs of debt and equity (and thus its WACC) will increase.

## SelfTest

Name three factors that affect the cost of capital and that are beyond the firm's control.

What are three factors under the firm's control that can affect its cost of capital?

Suppose interest rates in the economy increase. How would such a change affect the costs of both debt and common equity based on the CAPM?

# 10-9 Adjusting the Cost of Capital for Risk

As you will see in Chapters 11 and 12, the cost of capital is a key element in the capital budgeting process. Projects should be accepted if and only if their estimated returns exceed their costs of capital. Thus, the cost of capital is a "hurdle rate"—a project's expected rate of return must "jump the hurdle" for it to be accepted. Moreover, investors require higher returns on riskier investments. Consequently, companies that are raising capital to take on risky projects will have higher costs of capital than companies that are investing in safer projects.

Figure 10.1 illustrates the trade-off between risk and the cost of capital. Firm L is in a low-risk business and has a WACC of 8%. Firm A is an average-risk business

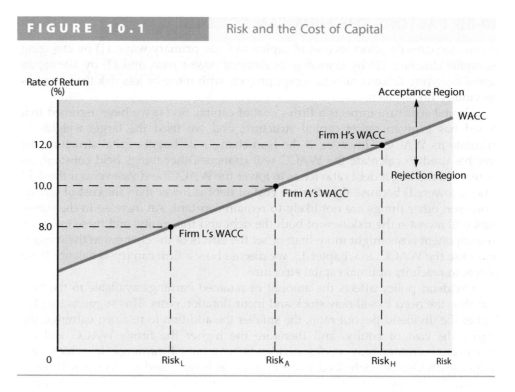

**FIGURE 10.1** Risk and the Cost of Capital

with a WACC of 10%, whereas Firm H's business is exposed to greater risk and consequently has a WACC of 12%. Thus, Firm L will accept a typical project if its expected return is above 8%. Firm A's hurdle rate is 10%, whereas the corresponding hurdle rate for Firm H is 12%.

It's important to remember that the costs of capital for Firms L, A, and H in Figure 10.1 represent the overall, or composite, WACCs for the three firms and thus apply only to "typical" projects for each firm. However, different projects often have different risks, even for a given firm. *Therefore, each project's hurdle rate should reflect the risk of the project, not the risk associated with the firm's average project as reflected in its composite WACC.* Empirical studies do indicate that firms consider the risks of individual projects, but the studies also indicate that most firms regard most projects as having about the same risk as the firm's average existing assets. Therefore, the WACC is used to evaluate most projects, but if a project has an especially high or low risk, the WACC will be adjusted up or down to account for the risk differential.

For example, assume that Firm A (the average-risk firm with a composite WACC of 10%) has two divisions, L and H. Division L has relatively little risk, and if it were operated as a separate firm, its WACC would be 7%. Division H has higher risk, and its divisional cost of capital is 13%. Because the two divisions are of equal size, Firm A's composite WACC is calculated as 0.50(7%) + 0.50(13%) = 10%. However, it would be a mistake to use this 10% WACC for either division. To see this point, assume that Division L is considering a relatively low-risk project with an expected return of 9%, and Division H is considering a higher-risk project with an expected return of 11%. As shown in Figure 10.2, Division L's project should be accepted because its return is above its risk-based cost of capital, whereas Division H's project should be rejected. If the 10% corporate WACC was used by each division, the decision would be reversed: Division H would incorrectly accept its project, and Division L would incorrectly reject its project. In general, failing to adjust for differences in risk would lead the firm to accept too many risky projects and reject too many safe ones. Over time, the firm would become riskier, its WACC would increase, and its shareholder value would suffer. We return to these issues in Chapter 12, when we consider different approaches for measuring project risk.

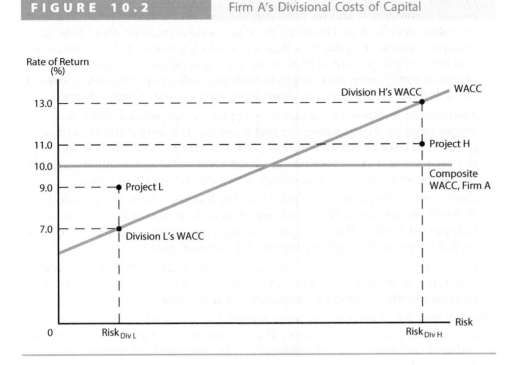

**FIGURE 10.2** Firm A's Divisional Costs of Capital

## SelfTest

Why is the cost of capital sometimes referred to as a "hurdle rate"?

How should firms evaluate projects with different risks?

Should all divisions within the same firm use the firm's composite WACC for evaluating all capital budgeting projects? Explain.

# 10-10 Some Other Problems with Cost of Capital Estimates

A number of issues related to the cost of capital have not been mentioned or were glossed over in this chapter. These topics are covered in advanced finance courses, but they deserve mention now to alert you to potential dangers and to provide a preview of some matters covered in advanced courses.

1. *Depreciation-generated funds.*[21] The largest single source of capital for many firms is depreciation, yet we have not discussed how the cost of this capital is determined. In brief, depreciation cash flows can either be reinvested or returned to investors (stockholders *and* creditors). The cost of depreciation-generated funds is thus an opportunity cost; and it is approximately equal to the WACC from retained earnings, preferred stock, and debt. Therefore, we can ignore it in our estimate of the WACC.

---

[21]See Table 3.3, the statement of cash flows, for an illustration of the cash flows provided from depreciation. Refer to advanced finance textbooks for a discussion on the treatment of depreciation-generated funds.

2. *Privately owned firms.* Our discussion of the cost of equity focused on publicly owned corporations, and we have concentrated on the rate of return required by public stockholders. However, there is a serious question about how to measure the cost of equity for a firm whose stock is not traded. Tax issues are also especially important in these cases. As a general rule, the same principles of cost of capital estimation apply to both privately held and publicly owned firms, but the problems of obtaining input data are somewhat different.

3. *Measurement problems.* We cannot overemphasize the practical difficulties encountered when estimating the cost of equity. It is very difficult to obtain good input data for the CAPM, for g in the formula $\hat{r}_s = D_1/P_0 + g$, and for the risk premium in the formula $r_s =$ Bond yield + Risk premium. As a result, we can never be sure of the accuracy of our estimated cost of capital.

4. *Costs of capital for projects of differing risk.* We touched briefly on the fact that different projects can differ in risk and thus in their required rates of return. However, it is difficult to measure a project's risk (hence, to adjust the cost of capital for capital budgeting projects with different risks).

5. *Capital structure weights.* In this chapter, we took as given the target capital structure and used it to calculate the WACC. As we shall see in Chapter 13, establishing the target capital structure is a major task in itself.

Although this list of problems appears formidable, the state of the art in cost of capital estimation is not in bad shape. The procedures outlined in this chapter can be used to obtain costs of capital estimates that are sufficiently accurate for practical purposes, so the problems listed previously merely indicate the desirability of refinements. The refinements are not unimportant, but the problems noted do not invalidate the usefulness of the procedures outlined in this chapter.

## SelfTest

Identify some problem areas in cost of capital analysis. Do these problems invalidate the cost of capital procedures discussed in this chapter? Explain.

# TYING IT ALL TOGETHER

We began this chapter by discussing the concept of the weighted average cost of capital. We then discussed the three major capital components (debt, preferred stock, and common equity) and the procedures used to estimate each component's cost. Next, we calculated the WACC, which is a key element in capital budgeting. A key issue here is the weights that should be used to find the WACC. In general, companies consider a number of factors and then establish a target capital structure that is used to calculate the WACC. We discuss the target capital structure and its affect on the WACC in more detail in Chapter 13.

The cost of capital is a key element in capital budgeting decisions, our focus in the following chapters. Indeed, capital budgeting as it should be done is impossible without a good estimate of the cost of capital; so you need to have a good understanding of cost of capital concepts before you continue to the next chapter, where we discuss capital budgeting basics.

# Self-Test Questions and Problems

(Solutions Appear in Appendix A)

**ST-1 KEY TERMS** Define each of the following terms:

a. Target capital structure; capital components
b. Before-tax cost of debt, $r_d$; after-tax cost of debt, $r_d(1 - T)$
c. Cost of preferred stock, $r_p$
d. Cost of retained earnings, $r_s$; cost of new common stock, $r_e$
e. Weighted average cost of capital, WACC
f. Flotation cost, F; flotation cost adjustment; retained earnings breakpoint

**ST-2 WACC** Lancaster Engineering Inc. (LEI) has the following capital structure, which it considers to be optimal:

| | |
|---|---|
| Debt | 25% |
| Preferred stock | 15 |
| Common equity | 60 |
| | 100% |

LEI's expected net income this year is $34,285.72; its established dividend payout ratio is 30%; its federal-plus-state tax rate is 40%; and investors expect future earnings and dividends to grow at a constant rate of 9%. LEI paid a dividend of $3.60 per share last year, and its stock currently sells for $54.00 per share. LEI can obtain new capital in the following ways:

- New preferred stock with a dividend of $11.00 can be sold to the public at a price of $95.00 per share.

- Debt can be sold at an interest rate of 12%.

a. Determine the cost of each capital component.

b. Calculate the WACC.

c. LEI has the following investment opportunities that are average-risk projects:

| Project | Cost at t = 0 | Rate of Return |
|---------|---------------|----------------|
| A | $10,000 | 17.4% |
| B | 20,000 | 16.0 |
| C | 10,000 | 14.2 |
| D | 20,000 | 13.2 |
| E | 10,000 | 12.0 |

Which projects should LEI accept? Why? Assume that LEI does not want to issue any new common stock.

# Questions

**10-1** How would each of the following scenarios affect a firm's cost of debt, $r_d(1 - T)$; its cost of equity, $r_s$; and its WACC? Indicate with a plus (+), a minus (−), or a zero (0) whether the factor would raise, lower, or have an indeterminate effect on the item in question. Assume for each answer that other things are held constant, even though in some instances this would probably not be true. Be prepared to justify your answer but recognize that several of the parts have no single correct answer. These questions are designed to stimulate thought and discussion.

| | | Effect on | | |
|---|---|---|---|---|
| | | $r_d(1-T)$ | $r_s$ | WACC |
| a. | The corporate tax rate is lowered. | _____ | _____ | _____ |
| b. | The Federal Reserve tightens credit. | _____ | _____ | _____ |
| c. | The firm uses more debt; that is, it increases its debt ratio. | _____ | _____ | _____ |
| d. | The dividend payout ratio is increased. | _____ | _____ | _____ |
| e. | The firm doubles the amount of capital it raises during the year. | _____ | _____ | _____ |
| f. | The firm expands into a risky new area. | _____ | _____ | _____ |
| g. | The firm merges with another firm whose earnings are countercyclical both to those of the first firm and to the stock market. | _____ | _____ | _____ |
| h. | The stock market falls drastically, and the firm's stock price falls along with the rest. | _____ | _____ | _____ |
| i. | Investors become more risk-averse. | _____ | _____ | _____ |
| j. | The firm is an electric utility with a large investment in nuclear plants. Several states are considering a ban on nuclear power generation. | _____ | _____ | _____ |

10-2 Assume that the risk-free rate increases, but the market risk premium remains constant. What impact would this have on the cost of debt? What impact would it have on the cost of equity?

10-3 How should the capital structure weights used to calculate the WACC be determined?

10-4 Suppose a firm estimates its WACC to be 10%. Should the WACC be used to evaluate all of its potential projects, even if they vary in risk? If not, what might be "reasonable" costs of capital for average-, high-, and low-risk projects?

10-5 The WACC is a weighted average of the costs of debt, preferred stock, and common equity. Would the WACC be different if the equity for the coming year came solely in the form of retained earnings versus some equity from the sale of new common stock? Would the calculated WACC depend in any way on the size of the capital budget? How might dividend policy affect the WACC?

# Problems

**Easy Problems 1–5**

10-1 **AFTER-TAX COST OF DEBT** The Holmes Company's currently outstanding bonds have an 8% coupon and a 10% yield to maturity. Holmes believes it could issue new bonds at par that would provide a similar yield to maturity. If its marginal tax rate is 40%, what is Holmes' after-tax cost of debt?

10-2 **COST OF PREFERRED STOCK** Torch Industries can issue perpetual preferred stock at a price of $57.00 a share. The stock would pay a constant annual dividend of $6.00 a share. What is the company's cost of preferred stock, $r_p$?

10-3 **COST OF COMMON EQUITY** Pearson Motors has a target capital structure of 30% debt and 70% common equity, with no preferred stock. The yield to maturity on the company's outstanding bonds is 9%, and its tax rate is 40%. Pearson's CFO estimates that the company's WACC is 10.50%. What is Pearson's cost of common equity?

**10-4** **COST OF EQUITY WITH AND WITHOUT FLOTATION** Jarett & Sons's common stock currently trades at $30.00 a share. It is expected to pay an annual dividend of $1.00 a share at the end of the year ($D_1 = \$1.00$), and the constant growth rate is 4% a year.

    a. What is the company's cost of common equity if all of its equity comes from retained earnings?

    b. If the company issued new stock, it would incur a 10% flotation cost. What would be the cost of equity from new stock?

**10-5** **PROJECT SELECTION** Midwest Water Works estimates that its WACC is 10.5%. The company is considering the following capital budgeting projects:

| Project | Size | Rate of Return |
|---------|------|----------------|
| A | $1 million | 12.0% |
| B | 2 million | 11.5 |
| C | 2 million | 11.2 |
| D | 2 million | 11.0 |
| E | 1 million | 10.7 |
| F | 1 million | 10.3 |
| G | 1 million | 10.2 |

Assume that each of these projects is just as risky as the firm's existing assets and that the firm may accept all the projects or only some of them. Which set of projects should be accepted? Explain.

**Intermediate Problems 6–13**

**10-6** **COST OF COMMON EQUITY** The future earnings, dividends, and common stock price of Callahan Technologies Inc. are expected to grow 6% per year. Callahan's common stock currently sells for $22.00 per share; its last dividend was $2.00; and it will pay a $2.12 dividend at the end of the current year.

    a. Using the DCF approach, what is its cost of common equity?

    b. If the firm's beta is 1.2, the risk-free rate is 6%, and the average return on the market is 13%, what will be the firm's cost of common equity using the CAPM approach?

    c. If the firm's bonds earn a return of 11%, based on the bond-yield-plus-risk-premium approach, what will be $r_s$? Use the midpoint of the risk premium range discussed in Section 10-5 in your calculations.

    d. If you have equal confidence in the inputs used for the three approaches, what is your estimate of Callahan's cost of common equity?

**10-7** **COST OF COMMON EQUITY WITH AND WITHOUT FLOTATION** The Evanec Company's next expected dividend, $D_1$, is $3.18; its growth rate is 6%; and its common stock now sells for $36.00. New stock (external equity) can be sold to net $32.40 per share.

    a. What is Evanec's cost of retained earnings, $r_s$?

    b. What is Evanec's percentage flotation cost, F?

    c. What is Evanec's cost of new common stock, $r_e$?

**10-8** **COST OF COMMON EQUITY AND WACC** Palencia Paints Corporation has a target capital structure of 35% debt and 65% common equity, with no preferred stock. Its before-tax cost of debt is 8%, and its marginal tax rate is 40%. The current stock price is $P_0 = \$22.00$. The last dividend was $D_0 = \$2.25$, and it is expected to grow at a 5% constant rate. What is its cost of common equity and its WACC?

**10-9** **WACC** The Paulson Company's year-end balance sheet is shown below. Its cost of common equity is 14%, its before-tax cost of debt is 10%, and its marginal tax rate is 40%. Assume that the firm's long-term debt sells at par value. The firm's total debt, which is the sum of the company's short-term debt and long-term debt, equals $1,167. The firm has

576 shares of common stock outstanding that sell for $4.00 per share. Calculate Paulson's WACC using market-value weights.

| Assets | | Liabilities and Equity | |
|---|---|---|---|
| Cash | $ 120 | Accounts payable and accruals | $ 10 |
| Accounts receivable | 240 | Short-term debt | 47 |
| Inventories | 360 | Long-term debt | 1,120 |
| Plant and equipment, net | 2,160 | Common equity | 1,703 |
| Total assets | $2,880 | Total liabilities and equity | $2,880 |

10-10 **WACC** Olsen Outfitters Inc. believes that its optimal capital structure consists of 55% common equity and 45% debt, and its tax rate is 40%. Olsen must raise additional capital to fund its upcoming expansion. The firm will have $4 million of retained earnings with a cost of $r_s = 11\%$. New common stock in an amount up to $8 million would have a cost of $r_e = 12.5\%$. Furthermore, Olsen can raise up to $4 million of debt at an interest rate of $r_d = 9\%$ and an additional $5 million of debt at $r_d = 13\%$. The CFO estimates that a proposed expansion would require an investment of $8.2 million. What is the WACC for the last dollar raised to complete the expansion?

10-11 **WACC AND PERCENTAGE OF DEBT FINANCING** Hook Industries's capital structure consists solely of debt and common equity. It can issue debt at $r_d = 11\%$, and its common stock currently pays a $2.00 dividend per share ($D_0 = \$2.00$). The stock's price is currently $24.75, its dividend is expected to grow at a constant rate of 7% per year, its tax rate is 35%, and its WACC is 13.95%. What percentage of the company's capital structure consists of debt?

10-12 **WACC** Empire Electric Company (EEC) uses only debt and common equity. It can borrow unlimited amounts at an interest rate of $r_d = 9\%$ as long as it finances at its target capital structure, which calls for 35% debt and 65% common equity. Its last dividend ($D_0$) was $2.20, its expected constant growth rate is 6%, and its common stock sells for $26. EEC's tax rate is 40%. Two projects are available: Project A has a rate of return of 12%, and Project B's return is 11%. These two projects are equally risky and about as risky as the firm's existing assets.

a. What is its cost of common equity?
b. What is the WACC?
c. Which projects should Empire accept?

10-13 **COST OF COMMON EQUITY WITH FLOTATION** Banyan Co.'s common stock currently sells for $46.75 per share. The growth rate is a constant 6%, and the company has an expected dividend yield of 5%. The expected long-run dividend payout ratio is 20%, and the expected return on equity (ROE) is 7.5%. New stock can be sold to the public at the current price, but a flotation cost of 5% would be incurred. What would be the cost of new equity?

**Challenging Problems 14–20**

10-14 **COST OF PREFERRED STOCK INCLUDING FLOTATION** Travis Industries plans to issue perpetual preferred stock with an $11.00 dividend. The stock is currently selling for $108.50, but flotation costs will be 5% of the market price, so the net price will be $103.08 per share. What is the cost of the preferred stock, including flotation?

10-15 **WACC AND COST OF COMMON EQUITY** Kahn Inc. has a target capital structure of 60% common equity and 40% debt to fund its $10 billion in operating assets. Furthermore, Kahn Inc. has a WACC of 13%, a before-tax cost of debt of 10%, and a tax rate of 40%. The company's retained earnings are adequate to provide the common equity portion of its capital budget. Its expected dividend next year ($D_1$) is $3, and the current stock price is $35.

a. What is the company's expected growth rate?
b. If the firm's net income is expected to be $1.1 billion, what portion of its net income is the firm expected to pay out as dividends? (Hint: Refer to Equation 9.4 in Chapter 9.)

**10-16** **COST OF COMMON EQUITY** The Bouchard Company's EPS was $6.50 in 2016, up from $4.42 in 2011. The company pays out 40% of its earnings as dividends, and its common stock sells for $36.00.

a. Calculate the past growth rate in earnings. (Hint: This is a 5-year growth period.)

b. The last dividend was $D_0 = 0.4(\$6.50) = \$2.60$. Calculate the next expected dividend, $D_1$, assuming that the past growth rate continues.

c. What is Bouchard's cost of retained earnings, $r_s$?

**10-17** **CALCULATION OF g AND EPS** Sidman Products's common stock currently sells for $60.00 a share. The firm is expected to earn $5.40 per share this year and to pay a year-end dividend of $3.60, and it finances only with common equity.

a. If investors require a 9% return, what is the expected growth rate?

b. If Sidman reinvests retained earnings in projects whose average return is equal to the stock's expected rate of return, what will be next year's EPS? (Hint: Refer to Equation 9.4 in Chapter 9.)

**10-18** **WACC AND OPTIMAL CAPITAL BUDGET** Adamson Corporation is considering four average-risk projects with the following costs and rates of return:

| Project | Cost | Expected Rate of Return |
|---------|------|-------------------------|
| 1 | $2,000 | 16.00% |
| 2 | 3,000 | 15.00 |
| 3 | 5,000 | 13.75 |
| 4 | 2,000 | 12.50 |

The company estimates that it can issue debt at a rate of $r_d = 10\%$, and its tax rate is 30%. It can issue preferred stock that pays a constant dividend of $5.00 per year at $50.00 per share. Also, its common stock currently sells for $38.00 per share; the next expected dividend, $D_1$, is $4.25, and the dividend is expected to grow at a constant rate of 5% per year. The target capital structure consists of 75% common stock, 15% debt, and 10% preferred stock.

a. What is the cost of each of the capital components?

b. What is Adamson's WACC?

c. Only projects with expected returns that exceed WACC will be accepted. Which projects should Adamson accept?

**10-19** **ADJUSTING COST OF CAPITAL FOR RISK** Ziege Systems is considering the following independent projects for the coming year:

| Project | Required Investment | Rate of Return | Risk |
|---------|---------------------|----------------|------|
| A | $4 million | 14.0% | High |
| B | 5 million | 11.5 | High |
| C | 3 million | 9.5 | Low |
| D | 2 million | 9.0 | Average |
| E | 6 million | 12.5 | High |
| F | 5 million | 12.5 | Average |
| G | 6 million | 7.0 | Low |
| H | 3 million | 11.5 | Low |

Ziege's WACC is 10%, but it adjusts for risk by adding 2% to the WACC for high-risk projects and subtracting 2% for low-risk projects.

a. Which projects should Ziege accept if it faces no capital constraints?

b. If Ziege can only invest a total of $13 million, which projects should it accept, and what would be the dollar size of its capital budget?

c. Suppose Ziege can raise additional funds beyond the $13 million, but each new increment (or partial increment) of $5 million of new capital will cause the WACC to increase by 1%. Assuming that Ziege uses the same method of risk adjustment, which projects should it now accept, and what would be the dollar size of its capital budget?

10-20 **WACC** The following table gives Foust Company's earnings per share for the last 10 years. The common stock, 7.8 million shares outstanding, is now (1/1/17) selling for $65.00 per share. The expected dividend at the end of the current year (12/31/17) is 55% of the 2016 EPS. Because investors expect past trends to continue, g may be based on the historical earnings growth rate. (Note that 9 years of growth are reflected in the 10 years of data.)

| Year | EPS | Year | EPS |
|------|------|------|------|
| 2007 | $3.90 | 2012 | $5.73 |
| 2008 | 4.21 | 2013 | 6.19 |
| 2009 | 4.55 | 2014 | 6.68 |
| 2010 | 4.91 | 2015 | 7.22 |
| 2011 | 5.31 | 2016 | 7.80 |

The current interest rate on new debt is 9%; Foust's marginal tax rate is 40%; and its target capital structure is 40% debt and 60% equity.

a. Calculate Foust's after-tax cost of debt and common equity. Calculate the cost of equity as $r_s = D_1/P_0 + g$.
b. Find Foust's WACC.

# Comprehensive/Spreadsheet Problem

10-21 **CALCULATING THE WACC** Here is the condensed 2016 balance sheet for Skye Computer Company (in thousands of dollars):

| | 2016 |
|---|------|
| Current assets | $2,000 |
| Net fixed assets | 3,000 |
| Total assets | $5,000 |
| | |
| Accounts payable and accruals | $ 900 |
| Short-term debt | 100 |
| Long-term debt | 1,100 |
| Preferred stock (10,000 shares) | 250 |
| Common stock (50,000 shares) | 1,300 |
| Retained earnings | 1,350 |
| Total common equity | $2,650 |
| Total liabilities and equity | $5,000 |

Skye's earnings per share last year were $3.20. The common stock sells for $55.00, last year's dividend ($D_0$) was $2.10, and a flotation cost of 10% would be required to sell new common stock. Security analysts are projecting that the common dividend will grow at an annual rate of 9%. Skye's preferred stock pays a dividend of $3.30 per share, and its preferred stock sells for $30.00 per share. The firm's before-tax cost of debt is 10%, and its marginal tax rate is 35%. The firm's currently outstanding 10% annual coupon rate, long-term debt sells at par value. The market risk premium is 5%, the risk-free rate is 6%, and Skye's beta is 1.516. The firm's total debt, which is the sum of the company's short-term debt and long-term debt, equals $1.2 million.

a. Calculate the cost of each capital component, that is, the after-tax cost of debt, the cost of preferred stock, the cost of equity from retained earnings, and the cost of newly issued common stock. Use the DCF method to find the cost of common equity.

b. Now calculate the cost of common equity from retained earnings, using the CAPM method.

c. What is the cost of new common stock based on the CAPM? (Hint: Find the difference between $r_e$ and $r_s$ as determined by the DCF method, and add that differential to the CAPM value for $r_s$.)

d. If Skye continues to use the same market-value capital structure, what is the firm's WACC assuming that (1) it uses only retained earnings for equity? (2) If it expands so rapidly that it must issue new common stock?

 **INTEGRATED CASE**

## COLEMAN TECHNOLOGIES INC.

**10-22** **COST OF CAPITAL** Coleman Technologies is considering a major expansion program that has been proposed by the company's information technology group. Before proceeding with the expansion, the company must estimate its cost of capital. Suppose you are an assistant to Jerry Lehman, the financial vice president. Your first task is to estimate Coleman's cost of capital. Lehman has provided you with the following data, which he believes may be relevant to your task.

- The firm's tax rate is 40%.

- The current price of Coleman's 12% coupon, semiannual payment, noncallable bonds with 15 years remaining to maturity, is $1,153.72. Coleman does not use short-term, interest-bearing debt on a permanent basis. New bonds would be privately placed with no flotation cost.

- The current price of the firm's 10%, $100.00 par value, quarterly dividend, perpetual preferred stock is $111.10.

- Coleman's common stock is currently selling for $50.00 per share. Its last dividend ($D_0$) was $4.19, and dividends are expected to grow at a constant annual rate of 5% in the foreseeable future. Coleman's beta is 1.2, the yield on T-bonds is 7%, and the market risk premium is estimated to be 6%. For the bond-yield-plus-risk-premium approach, the firm uses a risk premium of 4%.

- Coleman's target capital structure is 30% debt, 10% preferred stock, and 60% common equity.

To structure the task somewhat, Lehman has asked you to answer the following questions.

a. 1. What sources of capital should be included when you estimate Coleman's WACC?
   2. Should the component costs be figured on a before-tax or an after-tax basis?
   3. Should the costs be historical (embedded) costs or new (marginal) costs?

b. What is the market interest rate on Coleman's debt and its component cost of debt?

c. 1. What is the firm's cost of preferred stock?
   2. Coleman's preferred stock is riskier to investors than its debt, yet the preferred's yield to investors is lower than the yield to maturity on the debt. Does this suggest that you have made a mistake? (Hint: Think about taxes.)

d. 1. Why is there a cost associated with retained earnings?

   2. What is Coleman's estimated cost of common equity using the CAPM approach?

e. What is the estimated cost of common equity using the DCF approach?

f. What is the bond-yield-plus-risk-premium estimate for Coleman's cost of common equity?

g. What is your final estimate for $r_s$?

h. Explain in words why new common stock has a higher cost than retained earnings.

i. 1. What are two approaches that can be used to adjust for flotation costs?

   2. Coleman estimates that if it issues new common stock, the flotation cost will be 15%. Coleman incorporates the flotation costs into the DCF approach. What is the estimated cost of newly issued common stock, considering the flotation cost?

j. What is Coleman's overall, or weighted average, cost of capital (WACC)? Ignore flotation costs.

k. What factors influence Coleman's composite WACC?

l. Should the company use the composite WACC as the hurdle rate for each of its projects? Explain.

# TAKING A CLOSER LOOK

## CALCULATING 3M's COST OF CAPITAL

*Use online resources to work on this chapter's questions. Please note that website information changes over time, and these changes may limit your ability to answer some of these questions.*

In this chapter, we described how to estimate a company's WACC, which is the weighted average of its costs of debt, preferred stock, and common equity. Most of the data we need to do this can be found from various data sources on the Internet. Here we walk through the steps used to calculate Minnesota Mining & Manufacturing's (MMM) WACC.

## DISCUSSION QUESTIONS

1. As a first step, we need to estimate what percentage of MMM's capital comes from debt, preferred stock, and common equity. This information can be found on the firm's latest annual balance sheet. (As of year end 2014, MMM had no preferred stock.) Total debt includes all interest-bearing debt and is the sum of short-term debt and long-term debt.

   a. Recall that the weights used in the WACC are based on the company's target capital structure. If we assume that the company wants to maintain the same mix of capital that it currently has on its balance sheet, what weights should you use to estimate the WACC for MMM?

   b. Find MMM's market capitalization, which is the market value of its common equity. Using the sum of its short-term debt and long-term debt from the balance sheet (we assume that the market value of its debt equals its book value) and its market capitalization, recalculate the firm's debt and common equity weights to be used in the WACC equation. These weights are approximations of market-value weights. Be sure not to include accruals in the debt calculation.

2. Once again we can use the CAPM to estimate MMM's cost of equity. From the Internet, you can find a number of different sources for estimates of beta—select the measure that you think is best, and combine this with your estimates of the risk-free rate and the market risk premium to obtain an estimate of its cost of equity. (See the Taking a Closer Look problem in Chapter 8 for more details.) What is your estimate for MMM's cost of equity? Why might it not make much sense to use the DCF approach to estimate MMM's cost of equity?

3. Next, we need to calculate MMM's cost of debt. We can use different approaches to estimate it. One approach is to take the company's interest expense and divide it by total debt (which is the sum of short-term debt and long-term debt). This approach only works if the historical cost of debt equals the yield to maturity in today's market (i.e., if MMM's outstanding bonds are trading at close to par). This approach may produce misleading estimates in years in which MMM issues a significant amount of new debt. For example, if a company issues a great deal of debt at the end of the year, the full amount of debt will appear on the year-end balance sheet, yet we still may not see a sharp increase in annual interest expense because the debt was outstanding for only a small portion of the entire year. When this situation occurs, the estimated cost of debt will likely understate the true cost of debt. Another approach is to try to find this number in the notes to the company's annual report by accessing the company's home page and its Investor Relations section. Alternatively, you can go to other external sources, such as bondsonline.com, for corporate bond spreads, which can be used to find estimates of the cost of debt. Finally, you can also go to Morningstar.com, which will provide yield to maturity information on the firm's various bond issues. A longer-term issue's YTM could provide an estimate of the firm's current cost of debt to be used in the WACC calculation. Remember that you need the after-tax cost of debt to calculate a firm's WACC, so you will need MMM's tax rate (which has averaged around 30% in recent years). What is your estimate of MMM's after-tax cost of debt?

4. a. What is your estimate of MMM's WACC using the book-value weights calculated in question 1a?

   b. What is your estimate of MMM's WACC using the market-value weights calculated in question 1b?

   c. Explain the difference between the two WACC estimates. Which estimate do you prefer? Explain your answer.

   d. How confident are you in the estimate chosen in part c? Explain your answer.

## Solutions to Self-Test Questions and Problems

**ST-1**  Refer to the marginal glossary definitions or relevant chapter sections to check your responses.

**ST-2**  a. Component costs are as follows:

Common: $r_s = \dfrac{D_1}{P_0} + g = \dfrac{D_0(1+g)}{P_0} + g$

$\qquad\quad = \dfrac{\$3.60(1.09)}{\$54} + 0.09$

$\qquad\quad = 0.0727 + 0.09 = 16.27\%$

Preferred: $r_p = \dfrac{\text{Preferred dividend}}{P_p} = \dfrac{\$11}{\$95} = 11.58\%$

Debt: $r_d(1 - T) = 12\%(0.6) = 7.20\%$

b. WACC calculation:

$\text{WACC} = w_d r_d(1 - T) + w_p r_p + w_c r_s$

$\qquad\quad = 0.25(7.2\%) + 0.15(11.58\%) + 0.60(16.27\%) = 13.30\%$

c. $\dfrac{\text{Retained earnings}}{\text{breakpoint}} = \dfrac{\text{Addition to retained earnings for the year}}{\text{Equity fraction}}$

$\qquad\quad = \dfrac{0.7(\$34,285.72)}{0.6} = \$40,000$

At a capital budget greater than $40,000, new common stock would have to be issued, and the firm's WACC would increase above 13.3%. Therefore, only Projects A, B, and C can be accepted for a total capital budget of $40,000.

## Answers to Selected End-of-Chapter Problems

**10-2** $r_p = 10.53\%$

**10-4** a. $r_s = 7.33\%$

b. $r_e = 7.70\%$

**10-6** a. $r_s = 15.6\%$

b. $r_s = 14.4\%$

c. $r_s = 15\%$

d. $r_{s\,Avg} = 15.0\%$

**10-8** $r_s = 15.74\%$; WACC $= 11.91\%$

**10-10** WACC $= 9.31\%$

**10-12** a. $r_s = 14.97\%$

b. WACC $= 11.62\%$

c. Project A

**10-14** 10.67%

**10-16** a. $g = 8\%$

b. $D_1 = \$2.81$

c. $r_s = 15.81\%$

**10-18** a. $r_d(1 - T) = 7\%$; $r_p = 10\%$;

$r_s = 16.18\%$

b. WACC $= 14.19\%$

c. Projects 1 and 2 will be accepted

**10-20** a. $r_d(1 - T) = 5.4\%$; $r_s = 14.6\%$

b. WACC $= 10.92\%$

## Selected Equations and Tables

$$\text{WACC} = \begin{pmatrix} \% \\ \text{of} \\ \text{debt} \end{pmatrix}\begin{pmatrix} \text{After-tax} \\ \text{cost of} \\ \text{debt} \end{pmatrix} + \begin{pmatrix} \% \text{ of} \\ \text{preferred} \\ \text{stock} \end{pmatrix}\begin{pmatrix} \text{Cost of} \\ \text{preferred} \\ \text{stock} \end{pmatrix} + \begin{pmatrix} \% \text{ of} \\ \text{common} \\ \text{equity} \end{pmatrix}\begin{pmatrix} \text{Cost of} \\ \text{common} \\ \text{equity} \end{pmatrix}$$

$$= w_d r_d(1 - T) + w_p r_p + w_c r_s$$

After-tax cost of debt = Interest rate on new debt − Tax savings

$$= r_d - r_d T$$
$$= r_d(1 - T)$$

Component cost of preferred stock $= r_p = \dfrac{D_p}{P_p}$

Required rate of return = Expected rate of return

$$r_s = r_{RF} + RP = D_1/P_0 + g = \hat{r}_s$$

$$r_s = r_{RF} + (RP_M)b_i$$
$$= r_{RF} + (r_M - r_{RF})b_i$$

$r_s$ = Bond yield + Risk premium

$$P_0 = \dfrac{D_1}{(1 + r_s)^1} + \dfrac{D_2}{(1 + r_s)^2} + \cdots + \dfrac{D_\infty}{(1 + r_s)^\infty}$$
$$= \sum_{t=1}^{\infty} \dfrac{D_t}{(1 + r_s)^t}$$

$$P_0 = \dfrac{D_1}{r_s - g}$$

$$r_s = \hat{r}_s = \dfrac{D_1}{P_0} + \text{Expected } g$$

Cost of equity from new stock $= r_e = \dfrac{D_1}{P_0(1 - F)} + g$

$$\dfrac{\text{Flotation cost}}{\text{adjustment}} = \dfrac{\text{Adjusted}}{\text{DCF cost}} - \dfrac{\text{Pure}}{\text{DCF cost}}$$

$$\dfrac{\text{Cost of}}{\text{external equity}} = r_s + \dfrac{\text{Flotation cost}}{\text{adjustment}}$$

$$\dfrac{\text{Retained earnings}}{\text{breakpoint}} = \dfrac{\text{Addition to retained earnings for the year}}{\text{Equity fraction}}$$

# Chapter 11

# The Basics of Capital Budgeting

CHAPTER

© Ivan Cholakov/Shutterstock.com

## Competition in the Aircraft Industry: Airbus versus Boeing

Changing technology and market conditions often present executives with opportunities to invest in major projects, the success of which may go a long way toward determining their company's future success. For example, in recent years, Ford made the dramatic decision to shift to an aluminum base for its immensely popular F-150 pick-up; Apple decided after much fanfare to produce its Apple Watch; and Airbus (a unit of the European Aeronautic Defence & Space Co., EADS) unveiled the A350 XWB plane (where XWB stands for extra-wide body).

As you might expect, these projects require billions of dollars of capital to develop, and along the way the companies make many detailed calculations when forecasting crucial factors such as development costs, operating costs, and anticipated demand. These forecasts are further complicated by the fact that market conditions can dramatically change, and that companies don't operate in a vacuum—their key competitors are often making similar decisions, and the future cash flows will typically depend on who "wins the game" by developing the best product or service. Among these notable battles is the contest between Samsung, Apple, and others to develop smartphone technology, and the ongoing clash between Airbus and Boeing, where both companies have recently made major commitments toward investing in the next generation of aircraft.

Typically in these types of projects, Boeing and Airbus project negative cash flows for the first 5 or 6 years, and then positive cash flows for the following 20 years. Given their forecasted cash flows, both managements decided that taking on the projects would increase each company's intrinsic value. But given the inherent risks in this business and the fact that the planes will compete with one another, both Boeing's and Airbus's financial analysts recognized that their forecasts were subject to considerable errors.

For example, a recent *New York Times* article chronicles the different approaches that the two companies have taken. Airbus has chosen to emphasize its huge wide-body plane, in order to accommodate large flights between major international cities. Boeing has chosen instead to emphasize somewhat smaller planes that can better accommodate direct travel between non-hub airports. Although it is too early to declare a "winner," the article does highlight that while the Airbus 350 has attracted a lot of interest, it has so far struggled to obtain the number of orders that it had initially projected.

While these large-scale projects receive a great deal of attention; many companies also make a great many routine investment decisions every year, ranging from buying new trucks or machinery to purchasing computers and software to optimize inventory management. Although each project has its own unique characteristics, the same techniques described in this chapter are used to analyze projects of all types and sizes.

Sources: "Airbus Unveils First Passenger-Ready A350 XWB Plane," edition.cnn.com/business, January 3, 2014; Christopher Drew and Jad Mouawad, "Boeing Fix for Battery Is Approved by F.A.A.," *The New York Times*, April 20, 2013, p. B1; Jack Harty, "Countdown to Launch: The Airbus A350 XWB," *Airways News* (airwaysnews.com/blog), May 8, 2013; Peter Sanders and Daniel Michaels, "Winds of Change for Boeing, Airbus," *The Wall Street Journal* (online.wsj.com), March 16, 2010; and Jad Mouawad, "Oversize Expectations for the Airbus A380," *The New York Times* (www.nytimes.com), August 9, 2014.

# PUTTING THINGS IN PERSPECTIVE

In the last chapter, we discussed the cost of capital. Now we turn to investment decisions involving fixed assets, or *capital budgeting*. Here *capital* refers to long-term assets used in production, while a *budget* is a plan that outlines projected expenditures during some future period. Thus, the *capital budget* is a summary of planned investments in long-term assets, and **capital budgeting** is the whole process of analyzing projects and deciding which ones to include in the capital budget. Boeing, Airbus, and other companies use the techniques in this chapter when deciding to accept or reject proposed capital expenditures.

*Capital Budgeting*
The process of planning expenditures on assets with cash flows that are expected to extend beyond one year.

When you finish this chapter, you should be able to:

- **Discuss capital budgeting.**
- **Calculate and use the major capital budgeting decision criteria, which are NPV, IRR, MIRR, and payback.**
- **Explain why NPV is the best criterion and how it overcomes problems inherent in the other methods.**

With an understanding of the theory of capital budgeting developed in this chapter, which uses simplified examples, you will be ready for the next chapter, where we discuss how cash flows are estimated, how risk is measured, and how capital budgeting decisions are made.

## 11-1 An Overview of Capital Budgeting

The same concepts used in security valuation are also used in capital budgeting, but there are two major differences. First, stocks and bonds exist in the security markets, and investors select from the available set; firms, however, create capital budgeting projects. Second, for most securities, investors have no influence on the cash flows produced by their investments, whereas corporations have a major influence on projects' results. Still, in both security valuation and capital budgeting, we forecast a set of cash flows, find the present value of those flows, and make the investment only if the PV of the inflows exceeds the investment's cost.

A firm's growth, and even its ability to remain competitive and to survive, depends on a constant flow of ideas relating to new products, to improvements in existing products, and to ways of operating more efficiently. Accordingly, well-managed firms go to great lengths to develop good capital budgeting proposals. For example, the executive vice president of one successful corporation said that his company takes the following steps to generate projects:

*Our R&D department constantly searches for new products and ways to improve existing products. In addition, our Executive Committee, which consists of senior executives in marketing, production, and finance, identifies the products and markets in which our company should compete, and the Committee sets long-run targets for each division. These targets, which are spelled out in the corporation's* **strategic business plan**, *provide a general guide to the operating executives who must meet them. The operating executives then seek new products, set expansion plans for existing products, and look for ways to reduce production and distribution costs. Because bonuses and promotions are based on each unit's ability to meet or exceed its targets, these economic incentives encourage our operating executives to seek out profitable investment opportunities.*

*Although our senior executives are judged and rewarded on the basis of how well their units perform, people further down the line are given bonuses and stock options for suggestions that lead to profitable investments. Additionally, a percentage of our corporate profit is set aside for distribution to nonexecutive employees, and we have an Employees' Stock Ownership Plan (ESOP) to provide further incentives. Our objective is to encourage employees at all levels to keep an eye out for good ideas, especially those that lead to capital investments.*

**Strategic Business Plan**

A long-run plan that outlines in broad terms the firm's basic strategy for the next 5 to 10 years.

Analyzing capital expenditure proposals is not costless—benefits can be gained, but analysis does have a cost. For certain types of projects, an extremely detailed analysis may be warranted, while for other projects, simpler procedures are adequate. Accordingly, firms generally categorize projects and then analyze them in each category somewhat differently:

1. *Replacement: needed to continue current operations.* One category consists of expenditures to replace worn-out or damaged equipment required in the production of profitable products. The only questions here are should the operation be continued and if so, should the firm continue to use the same production processes? If the answers are yes, the project will be approved without going through an elaborate decision process.

2. *Replacement: cost reduction.* This category includes expenditures to replace serviceable but obsolete equipment and thereby to lower costs. These decisions are discretionary, and a fairly detailed analysis is generally required.

3. *Expansion of existing products or markets.* These are expenditures to increase output of existing products or to expand retail outlets or distribution facilities in markets now being served. Expansion decisions are more complex because they require an explicit forecast of growth in demand, so a more detailed analysis is required. The go/no-go decision is generally made at a higher level within the firm.

4. *Expansion into new products or markets.* These investments relate to new products or geographic areas, and they involve strategic decisions that could change the fundamental nature of the business. Invariably, a detailed analysis is required, and the final decision is generally made at the top level of management.

5. *Safety and/or environmental projects.* Expenditures necessary to comply with government orders, labor agreements, or insurance policy terms fall into this category. How these projects are handled depends on their size, with small ones being treated much like the Category 1 projects.

6. *Other projects.* This catch-all includes items such as office buildings, parking lots, and executive aircraft. How they are handled varies among companies.

7. *Mergers.* In a merger, one firm buys another one. Buying a whole firm is different from buying an asset such as a machine or investing in a new airplane, but the same principles are involved. The concepts of capital budgeting underlie merger analysis.

In general, relatively simple calculations, and only a few supporting documents, are required for replacement decisions, especially maintenance investments in profitable plants. More detailed analyses are required for cost-reduction projects, for expansion of existing product lines, and especially for investments in new products or areas. Also, within each category, projects are grouped by their dollar costs: Larger investments require increasingly detailed analysis and approval at higher levels. Thus, a plant manager might be authorized to approve maintenance expenditures up to $10,000 using a relatively unsophisticated analysis, but the full board of directors might have to approve decisions that involve amounts greater than $1 million or expansions into new products or markets.

If a firm has capable and imaginative executives and employees and if its incentive system is working properly, many ideas for capital investment will be advanced. Some ideas will be good ones, but others will not. Therefore, procedures must be established for screening projects. Companies use, and we discuss, the following criteria for deciding to accept or reject projects:[1]

1. Net present value (NPV)

2. Internal rate of return (IRR)

3. Modified internal rate of return (MIRR)

4. Regular payback

5. Discounted Payback

The NPV is the best method, primarily because it addresses directly the central goal of financial management—maximizing shareholder wealth. However, all of the methods provide useful information, and all are used in practice at least to some extent.

## Self Test

How is capital budgeting similar to security valuation? How is it different?

What are some ways that firms generate ideas for capital projects?

Identify the major project classification categories, and explain how and why they are used.

What is the single best capital budgeting decision criterion? Explain.

# 11-2 Net Present Value (NPV)

We saw in Chapter 3 that there is a difference between cash flows and accounting income, and we noted that investors are particularly concerned with *free cash flow.* Recall that free cash flow represents the net amount of cash that is available for all investors after taking into account the necessary investments in fixed assets (capital expenditures) and net operating working capital.

---

[1]Two other rarely used criteria, the Profitability Index and the Accounting Rate of Return, are covered in Chapter 12 and Web Extension 12A of Eugene F. Brigham and Phillip R. Daves, *Intermediate Financial Management*, 12th edition (Mason, OH: Cengage Learning, 2016).

*Net Present Value (NPV)*

A method of ranking investment proposals using the NPV, which is equal to the present value of the project's free cash flows discounted at the cost of capital.

In Chapter 9, we demonstrated that the value of the firm is equal to the present value of the free cash flows the firm produces for its investors over time. Similarly, the value of a project is equal to its **net present value (NPV)**, which is simply the present value of the project's free cash flows discounted at the cost of capital. The NPV tells us how much a project contributes to shareholder wealth—the larger the NPV, the more value the project adds; and added value means a higher stock price.[2] Thus, NPV is the best selection criterion.

The most difficult aspect of capital budgeting is estimating the relevant cash flows. For simplicity, the cash flows are treated as a given in this chapter, which allows us to focus on the rules for making capital budgeting decisions. However, in Chapter 12, we discuss cash flow estimation in detail.

We use the data for Projects S and L shown in Table 11.1 to illustrate the calculation. The S stands for *short*; the L, for *long*. Project S is a short-term project in the sense that more of its cash inflows come early, while L has more total cash inflows but they come in later in its life. The projects are equally risky, and they both have a 10% cost of capital. Furthermore, the cash flows have been adjusted to reflect depreciation, taxes, and salvage values. The investment outlays shown as $CF_0$ include fixed assets and any necessary investments in working capital, and cash flows come in at the end of the year. Finally, we show the table with an "Excel look," which simply means adding row and column headings to a "regular" table. All of the calculations can be done easily with a financial calculator; but because some students may want to work with Excel, we show how problems would be set up in Excel. Do keep in mind, though, that Excel is not necessary.

We find the NPVs as follows:

1. The present value of each cash flow is calculated and discounted at the project's risk-adjusted cost of capital, r = 10% in our example.

2. The sum of the discounted cash flows is defined as the project's NPV.

The equation for the NPV, set up with input data for Project S, is as follows:

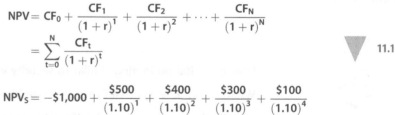

$$NPV = CF_0 + \frac{CF_1}{(1+r)^1} + \frac{CF_2}{(1+r)^2} + \cdots + \frac{CF_N}{(1+r)^N}$$

$$= \sum_{t=0}^{N} \frac{CF_t}{(1+r)^t} \qquad \qquad 11.1$$

$$NPV_S = -\$1{,}000 + \frac{\$500}{(1.10)^1} + \frac{\$400}{(1.10)^2} + \frac{\$300}{(1.10)^3} + \frac{\$100}{(1.10)^4}$$

$$= -\$1{,}000 + \$454.55 + \$330.58 + \$225.39 + \$68.30$$

$$= \$78.82$$

Here $CF_t$ is the expected cash flow at Time t; r is the project's risk-adjusted cost of capital (or WACC); and N is its life. Projects generally require an initial investment—for example, developing the product, buying the equipment needed to manufacture it, building a factory, and stocking inventory. The initial investment is a negative cash flow. For Projects S and L, only $CF_0$ is negative, but for large projects such as Boeing's Dreamliner or Airbus's A350 XWB, outflows occur for several years before cash inflows ever begin.

Figure 11.1 shows the cash flow time line for Project S, the PV of each cash flow, and the sum of the PVs, which is by definition the NPV. The cost, at t = 0, is −$1,000.

---

[2]We could divide the NPV by the number of shares outstanding to estimate a project's effect on the stock price. However, given the lag between project acceptance and visible effects on earnings, this is rarely done for routine projects. However, for major projects, this procedure is useful.

Data on Projects S and L          TABLE 11.1

|    | A | B | C | D | E | F | G |
|----|---|---|---|---|---|---|---|
| 13 | WACC for both projects = | | 10% | | | | |
| 14 | | Initial Cost | After-Tax, End-of-Year Cash Inflows, CF$_t$ | | | | Total |
| 15 | Year | 0 | 1 | 2 | 3 | 4 | Inflows |
| 16 | Project S | −$1,000 | $500 | $400 | $300 | $100 | $1,300 |
| 17 | Project L | −$1,000 | $100 | $300 | $400 | $675 | $1,475 |

The first positive cash flow is $500, and with a regular calculator, you could find its PV as $500/(1.10)^1 = $454.55$. You could also find the PV of the $500 with a financial calculator. Other PVs could be found similarly, and the end result would be the numbers in the left column of the diagram. When we sum those numbers, the result is $78.82, which is NPV$_S$. Note that the initial cost, the −$1,000, is not discounted because it occurs at Time 0. The NPV for Project L, $100.40, could be found similarly.

The step-by-step procedure shown in Figure 11.1 is useful for illustrating how the NPV is calculated, but in practice (and on exams), it is far more efficient to use a financial calculator or Excel. Different calculators are set up somewhat differently, but as we discussed in Chapter 5, they all have a "cash flow register" that can be used to evaluate uneven cash flows such as those for Projects S and L. Equation 11.1 is programmed into these calculators, and all you must do is enter the cash flows (with the correct signs) along with $r = I/YR = 10$. Once the data have been entered and you press the NPV key, the answer, 78.82, appears on the screen.[3]

FIGURE 11.1          Finding the NPV for Projects S and L

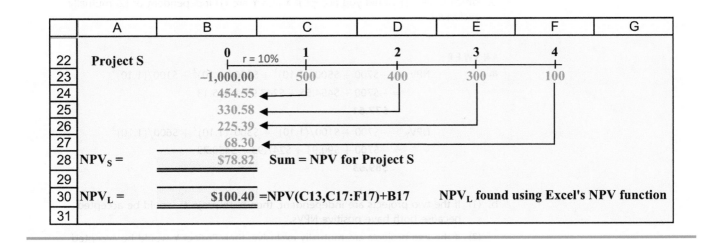

[3]The keystrokes for finding the NPV are shown for several calculators in the calculator tutorials provided on the text's website, www.cengagebrain.com.

If you are familiar with Excel, you can use Excel's NPV function to find the NPVs for S and L:[4]

$$NPV_S = \$78.82$$
$$NPV_L = \$100.40$$

The calculations used to obtain these values are provided in the chapter's Excel model, as shown in Figure 11.1. If you want to know something about Excel, you should review the model, because this is the way most people in practice find NPVs.

Before using these NPVs in the decision process, we need to know whether Projects S and L are **independent** or **mutually exclusive**. Independent projects are projects whose cash flows are not affected by one another. If Walmart was considering a new store in Boise and another in Atlanta, the projects would be independent; and if both had positive NPVs, Walmart should accept both. Mutually exclusive projects, on the other hand, are projects where if one project is accepted, the other must be rejected. A conveyor belt system to move goods in a warehouse and a fleet of forklifts used for the same purpose would be mutually exclusive—accepting one implies rejecting the other.

*Independent Projects*
Projects with cash flows that are not affected by the acceptance or non-acceptance of other projects.

*Mutually Exclusive Projects*
A set of projects where only one can be accepted.

quick question

Projects X and Y have the following cash flows:

| | End-of-Year Cash Flows | | | | |
| --- | --- | --- | --- | --- | --- |
| | **0** | **1** | **2** | **3** | **WACC = r = 10%** |
| X | −$700 | $500 | $300 | $100 | |
| Y | −$700 | $100 | $300 | $600 | |

QUESTION:

a. If a 10% cost of capital is appropriate for both projects, what are their NPVs?

b. Which project(s) would you accept if X and Y are (1) independent or (2) mutually exclusive?

ANSWER:

a.
$$NPV_X = -\$700 + \$500/(1.10)^1 + \$300/(1.10)^2 + \$100/(1.10)^3$$
$$= -\$700 + \$454.55 + \$247.93 + \$75.13$$
$$= \mathbf{\$77.61}$$

$$NPV_Y = -\$700 + \$100/(1.10)^1 + \$300/(1.10)^2 + \$600/(1.10)^3$$
$$= -\$700 + \$90.91 + \$247.93 + \$450.79$$
$$= \mathbf{\$89.63}$$

b. (1) If the two projects are independent, then both projects would be accepted because both have positive NPVs.

(2) If the two projects are mutually exclusive, then Project Y would be accepted because it has the larger positive NPV.

---

[4]Excel's NPV function has the following format: = NPV (rate, $CF_1$ to $CF_N$). Notice that the NPV function (shown in Figure 11.1) does not include the initial outlay at Time 0. Excel's NPV function assumes that the first cell reference in the cash flow range given refers to the cash flow at Time 1. Thus, the initial outlay must be subtracted from the value obtained using Excel's NPV function to calculate the project's NPV.

What should be the decision if Projects S and L are independent? In this case, both should be accepted because both have positive NPVs and thus add value to the firm. However, if they are mutually exclusive, Project L should be chosen because it has the higher positive NPV and thus adds more value than S. Here is a summary of the NPV decision rules:

- *Independent projects.* If NPV exceeds zero, accept the project.
- *Mutually exclusive projects.* Accept the project with the highest positive NPV. If no project has a positive NPV, reject them all.

Because projects must be either independent or mutually exclusive, one or the other of these rules applies to every project.

## Self Test

Why is the NPV the primary capital budgeting decision criterion?

Differentiate between independent and mutually exclusive projects.

# 11-3 Internal Rate of Return (IRR)

In Chapter 7, we discussed the yield to maturity on a bond, and we explained that if you hold it to maturity, you will earn the YTM on your investment. The YTM is found as the discount rate that forces the PV of the cash inflows to equal the price of the bond. This same concept is involved in capital budgeting when we calculate a project's **internal rate of return (IRR)**:

*A project's IRR is the discount rate that forces the PV of its inflows to equal its cost. This is equivalent to forcing the NPV to equal zero. The IRR is an estimate of the project's rate of return, and it is comparable to the YTM on a bond.*

**Internal Rate of Return (IRR)**

The discount rate that forces a project's NPV to equal zero.

To calculate the IRR, we begin with Equation 11.1 for the NPV, replace r in the denominator with the term IRR, and set the NPV equal to zero. This transforms Equation 11.1 into Equation 11.2, the one used to find the IRR. The rate that forces NPV to equal zero is the IRR:[5]

$$NPV = CF_0 + \frac{CF_1}{(1 + IRR)^1} + \frac{CF_2}{(1 + IRR)^2} + \cdots + \frac{CF_N}{(1 + IRR)^N} = 0$$

$$0 = \sum_{t=0}^{N} \frac{CF_t}{(1 + IRR)^t}$$

11.2

$$NPV_s = 0 = -\$1,000 + \frac{\$500}{(1 + IRR)^1} + \frac{\$400}{(1 + IRR)^2} + \frac{\$300}{(1 + IRR)^3} = \frac{\$100}{(1 + IRR)^4}$$

Figure 11.2 illustrates the process of finding the IRR for Project S. Three procedures can be used:

1. *Trial and error.* We could use a trial-and-error procedure—try a discount rate; see if the equation solves to zero; and if it doesn't, try a different rate. We could then continue until we found the rate that forces the NPV to zero; that rate would be the IRR. For Project S, the IRR is 14.489%. Note, though, that the trial-and-error procedure is so time-consuming that before computers and financial calculators were available, the IRR was rarely used. It's useful to

[5]For a large, complex project like Boeing's Dreamliner, costs are incurred for several years before cash inflows begin. That means that we have a number of negative cash flows before the positive cash flows start.

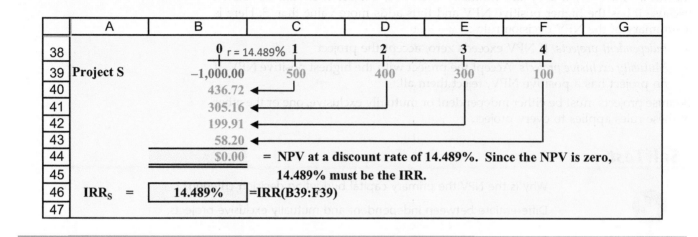

**FIGURE 11.2**     Finding the IRR for Project S

think about the trial-and-error procedure, but it's far better to use a calculator or Excel to do the actual calculations.

2. *Calculator solution.* Enter the cash flows in the calculator's cash flow register just as we did to find the NPV; then press the button labeled "IRR." Instantly, you get the IRR. Here are the values for Projects S and L:[6]

$$IRR_S = 14.489\%$$
$$IRR_L = 13.549\%$$

3. *Excel solution.* It is even easier to find IRRs using Excel's IRR function, as we demonstrate in the chapter model and illustrate in Figure 11.2.

## quick question

The cash flows for Projects X and Y are as follows:

**End-of-Year Cash Flows**

| | 0 | 1 | 2 | 3 | WACC = r = 10% |
|---|---|---|---|---|---|
| X | −$700 | $500 | $300 | $100 | |
| Y | −$700 | $100 | $300 | $600 | |

QUESTIONS:

a. What are the projects' IRRs?
b. Which project(s) would the IRR method select if the firm had a 10% cost of capital and the projects were (1) independent or (2) mutually exclusive?

---

[6]See the calculator tutorials on the text's website, www.cengagebrain.com. Note that once the cash flows have been entered in the cash flow register, you can find the NPV and the IRR. To find the NPV, enter the interest rate (I/YR) and then press the NPV key. Then with no further entries, press the IRR key to find the IRR. Thus, once you set up the calculator to find the NPV, it is easy to find the IRR. This is one reason most firms calculate both the NPV and the IRR. If you calculate one, it is easy to calculate the other; and both provide information that decision makers find useful. The same is true with Excel.

ANSWERS:

a. Using a financial calculator, you would enter each cash flow into the calculator's cash flow register and press the IRR key to find the answer.

*Project X*

Enter the data in your financial calculator as follows: $CF_0 = -700$; $CF_1 = 500$; $CF_2 = 300$; $CF_3 = 100$; ■ IRR = **18.01%**.

*Project Y*

Enter the data in your financial calculator as follows, making sure to clear your registers first: $CF_0 = -700$; $CF_1 = 100$; $CF_2 = 300$; $CF_3 = 600$; ■ IRR = **15.56%**.

b. (1) If both projects were independent, both projects would be accepted because both IRRs are greater than the firm's WACC.

(2) If both projects were mutually exclusive, using the IRR method Project X would be chosen because its IRR is greater than the IRR of Project Y, and it is greater than the firm's WACC.

Why is the discount rate that causes a project's NPV to equal zero so special? The reason is that the IRR is an estimate of the project's rate of return. If this return exceeds the cost of the funds used to finance the project, the difference will be an additional return (in a sense a "bonus") that goes to the firm's stockholders and causes the stock price to rise. Project S has an estimated return of 14.489% versus a 10% cost of capital, so it provides an additional return of 4.489% above its cost of capital. On the other hand, if the IRR is less than the cost of capital, stockholders must make up the shortfall, which will hurt the stock price.

Note again that the IRR formula, Equation 11.2, is simply the NPV formula, Equation 11.1, solved for the particular discount rate that forces the NPV to equal zero. Thus, the same basic equation is used for both methods. The only difference is that with the NPV method the discount rate is given, and we find the NPV; with the IRR method the NPV is set equal to zero, and we find the interest rate that produces this equality.

As we noted earlier, projects should be accepted or rejected depending on whether their NPVs are positive. However, the IRR is sometimes used (improperly we believe) to rank projects and make capital budgeting decisions. When this is done, here are the decision rules:

- *Independent projects.* If IRR exceeds the project's WACC, accept the project. If IRR is less than the project's WACC, reject it.

- *Mutually exclusive projects.* Accept the project with the highest IRR, provided that IRR is greater than WACC. Reject all projects if the best IRR does not exceed WACC.

The IRR is logically appealing—it is useful to know the rates of return on proposed investments. However, as we demonstrate in Section 11-7, NPV and IRR can produce conflicting conclusions when a choice is being made between mutually exclusive projects; and when conflicts occur, the NPV is generally better.

## SelfTest

In what sense is a project's IRR similar to the YTM on a bond?

## WHY NPV IS BETTER THAN IRR

Buffett University recently hosted a seminar on business methods for managers. A finance professor covered capital budgeting, explaining how to calculate the NPV and stating that it should be used to screen potential projects. In the Q&A session, Ed Wilson, the treasurer of an electronics firm, said that his firm used the IRR primarily because the CFO and the directors understood the selection of projects based on their rates of return but didn't understand the NPV. Ed had tried to explain why the NPV was better, but he simply confused everyone; so the company stuck with the IRR. Now a meeting on the firm's capital budget is approaching, and Ed asked the professor for a simple way to explain why the NPV is better.

The professor recommended the following extreme example. A firm with adequate access to capital and a 10% WACC is choosing between two equally risky, mutually exclusive projects. Project Large calls for investing $100,000 and then receiving $50,000 per year for 10 years, while Project Small calls for investing $1 and receiving $0.60 per year for 10 years. Each project's NPV and IRR are shown in the table in the top right column. The IRR says choose S, but the NPV says take L. Intuitively, it's obvious that the firm would be better off choosing the large project in spite of its lower IRR. With a cost of capital of only 10%,

| Project Large (L) | Project Small (S) |
|---|---|
| $CF_0 = -\$100,000$ | $CF_0 = -\$1.00$ |
| $CF_{1-10} = \$50,000$ | $CF_{1-10} = \$0.60$ |
| $I/YR = 10$ | $I/YR = 10$ |
| $\boxed{NPV = \$207,228.36}$ | $NPV = \$2.69$ |
| $IRR = 49.1\%$ | $\boxed{IRR = 59.4\%}$ |

a 49% rate of return on a $100,000 investment is more profitable than a 59% return on a $1 investment.

When Ed gave this example in his firm's executive meeting on the capital budget, the CFO argued that this example was extreme and unrealistic, and that no one would choose S in spite of its higher IRR. Ed agreed, but he asked the CFO where the line should be drawn between realistic and unrealistic examples. When Ed received no answer, he went on to say that (1) it's hard to draw this line and (2) the NPV is always better because it tells us how much value each project will add to the firm, and value is what the firm should maximize. The president was listening, and he declared Ed the winner. The company switched from using IRR to NPV, and Ed is now the CFO.

## 11-4 Multiple Internal Rates of Return[7]

A problem with the IRR is that under certain conditions a project may have more than one IRR. First, note that a project is said to have *normal* cash flows if it has one or more cash outflows (costs) followed by a series of cash inflows. If, however, a cash *outflow* occurs sometime after the inflows have commenced, meaning that the signs of the cash flows change *more than once*, the project is said to have *nonnormal* cash flows. Examples follow:

```
Normal :    −  +  +  +  +  +   or   −  −  −  +  +  +  +  +
Nonnormal : −  +  +  +  +  −   or   −  +  +  +  −  +  +  +
```

An example of a project with nonnormal cash flows would be a strip coal mine where the company spends money to purchase the property and prepare the site for mining, has positive inflows for several years, and then the company spends more money to return the land to its original condition. In such a case, the project might have two IRRs, that is, **multiple IRRs**.[8]

**Multiple IRRs**

The situation where a project has two or more IRRs.

---

[7]This section is relatively technical, but it can be omitted without loss of continuity.

[8]Equation 11.2 is a polynomial of degree n; so it has n different roots, or solutions. All except one of the roots is an imaginary number when investments have normal cash flows (one or more cash outflows followed by cash inflows). So in the normal case, only one value of IRR appears. However, the possibility of multiple real roots (hence multiple IRRs) arises when negative cash flows occur after the project has been placed in operation.

To illustrate multiple IRRs, suppose a firm is considering a potential strip mine (Project M) that has a cost of $1.6 million and will produce a cash flow of $10 million at the end of Year 1. Then at the end of Year 2, the firm must spend $10 million to restore the land to its original condition. Therefore, the project's expected cash flows (in millions) are as follows:

| | Year 0 | End of Year 1 | End of Year 2 |
|---|---|---|---|
| Cash flows | −$1.6 | +$10 | −$10 |

We can substitute these values into Equation 11.2 and solve for the IRR:

$$NPV = \frac{-\$1.6 \text{ million}}{(1 + IRR)^0} + \frac{\$10 \text{ million}}{(1 + IRR)^1} + \frac{-\$10 \text{ million}}{(1 + IRR)^2} = 0$$

NPV equals 0 when IRR = 25%, but it also equals 0 when IRR = 400%.[9] Therefore, Project M has an IRR of 25% and another of 400%, and we don't know which one to use. This relationship is depicted graphically in Figure 11.3.[10] The graph is constructed by plotting the project's NPV at different discount rates.

**FIGURE 11.3**      Graph for Multiple IRRs: Project M

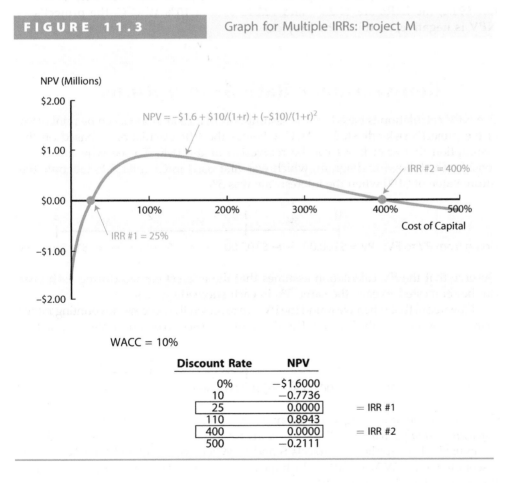

| Discount Rate | NPV | |
|---|---|---|
| 0% | −$1.6000 | |
| 10 | −0.7736 | |
| 25 | 0.0000 | = IRR #1 |
| 110 | 0.8943 | |
| 400 | 0.0000 | = IRR #2 |
| 500 | −0.2111 | |

[9]If you attempt to find Project M's IRR with an HP calculator, you will get an error message, while TI calculators give only the IRR that's closest to zero. When you encounter either situation, you can find the approximate IRRs by calculating NPVs using several different values for r = I/YR, plotting NPV on the vertical axis with the corresponding discount rate on the horizontal axis of a graph, and seeing about where NPV = 0. The intersection with the X-axis provides a rough idea of the IRRs' values. With some calculators and with Excel, you can find both IRRs by entering guesses, as explained in the calculator and Excel tutorials on the text's website, www.cengagebrain.com.

[10]Figure 11.3 is called an NPV profile. Profiles are discussed in more detail in Section 11-7.

Note that no dilemma regarding Project M would arise if the NPV method was used; we would simply find the NPV and use it to evaluate the project. We would see that if Project M's cost of capital was 10%, its NPV would be −$0.7736 million, and the project should be rejected. However, if r was between 25% and 400%, NPV would be positive, but those numbers would not be realistic or useful for anything.

## Self Test

What condition regarding cash flows would cause more than one IRR to exist?

Project MM has the following cash flows:

| | End-of-Year Cash Flows | | |
|---|---|---|---|
| 0 | 1 | 2 | 3 |
| −$1,000 | $2,000 | $2,000 | −$3,350 |

Calculate MM's NPV at discount rates of 0%, 10%, 12.2258%, 25%, 122.1470%, and 150%. What are MM's IRRs? If the cost of capital is 10%, should the project be accepted or rejected? **(NPVs range from −$350 to +$164.8 and then back down to −$94.4; the IRRs are 12.23% and 122.15%. At a 10% WACC, the project's NPV is negative, so reject the project.)**

# 11-5 Reinvestment Rate Assumptions[11]

The NPV calculation is based on the assumption that cash inflows can be reinvested at the project's risk-adjusted WACC, whereas the IRR calculation is based on the assumption that cash flows can be reinvested at the IRR. To see why this is so, consider the following diagram, which was first used in Chapter 5 to illustrate the future value of $100 when the interest rate was 5%.

|  | 0 | 5% | 1 | 5% | 2 | 5% | 3 |
|---|---|---|---|---|---|---|---|

Going from PV to FV:  PV = $100.00 ⟶ $105.00 ⟶ $110.25 ⟶ $115.76 = FV

Observe that the FV calculation assumes that the interest earned during each year can be reinvested to earn the same 5% in each succeeding year.

Now recall that when we found the PV, we reversed the process, discounting rather than compounding at the 5% rate. This diagram was used to demonstrate this point:

|  | 0 | 5% | 1 | 5% | 2 | 5% | 3 |
|---|---|---|---|---|---|---|---|

Going from FV to PV:  PV = $100.00 ◀—$105.00 ◀— $110.25 ◀— $115.76 = FV

This led to the following conclusion: *When we calculate a present value, we are implicitly assuming that cash flows can be reinvested at a specified interest rate, 5% in our example.* This applies to Projects S and L: When we calculated their NPVs, we discounted at the WACC, 10%, which means that we were assuming that their cash flows could be reinvested at 10%.

Now consider the IRR. In Section 11-3, we presented a cash flow diagram set up to show the PVs of the cash flows when discounted at the IRR. We saw that for

---

[11]This section gives a theoretical explanation of the key difference between NPV and IRR. However, it is relatively technical; so if time is a constraint, professors may decide to have students skip it and just read the box titled "Why NPV Is Better Than IRR," which appears in Section 11-3.

Project S the sum of the PVs is equal to the cost at a discount rate of 14.489%; so by definition, 14.489% is the IRR for Project S. Now we can ask this question: What reinvestment rate is built into the IRR?

*Because discounting at a given rate assumes that cash flows can be reinvested at that same rate, the IRR assumes that cash flows are reinvested at the IRR.*

The NPV assumes reinvestment at the WACC, while the IRR assumes reinvestment at the IRR. Which assumption is more reasonable? For most firms, assuming reinvestment at the WACC is more reasonable for the following reasons:

- If a firm has reasonably good access to the capital markets, it can raise all the capital it needs at the going rate, which in our example is 10%.
- Because the firm can obtain capital at 10%, if it has investment opportunities with positive NPVs, it should take them on, and it can finance them at a 10% cost.
- If the firm uses internally generated cash flows from past projects rather than external capital, this will save it the 10% cost of capital. Thus, 10% is the *opportunity cost* of the cash flows, and that is the effective return on reinvested funds.

To illustrate, suppose a project's IRR is 50%; the firm's WACC is 10%; and the firm has adequate access to the capital markets. Thus, the firm can raise the capital it needs at the 10% rate. Unless the firm is a monopoly, the 50% return would attract competition, which would make it difficult to find new projects with similar high returns, which is what the IRR assumes. Moreover, even if the firm does find such projects, it could take them on with external capital that costs 10%. The logical conclusion is that the original project's cash flows will save the 10% cost of the external capital, and that is the effective return on those flows.

If a firm does not have good access to external capital and if it has many potential projects with high IRRs, it might be reasonable to assume that a project's cash flows could be reinvested at a rate close to its IRR. However, that situation rarely exists: Firms with good investment opportunities generally *do* have good access to debt and equity markets.

Our conclusion is that the assumption built into the IRR—that cash flows can be reinvested at the IRR—is flawed, whereas the assumption built into the NPV—that cash flows can be reinvested at the WACC—is generally correct. Moreover, if the true reinvestment rate is less than the IRR, the true rate of return on the investment must be less than the calculated IRR; thus, the IRR is misleading as a measure of a project's profitability. This point is discussed further in the next section.

## Self *Test*

Why is it true that a reinvestment rate is implicitly assumed whenever we find the present value of a future cash flow? Would it be possible to find the PV of a FV without specifying an implicit reinvestment rate?

What reinvestment rate is built into the NPV calculation? The IRR calculation?

For a firm that has adequate access to capital markets, is it more reasonable to assume reinvestment at the WACC or the IRR? Explain.

# 11-6 Modified Internal Rate of Return (MIRR)[12]

It is logical for managers to want to know the expected rate of return on investments, and this is what the IRR is supposed to tell them. However, the IRR is based on the assumption that projects' cash flows can be reinvested at the IRR. *This assumption is generally incorrect, and this causes the IRR to overstate the project's*

---

[12]Again, this section is relatively technical, but it too can be omitted without loss of continuity.

*true return.*[13] Given this fundamental flaw, is there a percentage evaluator that is better than the regular IRR? The answer is yes—we can modify the IRR to make it a better measure of profitability.

**Modified IRR (MIRR)**
The discount rate at which the present value of a project's cost is equal to the present value of its terminal value, where the terminal value is found as the sum of the future values of the cash inflows, compounded at the firm's cost of capital.

This new measure, the **modified IRR (MIRR)**, is illustrated for Project S in Figure 11.4. It is similar to the regular IRR except that it is based on the assumption that cash flows are reinvested at the WACC (or some other explicit rate if that is a more reasonable assumption). Refer to Figure 11.4 as you read about its construction.

1. Project S has just one outflow, a negative $1,000 at t = 0. Because it occurs at Time 0, it is not discounted and its PV is −$1,000. If the project had additional outflows, we would find the PV at t = 0 for each one and sum them to arrive at the PV of total costs for use in the MIRR calculation.

2. Next, we find the future value of each *inflow* compounded at the WACC out to the "terminal year," which is the year the last inflow is received. We assume that cash flows are reinvested at the WACC. For Project S, the first cash flow, $500, is compounded at WACC = 10% for 3 years and it grows to $665.50. The second inflow, $400, grows to $484.00; the third inflow grows to $330.00. The last inflow is received at the end, so it is not compounded at all. The sum of the future values, $1,579.50, is called the "terminal value," or TV.

3. We now have the cost at t = 0, −$1,000, and the TV at Year 4, $1,579.50. There is some discount rate that will cause the PV of the terminal value to equal the cost. *That interest rate is defined as the MIRR.* In a calculator, enter N = 4, PV = −1000, PMT = 0, and FV = 1579.50. Then when you press the I/YR key, you get the MIRR, 12.11%.

4. The MIRR can be found in a number of ways. Figure 11.4 illustrates how the MIRR is calculated: We compound each cash inflow, sum them to determine the TV, and then find the rate that causes the PV of the TV to equal the cost. That rate is 12.11%. However, some of the better calculators have a built-in MIRR function that streamlines the process. In Excel, you can use either the RATE or MIRR function to calculate the MIRR, as shown in Figure 11.4.[14] We explain how to use the calculator function in the calculator tutorials, and we explain how to find MIRR with Excel in the chapter Excel model.[15]

---

[13]The IRR overstates the expected return for accepted projects because cash flows cannot generally be reinvested at the IRR. Therefore, the average IRR for accepted projects is greater than the true expected rate of return. This imparts an upward bias on corporate projections based on IRRs.

[14]Excel's MIRR function allows you to enter a different reinvestment rate from the WACC for the cash inflows. However, we assume reinvestment at the WACC, so the WACC is entered twice in the Excel MIRR function, shown in Figure 11.4.

[15]Equation 11.2a summarizes these steps.

$$\sum_{t=0}^{N} \frac{COF_t}{(1+r)^t} = \frac{\sum_{t=0}^{N} CIF_t(1+r)^{N-t}}{(1+MIRR)^N}$$

$$PV\ costs = \frac{TV}{(1+MIRR)^N}$$

11.2a

$COF_t$ is the cash outflow at time t, and $CIF_t$ is the cash inflow at time t. The left term is the PV of the investment outlays when discounted at the cost of capital; the numerator of the second term is the compounded value of the inflows, assuming the inflows are reinvested at the cost of capital. The MIRR is the discount rate that forces the PV of the TV to equal the PV of the costs.

Also, note that there are alternative definitions for the MIRR. One difference relates to whether negative cash flows, after the positive cash flows begin, should be compounded and treated as part of the TV or discounted and treated as a cost. A related issue is whether negative and positive flows in a given year should be netted or treated separately. For a complete discussion, see William R. McDaniel, Daniel E. McCarty, and Kenneth A. Jessell, "Discounted Cash Flow with Explicit Reinvestment Rates: Tutorial and Extension," *The Financial Review*, vol. 23, no. 3 (August 1988), pp. 369–385; and David M. Shull, "Interpreting Rates of Return: A Modified Rate of Return Approach," *Financial Practice and Education*, vol. 10 (Fall 1993), pp. 67–71.

**FIGURE 11.4**     Finding the MIRR for Project S, WACC = 10%

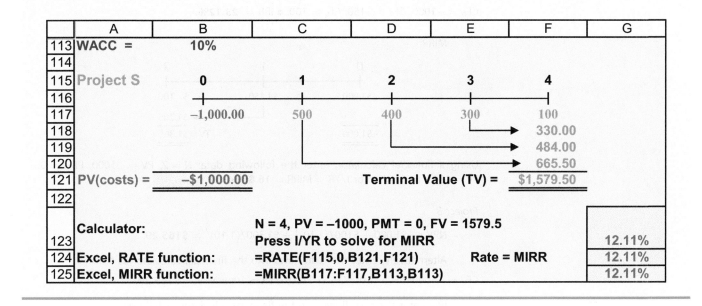

The MIRR has two significant advantages over the regular IRR. First, whereas the regular IRR assumes that the cash flows from each project are reinvested at the IRR, the MIRR assumes that cash flows are reinvested at the cost of capital (or some other explicit rate). Because reinvestment at the IRR is generally not correct, the MIRR is generally a better indicator of a project's true profitability. Second, the MIRR eliminates the multiple IRR problem—there can never be more than one MIRR, and it can be compared with the cost of capital when deciding to accept or reject projects.

## quick question

Projects A and B have the following cash flows:

**End-of-Year Cash Flows**

|  | 0 | 1 | 2 |
|---|---|---|---|
| Project A | −$1,000 | $1,150 | $100 |
| Project B | −$1,000 | $100 | $1,300 |

Their cost of capital is 10%.

QUESTIONS:

a. What are the projects' NPVs, IRRs, and MIRRs?

b. Which project would each method select if the projects were mutually exclusive?

---

ANSWER:

a. *Project A*
$$NPV: -\$1,000 + \$1,150/(1.10)^1 + \$100(1.10)^2 = \mathbf{\$128.10}$$

Alternatively, enter the cash flows into the financial calculator as follows:
$CF_0 = -1000$; $CF_1 = 1150$; $CF_2 = 100$; $I/YR = 10$; ∎ NPV = **$128.10**.

IRR: Enter the cash flows into the financial calculator as follows:

$CF_0 = -1000$; $CF_1 = 1150$; $CF_2 = 100$; ■ IRR = **23.12%**.

MIRR:

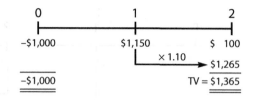

Using a financial calculator, enter the following data: N = 2; PV = −1000; PMT = 0; FV = 1365; and solve for I/YR = MIRR = **16.83%**.

*Project B*

$$NPV: -\$1,000 + \$100/(1.10)^1 + \$1,300/(1.10)^2 = \mathbf{\$165.29}.$$

Alternatively, enter the cash flows into the financial calculator as follows:

$CF_0 = -1000$; $CF_1 = 100$; $CF_2 = 1300$; I/YR = 10; ■ NPV = **$165.29**.

IRR: Enter the cash flows into the financial calculator as follows:

$CF_0 = -1000$; $CF_1 = 100$; $CF_2 = 1300$; ■ IRR = **19.13%**.

MIRR:

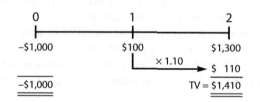

Using a financial calculator, enter the following data: N = 2; PV = −1000; PMT = 0; FV = 1410; and solve for I/YR = MIRR = **18.74%**.

b. Here's a summary of the results. The project chosen under each method is highlighted.

| | **Project A** | **Project B** |
|---|---|---|
| NPV | $128.10 | $165.29 |
| IRR | 23.12% | 19.13% |
| MIRR | 16.83% | 18.74% |

Using the NPV and MIRR criteria, you would select Project B; however, if you use the IRR criteria you would select Project A. Because Project B adds the most value to the firm, B should be chosen.

Our conclusion is that the MIRR is better than the regular IRR; however, this question remains: Is MIRR as good as the NPV? Here are our conclusions:

- For *independent* projects, the NPV, IRR, and MIRR always reach the same accept/reject conclusion, so the three criteria are equally good when evaluating independent projects.

- However, if projects are *mutually exclusive* and they differ in size, conflicts can arise. In such cases, the NPV is best because it selects the project that maximizes value.[16]
- Our overall conclusions are that (1) The MIRR is superior to the regular IRR as an indicator of a project's "true" rate of return. (2) NPV is better than IRR and MIRR when choosing among competing projects.

## Self Test

What's the primary difference between the MIRR and the regular IRR?

Which provides a better estimate of a project's "true" rate of return, the MIRR or the regular IRR? Explain.

## 11-7 NPV Profiles

Figure 11.5 presents the **net present value profile** for Project S. To make the profile, we find the project's NPV at a number of different discount rates and then plot those values to create a graph. Note that at a zero cost of capital, the NPV is simply the net total of the undiscounted cash flows, $1,300 − $1,000 = $300. This value is plotted as the vertical axis intercept. Also recall that the IRR is the discount rate that causes the NPV to equal zero, so the discount rate at which the profile line crosses the horizontal axis is the project's IRR. When we connect the data points, we have the NPV profile.[17]

**Net Present Value Profile**
A graph showing the relationship between a project's NPV and the firm's cost of capital.

Now consider Figure 11.6, which shows two NPV profiles—one for Project S and one for L—and note the following points:

- The IRRs are fixed, and S has the higher IRR regardless of the cost of capital.
- However, the NPVs vary depending on the actual cost of capital.
- The two NPV profile lines cross at a cost of capital of 11.975%, which is called the **crossover rate**. The crossover rate can be found by calculating the IRR of the differences in the projects' cash flows, as demonstrated below:

**Crossover Rate**
The cost of capital at which the NPV profiles of two projects cross and, thus, at which the projects' NPVs are equal.

|  | 0 | 1 | 2 | 3 | 4 |
|---|---|---|---|---|---|
| Project S | −$1,000 | $500 | $400 | $300 | $100 |
| −Project L | −$1,000 | $100 | $300 | $400 | $675 |
| $\Delta = CF_S − CF_L$ | $ 0 | $400 | $100 | −$100 | −$575 |

| IRR $\Delta$ = | 11.975% = Crossover rate |
|---|---|

- Project L has the higher NPV if the cost of capital is less than the crossover rate, but S has the higher NPV if the cost of capital is greater than that rate.

---

[16]See Brigham and Daves, *Intermediate Financial Management*, 12th edition (Mason, OH: Cengage Learning, 2016), Section 12-6.

[17]Notice that the NPV profile is curved—it is *not* a straight line. NPV approaches $CF_0$, which is the −$1,000 project cost, as the discount rate increases toward infinity. At an infinitely high cost of capital, all the PVs of the inflows would be zero; so NPV at r = ∞ must be $CF_0$. We should also note that under certain conditions, the NPV profiles can cross the horizontal axis several times or never cross it. This point was discussed in Section 11-4.

**FIGURE 11.5** NPV Profile for Project S

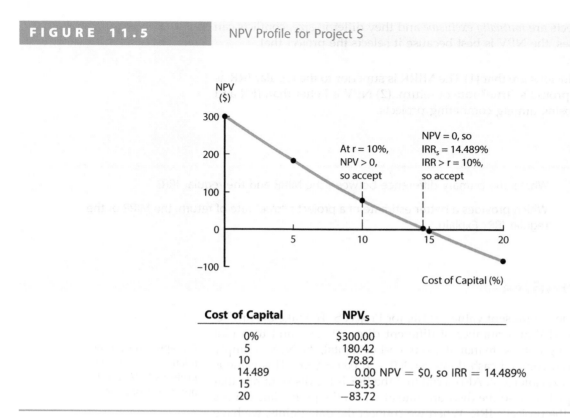

| Cost of Capital | NPV$_S$ |
|---|---|
| 0% | $300.00 |
| 5 | 180.42 |
| 10 | 78.82 |
| 14.489 | 0.00  NPV = $0, so IRR = 14.489% |
| 15 | −8.33 |
| 20 | −83.72 |

Notice that Project L has the steeper slope, indicating that a given increase in the cost of capital causes a larger decline in NPV$_L$ than in NPV$_S$. To see why this is so, recall that L's cash flows come in later than those of S. Therefore, L is a long-term project and S is a short-term project. Next, recall the equation for the NPV:

$$NPV = CF_0 + \frac{CF_1}{(1+r)^1} + \frac{CF_2}{(1+r)^2} + \cdots + \frac{CF_N}{(1+r)^N}$$

Now recognize that the impact of an increase in the cost of capital is much greater on distant than near-term cash flows, as we demonstrate here:

*Effect of doubling r on a Year 1 cash flow:*

$$\text{PV of \$100 due in 1 year @ } r = 5\%: \frac{\$100}{(1.05)^1} = \$95.24$$

$$\text{PV of \$100 due in 1 year @ } r = 10\%: \frac{\$100}{(1.10)^1} = \$90.91$$

$$\text{Percentage decline due to higher } r = \frac{\$95.24 - \$90.91}{\$95.24} = 4.5\%$$

*Effect of doubling r on a Year 20 cash flow:*

$$\text{PV of \$100 due in 20 years @ } r = 5\%: \frac{\$100}{(1.05)^{20}} = \$37.69$$

$$\text{PV of \$100 due in 20 years @ } r = 10\%: \frac{\$100}{(1.10)^{20}} = \$14.86$$

$$\text{Percentage decline due to higher } r = \frac{\$37.69 - \$14.86}{\$37.69} = 60.6\%$$

**FIGURE 11.6**   NPV Profiles for Projects S and L

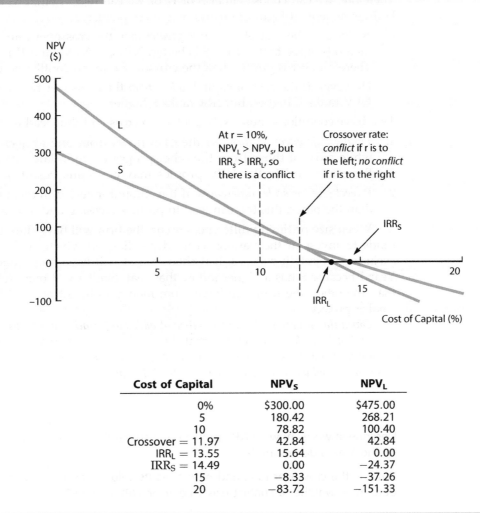

| Cost of Capital | NPV$_S$ | NPV$_L$ |
|---|---|---|
| 0% | $300.00 | $475.00 |
| 5 | 180.42 | 268.21 |
| 10 | 78.82 | 100.40 |
| Crossover = 11.97 | 42.84 | 42.84 |
| IRR$_L$ = 13.55 | 15.64 | 0.00 |
| IRR$_S$ = 14.49 | 0.00 | −24.37 |
| 15 | −8.33 | −37.26 |
| 20 | −83.72 | −151.33 |

Thus, a doubling of the discount rate results in only a 4.5% decline in the PV of a Year 1 cash flow, but the same discount rate increase causes the PV of a Year 20 cash flow to fall by more than 60%. *Therefore, if a project has most of its cash flows coming in the later years, its NPV will decline sharply if the cost of capital increases; but a project whose cash flows come earlier will not be severely penalized by high capital costs.* Most of Project L's cash flows come in its later years; so if the cost of capital is high, L is hurt much worse than Project S. Therefore, Project L's NPV profile has the steeper slope.

Sometimes the NPV and IRR methods produce conflicting results. We can use NPV profiles to see when conflicts can and cannot arise. If an independent project with normal cash flows is being evaluated, the NPV and IRR criteria always lead to the same accept/reject decision: If NPV says accept, IRR also says accept, and vice versa. To see why this is so, look at Figure 11.5 and notice that (1) The IRR says accept if the project's cost of capital is less than (or to the left of) the IRR. (2) If the cost of capital is less than the IRR, the NPV will be positive. Thus, at any cost of capital less than 14.489%, Project S will be recommended by both the NPV and IRR criteria; but both methods reject the project if the cost of capital is greater than 14.489%. A similar graph could be used for Project L or any other normal project, and we would always reach the same conclusion: *For normal, independent projects, if the IRR says accept, so will the NPV.*

Assume that Projects S and L are mutually exclusive rather than independent. Therefore, we can choose either S or L, or we can reject both; but we can't accept both. Now look at Figure 11.6 and note these points:

- As long as the cost of capital is *greater than* the crossover rate, 11.975%, both methods agree that Project S is better: $NPV_S > NPV_L$ and $IRR_S > IRR_L$. Therefore, if r is *greater* than the crossover rate, no conflict occurs.

- However, if the cost of capital is *less than* the crossover rate, a conflict arises: NPV ranks L higher, but IRR ranks S higher.

Two basic conditions cause NPV profiles to cross and thus lead to conflicts:[18]

1. *Timing differences.* If most of the cash flows from one project come in early while most of those from the other project come in later, as occurred with Projects S and L, the NPV profiles may cross and result in a conflict.

2. *Project size (or scale) differences.* If the amount invested in one project is larger than the other, this too can lead to profiles crossing and a resulting conflict.

When size or timing differences occur, the firm will have different amounts of funds to invest in the various years depending on which of the two mutually exclusive projects it chooses. If it chooses S, it will have more funds to invest in Year 1 because S has a higher inflow that year. Similarly, if one project costs more than the other, the firm will have more money to invest at $t = 0$ if it selects the smaller project.

*Given this situation, the rate of return at which differential cash flows can be reinvested is a critical issue.* We saw earlier that the NPV assumes reinvestment at the cost of capital and that this is generally the best assumption. Therefore, *when conflicts exist between mutually exclusive projects, use the NPV method.*

## SelfTest

Describe in words how an NPV profile is constructed. How are the intercepts of the X- and Y-axes determined?

What is the crossover rate, and how does its value relative to the cost of capital determine whether a conflict exists between NPV and IRR?

What two characteristics can lead to conflicts between the NPV and the IRR when evaluating mutually exclusive projects?

# 11-8 Payback Period

**Payback Period**
The length of time required for an investment's cash flows to cover its cost.

NPV is the most commonly used method for capital budgeting today; but historically, the first selection criterion used was the **payback period**, defined as the number of years required to recover the funds invested in a project from its cash flows. Equation 11.3 is used for the calculation, and the process is diagrammed in Figure 11.7. We start with the project's cost, a negative value, and then add the cash inflow for each year until the cumulative cash flow turns positive. The payback year is the year prior to full recovery plus a fraction equal to the shortfall at the end of that year divided by the cash flow during the full recovery year:[19]

---

[18]Of course, mutually exclusive projects can differ with respect to both scale and timing. Also, if mutually exclusive projects have different lives (as opposed to different cash flow patterns over a common life), this introduces further complications; and for meaningful comparisons, some mutually exclusive projects must be evaluated over a common life. This point is discussed later in Web Appendix 12E on the text's website, www.cengagebrain.com.

[19]Equation 11.3 assumes that cash flows come in uniformly during the full recovery year.

**FIGURE 11.7**   Payback Calculations

| Project S | Years | 0 | 1 | 2 | 3 | 4 |
|---|---|---|---|---|---|---|
| | Cash flow | −1,000 | 500 | 400 | 300 | 100 |
| | Cumulative cash flow | −1,000 | −500 | −100 | 200 | 300 |

Payback S = 2 + 100/300 =   2.33

| Project L | Years | 0 | 1 | 2 | 3 | 4 |
|---|---|---|---|---|---|---|
| | Cash flow | −1,000 | 100 | 300 | 400 | 675 |
| | Cumulative cash flow | −1,000 | −900 | −600 | −200 | 475 |

Payback L = 3 + 200/675 =   3.30

$$\text{Payback} = \frac{\text{Number of}}{\text{years prior to}} + \frac{\text{Unrecovered cost at start of year}}{\text{Cash flow during full recovery year}} \qquad \blacktriangledown \ \ 11.3$$

The shorter the payback, the better the project. Therefore, if the firm requires a payback of three years or less, S would be accepted, but L would be rejected. If the projects were mutually exclusive, S would be ranked over L because of its shorter payback.

The payback has three flaws: (1) All dollars received in different years are given the same weight (i.e., the time value of money is ignored). (2) Cash flows beyond the payback year are given no consideration regardless of how large they might be. (3) Unlike the NPV, which tells us how much wealth a project adds, and the IRR, which tells us how much a project yields over the cost of capital, the payback merely tells us when we will recover our investment. There is no necessary relationship between a given payback and investor wealth maximization, so we do not know what an acceptable payback is. The firm might use two years, three years, or any other number as the minimum acceptable payback; but the choice is arbitrary.

To counter the first criticism, analysts developed the **discounted payback**. Here cash flows are discounted at the WACC; then those discounted cash flows are used to find the payback. In Figure 11.8, we calculate the discounted paybacks for S and L assuming that both have a 10% cost of capital. Each inflow is divided by $(1 + r)^t = (1.10)^t$, where t is the year in which the cash flow occurs and r is the project's cost of capital; and those PVs are used to find the payback. Project S's discounted payback is 2.95, while L's is 3.78.

Note that the payback is a "break-even" calculation in the sense that if cash flows come in at the expected rate, the project will break even. However, because the regular payback doesn't consider the cost of capital, it doesn't specify the true break-even year. The discounted payback does consider capital costs, but it still disregards cash flows beyond the payback year, which is a serious flaw. Further, if mutually exclusive projects vary in size, both payback methods can conflict with the NPV, which might lead to a poor choice. Finally, there is no way of telling how low the paybacks must be to justify project acceptance.

Although the payback methods have faults as ranking criteria, they do provide information about *liquidity* and *risk*. The shorter the payback, other things held constant, the greater the project's liquidity. This factor is often important for smaller

**Discounted Payback**
The length of time required for an investment's cash flows, discounted at the investment's cost of capital, to cover its cost.

**FIGURE 11.8**      Discounted Payback Calculations at 10% Cost of Capital

| Project S | Years | 0 | 1 | 2 | 3 | 4 |
|---|---|---|---|---|---|---|
| Cash flow | | −1,000 | 500 | 400 | 300 | 100 |
| Discounted cash flow | | −1,000 | 455 | 331 | 225 | 68 |
| Cumulative discounted CF | | −1,000 | −545 | −215 | 11 | 79 |

Discounted payback S = 2 + 215/225 =     2.95

| Project L | Years | 0 | 1 | 2 | 3 | 4 |
|---|---|---|---|---|---|---|
| Cash flow | | −1,000 | 100 | 300 | 400 | 675 |
| Discounted cash flow | | −1,000 | 91 | 248 | 301 | 461 |
| Cumulative discounted CF | | −1,000 | −909 | −661 | −361 | 100 |

Discounted payback L = 3 + 361/461 =     3.78

firms that don't have ready access to the capital markets. Also, cash flows expected in the distant future are generally riskier than near-term cash flows, so the payback is used as one *risk indicator*.

### SelfTest

What information does the payback convey that is absent from the other capital budgeting decision methods?

What three flaws does the regular payback have? Does the discounted payback correct all of these flaws? Explain.

Project P has a cost of $1,000 and cash flows of $300 per year for 3 years plus another $1,000 in Year 4. The project's cost of capital is 15%. What are Project P's regular and discounted paybacks? **(3.10, 3.55)** If the company requires a payback of 3 years or less, would the project be accepted? Would this be a good accept/reject decision considering the NPV and/or the IRR? **(NPV = $256.72, IRR = 24.78%)**

## 11-9 Conclusions on Capital Budgeting Methods

We have discussed five capital budgeting decision criteria—NPV, IRR, MIRR, payback, and discounted payback. We compared these methods with one another and highlighted their strengths and weaknesses. In the process, we may have created the impression that "sophisticated" firms should use only one method, the NPV. However, virtually all capital budgeting decisions are analyzed by computer, so it is easy to calculate all five decision criteria. In making the accept/reject decision, large, sophisticated firms such as Boeing and Airbus generally calculate and consider all five measures because each provides a somewhat different piece of information about the decision.

NPV is the single best criterion because it provides a direct measure of value the project adds to shareholder wealth. IRR and MIRR measure profitability expressed as a percentage rate of return, which is useful to decision makers. Further, IRR and MIRR contain information concerning a project's "safety margin." To illustrate, consider a firm whose WACC is 10% that must choose between these two mutually exclusive projects: SS (for small), which costs $10,000 and is expected to return $16,500 at the end of one year, and LL (for large), which costs $100,000 and has an expected payoff of $115,550 after one year. SS has a huge IRR, 65%, while LL's IRR is a more modest 15.6%. The NPV paints a somewhat different picture—at the 10% cost of capital, SS's NPV is $5,000 while LL's is $5,045. By the NPV rule, we would choose LL. However, SS's IRR indicates that it has a much larger margin for error: Even if its cash flow was 39% below the $16,500 forecast, the firm would still recover its $10,000 investment. On the other hand, if LL's inflows fell by only 13.5% from its forecasted $115,550, the firm would not recover its investment. Further, if neither project generated any cash flows, the firm would lose only $10,000 on SS but $100,000 if it accepted LL.

The modified IRR has all the virtues of the IRR, but it incorporates a better reinvestment rate assumption and avoids the multiple rate of return problem. So if decision makers want to know projects' rates of return, the MIRR is a better indicator than the regular IRR.

Payback and discounted payback provide indications of a project's *liquidity* and *risk*. A long payback means that investment dollars will be locked up for a long time; hence, the project is relatively illiquid. In addition, a long payback means that cash flows must be forecasted far out into the future, and that probably makes the project riskier than one with a shorter payback. A good analogy for this is bond valuation. An investor should never compare the yields to maturity on two bonds without also considering their terms to maturity because a bond's risk is significantly influenced by the number of years remaining until its maturity. The same holds true for capital projects.

In summary, the different measures provide different types of information. Because it is easy to calculate all of them, all should be considered when capital budgeting decisions are being made. For most decisions, the greatest weight should be given to the NPV, but it would be foolish to ignore the information provided by the other criteria.

## SelfTest

Describe the advantages and disadvantages of the five capital budgeting methods discussed in this chapter.

Should capital budgeting decisions be made solely on the basis of a project's NPV? Explain.

# 11-10 Decision Criteria Used in Practice

Surveys designed to find out which of the criteria managers actually use have been taken over the years. Surveys prior to 1999 asked companies to indicate which method they gave the most weight, while the most recent survey, in 1999, asked what method(s) managers actually calculated and used. A summary of all these surveys is shown in Table 11.2, and it reveals some interesting trends.

First, the NPV criterion was not used significantly before 1980; but by 1999, it was close to the top in usage. Moreover, informal discussions with companies suggest that if a survey were to be taken in 2015, NPV would be at the top of this list. Second, the IRR method is widely used, but its recent growth is less dramatic than that of NPV. Third, payback was the most important criterion years ago, but its use as the primary criterion had fallen drastically by 1980. Companies still use payback because it is easy to calculate and it does provide some information, but it

**TABLE 11.2**  Capital Budgeting Methods Used in Practice

|  | Primary Criterion | | | Calculate and Use |
|---|---|---|---|---|
|  | **1960** | **1970** | **1980** | **1999** |
| NPV | 0% | 0% | 15% | 75% |
| IRR | 20 | 60 | 65 | 76 |
| Payback | 35 | 15 | 5 | 57 |
| Discounted Payback | NA | NA | NA | 29 |
| Other | 45 | 25 | 15 | NA |
| Totals | 100% | 100% | 100% |  |

Sources: The 1999 data are from John R. Graham and Campbell R. Harvey, "The Theory and Practice of Corporate Finance: Evidence from the Field," *Journal of Financial Economics*, vol. 60, nos. 2 and 3 (2001), pp. 187–244. Data from prior years are our estimates based on averaging data from these studies: J. S. Moore and A. K. Reichert, "An Analysis of the Financial Management Techniques Currently Employed by Large U.S. Corporations," *Journal of Business Finance and Accounting*, vol. 10, no. 4 (Winter 1983), pp. 623–645; and M. T. Stanley and S. R. Block, "A Survey of Multinational Capital Budgeting," *The Financial Review*, vol. 19, no. 1 (March 1984), pp. 36–51.

is rarely used today as the primary criterion. Fourth, "other methods," primarily the accounting rate of return and the profitability index, have been fading due to the increased use of IRR and especially NPV.

These trends are consistent with our evaluation of the various methods. NPV is the best single criterion, but all of the methods provide useful information and all are easy to calculate; thus, all are used, along with judgment and common sense. We will have more to say about all this in the next chapter.

## Self*Test*

What trends in capital budgeting methodology can be seen from Table 11.2?

# TYING IT ALL TOGETHER

In this chapter, we described five techniques—NPV, IRR, MIRR, payback, and discounted payback—that are used to evaluate proposed capital budgeting projects. NPV is the best single measure as it tells us how much value each project contributes to shareholder wealth. Therefore, NPV is the method that should be given the greatest weight in capital budgeting decisions. However, the other approaches provide useful information; and in this age of computers, it is easy to calculate all of them. Therefore, managers generally look at all five criteria when deciding to accept or reject projects and when choosing among mutually exclusive projects.

In this chapter, we took the cash flows given and used them to illustrate the different capital budgeting methods. As you will see in the next chapter, estimating cash flows is a major task. Still, the framework established in this chapter is critically important for sound capital budgeting analyses; and at this point, you should:

- Understand capital budgeting.
- Know how to calculate and use the major capital budgeting decision criteria, which are NPV, IRR, MIRR, and payback.

- Understand why NPV is the best criterion and how it overcomes problems inherent in the other methods.
- Recognize that while NPV is the best method, the other methods do provide information that decision makers find useful.

## Self-Test Questions and Problems

(Solutions Appear in Appendix A)

**ST-1 KEY TERMS** Define the following terms:

a. Capital budgeting; strategic business plan
b. Net present value (NPV)
c. Internal rate of return (IRR)
d. NPV profile; crossover rate
e. Mutually exclusive projects; independent projects
f. Nonnormal cash flows; normal cash flows; multiple IRRs
g. Modified internal rate of return (MIRR)
h. Payback period; discounted payback

**ST-2 CAPITAL BUDGETING CRITERIA** You must analyze two projects, X and Y. Each project costs $10,000, and the firm's WACC is 12%. The expected cash flows are as follows:

| | 0 | 1 | 2 | 3 | 4 |
|---|---|---|---|---|---|
| Project X | −$10,000 | $6,500 | $3,000 | $3,000 | $1,000 |
| Project Y | −$10,000 | $3,500 | $3,500 | $3,500 | $3,500 |

a. Calculate each project's NPV, IRR, MIRR, payback, and discounted payback.
b. Which project(s) should be accepted if they are independent?
c. Which project(s) should be accepted if they are mutually exclusive?
d. How might a change in the WACC produce a conflict between the NPV and IRR rankings of the two projects? Would there be a conflict if WACC were 5%? (Hint: Plot the NPV profiles. The crossover rate is 6.21875%.)
e. Why does the conflict exist?

## Questions

**11-1** How are project classifications used in the capital budgeting process?

**11-2** What are three potential flaws with the regular payback method? Does the discounted payback method correct all three flaws? Explain.

**11-3** Why is the NPV of a relatively long-term project (one for which a high percentage of its cash flows occurs in the distant future) more sensitive to changes in the WACC than that of a short-term project?

**11-4** What is a mutually exclusive project? How should managers rank mutually exclusive projects?

**11-5** If two mutually exclusive projects were being compared, would a high cost of capital favor the longer-term or the shorter-term project? Why? If the cost of capital declined, would that lead firms to invest more in longer-term projects or shorter-term projects? Would a decline (or an increase) in the WACC cause changes in the IRR ranking of mutually exclusive projects? Explain.

11-6    Discuss the following statement: If a firm has only independent projects, a constant WACC, and projects with normal cash flows, the NPV and IRR methods will always lead to identical capital budgeting decisions. What does this imply about the choice between IRR and NPV? If each of the assumptions were changed (one by one), how would your answer change?

11-7    Why might it be rational for a small firm that does not have access to the capital markets to use the payback method rather than the NPV method?

11-8    Project X is very risky and has an NPV of $3 million. Project Y is very safe and has an NPV of $2.5 million. They are mutually exclusive, and project risk has been properly considered in the NPV analyses. Which project should be chosen? Explain.

11-9    What reinvestment rate assumptions are built into the NPV, IRR, and MIRR methods? Give an explanation for your answer.

11-10   A firm has a $100 million capital budget. It is considering two projects, each costing $100 million. Project A has an IRR of 20% and an NPV of $9 million; it will be terminated after 1 year at a profit of $20 million, resulting in an immediate increase in EPS. Project B, which cannot be postponed, has an IRR of 30% and an NPV of $50 million. However, the firm's short-run EPS will be reduced if it accepts Project B because no revenues will be generated for several years.

   a.   Should the short-run effects on EPS influence the choice between the two projects?
   b.   How might situations like this influence a firm's decision to use payback?

## Problems

**Easy Problems 1–6**

11-1    **NPV**   Project L costs $65,000, its expected cash inflows are $12,000 per year for 9 years, and its WACC is 9%. What is the project's NPV?

11-2    **IRR**   Refer to problem 11-1. What is the project's IRR?

11-3    **MIRR**   Refer to problem 11-1. What is the project's MIRR?

11-4    **PAYBACK PERIOD**   Refer to problem 11-1. What is the project's payback?

11-5    **DISCOUNTED PAYBACK**   Refer to problem 11-1. What is the project's discounted payback?

11-6    **NPV**   Your division is considering two projects with the following cash flows (in millions):

| | 0 | 1 | 2 | 3 |
|---|---|---|---|---|
| Project A | −$25 | $5 | $10 | $17 |
| Project B | −$20 | $10 | $9 | $6 |

   a.   What are the projects' NPVs assuming the WACC is 5%? 10%? 15%?
   b.   What are the projects' IRRs at each of these WACCs?
   c.   If the WACC was 5% and A and B were mutually exclusive, which project would you choose? What if the WACC was 10%? 15%? (Hint: The crossover rate is 7.81%.)

**Intermediate Problems 7–13**

11-7    **CAPITAL BUDGETING CRITERIA**   A firm with a 14% WACC is evaluating two projects for this year's capital budget. After-tax cash flows, including depreciation, are as follows:

| | 0 | 1 | 2 | 3 | 4 | 5 |
|---|---|---|---|---|---|---|
| Project M | −$30,000 | $10,000 | $10,000 | $10,000 | $10,000 | $10,000 |
| Project N | −$90,000 | $28,000 | $28,000 | $28,000 | $28,000 | $28,000 |

   a.   Calculate NPV, IRR, MIRR, payback, and discounted payback for each project.
   b.   Assuming the projects are independent, which one(s) would you recommend?

    c. If the projects are mutually exclusive, which would you recommend?

    d. Notice that the projects have the same cash flow timing pattern. Why is there a conflict between NPV and IRR?

**11-8** **CAPITAL BUDGETING CRITERIA: ETHICAL CONSIDERATIONS** A mining company is considering a new project. Because the mine has received a permit, the project would be legal; but it would cause significant harm to a nearby river. The firm could spend an additional $10 million at Year 0 to mitigate the environmental problem, but it would not be required to do so. Developing the mine (without mitigation) would cost $60 million, and the expected cash inflows would be $20 million per year for 5 years. If the firm does invest in mitigation, the annual inflows would be $21 million. The risk-adjusted WACC is 12%.

    a. Calculate the NPV and IRR with and without mitigation.

    b. How should the environmental effects be dealt with when this project is evaluated?

    c. Should this project be undertaken? If so, should the firm do the mitigation?

**11-9** **CAPITAL BUDGETING CRITERIA: ETHICAL CONSIDERATIONS** An electric utility is considering a new power plant in northern Arizona. Power from the plant would be sold in the Phoenix area, where it is badly needed. Because the firm has received a permit, the plant would be legal; but it would cause some air pollution. The company could spend an additional $40 million at Year 0 to mitigate the environmental problem, but it would not be required to do so. The plant without mitigation would cost $240 million, and the expected cash inflows would be $80 million per year for 5 years. If the firm does invest in mitigation, the annual inflows would be $84 million. Unemployment in the area where the plant would be built is high, and the plant would provide about 350 good jobs. The risk-adjusted WACC is 17%.

    a. Calculate the NPV and IRR with and without mitigation.

    b. How should the environmental effects be dealt with when evaluating this project?

    c. Should this project be undertaken? If so, should the firm do the mitigation? Why or why not?

**11-10** **CAPITAL BUDGETING CRITERIA: MUTUALLY EXCLUSIVE PROJECTS** A firm with a WACC of 10% is considering the following mutually exclusive projects:

| | 0 | 1 | 2 | 3 | 4 | 5 |
|---|---|---|---|---|---|---|
| Project 1 | −$200 | $75 | $75 | $75 | $190 | $190 |
| Project 2 | −$650 | $250 | $250 | $125 | $125 | $125 |

Which project would you recommend? Explain.

**11-11** **CAPITAL BUDGETING CRITERIA: MUTUALLY EXCLUSIVE PROJECTS** Project S costs $17,000, and its expected cash flows would be $5,000 per year for 5 years. Mutually exclusive Project L costs $30,000, and its expected cash flows would be $8,750 per year for 5 years. If both projects have a WACC of 12%, which project would you recommend? Explain.

**11-12** **IRR AND NPV** A company is analyzing two mutually exclusive projects, S and L, with the following cash flows:

| | 0 | 1 | 2 | 3 | 4 |
|---|---|---|---|---|---|
| Project S | −$1,000 | $870 | $250 | $25 | $25 |
| Project L | −$1,000 | $0 | $250 | $400 | $845 |

The company's WACC is 8.5%. What is the IRR of the *better* project? (Hint: The better project may or may not be the one with the higher IRR.)

**11-13**    **MIRR**   A firm is considering two mutually exclusive projects, X and Y, with the following cash flows:

| | 0 | 1 | 2 | 3 | 4 |
|---|---|---|---|---|---|
| Project X | −$1,000 | $110 | $300 | $430 | $700 |
| Project Y | −$1,000 | $1,100 | $90 | $55 | $50 |

The projects are equally risky, and their WACC is 11%. What is the MIRR of the project that maximizes shareholder value?

**Challenging Problems 14–22**

**11-14**    **CHOOSING MANDATORY PROJECTS ON THE BASIS OF LEAST COST**   Kim Inc. must install a new air conditioning unit in its main plant. Kim must install one or the other of the units; otherwise, the highly profitable plant would have to shut down. Two units are available, HCC and LCC (for high and low capital costs, respectively). HCC has a high capital cost but relatively low operating costs, while LCC has a low capital cost but higher operating costs because it uses more electricity. The costs of the units are shown here. Kim's WACC is 7%.

| | 0 | 1 | 2 | 3 | 4 | 5 |
|---|---|---|---|---|---|---|
| HCC | −$600,000 | −$50,000 | −$50,000 | −$50,000 | −$50,000 | −$50,000 |
| LCC | −$100,000 | −$175,000 | −$175,000 | −$175,000 | −$175,000 | −$175,000 |

a. Which unit would you recommend? Explain.
b. If Kim's controller wanted to know the IRRs of the two projects, what would you tell him?
c. If the WACC rose to 15% would this affect your recommendation? Explain your answer and the reason this result occurred.

**11-15**    **NPV PROFILES: TIMING DIFFERENCES**   An oil-drilling company must choose between two mutually exclusive extraction projects, and each costs $12 million. Under Plan A, all the oil would be extracted in 1 year, producing a cash flow at t = 1 of $14.4 million. Under Plan B, cash flows would be $2.1 million per year for 20 years. The firm's WACC is 12%.

a. Construct NPV profiles for Plans A and B, identify each project's IRR, and show the approximate crossover rate.
b. Is it logical to assume that the firm would take on all available independent, average-risk projects with returns greater than 12%? If all available projects with returns greater than 12% have been undertaken, does this mean that cash flows from past investments have an opportunity cost of only 12% because all the company can do with these cash flows is to replace money that has a cost of 12%? Does this imply that the WACC is the correct reinvestment rate assumption for a project's cash flows? Why or why not?

**11-16**    **NPV PROFILES: SCALE DIFFERENCES**   A company is considering two mutually exclusive expansion plans. Plan A requires a $40 million expenditure on a large-scale integrated plant that would provide expected cash flows of $6.4 million per year for 20 years. Plan B requires a $12 million expenditure to build a somewhat less efficient, more labor-intensive plant with expected cash flows of $2.72 million per year for 20 years. The firm's WACC is 10%.

a. Calculate each project's NPV and IRR.
b. Graph the NPV profiles for Plan A and Plan B and approximate the crossover rate.
c. Calculate the crossover rate where the two projects' NPVs are equal.
d. Why is NPV better than IRR for making capital budgeting decisions that add to shareholder value?

**11-17**    **CAPITAL BUDGETING CRITERIA**   A company has an 11% WACC and is considering two mutually exclusive investments (that cannot be repeated) with the following cash flows:

| | 0 | 1 | 2 | 3 | 4 | 5 | 6 | 7 |
|---|---|---|---|---|---|---|---|---|
| Project A | −$300 | −$387 | −$193 | −$100 | $600 | $600 | $850 | −$180 |
| Project B | −$405 | $134 | $134 | $134 | $134 | $134 | $134 | $0 |

a. What is each project's NPV?

b. What is each project's IRR?

c. What is each project's MIRR? (Hint: Consider Period 7 as the end of Project B's life.)

d. From your answers to parts a, b, and c, which project would be selected? If the WACC was 18%, which project would be selected?

e. Construct NPV profiles for Projects A and B.

f. Calculate the crossover rate where the two projects' NPVs are equal.

g. What is each project's MIRR at a WACC of 18%?

11-18 **NPV AND IRR** A store has 5 years remaining on its lease in a mall. Rent is $2,000 per month, 60 payments remain, and the next payment is due in 1 month. The mall's owner plans to sell the property in a year and wants rent at that time to be high so that the property will appear more valuable. Therefore, the store has been offered a "great deal" (owner's words) on a new 5-year lease. The new lease calls for no rent for 9 months, then payments of $2,600 per month for the next 51 months. The lease cannot be broken, and the store's WACC is 12% (or 1% per month).

a. Should the new lease be accepted? (Hint: Make sure you use 1% per month.)

b. If the store owner decided to bargain with the mall's owner over the new lease payment, what new lease payment would make the store owner indifferent between the new and old leases? (Hint: Find FV of the old lease's original cost at t = 9; then treat this as the PV of a 51-period annuity whose payments represent the rent during months 10 to 60.)

c. The store owner is not sure of the 12% WACC—it could be higher or lower. At what *nominal* WACC would the store owner be indifferent between the two leases? (Hint: Calculate the differences between the two payment streams; then find its IRR.)

11-19 **MULTIPLE IRRS AND MIRR** A mining company is deciding whether to open a strip mine, which costs $2 million. Cash inflows of $13 million would occur at the end of Year 1. The land must be returned to its natural state at a cost of $12 million, payable at the end of Year 2.

a. Plot the project's NPV profile.

b. Should the project be accepted if WACC = 10%? if WACC = 20%? Explain your reasoning.

c. Think of some other capital budgeting situations in which negative cash flows during or at the end of the project's life might lead to multiple IRRs.

d. What is the project's MIRR at WACC = 10%? At WACC = 20%? Does MIRR lead to the same accept/reject decision for this project as the NPV method? Does the MIRR method *always* lead to the same accept/reject decision as NPV? (Hint: Consider mutually exclusive projects that differ in size.)

11-20 **NPV** A project has annual cash flows of $5,000 for the next 10 years and then $9,000 each year for the following 10 years. The IRR of this 20-year project is 8.52%. If the firm's WACC is 8%, what is the project's NPV?

11-21 **MIRR** Project A costs $1,000, and its cash flows are the same in Years 1 through 10. Its IRR is 16%, and its WACC is 8%. What is the project's MIRR?

11-22 **MIRR** A project has the following cash flows:

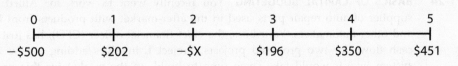

This project requires two outflows at Years 0 and 2, but the remaining cash flows are positive. Its WACC is 10%, and its MIRR is 14.14%. What is the Year 2 cash outflow?

## Comprehensive/Spreadsheet Problem

**11-23** **CAPITAL BUDGETING CRITERIA** Your division is considering two projects. Its WACC is 10%, and the projects' after-tax cash flows (in millions of dollars) would be as follows:

| | 0 | 1 | 2 | 3 | 4 |
|---|---|---|---|---|---|
| Project A | −$30 | $5 | $10 | $15 | $20 |
| Project B | −$30 | $20 | $10 | $8 | $6 |

a. Calculate the projects' NPVs, IRRs, MIRRs, regular paybacks, and discounted paybacks.

b. If the two projects are independent, which project(s) should be chosen?

c. If the two projects are mutually exclusive and the WACC is 10%, which project(s) should be chosen?

d. Plot NPV profiles for the two projects. Identify the projects' IRRs on the graph.

e. If the WACC was 5%, would this change your recommendation if the projects were mutually exclusive? If the WACC was 15%, would this change your recommendation? Explain your answers.

f. The crossover rate is 13.5252%. Explain what this rate is and how it affects the choice between mutually exclusive projects.

g. Is it possible for conflicts to exist between the NPV and the IRR when *independent* projects are being evaluated? Explain your answer.

h. Now look at the regular and discounted paybacks. Which project looks better when judged by the paybacks?

i. If the payback was the only method a firm used to accept or reject projects, what payback should it choose as the cutoff point, that is, reject projects if their paybacks are not below the chosen cutoff? Is your selected cutoff based on some economic criteria, or is it more or less arbitrary? Are the cutoff criteria equally arbitrary when firms use the NPV and/or the IRR as the criteria? Explain.

j. Define the MIRR. What's the difference between the IRR and the MIRR, and which generally gives a better idea of the rate of return on the investment in a project? Explain.

k. Why do most academics and financial executives regard the NPV as being the single best criterion and better than the IRR? Why do companies still calculate IRRs?

# INTEGRATED CASE

## ALLIED COMPONENTS COMPANY

**11-24** **BASICS OF CAPITAL BUDGETING** You recently went to work for Allied Components Company, a supplier of auto repair parts used in the after-market with products from Daimler AG, Ford, Toyota, and other automakers. Your boss, the chief financial officer (CFO), has just handed you the estimated cash flows for two proposed projects. Project L involves adding a new item to the firm's ignition system line; it would take some time to build up the market for this product, so the cash inflows would increase over time. Project S involves an add-on to an existing line, and its cash flows would decrease over time. Both projects have 3-year lives because Allied is planning to introduce entirely new models after 3 years.

Here are the projects' after-tax cash flows (in thousands of dollars):

| | 0 | 1 | 2 | 3 |
|---|---|---|---|---|
| Project L | −$100 | $10 | $60 | $80 |
| Project S | −$100 | $70 | $50 | $20 |

Depreciation, salvage values, net operating working capital requirements, and tax effects are all included in these cash flows. The CFO also made subjective risk assessments of each project, and he concluded that both projects have risk characteristics that are similar to the firm's average project. Allied's WACC is 10%. You must determine whether one or both of the projects should be accepted.

a. What is capital budgeting? Are there any similarities between a firm's capital budgeting decisions and an individual's investment decisions?

b. What is the difference between independent and mutually exclusive projects? Between projects with normal and nonnormal cash flows?

c. 1. Define the term *net present value (NPV)*. What is each project's NPV?

   2. What is the rationale behind the NPV method? According to NPV, which project(s) should be accepted if they are independent? Mutually exclusive?

   3. Would the NPVs change if the WACC changed? Explain.

d. 1. Define the term *internal rate of return (IRR)*. What is each project's IRR?

   2. How is the IRR on a project related to the YTM on a bond?

   3. What is the logic behind the IRR method? According to IRR, which project(s) should be accepted if they are independent? Mutually exclusive?

   4. Would the projects' IRRs change if the WACC changed?

e. 1. Draw NPV profiles for Projects L and S. At what discount rate do the profiles cross?

   2. Look at your NPV profile graph without referring to the actual NPVs and IRRs. Which project(s) should be accepted if they are independent? Mutually exclusive? Explain. Are your answers correct at any WACC less than 23.6%?

f. 1. What is the underlying cause of ranking conflicts between NPV and IRR?

   2. What is the reinvestment rate assumption, and how does it affect the NPV versus IRR conflict?

   3. Which method is best? Why?

g. 1. Define the term *modified IRR (MIRR)*. Find the MIRRs for Projects L and S.

   2. What are the MIRR's advantages and disadvantages as compared to the NPV?

h. 1. What is the payback period? Find the paybacks for Projects L and S.

   2. What is the rationale for the payback method? According to the payback criterion, which project(s) should be accepted if the firm's maximum acceptable payback is 2 years, if Projects L and S are independent? If Projects L and S are mutually exclusive?

   3. What is the difference between the regular and discounted payback methods?

   4. What are the two main disadvantages of discounted payback? Is the payback method useful in capital budgeting decisions? Explain.

i. As a separate project (Project P), the firm is considering sponsoring a pavilion at the upcoming World's Fair. The pavilion would cost $800,000, and it is expected to result in $5 million of incremental cash inflows during its 1 year of operation. However, it would then take another year, and $5 million of costs, to demolish the site and return it to its original condition. Thus, Project P's expected cash flows (in millions of dollars) look like this:

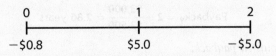

| | 0 | 1 | 2 |
|---|---|---|---|
| | −$0.8 | $5.0 | −$5.0 |

The project is estimated to be of average risk, so its WACC is 10%.

1. What is Project P's NPV? What is its IRR? Its MIRR?

2. Draw Project P's NPV profile. Does Project P have normal or nonnormal cash flows? Should this project be accepted? Explain.

# Solutions to Self-Test Questions and Problems

**ST-1**  Refer to the marginal glossary definitions or relevant chapter sections to check your responses.

**ST-2**  a. *Net present value (NPV):*

$$NPV_X = -\$10,000 + \frac{\$6,500}{(1.12)^1} + \frac{\$3,000}{(1.12)^2} + \frac{\$3,000}{(1.12)^3} + \frac{\$1,000}{(1.12)^4} = \$966.01$$

$$NPV_Y = -\$10,000 + \frac{\$3,500}{(1.12)^1} + \frac{\$3,500}{(1.12)^2} + \frac{\$3,500}{(1.12)^3} + \frac{\$3,500}{(1.12)^4} = \$630.72$$

Alternatively, using a financial calculator, input the cash flows into the cash flow register, enter $I/YR = 12$, and then press the NPV key to obtain $NPV_X = \$966.01$ and $NPV_Y = \$630.72$.

*Internal rate of return (IRR):*
To solve for each project's IRR, find the discount rates that equate each NPV to zero:

$$IRR_X = 18.0\%$$
$$IRR_Y = 15.0\%$$

*Modified internal rate of return (MIRR):*
To obtain each project's MIRR, begin by finding each project's terminal value (TV) of cash inflows:

$$TV_X = \$6,500(1.12)^3 + \$3,000(1.12)^2 + \$3,000(1.12)^1 + \$1,000 = \$17,255.23$$
$$TV_Y = \$3,500(1.12)^3 + \$3,500(1.12)^2 + \$3,500(1.12)^1 + \$3,500 = \$16,727.65$$

Now, each project's MIRR is the discount rate that equates the PV of the TV to each project's cost, $10,000:

$$MIRR_X = 14.61\%$$
$$MIRR_Y = 13.73\%$$

*Payback:*
To determine the payback, construct the cumulative cash flows for each project:

| | Cumulative Cash Flows | |
| --- | --- | --- |
| Year | Project X | Project Y |
| 0 | ($10,000) | ($10,000) |
| 1 | (3,500) | (6,500) |
| 2 | (500) | (3,000) |
| 3 | 2,500 | 500 |
| 4 | 3,500 | 4,000 |

$$Payback_X = 2 + \frac{\$500}{\$3,000} = 2.17 \text{ years}$$

$$Payback_Y = 2 + \frac{\$3,000}{\$3,500} = 2.86 \text{ years}$$

*Discounted payback:*
To determine the discounted payback, construct the cumulative discounted cash flows at the firm's WACC of 12% for each project:

**Project X**

| Years | 0 | 1 | 2 | 3 | 4 |
|---|---|---|---|---|---|
| Cash Flow | −10,000 | 6,500 | 3,000 | 3,000 | 1,000 |
| Discounted Cash Flow | −10,000 | 5,803.57 | 2,391.58 | 2,135.34 | 635.52 |
| Cumulative Discounted Cash Flow | −10,000 | −4,196.43 | −1,804.85 | +330.49 | +966.01 |

Discounted Payback$_X$ = 2 + \$1,804.85/\$2,135.34 = 2.85 years

**Project Y**

| Years | 0 | 1 | 2 | 3 | 4 |
|---|---|---|---|---|---|
| Cash Flow | −10,000 | 3,500 | 3,500 | 3,500 | 3,500 |
| Discounted Cash Flow | −10,000 | 3,125.00 | 2,790.18 | 2,491.23 | 2,224.31 |
| Cumulative Discounted Cash Flow | −10,000 | −6,875.00 | −4,084.82 | −1,593.59 | +630.72 |

Discounted Payback$_Y$ = 3 + \$1,593.59/\$2,224.31 = 3.72 years

b. The following table summarizes the project rankings by each method:

| | Project That Ranks Higher |
|---|---|
| NPV | X |
| IRR | X |
| MIRR | X |
| Payback | X |
| Discounted payback | X |

Note that all methods rank Project X over Project Y. In addition, both projects are acceptable under the NPV, IRR, and MIRR criteria. Thus, both projects should be accepted if they are independent.

c. In this case, we would choose the project with the higher NPV at r = 12%, or Project X.

d. To determine the effects of changing the cost of capital, plot the NPV profiles of each project. The crossover rate occurs between 6% and 7% (≈ 6.22%). See the graph on the next page.

   If the firm's cost of capital is less than 6.22%, a conflict exists because NPV$_Y$ > NPV$_X$, but IRR$_X$ > IRR$_Y$. Therefore, if r were 5%, a conflict would exist. Note, however, that when r = 5.0%, MIRR$_X$ = 10.64% and MIRR$_Y$ = 10.83%; hence, the modified IRR ranks the projects correctly, even if r is to the left of the crossover point because the size of the projects is equal.

e. The basic cause of the conflict is differing reinvestment rate assumptions between NPV and IRR. NPV assumes that cash flows can be reinvested at the cost of capital, while IRR assumes reinvestment at the (generally) higher IRR. The high reinvestment rate assumption under IRR makes early cash flows especially valuable, and hence short-term projects look better than long-term projects under IRR.

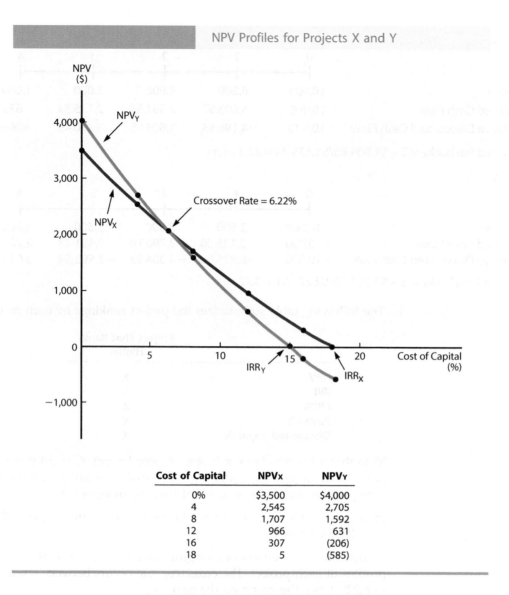

NPV Profiles for Projects X and Y

| Cost of Capital | NPVx | NPVy |
|---|---|---|
| 0% | $3,500 | $4,000 |
| 4 | 2,545 | 2,705 |
| 8 | 1,707 | 1,592 |
| 12 | 966 | 631 |
| 16 | 307 | (206) |
| 18 | 5 | (585) |

## Answers to Selected End-of-Chapter Problems

**11-2** IRR = 11.57%

**11-4** 5.42 yrs.

**11-6** a. 5%: $NPV_A$ = $3.52; $NPV_B$ = $2.87
10%: $NPV_A$ = $0.58; $NPV_B$ = $1.04
15%: $NPV_A$ = −$1.91; $NPV_B$ = −$0.55
b. $IRR_A$ = 11.10%; $IRR_B$ = 13.18%
c. 5%: Choose A; 10%: Choose B; 15%: Do not choose either one

**11-8** a. Without mitigation: NPV = $12.10 million; IRR = 19.86%;
With mitigation: NPV = $5.70 million; IRR = 15.24%

**11-10** Project 1; $NPV_1$ = $234.26

**11-12** $IRR_L$ = 12.70%

**11-14** a. HCC; PV = −$805,009.87
c. LCC; PV = −$686,627.14

**11-16** a. $NPV_A$ = $14,486,808; $NPV_B$ = $11,156,893
$IRR_A$ = 15.03%; $IRR_B$ = 22.26%
c. Crossover rate ≈ 11.71%

**11-18** a. No; $PV_{Old}$ = −$89,910.08;
$PV_{New}$ = −$94,611.45
b. $2,470.80
c. 22.94%

**11-20** $2,698.89

**11-22** $250.01

## Selected Equations and Tables

$$NPV = CF_0 + \frac{CF_1}{(1+r)^1} + \frac{CF_2}{(1+r)^2} + \cdots + \frac{CF_N}{(1+r)^N}$$

$$= \sum_{t=0}^{N} \frac{CF_t}{(1+r)^t}$$

$$CF_0 + \frac{CF_1}{(1+IRR)^1} + \frac{CF_2}{(1+IRR)^2} + \cdots + \frac{CF_N}{(1+IRR)^N} = 0$$

$$\sum_{t=0}^{N} \frac{CF_t}{(1+IRR)^t} = 0$$

$$\sum_{t=0}^{N} \frac{COF_t}{(1+r)^t} = \frac{\sum_{t=0}^{N} CIF_t(1+r)^{N-t}}{(1+MIRR)^N}$$

$$PV\ costs = \frac{TV}{(1+MIRR)^N}$$

$$Payback = Number\ of\ years\ prior\ to\ full\ recovery + \frac{Unrecovered\ cost\ at\ start\ of\ year}{Cash\ flow\ during\ full\ recovery\ year}$$

# Appendix A

## Solutions to Self-Test Questions and Problems

*Note:* Except for Chapter 1, we do not show an answer for ST-1 problems because they are verbal rather than quantitative in nature.

## Chapter 1

**ST-1** Refer to the marginal glossary definitions or relevant chapter sections to check your responses.

## Chapter 3

**ST-2**  a.

| | |
|---|---|
| EBIT | $5,000,000 |
| Interest | 1,000,000 |
| EBT | $4,000,000 |
| Taxes 40% | 1,600,000 |
| Net income | $2,400,000 |

b. Current liabilities = Accounts payable + Accruals + Notes payable
   = $3,000,000 + $1,000,000 + $2,000,000
   = $6,000,000

NOWC = Current assets − (Current liabilities − Notes payable)
     = $14,000,000 − ($6,000,000 − $2,000,000)
     = $10,000,000

c. NWC = Current assets − Current liabilities
       = $14,000,000 − $6,000,000
       = $8,000,000

d. $\text{FCF} = \left(\text{EBIT}(1-\text{T}) + \text{Depreciation}\right) - \left(\begin{array}{c}\text{Capital} \\ \text{expenditures}\end{array} + \begin{array}{c}\text{Increase in net operating} \\ \text{working capital}\end{array}\right)$

= [$5,000,000(0.6) + $1,000,000] − [$4,000,000 + 0]
= $4,000,000 − $4,000,000
= $0

Note that capital expenditures are equal to the change in net plant and equipment plus the annual depreciation expense.

e. Rattner's end-of-year Statement of Stockholders' Equity is calculated as follows:

**Statement of Stockholders' Equity**

| | Common Stock | | Retained | Total Stockholders' |
|---|---|---|---|---|
| | Shares | Amount | Earnings | Equity |
| Balances, beginning of year | 500,000 | $5,000,000 | $11,200,000 | $16,200,000 |
| Net income | | | 2,400,000 | |
| Cash dividends | | | −1,200,000 | |
| Addition to retained earnings | | | | 1,200,000 |
| Balances, end of year | 500,000 | $5,000,000 | $12,400,000 | $17,400,000 |

A-1

f.  MVA $=$ (P$_0$ $\times$ Number of shares) $-$ Book value of equity
    $=$ ($52 $\times$ 500,000) $-$ $17,400,000
    $=$ $8,600,000

g. Before we can calculate the firm's EVA, we need to calculate the firm's total invested capital. We know that the firm uses no preferred stock, and we know that Assets = Liabilities + Equity. From the information provided in the problem we know:

|  |  | | |
|---|---|---|---|
| | | Accounts payable | $ 3,000,000 |
| | | Accruals | 1,000,000 |
| | | Notes payable | 2,000,000 |
| Current assets | $14,000,000 | Current liabilities | $ 6,000,000 |
| | | Long-term debt | ? |
| Net fixed assets | 15,000,000 | Common equity | 17,400,000 |
| Total assets | $29,000,000 | Total liabilities & equity | $29,000,000 |

We calculated common equity in part e, so the only value we don't know on the balance sheet is long-term debt. However, we have enough information to calculate it:

Long-term debt   $=$ $29,000,000 $-$ $17,400,000 $-$ $6,000,000
Long-term debt   $=$ $5,600,000

Now, we can find the firm's total invested capital:

Total invested capital = Notes payable + Long-term debt + Common equity
Total invested capital = $2,000,000 + $5,600,000 + $17,400,000
Total invested capital = $25,000,000

Now, we can calculate the firm's EVA:

EVA $=$ EBIT(1 $-$ T) $-$ [Total invested capital $\times$ After-tax % cost of capital]
EVA $=$ $5,000,000(0.6) $-$ [$25,000,000 $\times$ 0.09]
EVA $=$ $3,000,000 $-$ $2,250,000 $=$ $750,000

## Chapter 4

**ST-2** Billingsworth paid $2 in dividends and retained $2 per share. Because total retained earnings rose by $12 million, there must be 6 million shares outstanding. With a book value of $40 per share, total common equity must be $40(6 million) = $240 million. Because Billingsworth has $120 million of total debt, its total debt to total capital ratio must be 33.3%:

$$\frac{\text{Total debt}}{\text{Total debt} + \text{Equity}} = \frac{\$120 \text{ million}}{\$120 \text{ million} + \$240 \text{ million}}$$
$$= 0.333 = 33.3\%$$

**ST-3** a. In answering questions such as this, always begin by writing down the relevant definitional equations, and then start filling in numbers. Note that the extra zeros indicating millions have been deleted in the following calculations.

(1)  DSO $= \dfrac{\text{Accounts receivable}}{\text{Sales}/365}$

40.55 $= \dfrac{\text{A/R}}{\text{Sales}/365}$

A/R $=$ 40.55($2.7397) $=$ $111.1 million

(2)  Current ratio $= \dfrac{\text{Current assets}}{\text{Current liabilities}} = 3.0$

$= \dfrac{\text{Current assets}}{\$105.5} = 3.0$

Current assets $= 3.0(\$105.5) = \$316.50$ million

(3) Total assets $=$ Current assets $+$ Fixed assets
$= \$316.5 + \$283.5 = \$600$ million

(4) ROA $=$ Profit margin $\times$ Total assets turnover

$= \dfrac{\text{Net income}}{\text{Sales}} \times \dfrac{\text{Sales}}{\text{Total assets}}$

$= \dfrac{\$50}{\$1,000} \times \dfrac{\$1,000}{\$600}$

$= 0.05 \times 1.667 = 0.083333 = 8.3333\%$

(5)  ROE $=$ ROA $\times \dfrac{\text{Assets}}{\text{Equity}}$

$12.0\% = 8.3333\% \times \dfrac{\$600}{\text{Equity}}$

Equity $= \dfrac{(8.3333\%)(\$600)}{12.0\%}$

Equity $= \$416.67$ million

(6) Current assets $=$ Cash and equivalents $+$ Accounts receivable $+$ Inventories
$\$316.5 = \$100.0 + \$111.1 +$ Inventories
Inventories $= \$105.4$ million

Quick ratio $= \dfrac{\text{Current assets} - \text{Inventories}}{\text{Current liabilities}}$

$= \dfrac{\$316.5 - \$105.4}{\$105.5} = 2.00$

(7) Total assets $=$ Total claims $= \$600$ million

Current liabilities $+$ Long-term debt $+$ Equity $= \$600$ million
$\$105.5 +$ Long-term debt $+ \$416.67 = \$600$ million
Long-term debt $= \$600 - \$105.5 - \$416.67 = \$77.83$ million

Note: We could have found equity as follows:

ROE $= \dfrac{\text{Net income}}{\text{Equity}}$

$12.0\% = \dfrac{\$50}{\text{Equity}}$

Equity $= \$50/0.12$

Equity $= \$416.67$ million

Then we could have gone on to find long-term debt.

b. Kaiser's average sales per day were $\$1,000/365 = \$2.74$ million. Its DSO was 40.55, so A/R $= 40.55(\$2.74) = \$111.1$ million. Its new DSO of 30.4 would cause A/R $= 30.4(\$2.74) = \$83.3$ million. The reduction in receivables would be $\$111.1 - \$83.3 = \$27.8$ million, which would equal the amount of cash generated.

(1)  New equity $=$ Old equity $-$ Stock bought back
$= \$416.7 - \$27.8$
$= \$388.9$ million

Thus,

$$\text{New ROE} = \frac{\text{Net income}}{\text{New equity}}$$

$$= \frac{\$50}{\$388.9}$$

$$= 12.86\% \text{ (versus old ROE of 12.0\%)}$$

(2)   $$\text{New ROA} = \frac{\text{Net income}}{\text{Total assets} - \text{Reduction in A/R}}$$

$$= \frac{\$50}{\$600 - \$27.8}$$

$$= 8.74\% \text{ (versus old ROA of 8.33\%)}$$

(3) Total debt before the asset reduction is the same as total debt after the asset reduction. Neither notes payable nor long-term debt was impacted by the asset reduction. However, after the asset reduction equity has declined, so total capital has declined.

$$\text{Total debt} = \text{Notes payable} + \text{Long-term debt}$$
$$\$97.8 = \$20 + \$77.8$$

$$\text{New total assets} = \text{Old total assets} - \text{Reduction in A/R}$$
$$= \$600 - \$27.8$$
$$= \$572.2 \text{ million}$$

*Before asset reduction:*

$$\text{Total capital} = \text{Total debt} + \text{Old equity}$$
$$= \$97.8 + \$416.7$$
$$= \$514.5 \text{ million}$$

*After asset reduction:*

$$\text{Total capital} = \text{Total debt} + \text{New equity}$$
$$= \$97.8 + \$388.9$$
$$= \$486.7 \text{ million}$$

Therefore,   $$\frac{\text{Total debt}}{\text{Old total capital}} = \frac{\$97.8}{\$514.5} = 19.0\%$$

and   $$\frac{\text{Total debt}}{\text{New total capital}} = \frac{\$97.8}{\$486.7} = 20.1\%$$

# Chapter 5

**ST-2**   a.

$1,000 is being compounded for 3 years, so your balance on January 1, 2019, is $1,259.71:

$$FV_N = PV(1 + I)^N = \$1,000(1 + 0.08)^3 = \$1,259.71$$

Alternatively, using a financial calculator, input $N = 3$, $I/YR = 8$, $PV = -1000$, $PMT = 0$, and $FV = ?$ Solve for $FV = \$1,259.71$.

b.

```
  1/1/16      1/1/17      1/1/18      1/1/19
     2%
  ├──┼──┼──┼──┼──┼──┼──┼──┼──┼──┼──┼──┤
  -1,000                           FV = ?
```

$$FV_N = PV\left(1 + \frac{I_{NOM}}{M}\right)^{MN} = FV_{12} = \$1,000(1.02)^{12} = \$1,268.24$$

Alternatively, using a financial calculator, input $N = 12$, $I/YR = 2$, $PV = -1000$, $PMT = 0$, and $FV = ?$ Solve for $FV = \$1,268.24$.

c.

```
  1/1/16      1/1/17      1/1/18      1/1/19
        8%
  ├───────────┼───────────┼───────────┤
           -333.333   -333.333   -333.333
```

Using a financial calculator, input $N = 3$, $I/YR = 8$, $PV = 0$, $PMT = -333.333$, and $FV = ?$ Solve for $FV = \$1,082.13$.

d.

```
  1/1/16      1/1/17      1/1/18      1/1/19
        8%
  ├───────────┼───────────┼───────────┤
 -333.333   -333.333   -333.333    FV = ?
```

Using a financial calculator in begin mode, input $N = 3$, $I/YR = 8$, $PV = 0$, $PMT = -333.333$, and $FV = ?$ Solve for $FV = \$1,168.70$.

e.

```
  1/1/16      1/1/17      1/1/18      1/1/19
        8%
  ├───────────┼───────────┼───────────┤
             ?           ?           ?
                                  FV = 1,259.71
```

Using a financial calculator, input $N = 3$, $I/YR = 8$, $PV = 0$, $FV = 1259.71$, and $PMT = ?$ Solve for $PMT = -\$388.03$. Therefore, you would have to make three payments of $388.03 beginning on January 1, 2017.

**ST-3** a. Set up a time line like the one in the preceding problem:

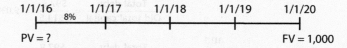

```
  1/1/16      1/1/17      1/1/18      1/1/19      1/1/20
        8%
  ├───────────┼───────────┼───────────┼───────────┤
  PV = ?                                        FV = 1,000
```

Note that your deposit will grow for 4 years at 8%. The deposit on January 1, 2016, is the PV, and the FV is $1,000. Using a financial calculator, input $N = 4$, $I/YR = 8$, $PMT = 0$, $FV = 1000$, and $PV = ?$ Solve for $PV = -\$735.03$.

$$PV = \frac{FV_N}{(1 + I)^N} = \frac{\$1,000}{(1.08)^4} = \$735.03$$

b.

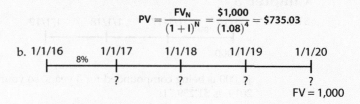

```
  1/1/16      1/1/17      1/1/18      1/1/19      1/1/20
        8%
  ├───────────┼───────────┼───────────┼───────────┤
             ?           ?           ?           ?
                                              FV = 1,000
```

Here, we are dealing with a 4-year annuity whose first payment occurs 1 year from today, on January 1, 2017, and whose future value must equal $1,000. You should modify the time line to help visualize the situation. Using a financial calculator, input $N = 4$, $I/YR = 8$, $PV = 0$, $FV = 1000$, and $PMT = ?$ Solve for $PMT = -\$221.92$.

c.  This problem can be approached in several ways. Perhaps the simplest is to ask this question: "If I received $750 on January 1, 2017, and deposited it to earn 8%, would I have the required $1,000 on January 1, 2020?" The answer is no.

```
1/1/16        1/1/17      1/1/18      1/1/19       1/1/20
├───────────┼──────────┼──────────┼───────────┤
       8%
           −750                                  FV = ?
```

$$FV_3 = \$750(1.08)(1.08)(1.08) = \$944.78$$

This indicates that you should let your father make the payments of $221.92 rather than accept the lump sum of $750 on January 1, 2017.

You could also compare the $750 with the PV of the payments, as shown below:

```
1/1/16        1/1/17      1/1/18      1/1/19       1/1/20
├───────────┼──────────┼──────────┼───────────┤
       8%
           −221.92     −221.92    −221.92      −221.92
           PV = ?
```

Using a financial calculator, input N = 4, I/YR = 8, PMT = −221.92, FV = 0, and PV = ? Solve for PV = $735.03.

This is less than the $750 lump sum offer, so your initial reaction might be to accept the lump sum of $750. However, this would be a mistake. The problem is that when you found the $735.03 PV of the annuity, you were finding the value of the annuity *today*, on January 1, 2016. You were comparing $735.03 today with the lump sum of $750 one year from now. This is, of course, not correct. What you should have done was take the $735.03, recognize that this is the PV of an annuity as of January 1, 2016, multiply $735.03 by 1.08 to get $793.83, and compare $793.83 with the lump sum of $750. You would then take your father's offer to make the payments of $221.92 rather than take the lump sum on January 1, 2017.

d.
```
1/1/16        1/1/17      1/1/18      1/1/19       1/1/20
├───────────┼──────────┼──────────┼───────────┤
       I = ?
           −750                                   1,000
```

Using a financial calculator, input N = 3, PV = −750, PMT = 0, FV = 1000, and I/YR = ? Solve for I/YR = 10.0642%.

e.
```
1/1/16        1/1/17      1/1/18      1/1/19       1/1/20
├───────────┼──────────┼──────────┼───────────┤
       I = ?
           −200       −200        −200         −200
                                              FV = 1,000
```

Using a financial calculator, input N = 4, PV = 0, PMT = −200, FV = 1000, and I/YR = ? Solve for I/YR = 15.09%.

You might be able to find a borrower willing to offer you a 15% interest rate, but there would be some risk involved—he or she might not actually pay you the $1,000!

f.

| 1/1/16 | | 1/1/17 | | 1/1/18 | | 1/1/19 | | 1/1/20 |
|--------|--|--------|--|--------|--|--------|--|--------|
| | 4% | | | | | | | |
| | | −400 | ? | ? | ? | ? | ? | ? |
| | | | | | | | | FV = 1,000 |

Find the future value of the original \$400 deposit:

$$FV_6 = PV(1.04)^6 = \$400(1.2653) = \$506.13$$

This means that on January 1, 2020, you need an additional sum of \$493.87:

$$\$1,000.00 - \$506.13 = \$493.87$$

This will be accumulated by making 6 equal payments that earn 8% compounded semiannually, or 4% each 6 months. Using a financial calculator, input $N = 6$, $I/YR = 4$, $PV = 0$, $FV = 493.87$, and $PMT = ?$ Solve for $PMT = -\$74.46$.

Alternatively, input $N = 6$, $I/YR = 4$, $PV = -400$, $FV = 1000$, and $PMT = ?$ Solve for $PMT = -\$74.46$. Note that the sign on the PV amount entered in the calculator was negative because the initial deposit will offset the total amount needed. If the signs on both the FV and PV amounts had been the same, you would have calculated a larger payment than was necessary.

g. $\text{Effective annual rate} = \left(1 + \dfrac{I_{NOM}}{M}\right)^M - 1.0$

$$= \left(1 + \dfrac{0.08}{2}\right)^2 - 1 = (1.04)^2 - 1$$

$$= 1.0816 - 1 = 0.0816 = 8.16\%$$

$APR = I_{PER} \times M$

$$= 0.04 \times 2 = 0.08 = 8\%$$

**ST-4**    Bank A's effective annual rate is 8.24%:

$\text{Effective annual rate} = \left(1 + \dfrac{0.08}{4}\right)^4 - 1.0$

$$= (1.02)^4 - 1$$

$$= 1.0824 - 1$$

$$= 0.0824 = 8.24\%$$

Now Bank B must have the same effective annual rate:

$$\left(1 + \dfrac{I_{NOM}}{12}\right)^{12} - 1.0 = 0.0824$$

$$\left(1 + \dfrac{I_{NOM}}{12}\right)^{12} = 1.0824$$

$$1 + \dfrac{I_{NOM}}{12} = (1.0824)^{1/12}$$

$$1 + \dfrac{I_{NOM}}{12} = 1.00662$$

$$\dfrac{I_{NOM}}{12} = 0.00662$$

$$I_{NOM} = 0.07944 = 7.94\%$$

Thus, the two banks have different quoted rates—Bank A's quoted rate is 8%, while Bank B's quoted rate is 7.94%; however, both banks have the same effective annual rate of 8.24%. The difference in their quoted rates is due to the difference in compounding frequency.

# Chapter 6

**ST-2**    a.  **Average inflation over 4 years** $= (2\% + 2\% + 2\% + 4\%)/4 = 2.5\%$

b.  $T_4 = r_{RF} + MRP_4$
$= r^* + IP_4 + MRP_4$
$= 3\% + 2.5\% + (0.1)3\%$
$= 5.8\%$

c.  $C_{4,BBB} = r^* + IP_4 + MRP_4 + DRP + LP$
$= 3\% + 2.5\% + 0.3\% + 1.3\% + 0.5\%$
$= 7.6\%$

d.  $T_8 = r^* + IP_8 + MRP_8$
$= 3\% + (3 \times 2\% + 5 \times 4\%)/8 + 0.7\%$
$= 3\% + 3.25\% + 0.7\%$
$= 6.95\%$

e.  $C_{8,BB} = r^* + IP_8 + MRP_8 + DRP + LP$
$= 3\% + 3.25\% + 0.7\% + 1.3\% + 0.5\%$
$= 8.75\%$

f.      $T_9 = r^* + IP_9 + MRP_9$
$7.3\% = 3\% + IP_9 + 0.8\%$
$IP_9 = 3.5\%$
$3.5\% = (3 \times 2\% + 5 \times 4\% + X)/9$
$31.5\% = 6\% + 20\% + X$
$5.5\% = X$

$X =$ Inflation in Year 9 $= 5.5\%$

**ST-3**    $T_1 = 6\%$; $T_2 = 6.2\%$; $T_3 = 6.3\%$; $T_4 = 6.5\%$; MRP $= 0$

a. Yield of 1-year security, 1 year from now, is calculated as follows:

$$(1.062)^2 = (1.06)(1 + X)$$
$$\frac{(1.062)^2}{1.06} = 1 + X$$
$$1.064 = 1 + X$$
$$6.4\% = X$$

b. Yield of 1-year security, 2 years from now, is calculated as follows:

$$(1.063)^3 = (1.06)^2(1 + X)$$
$$\frac{(1.063)^3}{(1.062)^2} = 1 + X$$
$$1.065 = 1 + X$$
$$6.5\% = X$$

c. Yield of 2-year security, 1 year from now, is calculated as follows:

$$(1.063)^3 = (1.06)(1 + X)^2$$
$$\frac{(1.063)^3}{1.06} = (1 + X)^2$$
$$1.13317 = (1 + X)^2$$
$$(1.13317)^{1/2} = 1 + X$$
$$6.45\% = X$$

d. Yield of 3-year security, 1 year from now, is calculated as follows:

$$(1.065)^4 = (1.06)(1 + X)^3$$
$$\frac{(1.065)^4}{1.06} = (1 + X)^3$$
$$1.213648 = (1 + X)^3$$
$$(1.213648)^{1/3} = 1 + X$$
$$6.67\% = X$$

# Chapter 7

**ST-2**  a. Pennington's bonds were sold at par; therefore, the original YTM equaled the coupon rate of 12%.

b. $$V_B = \sum_{t=1}^{50} \frac{\$120/2}{\left(1 + \dfrac{0.10}{2}\right)^t} + \frac{\$1,000}{\left(1 + \dfrac{0.10}{2}\right)^{50}}$$

With a financial calculator, input the following: $N = 50$, $I/YR = 5$, $PMT = 60$, $FV = 1000$, and $PV = ?$ Solve for $PV = \$1,182.56$.

c. **Current yield = Annual coupon payment/Price**
$$= \$120/\$1,182.56$$
$$= 0.1015 = 10.15\%$$

**Capital gains yield = Total yield − Current yield**
$$= 10\% - 10.15\% = -0.15\%$$

**Total return = YTM = 10%**

d. With a financial calculator, input the following: $N = 13$, $PV = -916.42$, $PMT = 60$, $FV = 1000$, and $r_d/2 = I/YR = ?$ Calculator solution = $r_d/2 = 7.00\%$; therefore, $r_d = YTM = 14.00\%$.

**Current yield = $120/$916.42 = 13.09%**
**Capital gains yield = 14% − 13.09% = 0.91%**
**Total return = YTM = 14.00%**

e. The following time line illustrates the years to maturity of the bond:

```
1/1/15      7/1/15      1/1/16      7/1/16      1/1/17                    12/31/21
  ├──────────┼──────────┼──────────┼──────────┼───────  • • •  ──────────┤
  3/1/15
```

Thus, on March 1, 2015, there were 13 2/3 periods left before the bond matured. Bond traders actually use the following procedure to determine the price of the bond:

(1) Find the price of the bond on the next coupon date, July 1, 2015. Using a financial calculator, input N = 13, I/YR = 7.75, PMT = 60, FV = 1000, and PV = ? Solve for PV = $859.76.

(2) Add the coupon, $60, to the bond price to get the total value of the bond on the next interest payment date: $859.76 + $60.00 = $919.76.

(3) Discount this total value back to the purchase date (March 1, 2015). Using a financial calculator, input N = 4/6, I/YR = 7.75, PMT = 0, FV = 919.76, and PV = ? Solve for PV = $875.11.

(4) Therefore, you would have written a check for $875.11 to complete the transaction. Of this amount, $20 = (1/3)($60) would represent accrued interest and $855.11 would represent the bond's basic value. This breakdown would affect both your taxes and those of the seller.

(5) This problem could be solved *very* easily using a spreadsheet or a financial calculator with a bond valuation function, such as the HP-12C or the HP-17BII. This is explained in the calculator manual under the heading, "Bond Calculations."

**ST-3**  a.  (1)  $100,000,000/10 = $10,000,000 per year, or $5 million each 6 months.

(2) VDC will purchase bonds on the open market if they're selling at less than par. So, the sinking fund payment will be less than $5,000,000 each period.

b. The debt service requirements will decline. As the amount of bonds outstanding declines, so will the interest requirements (amounts given in millions of dollars). If the bonds are called at par, the total bond service payments are calculated as follows:

| Semiannual Payment Period (1) | Sinking Fund Payment (2) | Outstanding Bonds on which Interest Is Paid (3) | Interest Payment[a] (4) | Total Debt Service (2) + (4) = (5) |
|---|---|---|---|---|
| 1 | $5 | $100 | $6.0 | $11.0 |
| 2 | 5 | 95 | 5.7 | 10.7 |
| 3 | 5 | 90 | 5.4 | 10.4 |
| ⋮ | ⋮ | ⋮ | ⋮ | ⋮ |
| 20 | 5 | 5 | 0.3 | 5.3 |

[a]Interest is calculated as (0.5)(0.12)(column 3); for example, Interest in Period 2 = (0.5)(0.12)($95) = $5.7.

The company's total cash bond service requirement will be $21.7 million per year for the first year. For both options, interest will decline by 0.12($10,000,000) = $1,200,000 per year for the remaining years. The total debt service requirement for the open market purchases cannot be precisely determined, but the amounts would be less than what's shown in column 5 of the table above.

c. Here we have a 10-year 7% annuity whose compound value is $100 million, and we are seeking the annual payment, PMT. The solution can be obtained with a financial calculator. Input N = 10, I/YR = 7, PV = 0, and FV = 100000000, and press the PMT key to obtain $7,237,750. This amount is not known with certainty as interest rates over time will change, so the amount could be higher (if interest rates fall) or lower (if interest rates rise).

d. Annual debt service costs will be $100,000,000(0.12) + $7,237,750 = $19,237,750.

e. If interest rates rose, causing the bond's price to fall, the company would use open market purchases. This would reduce its debt service requirements.

# Chapter 8

**ST-2** a. The average rate of return for each stock is calculated simply by averaging the returns over the 5-year period. The average return for Stock A is:

$$r_{Avg\ A} = (-24.25\% + 18.50\% + 38.67\% + 14.33\% + 39.13\%)/5$$
$$= 17.28\%$$

The average return for Stock B is:

$$r_{Avg\ B} = (5.50\% + 26.73\% + 48.25\% + -4.50\% + 43.86\%)/5$$
$$= 23.97\%$$

The realized rate of return on a portfolio made up of Stock A and Stock B would be calculated by finding the average return in each year as $r_A$(% of Stock A) + $r_B$(% of Stock B) and then averaging these annual returns:

| Year | Portfolio AB's Return, $r_{AB}$ |
|------|-------------------------------|
| 2011 | (9.38%) |
| 2012 | 22.62 |
| 2013 | 43.46 |
| 2014 | 4.92 |
| 2015 | 41.50 |
|  | $r_{Avg}$ = 20.62% |

b. The standard deviation of returns is estimated, using Equation 8.2a, as follows:

$$\text{Estimated } \sigma = \sqrt{\frac{\sum_{t=1}^{N}(\bar{r}_t - \bar{r}_{Avg})^2}{N-1}}$$

For Stock A, the estimated σ is 25.84%:

$$\sigma_A = \sqrt{\frac{\begin{array}{c}(-24.25\% - 17.28\%)^2 + (18.50\% - 17.28\%)^2 + (38.67\% - 17.28\%)^2 + \\ (14.33\% - 17.28\%)^2 + (39.13\% - 17.28\%)^2\end{array}}{5-1}}$$
$$= 25.84\%$$

The standard deviations of returns for Stock B and for the portfolio are similarly determined, and they are as follows:

|  | Stock A | Stock B | Portfolio AB |
|---|---------|---------|--------------|
| **Standard deviation** | 25.84% | 23.15% | 22.96% |

c. Because the risk reduction from diversification is small ($\sigma_{AB}$ falls only to 22.96%), the most likely value of the correlation coefficient is 0.8.

If the correlation coefficient were −0.8, the risk reduction would be much larger. In fact, the correlation coefficient between Stocks A and B is 0.76.

d. If more randomly selected stocks were added to a portfolio, $\sigma_p$ would decline to somewhere in the vicinity of 20% (see Figure 8.6); $\sigma_p$ would remain constant only if the correlation coefficient were +1.0, which is most unlikely. $\sigma_p$ would decline to zero only if the correlation coefficient, $\rho$, were equal to zero and a large number of stocks were added to the portfolio, or if the proper proportions were held in a two-stock portfolio with $\rho = -1.0$.

**ST-3**  a. $b = (0.6)(0.70) + (0.25)(0.90) + (0.1)(1.30) + (0.05)(1.50)$
$= 0.42 + 0.225 + 0.13 + 0.075 = 0.85$

b. $r_{RF} = 4\%$; $RP_M = 5\%$; $b = 0.85$ **(calculated in part a)**
$r_p = 4\% + (5\%)(0.85)$
$= 8.25\%$

c. $b_N = (0.5)(0.70) + (0.25)(0.90) + (0.1)(1.30) + (0.15)(1.50)$
$= 0.35 + 0.225 + 0.13 + 0.225$
$= 0.93$

$r = 4\% + (5\%)(0.93)$
$= 8.65\%$

# Chapter 9

**ST-2**  a. This is not necessarily true. Because G plows back two-thirds of its earnings, its growth rate should exceed that of D, but D pays higher dividends ($3 versus $1). We cannot say which stock should have the higher price.

b. Again, we just do not know which price would be higher.

c. This is false. The changes in $r_d$ and $r_s$ would have a greater effect on G; its price would decline more.

d. The total expected return for D is $\hat{r}_D = D_1/P_0 + g = 12\% + 0\% = 12\%$. The total expected return for G will have $D_1/P_0$ less than 12% and g greater than 0%, but $\hat{r}_G$ should be neither greater nor smaller than D's total expected return, 12%, because the two stocks are stated to be equally risky.

e. We have eliminated a, b, c, and d, so e should be correct. On the basis of the available information, D and G should sell at about the same price, $25; thus, $\hat{r}_s = 12\%$ for both D and G. G's current dividend yield is $1/$25 = 4\%$. Therefore, g = 12\% − 4\% = 8\%.

**ST-3**  The first step is to solve for g, the unknown variable, in the constant growth equation. Because $D_1$ is unknown, but $D_0$ is known, substitute $D_0(1 + g)$ for $D_1$ as follows:

$$\hat{P}_0 = P_0 = \frac{D_1}{r_s - g} = \frac{D_0(1 + g)}{r_s - g}$$

$$\$36 = \frac{\$2.40(1 + g)}{0.12 - g}$$

Solving for g, we find the growth rate to be 5%:

$$\$4.32 - \$36g = \$2.40 + \$2.40g$$
$$\$38.4g = \$1.92$$
$$g = 0.05 = 5\%$$

The next step is to use the growth rate to project the stock price 5 years hence:

$$\hat{P}_5 = \frac{D_0(1 + g)^6}{r_s - g}$$
$$= \frac{\$2.40(1.05)^6}{0.12 - 0.05}$$
$$= \$45.95$$

(**Alternatively,** $\hat{P}_5 = \$36(1.05)^5 = \$45.95$)

Therefore, the firm's expected stock price 5 years from now, $\hat{P}_5$, is $45.95.

**ST-4** a. (1) Calculate the PV of the dividends paid during the supernormal growth period:

$$D_1 = \$1.1500(1.15) = \$1.3225$$
$$D_2 = \$1.3225(1.15) = \$1.5209$$
$$D_3 = \$1.5209(1.13) = \$1.7186$$

$$PV\ D = \frac{\$1.3225}{1.12} + \frac{\$1.5209}{(1.12)^2} + \frac{\$1.7186}{(1.12)^3}$$
$$= \$1.1808 + \$1.2125 + \$1.2233$$
$$= \$3.6166 \approx \$3.62$$

(2) Find the PV of the firm's stock price at the end of Year 3:

$$\hat{P}_3 = \frac{D_4}{r_s - g} = \frac{D_3(1 + g)}{r_s - g}$$
$$= \frac{\$1.7186(1.06)}{0.12 - 0.06}$$
$$= \$30.36$$

$$PV\ \hat{P}_3 = \frac{\$30.36}{(1.12)^3} = \$21.61$$

(3) Sum the two components to find the value of the stock today:

$$\hat{P}_0 = \$3.62 + \$21.61 = \$25.23$$

Alternatively, the cash flows can be placed on a time line as follows:

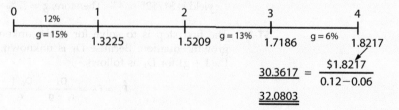

Enter the cash flows into the cash flow register (remembering that $CF_0 = 0$) and I/YR = 12, and press the NPV key to obtain $P_0 = \$25.23$.

b.
$$\hat{P}_1 = \frac{\$1.5209}{1.12} + \frac{\$1.7186}{(1.12)^2} + \frac{\$30.36}{(1.12)^2}$$
$$= \$1.3579 + \$1.3701 + \$24.2028$$
$$= \$26.9308 \approx \$26.93$$

(Calculator solution: $26.93)

$$\hat{P}_2 = \frac{\$1.7186}{1.12} + \frac{\$30.36}{1.12}$$
$$= \$1.5345 + \$27.1071$$
$$= \$28.6416 \approx \$28.64$$

(Calculator solution: $28.64)

c.

| Year | Dividend Yield $+$ | Capital Gains Yield | $=$ Total Return |
|------|-----------------|---------------------|--------------|
| 1 | $\dfrac{\$1.3225}{\$25.23} \approx 5.24\%$ | $\dfrac{\$26.93 - \$25.23}{\$25.23} \approx 6.74\%$ | $\approx 12\%$ |
| 2 | $\dfrac{\$1.5209}{\$26.93} \approx 5.65\%$ | $\dfrac{\$28.64 - \$26.93}{\$26.93} \approx 6.35\%$ | $\approx 12\%$ |
| 3 | $\dfrac{\$1.7186}{\$28.64} \approx 6.00\%$ | $\dfrac{\$30.36 - \$28.64}{\$28.64} \approx 6.00\%$ | $\approx 12\%$ |

# Chapter 10

**ST-2**    a. Component costs are as follows:

Common:    $r_s = \dfrac{D_1}{P_0} + g = \dfrac{D_0(1+g)}{P_0} + g$

$= \dfrac{\$3.60(1.09)}{\$54} + 0.09$

$= 0.0727 + 0.09 = 16.27\%$

Preferred:    $r_p = \dfrac{\text{Preferred dividend}}{P_p} = \dfrac{\$11}{\$95} = 11.58\%$

Debt:    $r_d(1 - T) = 12\%(0.6) = 7.20\%$

b. WACC calculation:

$\text{WACC} = w_d r_d(1 - T) + w_p r_p + w_c r_s$

$= 0.25(7.2\%) + 0.15(11.58\%) + 0.60(16.27\%) = 13.30\%$

c. $\dfrac{\text{Retained earnings}}{\text{breakpoint}} = \dfrac{\text{Addition to retained earnings for the year}}{\text{Equity fraction}}$

$= \dfrac{0.7(\$34,285.72)}{0.6} = \$40,000$

At a capital budget greater than $40,000, new common stock would have to be issued, and the firm's WACC would increase above 13.3%. Therefore, only Projects A, B, and C can be accepted for a total capital budget of $40,000.

# Chapter 11

**ST-2**   a. *Net present value (NPV):*

$$\text{NPV}_X = -\$10,000 + \frac{\$6,500}{(1.12)^1} + \frac{\$3,000}{(1.12)^2} + \frac{\$3,000}{(1.12)^3} + \frac{\$1,000}{(1.12)^4} = \$966.01$$

$$\text{NPV}_Y = -\$10,000 + \frac{\$3,500}{(1.12)^1} + \frac{\$3,500}{(1.12)^2} + \frac{\$3,500}{(1.12)^3} + \frac{\$3,500}{(1.12)^4} = \$630.72$$

Alternatively, using a financial calculator, input the cash flows into the cash flow register, enter I / YR = 12, and then press the NPV key to obtain $\text{NPV}_X = \$966.01$ and $\text{NPV}_Y = \$630.72$.

*Internal rate of return (IRR):*
To solve for each project's IRR, find the discount rates that equate each NPV to zero:

$$\text{IRR}_X = 18.0\%$$
$$\text{IRR}_Y = 15.0\%$$

*Modified internal rate of return (MIRR):*
To obtain each project's MIRR, begin by finding each project's terminal value (TV) of cash inflows:

$$\text{TV}_X = \$6,500(1.12)^3 + \$3,000(1.12)^2 + \$3,000(1.12)^1 + \$1,000 = \$17,255.23$$
$$\text{TV}_Y = \$3,500(1.12)^3 + \$3,500(1.12)^2 + \$3,500(1.12)^1 + \$3,500 = \$16,727.65$$

Now, each project's MIRR is the discount rate that equates the PV of the TV to each project's cost, $10,000:

$$\text{MIRR}_X = 14.61\%$$
$$\text{MIRR}_Y = 13.73\%$$

*Payback:*
To determine the payback, construct the cumulative cash flows for each project:

| | Cumulative Cash Flows | |
|---|---|---|
| Year | Project X | Project Y |
| 0 | ($10,000) | ($10,000) |
| 1 | (3,500) | (6,500) |
| 2 | (500) | (3,000) |
| 3 | 2,500 | 500 |
| 4 | 3,500 | 4,000 |

$$\text{Payback}_X = 2 + \frac{\$500}{\$3,000} = 2.17 \text{ years}$$

$$\text{Payback}_Y = 2 + \frac{\$3,000}{\$3,500} = 2.86 \text{ years}$$

*Discounted payback:*
To determine the discounted payback, construct the cumulative discounted cash flows at the firm's WACC of 12% for each project:

Project X

| Years | 0 | 1 | 2 | 3 | 4 |
|---|---|---|---|---|---|
| Cash Flow | −10,000 | 6,500 | 3,000 | 3,000 | 1,000 |
| Discounted Cash Flow | −10,000 | 5,803.57 | 2,391.58 | 2,135.34 | 635.52 |
| Cumulative Discounted Cash Flow | −10,000 | −4,196.43 | −1,804.85 | +330.49 | +966.01 |

Discounted Payback$_X$ = 2 + $1,804.85/$2,135.34 = 2.85 years

Project Y

| Years | 0 | 1 | 2 | 3 | 4 |
|---|---|---|---|---|---|
| Cash Flow | −10,000 | 3,500 | 3,500 | 3,500 | 3,500 |
| Discounted Cash Flow | −10,000 | 3,125.00 | 2,790.18 | 2,491.23 | 2,224.31 |
| Cumulative Discounted Cash Flow | −10,000 | −6,875.00 | −4,084.82 | −1,593.59 | +630.72 |

Discounted Payback$_Y$ = 3 + $1,593.59/$2,224.31 = 3.72 years

b. The following table summarizes the project rankings by each method:

| | Project That Ranks Higher |
|---|---|
| NPV | X |
| IRR | X |
| MIRR | X |
| Payback | X |
| Discounted payback | X |

Note that all methods rank Project X over Project Y. In addition, both projects are acceptable under the NPV, IRR, and MIRR criteria. Thus, both projects should be accepted if they are independent.

c. In this case, we would choose the project with the higher NPV at r = 12%, or Project X.

d. To determine the effects of changing the cost of capital, plot the NPV profiles of each project. The crossover rate occurs between 6% and 7% (≈ 6.22%). See the graph on the next page.

   If the firm's cost of capital is less than 6.22%, a conflict exists because NPV$_Y$ > NPV$_X$, but IRR$_X$ > IRR$_Y$. Therefore, if r were 5%, a conflict would exist. Note, however, that when r = 5.0%, MIRR$_X$ = 10.64% and MIRR$_Y$ = 10.83%; hence, the modified IRR ranks the projects correctly, even if r is to the left of the crossover point because the size of the projects is equal.

e. The basic cause of the conflict is differing reinvestment rate assumptions between NPV and IRR. NPV assumes that cash flows can be reinvested at the cost of capital, while IRR assumes reinvestment at the (generally) higher IRR. The high reinvestment rate assumption under IRR makes early cash flows especially valuable, and hence short-term projects look better than long-term projects under IRR.

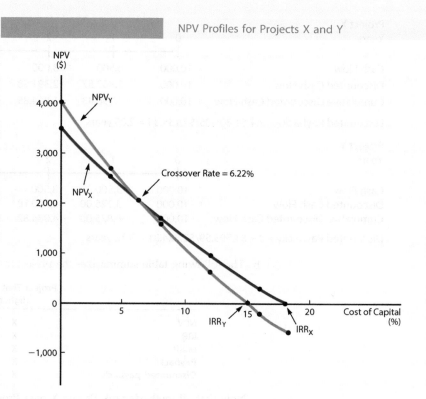

NPV Profiles for Projects X and Y

| Cost of Capital | NPVx | NPVy |
|---|---|---|
| 0% | $3,500 | $4,000 |
| 4 | 2,545 | 2,705 |
| 8 | 1,707 | 1,592 |
| 12 | 966 | 631 |
| 16 | 307 | (206) |
| 18 | 5 | (585) |

## Chapter 12

**ST-2**   a. Estimated investment requirements:

| | |
|---|---|
| **Price** | **($55,000)** |
| **Installation** | **( 10,000)** |
| **Change in net operating working capital** | **( 2,000)** |
| **Total investment outlay** | **($67,000)** |

b. Depreciation schedule:

Equipment cost = $65,000; MACRS 3-year class

| | Years | | |
|---|---|---|---|
| | **1** | **2** | **3** |
| **MACRS depreciation rates** | 33% | 45% | 15% |
| **Equipment depreciation expense** | $21,450 | $29,250 | $9,750 |

Note that the remaining book value of the equipment at the end of the project's life is 0.07 × $65,000 = $4,550.

c.

| | Year 0 | Year 1 | Year 2 | Year 3 |
|---|---|---|---|---|
| ***Investment Outlays:*** | | | | |
| Equipment purchase | ($65,000) | | | |
| Change in NOWC | (2,000) | | | |
| ***Operating Cash Flows over*** | | | | |
| ***Project's Life:*** | | | | |
| Revenues (4,000 × $50) | | $200,000 | $200,000 | $200,000 |
| Variable costs (70%) | | 140,000 | 140,000 | 140,000 |
| Fixed costs | | 30,000 | 30,000 | 30,000 |
| Depreciation | | 21,450 | 29,250 | 9,750 |
| EBIT | | $ 8,550 | $ 750 | $ 20,250 |
| Taxes on operating income (40%) | | 3,420 | 300 | 8,100 |
| AT project operating income | | $ 5,130 | $ 450 | $ 12,150 |
| Add back: Depreciation | | 21,450 | 29,250 | 9,750 |
| EBIT(1 − T) + Depreciation | | $ 26,580 | $ 29,700 | $ 21,900 |
| ***Terminal Cash Flows:*** | | | | |
| Salvage value | | | | 10,000 |
| Tax on salvage value | | | | (2,180) |
| AT salvage value | | | | $ 7,820 |
| Recovery of NOWC | | | | 2,000 |
| Project free cash flows | ($67,000) | $ 26,580 | $ 29,700 | $ 31,720 |

```
    0           1           2           3
    |    11%    |           |           |
    +-----------+-----------+-----------+
 -67,000     26,580      29,700      31,720
```

d. From the time line shown in part c, the project's NPV can be calculated as follows:

$$NPV = -\$67{,}000 + \$26{,}580/(1.11)^1 + \$29{,}700/(1.11)^2 + \$31{,}720/(1.11)^3$$
$$= \$4{,}245$$

Alternatively, using a financial calculator, you would enter the following data: $CF_0 = -67000$; $CF_1 = 26580$; $CF_2 = 29700$; $CF_3 = 31720$; $I/YR = 11$; and then solve for NPV = $4,245.

Because the NPV is positive, the project should be accepted.

e. Project analysis if unit sales turned out to be 20% below forecast:

Initial projection = 4,000 units; however, if unit sales turn out to be only 80% of forecast, then unit sales = 3,200.

| | Year 0 | Year 1 | Year 2 | Year 3 |
|---|---|---|---|---|
| ***Investment Outlays:*** | | | | |
| Equipment purchase | ($65,000) | | | |
| Change in NOWC | (2,000) | | | |
| ***Operating Cash Flows over*** | | | | |
| ***Project's Life:*** | | | | |
| Revenues (3,200 × $50) | | $160,000 | $160,000 | $160,000 |
| Variable costs (70%) | | 112,000 | 112,000 | 112,000 |
| Fixed costs | | 30,000 | 30,000 | 30,000 |
| Depreciation | | 21,450 | 29,250 | 9,750 |
| EBIT | | ($ 3,450) | ($ 11,250) | $ 8,250 |
| Taxes on operating income (40%) | | (1,380) | (4,500) | 3,300 |
| AT project operating income | | ($ 2,070) | ($ 6,750) | $ 4,950 |
| Add back: Depreciation | | 21,450 | 29,250 | 9,750 |
| EBIT(1 − T) + Depreciation | | $ 19,380 | $ 22,500 | $14,700 |

*(Continued)*

| | Year 0 | Year 1 | Year 2 | Year 3 |
|---|---|---|---|---|
| *Terminal Cash Flows:* | | | | |
| Salvage value | | | | 10,000 |
| Tax on salvage value | | | | (2,180) |
| AT salvage value | | | | $ 7,820 |
| Recovery of NOWC | | | | 2,000 |
| Project free cash flows | ($67,000) | $19,380 | $22,500 | $24,520 |

NPV calculation:

```
0          1          2          3
|----------|----------|----------|
   11%
-67,000   19,380    22,500    24,520
```

$$\text{NPV} = -\$67,000 + \$19,380/(1.11)^1 + \$22,500/(1.11)^2 + \$24,520/(1.11)^3$$
$$= -\$13,350$$

Alternatively, using a financial calculator, you would enter the following data: $CF_0 = -67000$; $CF_1 = 19380$; $CF_2 = 22500$; $CF_3 = 24520$; $I/YR = 11$; and then solve for NPV $= -\$13,350$.

Because the NPV is negative, the project should not be accepted. If unit sales were 20% below the forecasted level, the project would no longer be accepted.

f. *Best-case scenario:* Unit sales $= 4,800$; Variable cost % $= 65\%$

| | Year 0 | Year 1 | Year 2 | Year 3 |
|---|---|---|---|---|
| *Investment Outlays:* | | | | |
| Equipment purchase | ($65,000) | | | |
| Change in NOWC | (2,000) | | | |
| *Operating Cash Flows over Project's Life:* | | | | |
| Revenues (4,800 × $50) | | $240,000 | $240,000 | $240,000 |
| Variable costs (65%) | | 156,000 | 156,000 | 156,000 |
| Fixed costs | | 30,000 | 30,000 | 30,000 |
| Depreciation | | 21,450 | 29,250 | 9,750 |
| EBIT | | $ 32,550 | $ 24,750 | $ 44,250 |
| Taxes on operating income (40%) | | 13,020 | 9,900 | 17,700 |
| AT project operating income | | $ 19,530 | $ 14,850 | $ 26,550 |
| Add back: Depreciation | | 21,450 | 29,250 | 9,750 |
| EBIT(1 − T) + Depreciation | | $ 40,980 | $ 44,100 | $ 36,300 |
| *Terminal Cash Flows:* | | | | |
| Salvage value | | | | 10,000 |
| Tax on salvage value | | | | (2,180) |
| AT salvage value | | | | $ 7,820 |
| Recovery of NOWC | | | | 2,000 |
| Project free cash flows | ($67,000) | $ 40,980 | $ 44,100 | $ 46,120 |

Project NPV:

```
0          1          2          3
|----------|----------|----------|
   11%
-67,000   40,980    44,100    46,120
```

$$\text{NPV} = -\$67,000 + \$40,980/(1.11)^1 + \$44,100/(1.11)^2 + \$46,120/(1.11)^3$$
$$= \$39,434$$

Alternatively, using a financial calculator, you would enter the following data: $CF_0 = -67000$;  $CF_1 = 40980$;  $CF_2 = 44100$;  $CF_3 = 46120$; $I/YR = 11$; and then solve for NPV = $39,434.

*Base-case scenario:* The NPV was calculated in part d as $4,245.

*Worst-case scenario:* Unit sales = 3,200; Variable cost % = 75%

|  | Year 0 | Year 1 | Year 2 | Year 3 |
|---|---|---|---|---|
| *Investment Outlays:* | | | | |
| Equipment purchase | ($65,000) | | | |
| Change in NOWC | (2,000) | | | |
| *Operating Cash Flows over Project's Life:* | | | | |
| Revenues (3,200 × $50) | | $160,000 | $160,000 | $160,000 |
| Variable costs (75%) | | 120,000 | 120,000 | 120,000 |
| Fixed costs | | 30,000 | 30,000 | 30,000 |
| Depreciation | | 21,450 | 29,250 | 9,750 |
| EBIT | | ($ 11,450) | ($ 19,250) | $    250 |
| Taxes on operating income (40%) | | (4,580) | (7,700) | 100 |
| AT project operating income | | ($  6,870) | ($ 11,550) | $    150 |
| Add back: Depreciation | | 21,450 | 29,250 | 9,750 |
| EBIT(1 − T) + Depreciation | | $ 14,580 | $ 17,700 | $  9,900 |
| *Terminal Cash Flows:* | | | | |
| Salvage value | | | | 10,000 |
| Tax on salvage value | | | | (2,180) |
| AT salvage value | | | | $  7,820 |
| Recovery of NOWC | | | | 2,000 |
| Project free cash flows | ($67,000) | $ 14,580 | $ 17,700 | $ 19,720 |

Project NPV:

```
  0        1        2        3
  ├──11%───┼────────┼────────┤
-67,000  14,580   17,700   19,720
```

$$\text{NPV} = -\$67,000 + \$14,580/(1.11)^1 + \$17,700/(1.11)^2 + \$19,720/(1.11)^3$$
$$= -\$25,080$$

Alternatively, using a financial calculator, you would enter the following data: $CF_0 = -67000$;  $CF_1 = 14580$;  $CF_2 = 17700$;  $CF_3 = 19720$; $I/YR = 11$; and then solve for NPV = $-\$25,080$.

| Scenario | Probability | NPV |
|---|---|---|
| Best case | 25% | $39,434 |
| Base case | 50 | 4,245 |
| Worst case | 25 | −25,080 |
| | Expected NPV = | $  5,711 |

$$\sigma_{\text{NPV}} = \left[0.25(\$39,434 - \$5,711)^2 + 0.50(\$4,245 - \$5,711)^2 + 0.25(-\$25,080 - \$5,711)^2\right]^{1/2}$$
$$\sigma_{\text{NPV}} = [\$284,310,182 + \$1,074,578 + \$237,021,420]^{1/2}$$
$$\sigma_{\text{NPV}} = \$22,856$$
$$\text{CV}_{\text{NPV}} = \$22,856/\$5,711 = 4.0$$

g. The project's CV = 4.0, which is significantly larger than the firm's typical project CV. So, the WACC for this project should be adjusted upward, 11% + 3% = 14%.

To calculate the expected NPV, standard deviation, and coefficient of variation you would recalculate each scenario's NPV by discounting the project cash flows by 14% rather than 11%.

*Best-case scenario:*

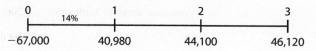

$$NPV = -\$67{,}000 + \$40{,}980/(1.14)^1 + \$44{,}100/(1.14)^2 + \$46{,}120/(1.14)^3$$
$$= \$34{,}011$$

Alternatively, using a financial calculator, you would enter the following data: $CF_0 = -67000$; $CF_1 = 40980$; $CF_2 = 44100$; $CF_3 = 46120$; $I/YR = 14$; and then solve for NPV = $34,011.

*Base-case scenario:*

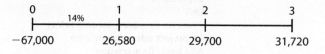

$$NPV = -\$67{,}000 + \$26{,}580/(1.14)^1 + \$29{,}700/(1.14)^2 + \$31{,}720/(1.14)^3$$
$$= \$579$$

Alternatively, using a financial calculator, you would enter the following data: $CF_0 = -67000$; $CF_1 = 26580$; $CF_2 = 29700$; $CF_3 = 31720$; $I/YR = 14$; and then solve for NPV = $579.

*Worst-case scenario:*

```
 0          1          2          3
 |   14%    |          |          |
-67,000   14,580    17,700    19,720
```

$$NPV = -\$67{,}000 + \$14{,}580/(1.14)^1 + \$17{,}700/(1.14)^2 + \$19{,}720/(1.14)^3$$
$$= -\$27{,}281$$

Alternatively, using a financial calculator, you would enter the following data: $CF_0 = -67000$; $CF_1 = 14580$; $CF_2 = 17700$; $CF_3 = 19720$; $I/YR = 14$; and then solve for NPV = −$27,281.

| Scenario | Probability | NPV |
|---|---|---|
| Best case | 25% | $34,011 |
| Base case | 50 | 579 |
| Worst case | 25 | −27,281 |
| | Expected NPV = | $ 1,972 |

$$\sigma_{NPV} = \left[0.25(\$34{,}011 - \$1{,}972)^2 + 0.50(\$579 - \$1{,}972)^2 + 0.25(-\$27{,}281 - \$1{,}972)^2\right]^{1/2}$$
$$\sigma_{NPV} = [\$256{,}624{,}380 + \$970{,}225 + \$213{,}934{,}502]^{1/2}$$
$$\sigma_{NPV} = \$21{,}715$$
$$CV_{NPV} = \$21{,}715/\$1{,}972 = 11.01$$

The expected NPV of the project is still positive, so the project would still be accepted, but it is a risky project.

# Chapter 13

**ST-2**   a. The following information is given in the problem:

Q = Units of output (sales) = 5,000
P = Average sales price per unit of output = $100
F = Fixed operating costs = $200,000
V = Variable costs per unit = $50
EBIT = Operating income = $50,000
Total assets = $500,000
Common equity = $500,000

(1)  Determine the new EBIT level if the change is made:

New EBIT = $P_2(Q_2) - F_2 - V_2(Q_2)$
New EBIT = $95(7,000) - $250,000 - $40(7,000)
       = $135,000

(2)  Determine the incremental EBIT:

$\Delta$EBIT = $135,000 - $50,000 = $85,000

(3)  Estimate the approximate rate of return on the new investment:

$$\Delta ROA = \frac{\Delta EBIT}{Investment} = \frac{\$85,000}{\$400,000} = 21.25\%$$

Because the ROA exceeds Olinde's average cost of capital, this analysis suggests that the firm should go ahead and make the investment.

b. The change would increase the break-even point. Still, with a lower sales price, it might be easier to achieve the higher new break-even volume.

$$\text{Old: } Q_{BE} = \frac{F}{P - V} = \frac{\$200,000}{\$100 - \$50} = 4,000 \text{ units}$$

$$\text{New: } Q_{BE} = \frac{F_2}{P_2 - V_2} = \frac{\$250,000}{\$95 - \$40} = 4,545 \text{ units}$$

c. The incremental ROA is:

$$ROA = \frac{\Delta Profit}{\Delta Sales} \times \frac{\Delta Sales}{\Delta Assets}$$

Using debt financing, the incremental profit associated with the investment is equal to the incremental profit found in part a minus the interest expense incurred as a result of the investment:

$\Delta$Profit = New profit − Old profit − Interest
       = $135,000 − $50,000 − 0.10($400,000)
       = $45,000

The incremental sales is calculated as:

$\Delta$Sales = $P_2Q_2 - P_1Q_1$
      = $95(7,000) − $100(5,000)
      = $665,000 − $500,000
      = $165,000

$$ROA = \frac{\$45,000}{\$165,000} \times \frac{\$165,000}{\$400,000} = 11.25\%$$

The return on the new investment still exceeds the average cost of capital, so the firm should make the investment.

**ST-3** a. Total capital = $5,000,000 and remains the same at all levels of debt; Tax rate = 35%; Original shares outstanding = 200,000; EBIT = $500,000 at all levels of debt.

From the data given in the problem, we can develop the following table:

| $w_d$ | $w_c$ | $r_d$ | EBIT | Interest[a] | Net Income[b] | Shares Outstanding[c] | EPS[d] |
|---|---|---|---|---|---|---|---|
| 0.00 | 1.00 | 5.00% | $500,000 | $ 0 | $325,000 | 200,000 | $1.63 |
| 0.25 | 0.75 | 6.00 | 500,000 | 75,000 | 276,250 | 150,000 | 1.84 |
| 0.50 | 0.50 | 8.30 | 500,000 | 207,500 | 190,125 | 100,000 | 1.90 |
| 0.75 | 0.25 | 11.00 | 500,000 | 412,500 | 56,875 | 50,000 | 1.14 |

*Notes:*

[a]Interest expense is calculated as $w_d \times$ Total capital $\times r_d$.

[b]Net income is calculated as $(\text{EBIT} - \text{Interest})(1 - T)$.

[c]Shares outstanding is calculated as Original shares outstanding at debt level = 0 − ($w_d \times$ Original shares outstanding at debt level = 0).

[d]EPS is calculated as Net income divided by Shares outstanding.

b. EPS is maximized at a capital structure consisting of 50% debt and 50% equity. At that capital structure, the firm's EPS is $1.90.

c. Tax rate = 35%; $r_{RF} = 3.5\%$; $b_U = 1.25$; $r_M - r_{RF} = 4.5\%$.

From data given in the problem, we can develop the following table:

| $w_d$ | $w_c$ | D/E | $r_d$ | $r_d(1 - T)$ | $b_L$[a] | $r_s$[b] | WACC[c] |
|---|---|---|---|---|---|---|---|
| 0.00 | 1.00 | 0.0000 | 5.00% | 3.25% | 1.25 | 9.13% | 9.13% |
| 0.25 | 0.75 | 0.3333 | 6.00 | 3.90 | 1.52 | 10.34 | 8.73 |
| 0.50 | 0.50 | 1.0000 | 8.30 | 5.40 | 2.06 | 12.78 | 9.09 |
| 0.75 | 0.25 | 3.0000 | 11.00 | 7.15 | 3.69 | 20.09 | 10.39 |

*Notes:*

[a]These beta estimates were calculated using the Hamada equation, $b_L = b_U[1 + (1 - T)(D/E)]$.

[b]These $r_s$ estimates were calculated using the CAPM, $r_s = r_{RF} + (r_M - r_{RF})b$.

[c]These WACC estimates were calculated with the following equation: WACC = $w_d(r_d)(1 - T) + (w_c)(r_s)$.

d. Carlisle's WACC is minimized at a capital structure consisting of 25% debt and 75% equity. At that capital structure, the firm's WACC is 8.73%.

e. The capital structure at which the firm's WACC is minimized is the optimal capital structure, that is, the capital structure at which the firm's value is maximized. For Carlisle, this capital structure consists of 25% debt and 75% equity. This is not the same capital structure at which EPS is maximized, because the additional risk taken on is not measured in the EPS calculation, but it is measured in the WACC calculation. (That is, the costs of debt and equity increase at additional debt levels, and those component costs are used in the WACC calculation.)

f. As an analyst (on the basis of these data), the recommendation to the firm would be to issue $1,250,000 of debt (calculated as $0.25 \times \$5,000,000$) with a 6% coupon rate (this is $r_d$ at this debt level) and use these funds to repurchase 50,000 shares of common stock.

# Chapter 14

**ST-2**  a.

| | |
|---|---|
| **Projected net income** | **$2,000,000** |
| **Less projected capital investments** | **800,000** |
| **Available residual** | **$1,200,000** |
| | |
| **Shares outstanding** | **200,000** |

**DPS = $1,200,000/200,000 shares = $6 = $D_1$**

b.  **EPS = $2,000,000/200,000 shares = $10**

**Payout ratio = DPS/EPS = $6/$10 = 60%, or**

**Total dividends/NI = $1,200,000/$2,000,000 = 60%**

c.  **Currently, $P_0 = \dfrac{D_1}{r_s - g} = \dfrac{\$6}{0.14 - 0.06} = \dfrac{\$6}{0.08} = \$75.00$**

Under the former circumstances, $D_1$ would be based on a 20% payout on an EPS of $10, or $0.2 \times \$10 = \$2$. With $r_s = 14\%$ and $g = 12\%$, we solve for $P_0$:

$$P_0 = \frac{D_1}{r_s - g} = \frac{\$2}{0.14 - 0.12} = \frac{\$2}{0.02} = \$100$$

Although CMC has suffered a severe setback, its existing assets will continue to provide a good income stream. More of these earnings should now be passed on to the shareholders, as the slowed internal growth has reduced the need for funds. However, the net result is a 25% decrease in the value of the shares.

d.  If the payout ratio were continued at 20%, even after internal investment opportunities had declined, the price of the stock would drop to $\$2/(0.14 - 0.06) = \$25$ rather than to $75.00. Thus, an increase in the dividend payout is consistent with maximizing shareholder wealth.

Because of the diminishing nature of profitable investment opportunities, the greater the firm's level of investment, the lower the average ROE. Thus, the more money CMC retains and invests, the lower its average ROE will be. We can determine the average ROE under different conditions as follows:

*Old situation (with founder active and a 20% payout):*

**g = (1.0 − Payout ratio)(Average ROE)**

**12% = (1.0 − 0.2)(Average ROE)**

**Average ROE = 12%/0.8 = 15% > $r_s$ = 14%**

Note that the *average* ROE is 15%, whereas the *marginal* ROE is presumably equal to 14%.

*New situation (with founder retired and a 60% payout as explained in part c):*

**g = 6% = (1.0 − 0.6)(ROE)**

**ROE = 6%/0.4 = 15% > $r_s$ = 14%**

This suggests that a new payout of 60% is appropriate and that the firm is taking on investments down to the point at which marginal returns are equal to the cost of capital. Note that if the 20% payout was maintained, the *average* ROE would be only 7.5%, which would imply a marginal ROE far below the 14% cost of capital.

# Chapter 15

**ST-2** The Calgary Company: Alternative Balance Sheets

|  | Restricted (40%) | Moderate (50%) | Relaxed (60%) |
|---|---|---|---|
| Current assets | $1,200,000 | $1,500,000 | $1,800,000 |
| Fixed assets | 600,000 | 600,000 | 600,000 |
| Total assets | $1,800,000 | $2,100,000 | $2,400,000 |
| Debt | $ 900,000 | $1,050,000 | $1,200,000 |
| Equity | 900,000 | 1,050,000 | 1,200,000 |
| Total liabilities and equity | $1,800,000 | $2,100,000 | $2,400,000 |

The Calgary Company: Alternative Income Statements

|  | Restricted | Moderate | Relaxed |
|---|---|---|---|
| Sales | $3,000,000 | $3,000,000 | $3,000,000 |
| EBIT | 450,000 | 450,000 | 450,000 |
| Interest (10%) | 90,000 | 105,000 | 120,000 |
| Earnings before taxes | $ 360,000 | $ 345,000 | $ 330,000 |
| Taxes (40%) | 144,000 | 138,000 | 132,000 |
| Net income | $ 216,000 | $ 207,000 | $ 198,000 |
| ROE | 24.0% | 19.7% | 16.5% |

**ST-3** a and b.

Income Statements for Year Ended December 31, 2016 (Thousands of Dollars)

|  | Vanderheiden Press | | Herrenhouse Publishing | |
|---|---|---|---|---|
|  | a | b | a | b |
| EBIT | $ 30,000 | $ 30,000 | $ 30,000 | $ 30,000 |
| Interest | 12,400 | 14,400 | 10,600 | 18,600 |
| Taxable income | $ 17,600 | $ 15,600 | $ 19,400 | $ 11,400 |
| Taxes (40%) | 7,040 | 6,240 | 7,760 | 4,560 |
| Net income | $ 10,560 | $ 9,360 | $ 11,640 | $ 6,840 |
| Equity | $100,000 | $100,000 | $100,000 | $100,000 |
| Return on equity | 10.56% | 9.36% | 11.64% | 6.84% |

The Vanderheiden Press has a higher ROE when short-term interest rates are high, whereas Herrenhouse Publishing does better when rates are lower.

c. Herrenhouse's position is riskier. First, its profits and return on equity are much more volatile than Vanderheiden's. Second, Herrenhouse must renew its large short-term loan every year, and if the renewal comes up at a time when money is very tight, when its business is depressed, or both, then Herrenhouse could be denied credit, which could put it out of business.

# Chapter 16

**ST-2**    To solve this problem, we define $\Delta S$ as the change in sales and g as the growth rate in sales, and then we use the three following equations:

$$\Delta S = S_0 g$$
$$S_1 = S_0(1 + g)$$
$$AFN = (A_0^*/S_0)(\Delta S) - (L_0^*/S_0)(\Delta S) - MS_1(1 - Payout)$$

Set AFN = 0, substitute in known values for $A_0^*/S_0$, $L_0^*/S_0$, M, payout, and $S_0$, and then solve for g:

$$0 = 1.6(\$100g) - 0.4(\$100g) - 0.10[\$100(1 + g)](1 - 0.45)$$
$$0 = \$160g - \$40g - 0.055(\$100 + \$100g)$$
$$0 = \$160g - \$40g - \$5.5 - \$5.5g$$
$$\$114.5g = \$5.5$$
$$g = \$5.5/\$114.5 = 0.048 = 4.8\%$$
$$g = \text{Maximum growth rate without external financing}$$

**ST-3**    Assets consist of cash, marketable securities, receivables, inventories, and fixed assets. Therefore, we can break the $A_0^*/S_0$ ratio into its components—cash/sales, inventories/sales, and so forth. Then,

$$\frac{A_0^*}{S_0} = \frac{A_0^* - \text{Inventories}}{S_0} + \frac{\text{Inventories}}{S_0} = 1.6$$

We know that the inventory turnover ratio is Sales/Inventories = 3 times, so Inventories/Sales = 1/3 = 0.3333. Further, if the inventory turnover ratio can be increased to 4 times, then the Inventory/Sales ratio will fall to 1/4 = 0.25, a difference of 0.3333 − 0.2500 = 0.0833. This, in turn, causes the $A_0^*/S_0$ ratio to fall from $A_0^*/S_0 = 1.6$ to $A_0^*/S_0 = 1.6 - 0.0833 = 1.5167$.

This change has two effects: First, it changes the AFN equation, and second, it means that Weatherford currently has excessive inventories. Because it is costly to hold excess inventories, Weatherford will want to reduce its inventory holdings by not replacing inventories until the excess amounts have been used. We can account for this by setting up the revised AFN equation (using the new $A_0^*/S_0$ ratio), estimating the funds that will be needed next year if no excess inventories are currently on hand, and then subtracting out the excess inventories that are currently on hand:

*Present conditions:*

$$\frac{\text{Sales}}{\text{Inventories}} = \frac{\$100}{\text{Inventories}} = 3$$

so

$$\text{Inventories} = \$100/3 = \$33.3 \text{ million at present}$$

*New conditions:*

$$\frac{\text{Sales}}{\text{Inventories}} = \frac{\$100}{\text{Inventories}} = 4$$

so

$$\text{New level of inventories} = \$100/4 = \$25 \text{ million}$$

Therefore,

$$\text{Excess inventories} = \$33.3 - \$25 = \$8.3 \text{ million}$$

*Forecast of funds needed:*

$$\Delta S = 0.2(\$100 \text{ million}) = \$20 \text{ million}$$

$$AFN = 1.5167(\$20) - 0.4(\$20) - 0.1(1 - 0.45)(\$120) - \$8.3$$
$$= \$30.3 - \$8 - \$6.6 - \$8.3$$
$$= \$7.4 \text{ million}$$

## Chapter 17

**ST-2**
$$\frac{\text{Euros}}{\text{C\$}} = \frac{\text{Euros}}{\text{US\$}} \times \frac{\text{US\$}}{\text{C\$}}$$

$$= \frac{€0.91}{\$1} \times \frac{\$1}{\text{C\$}1.25} = \frac{€0.91}{\text{C\$}1.25} = €0.7280 \text{ per Canadian dollar}$$

## Answers to Selected End-of-Chapter Problems

*Note:* This appendix presents some intermediate steps and final answers to selected end-of-chapter problems. Please note that your answer may differ slightly due to rounding differences. Also, some of the problems may have more than one correct solution depending upon the assumptions made in working the problem. Finally, where the selected problems involve a verbal discussion as well as numerical calculations, the verbal answer is not provided.

**3-2**    $800,000

**3-4**    $34,000,000

**3-6**    $22,000,000

**3-8**    a. $99,279
      b. 33%
      c. 26.47%

**3-10**   $71,600,000

**3-12**   a. $62,000
      b. $72,000

**3-14**   a. $NOWC_{2015} = \$56,000; NOWC_{2016} = \$65,220$
      b. $15,180
      c. CS = $40,000; RE = $46,220
      d. EVA = $15,078
      e. MVA = $13,780

**3-16**   a. $RE_{2015} = \$1,374$ million
      b. $1,600 million
      c. $15 million
      d. $620 million

**3-18**   a. $19,043.75
      b. 25%
      c. 18.49%

**4-2**    47.64%

**4-4**    M/B = 1.1765

**4-6**    ROE = 14.25%

**4-8**    NI = $451,562.50

**4-10**   $P_0 = \$72.22$

**4-12**   TIE = 6.00×

**4-14**   ROE = 9.33%

**4-16**   ΔROE = +6.94%

**4-18**   TIE = 6.22×

**4-20**   Accounts receivable = $49,085

**4-22**   Sales = $450,000; AR = $45,000;
      Inv = $90,000; FA = $150,000; CL = $75,000

**4-24**   a. Current ratio = 3.56×;
      Debt to total capital = 20.05%;
      DSO = 30.3 days; ROA = 6.00%;
      ROIC = 7.54%
      b. Firm: ROE = 3.4% × 1.77 × $450/$315
          = 8.6%

Industry: ROE = 3.0% × 3 × ROE/ROA
                 = 3.0% × 3 × 12.86%/9.00%
                 = 12.86%

**5-2**    PV = $10,929.80

**5-4**    N = 17.67 yrs.

**5-6**    $FVA_5 = \$4,420.51$; $FVA_{5\ Due} = \$4,641.53$

**5-8**    PMT = $811.06; EAR = 8.30%

**5-10**   a. $296.05
      b. $431.78
      c. $135.11
      d. $866.17; $1,263.30

**5-12**   a. 10%
      b. 10%
      c. 3%
      d. 11%

**5-14**   a. $6,616.38
      b. $1,109.99
      c. $2,800.00
      d(l). $7,542.67
      d(2). $1,187.68
      d(3). $2,800.00

**5-16**   $PV_{5\%} = \$12,000; PV_{10\%} = \$6,000$

**5-18**   a. Stream A: $1,505.84;
        Stream B: $1,522.73
      b. Stream A and Stream B: $1,750

**5-20**   Contract 2: PV = $12,358,739.18

**5-22**   a. $802.43
      b. Pymt 1: Int = $500; Princ = $302.43;
        Pymt 2: Int = $484.88; Princ = $317.55
      c. $984.88

**5-24**   a. $279.20
      b. $276.84
      c. $443.72

**5-26**   $17,290.89; $19,734.26

**5-28**   $I_{NOM} = 11.729145\% \approx 11.73\%$

**5-30**   a. A = 59.89 yrs.; L = 50.08 yrs.
      b. $12,649.64

**5-32**   $1,297.13

**5-34**   a. PMT = $7,372.64
      b. Yr.1: Int/Pymt = 20.62%; Princ/Pymt
          = 79.38%;
        Yr.2: Int/Pymt = 14.27%; Princ/Pymt
          = 85.73%;
        Yr.3: Int/Pymt = 7.41%; Princ/Pymt
          = 92.59%

**5-36**   a. $5,468.41
      b. $1,926.87

**5-38**   $580,191

**5-40**   $6,147

**6-2** 2.55%

**6-4** 2.65%

**6-6** 23.9%

**6-8** 8.36%

**6-10** 5.5%

**6-12** 0.47%

**6-14** a. $r_1$ in Yr. 2 = 5%

b. $I_1 = 2.2\%$; $I_2 = 4\%$

**6-16** 14%

**6-18** a. $r_{T1} = 9.20\%$; $r_{T2} = 8.40\%$; $r_{T3} = 7.60\%$;
$r_{T4} = 7.30\%$; $r_{T5} = 7.20\%$; $r_{T10} = 6.60\%$;
$r_{T20} = 6.30\%$

**7-2** a. 8.27%

b. $983.38

**7-4** YTM = $6.42%; YTC = 6.32%; most likely
yield = 6.32%

**7-6** a. Bond C: $1,108.82; $1,084.74; $1,058.69;
$1,030.50; $1,000.00

Bond Z: $729.61; $789.44; $854.17;
$924.21; $1,000.00

**7-8** 11.75%

**7-10** a. YTM = 10.595%

b. CY = 9.887%; CGY = 0.708%

**7-12** a. YTM = 6.50%; YTC = 3.72%

**7-14** a. 6 yrs.

b. YTC = 6.64%

**7-16** $1,071.06

**7-18** a. YTM = 8.22%

b. YTC = 7.91%

c. YTC = 7.91%

d. Yr. 7; YTC = 8.20%

**8-2** $b_p = 2.10$

**8-4** $r_M = 7.5\%$; $r = 6.7\%$

**8-6** a. $\hat{r}_B = 14\%$

b. $\sigma_A = 12.20\%$; $CV_B = 1.45$

**8-8** b = 1.1667

**8-10** 5.2%

**8-12** a. $r_i = 12.4\%$

b(1). $r_M = 11\%$; $r_i = 13.4\%$

b(2). $r_M = 9\%$; $r_i = 11.4\%$

c(1). $r_i = 15.2\%$

c(2). $r_i = 11.0\%$

**8-14** $b_N = 1.24$

**8-16** $r_p = 11.30\%$

**8-18** a. $0.5 million

d(1). $75,000

d(2). 15%

**8-20** a. $r_A = 11.30\%$; $r_B = 11.30\%$

b. $r_{p\ Avg} = 11.30\%$

c. $\sigma_A = 20.8\%$; $\sigma_B = 20.8\%$; $\sigma_p = 20.1\%$

d. $CV_A = CV_B = 1.84$; $CV_p = 1.78$

**9-2** $\hat{P}_0 = \$30.00$

**9-4** a. End of Yr. 2

b. $67.65

c. $59.88

**9-6** $r_p = 9.17\%$

**9-8** a. $114.29

b. $88.89

**9-10** $17.63

**9-12** a(1). $12.25

a(2). $15.63

a(3). $25.75

a(4). $43.75

b(1). Undefined

b(2). −$35.00, which is nonsense

**9-14** $P_0 = \$10.08$

**9-16** 2.25%

**9-18** a. $P_0 = \$54.11$; $D_1/P_0 = 3.55\%$; CGY = 6.45%

**9-20** $20.00

**9A-2** a. $P_0 = \$32.14$

b. $P_0 = \$37.50$

c. $P_0 = \$50.00$

d. $P_0 = \$78.28$

**10-2** $r_p = 10.53\%$

**10-4** a. $r_s = 7.33\%$

b. $r_e = 7.70\%$

**10-6** a. $r_s = 15.6\%$

b. $r_s = 14.4\%$

c. $r_s = 15\%$

d. $r_{s\ Avg} = 15.0\%$

**10-8** $r_s = 15.74\%$; WACC = 11.91%

**10-10** WACC = 9.31%

**10-12** a. $r_s = 14.97\%$

b. WACC = 11.62%

c. Project A

**10-14** 10.67%

**10-16** a. g = 8%

b. $D_1 = \$2.81$

c. $r_s = 15.81\%$

**10-18** a. $r_d(1 - T) = 7\%$; $r_p = 10\%$;
$r_s = 16.18\%$

b. WACC = 14.19%

c. Projects 1 and 2 will be accepted

**10-20** a. $r_d(1 - T) = 5.4\%$; $r_s = 14.6\%$

b. WACC = 10.92%

**11-2** IRR = 11.57%

**11-4** 5.42 yrs.

**11-6** a.  5%: $NPV_A = \$3.52$; $NPV_B = \$2.87$
10%: $NPV_A = \$0.58$; $NPV_B = \$1.04$
15%: $NPV_A = -\$1.91$; $NPV_B = -\$0.55$

b. $IRR_A = 11.10\%$; $IRR_B = 13.18\%$

c. 5%: Choose A; 10%: Choose B; 15%: Do
not choose either one

**11-8** a. Without mitigation: NPV = $12.10 million;
IRR = 19.86%;
With mitigation: NPV = $5.70 million;
IRR = 15.24%

**11-10** Project 1; $NPV_1 = \$234.26$

**11-12** $IRR_L = 12.70\%$

**11-14** a. HCC; PV = −$805,009.87

c. LCC; PV = −$686,627.14

**11-16**  a. $NPV_A = \$14,486,808$; $NPV_B = \$11,156,893$;
$IRR_A = 15.03\%$; $IRR_B = 22.26\%$
c. Crossover rate $\approx 11.71\%$

**11-18**  a. No; $PV_{Old} = -\$89,910.08$;
$PV_{New} = -\$94,611.45$
b. $2,470.80
c. 22.94%

**11-20**  $2,698.89

**11-22**  $250.01

**12-2**  a. $3,900,000
b. $3,000,000
c. $4,050,000; $\Delta = +\$150,000$

**12-4**  Yes, NPV = $4,156.54

**12-6**  a. SL: Deprec. = $200,000/yr.;
MACRS: $264,000; $360,000; $120,000;
$56,000
b. MACRS; $9,478.91

**12-8**  a. −$178,000
b. $52,135; $59,275; $92,590
c. No, NPV = −$8,783

**12-10**  Yes, NPV = $1,908.47

**12-12**  a. A: $6,750; B: $7,650; $\sigma_A = \$474.34$;
$CV_A = 0.0703$
b. Project B

**12-14**  a. NPV = $37,035.13; IRR = 15.30%;
MIRR = 12.81%; Payback = 3.33 yrs.
b. +20%: NPV = $77,975.63
−20%: NPV = −$3,905.37
c. E(NPV) = $34,800.21;
$\sigma_{NPV} = \$35,967.84$; CV = 1.03

**12-16**  a. −$792,750
b. Depr.$_{New}$: $235,000; $376,000;
$223,250; $141,000; $129,250
Depr.$_{Old}$: $120,000/yr.
$\Delta$Depr.: $115,000; $256,000; $103,250;
$21,000; $9,250
c. $206,000; $255,350; $201,888; $173,100;
$168,988 + $118,925 = $287,913
d. Yes; NPV = $11,819.67

**12-18**  a. A, B, C, D, E; $5,250,000
b. A, B, D, E; $4,000,000
c. B, C, D, E, F, G; $6,000,000

**13-2**  30% debt and 70% equity

**13-4**  $b_U = 0.9811$

**13-6**  a(1). −$38,000
a(2). $40,000
b. $Q_{BE} = 11,923$
c. $Q_{BE} = 7,750$
d. $Q_{BE} = 17,222$

**13-8**  $r_s = 13.35\%$

**13-10**  a. $FC_A = \$80,000$; $V_A = \$4.80/unit$;
$P_A = \$8.00/unit$

b. Firm B
c. 50,000 units

**13-12**  a. $EPS_{Old} = \$2.04$; New: $EPS_D = \$4.74$;
$EPS_S = \$3.27$
b. 339,750 units
c. $Q_{Old} = 316,957$ units;
$Q_{New, Debt} = 272,250$ units;
$Q_{New, Stock} = 204,750$ units

**14-2**  $P_0 = \$96.67$

**14-4**  $D_0 = \$5.37$

**14-6**  Payout = 36%

**14-8**  a. 12%
b. 18%
c. g = 6%; $r_s = 18\%$
d. 6%
e. 28,800 new shares; $0.13 per share

**15-2**  45.62 days; 30 days; $513,698.63

**15-4**  a. 51 days
b. $197,782.41 $\approx$ $197,782
c. 7.60×

**15-6**  a. 32 days
b. $313,600
c. $29,400
d(1). 27 days
d(2). $777,600

**15-8**  a. $ROE_T = 11.75\%$; $ROE_M = 10.80\%$;
$ROE_R = 9.16\%$

**15-10**  a. Oct. loan = $22,800
b. $111,300; $297,600; −$155,100;
−$22,800; $118,500; $187,800

**16-2**  AFN = $646,000

**16-4**  a. $133.50 million
b. 39.06%

**16-6**  $67 million; 5.01×

**16-8**  a. $825,000
b. $141,875

**16-10**  $34.338 million; 34.97 $\approx$ 35 days

**16-12**  a. $3,750,000,000
b. 21%
c. $31,500,000

**16-14**  a. 33%
b. NP = $3,553.2; Bonds = $6,598.8;
Stock = $2,514; RE = $28,284

**17-2**  32.04 yen per shekel

**17-4**  1 euro = $1.1765 or $1 = 0.8500 euro

**17-8**  13.0356 kronas per pound

**17-10**  $r_{NOM–U.S.} = 2.4989\%$

**17-12**  a. $1.528104
b. Discount

**17-14**  +$600,000

**17-16**  $490,534,351

# Appendix C

## Selected Equations and Tables

### Chapter 3

Stockholders' equity = Paid-in capital + Retained earnings

Stockholders' equity = Total assets − Total liabilities

Net working capital = Current assets − Current liabilities

Net operating working capital = (Current assets − Excess cash)
$$− (Current\ liabilities − Notes\ payable)$$

Total debt = Short-term debt + Long-term debt

Total liabilities = Total debt + Accounts payable + Accruals

Operating income (or EBIT) = Sales revenues − Operating costs

$$FCF = (EBIT(1 − T) + Depreciation) − \left( \begin{array}{c} Capital \\ expenditures \end{array} + \begin{array}{c} \Delta Net\ operating \\ working\ capital \end{array} \right)$$

$$MVA = (P_0 \times Shares\ outstanding) − Book\ value\ of\ total\ common\ equity$$

$$EVA = EBIT(1 − T) − \left( \begin{array}{ccc} Total \\ invested & \times & \begin{array}{c} After\text{-}tax \\ percentage \end{array} \\ capital & & cost\ of\ capital \end{array} \right)$$

**2015 Individual Tax Rates: Single Individuals**

| If Your Taxable Income Is | You Pay This Amount on the Base of the Bracket | Plus This Percentage on the Excess over the Base (Marginal Rate) | Average Tax Rate at Top of Bracket |
|---|---|---|---|
| Up to $9,225 | $      0 | 10.0% | 10.0% |
| $9,225–$37,450 | 922.50 | 15.0 | 13.8 |
| $37,450–$90,750 | 5,156.25 | 25.0 | 20.4 |
| $90,750–$189,750 | 18,481.25 | 28.0 | 24.3 |
| $189,750–$411,500 | 46,075.25 | 33.0 | 29.0 |
| $411,500–$413,200 | 119,401.25 | 35.0 | 29.0 |
| Over $413,200 | 119,996.25 | 39.6 | 39.6 |

**Married Couples Filing Joint Returns**

| If Your Taxable Income Is | You Pay This Amount on the Base of the Bracket | Plus This Percentage on the Excess over the Base (Marginal Rate) | Average Tax Rate at Top of Bracket |
|---|---|---|---|
| Up to $18,450 | 0 | 10.0% | 10.0% |
| $18,450–$74,900 | 1,845.00 | 15.0 | 13.8 |
| $74,900–$151,200 | 10,312.50 | 25.0 | 19.4 |
| $151,200–$230,450 | 29,387.50 | 28.0 | 22.4 |
| $230,450–$411,500 | 51,577.50 | 33.0 | 27.1 |
| $411,500–$464,850 | 111,324.00 | 35.0 | 28.0 |
| Over $464,850 | 129,996.50 | 39.6 | 39.6 |

C-1

**2015 Corporate Tax Rates**

| If a Corporation's Taxable Income Is | You Pay This Amount on the Base of the Bracket | Plus This Percentage on the Excess over the Base (Marginal Rate) | Average Tax Rate at Top of Bracket |
|---|---|---|---|
| Up to $50,000 | $        0 | 15% | 15.0% |
| $50,000–$75,000 | 7,500 | 25 | 18.3 |
| $75,000–$100,000 | 13,750 | 34 | 22.3 |
| $100,000–$335,000 | 22,250 | 39 | 34.0 |
| $335,000–$10,000,000 | 113,900 | 34 | 34.0 |
| $10,000,000–$15,000,000 | 3,400,000 | 35 | 34.3 |
| $15,000,000–$18,333,333 | 5,150,000 | 38 | 35.0 |
| Over $18,333,333 | 6,416,667 | 35 | 35.0 |

# Chapter 4

$$\text{Current ratio} = \frac{\text{Current assets}}{\text{Current liabilities}}$$

$$\text{Quick, or acid test, ratio} = \frac{\text{Current assets} - \text{Inventories}}{\text{Current liabilities}}$$

$$\text{Inventory turnover} = \frac{\text{Sales}}{\text{Inventories}}$$

$$\text{Days sales outstanding} (\text{DSO}) = \frac{\text{Receivables}}{\text{Average sales per day}} = \frac{\text{Receivables}}{\text{Annual sales}/365}$$

$$\text{Fixed assets turnover} = \frac{\text{Sales}}{\text{Net fixed assets}}$$

$$\text{Total assets turnover} = \frac{\text{Sales}}{\text{Total assets}}$$

$$\text{Total-debt-to-total-capital ratio} = \frac{\text{Total debt}}{\text{Total capital}} = \frac{\text{Total debt}}{\text{Total debt} + \text{Equity}}$$

$$\text{Total-liabilities-to-assets ratio} = \frac{\text{Total liabilities}}{\text{Total assets}}$$

$$\text{Debt-to-equity ratio} = \frac{\text{Total debt}}{\text{Equity}}$$

$$\text{Times-interest-earned} (\text{TIE}) = \frac{\text{EBIT}}{\text{Interest charges}}$$

$$\text{EBITDA coverage} = \frac{\text{EBITDA} + \text{Lease payments}}{\text{Interest} + \text{Principal payments} + \text{Lease payments}}$$

$$\text{Operating margin} = \frac{\text{EBIT}}{\text{Sales}}$$

$$\text{Profit margin} = \frac{\text{Net income}}{\text{Sales}}$$

$$\text{Return on total assets} (\text{ROA}) = \frac{\text{Net income}}{\text{Total assets}}$$

$$\text{Return on common equity} (\text{ROE}) = \frac{\text{Net income}}{\text{Common equity}}$$

$$\text{Return on invested capital} (\text{ROIC}) = \frac{\text{EBIT}(1 - \text{T})}{\text{Total invested capital}} = \frac{\text{EBIT}(1 - \text{T})}{\text{Debt} + \text{Equity}}$$

$$\text{Basic earning power (BEP)} = \frac{\text{EBIT}}{\text{Total assets}}$$

$$\text{Price/Earnings (P/E)} = \frac{\text{Price per share}}{\text{Earnings per share}}$$

$$\text{Book value per share} = \frac{\text{Common equity}}{\text{Shares outstanding}}$$

$$\text{Market/Book (M/B)} = \frac{\text{Market price per share}}{\text{Book value per share}}$$

$$\text{ROE} = \qquad\qquad \text{ROA} \qquad\qquad \times \text{Equity multiplier}$$

$$= \text{Profit margin} \times \text{Total assets turnover} \times \text{Equity multiplier}$$

$$= \frac{\text{Net income}}{\text{Sales}} \times \frac{\text{Sales}}{\text{Total assets}} \times \frac{\text{Total assets}}{\text{Total common equity}}$$

$$\text{EVA} = \text{Net income} - [\text{Equity} \times \text{Cost of equity}]$$

$$= (\text{Equity})[\text{Net income/Equity} - \text{Cost of equity}]$$

$$= (\text{Equity})(\text{ROE} - \text{Cost of equity})$$

# Chapter 5

$$\text{Future value} = \text{FV}_N = \text{PV}(1 + I)^N$$

$$\text{Present value} = \text{PV} = \frac{\text{FV}_N}{(1 + I)^N}$$

$$\text{FVA}_N = \text{PMT}(1 + I)^{N-1} + \text{PMT}(1 + I)^{N-2} + \text{PMT}(1 + I)^{N-3} + \cdots + \text{PMT}(1 + I)^0$$

$$= \text{PMT}\left[\frac{(1 + I)^N - 1}{I}\right]$$

$$\text{FVA}_{\text{due}} = \text{FVA}_{\text{ordinary}}(1 + I)$$

$$\text{PVA}_N = \text{PMT}/(1 + I)^1 + \text{PMT}/(1 + I)^2 + \cdots + \text{PMT}/(1 + I)^N$$

$$= \text{PMT}\left[\frac{1 - \dfrac{1}{(1 + I)^N}}{I}\right]$$

$$\text{PVA}_{\text{due}} = \text{PVA}_{\text{ordinary}}(1 + I)$$

$$\text{PV of a perpetuity} = \frac{\text{PMT}}{I}$$

$$\text{PV} = \frac{\text{CF}_1}{(1 + I)^1} + \frac{\text{CF}_2}{(1 + I)^2} + \cdots + \frac{\text{CF}_N}{(1 + I)^N}$$

$$= \sum_{t=1}^{N} \frac{\text{CF}_t}{(1 + I)^t}$$

$$\text{Periodic rate (I}_{\text{PER}}) = \frac{\text{Stated annual rate}}{\text{Number of payments per year}} = I/M$$

$$\text{Number of periods} = (\text{Number of years})(\text{Periods per year}) = NM$$

$$\text{Effective annual rate (EFF\%)} = \left(1 + \frac{\text{I}_{\text{NOM}}}{M}\right)^M - 1.0$$

# Chapter 6

**Quoted interest rate** $(r) = r^* + IP + DRP + LP + MRP$
$$= r_{RF} + DRP + LP + MRP$$

$r_{T\text{-bill}} = r_{RF} = r^* + IP$
$r_{T\text{-bond}} = r_t^* + IP_t + MRP_t$
$r_{C\text{-bond}} = r_t^* + IP_t + MRP_t + DRP_t + LP_t$

$r_{RF}$ **with cross-product term** $= r^* + IP + (r^* \times IP)$

# Chapter 7

**Bond's value** $= V_B = \dfrac{INT}{(1 + r_d)^1} + \dfrac{INT}{(1 + r_d)^2} + \cdots + \dfrac{INT}{(1 + r_d)^N} + \dfrac{M}{(1 + r_d)^N}$

$$= \sum_{t=1}^{N} \frac{INT}{(1 + r_d)^t} + \frac{M}{(1 + r_d)^N}$$

**Price of callable bond** $= \displaystyle\sum_{t=1}^{N} \frac{INT}{(1 + r_d)^t} + \frac{Call\ price}{(1 + r_d)^N}$

$$V_B = \sum_{t=1}^{2N} \frac{INT/2}{(1 + r_d/2)^t} + \frac{M}{(1 + r_d/2)^{2N}}$$

**Accrued interest = Coupon payment** $\times \left( \dfrac{\begin{array}{c}\text{Number of days since}\\ \text{last coupon payment}\end{array}}{\begin{array}{c}\text{Number of days}\\ \text{in coupon period}\end{array}} \right)$

**Dirty price = Clean price + Accrued interest**
**Invoice price = Quoted price + Accrued interest**

# Chapter 8

**Expected rate of return** $= \hat{r} = P_1 r_1 + P_2 r_2 + \cdots + P_N r_N$

$$= \sum_{i=1}^{N} P_i r_i$$

**Standard deviation** $= \sigma = \sqrt{\displaystyle\sum_{i=1}^{N} (r_i - \hat{r})^2 P_i}$

**Estimated** $\sigma = \sqrt{\dfrac{\displaystyle\sum_{t=1}^{N} (\bar{r}_t - \bar{r}_{Avg})^2}{N - 1}}$

**Coefficient of variation** $= CV = \dfrac{\sigma}{\hat{r}}$

$\hat{r}_p = w_1 \hat{r}_1 + w_2 \hat{r}_2 + \cdots + w_N \hat{r}_N$

$$= \sum_{i=1}^{N} w_i \hat{r}_i$$

$b_p = w_1 b_1 + w_2 b_2 + \cdots + w_N b_N$

$$= \sum_{i=1}^{N} w_i b_i$$

$RP_M = r_M - r_{RF}$

$RP_i = (RP_M) b_i$

$r_i = r_{RF} + (r_M - r_{RF}) b_i$

# Chapter 9

Value of stock $= \hat{P}_0 =$ PV of expected future dividends

$$= \frac{D_1}{(1+r_s)^1} + \frac{D_2}{(1+r_s)^2} + \cdots + \frac{D_\infty}{(1+r_s)^\infty}$$

$$= \sum_{t=1}^{\infty} \frac{D_t}{(1+r_s)^t}$$

Constant growth stock: $\hat{P}_0 = \dfrac{D_0(1+g)^1}{(1+r_s)^1} + \dfrac{D_0(1+g)^2}{(1+r_s)^2} + \cdots + \dfrac{D_0(1+g)^\infty}{(1+r_s)^\infty}$

$$= \frac{D_0(1+g)}{r_s - g} = \frac{D_1}{r_s - g}$$

Expected rate of return $=$ Expected dividend yield $+$ Expected growth rate, or capital gains yield

$$\hat{r}_s = \frac{D_1}{P_0} + g$$

Growth rate $= (1 - \text{Payout ratio})\,\text{ROE}$

Zero growth stock: $\hat{P}_0 = \dfrac{D}{r_s}$

Horizon value $= \hat{P}_N = \dfrac{D_{N+1}}{r_s - g}$

Nonconstant growth stock: $\hat{P}_0 = \dfrac{D_1}{(1+r_s)^1} + \dfrac{D_2}{(1+r_s)^2} + \cdots + \dfrac{D_N}{(1+r_s)^N}$

$$+ \frac{D_{N+1}}{(1+r_s)^{N+1}} + \cdots + \frac{D_\infty}{(1+r_s)^\infty}$$

$$= \frac{D_1}{(1+r_s)^1} + \frac{D_2}{(1+r_s)^2} + \cdots + \frac{D_N}{(1+r_s)^N} + \frac{\hat{P}_N}{(1+r_s)^N}$$

$$= \text{PV of nonconstant dividends} + \text{PV of horizon value, } \hat{P}_N$$

PV of horizon value, $\hat{P}_N = \dfrac{D_{N+1}/(r_s - g)}{(1+r_s)^N}$

Market value of company $= V_{company} =$ PV of expected future free cash flows

$$= \frac{FCF_1}{(1+WACC)^1} + \frac{FCF_2}{(1+WACC)^2} + \cdots + \frac{FCF_\infty}{(1+WACC)^\infty}$$

Horizon value $= V_{\text{Company at } t=N} = FCF_{N+1}/(WACC - g_{FCF})$

Market value of equity $=$ Book value $+$ PV of all future EVAs

$$V_p = \frac{D_p}{r_p}$$

$$\hat{r}_p = \frac{D_p}{V_p}$$

# Chapter 10

$$WACC = \begin{pmatrix} \% \\ \text{of} \\ \text{debt} \end{pmatrix} \begin{pmatrix} \text{After-tax} \\ \text{cost of} \\ \text{debt} \end{pmatrix} + \begin{pmatrix} \% \text{ of} \\ \text{preferred} \\ \text{stock} \end{pmatrix} \begin{pmatrix} \text{Cost of} \\ \text{preferred} \\ \text{stock} \end{pmatrix} + \begin{pmatrix} \% \text{ of} \\ \text{common} \\ \text{equity} \end{pmatrix} \begin{pmatrix} \text{Cost of} \\ \text{common} \\ \text{equity} \end{pmatrix}$$

$$= \qquad w_d r_d (1-T) \qquad + \qquad w_p r_p \qquad + \qquad w_c r_s$$

After-tax cost of debt = Interest rate on new debt − Tax savings
$$= r_d - r_d T$$
$$= r_d(1 - T)$$

Component cost of preferred stock $= r_p = \dfrac{D_p}{P_p}$

Required rate of return = Expected rate of return
$$r_s = r_{RF} + RP = D_1/P_0 + g = \hat{r}_s$$

$$r_s = r_{RF} + (RP_M)b_i$$
$$= r_{RF} + (r_M - r_{RF})b_i$$

$$r_s = \text{Bond yield} + \text{Risk premium}$$

$$P_0 = \dfrac{D_1}{(1 + r_s)^1} + \dfrac{D_2}{(1 + r_s)^2} + \cdots + \dfrac{D_\infty}{(1 + r_s)^\infty}$$
$$= \sum_{t=1}^{\infty} \dfrac{D_t}{(1 + r_s)^t}$$

$$P_0 = \dfrac{D_1}{r_s - g}$$

$$r_s = \hat{r}_s = \dfrac{D_1}{P_0} + \text{Expected } g$$

Cost of equity from new stock $= r_e = \dfrac{D_1}{P_0(1 - F)} + g$

$$\dfrac{\text{Flotation cost}}{\text{adjustment}} = \dfrac{\text{Adjusted}}{\text{DCF cost}} - \dfrac{\text{Pure}}{\text{DCF cost}}$$

$$\dfrac{\text{Cost of}}{\text{external equity}} = r_s + \dfrac{\text{Flotation cost}}{\text{adjustment}}$$

$$\dfrac{\text{Retained earnings}}{\text{breakpoint}} = \dfrac{\text{Addition to retained earnings for the year}}{\text{Equity fraction}}$$

# Chapter 11

$$NPV = CF_0 + \dfrac{CF_1}{(1 + r)^1} + \dfrac{CF_2}{(1 + r)^2} + \cdots + \dfrac{CF_N}{(1 + r)^N}$$
$$= \sum_{t=0}^{N} \dfrac{CF_t}{(1 + r)^t}$$

$$CF_0 + \dfrac{CF_1}{(1 + IRR)^1} + \dfrac{CF_2}{(1 + IRR)^2} + \cdots + \dfrac{CF_N}{(1 + IRR)^N} = 0$$
$$\sum_{t=0}^{N} \dfrac{CF_t}{(1 + IRR)^t} = 0$$

$$\sum_{t=0}^{N} \dfrac{COF_t}{(1 + r)^t} = \dfrac{\sum_{t=0}^{N} CIF_t(1 + r)^{N-t}}{(1 + MIRR)^N}$$

$$PV\ costs = \dfrac{TV}{(1 + MIRR)^N}$$

$$Payback = \text{Number of years prior to full recovery} + \dfrac{\text{Unrecovered cost at start of year}}{\text{Cash flow during full recovery year}}$$

# Chapter 12

**Taxes paid on salvaged assets = Tax rate × (Salvage value − Book value)**

**Recovery Allowance Percentage for Personal Property**

| Ownership Year | Class of Investment | | | |
| --- | --- | --- | --- | --- |
| | 3-Year | 5-Year | 7-Year | 10-Year |
| 1 | 33% | 20% | 14% | 10% |
| 2 | 45 | 32 | 25 | 18 |
| 3 | 15 | 19 | 17 | 14 |
| 4 | 7 | 12 | 13 | 12 |
| 5 | | 11 | 9 | 9 |
| 6 | | 6 | 9 | 7 |
| 7 | | | 9 | 7 |
| 8 | | | 4 | 7 |
| 9 | | | | 7 |
| 10 | | | | 6 |
| 11 | | | | 3 |
| | 100% | 100% | 100% | 100% |

# Chapter 13

$$\text{ROIC} = \frac{\text{EBIT}(1 - T)}{\text{Total invested capital}}$$

**Operating breakeven: EBIT = PQ − VQ − F = 0**

$$Q_{BE} = \frac{F}{P - V}$$

$$b_L = b_U[1 + (1 - T)(D/E)]$$

$$b_U = b_L/[1 + (1 - T)(D/E)]$$

$$r_s = r_{RF} + \frac{\text{Premium for}}{\text{business risk}} + \frac{\text{Premium for}}{\text{financial risk}}$$

**Net debt = Short-term debt + Long-term debt − Cash and equivalents**

# Chapter 14

**Dividends = Net income − Retained earnings required to help finance new investments**

**= Net income − [(Target equity ratio)(Total capital budget)]**

# Chapter 15

$$\frac{\text{Inventory}}{\text{conversion}} + \frac{\text{Average}}{\text{collection}} - \frac{\text{Payables}}{\text{deferral}} = \frac{\text{Cash}}{\text{conversion}}$$
$$\text{period} \qquad \text{period} \qquad \text{period} \qquad \text{cycle}$$

$$\text{Inventory conversion period} = \frac{\text{Inventory}}{\text{Cost of goods sold}/365}$$

$$\text{Average collection period (ACP or DSO)} = \frac{\text{Receivables}}{\text{Sales}/365}$$

$$\frac{\text{Payables}}{\text{deferral period}} = \frac{\text{Payables}}{\text{Purchases per day}} = \frac{\text{Payables}}{\text{Cost of goods sold}/365}$$

$$\text{Accounts receivable} = \text{Sales per day} \times \text{Length of collection period}$$
$$= (\text{ADS})(\text{DSO})$$

$$\begin{matrix}\text{Nominal annual} \\ \text{cost of} \\ \text{trade credit}\end{matrix} = \frac{\text{Discount \%}}{100 - \text{Discount \%}} \times \frac{365}{\begin{matrix}\text{Days credit is} \\ \text{outstanding}\end{matrix} - \begin{matrix}\text{Discount} \\ \text{period}\end{matrix}}$$

$$\text{Simple interest rate per day} = \frac{\text{Nominal rate}}{\text{Days in year}}$$

$$\text{Interest charge for month} = (\text{Rate per day})(\text{Amount of loan})(\text{Days in month})$$

$$\text{Approximate annual rate}_{\text{Add-on}} = \frac{\text{Interest paid}}{(\text{Amount received})/2}$$

# Chapter 16

$$\text{AFN} = \begin{matrix}\text{Projected} \\ \text{asset} \\ \text{increase}\end{matrix} - \begin{matrix}\text{Spontaneous} \\ \text{liabilities} \\ \text{increase}\end{matrix} - \begin{matrix}\text{Increase in} \\ \text{retained} \\ \text{earnings}\end{matrix}$$
$$= (A_0^*/S_0)\Delta S - (L_0^*/S_0)\Delta S - MS_1(1 - \text{Payout})$$

$$\begin{matrix}\text{Full} \\ \text{capacity} \\ \text{sales}\end{matrix} = \frac{\text{Actual sales}}{\begin{matrix}\text{Percentage of capacity} \\ \text{at which fixed assets} \\ \text{were operated}\end{matrix}}$$

$$\frac{\text{Target fixed assets}}{\text{Sales}} = \frac{\text{Actual fixed assets}}{\text{Full capacity sales}}$$

$$\begin{matrix}\text{Required level} \\ \text{of fixed assets}\end{matrix} = (\text{Target fixed assets}/\text{Sales})(\text{Projected sales})$$

# Chapter 17

$$\text{Direct quotation:} \frac{\text{U.S.\$ required}}{1 \text{ unit of foreign currency}}$$

$$\text{Indirect quotation:} \frac{\text{Units of foreign currency}}{1 \text{ U.S.\$}}$$

$$\frac{\text{Forward exchange rate}}{\text{Spot exchange rate}} = \frac{(1 + r_h)}{(1 + r_f)}$$

$$P_h = (P_f)(\text{Spot rate})$$

$$\text{Spot rate} = \frac{P_h}{P_f}$$

# Index